Children of Color

Children of Color

Psychological Interventions with Culturally Diverse Youth

Jewelle Taylor Gibbs

Larke Nahme Huang

and Associates

Forewords by

Stanley Sue, Ph.D.

Congressman George Miller

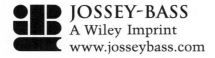

JOSSEY-BASS
A Wiley Imprint
www.josseybass.com

Published by Jossey-Bass
A Wiley Imprint
989 Market Street, San Francisco, CA 94103-1741   www.josseybass.com

Jossey-Bass books and products are available through most bookstores. To contact Jossey-Bass directly
call our Customer Care Department within the U.S. at 800-956-7739, outside the U.S. at 317-572-3986
or fax 317-572-4002.

Jossey-Bass also publishes its books in a variety of electronic formats. Some content that appears in
print may not be available in electronic books.

All of the names and identifying characteristics of the subjects of the case studies have been changed.
This book is not a substitute for counseling or legal, medical, or other professional advice, and the
reader should be aware that websites mentioned or referenced may have changed or disappeared
since this was written.

Library of Congress Cataloging-in-Publication Data

Gibbs, Jewelle Taylor.
    Children of color : psychological interventions with culturally
diverse youth / Jewelle Taylor Gibbs, Larke Nahme Huang, and associates;
forewords by Stanley Sue, George Miller.
        p.   cm.
An updated ed. previously published: San Francisco : Jossey-Bass, 1998.
Includes bibliographical references and index.
        ISBN 0-7879-6268-6 (alk. paper)
    1. Children of minorities—Mental health—United States.   I. Huang,
Larke.   II. Title.
        RJ507.M54G53   2003
        618.92′89′008900973—dc21   2002155394

Printed in the United States of America
SECOND EDITION
PB Printing   10 9 8 7 6 5 4 3

Contents

Foreword to the New Edition

In 2001, the Surgeon General of the United States issued a report titled *Mental Health: Culture, Race and Ethnicity,* which highlights four themes. First, culture counts in mental health. Culture is important in all phases of mental health from the fundamental experience of emotional distress, the expression of symptoms, and the identified stressors and resources to help-seeking patterns, utilization of services, and response to treatment. Second, disparities exist in the well-being of ethnic minority populations such as African Americans, Asian Americans, Latinos, and Native Americans. These disparities place ethnic minority groups at risk for mental health problems. The risk status of ethnic minority populations does not appear to be attributable to a higher incidence of mental disorders. Rather, disparities in the accessibility, availability, affordability, and cultural appropriateness of mental health services appear to be largely responsible for mental health disparities. Third, treatment can be very helpful. Although critical of the cultural appropriateness of mental health services, the Surgeon General indicated in his report that receiving mental health services for emotional distress was the best course of action. Fourth, little research is available that provides substantial knowledge of mental health issues, family resilience, effects of racism, and cultural competency in the delivery of services to ethnic minority populations.

This revised edition of Jewelle Taylor Gibbs and Larke Nahme Huang's book addresses the topics identified by the Surgeon General as the most important. The book is a highly successful and significant contribution to the mental health field dealing with ethnic minority children and families, especially in view of the rapidly growing ethnic minority populations. The new edition, with chapters written by leading authorities, is equally compelling in providing up-to-date knowledge of ethnic children and families, treatment and prevention intervention strategies to use, an integration of research and practice issues, insights into cultural competency, and the cultural, sociopolitical, and clinical context for understanding children of color and their families. New chapters have been included that cover Filipino Americans and Central Americans—two expanding populations that have not traditionally been given much attention in the literature. The book is pertinent to researchers and practitioners alike, be they psychologists, social workers, psychiatrists, nurses, graduate students, or other mental health providers. The specific cases analyzed by the chapter contributors are most enlightening. They point to how experts use their knowledge and skills to deal with cultural factors in assessment and therapy. There is much to learn from their analysis. Because the cases involve children and families of different ethnicities, readers can try to identify general principles in conducting culturally competent treatment, as well as specific procedures in working with clients from a particular ethnic group. In this edition, the authors and contributors focus more on policy implications for families of color, so the book is particularly valuable to practitioners and mental health administrators.

This book reveals the deep insights, thoughtfulness, and clinical wisdom of the editors and the chapter authors. It should be required reading in our graduate mental health training programs.

February 2003   STANLEY SUE, PH.D.
Professor of Psychology, Psychiatry,
and Asian American Studies
University of California, Davis

Reference

U.S. Department of Health and Human Services. *Mental Health: Culture, Race and Ethnicity.* Supplement to *Mental Health: A Report of the Surgeon General.* Rockville, Md.: U.S. Department of Health and Human Services, 2001.

Foreword

Over the last several decades, we in the United States have witnessed dramatic changes that have profoundly affected our young people and their families demographically, economically, socially, and psychologically and that pose enormous challenges to which the nation must respond. Perhaps nowhere are these changes more evident and compelling than in the rapidly increasing cultural and demographic diversity of our citizenry. Minority group members— blacks, Hispanics, American Indians, and Asians—constitute 14 percent of all adults in the country and 20 percent of children under seventeen. By the year 2000, it is projected that one-third of all school-age children will fall into this category.

This changing demographic tapestry in the United States promises not only the richness that diversity brings but also many difficult challenges in extending the American dream to all of our citizens. Historically, people of color have found themselves at the bottom of the economic and social order. They are disproportionately represented among the poor, the unemployed, the homeless, the sick, the inadequately educated, and those who are ill-prepared for full participation in American life. For children of color, the toll has been even greater. Infant mortality in the black community is double that in the white community, and the gap is widening. Half of all black children and one-third of all Hispanic children live in poverty. School dropout rates for minority youth remain at alarming levels, with rates reaching more than 60 percent in some urban areas.

Concomitant economic changes and increasing isolation of communities of color compound the challenges. The number of blue-collar manufacturing jobs—which allowed past generations of minorities and immigrants to climb into the economic mainstream—is declining. The opportunities now available to minority adults increasingly are in low-paying service-sector jobs that provide far fewer opportunities for upward mobility.

In addition, we have seen an upswing in race-related violence and other racially motivated incidents in diverse communities around the country. Apart from their tragic personal significance, incidents of racial antipathy give us important lessons about larger economic and demographic trends in our society and about the environments in which our children are growing up.

Children of color face daily challenges to their success and self-esteem. In investigations by the U.S. Select Committee on Children, Youth, and Families, we have documented the disparate treatment of minority and white children with mental health problems. The understanding and treatment of children's mental health is still in its infancy in America. Nearly ten million children suffer from mental health problems that need attention. Yet an estimated 70 to 80 percent of these children get inappropriate mental health services or no services at all. For children of color, the problems are even more severe. Due to a mental health system that is poorly funded and all too frequently insensitive to race and ethnic origin, these children are often misdiagnosed and mistreated, if they are treated at all.

The importance of addressing these issues cannot be overstated: they must be at the core of America's agenda. This book provides an important contribution to defining and making more visible these concerns, which have remained under wraps for far too long. Children are our future, and we must give them the opportunity to do a good job of it. They and the nation deserve no less.

February 1989
(for first edition)

CONGRESSMAN GEORGE MILLER
Chairman, Select Committee
on Children, Youth, and Families
U.S. House of Representatives

Preface

At the beginning of the twenty-first century, children and adolescents of color constitute the most rapidly expanding segment of the youth population in America, yet there is a serious dearth of literature available to enlighten clinicians, educators, health professionals, social workers, and policymakers about these children's problems and needs. When the first edition of this book was published in 1989, we recognized the need for a comprehensive text on the psychological assessment and treatment of ethnic minority children and adolescents—a group that had been generally neglected in the proliferation of textbooks on minority mental health in the 1980s. In general, these books focused on the mental health problems of minority adults and the implications of ethnicity for family therapy. However, all of the major ethnic minority groups are characterized by disproportionately youthful populations, as compared to the dominant white majority. Our experiences as clinicians, researchers, teachers, policy analysts, and consultants further emphasized the need for a book that would encompass theoretical, empirical, and clinical perspectives concerning the assessment and interventions for youth of color.

The response of mental health professionals, educators, and students to the first edition of the book was so positive that we revised it for an updated paperback edition in 1998. To date, there are still only a few books that address the unique problems and special needs of ethnic minority children and adolescents with psychological and behavioral problems. Although in recent years there has been an increase in the knowledge base about ethnic minority populations, this knowledge has been effectively translated into only a few comprehensive handbooks for use in the clinical intervention and training of mental health and human service professionals. Between 1990 and 2000, the population of nonwhite and Hispanic-speaking youth aged ten to nineteen in the United States increased from 31 to 36 percent of all U.S. youth, underscoring the need for educational and clinical resources relevant to this group (U.S. Bureau of the Census, 2001). In fact, ethnic minority youth now make up nearly 40 percent of the U.S. public school population and over 60 percent of the student population in many large urban school districts, with concomitant increases in academic and behavioral problems that teachers and counselors are unprepared to handle effectively (National Center for Educational Statistics, 2001). Thus this second edition of our book is designed to meet the needs of educators and professionals in the mental health and human service professions, including psychiatry, psychology, social work, psychiatric nursing, and counseling, who are faced with the challenges of working with this burgeoning population of racially and culturally diverse youth.

Purpose

This book is designed to fulfill several goals and to be useful in a wide variety of clinical, professional, and educational settings. First, its primary purpose is to present a well-balanced discussion of the issues involved in the clinical assessment and treatment of minority children and adolescents from four major ethnic groups and one emerging biracial-bicultural population group. A broad range of interventions is covered by the various contributors, from psychodynamic to social cognitive to systems-oriented approaches, with an ecological perspective providing a common thread across groups and serving to integrate the conventional with the more culture-based methods of intervention.

Second, a comparative, cross-cultural approach to the book will provide an overarching framework around which each chapter will be organized, enabling the reader to compare selected topics (for example, socialization practices, identity formation, coping strategies, assessment issues, treatment approaches) across ethnic groups.

Third, the book reflects a major commitment to an ecological perspective that recognizes the significant impact of social and environmental factors such as poverty, discrimination, immigration, and family structure on the adaptation and coping patterns of ethnic minority children and adolescents. We strongly believe that some knowledge of a group's history in the United States, traditional value system, family organization, and current demographic reality is essential for the accurate clinical assessment and effective intervention with youth from diverse ethnic backgrounds. Thus relevant background information is briefly summarized for each ethnic minority group in order to provide a sociocultural context that justifies the recommendations for differential strategies of assessment and treatment.

The most difficult aspect of planning the scope of this book was the initial decision concerning which groups to include and which groups to exclude. Our decision was to focus on children and adolescents from the four largest ethnic minority groups in the United States: African Americans, American Indians, Asian Americans, and Hispanic-Latino Americans. To acknowledge the diversity within each of these groups, we selected three of the largest subgroups among Asian Americans and Hispanic-Latino Americans: Chinese, Filipino, and Southeast Asians (representing the Asian American population) and Central American, Puerto Rican, and Mexican Americans (representing the Hispanic-Latino population). In addition, we have included a chapter on the rapidly increasing population of biracial and bicultural youth, who represent an emerging multiracial and multicultural population group.

These particular ethnic groups were selected for several reasons. First, they have been historically the largest minority groups with the longest period of residence in this country. Second, more literature and a greater range of reliable sources were available for writing about these groups. And third, these groups represent a range of demographic, linguistic, and acculturation differences. For example, in terms of population trends, Southeast Asians are rapidly increasing because they have high birth rates, whereas numbers of Japanese Americans, who were included in the earlier editions of our book, are stabilizing and perhaps even declining due to high rates of out-of-group marriage. The route of entry to the United States varies from American Indians and Alaskan Natives, who are indigenous peoples, to African Americans, who were imported as slaves, to the Japanese and Chinese Americans, who were imported as cheap laborers, to the most recent Southeast Asians and Central Americans, who were initially admitted as political refugees.

Along with these differences in migration history, a continuum of acculturation among these groups is reflected in linguistic and cultural patterns ranging from the bilingualism of many second-generation Spanish-speaking Americans to the rapid assimilation of many fourth-generation Filipino Americans. It is important to emphasize the wide diversity *within* each ethnic group; the attitudes, behaviors, and values of group members are strongly influenced by their degree of acculturation, their socioeconomic status (SES), and their ties with ethnic institutions and communities. For example, there may be greater differences between the first and third generations of Chinese Americans than between middle-class, acculturated Chinese and white Americans. Thus although our contributors have attempted to describe the traditional history, culture, and mental health attitudes and beliefs of these ethnic groups, we recognize that they are all in the process of continual change, acculturation, and adaptation to the dominant Anglo American society and that these generalizations are not equally applicable to all members of a specific ethnic minority group.

In addition, one chapter addresses the unique issues facing biracial and bicultural children and adolescents. Although there is very little in the clinical literature about these two groups, they are a rapidly growing segment of the youth population in this country, and we believe they pose particular challenges to mental health practitioners who may be unfamiliar with their developmental issues and social experiences. Moreover, the families of these racially and ethnically mixed youth successfully lobbied for expanded categories of racial categories in the U.S. census for the year 2000, thus challenging our society's traditional concepts of race and ethnicity. This chapter offers an initial attempt to consolidate the ethnographic, developmental, clinical, and empirical literature that provides useful information for clinicians who work with these youth.

Although we are aware that many other ethnic minority groups have established thriving communities and made significant contributions to American society since the end of World War II, such as Asian Indians, Caribbean blacks, Cubans, East Africans, and Koreans, among others, we have not been able to include all of these groups due to limitations of space and insufficient information concerning children's mental health issues. However, throughout this book there are sections on assessment and treatment that will have some relevance for these groups, as well as many research findings that are directly applicable to them.

In planning the topics to be included, we preferred to present more in-depth discussion about selected treatment modalities than to produce a survey text with a superficial coverage of all modalities of treatment for minority children and adolescents. Because most of these youth are seen in outpatient clinics and practice settings, the authors focus on appropriate individual and family treatment modalities. Few authors address the issues of residential treatment or hospitalization because these specialized settings frequently involve medication and more restrictive forms of intervention. Finally, psychological testing is not covered in this book because the issues of testing minority youth have been effectively addressed in many other texts.

The eleven chapters of the book are organized to reflect natural groupings within the broad category of ethnic minority populations, as well as historical differences in terms of their relationship to the dominant culture. First, Jewelle Taylor Gibbs and Larke Nahme Huang provide an introduction to the book and an overview of the issues. In this chapter, the coauthors describe the purpose and goals of the book, its conceptual framework, and its integrative cross-cultural perspective. Examples from each of the topical chapters are included to illustrate specific points and to highlight particular themes.

Nine topical chapters follow, each focusing on a particular ethnic minority group or emerging population. Authors of each chapter are psychologists who have both personal and professional knowledge and extensive clinical and research experience with the ethnic groups they describe. The content of these chapters adheres to a similar format: demographic data, epidemiological data regarding incidence of psychological and behavioral disorders (where available), historical information about entry or migration to the United States, significant issues of family structure and functioning, sociocultural issues in assessment (attitudes, values, and beliefs about mental health and illness; symptom patterns; help-seeking; and utilization patterns), and implications for effective intervention strategies and treatment techniques. Brief case vignettes are presented by the authors of each chapter to illustrate the appropriate role of sociocultural factors in the assessment of symptomatology, defensive strategies, and coping behaviors in emotionally troubled minority children and adolescents, for the purpose of developing specific treatment techniques and alternative intervention strategies.

In Chapter One, Teresa LaFromboise and Marivic R. Dizon propose a combination of indigenous and Western therapeutic methods to treat the psychological and behavioral problems of American Indian and Native Alaskan youth, whose problems often result from the poverty, social isolation, and cultural discontinuities of reservation or urban life.

In Chapter Two, Jewelle Taylor Gibbs delineates the mental health and psychosocial problems of African American adolescents, whose behavioral disorders often mask underlying psychological problems that are exacerbated by their disadvantaged SES and their lack of equal educational and employment opportunities.

In Chapter Three, Jewelle Taylor Gibbs examines the implications of biracial or bicultural heritage for the psychosocial adjustment of adolescents, whose identity development may be complicated by conflicts about their dual racial and cultural heritage.

In Chapter Four, Larke Nahme Huang, Yu-Wen Ying, and Girlyn F. Arganza describe the mental health issues for Chinese American children and adolescents and provide a unique model of "active exchange" in intervention with these youth and their families.

Pauline Agbayani-Siewert and Annalisa Vincente Enrile present a sociohistorical perspective on the experiences of the Filipino community in the United States in Chapter Five, providing a context for the conflicts over identity and assimilation among Filipino American youth.

Donna J. Ida and Pahoua Yang present an overview, in Chapter Six, of the adjustment issues facing Southeast Asian refugee and immigrant youth who have experienced the trauma of multiple separations and losses, forced relocation, and pressures for rapid acculturation to an unfamiliar society.

In Chapter Seven, Norita Vlach continues the theme of "fragmented identities" in delineating the multiple traumas of civil wars, family loss, and relocation experienced by many Central American immigrant and refugee youth.

In Chapter Eight, Kurt C. Organista points out the dual impact of biculturalism and bilingualism on the psychosocial development of Mexican American children, who often find themselves in conflict between the traditional Latino values of their parents and the contemporary values of Anglo American society.

Jaime E. Inclán and Mabel E. Quiñones echo many of these themes in Chapter Nine, as they characterize the mental health issues for Puerto Rican American youth. In this chapter and in Chapter Eight, the authors emphasize the importance of involving the family in any treatment program for a Hispanic child or adolescent.

In Chapter Ten, Larke Nahme Huang and Girlyn F. Arganza examine the major systems of care that provide mental health services to children and youth of color in terms of their capacity to deliver culturally competent services to these youth and their families. The following systems that serve youth with mental health needs are discussed: health care, mental health, education and special education, child welfare, and the juvenile justice system. This chapter concludes with the presentation of a proposed cultural competence model for these child-serving systems to improve outcomes for children of color.

In Chapter Eleven, Larke Nahme Huang and Jewelle Taylor Gibbs integrate the common themes developed in the topical chapters, highlighting the similarities and differences in mental health issues among the various groups of ethnic minority children and adolescents. In addition, they propose an ecological model of assessment and intervention that provides clinicians with a conceptual tool of clinical inquiry and assessment appropriate for these children and youth of color, who share certain common characteristics that set them apart from the dominant majority. Finally, they present a set of recommendations for further research on the mental health of ethnic minority youth, greater expansion and improvement in the training of mental health professionals to treat minority populations, and significant proposals to formulate policies to meet the needs of the expanding population of youth of color more effectively.

In summary, we feel that this book is an important contribution to the field of minority mental health for three reasons. First, it will fill a gap in the clinical literature on the treatment of ethnic minority children and adolescents, as so few books are currently available. Second, it will be a valuable tool for use in the training of all mental health and human service professionals, many of whom are required to learn about ethnic minority groups for their licensing examinations in psychiatry, psychology, social work, and family and marriage counseling. And third, it will be extremely useful for mental health and human service professionals in all public and private agencies which, according to current demographic trends and projections, will serve an increasingly higher proportion of ethnic minority populations well into the twenty-first century, even as people of color gradually gain majority status.

We should add one caveat to our readers: our goal is not to create "experts" or "specialists" in the field of minority mental health but to provide an introduction and a way of conceptualizing the mental health problems of ethnic minority youth. We hope that this book will not only expand the knowledge base of practitioners who work with these youth but will increase their sensitivity to the similarities and differences among and between groups in our diverse society. To that end, we especially appreciate the efforts of our contributors, who responded promptly and enthusiastically to our request to update their chapters with current demographic, epidemiological, and empirical data for this second edition.

Children and youth of color constitute one of the fastest-growing segments of the population, yet scant attention has been paid to their development by social scientists, little understanding of their special needs has been demonstrated by educators, and minimal awareness of their special problems has been expressed by mental health professionals. It is our hope that this second edition of our book will not only increase the accessibility of this important information but will further contribute to advancing our understanding of the needs of these youth, to improving the assessment of their mental health, and to developing more effective methods of intervention and treatment for their behavioral and psychological disorders.

February 2003

JEWELLE TAYLOR GIBBS
Stanford, California

LARKE NAHME HUANG
Washington, D.C.

References

National Center for Educational Statistics. *Education Statistics Digest: 2000.* Washington, D.C.: U.S. Department of Education, 2000.

U.S. Bureau of the Census. *Statistical Abstract of the United States: 2001.* Washington, D.C.: U.S. Department of Commerce, 2001.

Acknowledgments

Children of Color truly represents a collaborative undertaking, not only of the contributing authors but of many others who made direct and indirect contributions to the project. First, we would like to thank the contributing authors, whose enthusiasm and cooperation sustained us through the challenges inherent in such a project. We would also like to express our appreciation for the encouragement and support of our colleagues at the School of Social Welfare, University of California at Berkeley, and the Center for Child Health and Mental Health Policy at Georgetown University.

We owe thanks to several research assistants who assisted with the research on our chapters in current and previous editions of this book, including Laura Abrams, Helen Ahn, Teiasha Bankhead, Kathryn Chun, Holly Danforth, M. Clare Dunne, Alice Hines, Karen Huang, Mary Leong Lam, Huong Mai Le, Lawrence Liese, Joseph Merighi, Martha Sue Skinner, and Alberta Wu. We also want to acknowledge the helpful comments and insights offered by graduate students in our courses on minority mental health and participants in our workshops from 1981 through 1999. We further express our thanks to all of the office staff who were so cooperative in facilitating our work in countless ways. We owe a debt of gratitude to Alan Rinzler, the Jossey-Bass editor for this new edition, who shepherded us through the project with enthusiasm, patience, and valuable feedback.

For this new edition of the book, we particularly appreciate the support of the administrators and staff of the Research Institute for Comparative Studies of Race and Ethnicity at Stanford University, as well as the research assistance of senior Jennifer Marshall for the 2001–02 academic year.

Our special thanks go to Sharon Ikami, who typed several versions of this manuscript with professionalism, patience, and good humor. We wish to acknowledge the indirect contributions of the professors who taught us and the clinicians who supervised us during our graduate and postgraduate training in clinical and community psychology at the University of California at Berkeley (J.T.G.), Yale University (L.N.H.), Mt. Zion Hospital in San Francisco (J.T.G.), Stanford University (J.T.G.), George Washington University Medical Center (J.T.G.), and Langley Porter Psychiatric Institute, University of California Medical Center, San Francisco (L.N.H.).

We are grateful to our families and friends for their unwavering support and sustenance throughout the three editions of this book: Leonard and Dorothy Nahme, Andrew and Diana Huang, Donna and Charles Salcetti, Scott Ren Nahme, Ernestine Singletary, Phyllis Elperin, and all of the Taylor clan and the Gibbs extended family in the San Francisco Bay Area. To our respective spouses, James and Kirk, and to our children, Geoffrey, Lowell, Christina, and Kevin, we owe a special debt of gratitude for their patience and forbearance.

Finally, this volume is the culmination of a joint effort between two friends and colleagues from different ethnicities and backgrounds. We have learned much from and about each other, and in the spirit of diversity, our own lives have been enriched and the bonds of friendship and knowledge strengthened through this relationship.

J.T.G.
L.N.H.

Children of Color

Introduction and Overview
A Conceptual Framework for the Psychological Assessment and Treatment of Minority Youth

Jewelle Taylor Gibbs
Larke Nahme Huang

The field of community mental health, which emerged in the late 1960s, faces a number of critical challenges at the beginning of the twenty-first century. As the number of immigrants, refugees, and native-born people of color continues to increase dramatically in the population, the knowledge, skills, and intervention methods required for mental health providers to work effectively with these populations have not kept pace with the demographic changes. In his report, *Mental Health: Culture, Race and Ethnicity* (U.S. Department of Health and Human Services, 2001), the U.S. Surgeon General concludes that "many providers and researchers of all backgrounds are not fully aware of the impact of culture on mental health, mental illness, and mental health services" (p. 167).

Between 1980 and 2000, the proportion of people of color in the U.S. population has increased dramatically. Demographers accurately predicted that nonwhite and Hispanic-speaking youth under age eighteen would constitute 36 percent of the nation's youth population by the year 2000 and increase to 48 percent by 2020 (U.S. Bureau of the Census, 2001). These population changes and projected trends are largely the result of four factors: (1) increased immigration from Latin America, Asia, Africa, and the Caribbean, (2) higher birth rates of these immigrant groups and resident minority groups, (3) increased longevity of the minority population, and (4) lower birthrates of the resident white population.

These population trends have created a "demographic imperative" for the social institutions that serve youth to modify their traditional programs and services in order to serve these minority youth more effectively (Ozawa, 1986). The impact of this changing population has already been felt by schools, social services, health and mental health agencies, juvenile probation services, and all other family- and youth-oriented programs. For example, in 1998 nonwhite and Hispanic youth constituted 37 percent of the nation's public school population, over 40 percent of the students in states such as California, Florida, New York, and Texas, and well over 60 percent of the students in many large urban school districts throughout the country (National Center for Educational Statistics, 2001). However, as this minority youth population continues to grow, it has become increasingly clear that most of the human service and mental health professionals who serve them do not have adequate information, applicable training, or appropriate resources to address the youths' problems and needs. This problem is particularly acute in urban areas where high rates of poverty among these minority groups contribute to social isolation and social disorganization, further magnifying ethnic and cultural differences (Farley, 1997; Massey and Denton, 1993; Wilson, 1996).

In 1978, the President's Commission on Mental Health noted that low-income minority children and adolescents were particularly at risk for psychological disorders and behavioral problems because of their low socioeconomic status (SES), their often stressful environments, and their lack of access to mental health services. As the Surgeon General's report underscores, nearly three decades later this situation has not measurably improved, and children of color are still triply disadvantaged by their ethnicity, their poverty, and their social isolation (U.S. Department of Health and Human Services, 2001).

However, in an effort to address the mental health needs and counter the previous neglect of children of color, a growing number of clinical researchers and practitioners in the past two decades have contributed scholarly and practitioner books for providers who serve these youth and their families (Canino and Spurlock, 1994; Gibbs and Huang, 1989; Paniagua, 2001; Samuda, 1998; Vargas and Koss-Chioino, 1992).

The purpose of this book is to provide a balanced and comprehensive overview of psychological intervention with minority children and adolescents experiencing psychological and behavioral problems. Toward this objective, the book (1) provides basic demographic and sociocultural information about these minority youth, (2) presents data on the incidence of behavioral and psychological disorders in these groups, and (3) proposes an ecological and culturally sensitive framework for the psychosocial assessment and treatment of these youth. This book is not intended to present a comprehensive survey of all possible treatment modalities for children and adolescents but rather to focus on an in-depth coverage of clients seen in outpatient clinical settings, where the great majority of these young people are treated. Thus the contributors do not devote much attention to such topics as psychological testing, residential treatment, or psychiatric hospitalization.

The book focuses primarily on school-aged children and youth between the ages of ten through eighteen in four major ethnic minority groups in the United States: American Indians, African Americans, Asian Americans, and Hispanic-Latinos. In recognition of the diversity within the Asian and Hispanic-Latino populations, chapters are devoted to three of the largest ethnic groups within each of these categories: (1) Chinese American, Filipino American, and Southeast Asian youth (representing Asian Americans) and (2) Central American, Mexican American, and Puerto Rican youth (representing Hispanics-Latinos). In addition, one chapter examines the unique experiences and challenges of the fastest-growing group in the youth population: biracial and bicultural children and adolescents. Although the literature about this latter group is sparse, these children constitute a rapidly emerging segment of American society and pose particular challenges to mental health professionals who may be unfamiliar with their cultural and social experiences.

The choice of these groups was not random or capricious but based on several important considerations. First, the four ethnic groups are among the largest minority groups with a long period of residence in the United States. Second, there is a significant database on these groups that includes ethnographic, demographic, empirical, and clinical studies. Third, these groups represent a continuum of acculturation from the most assimilated (for example,

Filipino Americans) to the least assimilated (for example, South-east Asian refugees), with a wide spectrum between these extremes that reflects different patterns of migration, different degrees of bilingualism, and different levels of adaptation to mainstream customs, values, and behaviors. In addition, these groups represent contrasting demographic trends from Southeast Asians and Hispanic Americans, who are rapidly increasing in the population, to the Native American Indians and African Americans, who are experiencing slow growth rates or are declining in their relative proportion of the population.

Although we are aware that many other minority groups have more recently grown in size and made significant contributions to society, such as Asian Indians, Koreans, Cubans, Caribbean blacks, and Pacific Islanders, among others, we have not included all of these groups because of space limitations and inadequate databases concerning children's mental health issues and sociodemographic characteristics. However, throughout this book there are sections on assessment and treatment that will have some relevance for these groups, as well as many references that are directly applicable to them. Our decision was to select a few representative groups to discuss in depth rather than a larger number to discuss in more general terms.

It is also important to point out the diversity that exists within each of these groups in terms of migration history, SES, level of acculturation, lifestyle, values, and behaviors. Although we acknowledge this diversity, we have emphasized the shared history, cultural traditions, and social experiences of these groups relative to the dominant society. In some cases, there may be greater differences between Hispanic and non-Hispanic blacks, for example, or between American Indians from different tribal backgrounds than there would be between some members of these groups and white Americans. It is not our intention to create or reinforce stereotypes or myths about any of these groups but rather to present the available information that will inform mental health clinicians about some modal characteristics of their cultural heritage that will enable them to deliver more effective and culturally sensitive services to these youth and their families.

Cultural competence has been defined in various ways, but there is a general consensus in the field of mental health that this term

refers to "the delivery of services responsive to the cultural concerns of racial and ethnic minority groups, including their languages, histories, traditions, beliefs, and values . . . [it] underscores
the recognition of patients' cultures, and then develops a set of
skills, knowledge, and policies to deliver effective treatments" (U.S.
Department of Health and Human Services, 2001, p. 36).

Conceptual Framework

This book is organized around three primary conceptual perspectives: (1) a developmental perspective, (2) an ecological perspective,
and (3) a cross-cultural or minority mental health perspective. These
perspectives are described briefly next, followed by a discussion of
their relevance to the assessment and treatment of ethnic minority
children and adolescents.

Developmental Perspective — ethnic variations: behavior symbolic meaning societal responses

The developmental perspective provides a framework for examining the influence of race and ethnicity on the psychosocial tasks of
growing up in American society. Although maturational processes
are undeniably universal and occur with only minor variations
across racial and cultural groups, many social science researchers
have shown that these processes are subject to wide ethnic variations in their behavioral manifestations, their symbolic meanings,
and their societal responses (McLoyd, 1990; Phinney and Rotheram, 1987; Powell, Yamamoto, Romero, and Morales, 1983).

Erikson (1959) proposes that there are five psychosocial stages
from birth to late adolescence, each one posing a specific developmental challenge for the growing child to master. The outcomes for
each stage are determined by an interaction of the individual's personality attributes, relationships with significant others, and opportunities available in the environment. The psychosocial crises to be
resolved in the first five stages depend on a favorable interaction of
these three variables, which would result in sense of trust over mistrust in the infant, autonomy over shame and doubt in the toddler,
initiative over guilt in the preschool child, industry over inferiority
in the latency-aged child, and identity consolidation over identity
diffusion in the adolescent. In discussing these psychosocial crises,

Erikson points out that children from minority and low-income backgrounds may experience more difficulties in achieving these positive outcomes because of prejudice, discrimination, or barriers to full opportunity for personal growth.

It is important to note two major contributions of Erikson's theory to the study of minority children and youth, as well as to recognize certain limitations in the theory. First, this framework enables mental health clinicians to evaluate the child's level of psychosocial development at various age levels in terms of certain salient characteristics such as dependency, competence, interpersonal skills, and sense of personal identity. Second, this framework is useful for assessing the child's relationships with significant others (for example, parents, teachers, and peers) and adjustment to the environment (for example, home, school, and community).

Although Erikson's stage-related theory of psychosocial development is relevant for children reared in nuclear families in highly industrialized societies, his conceptual scheme may be less applicable to children reared in extended families in nonindustrial societies where the emphasis might be placed on different psychosocial outcomes. Awareness of this potential bias is an important caveat in assessing specific characteristics in children of recent immigrants, those reared on reservations, and those reared in other culturally homogeneous environments.

A second major limitation of Erikson's theory is its assumption that the self-concept and the self-esteem of minority children are significantly affected by the stigma of membership in a devalued ethnic group. This assumption is contradicted by the work of Mead (1934), who proposes that a child develops a self-concept and self-esteem from the reflected appraisals of family and close relatives and friends and not from the broader society, which only later affects the adolescent upon leaving the relative social insulation of family and ethnic community. Recent reports of surveys of the literature on the self-esteem of minority children and adolescents support the view that their level of self-esteem is as high or higher than their white peers (Rotheram-Borus, Dopkins, Sabate, and Lightfoot, 1996; Powell, 1985; Spencer and Dornbusch, 1990). Cross (1991) and Spencer and Markstrom-Adams (1990) further describe the complexity and diversity of identity formation among minority adolescents and the various factors that contribute to self-esteem for these youth. In spite of these limitations, Erikson's conceptual scheme provides the clinician with a framework for viewing important areas of psychosocial growth and development. By complementing this scheme with the ecological and cross-cultural perspectives, the clinician will obtain a more comprehensive and differentiated view of minority youth.

Ecological Perspective

The ecological perspective, as proposed by Bronfenbrenner (1979), is useful in viewing the growing child and adolescent as an active agent in a series of interlocking systems, ranging from the microsystems of the family and the school to the macrosystem of governmental, social, and economic policies. Each of these systems poses risks and opportunities for the child or adolescent interacting with the environment at successive developmental stages. This ecological perspective is especially relevant in analyzing the impact of poverty, discrimination, immigration, and social isolation on the psychosocial development and adjustment of minority children and youth.

Extensive research on poor families has shown that poverty has a negative impact on nearly all aspects of their children's lives, including nutrition, health care, housing, education, and recreation (Brooks-Gunn, Duncan, and Aber, 1997; Lynn and McGeary, 1990). When children are both poor *and* members of ethnic minority groups, the negative and long-term impact of poverty increases significantly (Farley, 1997; Wilson, 1996). Recent immigration status and language problems are additional sources of stress for children of immigrants and refugees, who must cope not only with adjustment to a strange new culture but with the loss of their native land and indigenous culture as well (Aronowitz, 1992; Gong-Guy, Craveks, and Paterson, 1991; Pawliuk and others, 1996).

Historical forces, economic factors, and political realities shape the macrosystem of minority youth. For example, Asian and Hispanic immigrants are often compared to European immigrants of the late nineteenth and early twentieth centuries, yet these contemporary nonwhite immigrants and their children encounter a very different set of attitudes and experiences from the dominant society than the earlier waves of white immigrants faced (Gibbs and

Bankhead, 2001; Gutierrez, 1996; Preston, Cain, and Bass, 1998; Perea, 1997). Second, structural changes in the economy and technological changes in the workforce have resulted in high rates of unemployment among minority adults, many of whom do not have the education or skills to compete in a highly industrialized urban economy (Farley, 1997). Third, since the demise of the U.S. government's War on Poverty, political attitudes have become more conservative, and there has been a backlash against affirmative action programs in employment and higher education. All of these trends have had a negative effect on low-income minority families, resulting in more stress, which, in turn, has diminished their ability to provide a stable and nurturant environment for their children (Edelman, 1987; Meyers, 1989). In spite of the ecological stressors, these families have demonstrated remarkable resiliency, creativity, and competence in meeting the tasks of socializing their children in an often hostile and alien environment.

The ecological perspective is also useful in the assessment of the child's psychosocial functioning in the family, the school, the peer group, and the community (Gustavsson and Balgopal, 1990; Spencer and Dornbusch, 1990). The impact of these systems on minority youth cannot be overestimated because they provide the environmental context in which their socialization occurs. As Vlach points out in her chapter on Central American refugee children, in families with a recent history of immigration, children and adolescents are often in conflict between two competing sets of values and norms that require them to develop one set of behaviors in the family setting and another set in school and community settings. When these behaviors are diametrically opposed, it inevitably leads to emotional stress and may be expressed in somatic symptoms, behavior disorders, school adjustment problems, delinquency, depression, or suicidal behavior (Baptiste, 1990; Chiu, Feldman, and Rosenthal, 1992; Evans and Lee, 1998; Lee, 1988; Rousseau, Drapeau, and Corin, 1996).

Cross-Cultural Perspective

The cross-cultural perspective, developed by anthropologists to establish a comparative framework for the analysis of all human societies, assumes that all behavior has meaning and serves some adaptive function; behavior is also governed by a set of rules and norms that promote stability and harmony within a society. Dysfunctional or deviant behavior, as defined by the group, disrupts group functioning and must be regulated by some type of institutionalized control mechanism—for example, shamans, spiritualists, faith healers, or mental health practitioners (Cervantes and Ramirez, 1992; Csordas, 1999; Kazarian and Evans, 1998; Kleinman, 1980).

This cross-cultural perspective has been employed by many minority mental health researchers in order to provide a comparative context for viewing psychological phenomena among diverse ethnic groups in the United States (Green, 1999; McGoldrick, Giordano, and Pearce, 1996; Paniagua, 2001; Sue and Sue, 1999). Although these efforts are still in their infancy, research on mental health in a variety of ethnic groups has encompassed a wide range of topics, including attitudes toward mental health and mental illness; belief systems about the causes of mental illness and dysfunctional behavior; differential symptomatology, defensive patterns, and coping strategies; help-seeking behaviors; utilization of services; and responsiveness to treatment.

Ethnicity and Mental Health

Research on minority mental health has documented the numerous ways in which ethnicity influences the psychological well-being of minority adults and families, but little attention has been paid to its influence on the developing child and adolescent (McLoyd and Steinberg, 1998; Evans and Lee, 1998; Leadbetter and Way, 1996; Powell, Yamamoto, Romero, and Morales, 1983; Phinney and Rotheram, 1987; Spencer and Dornbusch, 1990). Obviously, those influences are mediated to children through their parents and other significant adults in their immediate social environment.

First, ethnicity shapes the child's belief systems about what constitutes mental health and mental illness, both in terms of general criteria and specific behavioral traits.

Second, ethnicity influences the child's manifestation of symptoms, defensive styles, and patterns of coping with anxiety, depression, fear, guilt, and anger. Some ethnic groups reinforce "acting in" neurotic symptoms; others reward "acting out" characterological symptoms, and still others reward somatic symptoms; thus children learn patterns of illness and dysfunctional behavior that are culturally reinforced and tolerated.

3   Third, ethnicity largely determines help-seeking patterns that parents use to seek relief for children or adolescents with dysfunctional behaviors or symptoms. These help-seeking patterns may range from consulting a priest or minister, to a spiritualist or native healer, to an herbalist or acupuncturist, or to a tribal council or family elder.

4   Fourth, ethnicity is a major factor shaping the way the child or adolescent utilizes and responds to treatment. The level of initial trust and openness, the attitude toward self-disclosure, the willingness to discuss certain topics, the motivation to participate in insight-oriented treatment—all of these aspects of the treatment relationship are filtered through the screen of ethnicity.

Assessment   Sue and Sue (1977) have identified three variables that are important in assessing minority clients: (1) culture-bound variables, *Culture* (2) language-bound variables, and (3) class-bound variables. These *Language* variables are particularly relevant to children and adolescents *Class* whose daily lives are circumscribed by their family and community experiences. In order to conduct an adequate assessment of the young client, the clinician should have some knowledge of the cultural background, attitudes, norms, and childrearing practices of the family; some familiarity with the language, the immigration history, the belief systems, and the level of acculturation of the family; and an understanding of the impact of SES on the family's lifestyle, community experiences, opportunities, and aspirations (Canino and Spurlock, 1994; Isaacs and Benjamin, 1991; Lum, 1992; Vargas and Koss-Chioino, 1992).

Ethnicity, Social Class, and Adaptation

Ethnicity has been defined in various ways by various authors, but the term will be used here to mean "those who share a unique social and cultural heritage, that is passed on from generation to generation" (Mindel and Habenstein, 1981, p. 5). Fenton (1999) points out that ethnicity "refers to the social elaboration of collective identities whereby individuals see themselves as one among others like themselves" who mobilize their social transaction around "real or perceived differences of ancestry, culture and language" (p. 6). Despite his use of the term *race,* Fenton concurs with the contemporary scientific view that race is primarily a social construct rather than a biological reality and notes that it is frequently misused to justify political, economic, and social disparities and discrimination against people of color. The concepts of race and ethnicity are not identical but frequently overlap in common usage, as with references to Chinese Americans or black Americans (Fenton, 1999). Hispanics, however, are defined by their common cultural heritage (Mexican, or Central or Latin American) and their language (Spanish), but they can be white, black, or American Indian or a mixture of all three "races," as defined by the U.S. Bureau of the Census (2001).

Membership in an ethnic group provides a cultural identity and a set of prescribed values, norms, and social behaviors for an individual (Fenton, 1999; Phinney and Rotheram, 1987). Ethnic identity provides a significant framework through which the growing child views him- or herself, the world, and future opportunities. It also provides meaning to the child's subjective experiences, structure to interpersonal relationships, and form to behaviors and activities. For example, ethnicity may be a determining factor in the kind of family a child grows up in, which language he will speak first, what kind of neighborhood he lives in, what church he attends (if any), what kind of school he attends, and what role models are available.

Ethnic identity, when combined with membership in a minority race, creates a dual challenge to a child or adolescent (Phinney, 1990; Salett and Koslow, 1994). In a country where the dominant majority is Caucasian, there are many "white" ethnic groups such as Jews, Poles, Irish, and Italians (McGoldrick, Giordano, and Pearce, 1996). Members of these groups can practice their cultural customs in their homes and religious institutions, yet they can also blend into the mainstream social institutions such as schools, businesses, professions, and government. However, ethnic minority *Defined* groups are identifiable by their racial or linguistic differences. Minority groups have been defined as "those groups that have unequal access to power, that are considered in some way unworthy of sharing power equally, and that are stigmatized in terms of assumed inferior traits or characteristics" (Mindel and Habenstein,

1981, p. 8). Ethnic minority status has traditionally been associated with a more restricted range of options in education, employment, and lifestyle, as well as reduced opportunities for mobility and success in the wider society (Farley, 1997; Massey and Denton, 1993). Thus a child growing up in a minority family may be exposed to different family dynamics, different school experiences, and different community responses than a child from a white family.

Social class is another dimension that describes and defines a child's world by ascribing a specific position and value to her family's SES. The family's SES will largely determine the child's social environment, lifestyle, level of education attained, and occupational aspirations (Lynn and McGeary, 1990; Brooks-Gunn, Duncan, and Aber, 1997). For an adolescent, one's social class also influences the choice of friends, activities, and social roles. Thus membership in a social class provides a set of parameters within which the growing child and adolescent will experience a restricted range of opportunities, choices, and challenges in particular social contexts.

In American society, there is an important interrelationship between ethnicity, race, and social class; high status is associated with membership in white, Anglo-Saxon, middle-class families and low status with membership in nonwhite, ethnic minority, lower-class families (Farley, 1997; Hacker, 1992; Wilson, 1996). It follows that children and adolescents in many Asian, black, Hispanic, and Indian families are triply stigmatized in American society because they differ from the ideal norm in three major respects: (1) they are nonwhite by race (except for Hispanic-speaking whites), (2) they are non-Anglo Saxon by ethnicity, and (3) they are predominantly non-middle-class by socioeconomic status.

An Interactive Model

It is obvious that these three perspectives overlap considerably and may be conceived more parsimoniously as three interacting dimensions of the child's life experience. We propose that *ethnicity* is the overarching dimension that provides the child with a framework for perceiving and responding to the world; shapes the child's personal and social identity; establishes values, norms, and expectations for appropriate behaviors; and defines parameters for choices and opportunities for the child's social, educational, and occupational experiences. Ethnicity is a major influence on the child's socialization in the family, providing the structures through which developmental tasks are mediated (Phinney and Rotheram, 1987). Moreover, ethnicity has a significant impact on the way the child is perceived and treated in school, by peers, and in the broader community.

Further, it is important to point out that parents from different ethnic groups may use different criteria to measure independence, competence, and interpersonal skills, or they may differentially value these behaviors as relevant or irrelevant to the child's successful adaptation to the social environment (Garcia-Coll and others, 1996; Huang, 1994; Taylor, 1991). Thus their childrearing practices reflect broad diversity in the strategies and techniques employed to socialize children according to the belief system, values, and norms of their ethnic group.

de Anda (1984) describes the process of bicultural socialization through which minority parents teach their children how to function in two distinct sociocultural environments. She posits six factors that influence the outcome of this process of dual socialization: (1) the degree of overlap or commonality between the two cultures with regard to norms, values, perceptions, and beliefs; (2) the availability of cultural translators, mediators, and models; (3) the amount and type of corrective feedback provided by each culture regarding one's behaviors in the specific culture; (4) the congruence of conceptual style and problem solving of the minority individual with that of the mainstream culture; (5) the individual's degree of bilingualism; and (6) the degree of similarity in physical appearance to the mainstream culture. de Anda's model of bicultural socialization is an example of the incorporation of the developmental, ecological, and cross-cultural frameworks in conceptualizing the socialization of ethnic minority children.

Implications for Assessment

An understanding of these three overlapping perspectives offers a comprehensive framework for the clinician to assess the five major domains of the functioning of the child or adolescent: (1) the individual level of psychosocial adjustment, (2) relationships with family, (3) school adjustment and achievement, (4) relationships with peers, and (5) adaptation to the community (Guerra and Jagers, 1998; Kestenbaum and Williams, 1987; Oldham, Looney, and Blotcky, 1980; Looney and Lewis, 1983; Samuda, 1998; Sattler, 1992).

Assessment of Individual Psychosocial Adjustment

There are a number of areas in which these variations have significant implications for differences in the child's psychosocial adjustment and, by extension, implications for psychological evaluation. These areas are (1) physical appearance, affect, self-concept, and self-esteem, (2) interpersonal competence, (3) attitudes toward autonomy, (4) attitudes toward achievement, (5) management of aggression and impulse control, and (6) coping and defense mechanisms.

Physical Appearance

In evaluating the physical appearance of the minority child or adolescent, the clinician must bear in mind that low-income minority children often suffer from malnutrition, which causes stunted growth, low hemoglobin levels, and skin and hair problems (Homel and Burns, 1989; U.S. Congress, 1991). Diet can also affect their levels of energy, sleep, and elimination, so a complete physical examination may be indicated to rule out physiological causes of emotional and behavioral problems. In addition, variations from the preferred Anglo norms in height, weight, or physique can be a source of stress for minority adolescents. Even within communities of color, lighter shades of skin color and straighter hair are frequently valued, creating problems of low self-esteem and negative self-concepts for darker-skinned adolescents with curly hair (Miller and Rotheram-Borus, 1994; Robinson and Ward, 1995; Spencer and Dornbusch, 1990).

Affect

The affective expression in children is influenced by cultural norms so that some children appear to be more animated and others more reserved. Culturally appropriate norms of expressing affect should not be confused with lack of affect or depressed affect (Canino and Spurlock, 1994; Lum, 1992). Similarly, direct eye contact between children and adults is discouraged in some ethnic groups; the clinician should not interpret this as a sign of disrespect or evasiveness.

Self-Concept and Self-Esteem

Groups vary in the value they attach to particular characteristics and abilities, which become sources of self-concept and self-esteem for the child and adolescent (Spencer and Dornbusch, 1990; Rotheram-Borus, Dopkins, Sabate, and Lightfoot, 1996). It is important for the clinician to know the differential value placed on specific attributes within each ethnic group in order to evaluate the minority youth's criteria for self-evaluation.

Interpersonal Competence

Ethnic groups also vary in the values attached to certain kinds of interpersonal skills (Phinney and Rotheram, 1987). Behaviors that may be highly valued and reinforced in one group may be considered inappropriate in others (Savin-Williams and Berndt, 1990). Clinicians should be familiar with the norms of interpersonal competence in each group in order to determine whether or not a child or adolescent is behaving in socially appropriate ways in the sociocultural milieu.

Attitudes Toward Autonomy

Parents of different ethnic groups place differential emphasis on early training for independence and later encouragement of adolescent autonomy (Leadbetter and Way, 1996; Phinney and Rotheram, 1987; Spencer and Dornbusch, 1990). In evaluating parental attitudes toward autonomy, the clinician must have sufficient knowledge of the ethnic values toward independence training at each level of development in order to determine whether the family has respected or violated its own cultural norms with respect to the development of autonomy, whether the family's norms are in serious conflict with the norms of the child's school or community environment, and whether the degree of dependence or autonomy is adaptive in terms of the youth's overall life situation.

Attitudes Toward Achievement

Cultural attitudes toward educational achievement vary widely among these ethnic groups as a function of historical traditions, philosophical systems, opportunity structures, and school-related experiences (Chavez, Oetting, and Swaim, 1994; Irvine and Irvine, 1995; Fordham and Ogbu, 1986; Gilmore, 1985). The groups that have been cut off from their original cultures through slavery and forced relocation have been divorced from a meaningful connection with their past cultural achievements. Subjected further to continuing barriers to social mobility, these parents frequently subscribe to the value of education but find it difficult to demonstrate the connection between education and occupational success to their children. Often the achievement motive will be expressed in other ways for these youth, and their aspirations will be shaped accordingly.

In evaluating achievement attitudes and behaviors in minority youth, the clinician should not only examine traditional channels of educational achievement but should include other areas such as sports, music, and social relationships. When minority youth are referred for academic or behavioral problems in the classroom, their failure often reflects low teacher expectations, chaotic school environments, inflexible or inappropriate curricula, or inappropriate placement (Irvine and Irvine, 1995; Jones, 1988; Reed, 1988; Vega, Khoury, Zimmerman, Gil, and Warheit, 1995). The clinician should assess achievement motives, interests, aptitudes, and abilities and try to determine the most effective way to facilitate a match between the client's motives and abilities, on the one hand, and the available role models and opportunities on the other.

Management of Aggression and Impulse Control

There is great ethnic variation in the socialization practices used by families to teach children how to channel their aggression and sexual impulses (Leadbetter and Way, 1996; McGoldrick, Giordano, and Pearce, 1996; Phinney and Rotheram, 1987). Although some minority parents typically induce shame in order to teach children appropriate ways to manage their impulses, other parents prefer to induce guilt in order to achieve the same goals. Still other parents are more likely to use harsher methods of discipline to create external sanctions for inappropriate expressions of aggression and sexuality. These different approaches have implications for the development of internal controls, the ability to delay gratification, and the choice of subliminatory channels in these youth.

Coping and Defense Mechanisms

Parents from different ethnic groups employ culturally prescribed strategies to teach children how to cope with anxiety (Canino and Spurlock, 1994; Garmezy and Rutter, 1983; Glover and others, 1999; Kirmayer and Young, 1998; Leadbetter and Way, 1996; Pawliuk and others, 1996). The two basic strategies are to reinforce externalizing (acting-out) behaviors or internalizing (acting-in) behaviors as a defense against anxiety. Thus the clinician should be familiar with the cultural preference in handling anxiety, the defense mechanisms that are reinforced, and the adaptive strategies that are employed to handle stress.

An important caveat cannot be stated too frequently: the clinician should always use knowledge about a child's ethnic background as a *general* guide to psychosocial assessment but should always be mindful of the individual child's unique characteristics, situation, symptoms, defenses, and coping strategies. As the authors of Chapter Six (this volume) on Southeast Asian youth state, "Saying that culture accounts for everything is as dangerous as saying that culture plays no part in an individual's life."

Assessment of Family Relationships

Roles and functions of children in families vary according to the type of family structure, family size, family traditions, family communication patterns, and family expectations—all of which are influenced by the ethnicity and social class of the family (McGoldrick, Giordano, and Pearce, 1996; Phinney and Rotheram, 1987; Sue and Sue, 1999; Vargas and Koss-Chioino, 1992). Sex and birth order of the child frequently impose a set of norms and expectations that prescribe appropriate behaviors and attitudes for that child. Physical characteristics such as skin color, physical or mental disability, and certain personality traits may be irrelevant to the child's status in some families but highly salient in others. Socialization practices in the preschool years result in a broad spectrum of parent-child and sibling relationships in minority families (Phinney and Rotheram, 1987).

Family relationships in some ethnic groups tend to be defined in terms of age and sex role hierarchies, with a strong emphasis on filial obedience to parental authority, respect for elders, acceptance of male authority, loyalty to the extended family, and strong conformity to community norms and expectations (Garcia-Preto, 1996; Lee, 1996; Sue and Sue, 1999). Other ethnic groups are characterized by greater egalitarianism in age and sex roles, greater emphasis on shared household responsibilities, individual decision making, flexibility in marital roles, and moderate conformity to community norms and expectations (Billingsley, 1992; Sutton and Broken Nose, 1996).

In some ethnic families, children assume household chores and child care at earlier ages than is the norm among Anglo families. These roles should not be confused with the premature "parentified" role often assumed by the first-generation immigrant child, who may serve as an interpreter and mediator between parents and the dominant society (Felsman, Leong, Johnson, and Felsman, 1990; Lum, 1992). Parentified children are also found in single-parent families, where they may provide emotional support and companionship, as well as household help, to an overly stressed parent. The clinician should be able to make a distinction between children who are fulfilling supportive roles in accordance with their age and abilities and those who are acting inappropriately as substitute parents.

If family communication patterns are hierarchical, and children are not encouraged to express their opinions or to engage in free-flowing conversations, they may have problems adapting to the teacher's expectations of verbal participation in the classroom. Traditional communication patterns in some ethnic families, for example, are not wholly compatible with the demands of the American educational system, which rewards assertive behavior, verbal fluency, and competitiveness in students.

The ways in which parents use their authority and enforce discipline are reflected in the ways children respond to authority and to rule setting, which varies considerably among different ethnic groups (Phinney and Rotheram, 1987). The child who does not fit the ideal cultural familial norm may be scapegoated and identified as "the problem child" or "the difficult child" and may be perceived as the rule breaker and the norm violator. The role of the foster child or adopted child in a family may be the source of envy, anger, or ambivalence, thus exacerbating sibling rivalry and creating intrafamilial tension and disequilibrium (Popple and Leighninger, 1993). If parents displace their frustrations on the child as an interloper into the family system, the dynamics could precipitate psychological abandonment, physical and sexual abuse, or emotional neglect (Brassard, Hart, and Ziedenberg, 1987). A child subjected to any of these responses could be potentially at risk for disequilibrium and re-experiencing the trauma associated with earlier episodes of rejection and abuse in his or her previous family or foster homes.

School Adjustment and Achievement

As the second major institution of socialization for latency-aged children and adolescents in American society, school is an important arena for the evaluation of a child's adjustment (Hamburg, 1992; Irvine and Irvine, 1995). There are four broad areas in which the child's school adjustment should be measured: (1) psychological adjustment to the school setting, (2) behavioral adjustment in the school setting, (3) academic achievement, and (4) relationships with peers.

Psychological Adjustment lack of fit home | school

Minority children, particularly those from low-income families, often experience difficulties making the transition from the home to the school environment. A number of factors may account for this difficult transition: parental lack of education, negative parental attitudes or experiences with the school system, lack of familiarity with the norms and expectations of the classroom, language problems, and social-class differences (Abrams and Gibbs, 2002; Garcia, 1995). The lack of fit between the child's background or home culture and the school environment has been associated with poorer school performance (Bankston and Caldas, 1998; Comer, 1984; National Coalition of Advocates for Students, 1988) and an uneasy, sometimes disruptive parent-school relationship (Huang and Gibbs, 1992). Furthermore, for the latency-aged child, this lack of congruence may be reflected in separation anxiety, school phobia, somatic symptoms, sleeping and eating problems, enuresis, and depression.

In adolescents, school phobia or truancy may actually represent fear of a violent or chaotic school environment or fear of social rejection due to some cultural, racial, or economic difference from the majority of the student body. For many minority adolescents, the transition from elementary school to the middle school or junior high school is often stressful because they leave a neighborhood school where they form a majority of the students for a larger school where they may become a numerical minority— a process that is repeated in the transition from junior high to high school (Comer, 1988; Hamburg, 1992; National Center for Educational Statistics, 1996). The stress of being a minority adolescent in a dissonant social context has been discussed by Rosenberg (1979), who points out the potential negative effects of this situation on the self-concept and self-esteem of these teenagers. Such a transition also typically requires the adolescent to become accustomed to a new set of criteria for evaluating academic competence, social skills, and extracurricular abilities. These new standards of evaluation can create considerable anxiety and depression for minority students who have previously excelled in their own neighborhood schools but must adjust to new criteria that place them at an initial disadvantage (Darling-Hammond, 1998). School psychologists and social workers who evaluate students for placement in special classes need to take these various factors into account in order to avoid the misidentification of minority students, who are already overrepresented in classes for students with emotional problems and learning disabilities (Jones, 1988; Reed, 1988).

Immigrant and refugee youth from non-English-speaking homes face particularly daunting challenges of learning English as a second language while struggling to master the academic content of unfamiliar subjects. Advocates of "English only" as the language of instruction, fueled by the anti-immigration backlash of the 1990s, have succeeded in dismantling bilingual education programs in several states (Galindo, 1997; Gibbs and Bankhead, 2001; Tatlovich, 1997). Unfortunately, English immersion programs are not appropriate for many students classified as "limited English proficient" (LEP), thus creating a cycle of early academic difficulties, cultural alienation, and increased numbers of school dropouts (August and Hakuta, 1998; Garcia and Gonzalez, 1995).

Behavioral Adjustment

In the area of behavioral adjustment, minority children and adolescents are also overrepresented in special education classes for children with behavior problems (Jones, 1988; Reed, 1988). Although some children are socialized to internalize their anxiety through symptoms of depression, withdrawal, somatization, and phobic behaviors, others are reinforced for externalizing their anxiety through fighting, acting out, and engaging in delinquent behaviors. The incidence of school violence, delinquency, substance abuse, and gang activity is much higher in inner-city schools than in middle-class urban and suburban schools (Dryfoos, 1990; Fitzpatrick and Boldizar, 1993; Schubiner, Scott, and Tzelepis, 1993). Consequently, as more students display disruptive behaviors in the school setting, there are more disciplinary problems for teachers and fewer mental health professionals to handle the referrals. When these students are referred for problem behaviors, the clinician should conduct a careful assessment of their home situation (some do not have adequate sleeping or study facilities), their nutrition (some are hyperactive or lethargic due to poor diets), their family situation (some are victims of abuse, family violence, or absent parents), and their health status (some have undetected vision, hearing, or other physical problems) (Hamburg, 1992; U.S. Congress, 1991; U.S. Department of Health and Human Services, 2001). A careful evaluation of these students will reveal that behavior problems are usually symptomatic of more serious underlying psychological and physical problems that are often chronic and have been neglected because of poverty, lack of access to health care, and, in some cases, parental unawareness and neglect.

Academic Achievement

In the area of academic achievement, low-income minority children and adolescents have generally not performed as well on standardized achievement tests, in Carnegie units earned toward high school graduation, or in grade-point averages (Quality Education for Minorities Project, 1990; Reed, 1988). As a result, these minority students have had particular difficulties in achieving parity with the non-Hispanic white students in the public school system. Although this book does not tackle the controversy over the use of intelligence tests with minority students, other researchers have discussed the problems of norms and the inappropriate use of these tests with children from culturally different backgrounds (Hakuta and Garcia, 1989; Jones, 1988; Samuda, 1998). Through these test results, many minority students are mislabeled as educationally handicapped, placed in remedial classrooms, and channeled into educational programs that are neither challenging nor useful (Comer, 1988; Darling-Hammond, 1998). This mislabeling and misplacement probably contributes to the feelings of alienation among many minority students, who have higher dropout rates and higher rates of expulsions and suspensions than white students (Reed, 1988). This phenomenon is also applicable to students in ESL (English as a second language) classes, for whom these intelligence and placement tests are entirely inappropriate, yet educators use the results to place them in classes for slow learners or nonacademic tracks (August and Hakuta, 1998; Garcia and Gonzalez, 1995).

When clinicians assess the academic performance of minority youth, they should pay careful attention to the youths' verbal skills (they may have much greater fluency in their native language), to their attitudes toward school (they may feel stigmatized by placement in a special education class), to their motivation for learning (they may see no relationship between school and the real world), to their study habits (they may not have a safe and quiet place to study at home or a schedule for studying), and to their level of family support (their parents may not be able or willing to assist and reinforce efforts to succeed academically) (Comer, 1984; Irvine and Irvine, 1995; Kozol, 1991). Because poor academic achievement is more often a consequence of cultural, social, and environmental factors than lack of ability, a sensitive clinician can identify the factors that impede the performance of minority students. An educational team then can develop an intervention plan to improve students' academic skills.

Finally, the child's relationship with peers in the school setting should be evaluated because it is easier to obtain independent ratings of peer interactions in the school than in the community setting (Bankston and Caldas, 1998; Way, 1996). The clinician should assess the child's ability to form friendships, to display empathy, to engage in cooperative and competitive activities in the classroom and in extracurricular activities, to manage aggressive and sexual impulses, and to engage in socially appropriate same-sex and opposite-sex activities.

As minority children move into adolescence and enter schools with more heterogeneous student bodies, they are more likely to become aware of their particular ethnic or minority status and its associated degree of desirability (Phinney, 1990; Spencer and Dornbusch, 1990). Biracial and bicultural adolescents may have particular problems in joining a peer group because they do not fit into the rigid ethnic categories that define peer group membership in adolescence (Gibbs and Moskowitz-Sweet, 1991; Miller and Rotheram-Borus, 1994; Root, 1992). At this stage, it is also important to assess the formal and informal labels and identities of a peer group to which the adolescent belongs, as these labels supply valuable clues to the teen's self-perception and preferred activities. The minority teenager's choice of extracurricular activities and the level of involvement is also an important clue to self-confidence, sense of competence, and degree of comfort in relating to peers.

Peer Relationships in community

In addition to assessing a child's peer relations in the school setting, relationships with peers in the neighborhood and community should also be evaluated. Minority children and adolescents very often have two sets of peer relationships—one in the school setting and another in the community setting (Boykin and Ellison, 1995; Spencer and Dornbusch, 1990; Williams and others, 2002). Members of the latter group are more likely to form their own ethnic group in their immediate neighborhood, church, or community activities, for example, by celebrating Black History Week, the Chinese New Year, or Cinco de Mayo. Thus the usual question about "having a best friend" should include school and neighborhood to determine the primary locus of the child's peer affiliations. Minority children who are social isolates at a predominantly white school may be sociometric stars in their segregated neighborhood. Moreover, adolescents are increasingly more mobile and can select their friends from a wider geographical area, so inquiries should be made about the scope of their social networks. For teens referred for problem behaviors, substance abuse, and delinquency, the clinician should determine whether these behaviors represent individual maladaptation or whether they represent conformity to the peer group culture that exists in many inner-city ghettos and barrios. The choice of intervention for a teenager who is a socialized delinquent will be very different from that for one who is an antisocial delinquent (Thompson, 1990). Assessment of peer relationships should focus on the social skills of the adolescent, as defined by the ethnic group, that is, whatever criteria are used to measure social competence, group acceptance, and group leadership (Boykin and Ellison, 1995; Looney and Lewis, 1983).

In the area of peer relationships, sexual relationships in adolescence are an important area of assessment (Tolman, 1996). The clinician should inquire about dating practices, sexual orientation, involvement in sexual activity, attitudes toward contraception, knowledge about sexually transmitted diseases, and issues of intraracial versus interracial dating, particularly for biracial and bicultural youth.

Adaptation to the Community

The latency-aged child's experiences in the community usually revolve around church activities, youth groups, and language schools (Furstenberg and Hughes, 1995; Sanders, 1998). Involvement in these activities should be assessed to obtain a complete picture of the child's areas of interest, mobility in the community, sense of security about nonfamily activities, behavioral adjustment, and quality of relationships with other adult authority figures. Minority children are sometimes token members of community groups, including children's drama, dance, and music groups, which can be prestigious for their parents but stressful for them. They are sometimes scapegoated by other children, who subtly reward them for assuming the role of the group's clown, rebel, or victim. Alternately, a meaningful community activity can provide the minority child with a sense of competence and special skills that may not be available in the school or home situation. It is important for the clinician to determine the role and function of the child in community activities, which can either enhance development or can siphon off energy that could be used more productively in the regular school setting.

The adolescent's role in the community expands to include the possibility of work, organized sports and arts activities, and volunteer activities (Feldman and Elliott, 1990). If a teenager has a part-time or full-time job, it may be essential to assess job performance, interaction with employers and coworkers, and management of money. Minority adolescents often have problems finding jobs due to discrimination and other barriers, which has an impact on their sense of self-worth and on their ability to develop good work habits (Sum, Harrington, and Goedicke, 1987; Larson, 1988; U.S. Congress, 1991). If the adolescent is involved in any major activity such as an athletic team, a drama group, a rock band, or a volunteer group, the clinician should assess the impact of this activity on self-concept, sense of competence, and educational and occupational aspirations. The clinician should also determine whether this involvement has created any family conflicts, affected academic performance, or contributed to any dysfunctional behavior such as delinquency or drug abuse.

Finally, political, economic, and social policies in the wider society have increasingly affected the SES, life options, and general well-being of youth and families of color (Jaynes and Williams, 1989; Farley and Allen, 1989; Massey and Denton, 1993; Torrey-Purta, 1990). Government policies such as reforming welfare, limiting affirmative action, and instituting harsher penalties for juvenile offenders have diminished the educational and occupational opportunities for these youth, endangered their health and welfare, and threatened their social mobility in American society (Gibbs and Bankhead, 2001; Perea, 1997; Preston, Cain, and Bass, 1998; Orfield and Ashkinaze, 1991). Moreover, the current proposal to raise educational standards through standardized assessment tests, the failure of the nation's health system to solve the disparities in health care, and the persistent inequities in the juvenile justice system are all examples of macroenvironmental policies and practices that will potentially have harmful effects and further marginalize many minority youth.

Implications for Treatment

The distinction between assessment and treatment is often artificial because many clinicians believe that treatment begins with the first contact with the client. For the sake of this discussion, the assessment process is separated from treatment on the assumption that some children and adolescents will not be referred for psychological treatment per se but may be offered alternative options such as medication or environmental modification of a family, school, or peer system.

Because a number of studies have shown that minority clients have higher dropout rates than whites in the initial stages of treatment, clinicians should be particularly alert to the issues of involving minority children and youth in the treatment process after an initial diagnostic assessment and treatment recommendation has been completed (Sue and others, 1991). Clinicians who adopt the multidimensional conceptual framework outlined earlier will be more effective in selecting and implementing appropriate interventions for minority youth with psychological and behavioral problems. If these youth are referred for psychological treatment, we propose that certain issues must be addressed, irrespective of the therapeutic theoretical framework or the treatment modality (for example, individual, group, or family treatment). These issues, though common to all therapeutic encounters, take on special significance in the treatment of children of color, and they are discussed in depth in the chapters that follow. A brief summary highlights the issues that are salient to the culturally sensitive treatment of these youth.

Entry to Treatment

The initial task of the clinician is to relieve the child's anxiety and fears about treatment, particularly for minority youth who are less likely than white youth to have had experience with and knowledge about therapy. They may have entered treatment with negative attitudes about the helping professions, based on their families' previous experiences with the health and social welfare bureaucracy. Moreover, they may be concerned about being stigmatized by their families, teachers, and peers as "crazy," as formal mental health treatment is still a source of shame and embarrassment for many minority families (Canino and Spurlock, 1994; Lum, 1992; Sue and Sue, 1999).

In their initial contacts with these clients, clinicians have found several strategies to be effective. First, some minority youth respond favorably to a more informal, friendly style wherein the clinician chats with them to put them at ease. Called "*personalismo*" by the Hispanics and "interpersonal competence" by others, this approach defuses anxiety and establishes initial rapport with the client (Gibbs, 1985; Ramirez, 1998). Other youth, however, may prefer a more formal style of authority. Second, the traditional role relationships determined by sex and age should be respected if a child is initially interviewed with the family; this is a signal to the family that the clinician understands and respects their cultural norms, even if the family does not actually conform to those norms. Third, clinicians should offer a brief explanation of therapy, its similarity to familiar roles of healers in the culture (for example, *curandero,* or medicine man), and the expectation that it will bring some symptom relief to the client (Acosta, Yamamoto, and Evans, 1982).

Establishing a Relationship

Having overcome the initial barriers to treatment, the clinician faces the next challenge of establishing a therapeutic alliance with the minority youth. Major issues in the development of this relationship are establishing trust, facilitating open communication, and negotiating boundaries (Vargas and Koss-Chioino, 1992). Trust is a central issue in the treatment of minority clients, who have often been misperceived, mislabeled, and mistreated by other helping professionals. A certain degree of "cultural paranoia" is frequently expressed by these clients, who initially behave with suspicion and skepticism in clinical encounters (Gibbs, 1985; Ridley, 1984). Clinicians should consciously communicate warmth and acceptance of these clients, who may be expecting a distancing and superior attitude.

In order to facilitate open communication of information and feelings, the clinician should be willing to share some limited personal information. Minority clients vary in their degree of self-disclosure, but generally they are not as comfortable as Anglo clients in discussing their inner feelings and the intimate details of their lives. By respecting their pace of discussing culturally sensitive topics, the clinician will gradually build rapport and increase the clients' level of self-disclosure over the course of treatment.

As the treatment relationship develops, it will be important for the clinician to negotiate boundaries within which the treatment will occur. These boundaries are an extension of the treatment contract, but they focus more specifically on the client's expectations of the therapist. Because many of these clients are unfamiliar with the therapeutic process, as well as the relationship, it is important for clinicians to emphasize confidentiality, to define the relationship in business terms rather than social terms, and to structure sessions with flexible but clear guidelines. Negotiating boundaries in the treatment of minority youth and their families is a process of mutual accommodation between the clinical concerns of the therapist and the cultural norms of the clients.

Summary and Conclusion

This chapter has presented an overview of the issues in the assessment and treatment of minority children and adolescents from four major ethnic groups and one emerging group. Throughout this book, the mental health issues are viewed from three primary conceptual perspectives: developmental, ecological, and cross-cultural. Each contributor employs these perspectives with varying levels of emphasis, but all are committed to a person-in-environment approach to these issues. This multidimensional conceptual framework allows each author to analyze the interaction of sociocultural factors, developmental factors, and environmental forces on the psychosocial development of children and adolescents in their specific ethnic groups.

Children of color are described as a population at risk for behavioral and psychological problems because of their minority status, their often low SES, and their limited access to health and mental health services. Yet in spite of their greater vulnerability to problematic outcomes, the majority adapt successfully to their environments and grow up to function effectively as adults. Obviously, many of these children enjoy protective factors that provide effective buffers against the stresses of poverty, prejudice, and social isolation. These protective factors may include extended families, supportive kin and social networks, strong religious beliefs, and traditional sources of help or healing.

The remainder of this book is organized to reflect the experiences of minority groups who have followed different historical pathways in American society. Nine topical chapters follow, each focusing on a particular minority group or emerging population. Authors of each chapter are psychologists or mental health practitioners who have both personal and professional knowledge and extensive clinical experience with the ethnic groups they describe.

The content of these chapters adheres to a similar format: demographic data, epidemiological data regarding incidence of psychological and behavioral disorders (where available), historical information about entry or migration to the United States, significant issues of family structure and functioning, sociocultural issues in assessment (attitudes, values, and beliefs about mental health and illness; symptom patterns; help-seeking; and utilization patterns), and implications for effective intervention strategies and treatment techniques.

Brief case vignettes are presented by each author to illustrate the appropriate role of sociocultural factors in the assessment of symptomatology, defensive strategies, and coping behaviors in emotionally troubled minority children and adolescents, for the purpose of developing specific treatment techniques and alternative intervention strategies.

The remaining chapters are divided into five sections, each preceded with a brief introductory summary. In Part One, Chapter One focuses on American Indian youth, the indigenous population of Native Americans. In Part Two, African American youth and those of mixed racial or ethnic heritage are discussed to reflect their common experiences as members of minority groups who have experienced discrimination and unequal access to community resources.

The Asian American population groups are discussed in Part Three. Chinese American and Filipino American youth, described in Chapters Four and Five, respectively, trace their descent from immigrants categorized by Mindel and Habenstein (1981) as "early arriving ethnic minorities," who first emigrated to the United States before 1900. In Chapter Six, the adjustment challenges of Southeast Asian refugee and immigrant youth, more recent arrivals since the end of the Vietnam War in 1975, are discussed.

Part Four focuses on three Hispanic-Latino population groups. In Chapter Seven, Central American youth are presented as the most recent Hispanic population to arrive, some as refugees, others as immigrants, but all seeking a better future. Mexican American youth, many of whom are vulnerable to exploitation and marginalization as undocumented, are discussed in Chapter Eight. Puerto Rican youth, categorized by Mindel and Habenstein (1981) as belonging to a "recent and continuing ethnic minority" with divided loyalties between the U.S. mainland and their island common-wealth, are discussed in Chapter Nine.

Part Five encompasses the two final chapters, which deal with the current status of and future challenges in providing mental health services to ethnic minority children and adolescents. Chapter Ten examines the experiences and outcomes of children of color in various child-serving systems, such as child welfare and juvenile justice, and presents a model of culturally competent assessment and intervention for these service providers.

Chapter Eleven, the concluding chapter, highlights the challenges of providing culturally responsive mental health care to ethnically and culturally diverse youth and their families. Further, this chapter presents a series of policy, research, and training recommendations. Finally, the authors provide an ecological model of assessment and intervention to assist mental health practitioners in their work with these youth of color and their families.

At this point, we do not have enough valid and reliable data about some ethnic groups to constitute the final word on their mental health status problems or needs (U.S. Department of Health and Human Services, 2001). Yet as the minority populations continue to increase, we strongly feel that we cannot wait for more years of research to provide this information in order to address their mental health needs. We believe that this book represents an initial step in providing mental health practitioners and educators with a framework for understanding the impact of ethnicity and SES on the psychosocial development and adaptation of minority youth. Although we hope that clinicians will gain a better understanding of these youth and their families, we must caution them that they will not become experts in minority mental health simply by reading this book. Ideally, clinicians will become more knowledgeable about these particular ethnic groups and more sensitive to similarities and differences that exist among and between all human groups.

Children of color are rapidly increasing in American society, yet they remain literally and figuratively misunderstood, mislabeled, and mistreated. This book is a modest effort to increase the understanding of their needs, to improve the assessment of their problems, and to develop more effective methods of intervention and treatment for their behavioral and psychological disorders.

References

Abrams, L., and Gibbs, J. T. "Disrupting the Logic of Home-School Relations: Parent Involvement Strategies and Practices of Inclusion and Exclusion." *Urban Education,* 2002, *37*(3), 384–407.

Acosta, F. X., Yamamoto, J., and Evans, L. A. *Effective Psychotherapy for Low-Income and Minority Patients.* New York: Plenum, 1982.

American Public Welfare Association. *One Child in Four.* New York: American Public Welfare Association, 1986.

Aronowitz, M. "Adjustment of Immigrant Children as a Function of Parental Attitudes to Change." *International Migration Review,* 1992, *26,* 86–110.

August, D., and Hakuta, K. (eds.). *Educating Language-Minority Children.* Washington, D.C.: National Academy Press, 1998.

Bankston, C. L., and Caldas, S. J. "Family Structure, Schoolmates, and Racial Inequalities in School Achievement." *Journal of Marriage and the Family,* 1998, *60*(3), 715–723.

Baptiste, D. A., Jr. "The Treatment of Adolescents and Their Families in Cultural Transition: Issues and Recommendations." *Contemporary Family Therapy,* 1990, *12,* 3–22.

Billingsley, A. *Climbing Jacob's Ladder: The Enduring Legacy of African-American Families.* New York: Simon & Schuster, 1992.

Boykin, A. W., and Ellison, C. M. "The Multiple Ecologies of Black Youth Socialization: An Afrographic Analysis." In R. L. Taylor (ed.), *African-American Youth: Their Social and Economic Status in the United States.* New York: Praeger, 1995.

Brassard, M., Hart, S., and Ziedenberg, J. *Psychological Mistreatment of Children and Youth.* Elmsford, N.Y.: Pergamon Press, 1987.

Bronfenbrenner, U. *The Ecology of Human Development: Experiments by Nature and Design.* Cambridge, Mass.: Harvard University Press, 1979.

Brooks-Gunn, J., Duncan, G., and Aber, L. (eds.). *Neighborhood Poverty* (vol. 1). New York: Russell Sage Foundation, 1997.

Canino, I. A., and Spurlock, J. *Culturally Diverse Children and Adolescents: Assessment, Diagnosis and Treatment.* New York: Guilford Press, 1994.

Cervantes, J. M., and Ramirez, O. "Spirituality and Family Dynamics in Psychotherapy with Latino Children." In L. A. Vargas and J. D. Koss-Chioino (eds.), *Working with Culture: Psychotherapeutic Interventions with Ethnic Minority Children and Adolescents.* San Francisco: Jossey-Bass, 1992.

Chavez, E. L., Oetting, E. R., and Swaim, R. C. "Dropout and Delinquency: Mexican American and Caucasian Non-Hispanic Youth." *Journal of Clinical Child Psychology,* 1994, *23,* 47–55.

Chiu, M. L., Feldman, S., and Rosenthal, D. A. "The Influence of Immigration on Parental Behavior and Adolescent Distress in Chinese Families Residing in Two Western Nations." *Journal of Research on Adolescence,* 1992, *2,* 205–237.

Comer, J. P. "Home-School Relationships and How They Affect the Academic Success of Children." *Education and Urban Society,* 1984, *16*(3), 323–337.

Comer, J. P. "Educating Poor Minority Children." *Scientific American,* 1988, *259*(5), 42–48.

Cross, W. E. *Shades of Black: Diversity in African-American Identity.* Philadelphia: Temple University Press, 1991.

Csordas, T. J. "Ritual Healing and the Politics of Identity in Contemporary Navajo Society." *American Ethnologist,* 1999, *26,* 2–23.

Darling-Hammond, L. "New Standards, Old Inequalities: The Current Challenge for African-American Education." In L. A. Daniels (ed.), *The State of Black America.* New York: National Urban League, 1998.

de Anda, D. "Bicultural Socialization: Factors Affecting the Minority Experience." *Social Work,* 1984, *29,* 101–107.

Dryfoos, J. *Adolescents at Risk: Prevalence and Prevention.* New York: Oxford University Press, 1990.

Edelman, M. W. *Families in Peril: An Agenda for Social Change.* Cambridge, Mass.: Harvard University Press, 1987.

Erikson, E. H. "Identity and the Life Cycle." *Psychological Issues,* 1959, *1*(entire issue 1).

Evans, B., and Lee, B. K. "Culture and Child Psychopathology." In S. S. Kazarian and D. R. Evans (eds.), *Cultural Clinical Psychology: Theory, Research and Practice.* New York: Oxford University Press, 1998.

Farley, R. "Racial Trends and Differences in the United States 30 Years after the Civil Rights Decade." *Social Science Research,* 1997, *26,* 235–262.

Farley, R., and Allen, W. R. *The Color Line and the Quality of Life in America.* New York: Oxford University Press, 1989.

Feldman, S. S., and Elliott, G. R. (eds.). *At the Threshold: The Developing Adolescent.* Cambridge, Mass.: Harvard University Press, 1990.

Felsman, J. K., Leong, F. T., Johnson, M. C., and Felsman, I. C. "Estimates of Psychological Distress Among Vietnamese Refugees: Adolescents, Unaccompanied Minors, and Young Adults." *Social Science and Medicine,* 1990, *31,* 1251–1256.

Fenton, S. *Ethnicity, Class, and Culture.* Lanham, Md.: Rowman & Littlefield, 1999.

Fitzpatrick, K. M., and Boldizar, J. P. "The Prevalence and Consequences of Exposure to Violence Among African-American Youth." *Journal of the American Academy of Child and Adolescent Psychiatry,* 1993, *32,* 424–430.

Fordham, S., and Ogbu, J. "Black Student's School Success: Coping with the Burden of Acting White." *Urban Review,* 1986, *18*(3), 176–206.

Furstenberg, F. F. Jr., and Hughes, M. E. "Social Capital and Successful Development of At-Risk Youth." *Journal of Marriage and the Family,* 1995, *57,* 588–592.

Galindo, R. "Language Wars: The Ideological Dimensions of the Debates on Bilingual Education." *Bilingual Research Journal,* 1997, *21,* 163–201.

Garcia, E. "Language, Culture and Education." In L. Darling-Hammond (ed.), *Review of Research in Education.* Washington, D.C.: American Education Research Association, 1995.

Garcia, E., and Gonzalez, R. "Issues in Systemic Reform for Culturally and Linguistically Diverse Students." *Teachers College Record,* 1995, *96*(3), 418–431.

Garcia-Coll, C., and others. "An Integrative Model for the Study of Developmental Competencies in Minority Children." *Child Development,* 1996, *67,* 1891–1914.

Garcia-Preto, N. "Latino Families: An Overview." In M. McGoldrick, J. Giordano, and J. K. Pearce (eds.), *Ethnicity and Family Therapy.* New York: Guilford Press, 1996.

Garmezy, N., and Rutter, M. (eds.). *Stress, Coping and Development in Children.* New York: McGraw-Hill, 1983.

Gibbs, J. T. "Treatment Relationships with Black Clients: Interpersonal vs. Instrumental Strategies." In C. Germain (ed.), *Advances in Clinical Social Work Practice.* Silver Spring, Md.: National Association of Social Workers, 1985.

Gibbs, J. T., and Bankhead, T. *Preserving Privilege: California Politics, Propositions, and People of Color.* New York: Praeger, 2001.

Gibbs, J. T., and Huang, L. N. *Children of Color: Psychological Interventions with Minority Youth.* San Francisco: Jossey-Bass, 1989.

Gibbs, J. T., and Moskowitz-Sweet, G. "Clinical and Cultural Issues in the Treatment of Biracial and Bicultural Adolescents." *Families in Society,* 1991, *72*(10), 579–592.

Gilmore, P. "'Gimme Room': School Resistance, Attitudes, and Access to Literacy." *Journal of Education,* 1985, *167,* 111–128.

Glover, S. H., and others. "Anxiety Symptomatology in Mexican American Adolescents." *Journal of Child and Family Studies,* 1999, *8,* 47–57.

Gong-Guy, E., Craveks, R., and Paterson, T. "Clinical Issues in Mental Health Service Delivery to Refugees." *American Psychologist,* 1991, *46*(6), 642–648.

Green, J. W. *Cultural Awareness in the Human Services: A Multi-ethnic Approach.* (3rd ed.) Boston: Allyn & Bacon, 1999.

Guerra, N. G., and Jagers, R. "The Importance of Culture in the Assessment of Children and Youth." In V. C. McLoyd and L. Steinberg (eds.), *Studying Minority Adolescents: Conceptual, Methodological, and Theoretical Issues* (pp. 167–181). Mahwah, N.J.: Lawrence Erlbaum Associates, 1998.

Gustavsson, N. S., and Balgopal, P. R. "Violence and Minority Youth: An Ecological Perspective." In A. R. Stiffman and L. E. Davis (eds.), *Ethnic Issues in Adolescent Mental Health.* Thousand Oaks, Calif.: Sage, 1990.

Gutierrez, D. (ed.). *Between Two Worlds: Mexican Immigrants in the United States.* Wilmington, Del.: Scholarly Resources, 1996.

Hacker, A. *Two Nations: Black and White, Separate, Hostile, Unequal.* New York: Scribner, 1992.

Hakuta, K., and Garcia, E. "Bilingualism and Education." *American Psychologist,* 1989, *44*(2), 374–379.

Hamburg, D. A. *Today's Children: Creating a Future for a Generation in Crisis.* New York: Random House, 1992.

Homel, R., and Burns, A. "Environmental Quality and Well-Being in Children." *Social Indicators Research,* 1989, *21,* 133–158.

Huang, L. N. "An Integrative Approach to Clinical Assessment and Intervention with Asian American Adolescents." *Journal of Clinical Child Psychology,* 1994, *23,* 21–31.

Huang, L. N., and Gibbs, J. T. "Partners or Adversaries: Home-School Collaboration Across Culture, Race, and Ethnicity." In S. Christenson and J. Conoley (eds.), *Home-School Collaboration: Enhancing Children's Academic and Social Competence.* Silver Spring, Md.: National Association of School Psychologists, 1992.

Irvine, J. J., and Irvine, R. W. "Black Youth in School: Individual Achievement and Institutional/Cultural Perspectives." In R. L. Taylor (ed.), *African-American Youth: Their Social and Economic Status in the United States.* New York: Praeger, 1995.

Isaacs, M. R., and Benjamin, M. P. *Towards a Culturally Competent System of Care,* Vol. 2. Washington, D.C.: Georgetown University Child Development Center, 1991.

Jaynes, G. D., and Williams, R. M. *A Common Destiny: Blacks and American Society.* Washington, D.C.: National Academy Press, 1989.

Jones, R. (ed.). *Psychoeducational Assessment of Minority Group Children: A Casebook.* Berkeley, Calif.: Cobb & Henry, 1988.

Kazarian, S. S., and Evans, D. R. "Cultural Clinical Psychology." In S. S. Kazarian and D. R. Evans (eds.), *Cultural Clinical Psychology.* New York: Oxford University Press, 1998.

Kestenbaum, C., and Williams, D. (eds.). *Clinical Assessments of Children and Adolescents.* New York: New York University Press, 1987.

Kirmayer, L. J., and Young, A. "Culture and Somatization: Clinical, Epidemiological, and Ethnographic Perspectives." *Psychosomatic Medicine,* 1998, *60,* 420–430.

Kleinman, A. *Patients and Healers in the Context of Culture: An Exploration of the Borderland Between Anthropology, Medicine, and Psychiatry.* Berkeley, Calif.: University of California Press, 1980.

Kozol, J. *Savage Inequalities: Children in America's Schools.* New York: Crown Books, 1991.

Larson, T. E. "Employment and Unemployment of Young Black Men." In J. T. Gibbs (ed.), *Young, Black, and Male in America: An Endangered Species.* Dover, Mass.: Auburn House, 1988.

Leadbetter, B. J., and Way, N. (eds.). *Urban Girls: Resisting Stereotypes, Creating Identities.* New York: New York University Press, 1996.

Lee, E. "Cultural Factors in Working with Southeast Asian Refugee Adolescents." *Journal of Adolescence,* 1988, *11,* 167–179.

Lee, E. "Asian American Families: An Overview." In M. McGoldrick, J. Giordano, and J. K. Pearce (eds.), *Ethnicity and Family Therapy.* (2nd ed.) New York: Guilford Press, 1996.

Looney, J. G., and Lewis, J. M. "Competent Adolescents from Different Socioeconomic and Ethnic Contexts." *Adolescent Psychiatry,* 1983, *11,* 64–74.

Lum, D. *Social Work Practice and People of Color.* (2nd ed.) Pacific Grove, Calif.: Brooks/Cole, 1992.

Lynn, L. E., and McGeary, M. (eds.). *Inner-City Poverty in the United States.* Washington, D.C.: National Academy Press, 1990.

Massey, D. S., and Denton, N. A. *American Apartheid: Segregation and the Making of the Underclass.* Boston: Harvard University Press, 1993.

McGoldrick, M., Giordano, J., and Pearce, J. K. (eds.). *Ethnicity and Family Therapy.* (2nd ed.) New York: Guilford Press, 1996.

McLoyd, V. C. (ed.). "Minority Child Development: The Special Issue." *Child Development,* 1990, *61,* 263–266.

McLoyd, V. C., and Steinberg, L. (eds.). *Studying Minority Adolescents: Conceptual, Methodological, and Theoretical Issues.* Mahwah, N.J.: Lawrence Erlbaum Associates, 1998.

Mead, G. H. *Mind, Self, and Society.* Chicago: University of Chicago Press, 1934.

Meyers, H. F. "Urban Stress and the Mental Health of Afro-American Youth: An Epidemiologic and Conceptual Update." In R. L. Jones (ed.), *Black Adolescents* (pp. 123–152). Berkeley, Calif.: Cobb and Henry, 1989.

Miller, R. L., and Rotheram-Borus, M. J. "Growing Up Biracial in the United States." In E. P. Salett and D. R. Koslow (eds.), *Race, Ethnicity and Self.* Washington, D.C.: National Multicultural Institute, 1994.

Mindel, C. H., and Habenstein, R. W. (eds.). *Ethnic Families in America: Patterns and Variations.* (2nd ed.) New York: Elsevier, 1981.

National Center for Educational Statistics. *Educational Statistics Digest.* Washingon, D.C.: U.S. Department of Education, 1996.

National Center for Educational Statistics. *Educational Statistics Digest.* Washingon, D.C.: U.S. Department of Education, 2001.

National Coalition of Advocates for Students. *New Voices: Immigrant Students in the U.S. Public Schools.* Boston: National Coalition of Advocates for Students, 1988.

Oldham, D., Looney, J. G., and Blotcky, M. "Clinical Assessment of Symptoms in Adolescents." *American Journal of Orthopsychiatry,* 1980, *50,* 697–703.

Orfield, G., and Ashkinaze, C. *The Closing Door: Conservative Policy and Black Opportunity.* Chicago: University of Chicago Press, 1991.

Ozawa, M. "Nonwhites and the Demographic Imperative in Social Welfare Spending." *Social Work,* 1986, *31,* 440–446.

Paniagua, F. *Diagnosis in a Multicultural Context: A Casebook for Mental Health Professionals.* Thousand Oaks, Calif.: Sage, 2001.

Pawliuk, N., and others. "Acculturation Style and Psychological Functioning in Children of Immigrants." *American Journal of Orthopsychiatry,* 1996, *66,* 111–121.

Perea, J. F. (ed.). *Immigrants Out: The New Nativism and the Anti-Immigration Impulse in the United States.* New York: New York University Press, 1997.

Phinney, J. S., "Ethnic Identity in Adolescents and Adults: Review of Research." *Psychological Bulletin,* 1990, *108,* 499–514.

Phinney, J. S., and Rotheram, M. J. *Children's Ethnic Socialization: Pluralism and Development.* Thousand Oaks, Calif.: Sage, 1987.

Popple, P. R., and Leighninger, L. *Social Work, Social Welfare, and American Society.* Boston: Allyn and Bacon, 1993.

Powell, G. J. "Self-Concepts Among Afro-American Students in Racially Isolated Minority Schools: Some Regional Differences." *Journal of the American Academy of Child Psychiatry,* 1985, *24,* 142–149.

Powell, G. J., Yamamoto, J., Romero, A., and Morales, A. (eds.), *The Psychosocial Development of Minority Group Children.* New York: Brunner/Mazel, 1983.

President's Commission on Mental Health. *Mental Health in America: 1978,* Vol. 1. Washington, D.C.: U.S. Government Printing Office, 1978.

Preston, M. B., Cain, B. E., and Bass, S. (eds.). *Racial and Ethnic Politics in California,* Vol. 2. Berkeley, Calif.: Institute of Governmental Studies Press, University of California, 1998.

Quality Education for Minorities Project. *Education That Works: An Action Plan for the Education of Minorities.* Cambridge: Massachusetts Institute of Technology, 1990.

Ramirez, O. "Mexican American Children and Adolescents." In J. T. Gibbs and L. N. Huang (eds.), *Children of Color: Psychological Interventions with Culturally Diverse Youth* (pp. 215–239). San Francisco: Jossey-Bass, 1998.

Reed, R. "Education and Achievement of Young Black Males." In J. T. Gibbs (ed.), *Young, Black, and Male in America: An Endangered Species.* Dover, Mass.: Auburn House, 1988.

Ridley, C. R. "Clinical Treatment of the Nondisclosing Black Client: A Therapeutic Paradox." *American Psychologist,* 1984, *39,* 1234–1244.

Robinson, T. C., and Ward, J. V. "African American Adolescents and Skin Color." *Journal of Black Psychology, 21,* 1995, 156–274.

Root, M. P. (ed.). *Racially Mixed People in America.* Thousand Oaks, Calif.: Sage, 1992.

Rosenberg, M. *Conceiving the Self.* New York: Basic Books, 1979.

Rotheram-Borus, M. J., Dopkins, S., Sabate, N., and Lightfoot, M. "Personal and Ethnic Identity, Values, and Self-Esteem Among Black and Latino Adolescent Girls." In B. J. Leadbetter and N. Way (eds.), *Urban Girls: Resisting Stereotypes, Creating Identities.* New York: New York University Press, 1996.

Rousseau, C., Drapeau, A., and Corin, E. "School Performance and Emotional Problems in Refugee Children." *American Journal of Orthopsychiatry,* 1996, *66,* 239–251.

Salett, E. P., and Koslow, D. R., *Race, Ethnicity and the Self.* Washington, D.C.: National Multicultural Institute, 1994.

Samuda, R. *Psychological Testing of American Minorities: Issues and Consequences.* (2nd ed.) New York: Dodd, Mead, 1998.

Sanders, M. G. "The Effects of School, Family, and Community Support on the Academic Achievement of African American Adolescents." *Urban Education,* 1998, *33*(3), 385–409.

Sattler, J. M. *Assessment of Children.* (4th ed.) San Diego: Jerome M. Sattler, 1992.

Savin-Williams, P. C., and Berndt, T. J. "Friendship and Peer Relations." In S. S. Feldman and G. R. Elliott (eds.), *At the Threshold: The Developing Adolescent.* Cambridge, Mass.: Harvard University Press, 1990.

Schorr, W. *Common Decency: Domestic Policies after Reagan.* New Haven, Conn.: Yale University Press, 1986.

Schubiner, H., Scott, R., and Tzelepis, A. "Exposure to Violence Among Inner-City Youth." *Journal of Adolescent Health,* 1993, *14,* 214–219.

Spencer, M. B., and Dornbusch, S. M. "Challenges in Studying Minority Youth." In S. S. Feldman and C. R. Elliott (eds.), *At the Threshold: The Developing Adolescent.* Cambridge, Mass.: Harvard University Press, 1990.

Spencer, M. B., and Markstrom-Adams, C. M. "Identity Processes among Racial and Ethnic Minority Children in America." *Child Development,* 1990, *61,* 290–310.

Sue, D. W., and Sue, D. "Barriers to Effective Cross-Cultural Counseling." *Journal of Counseling Psychology,* 1977, *24,* 420–429.

Sue, D. W., and Sue, D. *Counseling the Culturally Different: Theory and Practice.* (3rd ed.) New York: Wiley, 1999.

Sue, S., and others. "Community Mental Health Services for Ethnic Minority Groups: A Test of the Cultural Responsiveness Hypothesis." *Journal of Consulting and Clinical Psychology,* 1991, *59*(4), 533–540.

Sum, A., Harrington, P. E., and Goedicke, W. "One-Fifth of the Nation's Teenagers: Employment Problems of Poor Youth in America, 1981–1985." *Youth and Society,* 1987, *18,* 195–237.

Sutton, C. T., and Broken Nose, M. A. "American Indian Families: An Overview." In M. McGoldrick, J. Giordano, and J. K. Pearce (eds.), *Ethnicity and Family Therapy* (2nd ed.). New York: Guilford Press, 1996.

Tatlovich, R. "Official English as Nativist Backlash." In J. F. Perea (ed.), *Immigrants Out: The New Nativism and the Anti-Immigration Impulse in the United States.* New York: New York University Press, 1997.

Taylor, R. L. "Poverty and Adolescent Black Males: The Subculture of Disengagement." In P. Edelman and J. Ladner (eds.), *Adolescence and Poverty: Challenge for the 1990s* (pp. 139–162). Washington, D.C.: Center for National Policy Press, 1991.

Thompson, C. L. "In Pursuit of Affirmation: The Antisocial Inner-City Adolescent." In A. R. Stiffman and L. E. Davis (eds.), *Ethnic Issues in Adolescent Mental Health.* Thousand Oaks, Calif.: Sage, 1990.

Tolman, D. L. "Adolescent Girls' Sexuality: Debunking the Myth of the Urban Girl." In B. L. Leadbetter and N. Way (eds.), *Urban Girls: Resisting Stereotypes, Creating Identities* (pp. 255–271). New York: New York University Press, 1996.

Torrey-Purta, J. "Youth in Relation to Social Institutions." In S. S. Feldman and G. R. Elliott (eds.), *At the Threshold: The Developing Adolescent.* Cambridge, Mass.: Harvard University Press, 1990.

U.S. Bureau of the Census. *Statistical Abstract of the U.S.* (121st ed.) Washington, D.C.: U.S. Department of Commerce, 2001.

U.S. Congress. *Adolescent Health.* Vol. 1. Washington, D.C.: Office of Technology Assessment, 1991.

U.S. Department of Health and Human Services. *Mental Health: Culture, Race and Ethnicity.* Supplement to *Mental Health: A Report of the Surgeon General.* Rockville, Md.: U.S. Department of Health and Human Services, 2001.

Vargas, L. A., and Koss-Chioino, J. D. (eds.). *Working with Culture: Psychotherapeutic Interventions with Ethnic Minority Children and Adolescents.* San Francisco: Jossey-Bass, 1992.

Vega, W. A., Khoury, E. L., Zimmerman, R. S., Gil, A. G., and Warheit, J. G. "Cultural Conflicts and Problem Behaviors of Latino Adolescents in Home and School Environments." *Journal of Community Psychology,* 1995, *23,* 167–179.

Way, N. "Between Experiences of Betrayal and Desire: Close Friendships Among Urban Adolescents." In B. J. Leadbetter and N. Way (eds.), *Urban Girls: Resisting Stereotypes, Creating Identities.* New York: New York University Press, 1996.

Williams, R., and others. "Friends, Family and Neighborhood: Understanding Academic Outcomes of African American Youth." *Urban Education,* 2002, *37*(3), 408–431.

Wilson, W. J. *When Work Disappears: The World of the New Urban Poor.* New York: Knopf, 1996.

Part One

Indigenous American Indian Population Groups

In this first section of the book, we focus on American Indians, also called Native Americans—the indigenous people of color in North America. It has been estimated that about one million indigenous people were spread in tribal groups throughout the continent in the sixteenth and seventeenth centuries when Spanish explorers and English settlers first arrived on the East Coast of the newly discovered continent.

By the end of the nineteenth century, Indians had been geographically isolated from the majority white population through the establishment of reservations. Many tribes were decimated by wars with the U.S. government, forced relocation, and epidemics of diseases imported from Europe; other tribes lost their economic livelihood and were politically disenfranchised and socially marginalized from the mainstream society. By 1850, the American Indian population had dwindled to 250,000, gradually reestablishing itself to 2.5 million by the year 2000 (see Tafoya and Del Vecchio, 1996).

American Indians had a number of characteristics that distinguished them from Anglo European settlers and from other, later-arriving immigrant groups. First, indigenous Indian societies were organized into tribal groups, clans, and smaller bands, with a wide diversity of languages, family structures, belief systems, customs, political-economic systems, and normative behaviors (see Sutton and Broken Nose, 1996).

Second, in their initial contacts with white settlers, Indians were immediately categorized as "the other," labeled as "uncivilized," and viewed as inferior to Europeans. Their racial and cultural differences set them apart as exotic and primitive.

Third, Indians were forced to accommodate, acculturate, or assimilate to Anglo-Saxon values and behavioral norms in order to gain acceptance and legitimacy in American society. Many responded to the pressures to relinquish their culture by exhibiting identity conflicts and self-destructive behaviors. The combination of cultural genocide and economic dislocation has contributed to high rates of poverty, social problems, community disorganization, and family dysfunction among Native Americans.

Fourth, American Indians have been victims of cultural exploitation and appropriation through the use of their images and cultural products; examples are "the noble savage," "the drunken Indian," and "the protector of the environment." Although these media images are often contradictory, they serve to reinforce primarily negative stereotypes about Indians (see Sutton and Broken Nose, 1996).

Sociocultural Characteristics

Some major cultural traditions, values, and practices of Native Americans have been summarized in Chapter One by Teresa L. LaFromboise and Marivic R. Dizon. Basic values that guide the behavior and daily life of Indian families include a strong belief in spirituality that pervades an individual's universe and protects the family, a respect for the earth and the natural environment as the source of all living things, and a belief that harmony between an individual and nature is essential to good mental and physical health.

In family and group relationships, American Indians believe that the extended family should operate as a mutual support system in which their family roles and obligations are determined by traditional relationships rather than by biological ties. Thus families and kinship networks function as natural sources of problem solving and social support. In relationships between peers and friendship groups, cooperation is stressed over competition, which has implications for the adaptation of Indian youth to American schools and jobs. Finally, in Indian communities parents have always recognized that "it takes a village to raise a child," so childrearing is a collaborative task in which grandparents and other relatives play an active role.

Implications for Assessment and Treatment

In Chapter One, LaFromboise and Dizon suggest some general principles that mental health practitioners will find useful in the assessment and treatment of American Indians, given their unique history in American society. With such a strong focus on the family as a central unit of Indian life, family therapy is indicated as one of the most effective forms of intervention for troubled Indian children and adolescents. LaFromboise and Dizon also describe other interventions that are particularly effective with Indian youth and their parents, such as social cognitive interventions, family network therapy, and traditional interventions such as use of the sweat lodge ceremonies, the "talking-circle," and the "four-circles." All are based on traditional healing ceremonies.

In the final decades of the twentieth century, Indian tribal groups have been reclaiming their reservation rights and developing self-sufficient economies based on the gaming industry, fishing, and natural resource development of their land. Indian elders and younger activists have spearheaded a movement to restore their cultural heritage by revising their tribal languages, reemphasizing their spiritual beliefs, and eliminating self-destructive behaviors such as alcoholism, substance abuse, and suicide, which they view as their communities' maladaptive responses to a history of chronic traumatic victimization and loss. These advocacy efforts to restore the rich heritage and the dignity of American Indians should contribute to fostering positive identities and promoting positive mental health among the first Americans.

References

Sutton, C. T., and Broken Nose, M. A. "American Indian Families: An Overview." In M. McGoldrick, J. Giordano, and J. K. Pearce (eds.), *Ethnicity and Family Therapy.* New York: Guilford Press, 1996.

Tafoya, N., and Del Vecchio, A. "Back to the Future: An Examination of the Native American Holocaust." In M. McGoldrick, J. Giordano, and J. K. Pearce (eds.), *Ethnicity and Family Therapy.* New York: Guilford Press, 1996.

Chapter One

American Indian Children and Adolescents

Teresa LaFromboise
Marivic R. Dizon

For centuries, American Indians have been uprooted, relocated, and socialized in attempts to integrate them into the dominant culture. Many demographic trends, such as the movement away from reservations, have tended to interfere with cultural practices and encourage assimilation. The survival of American Indian tribal cultures and identity, despite relocation, poverty, disease, and acculturation pressure, attests to the strength and flexibility of the first Americans.

Over the last three decades, mental health services delivered to American Indians have expanded and contracted, both in terms of general availability and range of care. Shifts in federal funding priorities, as well as crucial issues around determining the essential components of psychological treatment, have contributed to the change; often immediate need outstrips existing knowledge and resources for culturally sensitive, research-based treatment facilitation. A segment of the population in great need of attention is the American Indian youth population.

It is time to take stock of the resilience of American Indian people, their beliefs about health and healing, and their beliefs and knowledge concerning youth development. Toward this end, this chapter reviews the progress in the assessment and treatment of American Indian children and adolescents.

Demographic Data

The designator "American Indian" refers to all Native American people, including Alaska Natives, Aleuts, Eskimos, and *Métis* (mixed bloods). The terms *American Indian, Native American, Indian,* or *Native* are used interchangeably throughout this chapter to denote these varied peoples from distinctively diverse tribes. However, we realize the potential for inaccuracy in the use of these ethnic glosses and do not wish to convey disrespect to any group.

The Indian population, once estimated at several millions, is reduced, through what some have called cultural genocide, to 2.5 million, when those who identify themselves solely as American Indian and Alaska Native are counted. However, the population swells to 4.1 million when people who identify themselves as part American Indian and part Alaska Native include themselves in that count (Ogunwole, 2002). The population has grown by 13 percent since the 1990 census and can be characterized as diverse, young, and mobile. About 840,300 Indian people are under the age of eighteen (U.S. Bureau of the Census, 2002a). The median age is twenty-eight years for American Indians and Alaska Natives—significantly lower than the national average of thirty-five years (U.S. Bureau of the Census, 2002b).

There are 561 federally recognized tribes. Most maintain unique customs, traditions, social organizations, and ecological relationships. There are 210 distinct tribal languages still spoken today by Native peoples in the United States and Canada (Ambler, 2000; Krauss, 1996).

Identification of tribal membership is complicated by bureaucratic ambiguity and complex eligibility criteria for individuals of American Indian descent. Federal and state-managed treatment programs generally require one-quarter genealogically derived Indian blood for eligibility for service; community consensus or tribally defined membership are not accepted. However, the Indian Health Service offers services to

> persons of Indian descent belonging to the Indian community served by the local facilities and program. These include an individual "regarded as an Indian by the community in which he [or she] lives as evidenced by such factors as tribal membership, enroll-

ment, residence on tax-exempt land, ownership of restricted property, active participation, and other relevant factors." [Forquera, 2001, p. 8]

Private agencies and community programs generally respect the right of tribes to define membership.

In 2000, only 36 percent of American Indians and Alaska Natives lived on reservations or in other census-defined tribal areas (the historically Indian areas of Oklahoma), and 64 percent lived elsewhere in the United States (Forquera, 2001). The movement away from reservations has been attributed to limited employment and lack of educational opportunities, housing shortages, poverty, and substandard health care.

Among American Indians and Alaskan Natives as a whole, the three-year (1998–2000) average median household income was $31,799. This income was higher than the three-year average for African Americans ($28,679); it was not statistically different from that for Hispanics ($31,703) but lower than for non-Hispanic whites ($45,514) and for Asians and Pacific Islanders ($52,553) (DeNavas-Walt, Cleveland, and Roemer, 2001). On reservations, average income varies from tribe to tribe. About 26 percent of American Indians on reservations live in poverty, as compared to 23.9 percent of African Americans, 23.1 percent of Hispanics, 11.3 percent of Asian Americans–Pacific Islanders (AAPIs), and 9.9 percent of whites (Dalaker, 2001). Only 50 percent of Indians available for the workforce in Bureau of Indian Affairs (BIA) service areas are employed. Among those who are employed, 30 percent are earning wages below the poverty line (Bureau of Indian Affairs, 1997). However, on some reservations there is an emerging "middle class" due to income generated in the gaming industry. Increased opportunity from this new form of economic development, as well as the desire for togetherness, has lured some urban Indians back home to the reservations or rural Indian communities.

Sociocultural Environments and Well-Being

American Indians attain fewer years of formal education than members of other minority groups and whites (American Indian Research and Policy Institute, 2000). For some Indian children, lags in academic performance of one to two years in elementary school and two to four years in secondary school are not uncommon (Demmert and Bell, 1991). Thus it is not surprising that American Indian youth have the highest dropout rate among ethnic groups. About 35 to 50 percent never complete high school (Swisher, Hoisch, and Pavel, 1991). Only 21 percent of high school graduates enroll in college, compared to 36 percent from within the United States as a whole (Cunningham, 1996).

Scholastic functioning is hampered by educators unaccustomed to Indian ways of knowing; they also lack information on Native children's language deficits, neurosensory disorders, and other physically handicapping conditions (*otitis media* or middle ear disease, for example—a condition that is estimated to occur in over half of Indian children). American Indian children in public schools have a higher frequency of developmental disabilities (5.28 percent) than children of other minority groups (4 percent) and white children (3 percent) (Blum and others, 1992). Nationally, 11 percent of Native American children were identified as eligible for special education. Some reservations have reported that as many as 33 percent of students are schooled in special education classes (Dauphinais, 2000). Those with physical complications and learning, behavioral, or emotional problems are more likely to have significant social and emotional concerns than youth without these conditions (Blum, Potthoff, and Resnick, 1997).

Unfortunately, some Native Americans spiral downward from limited educational attainment to chronic unemployment to substance abuse to crime and homelessness. Indian people experience malnutrition, an alcoholism mortality rate 6.8 times higher, an incidence of cirrhosis of the liver 4.4 times higher, and a homicide rate 1.4 times higher than that of other racial-ethnic groups (Indian Health Service, 1997). In 1997, approximately 4 percent of Indian adults were under the care, custody, or control of the criminal justice system (Greenfeld and Smith, 1999). Although the homeless make up less than 1 percent of the general population, American Indians constitute 8 percent of the U.S. homeless population (U.S. Bureau of the Census, 1999). Their mortality rate is about 3.3 times higher than that of other groups for motor vehicle accidents. Their suicide rate is 1.7 times higher than that of other groups. In addition, environmental contamination continues to have a significant impact on Indian life expectancy (71.5 years or 6 percent lower than the white population) and prevalence of illness (Snipp, 1996).

Although there has been some reduction in the infant mortality rate in the postnatal period (one month to one year), this rate is 29 percent higher than that of the white population (May, 1996). Among American Indian and Alaskan Native children ages one through four, the two leading causes of death from 1995 through 1997 were unintentional injury and homicide. Between the ages of five and nine, the two leading causes of death were unintentional injury and malignant neoplasms or tumors. Between 1995 and 1997, the five leading causes of death among children and adolescents in the ten-to-fourteen age group, listed in descending order, were unintentional injury, homicide, suicide, malignant neoplasms, and heart disease. For adolescents fifteen to twenty-four, they were heart disease, malignant neoplasms, homicide, suicide, and unintentional injury. Many risk behaviors that emerge or are exhibited in adolescence are related to the leading causes of death among American Indian adults, such as liver disease, HIV, homicide, suicide, and unintentional injury (National Center for Health Statistics, 2002).

In a national study of adolescent health by Blum and others (1992), 18 percent of a sample of Indian youth had experienced some sort of abuse. Research findings on the concerns or worries of Native American school-age youth conducted by D'Andrea (1994) indicate that Lakota students worried quite often about someone forcing them to do sexual things they do not want to do and about violence in their home and neighborhood. Recent revelations about pedophilia among the clergy support the accounts of sexual molestation of Indian youth that have been suppressed for generations. Some investigators have noted the frequency with which Native perpetrators were initially abused themselves in substance-abusing families or while attending religious and BIA boarding schools (Fischler, 1985; Lujan, DeBruyn, May, and Bird, 1989). The traumatic experiences of abuse and neglect are often amplified by problems associated with alcohol abuse and high morbidity and mortality rates in the community (Irwin and Roll, 1995).

It is estimated that as many as 25 to 35 percent of Indian children have been forcibly removed from their homes for purposes of education (for example, to go to boarding schools), foster care, or adoption. When this occurred, Indian children were most often raised for some time by non-Indian caretakers in institutions and homes that "neither understood nor appreciated the cultural differences and needs in the tribal communities" (Mandrigal, 2001, p. 1506).

American Indians experience twice the rate of violence per capita that individuals from the general U.S. population do. The rate of violent crimes reported by American Indian females is nearly 50 percent higher than the rate reported by African American males. Of the violent victimizations that are experienced by American Indians, at least 70 percent are committed by persons who are not of the same racial or ethnic group. Twenty percent of Indian high school students attending BIA schools who responded to the Youth Risk Behavior Survey indicated that they had carried a weapon to school during the month. Fifty percent of the males and 30 percent of the females had been involved in a physical fight during the past year (Shaughnessy, Branum, and Everett-Jones, 2001). The arrest rates for violent crimes among Indian youth were about the same as for white youth and were about one-fifth those of African American youth (Greenfeld and Smith, 1999).

In recent years, organized gangs have branched out to reservations and rural communities adjacent to reservations. Across Indian country, tribal police have identified 180 gangs in operation (Shaughnessy, Branum, and Everett-Jones, 2001). In 1997, the Navajo Nation estimated that approximately sixty youth gangs existed on the reservation (Henderson, Kunitz, and Levy, 1999). Many believe that gangs are brought to the reservations by urban relatives who recruit adolescents to form new chapters for the dispersion of marijuana and hard drugs (Donnermeyer, Edwards, Chavez, and Beauvais, 1996). In a study of gang involvement among American Indian adolescents on three reservations in the Upper Midwest, Whitbeck, Hoyt, Chen, and Stubben (forthcoming) found that about one-third of fifth- through eighth-grade students had been asked to join a gang, and more than one-third had friends who were gang members. Gang involvement was associated with delinquency and substance abuse. Adolescents most susceptible to gang influence were those from single-parent and disorganized families. Baldridge (2001) reports that elders living on some reservations see gang activity and undisciplined children as real threats to their safety and have asked tribal governments to provide them with elderly protection teams.

Epidemiological Studies

In each of the following mental-health-related studies, there are reports of high rates of distress, according to diagnostic criteria refined on the general population.

Mental health problems must be considered in the context of the complicated economic, social, and political conditions in Indian communities. A study of American Indian youth thirteen to seventeen years of age who lived in the Northern Plains found that 29 percent of the sample received a diagnosis of at least one psychiatric disorder. The five most common disorders were alcohol dependence or abuse (11 percent), attention deficit–hyperactivity disorder (11 percent), marijuana dependence or abuse (9 percent), major depressive disorder (5 percent), and other substance dependence or abuse (4 percent). More than half (53.3 percent) of the youth that presented with a disruptive behavior disorder and 60 percent with any depressive disorder also had a substance use disorder (Beals and others, 1997).

Substance abuse was also a factor in a study of Appalachian children by Costello and his colleagues, who reported that American Indian children had a higher prevalence of substance use (9.0 percent) than white children (3.8 percent), yet fairly similar rates of psychiatric disorders (16.7 percent as opposed to 19.2 percent). Furthermore, substance use was comorbid with psychiatric disorder in 2.5 percent of Native American children, as opposed to 0.9 percent of white children in this sample. Family mental illness was found to be strongly associated with childhood disorder in both groups (Costello and others, 1997).

Depression is another major area of concern for both female and male American Indian youth (see Spencer and Thomas, 1992). Research has linked depression to substance use, learning problems, lethargy, antisocial behavior, and suicidal ideation among these youth. Research conducted by Novins and Mitchell (1997) showed that Indian adolescents who developed either isolated or recurrent chronic depressive symptoms were more likely to be female, had reported more stressful life events within the last six months, had lower self-esteem, and had higher levels of premorbid anxiety. Among the youth who developed this pattern of symptoms, many reported poorer school performance than did the nondepressed and isolated-depressed youth.

A study of Northern Plains youth who were detained showed that 10 percent of the participants had major depression and that females were more likely than males to suffer from depression (Duclos and others, 1998). A subsequent study with this population showed that 15.3 percent had an anxiety-depressive disorder, and 47.8 percent used mental health treatment services for emotional problems (Novins, Duclos, and others, 1999).

Anxiety disorders also figure prominently in mental health assessments of American Indians. In a national study of adolescent health (Blum and others, 1992), Indian youth expressed their anxiety as major worries about succeeding in school, being accepted by friends, losing their parents, handling economic survival issues of their families, and feeling concern over their eating habits. They reported a high level of disordered eating, with 35.2 percent of female students dieting between one and four times in the past year and 27.1 percent of females and 19.3 percent of males having induced vomiting.

Blum and his colleagues (1992) also found that, although the majority of American Indian and Alaska Native youth in the adolescent health study reported being in good emotional health, over 14 percent of females and 8.3 percent of males reported feeling so sad and hopeless in the last month that they wondered if anything was worthwhile; 6 percent said they had signs of severe emotional distress. This distress was related to high-risk behaviors, including sexual activity, pregnancy, poor school performance, and multiple school absences. Over 20 percent of the emotionally distressed youth in this sample had been sexually abused; 27 percent of female youth had been sexually abused, and almost 33 percent had experienced physical abuse. In this study, 17 percent of youth reported having attempted suicide (females, 21.6 percent; males, 11.8 percent). American Indian psychologists who work with young American Indian victims of abuse and neglect posit that emotional distress is related to feelings of fear, anger, guilt, shame, and grief, complicated by the shattering of self-esteem (Willis, Dobrec, and Sipes, 1992).

Indian youth come into contact with both legal and illegal drugs at an earlier age than white youth (Roski and others, 1997). Peer influence and peer pressures are significant predictors of early drug use (McMorris and others, under review; Roski and others, 1997). A study by Howard and others (1999) found inhalant use among 12.3 percent of a sample of fifth- and sixth-grade urban Indian youth.

Although Indian youth are reported to sustain the highest rates for alcohol and drug abuse (Bachman and others, 1991; Beauvais and Segal, 1992), a study by Beauvais and others (1996) revealed contradictory findings. In their survey study comparing 504 American Indian (202 male, 302 female), 1,052 Mexican American, and 459 white American adolescents, white American youth exceeded both Mexican American and American Indian youth in their use of alcohol. White American youth also exceeded American Indian youth in the number of occasions they admitted to drinking alcohol to intoxication.

Some research posits that substance abuse is a widely modeled means of coping with depression, anxiety, hostility, feelings of powerlessness, and stress reactions among Native people (Mail, 1995). However, a study of Indian and white adolescent alcohol use and emotional distress refutes this common "self-medication theory." Oetting, Swaim, Edwards, and Beauvais (1989) found that rather than self-medicate against anger, Indian youth who expressed their anger were linked to higher levels of self-esteem, which tended to reduce alcohol use. Their explanation for these findings was that expression of justifiable anger could serve as a protective factor when associated with institutional and situational oppression.

When gender differences in drug use have been examined, American Indian girls indicate higher rates of drug and alcohol use than boys (Bates, Wong Plemons, Jumper-Thurman, and Beauvais, 1997; McMorris and others, under review). A possible explanation for this finding is that girls are faced with "double jeopardy" because they encounter multiple social, economic, and cultural pressures on top of challenges associated with their cultural and gender role identities (McMorris and others, under review).

Alcohol abuse alone has critical consequences for young children in the form of fetal alcohol syndrome (FAS), which can lead to mental and psychosocial retardation (Uecker and Nadel, 1998).

The overall rate of FAS among Native Americans between 1980 and 1986 using a passive surveillance data-collection method was 2.97 per 1,000, compared to 0.6 per 1,000 African Americans, 0.09 for whites, 0.08 for Hispanics, and 0.03 for Asian Americans (Chavez, Cordero, and Becerra, 1988). The rate of FAS among Plains Indian tribes using active case ascertainment was 9.00 per 1,000 (May and Gossage, 2001). The consequences of FAS continue to affect youth well into adolescence and are manifested in poor impulse control, limited social and organizational skills, poor judgment, and difficulty recognizing and setting boundaries (LaDue, Streissguth, and Randels, 1992). These studies indicate that Indian youth have a significant problem with alcohol and drug abuse, often requiring dual diagnoses during assessment and special considerations in treatment planning.

Indian youth are sexually active and are concerned about the risks associated with sexual involvement. The study by Blum and others (1992) reveals that 30.9 percent of the seventh- through twelfth-grade youth (35.1 percent male; 27.0 percent female) say they have engaged in sexual intercourse, and 41.6 percent of adolescent girls who are sexually active report that they feel very worried about getting pregnant. Indian youth are also affected by AIDS and the HIV virus, with 1 percent of females and 1 percent of males in the thirteen- to nineteen-year-old age group diagnosed with AIDS and 2 percent of males and 10 percent of females diagnosed with the HIV infection (Centers for Disease Control and Prevention, 1999).

Indian youth experience traumatic loss of family and friends at a rate much higher than the general population because of accidental and premature death (Blum and others, 1992). They must also undergo long separations from family for medical treatment or educational and employment opportunities. Some believe that the prevalence of ongoing hardship and loss leads to cultural trauma or hopelessness and despair (Duran and Duran, 1995). The high incidence of suicide and accidental deaths among Indian youth attests to this phenomenon.

In a study on suicidality among adolescents in the Zuni pueblo, it was found that 30 percent of Zuni youth had attempted suicide (Howard-Pitney and others, 1992). A significant gender difference in suicide attempts was also found, with girls attempting suicide two to three times more often than boys. A study on suicide risk factors among Indian adolescents attending boarding school reports that 23 percent had attempted suicide (Manson, Beals, Dick, and Duclos, 1989). Blum and others (1992) found that youth who were at high risk for suicide had problems with drug abuse, had or caused a pregnancy, believed the family was uncaring, and had relatives or friends who had committed suicide. May (1987) asserts that Indian youth who come from tribes classified as traditional (maintaining the old ways) are less likely to commit suicide than youth from transitional (neither highly traditional nor modern) or acculturated tribes.

Despite considerable social and psychological risk, American Indian children often grow into adolescence with secure and strong identities and family and community affiliations (Fisher, Bacon, and Storck, 1998). In the national adolescent health study, 82 to 86 percent of Indian youth sampled reported that their parents cared "quite a bit" or "very much" about them (Blum, Potthoff, and Resnick, 1997). In another national study, Indian youth who reported a greater level of perceived caring by adults were less likely to feel bored, insecure, or depressed (Division of General Pediatrics and Adolescent Health, 1992). Studies of successful American Indian students found that most students considered their families to be their primary source of support and inspiration (Coggins, Williams, and Radin, 1996; Dodd, Garcia, Meccage, and Nelson, 1995; Whitbeck, Hoyt, Stubben, and LaFromboise, 2001).

American Indian Families: Strengths and Stresses

Complex and richly diverse, American Indian family life is difficult to describe. A key feature of contemporary American Indian families is the growing proportion of Indian children (slightly less than one-half) who reside with only one parent. American Indian women are less likely to ever marry and more likely to be divorced than women in the overall U.S. population. The extent of single parenthood, never marrying, and divorce appears to be higher on reservations with high unemployment and poverty rates. "The bottom line is that Indian women and children, especially those on reservations, are in more vulnerable social and economic situations than are all U.S. women and children" (Sandefur and Liebler, 1996, p. 213).

The number of intertribal and between-culture marriages continues to increase. The percentage of both American Indian men and women who married Indian partners fell from 54.2 percent to 41.2 percent for males (61 percent to 39.8 percent for females) between 1970 and 1990 (Snipp, 1996). To curb intertribal and between-culture marriages is quite a challenge, given the restricted range of available partners due to remote living conditions and restrictive clan relationships. This reality deeply troubles tribal members concerned about blood quantum, which can affect the tribal enrollment status of their children.

Indian communities have practiced informal caregiving through the extended family for centuries. Extended family members work together to help children develop a sense of personal worth and well-being. Even though there may be only one parent in the family, there are other adults in the household, including grandparents, aunts, uncles, and live-in partners. Time spent caring for, admiring, and playing with Indian children is cherished. Grandparents often willingly assume childrearing responsibilities, especially while the parents of young children are employed or away at college (Harris, Page, and Begay, 1988). Often parents seek the much-valued advice and assistance of older family members and elders because group consensus is a major value in important decision making and because great importance is still placed on age and life experiences (Joe and Malach, 1998).

The roles of specific family members and the structure of extended families vary across tribes and among families within tribes. Nonetheless, obvious contrasts emerge when Indian families are compared with families in the general population. Indian families often consist of members with differing levels of cultural involvement and traditionalism. For example, the grandparents may live on the reservation yet speak only English because of the negative experiences they have had with Native language use in boarding schools (Baldridge, 2001). Some of their grandchildren may be becoming bilingual due to Native language classes offered in tribal schools, whereas other grandchildren who live in the city may speak predominantly English. However, all members of the

family may be involved in enculturation activities such as participating in ceremonies and pow-wows, preparing Native foods, doing
beadwork, or hunting.

At this time, most Indian families function biculturally by
retaining some of the traditional ways of their tribes and blending
those ways with conventional American practices (National Indian
Child Welfare Association, 1986). For example, "an Indian baby
may start out in a traditional cradle board and disposable diapers
but is soon introduced to a baby walker and a stroller" (Joe and
Malach, 1998, p. 135). Even families heavily immersed in an American Indian lifestyle embrace other cultural traditions associated
with parenting. It is not uncommon to see a fusion of traditional
and nontraditional childrearing practices.

However, upon the birth of a child, attention to traditional childrearing practices may be amplified. Indian childrearing practices
are largely shaped by Indian worldviews, which regard children as
beloved gifts (Atkinson and Locke, 1995). Early introduction of
children to the spiritual life of the tribe fosters a loving respect for
nature, as well as independence and self-discipline. Tribal spirituality is the same as tribal life; the two are not deliberately separated
(Trujillo, 1999).

Early childhood is often marked by a variety of celebrations to
honor an infant's developmental milestones such as the first smile,
first laugh, first steps, or first attempts at using language (Buffalohead, 1988; Morey and Gilliam, 1974). Although American Indian
families celebrate these developments, they feel little pressure over
the timing of such events. Their beliefs involve acceptance of a
child's own readiness and restraint from pressuring a child to perform (Joe and Malach, 1998). Historically, children were seldom
physically punished in Indian households. After misbehaving, the
child might quickly experience disapproving words and "tsk-tsk"
sounds from the adults or may be ignored.

For some tribes, particularly those who still practice puberty rites,
there is no recognition of adolescence as a developmental stage. Cultural clashes concerning the Western-imposed social construction of
adolescence have arisen among the Navajo, for example, who still
initiate female children into womanhood during the *Kinaalda* ceremony. Goodluck (1998) indicates that Navajo girls must necessarily
shift gears between the traditional and the modern worlds from

child to adult or child to adolescent status depending upon context. The girls in her research who had participated in this coming of age ceremony valued their new adult status in the Navajo community despite the paradoxes they experienced when teachers and classmates referred to them as "teenagers."

Communication patterns in Indian families differ from tribe to tribe. In general, these patterns might be characterized as hierarchical and diffuse. For example, information about a youth's misbehavior might be passed from the mother to her parents and sisters or from the mother or father to an aunt or uncle who has been designated as responsible for guiding the youth's character development. Restitution for the wrongdoing on the part of the child may involve an apology to each of the family members who worry about the child or are embarrassed by the youth's misbehavior. This indirect line of communication serves to protect the bonds between parents and youth and reinforces extended family involvement in maintaining standards of behavior (Morey and Gilliam, 1974). Similarly, when a youth is worthy of praise for a significant accomplishment, one of the family members might share this information with others in the community through a person known as the "camp crier," who conveys good news about members of the community at pow-wows and other ceremonial gatherings.

Because autonomy is highly valued among American Indians, children are expected to make their own decisions and operate semi-independently at an early age (Joe and Malach, 1998). In this childrearing style, family members allow children choices and the freedom to experience the natural consequences of those choices. The impact of a child's behavior on others is also emphasized. This seemingly diffuse approach to childrearing has often been labeled as permissive or negligent by social service providers because it appears to them that Indian parents exercise minimal *observable* control over their children (Gray and Cosgrove, 1985).

Over the years, movement back and forth between urban and reservation areas has complicated Indian extended family functioning. Many who relocate to cities from reservations and other traditional Indian areas have felt detached and isolated from their families and other Indian social support networks. To combat this sense of alienation, they often seek support from other Indians, neighbors, and nonfamily members and, over time, reconstitute their extended family network (Ryan, 2000). "Politically, economically, and organizationally, urban Indian communities are now experiencing retribalization, and Indian people in cities are reconnecting with tribes" (Strauss and Valentino, 2001, p. 89).

American Indian families are, for the most part, quite resilient. *Resiliency* can be defined as a process in which a person is able to adapt, despite adverse circumstances. It is a process influenced by everyday life choices that also contributes to the ability to endure stressful experiences, develop competence, and create balance while striving for harmony (Cross, 1998; LaFromboise, Oliver, and Hoyt, forthcoming).

When the Indian Child Welfare Act was enacted in 1978, approximately 25 to 30 percent of Indian children were being placed in non-Indian homes for foster care or adoption. This act established the minimum federal standards and safeguards governing the placement of Indian children with the tribe as the first option when it is in the best interest of the child to be removed from his or her biological family. Indian leaders created this act because they recognized the potential for cultural extinction; removing so many Indian children from their communities meant that they would never learn their tribal customs, values, and traditions. Since that time, countless American Indian families have opened their homes to youth in need. By 1999, American Indian children accounted for only 1 percent of children in foster care (U.S. Department of Health and Human Services, 2001). This act reifies tribal sovereignty and recognizes the power of the extended family.

Many protective factors can be found within extended families to help prevent or delay the early onset of risk behaviors outlined in this chapter (Beauvais, 2000; Demmert, 2001). Protective factors currently under investigation with this population include cultural pride and involvement, ethnic identity, family cohesion, and family and community connectedness (LaFromboise, Oliver, and Hoyt, forthcoming).

Sociocultural Issues in Assessment

The psychological assessment of American Indian children and adolescents presents a perplexing array of considerations. This section highlights a number of assessment issues one must consider in working with Indian youth, including the testing situation, the use of standardized assessment instruments, and diagnostic procedures for the three psychological interventions presented later in the chapter.

Testing

Use of standardized tests with ethnic minority children remains controversial. Most assessment instruments have built-in biases; in fact, some argue that there is no such thing as a culturally unbiased instrument. Tests are designed and validated according to middle-class values and lifestyles and thus discriminate against other socioeconomic and non-dominant-culture groups (Helms, 1992; Plank, 2001). Primarily, the biases involve the assumptions that children readily engage in individual advancement and have a high degree of exposure to mainstream culture.

In the testing situation, a person seeking information in intake interviews and standardized assessment situations must consider the following: the testing environment; the biases, questioning style, and physical features of the test administrator; the biases inherent in the diagnostic instrument; and sociocultural factors that may affect the youth's perceptions of the assessment event and consequent performance. (See Sattler, 1998, for valuable information on the dynamics of cross-cultural and cross-ethnic interviewing with children and families.)

It is crucial that interpretations of assessment results take into account environmental factors that may facilitate or hinder the youth's response tendencies. These include the social organization that the test administrator represents, physical features and location of the testing room, and the presence or absence of contextually relevant materials (for example, pictorial stimuli of children with pale faces). The clinician must also be respectful while questioning and be aware of personal biases in noting, scoring, and interpreting responses to test items.

Deyhle (1986) believes that Navajo students do not fare well in test-taking situations because they do not believe that achievement is an individual accomplishment or that an individual should display accomplishments publicly. Although it is mostly outdated, the summary by Hynd and Garcia (1979) of behaviors of American

Indian children during diagnostic interviews that may negatively affect assessment outcome remain relevant today. Many Indian youth use nonassertive, nonspontaneous, and soft-spoken verbal interaction; they have limited eye contact, decreased performance with timed tasks, and reticence in relaying information; they perform skills selectively, based on the extent to which they might contribute to the betterment of the group. In addition, because many tribal cultures emphasize perfection, American Indian children may be apprehensive about creating a block design or enacting some other task without long periods of observation or previously established competence in performing the task.

Standardized test instructions assume a minimum vocabulary. They often use temporal concepts and terms that may be unusual to Indian worldviews. In addition, many tribal languages are vastly different from English in vocabulary and structure. Even when there is semantic equivalence, "language evokes a specific culture frame, with selective demand characteristics for the assessment of one's own behavior or the projection of personality variables" (Lefley, 1975, p. 36).

Special considerations also apply at the stage of making a psychological diagnosis. In the review of the *DSM-IV* titled "Outline for Cultural Formulation" (hereafter "the Outline"), Novins, Bechtold and others (1997) assert that the Outline provides clear guidelines for addressing cultural matters associated with American Indian youth in the assessment and treatment of mental health problems. However, they note several gaps in material for proper case formulation with American Indians not required by the Outline and illustrate additional relevant areas of coverage through case study presentations. They feel that the Outline fails to address the critical roles that development and the psychosocial context play in the formation of cultural identity. The Outline implies that cultural identity is fixed rather than fluid, depending on the identity of the parents and differences in cultural backgrounds between parents, as well as differences between the youth and biological, foster, step-, or adoptive parents. They also feel that challenges associated with adapting to and identifying with two or more cultures are overlooked.

We believe that a service provider considering social cognitive interventions who first conducts a functional analysis of the cognitive, behavioral, and social elements of disturbance associated with the target problem will ascertain most of the valuable cultural information advocated by Novins, Bechtold, and others (1997). Consideration is given to both external (social, environmental) and internal (cognitive, emotional) antecedents and consequences in social cognitive approaches (Bandura, 2002). Attention is paid particularly to the youth's personal and cultural schemata—beliefs about self and relationships with others—that may contribute to the onset and maintenance of the problem behavior. This analysis relies on the ability of the service provider to establish trust and credibility early in treatment. Another professional or extended family member or caregiver may be able to assist in interpreting cultural cognitions and designing culturally appropriate reinforcement regimens. However, the cultural elements of the relationship between the youth and the youth's caregivers and the service provider need to be included, in addition to comments about the assessment and treatment relationship (Novins, Bechtold, and others, 1997).

A service provider considering family systems therapies would search for information about how the presenting problem affects the identified client and other extended family members as individuals and as a social unit. Due to the importance of family in Indian life, clients should feel comfortable while a family history is being taken. Information about how families might be mobilized to support the client in dealing with problems can be gathered during network analysis (Attneave, 1969). Network analysis includes an assessment of the cultural fit between the family and the surrounding community, regardless of their absolute degree of acculturation.

A service provider considering Indian traditional methods can be aided by recent advances in writings on indigenous concepts of mental well-being (Csordas, 1999; Harrod, 1995) and the development of measurement scales specific to American Indian cultures (Oetting and Beauvais, 1990–1991). Mohatt and Blue (1982) used these methods to develop a scale to rate *tiospaye,* or degree of traditionality, among members of the Lakota Sioux nation. Oetting and Beauvais (1990–1991) have used the Cultural Identification Scale in a number of studies with American Indian youth. This scale allows an individual to identify independently with several ethnic identities simultaneously and accommodates changes in cultural identity depending on changing contexts. Recently Goodluck (1998) proposed a "strength-oriented" assessment perspective to better understand a young person's personal, ethnic, and tribal identity; experiences of being different ethnically and not fitting into the community; experiences with varied language use among family members; involvement in spiritual or religious practices; meaning attached to an Indian name; significance of ceremonies in one's life; and notions associated with various relationships within the family.

Intervention and Treatment

Little is known about the availability, access, organization, and financing of mental health services among Native Americans with established need (Manson, 2001). Generally, there are very low rates of service among those most is need of care (Manson, 2001; U.S. Department of Health and Human Services, 2001).

Tribal diversity makes it difficult to generalize about therapeutic issues. It is clear that Indian youth may have different values (for example, connectedness, balance) than youth from other cultures. Some tribes may actively discourage qualities important to mainstream culture such as individualism and competitiveness. The Coyote Stories, for example, carried from one generation to the next, warn of the danger associated with excessively individualistic and manipulative behavior.

Does it follow that American Indian youth considering counseling or being referred for treatment have different needs and expectations than clients from the dominant culture? Recent research lends empirical evidence to the consideration of culture in the application of individual, group, family, school, and community-based interventions, as well as assessment procedures with Indian children and adolescents.

Traditional tribal and pan-Indian beliefs and practices continue to be helpful in looking at the help-seeking patterns and preferences of American Indian adolescents. American Indian adults from all lifestyles follow a predictable pattern of accessing psychological services. The family is the first helping source sought; extended family and social network are next; then spiritual leaders and tribal leaders are approached. Finally, as a last resort the formal service delivery system (tribal, state, federal, and private programs) is contacted for assistance. It is generally thought that Indian adolescents follow a similar pattern. However, many also find their way to psychological services in educational settings or through the juvenile justice system.

Two studies involving American Indian adolescents highlight the role of peers as valuable helping resources. Bee-Gates, Howard-Pitney, LaFromboise, and Rowe (1996) found that both male and female Zuni high school students were most likely to seek help from a friend, parent, or relative for personal problems and to use professional help sources primarily for academic and career problems. Dauphinais, LaFromboise, and Rowe (1980) found that Indian youth in Oklahoma preferred to talk with friends and parents when they had problems rather than with school counselors or other support personnel. They generally sought psychological services only when school officials or tribal judges referred them there.

Among those detained in a juvenile detention center located on a Northern Plains reservation, 23.7 percent received services for substance use and 29.6 percent for emotional problems from traditional healers and pastoral counselors. However, the vast majority of youth in this center who suffered from psychiatric disorders did not use the alcohol, drug, and mental health services available in the detention center (Novins, Duclos, and others, 1999).

Once an Indian youth finally seeks help, it is very unlikely that the service provider has been trained to work with children or adolescents (Manson, 2001). Only 28 (14 percent) of the 198 direct care professionals in the Indian Health Service in 1993 were trained to work with children or adolescents. Only 6 percent of the clinically trained psychologists in the United States are American Indian or Alaska Native (West and others, 2000), and only seventeen of them are employed by the IHS (J. Davis-Hueston, personal communication, June 2, 2001, cited in Gone, forthcoming).

It would seem that Indian adolescents prefer to talk with counselors who come from their own cultural background. Studies of Indian adolescent assessments of positive counselor attributes have rendered conflicting findings over the importance attached to counselor race. Some studies found a strong preference for an Indian person (BigFoot-Sipes and others, 1992; Dauphinais, Dauphinais, and Rowe, 1981). BigFoot-Sipes and others (1992) found that American Indian female high school students prefer a female Indian counselor with attitudes and values similar to theirs, and male high school students most prefer an Indian counselor of either sex whose personality is similar to their own. However, other studies (LaFromboise and Dixon, 1981; LaFromboise, Dauphinais, and Rowe, 1980) do not confirm these results.

Trustworthiness is obviously important in every counseling relationship, regardless of the client's race or cultural background. This counselor attribute is crucial for Indian clients, who have learned from past experience that authorities purporting to give help may have ulterior motives (LaFromboise and Dixon, 1981; U.S. Department of Health and Human Services, 2001).

In general, Indian youth are looking for someone who understands the practical aspects of their culture and can give them sound practical advice about their lives, not someone who reflects and restates their feelings for purpose of analysis (Dauphinais, Dauphinais, and Rowe, 1981). In fact, a study by LaFromboise, Davis, and Rowe (1985) indicates that in many cases conventional psychological training is not necessary for one to be a good counselor with American Indian adolescents.

Probing questions on the part of the counselor may appear to be rude. Thus counselors may help American Indian youth feel more comfortable by modeling self-disclosure and explaining how counseling generally takes place. In any case, counselors must demonstrate patience and not offer interpretations unless asked to do so. Counselors do need to describe options and suggest solutions to problems. However, they must realize that Indian youth will know and discover what is best on their own (Garrett and Garrett, 1994).

Compared to the research on preferred helper attributes and various counseling process issues, little empirical evidence exists on the comparative efficacy of psychological interventions with American Indian youth. The three therapeutic approaches outlined next—social cognitive interventions, traditional healing, and family systems theory—are by no means the only interventions available to service providers working with American Indian youth. Although there are major differences among these treatment approaches, they have one important commonality: they incorporate the Native American youth's environment or social context into treatment and therefore better accommodate Indian cultural practices.

Social Cognitive Interventions

Social cognitive interventions have been considered less culturally biased than other approaches because they recognize the impact of culture on personal agency or confidence in people's ability to act on their own behalf, to influence others to act on their behalf, and to act in concert with others to shape their future (Bandura, 2002). This is particularly important in light of tribal differences. Because social cognitive interventions include the examination of belief systems associated with target behaviors, they have a heuristic appeal for accommodating cultural values and expectations (LaFromboise and Rowe, 1983; Willis, Dobrec, and Sipes, 1992). A counselor working with the American Indian youth is well advised to research the specific cultural practices and traditions of the tribes represented in his or her clientele. Generalizing about Indian cultural practices or making assumptions about tribal-specific conventions such as family structure may be insulting to the client and damaging to the therapeutic process.

External stimuli and reinforcers in a Native American social environment may differ dramatically from stimuli and reinforcement in the dominant culture. Consequently, a therapist working with Indian clients must be sensitive to the important philosophical differences between traditional cultures and the dominant culture. Dell (1980) describes an intervention for families and children based on Hopi worldviews that illustrates the importance of understanding Indian culture before designing an intervention or attempting to analyze stimuli and reinforcers.

Essentially, the Hopi feel that repetitive "bad" behaviors have a cumulative effect and that accrual of these behaviors leads to eventual change (Dell, 1980). A Hopi parent might therefore welcome the repetition of negative behavior as a sign of imminent change. A therapist unaware of Hopi philosophy might point out that the parents appear to be reinforcing poor behavior with their continual optimism and refusal to intervene. But an intervention designed to eliminate these reinforcing behaviors would strike at the underpinnings of Hopi philosophy. Tailoring an intervention to the particular tribe while reinforcing the importance of Hopi optimism regarding outcome reduces the client's justified concern that psychological interventions might dilute culture-specific behaviors and norms and allows the therapist to enlist tribal beliefs and traditions as resources.

It is important that the therapist balance the need for successfully establishing trust and the need for effecting change. Some Indian clients may expect immediate results and will be frustrated by a slow rate of change. In addition, they may be quite reticent, expecting the therapist to supply the therapeutic answers. Asking Indian clients to keep behavior logs or to solicit help from the extended family may actively engage them in therapy earlier and allow some immediate insight or feedback on the nature of the problem.

The following case illustrates the use of a social cognitive intervention.

Case Study: Mark

Mark, a fourteen-year-old Indian male of average intelligence, has been acting out for more than a year. Often truant and rumored to be gang-involved, Mark is hardly engaged in his academic work. He uses drugs and alcohol, has had several violent encounters with fellow students, and has been in minor trouble with local authorities. Mark has lived with his maternal aunt and uncle on the reservation for the last ten years. His mother is a chronic alcoholic, and Mark rarely sees her. The identity of Mark's father in unknown. Recently, Mark's uncle lost his job and began to disappear for days on end. A school counselor who has become increasingly concerned about his antisocial behavior and apparent depression has referred Mark.

Clearly, an initial goal in therapy with Mark would be to establish the therapist's credibility and trustworthiness. A variety of techniques are available, but strategies for engaging Mark in therapy may depend on tribal and family tradition. Conferences with the family and enlistment of the support of extended family or community members are crucial. In particular, relatives may help to ensure that Mark attends therapy sessions. In addition, community leaders, tribal elders, or other adults with whom Mark interacts might be consulted. The power of the extended family or tribe should not be underestimated.

Early in therapy, American Indian clients may feel more comfortable if the therapist practices some self-disclosure. Mark should not be pushed to make disclosures or assume a familiarity that he does not feel. Considerable time could be spent developing a definition of the problem from Mark's personal and cultural point of view. Asking Mark to help define the problem and provide input for establishing treatment goals may increase comfort and trust during the early stages of therapy.

The therapeutic problem, when defined through cognitive and behavioral assessment techniques, would involve exploring Mark's thoughts about himself and the cues and reinforcements for his negative behavior. His substance abuse may be a way of coping with peer and family pressure, or it may be the only way he has learned to make himself "feel good." In addition, Mark may be struggling with identity issues, involving both his paternity, his desire to belong, and his need to function adequately in Indian and mainstream cultures. His inability to function in either environment may be painful enough to prompt his angry behavior.

The counselor's goal in therapy would be to influence Mark to change his irrational thoughts, internal dialogue, and negative self-assessments by means of self-monitoring, discrimination training, behavior change, and social validation. Typical intervention strategies might include identifying the origin of his negative beliefs about himself (particularly if they are internalized from the dominant culture), exploring the effects of negative stereotypes about Indian drinking patterns, recording his irrational thoughts to help him discover self-statements that contradict these negative cognitions, verbal persuasion, modeling of positive thoughts and appropriate drinking behavior from tribal leaders, and specific techniques such as problem solving and increasing pleasant activities.

Because school is a problematic environment for Mark, a specific subgoal of therapy might involve rehearsal of school situations, starting with those in which he is comfortable (for example, talking with a friend) in order to develop his coping skills. With the rehearsal of ever-more-stressful scenarios, Mark's confidence will increase, ultimately improving his performance. Through consultation with Mark's teachers, methods of classroom participation might be modified to include cooperative learning activities that structure small-group activities and presentations rather than individual presentations to the entire class (Deyhle and Swisher, 1997).

In general, cognitive behavior therapy should not replace Indian social controls or therapeutic processes but should expand the adolescent's repertoire of coping options. For Mark, participation in social events such as basketball tournaments, rodeos, and enculturation activities such as drum groups and pow-wows would be an important first step in helping him reaffirm his Indian identity. Gradually, the therapist would hope to see an increase in Mark's self-esteem, the confirmation of personal identity and the emergence of a stronger Indian identity, improved academic performance, and comfortable and effective interactions in diverse and multicultural contexts.

In addition to individual therapy, social cognitive group interventions have been used successfully to engage youth in prosocial activities in the areas of life-skills development (LaFromboise, 1996) and refusal skills to avoid substance abuse and tobacco use (Schinke, Tepavac, and Cole, 2000). Social cognitive interventions presented in a group format may be particularly effective because they reduce the emphasis on individual disclosure, which may be difficult for some Indian adolescents, and introduce an expectation of shared responsibility. Because collective approaches are used in many Native communities, social cognitive groups may draw on an already familiar and powerful cultural ethic.

Systems Interventions for Families

Therapies based on systems theory effectively integrate ongoing strengths inherent in Indian extended-family networking. Systems theory includes a variety of specific therapeutic interventions, including family therapy, transgenerational interventions, and psychoeducation. These interventions share the assumption that the individual and the environment have continuous reciprocal interactions—that a client is one portion of a dynamic and interrelated whole. Systems theory argues that the most helpful therapeutic interventions are those that enhance an individual's interaction with others or with the environment and therefore ensure lasting changes outside the context of the therapeutic relationship. This approach takes advantage of the potentially supportive extended family while seeing that family members become aware of their own maladaptive patterns that may contribute to an individual's dysfunction.

The extended family, rather than conventional service delivery agencies, has remained the forum for problem solving and support in Indian communities, and most traditional interventions involve the extended family to ensure success (Napoliello and Sweet, 1992). A therapist who persists in focusing primarily on an Indian youth's relationship within the nuclear family may be missing important contributions from more distant family members.

Defining the family may be a difficult task for some Indian families, and the therapist must make sure that the client has salient family members included in therapy. Asking Indian youth questions to create a genogram, draw a portrait of the family, or tell a short story about their family may elicit important information about family function. Generally, family members who have a reasonable amount of contact with the client (for example, living in the same household) should be included in systems analysis.

The willing participation of all members of the family (particularly the men) in the intervention may be difficult to obtain. Family therapy is perceived by some as extremely intrusive and a violation of privacy. Unwilling family members may believe that they need to protect the family system from disclosure of personal family history (P. Running Wolf, personal communication, November 10, 1993). Engaging the family in therapy may require the support of the Indian community, persistent requests by the therapist or referring agency, or frequent visits to the home to establish trust and rapport before beginning treatment.

Some tribal mental health programs provide brief family therapy from an eclectic systems approach. The integration of tradition and conventional therapeutic practices appears to be a major theme of some exemplary models of Indian family therapy. For example, Tafoya (1989) combined traditional Indian therapeutic techniques with Western psychological models. Using a traditional story, he created a paradigm of the way Native Americans conceptualize relationships, responsibilities, learning, and teaching. He identified these four areas as the core elements of family therapy. He also integrated American Indian family systems into modified interventions stemming from conventional counseling practices. Schact, Tafoya, and Mirabla (1989) developed a home-based family therapy approach for families who are unable or unwilling to use clinic-based services. Besides providing a collection of highly plausible interventions, distinct family types such as "fringe families" and "two-world families" are delineated and pertinent family therapy techniques suggested. This model is unique in identifying beliefs through traditional healing ceremonies that are collaboratively provided in the home by the therapist. This model redefines the home as a place of healing.

Once key family members are attending therapy, they should be asked to define the family and its structure, addressing such issues as hierarchy, triangulation, and alliances. The therapist must keep in mind that extended family interchanges and interdependence is encouraged in many Indian families, in contrast to the independence valued by Anglo families. The therapist who labels Indian families "enmeshed" often mistakes interdependence for inadequate boundaries. Further, therapists should be sensitive to problems in defining family and alliances. In particular, intergenerational conflicts around traditional practices, inappropriate family expectations (for example, that students should miss school to attend tribal events), and independence issues may be problematic. Family sculpting is a useful tool for clarifying relationships within the family and for demonstrating a variety of possible relationships in Indian families. Drawing, storytelling, or using family models may elicit information about structure and alliances without being threatening.

Family roles, often crucial in systems therapy, may be quite different in Indian families. The youth may feel as if he or she had several "parents" in the forms of grandparents, aunts, uncles, and cousins and may use all of these as role models. The systems therapist working with an Indian family must explore the degree to which the family uses extended family roles and the nature of these roles.

Family values may also reflect the values of American Indian culture. Reverence for elders, emphasis on interdependence and community, and the ethic of sharing are all values typical of traditional Indian culture. The therapist who insists on promoting Anglo values in therapy is likely to meet substantial resistance and may not be acting in the best interest of the client. Instead, an intervention that focuses on increasing the cooperation, connectedness, and patience of the child may be a more culturally consonant approach.

In the case of Mark, a therapist conducting a systems intervention might want to assemble Mark's extended family in hopes of defining and solving his specific problems and eliciting the cooperation and support of family members (Attneave, 1969). In addition, the therapist might explore ways in which the family contributes to or reinforces Mark's current maladaptive behavior. Particularly helpful may be the cultural belief that the behavior of any single-family member reflects on the entire family and is therefore the concern and responsibility of all family members. In addition, other significant community members may be helpful resources for Mark, assisting in monitoring, supporting, and rewarding positive behavior.

Traditional Native American Interventions

Several traditional interventions may be used effectively in the treatment of Native American youth, particularly when youth present culturally specific explanations for their problems. Any of these could be incorporated into Mark's treatment. A counselor's decision to collaborate with a traditional healer usually begins with an assessment of the client's desire for ceremonial healing. These ceremonies are conducted either before or in conjunction with therapy.

Sweat lodge ceremonies are frequently conducted among American Indian groups for purification and prevention purposes. Participation in the sweat lodge consists of preparatory fasting, prayer, and offerings throughout serial purification sessions, which are referred to as "rounds." The ceremony lasts several hours; participants make offerings for health and balance in life (Manson, Walker, and Kivlahan, 1987). This practice helps promote group unity and a commitment to positive cultural values; it can also help integrate a recovering individual back into the wider community. (See Garrett and Osborne [1995] for use of the sweat lodge as metaphor for group work.)

The Native American Church can also be a source of support and intervention for Native American youth (Aberle, 1966; Office for Substance Abuse Prevention, 1990). This religious tradition stresses abstinence from alcohol use, as well as other values that promote health and wellness and encourage the preservation of cultural values. The development of a strong social support system is encouraged, and one-to-one counseling relationships and group meetings are spaces where religious members are encouraged to express their thoughts and feelings.

Manson, Walker, and Kivlahan (1987) suggest two other American Indian treatment strategies based on traditional healing practices: (1) the "four circles" (Figure 1.1) and (2) the "talking circle." The four circles intervention involves the symbolic organization of the important relationships in one's life: the centermost of four concentric circles represents the creator; the second circle symbolizes the relationships with a close friend or partner; the third represents the extended or immediate family; and the fourth signifies tribal members. Four circles is a pictorial search for balance in relationships and is a useful tool for clarifying and prioritizing allegiances and social responsibility.

The talking circle intervention resembles conventional group therapy. The participants form a circle and remain in the circle until the ceremony is complete. Sage or sweetgrass is burned to produce purifying smoke and provide direction for the group conversation. The leader begins by sharing feelings or thoughts about the group. Each participant is free to speak, and no one is allowed to interrupt. Often a sacred object is circulated, and the ceremony ends with a joining of hands in prayer. Unlike conventional group therapy, the leader does not offer ongoing remarks about the process of the group or individual contributions to the group.

These traditional practices might be particularly effective in a case like Mark's, in which an adolescent is struggling to assert his tribal identity and feelings of self-worth. A traditional intervention like the talking circle would reaffirm Mark's Indian identity and acceptance by the group. It could also offer him the opportunity to share his frustrations and concerns with concerned community

Figure 1.1. Four Circles Review of Important Relationships.

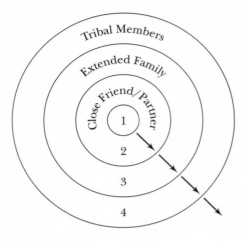

Four Circles Review of Important Relationships

1. The Creator
2. Close friend or partner
3. Extended family (cousins, aunts, uncles, and so on)
4. Tribal members

members. In turn, older participants in the talking circle could model behaviors or make suggestions that might help Mark cope with diverse cultural demands and enhance his self-esteem. Finally, the fact that a number of community members would engage in this level of support would enhance his estimate of self-worth. This integration of traditional healing with contemporary psychotherapy can solidify social support, facilitate communication with and cooperation from the community, and offer opportunity for healing.

All the techniques just described can be adapted in a multimodal intervention and used effectively with American Indian youth. Multidimensional therapy is a broad-based clinical approach that that can be used to treat mental and emotional illnesses among American Indian adolescents (Topper, 1992). This approach combines principles from both Western health care and traditional Navajo treatment and views patients from several perspectives (medical, psychological, socioeconomic, and cultural-historical). A strength of this approach is that it provides an interdisciplinary method of evaluation and treatment that takes into account both the context of the patient's life and the content of his or her culture. This is a particularly effective approach for youth with complex problems who live either on reservations or in inner cities where multiple systems, institutions, and caretakers are directly involved in their life. The case of Carol illustrates this blended approach.

> A group of adolescents, mostly males, had gathered in a remote area of the reservation for a drinking party. After the late-night affair, a distant cousin raped Carol—a twelve-year-old member of the group. She reported the incident to her parents. They felt, however, that she had "brought the problem on herself" and refused to take any action. Carol was referred to therapy by school authorities because of noticeable weight loss and symptoms of depression.

An approach that combines a variety of intervention techniques might help Carol. Therapy could explore her negative thoughts, particularly those relating to having been violated and to feeling dirty. The tribe's attitude toward early sexual activity and possible strong taboos against incest and forced copulation might be revealed as the cause of Carol's depression. The therapist might also incorporate behavioral techniques to relieve depression and improve Carol's eating habits. Such techniques might include increasing Carol's physical activity, monitoring her diet, and constructing a system of rewards for weight gain and positive interaction with others.

Meanwhile, traditional interventions such as a sweat lodge ceremony or a talking circle with female relatives might be particularly effective in Carol's case. The sweat lodge ritual could help relieve Carol's feeling of dirtiness or guilt through purification. The talking circle would provide the opportunity for Carol to obtain support and reinforcement and give her a safe forum in which to express anger and pain. Systems therapy could focus on family interactions and provide an understanding of her parents' reaction to Carol's rape.

Defining the family is an important task. Carol's mother and father may not have been her primary caretakers; other adults may have been equally supportive or influential in Carol's life. For whatever reason, Carol's family may be resistant to traditional interventions or to conventional therapeutic techniques. Nonetheless, assembling even part of the family is beneficial. Parent-child inter-action, family roles, the impact of the rape, and individual family members' attitudes should all be explored.

School- and Community-Based Programs

Finally, both Carol and Mark could benefit from culturally tailored school- or community-based interventions. Programs implemented to date to support Native American youth focus on targeted problems or specifically address the prevention of risk behaviors, including alcohol and drug abuse, HIV infection, youth violence, and suicide. Research findings that support the importance of cultural identity as a protective factor against substance abuse and substance-related problem behavior has emphasized the role of culture and the strengthening of bicultural identity within these programs (Sanchez-Way and Johnson, 2000).

The key to successful intervention and prevention efforts lies in locally developed and implemented programs that are based on multiple systems and use community resources and strengths. Jumper-Thurman and others (2001) created the Community Readiness Model, which is a tool that can help community members assess a community's level of readiness to initiate prevention strategies. Although this model was developed specifically for alcohol and drug abuse prevention, it can be applied to many types of community-based prevention initiatives.

The Zuni pueblo, for example, has been successful in implementing a community-based program that promotes general health and well-being, as well as a school-based program that addresses the prevention of suicide. LaFromboise and Howard-Pitney (1995) evaluated the Zuni Life Skills Development Curriculum—a school-based life-skills development program that was also implemented in the Zuni tribal high school—with the purpose of reducing factors associated with suicidal behavior. This program merges a social cognitive, life-skills-development approach with peer helping. A key strength of the curriculum is that it is culturally tailored to be compatible with Zuni values, beliefs, and attitudes. This life-skills intervention proved to be effective in reducing suicide probability and hopelessness and in enhancing youths' problem-solving and suicide-intervention skills.

The Zuni pueblo also established a community-based primary prevention project aimed at reducing the prevalence of diabetes risk factors among high school youth (Teufel and Ritenbaugh, 1998). Through the creation of the Zuni Wellness Center that is located within the tribal high school, the community helps promote positive healthy behaviors by exposing youth to an environment that supports healthy choices (nutrition, exercise, and so on). Besides having a culturally relevant program, engaging families in the implementation of prevention programs is also important. Beauvais (2000) argues that American Indian families play a key role in the successful prevention of drug and alcohol abuse, and those schools alone cannot address this problem. Compared with non-Indian youth, American Indian families have been shown to be more influential in the lives of children, and therefore families need to be included in any prevention efforts.

In the Great Lakes Region, the First American Prevention Center—a tribally chartered organization of the Red Cliff Band of Lake Superior Chippewa—created the Parent, School, and Community Partnership Program. This program was found to help reduce the prevalence, use, and expectation of use of tobacco, alcohol, marijuana, and inhalants among Native American youth residing on or near three reservations in the Great Lakes region (Petoskey, Van Stelle, and De Jong, 1998). The interventions implemented within this program included the following:

- The Red Cliff Wellness Curriculum—a K–12 school-based and culturally based substance abuse curriculum that incorporated tribal legends and cooperative learning techniques
- A teacher training program that provided hands-on training and technical assistance for implementation of the curriculum
- Leadership through a core group of trainers who took the lead in promoting community health
- A community strategy that addressed spiritual, family, and cultural perspectives on substance abuse and helped build the skills of community members to organize and advocate for community change

Several other Indian organizations and programs are addressing youth risk behaviors on a national scale. The Association of

American Indian Physicians and the National Native American AIDS Prevention Center are two national organizations that raise awareness about the HIV-AIDS epidemic through the establishment of HIV-AIDS prevention programs (Roubideaux, 2000; Westberg, 1997). The National Indian Fetal Alcohol Syndrome Prevention Program was designed to provide Native American communities with the skills and strategies to initiate primary, secondary, and tertiary prevention measures all across the nation (May and Hymbaugh, 1989).

The Office of Juvenile Justice and Delinquency Program runs the Tribal Youth Program. This program was created in response to an increase in youth violence in many American Indian communities. This program is dedicated to the prevention and control of juvenile crime and to the improvement of the juvenile justice system in Indian communities (Andrews, 2000). The Center for Substance Abuse Prevention (a part of the Substance and Mental Health Services Administration) has funded more than four hundred demonstration grant programs for high-risk youth (Sanchez-Way and Johnson, 2000).

Summary and Conclusion

Although great strides have been made toward understanding and addressing the problems facing Indian youth today, extensive work still needs to be done to offset the impact of trauma, poverty, negative social indicators, and poorly coordinated service delivery systems (Gone, forthcoming; Manson, 2001). Indian cultural beliefs and practices concerning development and well-being still prevail. American Indians not only assert that children are their most vital natural resource but they acknowledge children's importance daily through renewed efforts at blending effective parenting practices. Indian people realize that the pressures for acculturation will not diminish and that they must continue to work diligently for personal strength through traditional practices. Even though Native Americans are moving off the reservation in increasing numbers, they maintain extended family structures through frequent visits back to the reservation and reconstitution of the extended family with other off-reservation Indians while living in the city. Unfortunately, professional helpers who fail to see the value of communal support systems in protecting against contemporary life challenges can misunderstand this family structure and method of functioning.

Some progress has been made in the refinement of psychological interventions with American Indians. However, the cultural adaptation of psychological interventions must be accompanied by empirical validation of modified treatment procedures, particularly in the development of community-based programs for youth (Eccles and Gootman, 2002). Further progress toward identifying effective areas of intervention with Indian youth depends on increased research on the effectiveness of individual family systems or school and community-based approaches that take into account local beliefs about health and well-being.

It is time to reverse the emphasis on pathology in research and treatment with American Indians. Social cognitive interventions, systems approaches, and American Indian traditional healing methods are recommended because of their ability to focus on American Indian cultural attributes and strengths. We propose that Indian traditional beliefs and healing practices be incorporated into conventional treatment programs whenever they are desired by the client and deemed appropriate by the community. Social cognitive interventions in particular lend themselves to application in educational settings with American Indian youth.

Research considerations of particular relevance to Indian youth include the need to better understand critical antecedents of academic apathy; the need to better understand the process of American Indian and multiracial identity development; the need to delineate more tribal-specific behavioral manifestations of depression, anxiety, and anger; and the need to better understand the role of enculturation on risk and protective factors associated with youth development.

Studies have shown that clinical treatment need not involve professionally trained caregivers to be effective with Indian youth. In fact, it has been suggested that the natural skills of Indian helpers may be obviated by conventional clinical training experiences that impart Rogerian-style interviewing skills (Dauphinais, Dauphinais, and Rowe, 1981). Ways of legitimizing the work of Indian community advisers (for example, as Community Health Representatives) and strategies for incorporating their helping style into individual, family, and community-based interventions should be explored (see Gone [forthcoming] for his proposal for a tribal-based mental health workers training program). Increased collaboration between service providers and traditional healers is both exciting and challenging. Furthermore, American Indians should be encouraged to help fill the desperate need for leadership in the mental health and youth development arenas. Native American psychologists would seem to be uniquely qualified to help mobilize community solutions to community problems. According to Thomason (1999), academic institutions and professional schools of psychology should step up their necessary involvement in the field through accelerated recruitment and retention efforts, incentives for faculty outreach to reservations, and establishment of Native American resource centers on university campuses.

References

Aberle, D. F. *The Peyote Religion Among the Navajo.* Chicago, Ill.: Aldine, 1966.

Ambler, M. J. (ed.). "Native Language" [Special issue]. *Tribal College. Journal of American Indian Higher Education,* 2000, *11*(3).

American Indian Research and Policy Institute. Available online at www.airpi.org/, 2000.

Andrews, C. "OJJDP Tribal Youth Program." *Journal of the Office of Juvenile Justice and Delinquency Prevention,* 2000, *12*(2), 9–19.

Atkinson, R., and Locke, P. "The Lakota View of the Child." *The Maine Scholar: A Journal of Ideas and Public Affairs,* 1995, *8*, 207–220.

Attneave, C. L. "Therapy in Tribal Settings and Urban Network Intervention." *Family Process,* 1969, *8*, 192–210.

Bachman, J. G., and others. "Racial/Ethnic Differences in Smoking, Drinking, and Illicit Drug Use Among American High School Seniors, 1976–1989." *American Journal of Public Health,* 1991, *81*, 372–377.

Baldridge, D. "Indian Elders: Family Traditions in Crisis." *American Behavioral Scientist,* 2001, *44*, 1515–1527.

Bandura, A. "Social Cognitive Theory in Cultural Context." *Applied Psychology,* 2002, *51*, 269–290.

Bates, S. C., Wong Plemons, B., Jumper-Thurman, P., and Beauvais, F. "Volatile Solvent Use: Patterns by Gender and Ethnicity Among School Attenders and Dropouts." In F. Beauvais and J. E. Trimble (eds.), *Sociocultural Perspectives on Volatile Solvent Use.* New York: Harrington Park Press, 1997.

Beals, J., and others. "Psychiatric Disorder Among American Indian Adolescents: Prevalence in Northern Plains Youth." *Journal of the American Academy of Child and Adolescent Psychiatry,* 1997, *36,* 1252–1259.

Beauvais, F. "Indian Adolescence: Opportunity and Challenge." In R. Montmeyer, G. Adams, and T. Gullotta (eds.), *Adolescent Diversity in Ethnic, Economic and Cultural Contexts.* Thousand Oaks, Calif.: Sage, 2000.

Beauvais, F., and Segal, B. "Drug Use Patterns Among American Indian and Alaskan Native Youth: Special Rural Populations." *Drugs and Society,* 1992, *7*(1, 2), 77–94.

Beauvais, F., and others. "Drug Use, Violence, and Victimization Among White American, Mexican American, and American Indian Dropouts, Students with Academic Problems, and Students in Good Academic Standing." *Journal of Counseling Psychology,* 1996, *43,* 292–299.

Bee-Gates, D., Howard-Pitney, B., LaFromboise, T., and Rowe, W. "Help-Seeking Behavior of Native American Indian High School Students." *Professional Psychology: Research and Practice,* 1996, *27,* 495–499.

BigFoot-Sipes, D., and others. "American Indian Secondary School Students' Preference for Counselors." *Journal of Multicultural Counseling and Development,* 1992, *20,* 113–122.

Blum, R. W., Potthoff, S. J., and Resnick, M. D. "The Impact of Chronic Conditions on Native American Adolescents." *Families, Systems, and Health,* 1997, *15*(3), 275–282.

Blum, R. W., and others. "American Indian-Alaska Native Youth Health." *Journal of American Medical Association,* 1992, *267,* 1637–1644.

Buffalohead, P. *Cherish the Children: Parenting Skills for Indian Mothers with Young Children.* Minneapolis: Minnesota Indian Women's Resource Center, 1988.

Bureau of Indian Affairs. *Indian Labor Force Report: Portrait 1997.* Washington, D.C.: Bureau of Indian Affairs, 1997.

Bureau of Justice Statistics. *American Indians and Crime.* Washington, D.C.: U.S. Government Printing Office, 1999.

Centers for Disease Control and Prevention. *HIV/AIDS Surveillance Report.* Atlanta: U.S. Department of Health and Human Services, 1999, *11*(1), 1–42.

Chavez, G. F., Cordero, J. F., and Becerra, J. S. "Leading Major Congenital Malformations Among Minority Groups in the United States, 1981–1986." *Morbidity and Mortality Weekly Report, Centers for Disease Control and Prevention Surveillance Summary,* 1988, *37,* 17–24.

Coggins, K., Williams, E., and Radin, N. *The Traditional Tribal Values of Ojibwa Parents and the School Performance of Their Children: An Exploratory Study.* Ann Arbor: University of Michigan, 1996. (ED 400 116)

Costello, E. J., and others. "Psychiatric Disorders Among American Indian and White Youth in Appalachia: The Great Smoky Mountains Study." *American Journal of Public Health,* 1997, *87,* 827–832.

Cross, T. L. "Understanding Family Resiliency from a Relational Worldview." In H. I. McCubbin, E. A. Thompson, A. I. Thompson, and J. E. Fromer (eds.), *Resiliency in Native American and Immigrant Families.* Thousand Oaks, Calif.: Sage, 1998.

Csordas, T. J. "Ritual Healing and the Politics of Identity in Contemporary Navajo Society." *American Ethnologist,* 1999, *26,* 3–23.

Cunningham, P. J. "Health Care Utilization, Expenditures, and Insurance Coverage for American Indians and Alaska Natives Eligible for the Indian Health Service." In G. Sandefur, R. R. Rindfuss, and B. Cohen (eds.), *Changing Numbers, Changing Needs: American Indian Demography and Public Health.* Washington, D.C.: National Academy Press, 1996.

Dalaker, J. "Poverty in the United States: 2000." *Current Population Reports: Consumer Income.* Washington, D.C.: U.S. Bureau of the Census, 2001.

D'Andrea, M. "The Concerns of Native American Youth." *Journal of Multicultural Counseling and Development,* 1994, *22,* 173–181.

Dauphinais, P. "Slowing the Flood of Special Education Referrals." *Tribal College: Journal of American Indian Higher Education,* 2000, *11*(4), 14–17.

Dauphinais, P., Dauphinais, L., and Rowe, W. "Effects of Race and Communication Style on Indian Perceptions of Counselor Effectiveness." *Counselor Education and Supervision,* 1981, *21,* 72–80.

Dauphinais, P., LaFromboise, T., and Rowe, W. "Perceived Problems and Sources of Help for American Indian Students." *Counselor Education and Supervision,* 1980, *20,* 37–44.

Dell, P. F. "The Hopi Family Therapist and the Aristotelian Parents." *Journal of Marital and Family Therapy,* 1980, *6,* 123–130.

Demmert, W. G. *Improving Academic Performance Among Native American Students: A Review of the Research Literature.* Charleston, W.Va.: ERIC Clearinghouse on Rural Education and Small Schools, 2001.

Demmert, W. G., and Bell, T. H. *Indian Nation at Risk: An Educational Strategy for Action.* Washington, D.C.: U.S. Department of Education, 1991.

DeNavas-Walt, C., Cleveland, R. W., and Roemer, M. I. *Money Income in the United States: 2000.* Washington, D.C.: U.S. Bureau of the Census, U.S. Department of Commerce, 2001.

Deyhle, D. "Success and Failure: A Micro-Ethnographic Comparison of

Navajo and Anglo Students' Perceptions of Testing." *Curriculum Inquiry,* 1986, *16*(4), 365–389.

Deyhle, D., and Swisher, K. "Research in American Indian and Alaska Native Education: From Assimilation to Self-Determination." In M. Apple (ed.), *Review of Research in Education.* Washington, D.C.: American Educational Research Association, 1997.

Division of General Pediatrics and Adolescent Health. *The State of Native American Youth Health.* Minneapolis: University of Minnesota Health Center, 1992.

Dodd, J. M., Garcia, F. M., Meccage, C., and Nelson, J. R. "American Indian Student Retention." *National Association of Student Personnel Administrators Journal,* 1995, *33*(10), 72–78.

Donnermeyer, J., Edwards, R., Chavez, E., and Beauvais, R. "Involvement of American Indian Youth in Gangs." *Free Inquiry,* 1996, *24,* 167–174.

Duclos, C. W., and others. "Prevalence of Common Psychiatric Disorders Among American Indian Adolescent Detainees." *Journal of the American Academy of Child and Adolescent Psychiatry,* 1998, *37,* 866–873.

Duran, E., and Duran, B. *Native American Postcolonial Psychology.* Albany, N.Y.: State University of New York, 1995.

Eccles, J., and Gootman, J. A. (eds.). *Community Programs to Promote Youth Development.* Washington, D.C.: National Academy Press, 2002.

Fischler, R. "Child Abuse and Neglect in American Indian Communities." *Child Abuse and Neglect,* 1985, *9,* 95–106.

Fisher, P. A., Bacon, J. G., and Storck, M. "Teacher, Parent, and Youth Reports of Problem Behaviors Among Rural American Indian and Caucasian Adolescents. *American Indian and Alaska Native Mental Health Research,* 1998, *8*(2), 1–23.

Forquera, R. *Urban Indian Health.* Menlo Park, Calif.: Henry J. Kaiser Family Foundation, 2001.

Garrett, J. T., and Garrett, M. W. "The Path of Good Medicine: Understanding and Counseling Native Americans." *Journal of Multicultural Counseling and Development,* 1994, *22,* 134–144.

Garrett, M. T., and Osborne, W. L. "The Native American Sweat Lodge as Metaphor for Group Work." *Journal for Specialists in Group Work,* 1995, *20,* 33–39.

Gilbert, W. S. "Bridging the Gap Between High School and College." *Journal of American Indian Education,* 2000, *39*(3), 36–58.

Gone, J. P. "American Indian Mental Health Service Delivery: Persistent Challenges and Future Prospects." In J. S. Mio and G. Y. Iwamasa (eds.), *Multicultural Mental Health Research and Resistance: Continuing Challenges of the New Millennium.* New York: Brunner-Routledge, forthcoming.

Goodluck, C. T. "Understanding Navajo Ethnic Identity: Weaving the Meaning Through the Voices of Young Girls." Doctoral dissertation. *Dissertation Abstracts International, 59* (08A). (UMI No. 9902397). Denver: University of Denver, 1998.

Gray, E., and Cosgrove, J. "Ethnocentric Perception of Childrearing Practices in Protective Services." *Child Abuse and Neglect,* 1985, *9,* 389–396.

Greenfeld, L. A., and Smith, S. K. *American Indians and Crime.* Washington, D.C.: U.S. Department of Justice, Bureau of Justice Statistics, 1999.

Harris, M. B., Page, P., and Begay, C. "Attitudes Toward Aging in a Southwestern Sample: Effects of Ethnicity, Age, and Sex." *Psychological Reports,* 1988, *62,* 735–746.

Harrod, H. L. *Becoming and Remaining a People: Native American Religions on the Northern Plains.* Tucson: University of Arizona Press, 1995.

Helms, J. E. "Why Is There No Study of Cultural Equivalence in Standardized Cognitive-Ability Testing?" *American Psychologist,* 1992, *47,* 1083–1101.

Henderson, E., Kunitz, S. J., and Levy, J. E. "The Origins of Navajo Youth Gangs." *American Indian Culture and Research Journal,* 1999, *23*(3), 243–264.

Howard, M. O., and others. "Inhalant Use Among Urban American Indian Youth." *Addiction,* 1999, *94,* 83–95.

Howard-Pitney, B., and others. "Psychological and Social Indicators of Suicide Ideation and Suicide Attempts in Zuni Adolescents." *Journal of Consulting and Clinical Psychology,* 1992, *60,* 473–476.

Hynd, G. W., and Garcia, W. I. "Intellectual Assessment of the Native American Student." *School Psychology Digest,* 1979, *8,* 446–454.

Indian Health Service. *Trends in Indian Health.* Washington, D.C.: Indian Health Service, 1997.

Irwin, M. H., and Roll, S. "The Psychological Impact of Sexual Abuse of Native American Boarding-School Children." *Journal of the American Academy of Psychoanalysis,* 1995, *23,* 461–473.

Joe, J. R., and Malach, R. S. "Families with Native American Roots." In E. W. Lynch and M. J. Hanson (eds.), *Developing Cross-Cultural Competence: A Guide for Working with Children and Families.* Baltimore: Paul H. Brookes, 1998.

Jumper-Thurman, P., and others. "Using the Community Readiness Model in Native Communities." In J. E. Trimble and F. Beauvais (eds.), *Health Promotion and Substance Abuse Prevention Among American Indian and Alaska Native Communities: Issues in Cultural Competence.* Special Collaborative Monograph, Cultural Competence

Series, no. 9. Rockville, Md.: Center for Substance Abuse and Prevention, 2001.

Krauss, M. "Status of Native American Language Endangerment." In G. Cantoni (ed.), *Stabilizing Indigenous Languages*. Flagstaff, Ariz.: Center for Excellence in Education, Northern Arizona University, 1996. Available online at www.ncbe.gwu.edu/miscpubs/stabilize/I-needs/status.htm/

LaDue, R. A., Streissguth, A. P., and Randels, S. P. "Clinical Considerations Pertaining to Adolescents and Adults with Fetal Alcohol Syndrome." In T. B. Sonderegger (ed.), *Perinatal Substance Abuse: Research Findings and Clinical Implications*. Baltimore: Johns Hopkins University Press, 1992.

LaFromboise, T. *American Indian Life Skills Development Curriculum*. Madison, Wisc.: University of Wisconsin Press, 1996.

La Fromboise, T. D., Dauphinais, P., and Rowe, W. "Indian Students' Perceptions of Positive Helper Attributes." *Journal of American Indian Education*, 1980, *19*, 11–16.

LaFromboise, T. D., Davis, B., and Rowe, W. "Verbal Response Patterns of Effective Indian Helpers." Paper presented at the annual meeting of the American Psychological Association, Los Angeles, August 1985.

LaFromboise, T. D., and Dixon, D. "American Indian Perceptions of Trustworthiness in Counseling Interview." *Journal of Counseling Psychology*, 1981, *28*, 135–139.

LaFromboise, T., and Howard-Pitney, B. "The Zuni Life Skills Development Curriculum: Description and Evaluation of a Suicide Prevention Program." *Journal of Counseling Psychology*, 1995, *42*, 479–486.

LaFromboise, T. D., Oliver, L., and Hoyt, D. "Strengths and Resilience of American Indian Adolescents." In L. Whitbeck (ed.), *This Is Not Our Way: Traditional Culture and Substance Use Prevention in American Indian Adolescents and Their Families*, forthcoming.

LaFromboise, T. D., and Rowe, W. "Skills Training for Bicultural Competence: Rationale and Application." *Journal of Counseling Psychology*, 1983, *30*, 589–595.

Lefley, H. P. "Differential Self-Concept in American Indian Children as a Function of Language and Examiner." *Journal of Personality and Social Psychology*, 1975, *31*, 36–41.

Lujan, C., DeBruyn, L. M., May, P. A., and Bird, M. E. "Profile of Abused and Neglected American Indian Children in the Southwest." *Child Abuse and Neglect*, 1989, *13*, 449–461.

Mail, P. D. "Early Modeling of Drinking Behavior by Native American

Elementary School Children Playing Drunk." *The International Journal of the Addictions,* 1995, *30,* 1187–1197.

Mandrigal, L. "Indian Child and Welfare Act: Partnership for Preservation." *American Behavioral Scientist,* 2001, *44,* 1505–1511.

Manson, S. M. "Behavioral Health Services for American Indians: Need, Use, and Barriers to Effective Care." In M. Dixon and Y. Roubideaux (eds.), *Promises to Keep: Public Health Policy for American Indians and Alaska Natives in the 21st Century.* Washington, D.C.: American Public Health Association Press, 2001.

Manson, S., Beals, J., Dick, R., and Duclos, C. "Risk Factors for Suicide Among Indian Adolescents at a Boarding School." *Public Health Reports,* 1989, *104,* 609–614.

Manson, S. M., Walker, R. D., and Kivlahan, D. R. "Psychiatric Assessment and Treatment of American Indians and Alaska Natives." *Hospital and Community Psychiatry,* 1987, *38,* 165–173.

May, P. A. "Suicide and Self-Destruction Among American Indian Youths." *American Indian and Alaska Native Mental Health Research,* 1987, *1,* 52–69.

May, P. A. "Overview of Alcohol Abuse Epidemiology for American Indian Populations." In G. Sandefur, R. R. Rindfuss, and B. Cohen (eds.), *Changing Numbers, Changing Needs: American Indian Demography and Public Health.* Washington, D.C.: National Academy Press, 1996.

May, P. A., and Gossage, J. P. "Estimating the Prevalence of Fetal Alcohol Syndrome: A Summary." *Alcohol Research and Health,* 2001, *25*(3), 159–167.

May, P. A., and Hymbaugh, K. J. "A Macro-Level Fetal Alcohol Syndrome Prevention Program for American Indians and Alaska Natives: Description and Evaluation." *Journal of Studies on Alcohol,* 1989, *16,* 218–244.

McMorris, B. J., and others. *Parents, Peers, and Precociousness: Disentangling Factors Associated with Early Alcohol Use Among Native American Girls and Boys,* under review.

Mohatt, G., and Blue, A. W. "Primary Prevention as It Relates to Traditionality and Empirical Measures of Social Deviance." In S. Manson (ed.), *New Directions in Prevention Among American Indian and Alaska Native Communities.* Portland: Oregon Health Sciences University, 1982.

Morey, S. M., and Gilliam, O. J. (eds.). *Respect for Life: The Traditional Upbringing of American Indian Children.* New York: Myrin Institute, 1974.

Napoliello, A. L., and Sweet, E. S. "Salvador Minuchin's Structural Family Therapy and Its Application to Native Americans." *Family Therapy,* 1992, *19,* 155–165.

National Center for Health Statistics. *Ten Leading Causes Of Death: American Indian and Alaskan Natives (Both Sexes, Males or Females, 1995–97).* Atlanta: Office of Statistics and Programming, National Center for Injury Prevention and Control, Centers for Disease Control and Prevention, 2002.

National Indian Child Welfare Association. *Positive Indian Parenting: Honoring Our Children by Honoring Our Traditions.* Portland, Oreg.: National Indian Child Welfare Association, 1986.

Novins, D. K., Beals, J., Roberts, R. E., and Manson, S. M. "Factors Associated with Suicide Ideation Among American Indian Adolescents: Does Culture Matter?" *Suicide and Life-Threatening Behavior,* 1999, *29,* 332–346.

Novins, D. K., Bechtold, D. W., and others. "The DSM-IV Outline for Cultural Formulation: A Critical Demonstration with American Indian Children." *Journal of American Academy of Child and Adolescent Psychiatry,* 1997, *38,* 1102–1108.

Novins, D. K., Duclos, C. W., and others. "Utilization of Alcohol, Drug, and Mental Health Treatment Services Among American Indian Adolescent Detainees." *Journal of the American Academy of Child and Adolescent Psychiatry,* 1999, *38,* 1102–1108.

Novins, D. K., and Mitchell, C. M. "Future Depressive Symptomatology: Predictive Factors Among American Indian Adolescents." Paper presented at the annual meeting of the American Academy of Child and Adolescent Psychiatry, Toronto, 1997.

Oetting, E. R., and Beauvais, F. "Orthogonal Cultural Identification Theory: The Cultural Identification of Minority Adolescents." *The International Journal of the Addictions,* 1990-1991, *25,* 655–685.

Oetting, E. R., Swaim, R. C., Edwards, R. W., and Beauvais, F. "Indian and Anglo Adolescent Alcohol Use and Emotional Distress: Path Models." *American Journal of Drug and Alcohol Abuse,* 1989, *15,* 153–172.

Office for Substance Abuse Prevention. *Breaking New Ground for American Indian and Alaska Native Youth at Risk: Program Summaries.* U.S. Department of Health and Human Services, 1990.

Ogunwole, S. *The American Indian and Alaska Native Population: 2000.* Washington, D.C.: U.S. Bureau of the Census, U.S. Department of Commerce, 2002.

Petoskey, E. L., Van Stelle, K. R., and De Jong, J. A. "Prevention Through Empowerment in a Native American Community." *Drugs and Society,* 1998, *12*(1/2), 147–162.

Plank, G. A. "Application of the Cross Battery Approach in the Assessment of American Indian Children: A Viable Alternative." *American Indian and Alaska Native Mental Health Research,* 2001, *10*(1), 21–33.

Roski, J., and others. "Psychosocial Factors Associated with Alcohol Use Among Young Adolescent American Indians and Whites." *Journal of Child and Adolescent Substance Abuse,* 1997, 7(2), 1–18.

Roubideaux, Y. K. "AAIP HIV/AIDS Prevention/Awareness Program." *Association of American Indian Physicians Newsletter,* 2000, 1–11.

Ryan, R. (prod.). *The Healing Road: Professional Helping in Native America.* Motion picture available from Microtraining Associates, 25 Burdette Avenue, Framingham, MA 01702, 2000.

Sanchez-Way, R., and Johnson, S. "Cultural Practices in American Indian Prevention Programs." *Juvenile Justice,* 2000, 7(2), 20–30.

Sandefur, G. D., and Liebler, C. A. "The Demography of American Indian Families." In G. Sandefur, R. R. Rindfuss, and B. Cohen (eds.), *Changing Numbers, Changing Needs: American Indian Demography and Public Health.* Washington, D.C.: National Academy Press, 1996.

Sattler, J. M. *Clinical and Forensic Interviewing of Children and Families.* San Diego, Calif.: Jerome M. Sattler, 1998.

Schacht, A. J., Tafoya, N., and Mirabla, K. "Home-Based Therapy with American Indian Families." *American Indian and Alaska Native Mental Health Research,* 1989, *3*(2), 27–42.

Schinke, S. P., Tepavac, L., and Cole, K. C. "Preventing Substance Use Among Native American Youth: Three-Year Results." *Addictive Behaviors,* 2000, *25,* 387–397.

Shaughnessy, L., Branum, C., and Everett-Jones, S. *2001 Youth Risk Behavior Survey of High School Students Attending Bureau Funded Schools.* Available online at the Bureau of Indian Affairs Web site: www indianedu research.net/youthrisk.pdf/, 2001.

Snipp, C. M. "The Size and Distribution of the American Indian Population: Fertility, Mortality, Residence, and Migration." In G. Sandefur, R. R. Rindfuss, and B. Cohen (eds.), *Changing Numbers, Changing Needs: American Indian Demography and Public Health.* Washington, D.C.: National Academy Press, 1996.

Spencer, J., and Thomas, J. "Psychiatric Diagnostic Profiles in Hospitalized Adolescent and Adult Navajo Indians." *Social Psychiatry and Epidemiology,* 1992, *27,* 226–229.

Strauss, T., and Valentino, D. "Retribalization in Urban Indian Communities." In S. Lobo and K. Peters (eds.), *American Indians and the Urban Experience.* Walnut Creek, Calif.: Altamira Press, 2001.

Swisher, K. G., Hoisch, M., and Pavel, D. M. *American Indian/Alaskan*

Native Dropout Study. Washington, D.C.: National Education Association, 1991.

Tafoya, T. "Circles and Cedar: Native Americans and Family Therapy." *Minorities and Family Therapy.* Binghamton, N.Y.: Haworth House, 1989.

Teufel, N. I., and Ritenbaugh, C. K. "Development of a Primary Prevention Program: Insight Gained in the Zuni Diabetes Prevention Program." *Clinical Pediatrics,* 1998, *37,* 131–141.

Thomason, T. "Improving the Recruitment and Retention of Native American Students in Psychology." *Cultural Diversity and Ethnic Minority Psychology,* 1999, *5,* 308–316.

Topper, M. D. "Multidimensional Therapy: A Case Study of a Navajo Adolescent with Multiple Problems." In L. Vargas and J. D. Koss-Chioino (eds.), *Working with Culture: Psychotherapeutic Interventions with Ethnic Minority Children and Adolescents.* San Francisco: Jossey-Bass, 1992.

Trujillo, A. "Psychotherapy with Native Americans: A View into the Role of Religion and Spirituality." In P. S. Richards and A. E. Bergin (eds.), *Handbook of Psychotherapy and Religious Diversity.* Washington, D.C.: American Psychological Association, 1999.

Uecker, A., and Nadel, L. "Spatial But Not Object Memory Impairments in Children with Fetal Alcohol Syndrome." *American Journal of Mental Retardation,* 1998, *103*(1), 12–18.

U.S. Bureau of the Census. *National Survey of Homeless Assistance Providers and Clients.* Washington, D.C.: U.S. Department of Commerce, 1999.

U.S. Bureau of the Census. *American Indian and Alaska Native Population, by Age and Sex for the United States: 2000.* Washington, D.C.: U.S. Department of Commerce, 2002a.

U.S. Bureau of the Census. *Total Population by Age and Sex for the United States: 2000.* Washington, D.C.: U.S. Department of Commerce, 2002b.

U.S. Department of Health and Human Services. *Mental Health: Culture, Race and Ethnicity.* Supplement to *Mental Health: A Report of the Surgeon General.* Rockville, Md.: U.S. Department of Health and Human Services, 2001.

West, J., and others. "Mental Health Practitioners and Trainees." In R. W. Manderscheid and M. J. Henderson (eds.), *Mental Health, United States, 2000.* Rockville, MD: U. S. Department of Health and Human Services, 2000.

Westberg, J. "Native Organizations Battle Against the Spread of AIDS." *Winds of Change,* 1997, 79–84.

Whitbeck, L. B., Hoyt, D. R., Chen, X., and Stubben, J. D. "Predictors of Gang Involvement Among American Indian Adolescents." *Journal of Gang Research,* forthcoming.

Whitbeck, L. B., Hoyt, D. R., Stubben, J. D., and LaFromboise, T. "Traditional Culture and Academic Success Among American Indian Children in the Upper Midwest." *Journal of American Indian Education,* 2001, *40*(2), 48–60.

Willis, D. J., Dobrec, A., and Sipes, D. "Treating American Indian Victims of Abuse and Neglect." In L. Vargas and J. D. Koss-Chioino (eds.), *Working with Culture: Psychotherapeutic Interventions with Ethnic Minority Children and Adolescents.* San Francisco: Jossey-Bass, 1992.

Part Two

African American and Racially Mixed Population Groups

In this section of the book, we focus on African Americans and youth who are racially and culturally mixed—two populations of color dating back to the seventeenth century. In Chapter Two, Jewelle Taylor Gibbs points out that African Americans trace their history to the arrival of the first slave ships in Jamestown, Virginia, in 1619—the year before the Pilgrims landed on Plymouth Rock, Massachusetts, in 1620. Until the international slave trade was abolished in 1807, most of the millions of slaves forcibly brought to the United States were imported from West and Central Africa. By the end of the Civil War in 1865, there were more than four million emancipated blacks in the U.S. population (see Franklin and Moss, 1988).

Like the American Indians, these slaves came from tribal societies that were highly diversified in culture, language, political economies, and belief systems (see Gibbs, 1998). Due to their physical appearance and unfamiliar customs, they were also viewed as uncivilized, primitive, and inferior to Europeans, providing the rationale for them to be treated as subhumans in both the law and in civil society. After "emancipation" and a brief period of reconstruction, African Americans endured nearly a century of legal discrimination, economic exploitation, and political disenfranchisement, particularly in the southern states, until the Civil Rights Acts of 1964 and 1965 were passed.

Since World War II, the African American community has become increasingly diverse, as newer black immigrants from the Caribbean Islands and various African countries have arrived with their own languages and customs, while gradually becoming incorporated into the broader community of the African diaspora (see Drake, 1987). This heterogeneous black population has also achieved significant gains in educational and occupational status, average income, and access to mainstream American economic and political institutions.

Despite these gains, African Americans still have high rates of poverty, with a hard-core urban underclass who are characterized by chronic high unemployment, deteriorating community institutions, and social problems. In turn, black youth in these distressed communities are at risk for school failure, delinquency, and self-destructive behaviors (see Gibbs, 1988). In spite of these circumstances, resilience and strengths may be found in these communities and can provide the foundation for building effective interventions.

Sociocultural Characteristics

Gibbs points out that since the era of slavery, the African American church has been the central institution serving the social and emotional needs of black families. Thus African Americans place a high value on religion and spirituality in their worldview. Childrearing has also been traditionally viewed as the collective responsibility of the extended family, in which grandparents now play an increasingly significant role in raising children. Although education has been viewed by middle-class families as the route to mobility, low-income families have had greater difficulties in gaining access to high-quality schools, and many of their children have been alienated from the educational system as a result. Black families have also encouraged flexible sex roles and resilient coping skills in their children to prepare them to cope with an often hostile and unpredictable society.

Although hard work, patience, forbearance, and personal dignity have traditionally been valued in black families, the protests of the civil rights movement have empowered younger blacks to be more assertive about demanding equal rights and equal access to all institutions in American society.

In Chapter Three, Gibbs describes the unique set of developmental challenges that biracial and bicultural youth must negotiate in order to establish positive identities. However, racially and culturally mixed children are not a new phenomenon in American society but trace their origins back to the earliest contacts between indigenous Indians and white settlers and later to the widespread miscegenation between African slaves and their white masters and overseers. Until recently, racially mixed people had been forced to categorize themselves as "blacks" if they had a minuscule degree of African ancestry (the "one-drop" hypodescent rule) or "Indios" if they had at least one-quarter or more of "Indian blood" (hyperdescent rule). However, since 1980 this population has grown so rapidly and gained so much visibility in the society that they successfully advocated for a special designation in the 2000 federal census: the right to label themselves in multiple racial-ethnic categories.

Many of these mixed children are actually multiracial and multicultural, growing up in families with two parents of mixed racial or ethnic backgrounds. For a significant number of these youth, the transition from adolescence to adulthood precipitates identity conflicts about who they are, where they fit, how they behave, and what their future holds as they struggle to incorporate the salient characteristics of their dual racial or ethnic heritages. These youth are confronted with unique development challenges that may precipitate problematic behaviors or stimulate resilient and adaptive coping strategies.

From another perspective, this emerging population of multiracial and multicultural youth has challenged our society's conceptions of racial and ethnic boundaries (Root, 1996). They represent the vanguard of a multiracial, multicultural society that will make the term *minority groups* obsolete and may ultimately produce a nation in which race and ethnicity are irrelevant (see Hollinger, 1995).

Implications for Mental Health

In conducting an assessment of African American youth and their families, Gibbs recommends that clinicians evaluate their exposure to traumatic events, their experiences with racial integration, their coping skills, and their access to opportunities in the community, as well as current symptomatology and history of problem behaviors.

An assessment of biracial and bicultural youth should focus on their identity issues, their experiences in the schools and community, their family's attitudes toward their mixed race or ethnicity, and their coping strategies to reconcile and incorporate their dual or multiple racial-ethnic heritages.

Family therapy is an important modality for African American and racially mixed youth, as parental communication and support are essential in the successful resolution of their problems. Group therapy and psychoeducational interventions have also proven to be effective with delinquent and substance-abusing youth of color, whereas older youth may benefit from individual psychotherapy to support their adaptive coping strategies in their transition to adulthood.

References

Drake, S. C. *Black Folk Here and There.* Vol. 1. Los Angeles: Center for Afro-American Studies, University of California, Los Angeles, 1987.

Franklin, J. H., and Moss, A. A., Jr. *From Slavery to Freedom: A History of Negro Americans.* (6th ed.) New York: Knopf, 1988.

Gibbs, J. L., Jr. (ed.). *Peoples of Africa.* Prospect Heights, Ill.: Waveland Press, 1988.

Gibbs, J. T. (ed.). *Young, Black and Male in America: An Endangered Species.* Westport, Conn.: Greenwood Press, 1998.

Hollinger, D. A. *Postethnic America.* New York: Basic Books, 1995.

Root, M. P. (ed.). *The Multiracial Experience: Racial Borders as the New Frontier.* Thousand Oaks, Calif.: Sage, 1996.

Chapter Two

African American Children and Adolescents

Jewelle Taylor Gibbs

African American adolescents are one of the most vulnerable and victimized groups in contemporary American society. They have been mislabeled and miseducated by the schools, mishandled by the juvenile justice system, mistreated by mental health agencies, and neglected by the social welfare bureaucracy until very recently. Their plight has been minimized by health care professionals and ignored by policymakers; they have been labeled an "endangered species" (Gibbs, 1984, 1988b), members of a growing "underclass" (Glasgow, 1981; Wilson, 1987; Massey and Denton, 1993), and "at high risk for a variety of self-destructive and anti-social behaviors" (Dryfoos, 1990, p. 109).

As a result of generations of discrimination and deprivation, African American adolescents have developed high rates of psychological and behavioral disorders, as well as certain problematic psychosocial behaviors. However, in spite of the high incidence of these problem behaviors, many African American youth have managed to become competent, well-functioning young adults.

The purpose of this chapter is to present an overview of the psychological and psychosocial problems of African American adolescents, to discuss issues of assessment and diagnosis, and to describe intervention strategies that are appropriate and effective for this group. This chapter focuses on African American adolescents and youth aged ten to nineteen, which includes the school years from junior high school through college. In addition, the discussion focuses primarily on non-Hispanic, African American youth who are identified as African American rather than Caribbean in their ethnic heritage because the former group constitutes the great majority of black Americans.

The mental health problems and needs of these African American youth are discussed in the context of the historical, social, economic, and political factors that have shaped their experiences in American society. Further, the cultural values and adaptive behaviors that many African Americans have developed in response to these experiences are described.

The overarching conceptual framework of the chapter is a combination of two major perspectives: (1) an ego-psychology perspective on adolescent development (Erikson, 1950, 1959) and (2) an ecological perspective on the social environment in which this development occurs (Bronfenbrenner, 1979; Garbarino, 1982). Only through some comprehension of the complex socioeconomic and political forces impinging on African American youth and their families is it possible to understand their adaptive and maladaptive behaviors (Gibbs, 1988b; Jones, 1989; Taylor, 1995).

Moreover, it is essential for mental health professionals to be cognizant of the historical forces of slavery, discrimination, and segregation that produced a "separate and unequal" universe for African Americans, reinforcing the development of a black subculture with its own set of values, belief systems, and behavioral norms (Billingsley, 1992; Frazier, 1966). Thus this author proposes that the assessment and treatment of the psychological, behavioral, and psychosocial problems of African American youth should be carried out with particular attention to the interaction of intrapsychic, interpersonal, familial, cultural, and environmental factors— all of which have a significant impact on adolescent development, adaptation, and dysfunction.

Demographic Information

In 2000, there were approximately 6,225,000 African American youth aged ten to nineteen—3,172,000 of whom were in the fifteen- to nineteen-year age bracket (U.S. Bureau of the Census, 2001). The ten- to nineteen-year-old group constitutes 14.7 percent of the total youth population, with an equal ratio of males to females. Because youth from twenty to twenty-four constitute over 40 percent of the total African American population, the median age for African Americans is 30.3 years, compared to a white median age of 36.9 (U.S. Bureau of the Census, 2001). Thus the African American population is a relatively youthful population, which has important implications for mental health policies, programs, and services that are targeted to the African American community.

In 1999, one-third (32.7 percent) of African American youth under eighteen lived in families below the poverty line, whereas nearly two-thirds (63.1 percent) of those in female-headed households were poor (U.S. Bureau of the Census, 2001). Nearly three of every five African American children live in female-headed families, which were five times more likely to be welfare-dependent than two-parent families. Although over one-third of African American youth live in two-parent families, the remaining group also has higher rates than white youth of out-of-home placements in foster homes and institutions.

The median income of all African American families in 1999 was $31,778, which is 62 percent of the white family income of $51,224 (U.S. Bureau of the Census, 2001). However, there were striking disparities between the median income of intact families with two parents employed ($26,583) and female-headed families ($9,300). Thus middle-class status for most African American youth is related to having two employed parents and a stable economy. The unemployment rate among African American adults is more than twice as high as the unemployment rate for white adults (U.S. Bureau of the Census, 2001). In 2001, the unemployment rate for African American teenagers sixteen to nineteen was over 13.1 percent, more than twice as high as the rate for white teenagers.

By 2000, 78.5 percent of all African Americans had completed high school, and 16.5 percent had completed college or graduate school, compared to 85 and 26 percent of whites, respectively (National Center for Educational Statistics, 2001). High school dropout rates for blacks sixteen to twenty-four years old have dropped from 22.0 percent in 1970 to 12.6 percent in 1999 (U.S. Bureau of the Census, 2001). However, for school-age youth aged fifteen to nineteen, only 4.7 percent of black students dropped out of school during the 1998–99 academic year.

Finally, African American youth were more likely than white youth to live in deteriorating, central-city neighborhoods and in substandard housing with poor sanitation. They were more likely to be located in urban areas with depressed economies, where they have much less access to adequate health and mental health facilities (Farley, 1997; Massey and Denton, 1993).

As several researchers have pointed out, these social and economic characteristics of inner-city neighborhoods generate chronic levels of stress for African American youth and their families (McLoyd, 1990; Myers, 1989). Thus an understanding of these ecological realities is essential for clinicians who deliver mental health services to African American youth (Dubow, Edwards, and Ippolito, 1997; Spencer, 1995).

Historical, Social, and Political Influences on Blacks in the United States

The current status of African Americans in the United States can be directly attributed to four major historical and social factors: (1) slavery, (2) segregation and discrimination, (3) poverty, and (4) urbanization (Franklin and Moss, 1988; Massey and Denton, 1993; Omi and Winant, 1986; Wilson, 1987). Moreover, these factors also contributed significantly to undermining the functioning of the African American family and major institutions of the African American community, which, in turn, created a hospitable environment for the development of social, psychological, and behavioral problems among African American youth.

The effects of nearly 250 years of slavery on the African American family have been widely debated, but there is general agreement that slavery had a deleterious impact on the structure and functioning of the family as a unit, particularly on the role of the African American male as the head of the household (Franklin and Moss, 1988; Frazier, 1966). The racial caste system, introduced by slavery, defined African Americans as inferior and subordinate to whites. This caste system has been reinforced by the educational and economic disparities between African Americans and whites, which have persisted since slavery was abolished in 1863 (Farley, 1997; Massey and Denton, 1993).

Even after legal segregation was eliminated by a series of Supreme Court decisions, culminating in the landmark school desegregation decision in 1954, discriminatory practices were still pervasive and pernicious, depriving African Americans of equal access to schools, jobs, housing, health care, political participation, recreation, and public facilities (Farley, 1997; Massey and Denton, 1993). By enforcing the status of second-class citizenship on African Americans, the dominant society created a "separate and unequal" society that developed its own institutions, subcultural values, and behavioral norms, forcing African American parents to develop childrearing strategies that would enable them to promote healthy development in their children in spite of their minority status (McAdoo and McAdoo, 1985; Spencer, Brookins, and Allen, 1985; Taylor, 1991).

A third factor that has significantly influenced the status of African American families is persistent poverty and low SES. African American families are still three times more likely to be poor than white families. Poverty obviously has multiple adverse effects on African American youth, placing them at greater risk for a range of health and mental health problems, conduct disorders, and psychosocial problems (Lynn and McGeary, 1990; Brooks-Gunn, Duncan, and Aber, 1997; McLoyd, 1990).

Fourth, the mass migration of African Americans between World Wars I and II from the rural South to industrial centers in the North transformed the African American population from a predominantly rural, agrarian group to an urban working class (Billingsley, 1992; Franklin and Moss, 1988). Although this rapid urbanization was accompanied by many positive benefits, including opportunities for educational and occupational mobility, it resulted in the development of huge ghettos in most urban areas, concentration of African American males in a few industries, and social and cultural isolation from the dominant society. These negative outcomes of urbanization laid the foundation for the subsequent development of the so-called underclass two decades later (Massey and Denton, 1993; Wilson, 1987).

The more recent social forces that have shaped the experience of African American youth and their families have included three major socioeconomic and political developments: (1) the civil rights movement, (2) the affirmative action legislation and backlash, and (3) the radical structural and technological changes in the American economy. The civil rights movement, which began with the Montgomery bus boycott in 1955 and ended with the passage of two major civil rights bills in 1964 and 1965, signaled a new era of militancy among African Americans to obtain their full rights as citizens (Branch, 1988). Participation by thousands of college youth in the movement provided positive role models and raised the expectations and aspirations of millions of African American youth.

After the successful passage of civil rights legislation, direct-action strategies were replaced in the early 1970s by legislative and administrative programs of affirmative action to promote equal opportunity in education and employment (Jaynes and Williams, 1989). However, these efforts were only moderately successful before a widespread backlash developed among whites, who perceived these efforts as "reverse racism" and an organized effort to deprive them of their privileged status (Orfield and Ashkinaze, 1991; Schorr, 1986). Reinforcement of this backlash since 1980 by a conservative political administration has had a particularly negative impact on African American youth, as their gains in employment rates and college enrollment rates achieved by the mid-1970s had been virtually wiped out by the late 1990s (Orfield and Ashkinaze, 1991).

Finally, the post–World War II structural and technological changes in the economy from a predominantly industrial and agricultural base to a high-technology and service base have had devastating effects on the African American community (Farley, 1997; Wilson, 1996). Northern industrial cities with large African American populations have suffered economic decline, while the suburbs and the Sunbelt cities have expanded their white-collar economies. The lack of fit between a largely unskilled African American labor market and the demands of a highly technical job market have resulted in high rates of unemployment, high rates of poverty, and high rates of family dysfunction, contributing to high levels of stress for African American youth and their families (Edelman, 1987; McLoyd, 1990; Wilson, 1996).

Cultural Attitudes, Values, and Norms of African American Families

The literature has identified four major values of African American families, all of which can be understood as adaptive responses to their historical and social experiences in American society. These values focus on (1) the importance of religion and the church, (2) the importance of the extended family and kinship networks, (3) the importance of flexible family roles, and (4) the importance of education (Billingsley, 1992; Staples and Johnson, 1993).

Role of Religion

In the African American community, the church is often the central focus of social and civic activity (Billingsley, 1992; Lincoln and Mamiya, 1990). Most African Americans are Protestants, and many participate in fundamentalist denominations (for example, Baptists, Methodists, Church of God) that stress asceticism, tithing, and religious piety. In recent years, the Black Muslims have made inroads in urban inner-city communities, while more liberal denominations have attracted upwardly mobile and professional African Americans (Jaynes and Williams, 1989). Even if African American families are not currently involved in a specific church, their religious heritage will shape their beliefs and values, their views on marital relationships and divorce, abortion, adoption, childrearing practices, and so on. Awareness of the client's religious background will increase the clinician's understanding of attitudes and values, which may affect treatment decisions. In addition, clinicians should identify the local African American ministers and view them as resources in helping clients cope with problems.

Role of Family

African Americans value their family ties and tend to maintain contact with a large network of relatives and fictive kin. Especially functional for low-income African American families, who exchange resources, services, and emotional support, knowledge of this pattern is valuable for the clinician, who can often mobilize relatives to offer support to a troubled adolescent (Billingsley, 1992; McAdoo, 1981; Stack, 1974). It is not unusual for parents to send adolescents to live with other relatives in order to change their environment or to defuse conflict in a family—a practice called child-lending or child-keeping.

Flexibility in Family Roles

Flexibility in family roles has always been an important aspect of African American family functioning, as most African American women have had to work in order to maintain an adequate standard of living for their families (Billingsley, 1992; Staples and Johnson, 1993). Thus parents have divided their responsibilities less in terms of traditional gender-based roles and more in terms of household function. Traditional childrearing patterns also foster early independence in male and female children, as well as less differentiation in roles and family tasks (Peters, 1981). Although these patterns vary according to socioeconomic level and rural-urban residence, recent empirical studies generally support the descriptive accounts of greater role flexibility and less gender-specific role functioning in African American families (Billingsley, 1992; Staples and Johnson, 1993). These findings have obvious implications for the assessment of African American families, as well as for the interpretation of gender-related behaviors in male and female adolescents.

Role of Education

African American families have historically valued hard work, education, and social mobility (Billingsley, 1992; Franklin and Moss, 1988). These values prompted the mass migrations from the rural agrarian South to the urban industrial North, which offered greater educational and economic opportunities to African Americans. In spite of widespread discrimination and poverty, many African American families have sacrificed to send their children to college and prepare them for professional careers, often to serve the African American community. Unfortunately, this impetus for higher education has slowed down in recent years due to several factors, including the social isolation of poor, inner-city African Americans who lack middle-class role models, the changing nature of the economy, and the government's declining commitment to affirmative action (Orfield and Ashkinaze, 1991; Wilson, 1996). These social changes have created a widening gap between middle-class African Americans, who are able to take advantage of educational opportunities, and poor African Americans, who are frequently not even aware of these opportunities.

Mental Health Issues of African American Youth

There are no large-scale epidemiological surveys of African American adolescent mental health problems, but there have been a few community surveys and clinical studies that provide estimates of the incidence of psychological and behavioral disorders in this population.

At-Risk Behaviors

In a study of ten-year trends of at-risk behaviors in a national sample of black and white high school seniors, African American youth reported fewer at-risk behaviors than white youth, with black females reporting the lowest number of behaviors, than all other sex-race groups (Benson and Donahue, 1989).

Depression

The incidence of depression among African American youth has been investigated by researchers in a variety of school and community samples (Kaplan, Landa, Weinhold, and Shenker, 1984; Schoenbach and others, 1983; Gibbs, 1986a; Roberts, Roberts, and Chen, 1997; Siegel and others, 1998). Rates of mild-to-moderate depression have ranged from 20 to 40 percent, whereas rates of severe depression have ranged from 5 to 15 percent in these non-clinical samples. Higher rates of depression have generally been found among females and lower-income African American adolescents in within-group studies. However, results conflict on whether there are significant differences in rates of depression between black, white, and Latino adolescents (U.S. Department of Health and Human Services, 2001).

Some of these studies have found that African American adolescents obtained comparable or lower scores on standardized depression scales and on self-report inventories than white, Asian, or Latino adolescents; a few studies have reported higher scores for blacks than whites. These conflicting results probably reflect differences in sampling design, measures used, and definitions of depression. In the Youth Risk Behavior Surveillance of 2001 (Centers for Disease Control and Prevention, 2002b), similar proportions of

African American and white high school students reported having felt sad or hopeless almost daily for two weeks or more in the past twelve months (28.8 percent and 26.5 percent, respectively), but Latino students were significantly more likely than blacks or whites to report these feelings (34.0 percent) in the past year.

Eating Disorders

Eating disorders such as anorexia nervosa or bulimia were very rare among African American youth, with only sixteen reported in the clinical literature through 1985 (Pumariega, Edwards, and Mitchell, 1984; Robinson and Andersen, 1985). However, since that time several researchers have reported an increased incidence of disordered eating symptoms and diagnoses among African American females, especially symptoms of bulimia among older adolescents and young adults who are well educated, but their overall rates are generally much lower than among white and Latino females (see review article by Crago, Shisslak, and Estes, 1996). Although black females were more likely than whites to be obese, they were less likely to binge and purge and more likely to use laxatives and diuretics than white females.

Conduct Disorders

Although the prevalence of conduct disorders among African American adolescents is not known, it can be safely said that they have disproportionately high rates of conduct problems in school and clinic settings (Costello and others, 1988; Mukuria, 2002; Reed, 1988). In their study of problem behaviors in a national sample of racially diverse students aged five to seventeen, McDermott and Spencer (1997) found varying patterns in teachers' ratings of six major behavioral symptom clusters among white, black, and Latino youth, with black youth exhibiting significantly higher ratings of oppositional-defiant and solitary-impulsive behaviors than the other two groups. African American teens are suspended or expelled more often than whites for fighting, extortion of money, verbal or physical abuse of teachers, vandalism, and truancy in junior high and high schools (Garibaldi and Bartley, 1988; Irvine and Irvine, 1995). Fine (1991) found that students with persistent discipline problems are more likely to drop out of school and to have limited job options.

Psychiatric Treatment

Psychiatric hospitalization rates of African American youth have traditionally been two to three times the rates for white youth (Myers, 1989). Studies of psychiatric treatment of African American youth suggest that they are underrepresented in outpatient settings and receive more severe diagnoses, yet remain in treatment for shorter periods of time than white youth. However, black youth are overrepresented in publicly funded residential treatment and inpatient psychiatric treatment facilities (see U.S. Department of Health and Human Services, 2001).

Suicide

Suicide is increasing among African American adolescents and is now, at the rate of 5.4 per 100,000, the third leading cause of death for black youth in the fifteen- to nineteen-year age group. Between 1980 and 1999, the suicide rate for black males in this age range nearly doubled from 5.6 to 10.0 per 100,000; the rate for black females only increased from 1.6 to 1.9 per 100,000 (Centers for Disease Control and Prevention, 2001). Data from the Youth Risk Behavior Survey in 2001 (Centers for Disease Control and Prevention, 2002b) showed that black female high school students reported lower rates than white or Latino females of suicide attempts or ideations, whereas black males reported higher rates of serious suicidal attempts than their white or Latino age-mates. Although suicide rates are much lower than homicide rates for black youth, they may be underestimated; many "undetermined deaths" may be misclassified as accidents due to the strong prohibition against suicide in the African American community (Shaffer and Fisher, 1981). Moreover, the symptoms of suicidal behavior in black youth are often masked by extreme anger, acting out, and engaging in high-risk behaviors, making it more difficult for clinicians to assess suicidal intent. Thus it is essential for clinicians to recognize "depressive equivalents" and high-risk behaviors as potential clues to suicidal behavior in African American youth and to conduct a suicide assessment whenever these symptoms are chronic or severe (Gibbs, 1988a; Weddle and McKenry, 1995).

Psychosocial Problems of African American Youth

Psychosocial problems of African American youth are reflected in the statistics on social indicators—those conditions that cause social or legal difficulties for the youth and usually have adverse consequences for the family and community, such as dropping out of school, juvenile delinquency, substance abuse, and unwed teenage pregnancy and parenthood. Although the causal sequence is not clear, many of these youth experience anxiety, depression, and other emotional distress in connection with these social problems. Yet studies of school-age African American youth have documented that they are less likely than white youth to have visited a mental health clinic or to have received psychological treatment across several institutional settings (Cuffe and others, 1995; U.S. Department of Health and Human Services, 2001).

School Dropout Rates

In the fall of 1998, 17.1 percent of all students enrolled in public elementary and secondary schools were African American (National Center for Educational Statistics, 2001). Over half (51.6 percent) of these students were enrolled in schools with predominantly black student populations, whereas 70.2 percent were enrolled in schools with 50 to 90 percent minority student bodies, continuing the trend toward more racially and ethnically segregated schools (Farley, 1997). Black students in central-city areas were also more likely to attend schools with building facilities rated as "inadequate" and environmental factors rated as "unsatisfactory" than students in urban fringe or small-town areas (National Center for Education Statistics, 2001).

Despite these adverse conditions for learning, dropout rates for African American youth ages sixteen to twenty-four have steadily declined from 27.9 percent in 1970 to 12.6 percent in 1999, as compared to 13.2 percent and 7.3 percent for white youth in that same three-decade period (National Center for Education Statistics, 2001).

However, the rates in many inner-city areas currently range from 30 to 50 percent, and some students leave school as early as eighth grade (Reed, 1988). Further, on national assessments of reading, mathematics, and science, the performance of black students consistently lags behind that of white and Asian students at all grade levels (Darling-Hammond, 1998; Williams and others, 2002). Handicapped by educational deficiencies, lack of vocational training, and lack of access to home computers, black youth dropouts have high unemployment rates and few opportunities for legitimate income.

Juvenile Delinquency

Official delinquency rates indicate that African American youth are more likely to be arrested than white youth for status offenses and index offenses. In 1960, black youth accounted for 19.6 percent of all juvenile arrests, but that had increased to 26.0 percent in 1997. They were also more likely to be arrested for serious felony offenses than any other race-sex category. Although black youth were more likely than white youth to be arrested, convicted, and incarcerated for the same category of offenses, a recent study concluded that there are no significant differences between black and white youth in their rates of self-reported delinquency (Krisberg and others, 1986). Other researchers have concluded that the juvenile justice system discriminates against African American youth at every stage of the process (Austin, Dimas, and Steinhart, 1992; Poe-Yamagata and Jones, 2000), but the racial disparities are greater at the initial stages of involvement in the system (Pope and Feyerherm, 1993; Snyder and Sickmund, 1999).

African American juvenile delinquents also have higher rates of depression and of psychological and neurological symptoms that are often undetected and undiagnosed (Dembo and others, 1990; Gibbs, 1982; Hutchinson, 1990). According to a report by the Coalition for Juvenile Justice (2000), 50 to 75 percent of incarcerated juveniles have a diagnosable mental health disorder, whereas it estimates that one out of five of these youth suffers from a serious mental disorder. Because black and other minority youth constitute two-thirds of the more than 100,000 juveniles confined in local detention and correctional facilities, it is clear that they suffer disproportionately from mental health problems (Cocozza, 1992).

Youth of color in juvenile and adult facilities are less likely than whites to undergo a thorough psychological assessment and less likely to receive any form of therapeutic treatment (Coalition for Juvenile Justice, 2000; Hutchinson, 1990). If they are evaluated, African American and other minority youth are more likely to be misdiagnosed or overdiagnosed. For example, black males are much more likely than white males to receive a diagnosis of conduct disorder, antisocial personality disorder, or a substance abuse disorder than an anxiety or depressive disorder. As Dembo (1988) points out, the juvenile justice system is increasingly the channel for "handling" African American youth with behavioral disorders, whereas white youth with similar behaviors are more likely to be referred for treatment in the mental health system. The system of entry obviously determines the nature and quality of the services offered, the assessment and diagnosis of the problem behaviors, and the effectiveness of the intervention used.

Substance Abuse

Community- and school-based surveys of drug and alcohol use have consistently shown that African American adolescents have comparable or lower rates than whites and Latinos of most illicit drug substances (National Institute of Drug Abuse, 2001; Centers for Disease Control and Prevention, 2002b).

In the 2001 Youth Risk Behavior Surveillance (Centers for Disease Control and Prevention, 2002b), African American high school students reported significantly lower rates than white or Hispanic students of both current and lifetime alcohol use and of episodic heavy drinking. Although the rates of marijuana use among the three groups were about the same, black students also reported significantly lower rates of current and lifetime use of cocaine, inhalants, heroin, and amphetamines. Contrary to popular stereotypes, black youth who stay in school have lower rates of overall substance use than their white, Latino, or American Indian counterparts. However, an important limitation of these school-based surveys is that school dropouts are not included, probably resulting in an underestimation of drug use in this age cohort, because dropouts are more likely to be involved in deviant activities.

Drug use for those inner-city black youth who are disengaged from school and work is particularly problematic because it is often linked to a total lifestyle that includes delinquency, violence, drug-selling, and chronic health problems (Brunswick and Rier, 1995; Centers and Weist, 1998). Consequently, when these youth are referred for treatment, they are usually involuntary clients with multiple social, behavioral, and psychological problems (Cocozza, 1992; Hutchinson, 1990).

Sexually Transmitted Diseases

African American adolescent females are particularly at risk for sexually transmitted diseases because of several sociocultural factors. First, tolerant attitudes in inner-city black communities toward premarital sexual experimentation contributes to an earlier age of initiation of sexual intercourse among black females (Anderson, 1995; Scott-Jones, Davis, Foster, and Hughes, 1995). Second, condom use is less frequent among girls who are engaged in multiple high-risk behaviors such as alcohol and drug use. Third, in response to widespread homophobic attitudes among African Americans, gay males frequently mask their sexual orientation and engage in heterosexual sex with unsuspecting females. Moreover, the 2001 Youth Risk Behavior Surveillance (Centers for Disease Control and Prevention, 2002b) found that African American high school students were significantly less likely than whites to have been taught about AIDS or HIV infection in their schools.

Currently, young African American intravenous drug users who use unsterilized needles, as well as those who engage in high-risk, unprotected sex with homosexual or bisexual males, face the threat of infection from the AIDS virus (Brunswick and Rier, 1995). From 1996 until 1998 non-Hispanic African American youth from eleven to nineteen had the highest rates of AIDS infection among all racial-ethnic youth groups in the United States, ranging from 4.31 per 100,000 (for males) and 2.76 (for females) in the fifteen- to seventeen-year-old age group, to 12.16 per 100,000 (for males) and 8.28 (for females) in the eighteen- to nineteen-year-old age group (Centers for Disease Control and Prevention, 2000). In December

2001, 51 percent of all youth between thirteen and nineteen who were diagnosed with AIDS were black; black youth also constituted 65 percent of all reported cases of children under thirteen years of age (Centers for Disease Control and Prevention, 2002a). Unfortunately, there are inadequate services for counseling African American youth, their families, and their sexual partners about the chronic course of the disease, the behavioral and sexual changes necessary, and the prolonged grieving process (Jemmott, Jemmott, Fong, and McCaffree, 1999). Black adolescents also had much higher rates than other racial-ethnic groups of sexually transmitted diseases such as chlamydia and gonorrhea, both of which can cause chronic pelvic pain and can result in ectopic pregnancies or infertility for females (Centers for Disease Control and Prevention, 2000). The psychological consequences of these diseases include depression, substance abuse, and psychotic reactions.

Teenage Pregnancy and Parenthood

Although the overall birthrate for teenagers fifteen to nineteen declined from 62.1 per 1,000 in 1991 to 45.9 per 1,000 in 2001, teen pregnancy and childbearing still remains a major psychosocial problem for African American teenagers, particularly because it is often followed by a number of negative social and psychological sequelae (Rosenheim and Testa, 1992; Ventura, Clarke, and Mathews, 1996). In 2000, the birth rate for black adolescent females ages fifteen to nineteen was 73.1 per 1,000, as compared to rates of 30.2 and 92.4 per 1,000 for white and Hispanic teenage females, respectively (National Center for Health Statistics, 2001). Fewer than one out of ten African American young women from age fifteen to nineteen had a child, but they were still 2.5 times more likely to give birth than their white same-age peers (National Center for Health Statistics, 2001). In 2000, about 79.1 percent of all births to adolescent females under age twenty occurred to unmarried mothers, with black females showing a rate of over 77.0 percent of out-of-wedlock births, compared to 24.5 and 74.2 percent among unmarried white and Hispanic females, respectively. African American teenage mothers had high rates of school dropouts, welfare dependency, and unemployment (Ventura, Clarke, and Mathews, 1996). They were also more likely than girls who delayed their first pregnancy to experience health problems, psychological problems, and family problems (Rosenheim and Testa, 1992). Several studies have indicated that these teen mothers need a range of comprehensive health, mental health, and educational-vocational services (Murry, 1996). Attempts to cope with teenage parenthood often result in psychological problems for both males and females, including depression, anxiety, anger, psychosomatic symptoms, and feelings of helplessness (Hendricks, 1980; Robinson, 1988). One of the major issues in counseling this group is that their own adolescent developmental needs are frequently in conflict with the needs of their infants and children.

It is interesting to note that statistics on African American youth psychosocial problems are much more accessible than statistics on their psychological problems. This may reflect an actual difference between African American and white youth in their patterns of response to anxiety and stress, or it may reflect differential treatment and bias in their patterns of referral for evaluation, that is, African American youth are more likely to be referred through the social welfare and juvenile justice systems and white youth through the mental health system (Coalition for Juvenile Justice, 2000; U.S. Department of Health and Human Services, 2001).

Sociocultural Issues in Assessment

The assessment of African American youth is discussed here from three vantage points: (1) theoretical perspectives, (2) sociocultural issues, and (3) levels of assessment.

First, the two theoretical perspectives that are useful in understanding the mental health issues of African American youth are the ego-oriented developmental theory of Erik Erikson (1950, 1959) and the ecological theory of Urie Bronfenbrenner (1979), as described in the Introduction. Both of these theories might predict differential outcomes for nonwhite and low-income youth, particularly because they are more likely than white and higher-income youth to experience greater socioeconomic deprivation, more prejudice and discrimination, and more restricted access to educational and vocational opportunities in American society. Accordingly, Erikson

(1959) suggests that teens growing up in these "disadvantaged" or minority families could develop "negative" identities and thus be "at risk" for dysfunctional or maladaptive behaviors.

Second, sociocultural factors must be considered in the assessment of all African American adolescents, particularly for those from residentially segregated and economically disadvantaged families. As the U.S. Surgeon General's report notes, there is a growing literature documenting differences between African Americans and whites in definitions of mental health and mental disorders, help-seeking behaviors, symptomatology, distribution of psychiatric disorders, and response to treatment (U.S. Department of Health and Human Services, 2001).

Third, the four levels of assessment necessary to obtain a comprehensive picture of the African American adolescent are (1) individual, (2) family, (3) school, and (4) community. These four levels of assessment are consistent with the dual individual and ecological theoretical perspective.

Individual Assessment

Erikson's view (Erikson, 1959) that African American adolescents may have greater difficulty in forming a positive identity because of negative societal feedback has been challenged by Chestang (1984), who distinguishes between "personal identity" and "racial identity" for African American youth, who have shown in a number of studies that they are able to separate their personal self-evaluations from the social evaluation of their racial identity (Cross, 1987; Rotheram-Borus, Dopkins, Sabate, and Lightfoot, 1996; Spencer, 1982). Because the process of identity formation is intimately connected to the development of a self-concept and a sense of competence, management of sexual and aggressive feelings, establishment of autonomy from parental control, and educational aspirations, the clinician should evaluate these areas of adjustment in African American adolescents.

Attitudes Toward Self

African American children and adolescents develop their self-concept and self-esteem from the reflected appraisals of parents, relatives, and peers in their own ethnic communities (Spencer, 1982). Prior to the

1970s, many clinical and empirical studies found that African American youth had negative self-concepts and low self-esteem (Clark and Clark, 1940; Goodman, 1964). However, more recent studies of nonclinical samples of African American youth have consistently found that their self-concepts and self-esteem are as positive or more positive than comparative samples of whites (Gibbs, 1985a; Phinney, Cantu, and Kurtz, 1997; Spencer, 1984). Contrary to predictions, black youth in segregated school settings frequently express higher levels of self-esteem than black youth in integrated settings (Powell, 1985). In fact, several researchers have found that a strong sense of black ethnic identification is positively related to higher levels of self-esteem for African American youth (Martinez and Dukes, 1997; Phinney, Cantu, and Kurtz, 1997).

Clinicians are more likely to find evidence of negative self-concepts and low levels of self-esteem among African American youth referred for behavioral or psychological problems. These youth may develop negative feelings about themselves because of their physical appearance, their atypical family structures, their lack of competence in culturally valued skills, or their feelings of racial victimization (Franklin, 1982; Gibbs, 1995). In assessing an African American adolescent's self-concept or self-esteem, the clinician should be cognizant of the significant sources of esteem for these youth, parental and peer reinforcement, and environmental factors (Phinney, Cantu, and Kurtz, 1997). For example, some studies indicate that athletic ability is a major source of esteem for African American male adolescents, whereas physical attractiveness and social skills are very important assets for African American females. Other abilities that are valued by both sexes are verbal skills (for example, "rapping"), assertiveness, and fashionable dressing (for example, "styling") (Anderson, 1990; Majors and Billson, 1992; Mancini, 1980).

Intellectual achievement is valued in some settings, whereas in other settings it is demeaned. High-achieving students in predominantly African American high schools are often ridiculed as "brainiacs" and accused of acting "like white folks" (Fordham and Ogbu, 1986; Williams and others, 2002). Boys who are physically small and girls who are precociously mature may become the targets of sarcasm and humor, sometimes causing them to develop overcompensatory behaviors. Social distinctions may be made on the basis of skin color or SES, which can have damaging effects on the adolescent's self-concept and self-esteem, particularly for African American females (Canino and Spurlock, 1994). Thus an assessment of African American adolescent self-esteem must take into account the adolescent's *subjective* evaluation of assets and liabilities, the reflected appraisal of parents, peers, and significant others in the social environment, and whether the environment is a consonant or dissonant context, that is, whether the adolescent is in a majority or minority social context (Rosenberg, 1979).

Affect

African American adolescents are characteristically described as expressive, lively, and extraverted (Gibbs, 1985a; Majors and Billson, 1992; Robinson and Ward, 1991). Yet in treatment situations, they often appear angry and hostile or sullen and withdrawn (Franklin, 1982; Gibbs, 1990; Ridley, 1984). Angry, hostile teenagers may express a great deal of negative affect and appear to be physically intimidating, especially older youth who are referred for delinquent behaviors and substance abuse. Outwardly uncommunicative and uncooperative, the unresponsive demeanor of these youth often masks underlying depression over family problems, school failure, interpersonal rejection, or self-destructive behaviors (Franklin, 1982; Gibbs, 1986a).

Speech and Language

African American adolescents tend to have good verbal skills, but those reared in African American neighborhoods often speak a variety of "Black English," which may be unfamiliar to non-African American clinicians (Fordham and Ogbu, 1986; Smitherman, 1994). Because many are able to switch back and forth from Black English to standard English, the clinician can usually communicate effectively by responding with flexibility and a willingness to clarify unfamiliar terms. Clinicians should also be aware that language serves many symbolic functions for African American youth, who use it as a means of artistic expression (as in rapping), as well as a means of verbal assault (for example, "playing the dozens") (Anderson, 1990; Majors and Billson, 1992). Language can also be a source of conflict in schools and in the workplace, placing them at a competitive disadvantage in both settings.

Interpersonal Relations

The quality and intensity of relationships among African American adolescents must be evaluated in the context of their social and cultural environment. Same-sex peer groups have very close bonds, with strong pressures to conform to group norms, particularly in situations where the peer group or gang also serves the functions of social identity and mutual protection (Anderson, 1990, 1995; Way, 1996). In areas with high rates of single-parent families and few community resources, peer group bonds among females function as social support networks (Staples and Johnson, 1993). However, these intense bonds can also cause intense rivalries and conflicts, reduce individual autonomy, and foster involvement in antisocial or self-destructive activities. For example, studies have found that high involvement of low-income African American teenagers in certain types of peer networks was inversely related to academic achievement and premarital sexual activity (Felner, Aber, Primavera, and Cauce, 1985). Moreover, the inner-city African American adolescent who is not a member of a cohesive peer group or gang is often excluded from activities, labeled negatively, and sometimes physically harassed (Anderson, 1990; Way, 1996).

Sexuality

Both the expression of sexuality and sexual relationships are major issues for African American adolescents. African American adolescents tend to initiate sexual activity about one year earlier, on the average, than white adolescents. In the 2001 Youth Risk Behavior Surveillance (Centers for Disease Control and Prevention, 2002b), African American high school students were significantly more likely than white or Hispanic students to report that they had initiated sexual intercourse before age thirteen, that they had sexual relations with four or more partners, and that they were currently sexually active. In a reversal of earlier trends, black teenagers were significantly more likely to report using condoms than white or Hispanic students. Although seven of ten black students reported using condoms, the 30 percent who do not use any form of contraception are placing themselves and their partners at high risk for sexually transmitted diseases, including HIV-AIDS, pregnancy, and other deleterious consequences. Despite these reports of condom use, African American teenage females have higher rates of unintended pregnancy and higher birth rates than white females (National Center for Health Statistics, 2001). Because African American adolescent females are often referred to counselors for issues of sexuality, pregnancy, and parenting, clinicians should be familiar with their cultural attitudes about premarital sexual activity, contraception, childbearing, and childrearing (Anderson, 1995; Dash, 1989; Scott-Jones, Davis, Foster, and Hughes, 1995).

Anxiety and Patterns of Defense

It is important to assess the level of anxiety, the ways in which it is expressed, and the situations in which it is most likely to occur. Anxiety may be triggered for African American youth by academic problems, family conflict, community violence, interpersonal or sexual relationships, or employment and career issues, so it is important for the clinician to assess the impact of all of these factors on the adolescent client. High levels of anxiety may not be evident in African American adolescents under direct observation, partly because culturally acceptable childrearing patterns, particularly in low-income African American families, often reinforce the externalization of anxiety in African American youth (Anderson, 1990; Taylor, 1991). Thus anxiety may be denied, projected, or displaced. Hyperactivity, acting out, and aggression in younger adolescents may be a clue to anxiety, whereas delinquent activity, substance abuse, and sexual promiscuity may be responses to underlying anxiety or depression in older adolescents (Gibbs, 1982; Paster, 1985). Some clinical studies of African American college students suggest that they may have fairly high rates of somatic symptoms, so clinicians should be alert to signs of physical distress and psychosomatic complaints as possible evidence of anxiety.

Coping and Adaptive Behaviors

African American adolescents have developed a number of coping skills and adaptive behaviors to compensate for their marginal minority status in this society (Spencer and Dornbusch, 1990; Leadbetter and Way, 1996). Young African American males have learned that athletic ability is one route to mobility, so many develop skills in a competitive sport (especially basketball, baseball, and track) that requires discipline, physical coordination, and motivation. Reinforced for social and interpersonal skills, young African American females may become sexually active as a route to premature parenthood, often foreclosing their educational and career opportunities (Anderson, 1995; Apfel and Seitz, 1996; Dash, 1989; Gibbs, 1992; Murry, 1996). In response to the uncertainties of their environment, many inner-city African American youth have developed a patterned set of behaviors known as "playing it cool" or "getting over." Researchers have identified a number of different coping styles that have enabled these youth to adapt to the realities of ghetto life yet may be maladaptive for success in mainstream society (Anderson, 1990; Majors and Billson, 1992). Nonetheless, they have consistently demonstrated much resilience, creativity, and persistence in the face of economic deprivation, social disorganization, and limited community resources—all of which reduce their opportunities and restrict their mobility.

The Family System

An assessment of the family environment of the African American adolescent should focus on the following factors: the structure and roles of the family, SES and living arrangements, degree of integration or acculturation, support system, communication patterns, and help-seeking patterns (Boyd-Franklin, 1989; Gwyn and Kilpatrick, 1981; Jones, 1992).

Family Structure and Roles

It will be helpful to the clinician to know whether the family is an intact nuclear family, a single-parent family with or without other adults in the household, or an extended family. Family structure not only helps to shape the psychosocial identity and social experiences of adolescents but may actually place constraints on the development of their social roles (Cauce and others, 1996; Salem, Zimmerman, and Nataro, 1998; Steinberg, 1987). For example, teenagers in single-parent families are often given more household and child-care responsibilities than those in two-parent families, creating potential detrimental effects on their health and school achievement. Teenagers living in extended families with several adult caretakers (for example, mothers, grandmothers, or aunts) may experience conflicts over discipline and autonomy because of unclear lines of parental authority. In their study of African American adolescents' perceptions of family climate, Dancy and Handal (1987) found that teenagers who perceived high levels of conflict in their families reported more psychological symptoms than those who perceived low levels of conflict.

SES and Living Arrangements

Occupational status and income of the parents are important indicators of the adolescent's SES, material resources, and lifestyle (Furstenberg and Hughes, 1995; McLoyd, 1990). Living arrangements should also be investigated to determine the size of the household, the sleeping arrangements, and the household responsibilities of the adolescent. Many low-income African American youth live in crowded households with very little privacy and inadequate sleeping and study facilities, and are exposed to negative role models—all of which frequently have negative consequences for their physical and mental health if there are not sufficient protective factors to counterbalance the risk factors (Furstenberg, 1993; Seidman and others, 1999).

Degree of Integration or Acculturation

The extent to which the family is integrated and has assimilated the values and norms of the mainstream culture is also relevant to treatment of African American youth (Billingsley, 1992; Jones, 1992). Adolescents with varying levels of exposure to integrated schools and neighborhoods may present different patterns of symptomatology, problem behaviors, and adaptation to the community (Gibbs, 1990; Powell, 1985).

Social Support System

The clinician should assess the wider kinship network and social support network of the adolescent's family. As noted earlier, church affiliation is an important source of social support for many African American families. Further, many African American families are involved in neighborhood associations, civic organizations, and fraternal lodges—all of which can be valuable sources of support (Jaynes and Williams, 1989). Urban African American families also sometimes send troubled teenagers to live temporarily with relatives in smaller communities in the South, so that northern-southern family ties are continually reinforced through mutual assistance (Billingsley, 1992; McAdoo, 1981).

Communication Patterns

Interaction in African American families also varies by SES and level of acculturation. In low-income families, there is some ethnographic evidence that parent-child communication tends to be authoritarian, critical, unidirectional, and confrontational (Bartz and Levine, 1978; Peters, 1981). African American parents and siblings sometimes engage in mutual teasing, sarcasm, and denigrating comments (Cauce and others, 1996; Ward, 1996). Overt expressions of affection, nurturance, support, and praise are not frequent in these families, and self-deprecating humor may be used as a protective mechanism to preserve one's self-esteem. Patterns of communication in middle-class families are more likely to be bidirectional, authoritative, and mutually supportive than in low-income families (Bartz and Levine, 1978; Billingsley, 1992; Peters, 1981).

Help-Seeking Patterns

African American families generally do not voluntarily seek psychiatric treatment for the emotional or behavioral problems of their children, who are more likely to be referred by schools, the juvenile court, and the child welfare system (Boyd-Franklin, 1989; Myers, 1989; U.S. Department of Health and Human Services, 2001). Although this varies by SES and level of acculturation, some studies show that African American families are more likely to seek counseling initially from family doctors, ministers, and friends or relatives than from mental health professionals (Neighbors, 1985).

School Assessment

The school as an instrument of education and socialization has long been a source of conflict and controversy for African American youth (Fordham and Ogbu, 1986; Irvine and Irvine, 1995; Williams and others, 2002). That these youth are frequently referred for school-related academic or behavioral problems is not surprising, but the clinician's task is to disentangle the client's presenting problems from factors in the school environment that may have substantially contributed to or exacerbated them.

School Environment

The milieu of the school can be a safe, orderly setting that facilitates learning and personal growth, or it can be a violent, chaotic setting that intimidates students and teachers and undermines both learning and social development (Dupper and Meyer-Adams, 2002; Elliott, Hamburg, and Williams, 1998). African American students may respond to these school environments with apathy and alienation, anger and hostility, and fear and anxiety, or by acting out and identifying with the antisocial elements in the school.

Educational Program

African American students are overrepresented in special education programs and nonacademic tracks. Frequently mislabeled in elementary school, many African American adolescents either drop out or are "pushed out" of high school after experiencing years of academic failure or low achievement, low teacher expectations, high rates of suspension, and chaotic school environments (Darling-Hammond, 1998; Fine, 1991; Irvine and Irvine, 1995). Clinicians who suspect that students are performing below their abilities should use a culturally sensitive measure such as the System of Multicultural Plural Assessment battery, to assess their ability levels (Samuda, 1998; Snowden and Todman, 1982). Should the clinician discover a discrepancy between the client's potential ability and the educational program, a recommendation for a more appropriate academic placement could be the most effective intervention.

Peer Relationships

Attitudes and behaviors of peers are very influential in shaping the school experiences of African American adolescents (Cauce, Felner, and Primavera, 1982; National Research Council, 1993; Way, 1996). Where the prevailing norms are anti-intellectual and college is not viewed as a realistic option, low-income African American teenagers have an especially difficult time if they are viewed as high achievers by their black peers (Fordham and Ogbu, 1986; Hare, 1988). Similarly, in many inner-city neighborhoods there are permissive attitudes toward early involvement in sexual activity and experimentation with drugs (Anderson, 1990; Murry, 1996). When students resist pressures to conform to these norms, they may be socially isolated and ridiculed. In these situations, clinicians should evaluate the students' psychological distress and ability to cope with the peer pressures, as well as the environmental supports or modifications necessary to reinforce their proactive behaviors.

Community Assessment

When African American children reach adolescence and venture out beyond their immediate social environment, they may have their first experience with racial discrimination. If they enter an integrated high school, seek a part-time job, or participate in community youth groups or athletic teams, African American teenagers begin to sense racism and barriers to their opportunities and aspirations (Boykin and Ellison, 1995; Franklin and Boyd-Franklin, 2000). Further, early exposure to unemployment, drugs, and illegal activities in inner-city communities often fosters cynicism, anger, and antisocial attitudes in these youth (Anderson, 1990; Centers and Weist, 1998; Gibbs, 1988b). In response to these environmental realities, African American youth often develop a sense of social isolation and hopelessness about their life chances, which increases their vulnerability to involvement in self-destructive activities such as drug abuse, unwed teenage pregnancy, suicide, and homicide (Dryfoos, 1990; Gibbs, 1988b).

Clinicians who evaluate youth referred for antisocial or self-destructive behavior need to assess their underlying feelings of alienation, depression, and rage in order to recommend appropriate treatment interventions (Franklin, 1982; Gibbs, 1990; Paster, 1985).

Intervention and Treatment

In this section, four modalities of treatment for African American adolescents are examined: (1) individual, (2) family, (3) group, and (4) crisis intervention.

Individual Treatment

Short-term ego-oriented psychotherapy is the model of individual treatment recommended for African American adolescents with nonpsychotic disorders who are usually seen in outpatient settings.

As described by Norman (1980), this approach is appropriate for this group because it focuses on problem solving, strengthens coping skills, and is time-limited. This approach is also useful for a wide range of adolescent problems ranging from anxiety and depression to identity conflicts and acting-out behaviors.

Entry to Treatment

From the African American adolescent's initial contact with the therapist, he will be judging the therapist's affect and behaviors while he is being evaluated. Thus it is important for the therapist to project warmth, genuineness, and positive regard for the client, being especially attentive to cues that the client is testing for signs of prejudice, superiority, disapproval, and rejection (Canino and Spurlock, 1994; Gibbs, 1985b; Ridley, 1984). Therapists should be aware that African American youth are sensitive to how they are addressed (avoid overfamiliarity and excessive patronizing), how they are engaged in conversation (avoid using ethnic slang and an overly simplistic vocabulary), how the office is furnished (they appreciate attractive decor, even if they live in projects), how the therapist is dressed (they believe that clothes reflect social status), and how respectful the therapist is toward them. The therapist should not keep the client waiting interminably and should not answer a string of phone calls during sessions (Franklin, 1982).

Clients will be more favorably disposed toward clinicians who demonstrate interpersonal competence rather than instrumental competence in the first sessions (Gibbs, 1985b). African American adolescents may initially approach treatment with a great deal of misapprehension, suspicion, and anxiety due to lack of knowledge or prior treatment experience. The therapist can minimize the client's anxiety by spending a few minutes at the beginning of the first session in informal conversation, followed by a brief description of the treatment process through a "role induction" technique (Frank and others, 1978) or a patient-orientation program (Acosta, Yamamoto, and Evans, 1982). The goal is to demystify the therapeutic process for these clients and to be certain that they fully understand the "talking cure" before treatment proceeds.

Like all adolescents, African American youth are rarely psychologically sophisticated and generally have trouble distancing themselves from their own behaviors, that is, their "observing egos" are much less developed than their "experiencing egos." They also tend to be less comfortable with self-disclosure than white adolescents, partly reflecting the African American cultural pattern of masking their true feelings and concerns from whites and authority figures (Jenkins, 1982; Pinderhughes, 1989; Ridley, 1984; Sanchez-Hucles, 1999). Moreover, African American adolescents often have a history of conflict with authority figures, so they may appear unusually resistant, sullen, or hostile in the early sessions because most have been referred by schools or social agencies.

To overcome this initial resistance and to establish rapport, the clinician needs to be fairly active, outgoing, directive, and open, encouraging adolescents to discuss their anger and ambivalent feelings about being referred for treatment, their fears about being labeled "crazy" by their peers, and their reluctance to reveal their true feelings and concerns to a stranger. By showing sensitivity to these issues and understanding of their cultural context, therapists can reassure clients that their concerns about treatment are fairly common among teenagers. At this point, the therapist should reiterate the role of confidentiality in treatment and its specific limitations with minors and in involuntary cases, so that clients can clarify any concerns about freely discussing their problems. The following case provides an example of these issues in the initial phase of treatment.

> Wanda, a fourteen-year-old African American female, was referred by her junior high school counselor because of her frequent somatic symptoms, her immature behaviors, and her problems in getting along with her peers. During her first session, Wanda seemed anxious and fearful and responded reluctantly when she was asked about her concerns. At the beginning of the second session, she blurted out that she "didn't want to be sent away to a special school." The therapist learned that Wanda's older brother had been abruptly institutionalized several years earlier for mental retardation when her mother remarried. Whenever her stepfather became angry with her, he would threaten to send her to join her brother. In order to please her very strict parents, Wanda had become excessively compliant at home but had frequent nightmares and physical symptoms. At school, she wasn't able to contain her anxiety, so she frequently did inappropriate things to get attention from her teachers and peers. After the therapist clarified the referral and explained her role and her interest in helping Wanda, the teenager was able to feel more comfortable,

to express her fears about being abandoned by her parents, and to set some short-term goals about improving her communication with her parents and reducing the frequency of her impulsive and inappropriate behaviors in the school setting.

Establishing the Working Alliance

To establish a working alliance with the African American adolescent, the clinician should proceed cautiously and anticipate a great number of "testing" behaviors, which may include males wearing hats and sunglasses in sessions, refusing to remove heavy coats and jackets, using obscene or provocative language, coming late for appointments, terminating the session prematurely, being unresponsive, and acting hostile and rebellious. These behaviors will quickly diminish and usually disappear as the teenager becomes more comfortable in the relationship.

During this phase of treatment, the adolescent will expend a great deal of energy in challenging the therapist's authority and ability to maintain control of the sessions (Franklin, 1982; Gibbs, 1985b). The therapist must avoid being drawn into a power struggle with the client while, at the same time, establishing structure and setting firm limits for the sessions. Male adolescent clients may try to intimidate the therapist with aggressive behaviors and sarcastic, street-style verbal responses; adolescent females may act in a seductive or sullen manner. Franklin (1982) describes three types of urban African American adolescent clients: (1) "reluctant talkers" who are difficult to engage in conversation, (2) "babblers" who control sessions by compulsively talking about superficial issues, and (3) "impressers" who brag about antisocial activities in an attempt to shock the therapist. Therapists should recognize some of these behaviors as "manipulative" but should avoid premature interpretations that will threaten the adolescent's fragile sense of self-esteem and weak defense mechanisms.

Therapists should understand that many African American adolescents have adopted a demeanor of "being cool" and a repertoire of street-smart behaviors in order to survive in an environment that is stressful, frequently chaotic, and unpredictable (Anderson, 1990; Majors and Billson, 1992). To facilitate rapport in the treatment relationship, clinicians should be familiar with the inner-city adolescent culture, with some of the slang, and with some of the characteristic behaviors. This does not imply that clinicians should use the language or engage in the behaviors, which would be condescending or patronizing to the client. Clinicians can also inquire about unfamiliar language or behaviors in order to determine whether these patterns are cultural or idiosyncratic in origin.

Humor is an important tool in forming a working alliance with the African American adolescent. African American culture has a highly developed oral tradition in which humor has always played a prominent role, as exemplified in many contemporary soul and rock songs, rapping, and routines of African American comedians (Anderson, 1990; Baugh, 2000; Smitherman, 1994). Humor can be employed to foster insight in a client who might not be responsive to dynamic interpretations of his underlying conflict but who can see the irony of his self-defeating behaviors.

The following case provides an example of therapeutic strategies to facilitate a working alliance with an African American adolescent.

John, a sixteen-year-old high school sophomore, was referred by his probation officer for excessive truancy, failing grades, and constant conflict with his mother. Born out of wedlock to a teenage mother, John had a two-year history of minor delinquency and was suspected of drug use. He had begun to act out shortly after the death of his grandmother, who had actually reared him while his mother worked in a nearby city. John was initially hostile and rude to the therapist, clearly communicating that he was there against his will and did not intend to cooperate. In addition to coming late, he hummed popular songs, leafed through magazines, frequently said he was wasting his time, and answered questions in a sarcastic and condescending manner. After several unproductive sessions, the therapist learned that John had a collection of classic rock and roll records, which he had enjoyed listening to with his grandmother. He was encouraged to talk about this collection, which led to lively discussions about his interest in music and his aspirations to be a disc jockey. After his initial resistance was overcome by setting limits on his disruptive behaviors and consistent reinforcement of his positive responses, the therapist was able to explore his unresolved feelings of grief over the loss of his grandmother, who had been very supportive of his school work and interests. The working alliance was further strengthened when the therapist consulted with John's school counselor about developing a work-study plan that would enable him to work part-time at a radio station while taking courses more closely related to his vocational interests.

Issues in Individual Treatment

Clinical treatment of African American adolescents must recognize the impact of the social and political environment on these youth, as well as the culturally patterned coping strategies and defensive behaviors they have developed in response to their chronic levels of environmental stress (Franklin and Boyd-Franklin, 2000; Myers, 1989; Paster, 1985).

Once the working alliance has been established, the clinician must remain continuously sensitive and alert to the interaction of the intrapsychic, interpersonal, and environmental aspects of the problem. The clinician should encourage clients to describe their problems or issues as they view them, to explore the subjective effects of the problems and the impact of their behaviors on others, and to identify specific ways to alleviate the symptoms and ameliorate the problems. The problem-solving strategies should be reasonable and achievable within each adolescent's social context.

The following cases provide examples of how these factors interact and influence the therapeutic interventions with black adolescents. These three cases illustrate frequent issues presented by these clients, for example, delinquent behavior, sexual problems, and aggressive behavior.

Bobby, a sixteen-year-old high school dropout, was referred by his probation officer while he was living in a group home. Bobby had been involved with the juvenile court system since the age of fourteen when he was first arrested, with two older boys, for burglarizing houses in his neighborhood. In treatment, Bobby was very "street-wise," manipulative, and defensive, avoiding discussion of his chaotic family and his failures in a succession of schools.

When the clinician learned that Bobby was a natural leader in the group home, she was able to support his efforts to obtain some athletic equipment and games for the residents. As he gained more confidence by organizing activities in the home, he became less defensive and was able to talk about his feelings of never having nice things and never being able to depend on his parents for anything. He was recruited into a neighborhood gang at the age of thirteen, and they became his substitute family. The male clinician provided him with a model of warmth, acceptance, and consistency, as well as a predictable environment in which limits were set on his manipulative behavior. A

few weeks after he confronted Bobby on the discrepancy between his obvious
ability and his school failures, Bobby announced that he was going back to
school "just to show these teachers and my parents that they were all wrong
about me. I ain't dumb. I just didn't feel like working too hard." By challenging Bobby's negative self-image and supporting his competent behaviors,
the clinician was able to help Bobby raise his self-esteem and his educational
aspirations.

Juanita, a fifteen-year-old high school sophomore, was referred by her parents
because she had recently become very depressed and withdrawn and had
seemed to lose interest in everything. Juanita was overweight and very mature
looking, but she seemed listless, slightly sullen, and unmotivated for treatment. In exploring the reasons for Juanita's recent mood change, the therapist
noted that she was very uncomfortable discussing the topics of boys and social
life but she became more animated when she talked about one special girlfriend. Through careful probing, her confused feelings about this relationship
emerged. After the therapist spent one session generally discussing the importance of having a "best friend" and normalizing her feelings, Juanita revealed
that she was "turned off" from boys after a party where she had smoked some
marijuana and two boys had fondled her, then later bragged about it to their
friends. She had felt very ashamed but was grateful to her girlfriend, who was
supportive. Following this session, Juanita formed a very positive relationship
with the therapist, whose warmth and empathy contrasted with her mother's
punitive and critical manner.

Andrew was a nineteen-year-old sophomore in a private, elite college. He was
referred to the counseling center for assaulting a white male student in his
dormitory. After initially seeming to be very suspicious and hostile toward the
female therapist, he formed a good working alliance with her, facilitated by a
positive transference that was not interpreted. Andrew reported that he had
attacked the student after a series of incidents in which several students had
made fun of his Southern accent, his Afro haircut, and his clothes—all of
which he interpreted as racist comments. The short-term treatment focused on
helping Andrew express his feelings about being a "token" African American
who always was under a microscope, his doubts about his ability to achieve in
the highly competitive environment, and his anger about being rejected by a
white girlfriend. His self-esteem and feelings of competence were enhanced
by encouraging him to identify the talents and skills that had gained him

admission to college and to review his actual college performance, which was above average. In addition, his own ambivalence toward socializing with other African American students was explored, and he was able to reevaluate and reframe his social options. Finally, the therapist helped Andrew to recognize situations that triggered his rather explosive temper and to develop more socially acceptable ways of channeling his anger.

Family Treatment

Family treatment, which is increasingly being viewed as an important modality for African American adolescents, has been described by several authors (Boyd-Franklin, 1989; Coner-Edwards and Spurlock, 1988; Jones, 1992; Sanchez-Hucles, 1999). Because many teenagers are struggling to separate from their families and to function autonomously, the clinician must make a careful assessment of the advantages and disadvantages of family therapy for a given client. It can be especially appropriate for pregnant teenagers and for those who are delinquent or predelinquent, depressed, and suicidal, as well as for substance abusers whose self-destructive behaviors may be symptomatic of a dysfunctional family system, a scapegoated teenager, or a breakdown in family communication. It is especially important to assess the family's involvement with all the systems affecting its social, economic, political, and cultural well-being (Boyd-Franklin, 1989).

An eclectic blend of structural and strategic techniques is particularly effective for African American families with children and adolescents, wherein attention is focused both on restructuring family roles, modifying family communication patterns, and changing social behaviors (Boyd-Franklin, 1989; Santisteban and others, 1997). Multisystemic therapy has also shown positive results on African American delinquents and other youth of color involved in the juvenile justice system (Henggeler, 1997; Sutphen, Thyer, and Kurtz, 1995). Frequently, parents have singled out one child to bear the brunt of their own frustrations and feelings of victimization, thus scapegoating the adolescent by projecting all of their own anxieties and displacing their anger toward society on this particular child. The adolescent, in turn, has responded by acting out the negative impulses in a way that both reinforces his unworthiness in the family and confirms his negative identity in the community.

Debbie, a pregnant sixteen-year-old school dropout, was referred by a counselor at her alternative high school because of depression. Debbie, who had a good academic record, had been pressured into a sexual relationship by her older boyfriend, but he had dropped her soon after she discovered her pregnancy. Against her parents' wishes, she had decided to have the baby and now felt that she didn't have any emotional support. Debbie's parents were an upwardly mobile, working-class couple who wanted her to go to college and were quite angry about her "lower-class behavior."

Family treatment, which was recommended after Debbie's evaluation, focused on helping Debbie and her parents express their mutual feelings of anger, disappointment, and shame over her pregnancy, to explore alternative options for the baby, and to reevaluate Debbie's educational and vocational goals. After her parents recognized that Debbie's pregnancy was partly a response to their rigid rules and excessive expectations, their anger dissipated and they were able to show her more positive concern and support. When Debbie understood that her academic success was symbolic of upward mobility to her hard-working but poorly educated parents, she actively engaged with them to make plans so she could obtain child care while she returned to her regular high school and pursued her plans to attend a local community college.

Group Treatment

Group treatment is a popular modality for adolescents, both in outpatient settings and residential treatment (Brandes and Gardner, 1991; Curry, 1991; Rose and Edleson, 1987). There are some special factors to consider in forming groups for African American adolescents: whether the group should be mixed by gender, by race, and by social class; whether the therapists should also be mixed by gender and race; and whether the group members should be selected by diagnostic category or balanced to reflect a diverse range of problems.

Psychoeducational groups are especially appropriate for delinquents, school dropouts, and other troubled African American youth who need a comprehensive treatment program that includes counseling, remedial education, and vocational training (Franklin, 1982; Hooper, Murphy, Devany, and Huttman, 2000). Such groups are an integral part of many alternative high schools and residential treatment centers; they are also a core element in the "street academies" pioneered by the National Urban League in the 1970s and the Afrocentric mentoring and manhood "rites of initiation" programs for high-risk urban youth in the 1980s (Mincy, 1994).

Group leaders should foster a sense of cohesiveness and support in addressing the similar problems of the group members, encourage the development of appropriate problem-solving skills to replace acting-out and self-destructive behaviors, and promote an identification with constructive role models. Preferably, African American males with sexual identity problems, impulse disorders, or acting-out problems should be assigned to groups with African American male therapists who can be positive role models and will not be intimidated by aggressive or seductive behaviors. African American females can also benefit from relating to an African American female clinician who can offer an alternative model for identification other than teenage motherhood as a route to adulthood.

Crisis Intervention

Crisis intervention is a modality that is particularly appropriate for adolescents who cannot control their violent impulses, those who suffer toxic effects from alcohol or drug abuse, those who are physically or sexually abused, those who are extremely depressed or suicidal, and those who have psychotic symptoms (Edwards, 1996; Landau-Stanton and Stanton, 1985; Paster, 1985).

African American teenagers who have experienced a severe trauma or have decompensated due to drugs or alcohol may present with extreme anxiety and paranoid symptomatology. As Ridley (1984) points out, many African American patients have a degree of "healthy cultural paranoia" due to their marginal status in society, yet this paranoid outlook has a tendency to become more pronounced under stress. Thus African American patients in crisis situations may appear very fearful and suspicious of the clinical staff, withhold pertinent information, engage in verbally abusive and threatening behaviors, and sometimes refuse medication or treatment. For those African American youth who are severely depressed or suicidal, being in the hospital emergency room may be a very frightening experience.

Sexual abuse and sexual exploitation of African American adolescents will probably increase as their ranks increase in the homeless population. As more African American youth become addicted to "crack" (the derivative of cocaine), there will be an increased number of cases of drug overdoses and victims of drug-related violence (Brunswick, 1988; Centers for Disease Control and Prevention, 2001). It is important for emergency room doctors to refer these youth for follow-up counseling to help them to deal with their feelings of anger, shame, low self-esteem, worthlessness, helplessness, and despair.

In crisis intervention with African American youth, the clinician's task is not only to allay the immediate symptoms of distress and restore the client's ability to function but to assess the family environment and social support system that is available when the client returns home. Effective treatment often requires the clinician to intervene in a number of systems that impinge on the lives of African American adolescents, including the family, the school, the workplace, the juvenile justice system, and the social welfare system.

The following case illustrates a comprehensive approach to crisis intervention for an older female adolescent.

> Mona, an eighteen-year-old high school dropout, was brought to the emergency room by her boyfriend after a suicide attempt. Mona had taken an overdose of sleeping pills, but she was conscious; she recovered after emergency treatment. She was admitted to the hospital on a forty-eight-hour hold for evaluation and follow-up. Mona had been very depressed for several weeks due to a number of traumatic events. First, she had had a miscarriage after being beaten by her boyfriend; then she lost her job as a grocery clerk; then her boyfriend threatened to leave her. She felt that her life was hopeless, and she could no longer cope with all her losses. The team of clinicians who evaluated her developed a plan that included four major aspects: (1) she was referred for outpatient counseling to deal with her grief over losing the baby; (2) she was referred for vocational counseling to discuss job training programs; (3) she was referred to a social service agency for temporary financial assistance; and (4) she and her boyfriend were encouraged to discuss the problems in their relationship, and her boyfriend made a commitment to stay with her until the immediate crisis was resolved.

Crisis intervention requires rapid assessment skills, sensitivity to the client's social and psychological problems, and knowledge of community resources that are accessible and affordable for African American clients.

Summary and Conclusion

The psychological and psychosocial problems of African American adolescents and youth have been described in this chapter. It is clear that African American youth are more likely to be identified for psychosocial than for psychological problems, although there is a close relationship between these two types of presenting problems. Because African American youth are more likely than white youth to be identified through the juvenile justice system, they are also less likely to undergo a thorough psychological assessment, less likely to receive a psychiatric diagnosis, less likely to obtain therapeutic treatment, and more likely to experience long-term psychological impairments and behavioral and social deficits or dysfunctions.

The multiple risk factors for African American youth have been described, as well as the impact of social and cultural experiences on their values, norms, and behaviors. Knowledge of these factors will enable clinicians to understand the sociocultural influences on their attitudes and beliefs about mental health, symptomatology, patterns of defense and coping strategies, help-seeking patterns, utilization of services, and responsiveness to therapeutic treatment.

Phases of the treatment process were discussed, with a focus on the initial phase, the development of the working alliance, and examples of common issues in treatment of African American adolescents. Finally, four modalities of treatment of African American youth were described: individual, family, group, and crisis intervention.

In summary, since 1980 some of the psychological and psychosocial problems of African American adolescents in America have increased rather than decreased, despite declining rates of poverty. These problems have been exacerbated by the growth of the underclass, continuing racial discrimination, economic dislocation, and social policy changes that have had disproportionate, deleterious effects on the African American community. Many of these problems could be reduced or eliminated if there were a coordinated effort of federal, state, and local governments to develop comprehensive and humane social and economic policies to eliminate racial discrimination in our society, to strengthen vulnerable families, and to provide adequate health and social services for all children and youth. In the absence of such policies and programs, African American youth will continue to need a wide range of social and mental health services to address their psychological and behavioral problems in a social environment and political climate, which are far less than optimal for their psychosocial development.

References

Acosta, F. X., Yamamoto, J., and Evans, J. A. *Effective Psychotherapy for Low-Income and Minority Patients.* New York: Plenum, 1982.

Anderson, E. *Streetwise: Race, Class, and Change in an Urban Community.* Chicago: University of Chicago Press, 1990.

Anderson, E. "Sex Codes and Family Life Among Poor Inner-city Youths." In R. L. Taylor (ed.), *African American Youth: Their Social and Economic Status in the United States.* New York: Praeger, 1995.

Apfel, N., and Seitz, V. "African American Adolescent Mothers, Their Families, and Their Daughters: A Longitudinal Perspective over Twelve Years." In B. J. Leadbetter and N. Way (eds.), *Urban Girls: Resisting Stereotypes, Creating Identities.* (pp. 149–170). New York: New York University Press, 1996.

Austin, J., Dimas, J., and Steinhart, D. *The Over-Representation of Minority Youth in the California Juvenile Justice System.* San Francisco: National Council on Crime and Delinquency, 1992.

Bartz, K. W., and Levine, E. S. "Childrearing by Black Parents: A Description and Comparison to Anglo and Chicano Parents." *Journal of Marriage and the Family,* 1978, *40,* 709–719.

Baugh, J. *Beyond Ebonics: Linguistic Pride and Racial Prejudice.* New York: Oxford University Press, 2000.

Benson, P. L., and Donahue, M. J. "Ten-Year Trends in At-Risk Behaviors: A National Study of Black Adolescents." *Journal of Adolescent Research,* 1989, *4,* 125–139.

Billingsley, A. *Climbing Jacob's Ladder: The Enduring Legacy of African-American Families.* New York: Simon & Schuster, 1992.

Boyd-Franklin, N. *Black Families in Therapy: A Multisystems Approach.* New York: Guilford Press, 1989.

Boykin, A. W., and Ellison, C. M. "The Multiple Ecologies of Black Youth Socialization: An Afrographic Analysis." In R. L. Taylor (ed.), *African-American Youth: Their Social and Economic Status in the United States.* New York: Praeger, 1995.

Branch, T. *Parting the Waters: America in the King Years, 1954–63.* New York: Simon & Schuster, 1988.

Brandes, N. S., and Gardner, M. L. (eds.). *Group Therapy for the Adolescent.* New York: Jason Aronson, 1991.

Bronfenbrenner, U. *The Ecology of Human Development: Experiments by Nature and Design.* Cambridge, Mass.: Harvard University Press, 1979.

Brooks-Gunn, J., Duncan, G., and Aber, L. *Neighborhood Poverty: Context and Consequences for Children* (vol. 1). New York: Russell Sage Foundation, 1997.

Brunswick, A. "Young Black Males and Substance Use." In J. T. Gibbs (ed.), *Young, Black, and Male in America: An Endangered Species.* Dover, Mass.: Auburn House, 1988.

Brunswick, A., and Rier, D. A. "Structural Strain: Drug Use Among African American Youth." In R. L. Taylor (ed.), *African American Youth: Their Social and Economic Status in the United States* (pp. 225–246). Westport, Conn.: Praeger, 1995.

Canino, I. A., and Spurlock, J. *Culturally Diverse Children and Adolescents: Assessment, Diagnosis and Treatment.* New York: Guilford Press, 1994.

Cauce, A. M., Felner, R., and Primavera, J. "Social Support in High-Risk Adolescents: Structural Components and Adaptive Impact." *American Journal of Community Psychology,* 1982, *10,* 417–428.

Cauce, A. M., and others. "African American Mothers and Their Adolescent Daughters: Closeness, Conflict, and Control." In B. J. Leadbetter and N. Way (eds.), *Urban Girls: Resisting Stereotypes, Creating Identities* (pp. 100–116). New York: New York University, 1996.

Centers, N. L., and Weist, M. D. "Inner City Youth and Drug Dealing: A Review of the Problem." *Journal of Youth and Adolescence,* 1998, *27*(3), 395–411.

Centers for Disease Control and Prevention. *Health, United States, 2000.* Hyattsville, Md.: National Center for Health Statistics, 2000.

Centers for Disease Control and Prevention. *Health, United States, 2001.* Hyattsville, Md.: National Center for Health Statistics, 2001.

Centers for Disease Control and Prevention. *HIV/AIDS Surveillance Report,* Sept. 24, 2002a, *13*(2). Rockville, Md.: National Center for HIV, STD, and TB Prevention. Available online at www.cdc.gov/hiv/stats/hasr/1302.htm

Centers for Disease Control and Prevention. "Youth Risk Behavior Surveillance—United States, 2001." *Morbidity and Mortality Weekly Report, 51*(SS-4), June 28, 2002b.

Cheatham, H. E., and Stewart, J. D. (eds.). *Black Families: Interdisciplinary Perspectives.* New Brunswick, N.J.: Transaction Books, 1990.

Chestang, L. "Racial and Personal Identity in the Black Experience." In

B. White (ed.), *Color in a White Society*. Silver Spring, Md.: National Association of Social Workers, 1984.

Clark, K. B., and Clark, M. "Skin Color as a Factor in Racial Identification of Negro Pre-School Children." *Journal of Social Psychology*, 1940, *2*, 154–167.

Coalition for Juvenile Justice. *Handle With Care: Serving the Mental Health Needs of Young Offenders*. Washington, D.C.: Coalition for Juvenile Justice, 2000.

Cocozza, J. J. (ed.). *Responding to the Mental Health Needs of Youth in the Juvenile Justice System*. Seattle, Wash.: National Coalition for the Mentally Ill in the Criminal Justice System, 1992.

Comer, J. P., and Hill, H. "Social Policy and the Mental Health of Black Children." *Journal of the American Academy of Child Psychiatry*, 1985, *24*, 175–181.

Coner-Edwards, A. F., and Spurlock, J. *Black Families in Crisis: The Middle-Class*. New York: Brunner/Mazel, 1988.

Costello, E. J., and others. "Psychiatric Disorders in Primary Care: Prevalence and Risk Factors." *Archives of General Psychiatry*, 1988, *45*, 107–116.

Crago, M., Shisslak, C. M., and Estes, L. S. "Eating Disturbances Among American Minority Groups: A Review." *International Journal of Eating Disorders*, 1996, *19*(3), 239–248.

Cross, W. E. "A Two-Factor Theory of Black Identity: Implications for the Study of Identity Development in Minority Children." In J. Phinney and M. J. Rotheram (eds.), *Children's Ethnic Socialization: Pluralism and Development*. Thousand Oaks, Calif.: Sage, 1987.

Cuffe, S. P., and others. "Race and Gender Differences in the Treatment of Psychiatric Disorders in Young Adolescents." *Journal of the American Academy of Child and Adolescent Psychiatry*, 1995, *34*(11), 1536–1543.

Curry, J. "Outcome Research on Residential Treatment: Implications and Suggested Directions." *American Journal of Orthopsychiatry*, 1991, *61*, 348–357.

Dancy, B., and Handal, P. "Perceived Family Climate, Psychological Adjustment and Peer Relationships of Black Adolescents: Implications for the Study of Identity Development in Minority Children." In J. Phinney and M. J. Rotheram (eds.), *Children's Ethnic Socialization: Pluralism and Development*. Thousand Oaks, Calif.: Sage, 1987.

Darling-Hammond, L. "New Standards, Old Inequalities: The Current Challenge for African-American Education." In L. A. Daniels (ed.), *The State of Black America, 1998*. New York: National Urban League, 1998.

Dash, L. *When Children Want Children: The Urban Crisis of Teenage Childbearing*. New York: Morrow, 1989.

Dembo, R. "Delinquency Among Black Male Youth." In J. T. Gibbs (ed.), *Young, Black, and Male In America: An Endangered Species.* Dover, Mass.: Auburn House, 1988.

Dembo, R., and others. "Examination of the Relationships among Drug Use, Emotional/Psychological Problems, and Crime Among Youths Entering a Juvenile Detention Center." *International Journal of the Addictions,* 1990, *25,* 1301–1340.

Dryfoos, J. *Adolescents At Risk: Prevalence and Prevention.* New York: Oxford University Press, 1990.

Dubow, E. F., Edwards, S., and Ippolito, M. F. "Life Stressors, Neighborhood Disadvantage, and Resources: A Focus on Inner-City Children's Adjustment." *Journal of Clinical Child Psychology,* 1997, *26*(2), 130–144.

Dupper, D. R., and Meyer-Adams, N. "Low-Level Violence: A Neglected Aspect of School Culture." *Urban Education,* 2002, *37*(3), 350–364.

Edelman, M. W. *Families in Peril: An Agenda for Social Change.* Cambridge, Mass.: Harvard University Press, 1987.

Edwards, V. R. "Clinical Case Management With Severely Mentally Ill African Americans." In P. Manoleas (ed.), *The Cross-Cultural Practice of Clinical Case Management in Mental Health,* 1996.

Elliott, D. S., Hamburg, B. A., and Williams, K. R. (eds.). *Violence in American Schools.* New York: Cambridge University Press, 1998.

Erikson, E. H. *Childhood and Society.* New York: Norton, 1950.

Erikson, E. H. "Identity and the Life Cycle." *Psychological Issues,* 1959, *1*(1), entire issue.

Farley, R. "Racial Trends and Differences in the United States 30 Years After the Civil Rights Decade." *Social Science Research,* 1997, *26,* 235–262.

Felner, R. D., Aber, M. S., Primavera, J., and Cauce, A. M. "Adaptation and Vulnerability in High-Risk Adolescents: An Examination of Environmental Mediators." *American Journal of Community Psychology,* 1985, *13,* 365–379.

Fine, M. *Framing Drop-Outs: Notes on the Politics of an Urban Public High School.* Albany: State University of New York, 1991.

Fordham, S., and Ogbu, J. "Black Students' School Success: Coping With the Burden of Acting White." *Urban Review,* 1986, *18*(3), 176–206.

Foster, M., and Perry, L. R. "Self-Valuation Among Blacks." *Social Work,* 1982, *27,* 60–66.

Frank, J. D., and others. *Effective Ingredients of Successful Psychotherapy.* New York: Brunner/Mazel, 1978.

Franklin, A. J. "Therapeutic Interventions with Urban Black Adolescents." In E. E. Jones and S. J. Korchin (eds.), *Minority Mental Health.* New York: Praeger, 1982.

Franklin, A. J., and Boyd-Franklin, N. "Invisibility Syndrome: A Clinical Model of Effects of Racism on African-American Males." *American Journal of Orthopsychiatry,* 2000, *70*(1), 33–41.

Franklin, J. H., and Moss, A. A. *From Slavery to Freedom: A History of American Negroes.* (6th ed.) New York: Knopf, 1988.

Frazier, E. F. *The Negro Family in the United States.* Chicago: University of Chicago Press, 1966.

Furstenberg, F. F., Jr. "How Families Manage Risk and Opportunity in Dangerous Neighborhoods." In W. J. Wilson (ed.), *Sociology and the Public Agenda* (pp. 231–258). Newbury Park, Calif.: Sage, 1993.

Furstenberg, F. F., Jr., and Hughes, M. E. "Social Capital and Successful Development Among At-Risk Youth." *Journal of Marriage and the Family,* 1995, *57,* 580–592.

Garbarino, J. *Children and Families in the Social Environment.* Hawthorne, N.Y.: Aldine de Gruyter, 1982.

Garibaldi, A. M., and Bartley, M. "Black Pushouts and Drop-Outs: Strategies for Reduction." *Educational Review,* 1988, *50,* 227–234.

Gibbs, J. T. "Depression and Suicidal Behavior Among Delinquent Females: Ethnic and Sociocultural Variations." *Journal of Youth and Adolescence,* 1981, *2,* 159–167.

Gibbs, J. T. "Personality Patterns of Delinquent Females: Ethnic and Sociocultural Variations." *Journal of Clinical Psychology,* 1982, *38*(1), 198–206.

Gibbs, J. T. "Black Adolescents and Youth: An Endangered Species." *American Journal of Orthopsychiatry,* 1984, *54,* 6–21.

Gibbs, J. T. "City Girls: Psychosocial Adjustment of Urban Black Adolescent Females." *A Scholarly Journal on Black Women,* 1985a, *2,* 28–36.

Gibbs, J. T. "Treatment Relationships with Black Clients: Interpersonal vs. Instrumental Strategies." In C. Germain (ed.), *Advances in Clinical Social Work Practice.* Silver Spring, Md.: National Association of Social Workers, 1985b.

Gibbs, J. T. "Assessment of Depression in Urban Adolescent Females: Implications for Early Intervention Strategies." *American Journal of Social Psychiatry,* 1986a, *6,* 50–56.

Gibbs, J. T. "Psychosocial Correlates of Sexual Attitudes and Behaviors in Urban Early Adolescent Females: Implications for Intervention." *Journal of Social Work and Human Sexuality,* 1986b, *5,* 81–97.

Gibbs, J. T. "Conceptual, Methodological and Sociocultural Issues in Black Youth Suicide: Implications for Assessment and Early Intervention." *Suicide and Life-Threatening Behavior,* 1988a, *18,* 73–89.

Gibbs, J. T. (ed.). *Young, Black and Male in America: An Endangered Species.* Dover, Mass.: Auburn House, 1988b.

Gibbs, J. T. "Mental Health Issues of Black Adolescents: Implications for Policy and Practice." In A. R. Stiffman and L. E. Davis (eds.), *Ethnic Issues in Adolescent Mental Health.* Thousand Oaks, Calif.: Sage, 1990.

Gibbs, J. T. "The Social Context of Teen-age Pregnancy and Parenting in the Black Community: Implications for Public Policy." In M. Rosenheim and M. Testa (eds.), *Early Parenthood and the Transition to Adulthood.* New Brunswick, N.J.: Rutgers University Press, 1992.

Gibbs, J. T. "Health and Mental Health of Black Adolescents." In R. L. Taylor (ed.), *African American Youth: Their Social and Economic Status in the United States* (pp. 71–90). Westport, Conn.: Praeger, 1995.

Glasgow, D. *The Black Underclass.* New York: Vintage Books, 1981.

Goodman, M. E. *Race Awareness in Young Children.* Reading, Mass.: Addison-Wesley, 1964.

Grier, W., and Cobbs, P. *Black Rage.* New York: Basic Books, 1968.

Gwyn, F. F., and Kilpatrick, A. C. "Family Therapy with Low-Income Blacks: A Tool or Turn-off?" *Social Casework,* 1981, *5,* 259–266.

Hare, B. R. "Black Youth at Risk." In J. D. Williams (ed.), *The State of Black America 1988.* New York: National Urban League, 1988.

Hendricks, L. E. "Unwed Adolescent Fathers: Problems They Face and Their Sources of Social Support." *Adolescence,* 1980, *15,* 862–869.

Henggeler, S. *Treating Serious Anti-Social Behavior in Youth: The MST Approach.* Washington, D.C.: Office of Juvenile Justice and Delinquency Prevention, 1997.

Hooper, S. R., Murphy, J., Devany, A., and Huttman, T. "Ecological Outcomes of Adolescents in a Psychoeducational Residential Treatment Facility." *American Journal of Orthopsychiatry,* 2000, *70*(4), 491–500.

Hutchinson, J. "Mental Health Issues for Incarcerated Black Youth." In J. A. Farrow and R. Jenkins (eds.), *East Coast Scientific Symposium on the Health of the Black Adolescent Male.* Rockville, Md.: U.S. Department of Health and Human Services, 1990.

Irvine, J. J., and Irvine, R. W. "Black Youth in School: Individual Achievement and Institutional/Cultural Perspectives." In R. L. Taylor (ed.), *African American Youth: Their Social and Economic Status in the United States.* New York: Praeger, 1995.

Jaynes, G. D., and Williams, R. M., Jr. (eds.). *A Common Destiny: Blacks and American Society.* Washington, D.C.: National Academy Press, 1989.

Jemmott, J. B., Jemmott, L. S., Fong, G. T., and McCaffree, K. "Reducing HIV-Risk Associated Sexual Behavior Among African American Adolescents: Testing the Generality of Intervention Efforts." *American Journal of Community Psychology,* 1999, *27*(2), 161–187.

Jenkins, A. *The Psychology of the Afro-American.* New York: Pergamon Press, 1982.

Jones, A. C. "Self-Esteem and Identity in Psychotherapy With Adolescents From Upwardly Mobile Middle-Class African American Families." In L. A. Vargas and J. D. Koss-Chioino (eds.), *Working With Culture: Psychotherapeutic Interventions With Ethnic Minority Children and Adolescents*. San Francisco: Jossey-Bass, 1992.

Jones, E. E., and Korchin, S. J. (eds.). *Minority Mental Health*. New York: Praeger, 1982.

Jones, R. L. (ed.). *Black Adolescents*. Berkeley, Calif.: Cobb & Henry, 1989.

Kaplan, S., Landa, B., Weinhold, C., and Shenker, I. "Adverse Health Behaviors and Depressive Symptomatology in Adolescents." *Journal of the American Academy of Child Psychiatry*, 1984, *23*, 595–601.

Krisberg, B., and others. *The Incarceration of Minority Youth*. Minneapolis: H. H. Humphrey Institute of Public Affairs, University of Minnesota, 1986.

Landau-Stanton, J., and Stanton, M. "Treating Suicidal Adolescents and Their Families." In M. Mirkin and S. Koman (eds.), *Handbook of Adolescents and Family Therapy*. New York: Gardner Press, 1985.

Leadbetter, B. J., and Way, N. (eds.). *Urban Girls: Resisting Stereotypes, Creating Identities*. New York: New York University Press, 1996.

Lincoln, C. E., and Mamiya, L. *The Black Church in the African-American Experience*. Durham, N.C.: Duke University Press, 1990.

Lynn, L. E., and McGeary, M. G. (eds.). *Inner-City Poverty in the United States*. Washington, D.C.: National Academy Press, 1990.

Majors, R., and Billson, J. M. *Cool Pose: The Dilemmas of Black Manhood in America*. New York: Lexington Books, 1992.

Mancini, J. K. *Strategic Styles: Coping in the Inner City*. Hanover, N.H.: University Press of New England, 1980.

Martinez, R. O., and Dukes, R. L. "The Effects of Ethnic Identity, Ethnicity, and Gender on Adolescent Well-Being." *Journal of Youth and Adolescence*, 1997, *26*(5), 503–516.

Massey, D. S., Condrane, G. A., and Denton, N. A. "The Effect of Residential Segregation on Black Social and Economic Well-Being." *Social Forces*, 1987, *66*, 29–56.

Massey, D. S., and Denton, N. A. *American Apartheid: Segregation and the Making of the Underclass*. Cambridge, Mass.: Harvard University Press, 1993.

McAdoo, H. *Black Families*. Thousand Oaks, Calif.: Sage, 1981.

McAdoo, H. P., and McAdoo, J. L. (eds.). *Black Children: Social, Educational, and Parental Environments*. Thousand Oaks, Calif.: Sage, 1985.

McDermott, P. A., and Spencer, M. B. "Racial and Social Class Prevalence of Psychopathology Among School-Age Youth in the United States." *Youth and Society*, 1997, *28*(4), 387–414.

McLoyd, V. C. "The Impact of Economic Hardship on Black Families and Children: Psychological Distress, Parenting, and Socioemotional Development." *Child Development,* 1990, *61,* 311–346.

Mincy, R. B. (ed.). *Nurturing Young Black Males: Challenges to Agencies, Programs, and Social Policy.* Washington, D.C.: The Urban Institute Press, 1994.

Mukuria, G. "Disciplinary Challenges: How Do Principals Address This Dilemma?" *Urban Education,* 2002, *37*(3), 432–452.

Murry, V. M. "Inner-City Girls of Color: Unmarried, Sexually Active Non-Mothers." In B. J. Leadbetter and N. Way (eds.), *Urban Girls: Resisting Stereotypes, Creating Identities.* (pp. 272–290). New York: New York University Press, 1996.

Myers, H. F. "Urban Stress and the Mental Health of Afro-American Youth: An Epidemiologic and Conceptual Update." In R. L. Jones (ed.), *Black Adolescents.* Berkeley, Calif.: Cobb and Henry, 1989.

National Center for Education Statistics. *Educational Statistics Digest, 2000.* Washington, D.C.: U.S. Department of Education, 2001.

National Center for Health Statistics. *Health, United States, 2000.* Hyattsville, Md.: Centers for Disease Control and Prevention, 2001.

National Institute of Drug Abuse. *National Household Survey on Drug Abuse, 2000.* Rockville, Md.: U.S. Department of Health and Human Services, 2001.

National Research Council. *Losing Generations: Adolescents in High-Risk Settings.* Washington, D.C.: National Academy of Sciences, 1993.

Neighbors, H. W. "Seeking Professional Help for Personal Problems: Black Americans' Use of Health and Mental Health Services." *Community Mental Health Journal,* 1985, *21,* 156–166.

Norman, J. S. "Short-Term Treatment with the Adolescent Client." *Social Casework,* 1980, *61,* 74–82.

Omi, M., and Winant, H. *Racial Formation in the United States: From the 1960s to the 1980s.* New York: Routledge, 1986.

Orfield, G., and Ashkinaze, C. *The Closing Door: Conservative Policy and Black Opportunity.* Chicago: University of Chicago Press, 1991.

Paster, V. "Adapting Psychotherapy for the Depressed, Unacculturated, Acting-Out Black Male Adolescent." *Psychotherapy,* 1985, *22*(25), 408–417.

Peters, M. F. "Parenting in Black Families with Young Children: A Historical Perspective." In H. McAdoo (ed.), *Black Families.* Thousand Oaks, Calif.: Sage, 1981.

Phinney, J. S. "Ethnic Identity in Adolescents and Adults: Review of Research." *Psychological Bulletin,* 1990, *108*(3), 499–514.

Phinney, J. S., Cantu, C. L., and Kurtz, D. A. "Ethnic and American Identity as Predictors of Self-Esteem Among African American, Latino, and White Adolescents." *Journal of Youth and Adolescence,* 1997, *26*(2), 165–185.

Pinderhughes, E. *Understanding Race, Ethnicity and Power: The Key to Efficacy in Clinical Practice.* New York: Free Press, 1989.

Poe-Yamagata, E., and Jones, M. A. *And Justice for Some: Differential Treatment of Minority Youth in the Justice System.* Washington, D.C.: Youth Law Center, 2000.

Pope, C. E., and Feyerherm, W. H. *Minorities in the Juvenile Justice System.* Washington, D.C.: Office of Juvenile Justice and Delinquency Prevention, 1993.

Powell, G. J. "Self-Concepts Among Afro-American Students in Racially Isolated Minority Schools: Some Regional Differences." *Journal of the American Academy of Child Psychiatry,* 1985, *24,* 142–149.

Pumariega, A., Edwards, P., and Mitchell, C. "Anexoria Nervosa in Black Adolescents." *Journal of the American Academy of Child Psychiatry,* 1984, *23,* 111–114.

Reed, R. "Education and Achievement of Young Black Males." In J. T. Gibbs (ed.), *Young, Black, and Male in America: An Endangered Species.* Dover, Mass.: Auburn House, 1988.

Ridley, C. R. "Clinical Treatment of the Nondisclosing Black Client: A Therapeutic Paradox." *American Psychologist,* 1984, *39,* 1234–1244.

Roberts, R. E., Roberts, C., and Chen, Y. R. "Ethnocultural Differences in Prevalence of Adolescent Depression." *American Journal of Community Psychology,* 1997, *25,* 95–110.

Roberts, R. E., and Sobhan, M. "Symptoms of Depression in Adolescence: A Comparison of Anglo, African, and Hispanic Americans." *Journal of Youth and Adolescence,* 1992, *21*(6), 639–651.

Robinson, B. *Teenage Fathers.* Lexington, Mass: Lexington Books, 1988.

Robinson, P., and Andersen, A. "Anorexia Nervosa in American Blacks." *Journal of Psychiatry Research,* 1985, *19,* 183–188.

Robinson, T., and Ward, J. V. "A Belief in Self Far Greater than Anyone's Disbelief: Cultivating Healthy Resistance Among African American Female Adolescents." In C. Gilligan, A. G. Rogers, and D. Tolman (eds.), *Women, Girls and Psychotherapy.* Binghamton, N.Y.: Harrington Park Press, 1991.

Rose, S. D., and Edleson, J. L. *Working With Children and Adolescents in Groups.* San Francisco: Jossey-Bass, 1987.

Rosenberg, M. *Conceiving the Self.* New York, Basic Books, 1979.

Rosenheim, M. K., and Testa, M. F. (eds.). *Early Parenthood and Coming of Age in the 1990s.* New Brunswick, N.J.: Rutgers University Press, 1992.

Rotheram-Borus, M. J., Dopkins, S., Sabate, N., and Lightfoot, M. "Personal and Ethnic Identity, Values, and Self-Esteem Among Black and Latino Girls." In B. J. Leadbetter and N. Way (eds.), *Urban Girls: Resisting*

Stereotypes, Creating Identities. (pp. 35–52). New York: New York University Press, 1996.

Salem, D. A., Zimmerman, M. A., and Nataro, P. C. "Effects of Family Structure, Family Process, and Father Involvement on Psychosocial Outcomes Among African American Adolescents." *Family Relations,* 1998, *47*(4), 331–341.

Samuda, R. *Psychological Testing of American Minorities: Issues and Consequences.* New York: Dodd, Mead, 1998.

Sanchez-Hucles, J. *The First Session With African Americans: A Step-By-Step Guide.* San Francisco: Jossey-Bass, 1999.

Santisteban, D. A., and others. "Brief Structural/Strategic Family Therapy with African American and Hispanic High-Risk Youth. *Journal of Community Psychology,* 1997, *25*(5), 453–471.

Schoenbach, V., and others. "Prevalence of Self-Reported Depressive Symptoms in Young Adolescents." *American Journal of Public Health,* 1983, *73,* 1281–1287.

Schorr, A. *Common Decency: Domestic Politics After Reagan.* New Haven, Conn.: Yale University Press, 1986.

Scott-Jones, D., Davis, A., Foster, M., and Hughes, T. "Sexual Activity, Pregnancy and Child-Bearing Among African-American Youth." In R. L. Taylor (ed.), *African American Youth: Their Social and Economic Status in the United States* (pp. 157–178). Westport, Conn.: Praeger, 1995.

Seidman, E., and others. "The Risk and Protective Functions of Perceived Family and Peer Microsystems Among Urban Adolescents in Poverty." *American Journal of Community Psychology,* 1999, *27*(2), 211–237.

Shaffer, D., and Fisher, P. "The Epidemiology of Suicide in Children and Young Adolescents." *Journal of the American Academy of Child Psychiatry,* 1981, *20,* 545–566.

Siegel, J. M., and others. "Adolescent Depressed Mood in a Multiethnic Sample." *Journal of Youth and Adolescence,* 1998, *27*(4), 413–427.

Smitherman, G. *Black Talk: Words and Phrases From the Hood to the Amen Corner.* Boston: Houghton Mifflin, 1994.

Snowden, L. R., and Todman, P. A. "The Psychological Assessment of Blacks: New and Needed Developments." In E. E. Jones and S. J. Korchin (eds.), *Minority Mental Health.* New York: Praeger, 1982.

Snyder, H. N., and Sickmund, M. *Juvenile Offenders and Victims: 1999 National Report.* Washington, D.C.: U.S. Department of Justice, Office of Juvenile Justice and Delinquency Prevention, 1999.

Spencer, M. B. "Personal and Group Identity of Black Children: An Alternative Synthesis." *Genetic Psychology Monographs,* 1982, *106,* 59–84.

Spencer, M. B. "Black Children's Race Awareness, Racial Attitudes, and Self-Concept: A Reinterpretation." *Journal of Child Psychology and Psychiatry,* 1984, *25*(3), 433–441.

Spencer, M. B. "Old Issues and New Theorizing About African-American Youth: A Phenomenological Variant of Ecological Systems Theory." In R. L. Taylor (ed.), *African American Youth: Their Social and Economic Status in the United States* (pp. 157–178). Westport, Conn.: Praeger, 1995.

Spencer, M. B., Brookins, G. K., and Allen, W. R. (eds.). *Beginnings: The Social and Affective Developments of Black Children.* Mahwah, N. J.: Lawrence Erlbaum Associates, 1985.

Spencer, M. B., and Dornbusch, S. M. "Challenges in Studying Minority Adolescents." In S. Feldman and G. R. Elliott (eds.), *At the Threshold: The Developing Adolescent.* Cambridge, Mass.: Harvard University Press, 1990.

Spencer, M. B., and Markstrom-Adams, C. M. "Identity Processes Among Racial and Ethnic Minority Children in America." *Child Development,* 1990, *61,* 290–310.

Stack, C. *All Our Kin: Strategies for Survival in a Black Community.* New York: Harper & Row, 1974.

Staples, R., and Johnson, L. B. *Black Families at the Crossroads: Challenges and Prospects.* San Francisco: Jossey-Bass, 1993.

Steinberg, L. "Single Parents, Step-Parents, and the Susceptibility of Adolescents to Antisocial Peer Pressure." *Child Development,* 1987, *587,* 269–439.

Sutphen, R. D., Thyer, B. A., and Kurtz, D. "Multisystemic Treatment of High-Risk Juvenile Offenders." *International Journal of Offender Therapy and Corrective Criminology,* 1995, *39,* 327–334.

Taylor, R. L. "Childrearing in African American Families." In J. Everett, S. J. Chipungu, and B. L. Leashore (eds.), *Child Welfare: An Afrocentric Perspective.* New Brunswick, N.J.: Rutgers University Press, 1991.

Taylor, R. L. (ed.). *African-American Youth: Their Social and Economic Status in the United States.* Westport, Conn.: Praeger, 1995.

U.S. Bureau of the Census. *Statistical Abstract of the United States: 2001.* (121st ed.) Washington, D.C.: U.S. Department of Commerce, 2001.

U.S. Department of Health and Human Services. *Mental Health: Culture, Race and Ethnicity:* Supplement to *Mental Health: A Report of the Surgeon General.* Rockville, Md.: U.S. Department of Health and Human Services, 2001.

Ventura, S. J., Clarke, S. C., and Mathews, T. J. "Recent Decline in Teenage Birth Rates in the United States: Variations by State, 1990–94." *Monthly Vital Statistics Report: Supplement,* 1996, *45*(5), entire issue.

Ward, J. V. "Raising Resisters: The Role of Truth Telling in the Psychological Development of African American Girls." In B. J. Leadbetter and N. Way (eds.), *Urban Girls: Resisting Stereotypes, Creating Identities.* (pp. 149–170). New York: New York University Press, 1996.

Way, N. "Between Experiences of Betrayal and Desire: Close Friendships Among Urban Adolescents." In B. J. Leadbetter and N. Way (eds.), *Urban Girls: Resisting Stereotypes, Creating Identities.* (pp. 149–170). New York: New York University Press, 1996.

Weddle, K. D., and McKenry, P. C. "Self Destructive Behaviors Among Black Youth: Suicide and Homicide." In R. L. Taylor (ed.), *African American Youth: Their Social and Economic Status in the United States* (pp. 157–178). Westport, Conn.: Praeger, 1995.

Williams, T. R., and others. "Friends, Family and Neighborhood: Understanding Academic Outcomes of African American Youth." *Urban Education,* 2002, *37*(3), 408–431.

Wilson, W. J. *The Truly Disadvantaged.* Chicago: University of Chicago Press, 1987.

Wilson, W. J. *When Work Disappears: The New World of the Urban Poor.* New York: Knopf, 1996.

Chapter Three

Biracial and Bicultural Children and Adolescents

Jewelle Taylor Gibbs

Since the early 1960s, American society has undergone some profound social, cultural, and demographic changes. As a natural consequence of the civil rights movement, the counterculture movement, and the Vietnam War protests, conventional social barriers have been weakened and contacts between diverse racial and ethnic groups greatly increased. As social interactions among members of different ethnic groups expanded, interracial and interethnic marriages and partnerships have inevitably increased (Cretser and Leon, 1982; Dalmage, 2000; Korgen, 1998; Root, 1992, 1996). These mixed marriages have produced a growing number of biracial and bicultural children, many of whom are now adolescents and young adults.

During the 1980s, this growing mixed-race population became more visible and more vocal in their advocacy for a distinctive ethnic label and official classification in the U.S. census (Daniel, 1992; Fernandez, 1996; Spencer, 1997). In 2000, for the first census in the twenty-first century, residents were allowed to identify themselves according to multiple ethnic-racial categories, yielding a surprising total of 6.8 million (2.4 percent) of racially or ethnically mixed people in the population (U.S. Bureau of the Census, 2001).

This chapter describes biracial and bicultural adolescents as an emerging population of young people who have some unique characteristics, some potential problems, and some special needs—all of which are related to their ambiguous ethnicity and their need to define their identities in a society where race has always been a significant social dimension (Bradshaw, 1992; Ramirez, 1996; Xie and Goyette, 1997). As this group has expanded in numbers, there has been a concomitant blurring of racial distinctions and an increasing societal tolerance toward interracial and interethnic marriage (Cretser and Leon, 1982; Daniel, 1992; Holinger, 1995). Despite these changes, we lack adequate information about these biracial youth, who are faced with the developmental task of integrating two ethnic identities and, frequently, two or more distinct cultural heritages (Gibbs and Moskowitz-Sweet, 1991; Kich, 1992; Poston, 1990). Because adolescence is the stage during which these issues emerge as major psychosocial tasks, it is important for mental health clinicians, educators, and other human service professionals who serve youth to understand the impact of biracial or bicultural identity on their attitudes, behaviors, and problems.

Demographic data on the population of biracial and bicultural children are subject to a number of statistical biases because the validity of self-professed racial labels on marriage applications and birth certificates is questionable, particularly for children born out of wedlock. Because the federal census only reports statistics on "Black/white" interracial couples and "Hispanic/non-Hispanic" couples, this chapter primarily focuses on children and adolescents who are offspring of those two specific groups of mixed marriages.

In the 2000 census, over 6.8 million people described themselves as "multiracial" by checking the option of belonging to "two or more races"; they now constitute 2.4 percent of the nation's population, a small but rapidly expanding segment of American society (U.S. Bureau of the Census, 2002).

According to the 2000 census, there were over 1,464,000 interracial married couples and 1,742,000 interethnic couples (Hispanic and non-Hispanic) in the United States (U.S. Bureau of the Census, 2002). Although the 363,000 "Black/White" married couples constituted only 24.8 percent of all interracial married couples in 2000, the actual number had increased more than five-fold from 65,000 in 1970. The majority of these families reside in urban areas of the North, Midwest, and West Coast, where they have found less overt racial prejudice and greater tolerance for diversity in family structures and lifestyles. Metropolitan areas with a significant number of interracial families are New York, Boston, Chicago, Minneapolis-St. Paul, Denver, Seattle, San Francisco, and Los Angeles (Brown and Douglass, 1996).

By the end of the 1990s, increasing numbers of multiracial and multicultural families had found a niche even in border and Southern cities such as Washington, D.C., Atlanta, Miami, and Houston. States with the highest number of mixed-race people are California, Hawaii, Florida, New York, and New Jersey.

Estimates of the number of biracial and bicultural children and adolescents in the United States have ranged from 600,000 to 5 million, but more recently, the population of racially and ethnically mixed children has been estimated at 2 million (Holmes, 1996). However, this probably understates the actual number due to methodological difficulties in identifying children from mixed racial or ethnic parentage from birth certificates or from visual appearance (Root, 1992; Spickard, 1992). They now constitute a visible and "critical mass" on many college campuses, where they have actively lobbied for Ethnic Studies Departments to establish courses on multicultural and multiracial people (Williams, Nakashima, Kich, and Daniel, 1996; Wilson, 1992).

Over a decade ago, a series about interracial families in the *Los Angeles Times* (Njeri, 1988) described the experiences of these families, the varied ways in which they cope with their uniqueness, and the complex challenges biracial teenagers face in their efforts to separate from their families and establish their own identities. Quoting from several of these articulate young people, Njeri noted the emerging sense of community among biracial persons and the perceived need for a new racial category to describe themselves.

Since that article appeared, public awareness and interest has grown about the emerging population of racially and ethnically mixed families and their children, inspiring a plethora of popular articles, books, and documentation on this phenomenon. With the growth of immigration from Asia and Latin America and the social mobility of native-born ethnic minority groups, the pace of interethnic marriages and sexual relationships also accelerated (U.S. Bureau of the Census, 2002).

In her two books about racially mixed families and individuals in the United States, Maria Root (1992, 1996) discusses and analyzes the variety of attitudes, experiences, and responses of interracial and interethnic families who represent the multiple combinations of

Asians, African Americans, American Indians, Latinos, and whites. Describing the proliferation of this polyglot population as "the new frontier" in the United States, she and her colleagues have produced a multidimensional and nuanced perspective on the variations, the strengths, and the challenges facing these families in American society (Root, 1996). Although this chapter focuses primarily on the offspring of African American and white and Latino and white couples, the issues they must confront and resolve are similar in nature, if not in severity, to those of other youth in interracial and interethnic families.

Historical Background

Interracial families are a relatively recent phenomenon in American society, primarily because of three historical factors. First, many states passed laws before and after the Civil War prohibiting marriage between whites and nonwhites. As Gay (1987) points out, these laws were based on theories of white supremacy and myths about racial mixing that were frequently supported by conservative political and religious writings. Second, even after the Supreme Court declared these antimiscegenation laws unconstitutional in 1967, social sanctions continued to operate against interracial marriages, and the costs of defying these sanctions were very high, including family disapproval and alienation, social exclusion, and discrimination in housing, employment, and public accommodations (Gay, 1987). Third, social and economic discrimination against blacks and other nonwhites resulted in the development of two essentially separate, castelike communities, so that blacks and whites had few opportunities for social relationships and shared activities (Franklin and Moss, 1988). Thus, although informal contacts and nonmarital sexual liaisons between whites and other racial-ethnic groups occurred despite these barriers, marriages between these groups were relatively rare before World War II, with the exception of American Indians and whites in some areas of the country with long traditions of white and Indian contact, whose offspring have been called half-breeds, *métis,* or mixed bloods (Root, 1992; Wilson, 1992).

After World War II and the Korean War, black and white servicemen brought home European and Asian war brides. Coinciding with a number of other significant changes in American society, these interracial couples settled in communities that seemed more hospitable to them and were generally more open to the other postwar innovations in economy, technology, and social structure. These communities included the newly expanded suburbs, with housing developments tailored to the needs of returning veterans and carrying low-interest mortgages. The Levittown planned communities in the Northeast were among the first to promote integrated middle-income housing.

During the postwar period of the late 1940s and early 1950s, landmark Supreme Court decisions overturned many of the legal underpinnings of discrimination in housing, public accommodations, and education—further generating a social climate of tolerance and equal opportunity that was beneficial for interracial and interethnic couples and families (Farley and Allen, 1989; Omi and Winant, 1986; Stuart and Abt, 1973).

After the Supreme Court outlawed school segregation in 1954 and the Montgomery, Alabama, bus boycott began in late 1955, the South witnessed a remarkable alliance between young blacks and whites, who mounted a successful decade of civil rights protests that culminated in two major federal civil rights bills in 1964 and 1965 (Albert and Hoffman, 1990; Branch, 1988; Chambers, 1968). Although these protests and the ensuing legislation met with much resistance, the important legacy of this era was the breaking down of institutional barriers to blacks, as well as the opening up of greater opportunities for interracial social interaction in educational, employment, recreational, and cultural settings (Jaynes and Williams, 1989). These opportunities inevitably led to more interracial dating and more interracial marriages, as can be inferred from the dramatic increase in the black-white marriage rate in the past three decades (Daniel, 1992; Porterfield, 1982; U.S. Bureau of the Census, 2001).

As noted earlier, the social upheaval brought about by the counterculture movement of the late 1960s and 1970s, the black student protests on white college campuses, and the Vietnam War protests was accompanied by significant shifts in black-white relationships and radically different norms of social behavior regarding sexuality, drug use, and marital patterns. Antiestablishment attitudes and massive rejection of middle-class norms among young whites and blacks fostered an environment of social and political experimentation, including interracial relationships, communes, and political organizations. In some liberal communities and on many college campuses, it became a sign of "radical chic" to date interracially, so that the incidence of black-white affairs and marriages rose, with a corresponding increase in numbers of biracial children (Cretser and Leon, 1982; Pope, 1985; Root, 1992, 1996).

In more recent years, the trend toward interracial marriages appears to have increased, perhaps for a number of reasons, including the greater number of unions between black females and white males, the weakened sanction against unions between black males and white females, and the general decrease in societal disapproval of interracial marriages (Gibbs and Hines, 1992; Thornton, 1996).

Since the 1980s, however, the trend toward interracial and interethnic marriages between whites and Asians and between whites and Latinos has outpaced marriages between blacks and whites (U.S. Bureau of the Census, 2002). In fact, a Gallup poll analysis of changes in American attitudes toward interracial marriage found that between 1968 and 1983 the proportion of people who expressed disapproval decreased from 72 percent to 50 percent. By 1991, a slight majority of Americans responded that they did not support antimiscegenation laws (Gallup Poll, cited in Thornton, 1996). Although nearly half of the American public may still disapprove of interracial marriage, the trend is clearly toward a more liberal viewpoint.

Social and Cultural Issues

One of the major issues for interracial families is the transmission of a coherent sense of a cultural heritage and an ethnic identity to their children. In contrast to other ethnic minority families, these parents do not share the same racial or cultural heritage, even if they are from the same socioeconomic background and educational level. Whites and blacks in America have different historical roots and social experiences and are reared in different subcultural contexts (Farley and Allen, 1989; Franklin and Moss, 1988; Hacker, 1992; Omi and Winant, 1986). As the descriptions in Chapter Two clearly show, the predominant influences shaping the experiences of blacks in America have been slavery, discrimination, and poverty. Blacks were forced to develop a "separate and un-equal" set of social institutions (for example, churches, schools, social and health services, small businesses, and fraternal, social, and political organizations) and have maintained many of these institutions, even after segregation was legally abolished. This quasi caste system required most blacks to become familiar with the insti-tutions of the dominant society to the extent that this knowledge facilitated their educational or economic activities, but few whites found it necessary or useful to acquire any knowledge about black cultural or social institutions. Even for most middle-class blacks, this legacy has left its imprint in many social, psychological, and behavioral characteristics that reflect an adaptation to prejudice and social exclusion (Cose, 1993; Grier and Cobbs, 1968; Pinder-hughes, 1982).

Whites, however, came to America voluntarily as immigrants or refugees and so were able to maintain much of their cultural her-itage while adjusting to a new country (Glazer and Moynihan, 1970). Regardless of their country of origin, white immigrants were eventually able to become fully acculturated and assimilated into the mainstream society through educational and economic mobil-ity. By contrast, the waves of nonwhite immigrants from Asia, Africa, the Caribbean, and Latin America have not been easily as-similated into the dominant society, even after they have become acculturated (Perea, 1997; Root, 1992, 1996; Takaki, 1994). These immigrants of color have faced widespread racial and ethnic dis-crimination, social marginalization, and cultural exclusion. Since the conservative backlash in the 1980s, they have been subjected to high levels of anti-immigrant rhetoric and behavior, as exem-plified by the passage of state and national legislation repealing or severely limiting affirmative action, bilingual education, and immi-grants' welfare benefits (Gibbs and Bankhead, 2001; Perea, 1997; Preston, Cain, and Bass, 1998).

Disparities in social and cultural backgrounds sometimes make it difficult for whites and people of color to communicate and to understand each other's viewpoints. Even more relevant to inter-racial and interethnic families, these background differences pose a special challenge to parents, who must transmit to their children knowledge about their family history and continuity, a positive sense about their dual cultural heritage, and an integrated sense of an ethnic identity (Phinney, 1990). As McGoldrick (1982) asserts,

> Ethnicity is a powerful influence in determining identity. A sense of belonging and of historical continuity is a basic psychological need. We may ignore it or cut it off by changing our names [and] rejecting our families and social backgrounds, but we do so to the detriment of our well-being. [p. 5]

Despite evidence of more liberal societal attitudes toward inter-racial and interethnic marriages, some studies of these couples and their children suggest that they frequently encounter problems of family disapproval, community acceptance, job discrimination, and social isolation (Brown, 1987, 1990; Gay, 1987; Herring, 1992; Ra-mirez, 1996). These studies have suggested or implied that biracial and bicultural youth are particularly vulnerable to differential treat-ment by their parents and relatives, social rejection by their peers, and ambivalent attention in their schools and communities. How-ever, more recent empirical studies have found that these youth are not significantly different in their psychosocial adjustment and family relationships than their monoracial-monoethnic peers of the same age (Cauce and others, 1992; Gibbs and Hines, 1992; Ker-win, Ponterotto, Jackson, and Harris, 1993). It is important to note that most of these studies are based on clinical samples or small community-based, nonrandom samples, limiting their generaliz-ability to all ethnically and racially mixed youth and their families. Nonetheless, the contrasting findings provide alternative perspec-tives for viewing the mental health issues for these youth.

Mental Health Issues

Biracial and bicultural children and adolescents have legitimate claims to majority and minority ethnicity, and yet society usually forces them to define and label themselves as members of a minor-ity group (Fernandez, 1996). The existence of a dual racial iden-tity or a dual cultural heritage may pose dilemmas for these youth as they enter adolescence (Benson, 1981; Sommers, 1964). Erik-son (1959) proposes that the central task of adolescence is to form a stable identity, which he describes as "a sense of personal sameness and historical continuity" (p. 89). He delineates a series of developmental tasks to be successfully negotiated in the development of a healthy and positive identity: development of a personal identity (sense of uniqueness and self-esteem), establishment of a sense of autonomy and independence from parents, development of the ability to relate to same-sex and other-sex peers, and commitment to a vocational choice.

Several African American authors have pointed out that identity formation for black adolescents may be a more difficult and problematic task, particularly in view of the messages they receive from the dominant society that they are members of a disadvantaged and devalued minority group (Erikson, 1968; Jenkins, 1982; Logan, 1981; Taylor, 1976). Chestang (1984) notes that blacks must integrate a "personal" and a "racial" identity in order to form a cohesive total identity. Recent history offers numerous examples of African American young adults who have overcome barriers of discrimination and the social devaluation by whites to achieve remarkable accomplishments that reflect an internal sense of coherence and personal worth. Examples are the musician Wynton Marsalis and the tennis-playing champions Venus and Serena Williams; there are countless other talented and successful men and women.

Empirical studies of biracial children indicate that their racial attitudes and self-concepts develop differently from those of either black or white children (Jacobs, 1992; Kich, 1992; Lyles, Yancy, Grace, and Carter, 1985; Payne, 1977; Poston, 1990). In one study, accurate racial identification decreased as skin color darkened, suggesting that the darker children had a more negative self-concept. However, other studies have found that biracial children have equivalent or higher self-esteem compared with their monoracial peers (Chang, 1974; Duffy, 1978). In his study of ten biracial children, Jacobs (1992) identifies three stages of racial identity development, with increasing levels of cognitive maturity from the first stage of pre-color constancy to the second stage of post-color constancy and racial ambivalence to the third stage of a unified biracial identity.

In the most rigorous empirical investigation of mixed-race children to date, Cooney and Radina (2000) evaluated nine indicators of psychosocial adjustment in a stratified random sample of 284 mixed-race youth in grades 7 through 12, drawn from the National

Longitudinal Study of Adolescent Health. Comparing mixed-race youth with two other groups of white-only and single-race minority youth (63.1 percent African Americans, 18.0 percent Latino, 18.0 percent Asian), the authors found that mixed-race youth were significantly different in fewer than half of the school, behavioral, and psychological variables assessed. Results of a multivariate regression analysis showed that mixed-race youth of both sexes were significantly more likely to have had psychological counseling in the past year than students in the comparison groups; these youth also had significantly higher rates of grade retention in school and higher rates of school suspension than their white peers. While mixed-race boys had higher depression scores than white boys, there were no significant differences in depression scores among mixed-race girls and their peers in the comparison groups. By contrast, mixed-race girls had significantly higher delinquency scores than white girls, but there were no differences among the three groups of boys in delinquency scores. The results of this study confirmed some of the findings from the earlier clinical and community studies that mixed-race youth, in contrast to white youth, experience more psychological and behavioral problems for which they may seek counseling, but it is unclear how many of these problems can be directly attributed to identity conflicts over their racially mixed status.

If identity formation is more problematic for black than white adolescents, then one can hypothesize that it would be even more difficult for adolescents with a biracial background (Kerwin, Ponterotto, Jackson, and Harris, 1993; Poston, 1990). By their teen years, these youth are fully cognizant of the differential prestige accorded to blacks and whites in America, the differential opportunities available to each group, and the advantages and disadvantages of belonging to each. Moreover, their normal identity conflicts will inevitably be exacerbated by their feelings of love and loyalty to each parent, especially when they can easily attribute ambivalent feelings toward either parent as a sign of racial rejection rather than as an expression of the normal separation process (Lyles, Yancy, Grace, and Carter, 1985; Sebring, 1985).

Two other sources of documentation for the identity conflicts and psychological challenges of biracial and bicultural individuals are autobiographical accounts and memoirs, which have appeared with increasing frequency in the past two decades. The social and personal struggles of mixed-race youth have been starkly described by authors such as Gregory Howard Williams (1995), James McBride (1996), and Lawrence Funderburg (1999). The impact of "passing for white" on three generations of a mixed-race family has also been sensitively chronicled by Shirlee Taylor Haizlip (1994).

Community surveys of biracial and bicultural children and adolescents have also produced conflicting findings. Whereas earlier researchers focused on the incidence of low self-esteem, confused racial or ethnic identity, and psychological or behavioral problems among these youth (Benson, 1981; Henriques, 1974; Ladner, 1977; Piskacek and Golub, 1973), more recent authors have emphasized their adaptability, resiliency, and creativity (Gay, 1987; Johnson and Nagoshi, 1986; Kerwin, Ponterotto, Jackson, and Harris, 1993; Poussaint, 1984) and their overall positive psychosocial adjustment (Cauce and others, 1992; Gibbs and Hines, 1992). Positive outcomes are predicted for those youth who are reared in supportive families, have a sense of competence and high self-esteem, and are involved in supportive schools and social networks (Gibbs and Hines, 1992; Lyles, Yancy, Grace, and Carter, 1985; Sebring, 1985; Wehlage and others, 1989).

Contemporary examples of biracial and bicultural young adults who appear to have successfully negotiated the challenges of a biracial and bicultural identity include the actress Halle Berry, golfer Tiger Woods, singer Mariah Carey, and basketball player Rick Fox. It is interesting to note that these are all well-known celebrities whose identities transcend race and ethnicity; they are, in fact, superstars.

Biracial and bicultural children in school settings have also been characterized as having a high incidence of academic and behavioral problems, as well as identity conflicts (Herring, 1992; McRoy and Freeman, 1986). Further, these problems have been noted among black or racially mixed children who have been adopted by white parents (McRoy, Zurcher, Lauderdale, and Anderson, 1984; Simon and Alstein, 1977; Silverman and Feigelman, 1981). Although the majority of these adopted children appear well adjusted, those who do have problems are more likely to reveal them as they enter adolescence.

Clinical studies of biracial children are sparse, but a pioneer study by Teicher (1968) notes that these children have problems of identification with the minority parent, sexual-identity conflicts, and problems of adjustment to a predominantly white environment. These observations have been supported by reports of clinicians who have treated a variety of biracial children, adolescents, college students, and interracial families (Adams, 1973; Brandell, 1988; Faulkner and Kich, 1983; Gibbs, 1987; Lyles, Yancy, Grace, and Carter, 1985; Sebring, 1985; Tizard and Phoenix, 1995). In addition, these latter studies have described a range of psychological and behavioral problems in these youth, including conduct disorders, substance abuse, academic problems, psychosomatic disorders, depression, and suicidal behaviors.

Finally, in a 1986 survey of fifty social service, mental health, special education, and probation agencies located in the San Francisco area, 60 percent of the thirty-one responding agencies reported that referrals of biracial adolescents had increased during the past ten years and that this group was overrepresented among their adolescent client population (Gibbs, 1987). These clients had been referred for a broad spectrum of problems similar to those described in the clinical literature. Not only had the incidence of referrals in this group increased but their presenting symptoms had become more severe. It was not clear from the study whether the actual incidence of biracial children seeking help had increased in these agencies or whether they had only increased in proportion to their overall increase in the community.

Despite the obvious limitations of clinical studies and the difficulty of drawing any generalizations from so few studies of biracial and bicultural children and adolescents, some issues have been identified across a wide range of studies, as well as some themes of potential problems and protective coping mechanisms. First, these biracial and bicultural youth must integrate dual racial or cultural identifications while learning to develop a positive self-concept and sense of competence. Second, as they enter adolescence, they must synthesize their earlier identifications into a coherent and stable sense of a personal identity, as well as a positive racial identity. In accomplishing this task, they must deal effectively with the related tasks of developing peer relationships, defining their sexual orientation and sexual preference, making a career choice, and separating from their parents—all of which may be more problematic for this group.

In conceptualizing the process of identity development for biracial and bicultural adolescents, I have proposed that they may experience conflicts in their efforts to resolve five major psychosocial tasks: (1) integrating their dual racial-ethnic identity, (2) negotiating their social marginality, (3) confronting their sexuality and choice of sexual partners, (4) separating from their parents, and (5) planning their educational or career aspirations (Gibbs, 1987; Gibbs and Moskowitz-Sweet, 1991). Both clinical studies and community surveys indicate that these conflicts may be expressed in a variety of psychological and behavioral symptoms, ranging from mild symptoms of anxiety and depression to moderate symptoms of academic underachievement and peer conflicts to severe symptoms of delinquency, substance abuse, and suicidal behaviors. At the milder end of the spectrum, these symptoms reflect a pattern of identity confusion, whereas the moderate level of symptomatology reflects a form of identity diffusion or foreclosure, and the severe symptoms reflect the formation of a negative identity (Hauser, 1972).

The consensus of clinicians is that teenagers who do experience difficulties in negotiating their identity process are those most likely to be referred for assessment and treatment (Gibbs and Hines, 1992; Lyles, Yancy, Grace, and Carter, 1985; Sebring, 1985). Further, some clinicians would predict that biracial-bicultural adolescents are at greater risk for problematic outcomes because of their potential vulnerability to conflicts in each of the central developmental tasks. Although there are no epidemiological data to support this hypothesis, clinical evidence suggests that an understanding of this important developmental process in racially and ethnically mixed adolescents will increase clinicians' sensitivity to their unique concerns and will enable them to serve this emerging group more effectively.

In the following section, these identity conflicts are illustrated with case vignettes and guidelines for assessment. The case examples are drawn from my experiences over a twenty-five-year period as a clinician, consultant, and supervisor in college mental health clinics, outpatient psychiatric clinics, and private practice. The clinical material is supplemented by interpretations of the developmental, empirical, and clinical studies summarized earlier.

Conflicts and Coping Strategies

In this section, I propose that the central issue for the clinician to assess in evaluating biracial adolescents is their underlying attitude toward their dual racial-ethnic heritage, which must be successfully integrated before they can resolve the developmental tasks in the four related areas of identity achievement. The defense mechanisms and coping strategies employed by these teenagers to handle these conflicts are also described. An ecological framework is used to examine four other important domains of assessment, encompassing individual, family, school, and peer areas.

Conflicts About Racial-Ethnic Identity

Racial or ethnic identity is the most widespread conflict encountered by clinicians when treating biracial adolescents who describe themselves variously as "half and half," "Heinz 57 varieties," "Oreos," "Coconuts," "Bananas," or "Apples." The basic question in this area is "Who am I?" In these cases, there has been a partial or complete failure to integrate both parental racial or ethnic backgrounds into a cohesive racial-ethnic identity. These teenagers may identify with the white parent as the symbol of the dominant majority, rejecting the nonwhite or Latino parent, even if there is a closer physical resemblance. Typically, the mixed-race teens whom clinicians see express ambivalent feelings toward the racial-ethnic background of both parents, alternately denigrating and praising the perceived attributes of both groups (Benson, 1981; Lyles, Yancy, Grace, and Carter, 1985; Sebring, 1985). As with other racially or ethnically mixed adolescents, they may experiment with passing as white or adopting an alternative identity as "jock," "punk rocker," "Moonie," or "druggie" (Daniel, 1992; Kich, 1992; Gibbs and Moskowitz-Sweet, 1991; Wilson, 1992).

Adolescent females are more likely to feel ashamed of their nonwhite physical traits, such as darker skin, curly hair, almond-shaped eyes, or broad facial features (Boyd-Franklin, 1989; Garrod, Ward, Robinson, and Kilkenny, 1999; Pinderhughes, 1982). As a consequence of incorporating negative attitudes and stereotypes about nonwhites, they often try to distance themselves from their ethnic peers in school and social situations, and they may reject any identification with their ethnic culture as it is expressed in the music, dance, and dress styles of those peers.

When biracial or bicultural teens have overidentified with their African American or Latino parents, the similar phenomenon of rejecting white culture and white friends is played out. This over-identification may take the form of adopting the attitudes, behaviors, styles of dress, and styles of speech stereotypically associated with low-income blacks or Latinos rather than with their own middle-class lifestyle, thus confusing race or ethnicity with SES. Because many of the biracial and bicultural adolescents referred for treatment are from middle-class families, these behaviors not only are quite dissonant with their family's lifestyle but they tend to result in a negative identity formation. In other words, the negative identity is associated with the dissonant and devalued social status of the minority parent's culture, which is not congruent with the reality of these clients' life experiences.

Thirteen-year-old Marcia, born out of wedlock to a white mother and black father, was referred by her white adoptive parents because of rebellious behavior, truancy, and stealing from family members. The parents also suspected she was sexually active and using drugs. In individual sessions, Marcia, who had very light skin but black facial features and hair, spoke of always feeling inferior to her younger sister, who was part Asian and had always been favored by the adoptive parents. Her behavioral problems had surfaced when she entered junior high school and felt she did not belong with any of the cliques, was rejected by former white neighborhood friends, and drifted into a group of "dopers" who were alienated from school and society. In family sessions, it was clear that Marcia had assumed the role of the "bad child," identifying with the negative stories she had been told about her black father, who had been imprisoned for drugs and burglary, and playing out an unspoken script to fulfill the negative expectations communicated to her by her parents. Marcia tried to resolve her racial identity conflict through assuming a negative identity and seeking out deviant peers whose antisocial behaviors reinforced that identity. By "acting just like my dad," Marcia was identifying with her natural black parent while punishing her adoptive white parents for their ambivalence toward her "blackness."

Linda, a seventeen-year-old high school senior, was the daughter of an Indian mother and Scotch-English father who had been a teacher at an Indian boarding school. Linda, who had inherited her father's freckled skin and red hair, had been the object of constant teasing and ridicule while growing up in a small Southwestern town just outside her mother's reservation. After she was admitted to college with a special scholarship for American Indian students, she asked for an appointment with her high school counselor. Appearing very nervous and unsure of herself, Linda said she wanted to discuss "something very personal" with the counselor. She revealed that she had not told her parents about the scholarship because they were very proud and would prefer to pay her college costs without financial aid. Sensing a deeper issue, the counselor asked Linda if she had any other reasons for rejecting the generous scholarship. Linda began to cry and confided that she planned to keep her "Indianness" a secret when she entered college and live the rest of her life as a white person. As she talked more about her decision to "pass for white," Linda revealed that she had always felt that Indians were inferior to white people because most of the ones she knew were poor, not well educated, and had so many social problems. She told the counselor that life was easier for white people, and she was just tired of people looking down on her as an Indian.

Conflicts About Social Marginality

A conflict about social marginality is inextricably related to the core identity conflict, but it can be assessed as a separate problem. The basic question in this area for these biracial teens is, "Where do I fit?" This question is especially salient as they enter adolescence and begin to participate in heterosexual social and extracurricular activities. During this phase of development, teens are particularly vulnerable to the twin terrors of anxiety about social acceptance and fear of social rejection.

In elementary school, these children may have had a close-knit peer group and satisfying social relationships. However, social problems often emerge when they enter junior high school and later go to high school. Typically, girls seem to experience more anxiety than boys about social acceptance, because they are more often excluded from social activities and extracurricular school activities.

In a developmental stage at which conformity is expected and valued, these biracial-bicultural teens are often rejected by both majority and minority peer groups because they are neither fish nor fowl, their physical appearance may be "exotic" or unusual, their family background is unorthodox, and they often feel torn between two competing sets of cultural norms and values (Benson, 1981; Garrod, Ward, Robinson, and Kilkenny, 1999; Porterfield, 1982; Williams, Nakashima, Kich, and Daniel, 1996).

Jill, the nineteen-year-old daughter of a black mother and white father, was from a well-do-to Eastern family. After growing up in a white neighborhood and attending an exclusive prep school, she enrolled in a West Coast university for a "change of scenery." Her first year was difficult because she preferred to socialize with the white students from similar backgrounds but felt that the black students were very hostile to her. After an unhappy affair with an older white male who physically abused her, she became very depressed and stopped going to classes. She was brought into the student mental health clinic by her roommate after she took an overdose of sleeping pills, and she was hospitalized for several days. Jill confided to the therapist that she felt as if she had a foot in two worlds but couldn't stand on both feet in the white world or the black. She was very angry with her parents "for treating me like I was white and not preparing me for the real world as a black person."

Jose, the fifteen-year-old son of an Anglo mother and a Mexican American father, was referred by his school counselor who was concerned about his failing grades and his frequent absences. Initially, Jose was very hostile and sarcastic to the therapist, speaking alternately to her in English and Spanish, wearing his baseball cap backwards, and slouching down in his chair with his hands in his baggy pants. Realizing that she was not intimidated by his behavior or appearance, he gradually became less defensive and revealed to her that he had been skipping school to "hang out" with a local Chicano gang. Over the course of several months, he was able to articulate his feelings of anger about being called a "Mars Bar" (brown outside, white inside) by his Latino friends at school because he lived in a predominantly white, middle-class neighborhood and was unfamiliar with the Chicano peer culture. Despite his parents' strong objections, he felt it was important to validate his Mexican identity by joining a gang and becoming a "true Cholo."

Conflicts About Sexuality

Conflicts about sexuality emerge in tandem with the conflicts of racial identity and social marginality. The basic question in this area is, "What is my sexual role?" This conflict finds expression in several ways—in issues of sexual orientation, gender identity, choice of sexual partners, and patterns of sexual activity. Uncertainties about gender identity and sexual orientation sometimes seem to be an extension of a more general identity confusion of biracial and bicultural adolescents. Females may exhibit very masculine mannerisms in speech, dress, and behavior long beyond the normal "tomboy" stage; males may appear effeminate and engage in traditionally feminine activities. Sexual orientation is a conflictual issue with some of these teens, particularly those who failed to make appropriate sex role identifications during the oedipal phase of development, perhaps as a result of negative feeling toward the nonwhite parent of the same sex.

Choice of sexual partners and patterns of sexual activity are also highly charged issues for these teens. Biracial females often perceive that their dating options are limited to black males—a group toward which they are often ambivalent and from which they frequently feel alienated. Although black males feel they have a broader range of options, they are also acutely aware of the risk of rejection from white females.

Patterns of sexual activity also tend to be an all-or-none situation. Sexual promiscuity represents for some biracial-bicultural adolescents a negative identification with their black or Latino heritage, whereas others may choose the path of celibacy and avoid the risks of sexual relations.

> Brenda, a sixteen-year-old eleventh-grader, was the daughter of a white mother and a black father who had divorced when she was ten. She physically resembled her father, with light-brown skin and dark curly hair, but she streaked her hair blond like her mother's. After she entered high school, she became friendly with a group of older teens who liked to party, were using drugs, and were sexually active. When she became pregnant after a casual date, she told her mother that boys expected her to have sex with them because she was black. She was referred for counseling from a family planning clinic.

> Maria, an eighteen-year-old college freshman, was the daughter of a working-class Puerto Rican mother and an Irish Catholic father from New York City. Although she had attended Catholic schools, she had been sexually active since the age of fifteen. After winning a scholarship to an elite college on the West Coast, she soon became homesick and requested an appointment to see the

college counselor. She reported that she felt like "a fish out of water," missed her friends, and thought college was a waste of time. Several of her friends had become pregnant right after high school graduation, so she felt left out of their conversations and experiences. After she returned from the Christmas holidays, she confided to the therapist that she was pregnant and wanted to keep her baby because a "good Puerto Rican girl" would never have an abortion. She withdrew from the college at the beginning of the spring semester, expressing mixed feelings about giving up her scholarship but excitement about the prospects of motherhood.

Conflicts over Autonomy

Biracial-bicultural adolescents may experience an exaggerated version of the normative adolescent separation-individuation conflict over the balance between autonomy and dependency in parent-teen relationships. The basic question in this area is, "Who is in charge of my life?"

Particularly vulnerable to external assaults on their self-esteem, these adolescents are often overprotected by their parents, who try to shelter them from the social realities of prejudice and discrimination. They may respond either by becoming overly dependent on their parents and using home as a haven against the mixed signals of society or by rebelling and establishing their independence prematurely.

Adolescents who prolong dependency on their parents are usually immature physically and socially, as expressed in their tendencies to be more obedient, more conforming, and more passive in their relationships with adults and peers than are those who become independent at an earlier age. Clinically, adolescents in this group appear to be more depressed or emotionally constricted and do not seem to be handling the task of separation very effectively, accepting the parental message that they need protection from a potentially hostile society.

The more rebellious adolescents assume an overt posture of pseudosophistication and maturity, engaging in more assertive, more confrontational, and more risk-oriented behaviors than do those who are not so rebellious. More frequently involved in delinquent behaviors, school problems, and interpersonal conflicts with parents, siblings, and peers, these teenagers challenge society to acknowledge them and to validate them, refusing to accept parental discipline or protection.

Diane, the fourteen-year-old only daughter of a white mother and a Chinese American father, both highly successful professionals, was referred with her parents for family counseling by their minister. Diane's parents reported that she had recently become very rebellious and hostile and was refusing to see most of her friends. Diane interrupted them several times so she could tell her side of the story, angrily accusing them of "treating her like a baby." The incident that precipitated their decision to seek help was a confrontation over the choice of Diane's high school. Her parents wanted Diane to attend a highly competitive public high school with a majority Asian American student body, but she wanted to enroll in a private prep school with a reputation for serving the socially elite in her West Coast community. After the therapist had de-escalated the debate, she encouraged Diane to discuss with her parents her feelings and thoughts about which school would be more appropriate for her. Still agitated, Diane blurted out that she didn't want to attend the public high school "with all those Asian computer geeks" but preferred to spend her high school years with "people like my mother's family," who know what's going on in the world. Although her father had a very pained expression on his face, he quickly responded that Diane had always identified with her mother's side of the family and always seemed slightly ashamed of her Asian roots.

Sam, the seventeen-year-old eldest son of a Vietnamese refugee family, was referred for psychological evaluation after he was arrested for a "home invasion" robbery with three of his friends. Born a few years after his parents had escaped from Vietnam as "boat people," Sam had grown up in America and had strenuously resisted his parents' efforts to rear him with traditional Vietnamese values. After his father died, his mother married a white man; Sam had dropped out of high school at age fifteen, joined a gang, and was estranged from his parents, who were storekeepers. In his evaluation interviews with the psychologist, he assumed a very defiant, streetwise attitude and expressed his intention to be a "big man" in his community. He showed no remorse over his serious offenses but bragged that he had learned to survive on his wits and admired the famous gangsters he had seen in the movies. When asked to describe his relationship with his mother and stepfather, he sarcastically responded that he wasn't one of the "punk Asian guys" who hid behind their mother's skirts and were afraid to stand up to white people. He admitted that his mother was ashamed of him but felt he had to live his own life, with or without her approval. He was clearly ambivalent about his white stepfather, grudgingly acknowledging that he had rescued his family from poverty after Sam's father died.

Conflicts over Educational and Occupational Aspirations

The source of conflicts over aspirations for many of these adolescents is their ambivalence toward achievement and upward mobility. The basic question for them is, "Where am I going?" Some biracial-bicultural teens, fearing rejection by their black, Latino, or Indian peers if they are perceived as "bookworms" or "nerds," lose interest in school achievement or activities (Fordham and Ogbu, 1986; Irvine and Irvine, 1995). Others become involved in truancy and deliberately fail their courses. For those teens who identify with white middle-class culture, academic achievement may be one area in which they excel in order to prove that they are as smart as their white peers. In the clinical setting, the more typical pattern is nonachievement, negative attitudes toward school, and unclear or unrealistic career aspirations.

The aspirations of many of these teens seem to be shaped by their unstated awareness of prejudice and discrimination toward their racial or ethnic minority group. In some cases, they apparently impose self-limiting constraints on their educational achievement and mobility aspirations in response to these perceptions.

David, a seventeen-year-old high school senior, was the son of a German American woman and an African American soldier. He had grown up on army bases in Europe until he moved to the States to complete high school. David had attended base schools where there were children of many nationalities, and he thought of himself as a "military brat." A good student, he particularly enjoyed athletics and tried out for several teams. His teammates were friendly at school but rarely included him when they were out on weekends after games. White girls rejected his overtures to date, and he gradually withdrew and lost interest in school. His parents encouraged him to apply to college, but he said he couldn't make up his mind about what he wanted to study. When his counselor referred him for treatment, he was quite apathetic and refused to talk. After a few sessions, he confided that he had always felt "more white than black" because he spoke German and had very light skin. He said he didn't like living in the States because "you have to choose to be something you would rather not be." He didn't want to go to college at this point because "most black people don't go to college, and anyway nobody expects me to set the world on fire."

Michael, the sixteen-year-old son of a white mother and an Indian father, was reared on the reservation until his parents divorced when he was twelve years old. He moved to a West Coast city with his mother, where he attended a racially mixed high school and lived in a lower-income neighborhood with very few American Indians. He was referred to the clinic for depression, drinking, and suicidal ideations after his mother found him drunk and threatening to kill himself unless they returned to the reservation. At first, the therapist found it difficult to establish rapport with Michael, who was sullen and unresponsive. After several sessions of nonverbal communication and playing board games, Michael gradually opened up and talked about his feelings of cultural alienation from urban middle-class life, his feelings of anger and betrayal over his parents' divorce, and his inability to hook up with any Indian friends. When the therapist confronted Michael about his drinking and experimentation with drugs, he responded very matter-of-factly: "That's what Indians do when they're depressed. That's why I'd rather go back home to the reservation, where people let you drink and die in peace."

In summary, these cases illustrate the types of identity conflicts experienced by biracial adolescents who are referred for psychological treatment. These conflicts may be (1) mild, resulting in some level of identity confusion and maladaptive behaviors, or (2) moderate, resulting in more symptoms of identity diffusion or identity foreclosure, or (3) severe, resulting in a negative identity with more serious behavioral problems.

It is important to emphasize, however, that clinicians should not assume that psychological or behavioral problems presented by biracial or bicultural adolescents are necessarily responses to conflicts over their ethnic identity. In fact, clinicians must be particularly cautious in inferring a causal relationship between biracial ethnicity and psychosocial maladaptation. Adolescents of all races may experience emotional distress because of normative developmental and social experiences, interpersonal relationships, academic problems, family conflicts, and a host of other causes. In assessing biracial-bicultural adolescents, clinicians must rule out all of these usual stressors before concluding that psychological symptoms are the result of ambivalence or rejection of their dual racial-ethnic heritage.

Defense Mechanisms and Coping Strategies

Given the adolescent's task of developing a stable identity, a biracial or bicultural background can create anxiety and confusion. If the adolescent is unable to integrate the racial or ethnic identities of both parents, he or she may feel pressure to assume one identity at the expense of the other, precipitating anxiety or guilt over rejecting one parent and identifying with the other.

The defense mechanisms and coping strategies employed by these adolescents to deal with anxiety may be maladaptive or adaptive, depending on their context and the function they serve in the adolescent's overall psychological adjustment. Many behavioral strategies are aimed at protecting the adolescents' low self-esteem and warding off the anxiety associated with their feelings of identity diffusion. To cope with their conflicts over racial-ethnic identity and social marginality, they employ denial (for example, "I'm not black; I'm mixed"), reaction formation ("I don't like to hang around with the Latino kids at school because they always segregate themselves"), and overidentification with the idealized racial group ("I prefer to go to white parties").

Their fears of social rejection may result in social withdrawal as "loners" or in overconformity to group norms, such as using drugs or joining gangs. They may be especially vulnerable to peer pressure to become involved in delinquency in order to achieve group membership and social acceptance.

To cope with their sexual identity conflicts, they employ two contrasting sets of defense mechanisms and behaviors. On the one hand, some exhibit a pattern of repression (for example, asceticism and lack of any interest in sexual activity) or sublimation (for example, excessive involvement in sports of extracurricular activities); on the other hand, others exhibit a pattern of promiscuity and, in a few instances, experimentation with homosexuality, bisexuality, or prostitution.

To cope with their autonomy-dependency conflicts, these youth may also adopt contrasting defenses and behaviors. Teens who use reversal to deal with their anxieties about separation from their parents behave in a pseudomature manner, insisting on independence from parental supervision and rejecting parental rules and values. This pattern may occur more frequently in single-parent homes and adoptive homes where the teenager is defending against fears of abandonment in a problematic or unstable family situation.

For those teens who employ regression as a defense, excessive dependency emerges, and they appear childish, clinging, and fearful. In families where parents have been extremely overprotective, teens may unconsciously choose to delay their second separation-individuation process.

Biracial and bicultural teens also use rationalization and projection or intellectualization and identification with the aggressor to cope with their conflicts over educational and career goals. Rationalization ("I'm not going to waste my time studying because I probably won't be able to get a good job anyway") and projection ("None of the teachers like me because I'm different") are defenses used more frequently by underachievers. These adolescents are also more likely to be negatively invested in their ethnic identity, to have problematic relationships with their teachers, to blame external causes for their erratic academic record, to have a record of truancy or acting-out behaviors in school, to express low aspirations for college, and to have no clearly articulated career goals.

Intellectualization ("I spend all my time studying and don't have energy to worry about what people think of my race or color") and identification with the aggressor ("White people run the country because they are smarter than Latinos") are sometimes employed as defenses by teens who are consistent overachievers. This group are more likely to be positively invested in their white identity, to feel committed to academic achievement, to be "super-students," to be heavily involved in extracurricular activities, and to express high aspirations for college and future career plans.

In evaluating this spectrum of defense mechanisms and coping strategies, three trends emerge. First, teens who assume a negative identity tend to exhibit more primitive defense mechanisms (for example, denial, acting out), and their coping strategies are more maladaptive and socially dysfunctional (for example, sexual promiscuity, low school achievement). Second, teens who develop a negative identity usually identify with the most devalued and deviant stereotypes about their ethnic minority heritage and then pattern their behaviors to achieve a self-fulfilling prophecy. Third, teens who identify with their white racial heritage tend to maintain an overt facade of adaptation to the majority culture but experience some degree of identity confusion, which exacts a high psychic cost. Thus they are more likely to be sexually and emotionally inhibited, overenmeshed with their families, and perfectionistic in school and community contexts.

Sociocultural Issues in Assessment

In the assessment of biracial and bicultural adolescents, it is important to evaluate four specific areas: (1) age-appropriate developmental behaviors and concerns, in contrast to identity conflicts and problems, (2) parental and family attitudes toward biracial identity, (3) school and community resources, and (4) peer relationships and social networks. As McRoy and Freeman (1986) suggest, the assessment of mixed-race children should have two goals: (1) to isolate the factors that influence the child's racial identity and (2) to identify environmental supports to reinforce a positive racial identity.

Age-Appropriate Behaviors and Concerns

Normal adolescents have a host of concerns that may induce periods of transitory anxiety or depression, minor rebelliousness in the family, and some fluctuations in school performance, peer relationships, and community activities. Such symptoms and mood shifts are not indicative of severe pathology or maladjustment (Oldham, Looney, and Blotcky, 1980).

However, more serious psychological or behavioral problems should not be confused with age-appropriate developmental problems and concerns. These behaviors should be evaluated for evidence of successful identity achievement, in contrast to identity foreclosure, identity diffusion, or negative identity. As described earlier, the latter three outcomes tend to be expressed in exaggerated, deviant, or self-destructive behaviors in the areas of personality functioning, family and peer relationships, school achievement, and antisocial activities.

These adolescents call attention to themselves because they are *oversocialized* (overachieving, constricted, and overconforming) or *undersocialized* (impulsive, antisocial, and alienated). Even if they are superficially adapted, they may be paying a high psychological price for their external conformity. Alternatively, their behaviors may be dysfunctional and maladaptive to the environment in which they are living.

Parental and Family Attitudes

Biracial adolescents often receive conflicting messages about their identity from parents and family members on both sides (Benson, 1981; Lyles, Yancy, Grace, and Carter, 1985; Porterfield, 1982; Xie and Goyette, 1997). This may be particularly true of white parents who cannot accept society's definition of their children as "black" and give them mixed messages about their skin color and non-white physical appearance. Some parents handle their child's biracial identity through denial, whereas others assume a Pollyanna-ish attitude, behaving as if the society were truly "color blind" and minimizing evidence of differential treatment. Assessment of parental racial attitudes is especially important in family treatment so that these attitudes can be confronted and clarified in order to provide clear, consistent, and positive feedback to children about both sides of their racial heritage. It is also essential to determine what steps parents have taken to expose their teens to both racial-ethnic backgrounds.

In this connection, attitudes of relatives and close family friends must also be assessed. Relatives might treat the child in an ambivalent, demeaning, or rejecting manner, or they may express their ambivalence by teasing the child or making racist statements about either parent's racial or ethnic background, physical traits, language fluency, or cultural practices.

School and Community Resources

Several researchers have proposed that biracial-bicultural children and adolescents are happier and better adjusted in schools and neighborhoods where there are other mixed families and minority families with similar socioeconomic backgrounds, primarily because they feel less visible and less isolated socially (Brown and Douglass, 1996; Gibbs and Hines, 1992; McRoy and Freeman, 1986).

In addition to the racial and socioeconomic composition of the school's student body, it is important to evaluate the racial-ethnic balance of the faculty and staff and their experience in teaching from a multicultural perspective, as well as dealing with children of varied racial and cultural backgrounds. Further, the community should be evaluated for its educational, cultural, and social resources that would be helpful to interracial families in supporting their efforts to develop positive identities in their adolescents, such as celebrations of ethnic holidays, special library collections and programs, ethnic arts festivals, and so on.

Peer Relationships and Social Networks

Because relations with peers are a particularly critical area for biracial and bicultural teens, it is important to evaluate not only the size and cohesiveness of their current social networks but the group dynamics to determine whether the adolescent is playing an unhealthy role or being scapegoated in order to be accepted by the group.

The adolescent's self-perception in relation to peer groups in the neighborhood and the school should be assessed. If the current relationships are not satisfactory, alternative group experiences such as youth organizations that promote multicultural goals and focus on building self-esteem and competence should be sought, as well as participation in interracial-intercultural family organizations such as I-Pride and the Association for Multi-Cultural Americans (Brown and Douglass, 1996).

Implications for Intervention and Treatment

The clinician must first develop a working relationship with the teenager, following the general principles of short-term, ego-oriented adolescent treatment (Norman, 1980). In addition, the clinician must be particularly sensitive to the possibility of mistrust and hostility based on racial factors in the therapeutic relationship (Gibbs, 1985; Ridley, 1984). In the case of Marcia, for example, the African American female therapist had to explore Marcia's negative transference

feelings toward her and confront her testing behaviors, simultaneously establishing a therapeutic climate of warmth and nonjudgmental acceptance to elicit Marcia's trust.

Second, the clinician must permit these teenagers to ventilate
feelings about their biracial identity and its meaning in our society
and must be able to provide confirmation and assurance that those
feelings are not irrational or paranoid (Gibbs, 1987; Lyles, Yancy,
Grace, and Carter, 1985; Sebring, 1985). In these sessions, the clinician must demonstrate cognizance of the social realities and must
be aware of his or her own attitudes and feelings about majority-
minority race relations. In the case of Jill, for example, the therapist's knowledge of the particular problems of middle-class African
American students on integrated college campuses was useful in
establishing rapport and encouraging Jill to express her ambivalence and anger toward both her white and black classmates.

Third, the clinician should help these teenagers build up their
self-esteem as unique individuals by identifying and supporting
their positive coping mechanisms, their abilities, and their interests that are independent of their racial heritage (Gibbs, 1987;
Lyles, Yancy, Grace, and Carter, 1985; Sebring, 1985). In this
process, the clinician will have to help these teenagers distinguish
between their own personal interests and abilities and those they
have adopted out of a stereotyped notion of their racial identity.
In David's case, for example, the therapist encouraged him to describe his interests in sports and languages. By reinforcing his basic
feelings of competence and exploring his individual aspirations,
she was able to help him sort out his own interests as distinct from
the negative ethnic stereotypes he had internalized.

Fourth, the clinician must help these adolescents see the link
between their confusion over their racial or ethnic identity with
their confusion in other areas of behavior or developmental tasks
(Gibbs, 1987; Sebring, 1985). It is important to challenge those
with foreclosed or negative identities so as to unlock their potential for growth in a positive direction. They should be encouraged
to discuss alternative scenarios for their current behaviors and to
project reasonable options for their future; they should be confronted with the realistic fact that continued dysfunctional or antisocial activities will result in a self-fulfilling prophecy for their
negative or foreclosed identities. Brenda's self-destructive behav-

iors, for example, though motivated by a need for social acceptance, represented a negative identification based on a stereotype of black female sexuality. The therapist focused on helping Brenda understand this connection and channel her considerable energies into more constructive activities.

Fifth, the clinician should encourage these youth to explore both sides of their racial-ethnic heritage in order to form a positive sense of identification with their ethnic and cultural roots (Lyles, Yancy, Grace, and Carter, 1985; Sebring, 1985). They can be assigned "homework" to read and report on heroes and achievements of both groups for school essays; assisted in drawing a family tree to illustrate the various facets of their heritage; encouraged to put together scrapbooks about their family, friends, and neighbors to illustrate the cultural diversity in their lives; and urged to participate in holiday celebrations and other community activities that recognize the contributions of both of their racial-ethnic groups.

Finally, parents and siblings should be involved in treatment if at all possible, particularly so that one child can avoid being stigmatized as the "family problem" (Gibbs, 1987; Lyles, Yancy, Grace, and Carter, 1985). If the teenager is seriously confused about his racial identity, he has probably received mixed signals from his immediate family. By exploring the parents' attitudes toward race and ethnicity in general and toward the teenager specifically, the therapist can attempt to clarify and modify attitudes so that a more supportive family environment can be developed.

In addition, the clinician can involve the entire family in activities that will promote individual self-esteem and family pride, such as recreational and cultural activities involving ethnic themes, church-based interracial-intercultural activities, and political activities to enhance the status of their ethnic minority group (Brown and Douglass, 1996; Ramirez, 1996).

Other strategies that are effective in working with these teenagers to help them consolidate their identities and improve their self-esteem include role playing, keeping diaries to record feelings and concerns, expressing conflictual feelings in creative writing or other forms of creative endeavor, storytelling about the past, and fantasizing about the future. More traditional psychodynamic techniques can also be supplemented by behavioral techniques such as contracting for short-term behavioral goals, giving homework assignments for specific behavioral change, and using self-monitoring to address negative attitudes and feelings.

Implications for Research, Clinical Training, and Practice

The increasing numbers of biracial and bicultural children and adolescents in the community pose a new set of challenges for mental health professionals. Given the inadequacy of classroom and clinical training in minority mental health in most professional schools, it will be necessary for clinicians to expand their knowledge in this area through continued education, workshops, in-service training, and consultation (Kerwin, Ponterotto, Jackson, and Harris, 1993; Thornton, 1996). It is also important for clinicians to examine their own attitudes toward interracial relationships so that they can confront their own prejudices in working with these youth and their families.

Graduate training programs for mental health professionals need to strengthen their course offerings in the area of minority mental health, integrate this information into their regular curriculum, sponsor colloquia on these topics, and provide clinical opportunities for students to gain experience and skills in working with these clients (Isaacs and Benjamin, 1991; U.S. Department of Health and Human Services, 2001).

Mental health providers must make greater efforts to diversify their professional staffs and to offer them continuing education in cultural awareness and sensitivity. Such efforts will enable these providers to develop the knowledge and skills to deliver culturally competent clinical assessment and treatment services to this population and to other clients from communities of color (Isaacs and Benjamin, 1991; U.S. Department of Health and Human Services, 2001).

Demographic trends suggest that rates of marriages between African Americans and whites will continue to rise as the two groups come into closer contact and as social attitudes continue to become more cosmopolitan (Root, 1996). Intermarriage between whites and other nonwhite ethnic groups will also increase as the proportion of people of color increases in the population because of immigration, high birth rates, and lower mortality rates. Thus the proportion of biracial children in our society will continue to rise, and, as they enter adolescence, they may prove to be particularly vulnerable to the vicissitudes of this developmental stage.

Summary and Conclusion

This chapter offers a conceptual framework for the understanding of the special issues that biracial-bicultural teenagers face, as well as a set of therapeutic goals and techniques for the effective treatment of these clients. As these youth proliferate in the population, many will manage to achieve truly integrated identities; others will experience transitory or chronic identity conflicts. This latter group will pose a growing challenge to mental health professionals in the twenty-first century.

More optimistically, the growth of this biracial and bicultural population, which has already forced the federal government to acknowledge their diversity, is part of the larger demographic shift that will result in parity between whites and people of color in the nation's population by 2050. As the merging of racial and ethnic groups produces children of all skin colors and physical features, their identities will be more ambiguous, and skin color will no longer be linked to race in ways that stigmatize and disempower individuals and groups (Bradshaw, 1992; Korgen, 1998). Moreover, the cognitive and cultural benefits of bilingualism will become more evident and more valued as the global economy will require millions of middle-class Americans to speak other languages in their businesses, professions, and social interactions.

In his book *Postethnic America,* Holinger (1995) predicts that by the middle of the twenty-first century, the nation's population will be so racially and culturally diverse that labels will be irrelevant and American society may finally lose its obsession with race and ethnicity. He concurs with several other scholars that racial identity will eventually become more fluid, pragmatic, and situational, that is, individuals will define themselves with identity labels that vary according to different contexts (family, work, community), different relationships (friends, colleagues, neighbors), and different goals (social, political, cultural). This racially and ethnically mixed population has already demonstrated its resilience and its determination to be acknowledged and treated with respect by the federal government, educational institutions, and employers who have, heretofore, forced them to accept unidimensional ethnic and racial labels. Should Holinger's prediction be realized, it would ultimately create a true multiracial, multicultural society in which racially and ethnically mixed people would be comfortable in their own skins and identity conflicts would be an unfamiliar phenomenon.

References

Adams, P. "Counseling with Interracial Couples and Their Children in the South." In I. R. Stuart and L. E. Abt (eds.), *Interracial Marriage: Expectations and Reality.* New York: Grossman, 1973.

Albert, P. J., and Hoffman, R. (eds.). *We Shall Overcome: Martin Luther King, Jr. and the Black Freedom Struggles.* New York: Pantheon Books, 1990.

Benson, S. *Ambiguous Ethnicity.* London: Cambridge University Press, 1981.

Bowles, D. D. "Bi-Racial Identity: Children Born to African-American and White Couples." *Clinical Social Work Journal,* 1993, *21,* 417–428.

Boyd-Franklin, N. *Black Families in Therapy: A Multisystems Approach.* New York: Guilford Press, 1989.

Bradshaw, C. K. "Beauty and the Beast: On Racial Ambiguity." In M. P. Root (ed.), *Racially Mixed People in America.* Thousand Oaks, Calif.: Sage, 1992.

Branch, T. *Parting the Waters: America in the King Years, 1954–63.* New York: Simon & Schuster, 1988.

Brandell, J. R. "Treatment of the Biracial Child: Theoretical and Clinical Issues." *Journal of Multicultural Counseling and Development,* 1988, *16,* 176–187.

Brown, N. G., and Douglass, R. E. "Making the Invisible Visible: The Growth of Community Network Organizations." In M. P. Root (ed.), *The Multiracial Experience: Racial Borders as the New Frontier* (pp. 323–340). Thousand Oaks, Calif.: Sage, 1996.

Brown, P. M. "Casework Contracts with Black-White Couples." *Social Casework,* 1987, *68,* 24–29.

Brown, P. M. "Biracial Identity and Social Marginality." *Child and Adolescent Social Work,* 1990, *7,* 319–337.

Cauce, A. M., and others. "Between a Rock and a Hard Place: Social Adjustment of Biracial Youth." In M. P. Root (ed.), *Racially Mixed People in America* (pp. 207–222). Thousand Oaks, Calif.: Sage, 1992.

Chambers, B. *Chronicles of Black Protest.* New York: New American Library, 1968.

Chang, T. "The Self-Concept of Children of Ethnically Different Marriages." *California Journal of Educational Research,* 1974, *25,* 245–253.

Chestang, L. "Racial and Personal Identity in the Black Experience." In B. White (ed.), *Color in a White Society*. Silver Spring, Md.: National Association of Social Work, 1984.

Cooney, T. M., and Radina, M. E. "Adjustment Problems in Adolescence: Are Multiracial Children at Risk?" *American Journal of Orthopsychiatry*, 2000, *70*(4), 433–444.

Cose, E. *The Rage of a Privileged Class*. New York: HarperCollins, 1993.

Cretser, G. A., and Leon, J. J. (eds.). *Intermarriage in the United States*. New York: Haworth Press, 1982.

Dalmage, H. M. *Tripping on the Color Line: Black-White Multiracial Families in a Racially Divided World*. New Brunswick, N.J.: Rutgers University Press, 2000.

Daniel, G. R. "Beyond Black and White: The New Multiracial Consciousness." In M. P. Root (ed.), *Racially Mixed People in America* (pp. 333–341). Thousand Oaks, Calif.: Sage, 1992.

Duffy, L. K. "The Interracial Individual: Self-Concept, Parental Interaction, and Ethnic Identity." Unpublished master's thesis, University of Hawaii, 1978.

Erikson, E. H. "Identity and the Life Cycle." *Psychological Issues*, 1959, *1*(1), 1–171.

Erikson, E. H. "Race and the Wider Identity." In E. H. Erikson, *Identity, Youth and Crisis*. New York: W. W. Norton, 1968.

Farley, R., and Allen, W. R. *The Color Line and the Quality of Life in America*. New York: Oxford University Press, 1989.

Faulkner, J., and Kich, G. "Assessment and Engagement Stages in Therapy with the Interracial Family." *Family Therapy Collections*, 1983, *6*, 78–90.

Fernandez, C. A. "Government Classification of Multiracial/Multiethnic People." In M. P. Root, *The Multiracial Experience: Racial Borders as the New Frontier* (pp. 323–340). Thousand Oaks, Calif.: Sage, 1996.

Fordham, S., and Ogbu, J. U. "Black Students' School Success: Coping with the Burden of 'Acting White.'" *Urban Review*, 1986, *18*(3), 176–206.

Franklin, J. H., and Moss, A. A., Jr. *From Slavery to Freedom: A History of Negro Americans*. (6th ed.). New York: Knopf, 1988.

Funderburg, L. *Black, White, Other: Biracial Americans Talk About Race and Identity*. New York: Morrow, 1999.

Garrod, A., Ward, J. V., Robinson, T. L., and Kilkenny, R. (eds.). *Souls Looking Back: Life Stories of Growing Up Black*. New York: Routledge, 1999.

Gay, K. *The Rainbow Effect: Interracial Families*. New York: Franklin Watts, 1987.

Gibbs, J. T. "Black Students/White Universities: Different Expectations." *Personnel and Guidance Journal*, 1973, *51*, 463–469.

Gibbs, J. T. "Treatment Relationships with Black Clients: Interpersonal vs. Instrumental Strategies." In C. Germain (ed.), *Advances in Clinical Social Work Practice.* Silver Spring, Md.: National Association of Social Work, 1985.

Gibbs, J. T. "Identity and Marginality: Issues in the Treatment of Biracial Adolescents." *American Journal of Orthopsychiatry,* 1987, *57*(2), 265–278.

Gibbs, J. T., and Bankhead, T. *Preserving Privilege: California Politics, Propositions, and People of Color.* New York: Praeger, 2001.

Gibbs, J. T., and Hines, A. M. "Negotiating Ethnic Identity: Issues for Black-White Biracial Adolescents." In M. P. Root (ed.), *Racially Mixed People in America* (pp. 223–238). Thousand Oaks, Calif.: Sage, 1992.

Gibbs, J. T., and Moskowitz-Sweet, G. "Clinical and Cultural Issues in the Treatment of Biracial and Bicultural Adolescents." *Families in Society,* 1991, *72*(10), 579–592.

Glazer, N., and Moynihan, D. P. *Beyond the Melting Pot.* Cambridge, Mass.: MIT Press, 1970.

Gordon, A. *Intermarriage.* Boston: Beacon Press, 1964.

Grier, W., and Cobbs, P. *Black Rage.* New York: Basic Books, 1968.

Hacker, A. *Two Nations: Black and White, Separate, Hostile, Unequal.* New York: Scribner, 1992.

Haizlip, S. T. *The Sweeter the Juice: A Family Memoir in Black and White.* New York: Simon & Schuster, 1994.

Hauser, S. "Black and White Identity Development: Aspects and Perspectives." *Journal of Youth and Adolescence,* 1972, *1,* 113–130.

Henriques, F. *Children of Conflict: A Study of Interracial Sex and Marriage.* New York: Dutton, 1974.

Herring, R. D. "Biracial Children: An Increasing Concern for Elementary and Middle-School Counselors." *Elementary School Guidance and Counseling,* 1992, *27,* 123–130.

Holinger, D. A. *Postethnic America: Beyond Multiculturalism.* New York: Basic Books, 1995.

Holmes, S. A. "Study Finds Rising Number of Black-White Marriages." *New York Times* (National Edition), July 4, 1996, p. A16.

Irvine, J. J., and Irvine, R. W. "Black Youth in School: Individual Achievement and Institutional/Cultural Perspectives." In R. L. Taylor (ed.), *African-American Youth: Their Social and Economic Status in the United States.* New York: Praeger, 1995.

Isaacs, M. R., and Benjamin, M. P. *Towards a Culturally Competent System of Care,* Vol. 2. Washington, D.C.: Georgetown University Child Development Center, 1991.

Jacobs, J. H. "Identity Development in Biracial Children." In M. P. Root (ed.), *Racially Mixed People in America* (pp. 223–238). Thousand Oaks, Calif.: Sage, 1992.

Jaynes, G. D., and Williams, R. M., Jr. (eds.). *A Common Destiny: Blacks and American Society.* Washington, D.C.: National Academy Press, 1989.

Jenkins, A. *The Psychology of the Afro-American.* New York: Pergamon Press, 1982.

Johnson, R. C., and Nagoshi, C. J. "The Adjustment of Offspring Within Group and Interracial/Intercultural Marriages: A Comparison of Personality Factor Scores." *Journal of Marriage and the Family,* 1986, *48,* 279–284.

Kerwin, C., Ponterotto, J. G., Jackson, B. L., and Harris, A. "Racial Identity in Biracial Children: A Qualitative Investigation." *Journal of Counseling Psychology,* 1993, *40,* 221–231.

Kich, G. K. "The Developmental Process of Asserting a Biracial, Bicultural Identity." In M. P. Root (ed.), *Racially Mixed People in America* (pp. 223–238). Thousand Oaks, Calif.: Sage, 1992.

Korgen, K. O. *From Black to Biracial: Transforming Racial Identity Among Americans.* New York: Praeger, 1998.

Ladner, J. A. *Mixed Families.* New York: Anchor Press, 1977.

Ladner, J. A. "Providing a Healthy Environment for Interracial Children." *Interracial Books for Children Bulletin,* 1984, *15,* 7–8.

Logan, S. L. "Race, Identity and Black Children: A Developmental Perspective." *Social Casework,* 1981, *62,* 47–56.

Lyles, M., Yancy, A., Grace, B., and Carter, J. "Racial Identity and Self-Esteem: Problems Peculiar to Bi-Racial Children." *Journal of the American Academy of Child Psychiatry,* 1985, *24,* 150–153.

Mathews, L. "More Than Identity Rides on a New Racial Category." *New York Times* (National Edition), July 6, 1996, p. A1.

McBride, J. *The Color of Water: A Black Man's Tribute to His White Mother.* New York: Riverhead Books, 1996.

McGoldrick, M. "Ethnicity and Family Therapy: An Overview." In M. McGoldrick, J. K. Pearce, and J. Giordano (eds.), *Ethnicity and Family Therapy.* New York: Guilford Press, 1982.

McRoy, R. G., and Freeman, E. "Racial Identity Issues Among Mixed-Race Children." *Social Work in Education,* 1986, *8,* 164–174.

McRoy, R. G., Zurcher, L. A., Lauderdale, M. L., and Anderson, R. E. "The Identity of Transracial Adoptees." *Social Casework,* 1984, *65,* 34–39.

Njeri, I. "A Sense of Identity." *Los Angeles Times,* June 5, 1988, p. C-1.

Norman, J. S. "Short-Term Treatment with the Adolescent Client." *Social Casework,* 1980, *61,* 74–82.

Oldham, D. G., Looney, J. G., and Blotcky, M. "Clinical Assessment of Symptoms in Adolescents." *American Journal of Orthopsychiatry*, 1980, *50*, 697–703.

Omi, M., and Winant, H. *Racial Formation in the United States: From the 1960s to the 1980s*. New York: Routledge, 1986.

Payne, R. "Racial Attitude Formation in Children of Mixed Black and White Heritage: Skin Color and Racial Identity." *Dissertation Abstracts International*, 1977, *38*(6-B), 2876.

Perea, J. F. (ed.). *Immigrants Out: The New Nativism and the Anti-immigration Impulse in the United States*. New York: New York University Press, 1997.

Phinney, J. S. "Ethnic Identity in Adolescents and Adults: Review of Research." *Psychological Bulletin*, 1990, *108*(3), 499–514.

Pinderhughes, E. "Afro-American Families and the Victim System." In M. McGoldrick, J. K. Pearce, and J. Giordano (eds.), *Ethnicity and Family Therapy*. New York: Guilford Press, 1982.

Piskacek, V., and Golub, M. "Children of Interracial Marriage." In I. R. Stuart and L. E. Abt (eds.), *Interracial Marriage: Expectations and Reality*. New York: Grossman, 1973.

Pope, B. R. "Black Men in Interracial Relationships: Psychological and Therapeutic Issues." *Journal of Multicultural Counseling and Development*, 1985, *5*, 10–16.

Porterfield, E. *Black and White Mixed Marriages*. Chicago: Nelson-Hall, 1978.

Porterfield, E. "Black Intermarriage in the United States." In G. A. Cretser and J. J. Leon (eds.), *Intermarriage in the United States*. New York: Haworth Press, 1982.

Poston, W. S. "The Biracial Identity Development Model: A Needed Addition." *Journal of Counseling & Development*, 1990, *69*, 152–155.

Poussaint, A. "Study of Interracial Children Presents Positive Picture." *Interracial Books for Children Bulletin*, 1984, *15*(6), 9–10.

Preston, M. B., Cain, B. E., and Bass, S. (eds.). *Racial and Ethnic Politics in California*, Vol. 2. Berkeley, Calif.: Institute of Governmental Studies Press, University of California, Berkeley, 1998.

Ramirez, D. A. "Multiracial Identity in a Color-Conscious World. In M. P. Root (ed.), *The Multiracial Experience: Racial Borders as the New Frontier*. Thousand Oaks, Calif.: Sage, 1996.

Ridley, C. R. "Clinical Treatment of the Nondisclosing Black Client: A Therapeutic Paradox." *Clinical Psychologist*, 1984, *39*, 1234–1244.

Root, M. P. *Racially Mixed People in America*. Thousand Oaks, Calif.: Sage, 1992.

Root, M. P. (ed.). *The Multiracial Experience: Racial Borders as the New Frontier.* Thousand Oaks, Calif.: Sage, 1996.

Sebring, D. "Considerations in Counseling Interracial Children." *Journal of Non-White Concerns in Personnel and Guidance,* 1985, *13,* 3–9.

Seiffge-Krenke, I., and Shulman, S. "Coping Style in Adolescence: A Cross-Cultural Study." *Journal of Cross-Cultural Psychology,* 1990, *21,* 351–377.

Silverman, A. R., and Feigelman, W. "The Adjustment of Black Children Adopted by White Families." *Social Casework,* 1981, *62,* 529–536.

Simon, R. J., and Alstein, H. *Transracial Adoption.* New York: Wiley, 1977.

Sommers, V. "The Impact of Dual Cultural Membership on Identity." *Psychiatry,* 1964, *27,* 332–344.

Spencer, J. M. *The New Colored People: The Mixed-Race Movement in America.* New York: New York University Press, 1997.

Spickard, P. R. "The Illogic of American Racial Categories." In M. P. Root (ed.), *Racially Mixed People in America* (pp. 12–23). Thousand Oaks, Calif.: Sage, 1992.

Stuart, I. R., and Abt, L. E. (eds.). *Interracial Marriage: Expectations and Reality.* New York: Grossman, 1973.

Takaki, R. (ed.). *From Different Shores: Perspectives on Race and Ethnicity in America.* New York: Oxford University Press, 1994.

Taylor, R. "Psychosocial Development Among Black Children and Youth: A Reconsideration." *American Journal of Orthopsychiatry,* 1976, *46,* 4–19.

Teicher, J. "Some Observations on Identity Problems in Children of Negro-White Marriages." *Journal of Nervous and Mental Disease,* 1968, *146,* 249–256.

Thornton, M. C. "Hidden Agendas, Identity Theories, and Multiracial People." In M. P. Root (ed.), *The Multiracial Experience: Racial Borders as the New Frontier* (pp. 101–120). Thousand Oaks, Calif.: Sage, 1996.

Tizard, B., and Phoenix, A. "The Identity of Mixed Parentage Adolescents." *Journal of Child Psychology and Psychiatry and Allied Disciplines,* 1995, *36,* 1399–1410.

U.S. Bureau of the Census. *Statistical Abstract of the United States, 1988.* (108th ed.) Washington, D.C.: U.S. Department of Commerce, 1987.

U.S. Bureau of the Census. *Statistical Abstract of the United States, 1996.* (116th ed.) Washington, D.C.: U.S. Department of Commerce, 1996.

U.S. Bureau of the Census. *Statistical Abstract of the United States, 2001.* (121st ed.) Washington, D.C.: U.S. Department of Commerce, 2001.

U.S. Bureau of the Census. *Statistical Abstract of the United States, 2002.* (122nd ed.) Washington, D.C.: U.S. Department of Commerce, 2002.

U.S. Department of Health and Human Services. *Mental Health: Culture, Race and Ethnicity.* Supplement to *Mental Health: A Report of the Surgeon General.* Rockville, Md.: U.S. Department of Health and Human Services, 2001.

Wehlage, G., and others. *Reducing the Risk: Schools as Communities of Support.* New York: Falmer Press, 1989.

Williams, G. H. *Life on the Color Line: The True Story of a White Boy Who Discovered He Was Black.* New York: Dutton, 1995.

Williams, T. K., Nakashima, C. L., Kich, G. K., and Daniel, G. R. "Being Different Together in the University Classroom: Multiracial Identity as Transgressive Education." In M. P. Root (ed.), *The Multiracial Experience: Racial Borders as the New Frontier* (pp. 359–379). Thousand Oaks, Calif.: Sage, 1996.

Wilson, T. P. "Blood Quantum: Native American Mixed Bloods." In M. P. Root (ed.), *Racially Mixed People in America* (pp. 108–125). Thousand Oaks, Calif.: Sage, 1992.

Xie, Y., and Goyette, K. "The Racial Identification of Biracial Children with One Asian Parent: Evidence from the 1990 Census." *Social Forces,* 1997, *76,* 547–570.

Part Three

Asian American Population Groups

In this section of the book, we focus on three of the over forty Asian American and Pacific Islander ethnic groups who have emigrated to the United States since the first half of the nineteenth century. The Chinese, who were first recruited in the 1840s as unskilled laborers to work in the fledgling California gold mining industry, and the Filipinos, who were recruited as farm workers in the 1920s and 1930s to develop California agribusiness, are called "early-arriving minorities" by Mindel and Habenstein (1981). By contrast, Southeast Asians are one of the most recent Asian groups to seek refuge in America, immigrating in large numbers from Vietnam, Laos, and Cambodia after 1975, when the Communists defeated the United States and its allies in the Vietnam War.

Sociocultural Characteristics

These three groups are representative of the diversity within the Asian American population, yet they also share some common cultural characteristics that have spread through the Asian Pacific region through centuries of exploration, commerce, and conquest. Between 1980 and 2000, the total Asian American population nearly tripled in the United States from 3,563,000 to 10,504,000 (U.S. Bureau of the Census, 2001).

Chinese and Southeast Asian American families have been strongly influenced by the philosophy of Confucianism and the Buddhist religion, although there are strong strains of Protestant

Christianity among the Chinese and Catholicism among the Vietnamese. Cambodians and Laotians practice aspects of Hinduism along with Buddhism, while the hill tribes of the Hmong and the Mien practice animism, with strong beliefs in supernatural forces (see Lee, 1996). Long-term occupation by both the Spanish and the American governments left a legacy of Catholicism and Western influences among Filipinos.

In Chapter Four, Larke Nahme Huang, Yu-Wen Ying, and Girlyn Arganza describe some of the Asian American values that are shared among these three groups, including a strong focus on the family as the most significant influence in their lives, shaping their identities, defining their age and sex roles, and circumscribing the boundaries of their social relationships. Asian children are generally reared to express loyalty, obedience, and obligation to their parents, elders, and extended family, even at the expense of their individual desires, needs, and aspirations. Parents also instill in their children a sense of family tradition and continuity, admonishing them not to bring dishonor or shame on their families and forbears. Males, elders, and older siblings are accorded great respect and deference by the women and younger members of the family.

Traditional childrearing values also emphasize hard work, thrift, achievement in school, conformity to community norms, self-sacrifice, and personal modesty. Although this formula has worked well for early-arriving Asian immigrants, including Japanese Americans, it has sometimes been problematic for the more recent Southeast Asian refugees, who have experienced the traumas of forced migrations, family losses, relocation camps, and brutal trips as "boat people." As Donna Ida and Pahoua Yang point out in Chapter Six, many of these youth have manifested symptoms of posttraumatic stress disorder (PTSD) and have exhibited maladaptive behaviors at home, school, and in the community.

Filipinos, the second-largest group of Asian Americans in this country, have often found it easier to assimilate due to their familiarity with the language and culture of the American mainland. Although their cultural worldview originates from Asian values and traditions, they have also incorporated many Western perspectives. Filipino society stresses smooth interpersonal relations and indirect nonconfrontational communication. In Chapter Five, Pauline Agbayani-Siewert and Annalisa Enrile note that, like the other

Asian groups, Filipinos are closely involved in their families through a pattern of mutual obligations and mutual reciprocity of gifts and favors. Moreover, they share the concerns of the Chinese and Southeast Asians about behaviors that bring shame on their families and violate the norms of the community.

Asian immigrants were the victims of racial prejudice in the early decades of their arrival in the United States, targeted by exclusionary legislation in the late nineteenth and early twentieth centuries, and persistent discriminatory treatment throughout the twentieth century (see Takaki, 1994). They have experienced economic exploitation in the gold mines and farmlands of the West Coast, internment during World War II (Japanese Americans), residential segregation, mob violence, and educational quotas in their journey to become full-fledged Americans. By the beginning of the twenty-first century, they had achieved enormous gains in educational and occupational attainment, family income, and residential integration. With their increasing mobility and visibility, they are also gaining political power and breaking down the final barriers to full participation in American society.

Implications for Assessment and Treatment

The overarching, shared cultural characteristics tend to mask the enormous heterogeneity of the Asian American population, with its range of languages, ethnic subcultures, religious preferences, economic systems, immigration patterns, family structures, socioeconomic issues, and cultural worldviews (see Lee, 1996). However, the unique characteristics of each group, as well as their shared characteristics, should be taken into account in the assessment and treatment of Asian American children and youth.

It is important for the clinician to remember several factors in the treatment of Asian American families and their children. First, it is important to respect age and gender roles in establishing rapport with these families. Second, it is important to recognize that the family is the central unit of the culture, so the therapist must view the child or adolescent in the context of the family and gain the trust of the parents if the treatment is to proceed successfully. Third, generational issues may be at the root of many parent-child conflicts, as bicultural Asian American youth attempt to establish their own identities and norms that challenge the traditional values and worldviews of their parents and community elders.

References

Lee, E. "Asian American Families: An Overview." In M. McGoldrick, J. Giordano, and J. K. Pearce (eds.), *Ethnicity and Family Therapy.* (2nd ed.) New York: Guilford Press, 1996.

Mindel, C. H., and Habenstein, R. W. (eds.). *Ethnic Families in America: Patterns and Variations.* New York: Elsevier, 1981.

Takaki, R. (ed.). *From Different Shores: Perspectives on Race and Ethnicity in America.* Boston: Little, Brown, 1994.

U.S. Bureau of the Census. *Statistical Abstract of the United States, 2001.* (121st ed.) Washington, D.C.: U.S. Department of Commerce, 2001.

Chapter Four

Chinese American Children and Adolescents

Larke Nahme Huang
Yu-Wen Ying
Girlyn F. Arganza

Chinese Americans are the largest Asian group in the United States; more than 20 percent of nearly 12 million people identified themselves as Asians in the year 2000 census. This translates to 2.7 million people who reported being Chinese or a combination of Chinese and other races or Asian groups residing in the United States. Although the year 2000 census data on race are not directly comparable with data from the 1990 census because of different racial designations and options in 2000, these most recent data indicate a significant growth in this population, which was reported as 1,648,696 persons in 1990. With these rapid population changes, mental health needs and concerns rise, and changes occur in the mental health profile of this population.

Although there have been many generations of Chinese in the United States, they are still primarily an immigrant group; just over half remain linguistically isolated, which means that no one in the household over the age of fourteen speaks English very well. The educational and developmental needs of these children are unique and are characterized by the stress of acculturation and intergenerational conflict. The poverty rate for Chinese Americans is 14 percent (U.S. Bureau of the Census, 1990). Rates are higher in urban areas in spite of multiple wage earners in a household.

However, there are collective strengths in this population. Chinese strive to retain the inherent strengths of an extended family unit; they attain among the highest education levels, have relatively high median household income rates, and have established ethnic networks of social and economic support. These various factors enter into the mental health picture for Chinese Americans.

In 1978, the Special Populations Task Force of the President's Commission on Mental Health (1978) concluded that ethnic minorities are underserved or inappropriately served by existing mental health services and that utilization rates are not reliable indicators of need in minority communities. Two decades later, the Surgeon General's report, *Mental Health: Culture, Race and Ethnicity* (U.S. Department of Health and Human Services, 2001) concluded that the mental health field, more so than other areas of health care, is plagued by disparities in the availability of and access to its services and that for culturally, ethnically, and racially diverse populations, effective mental health treatments are even less available. Ethnic minority clients often find mental health services strange, intimidating, stigmatizing, and unhelpful. Chinese Americans, in particular, tend to use mental health services only as a last resort, when family and community resources have been exhausted.

Cultural definitions of mental health problems vary considerably within the Chinese community and most dramatically between Asian and Western cultures. These conceptualizations often direct one's search for resolution, so that if the disorder is thought to result from weak will or organic factors, a teacher, elder, or physician may be sought rather than a psychiatrist, psychologist, or mental health worker. These unconventional help-seeking patterns further obscure the true incidence of psychological concerns in this population and necessitate more culturally appropriate forms of outreach and structuring of services.

The objective of this chapter is to familiarize the reader with the Chinese American population in the United States and to highlight mental health issues and intervention strategies for children and adolescents in this population. This task is "easier said than done," as Chinese Americans are an extremely heterogeneous group—socially, politically, and culturally. Although it is impossible to provide a picture of the typical Chinese American, it is reasonable to try to present a framework for examining the Chinese experience in America. One such framework that allows for multiple levels of analysis is an ecological systems approach (Bronfenbrenner, 1979), which enables one to examine the interaction between individual and environment. So, for example, to understand the experience of Chinese American youth in this country, it is necessary not only to understand childrearing strategies of Chinese and Chinese American parents but to comprehend the impact of restrictive immigration laws in the 1900s, of miscegenation and exclusion laws, which were only repealed in the 1960s, and of racism and discrimination. These larger societal issues have an impact on Chinese American families, the composition of these families, their descendants, and the community as a whole. Similarly, Confucian traditions that are passed from one generation to the next, though becoming increasingly diluted and "Westernized," still impose an Eastern philosophy of order on the family. Although these events and traditions will have varying effects, depending on the degree of acculturation, they represent levels of analysis critical to an understanding of Chinese American youth and their manifestation of psychological problems.

To begin to understand these youth, it is first necessary to obtain an overview of the Chinese in the United States, critical events in their history and patterns of migration, and traditions carried from China and other Asian countries that have influenced family formation in this country.

The Chinese in America

According to the 2000 census, there are 2,700,000 Chinese or mixed-race Chinese residing in the United States, of whom the majority are foreign-born (U.S. Bureau of the Census, 2000). This is a population still in the process of acculturating and establishing a Chinese American culture; the migration process is still a fresh experience, and integration of the "old" with the "new" is ongoing. The rate of immigration has significantly increased since the elimination of quotas on immigrants from Asia in 1965, and it is expected to continue to rise into the next century.

The largest numbers of Chinese Americans are found in California (1,122,187), New York (451,859), Hawaii (170,803), Texas (121,588), New Jersey (110,263), Massachusetts (92,380), and Illinois (86,095) (U.S. Bureau of the Census, 2000). This represents a slightly more dispersed population than reported in the 1990 census that reported Chinese Americans primarily along the West and East coasts around major metropolitan centers.

The median age of Chinese Americans is 32.8 years. Youth make up 23 to 27 percent of the population (this varies according to whether "Chinese-only" or "mixed-race Chinese" is used as the total population number), with adolescents ages ten to seventeen making up 38 percent of this population (U.S. Bureau of the Census, 2000). The youth population is fairly evenly split by gender.

Education is highly valued within this culture, which is demonstrated in the high percentage of school enrollees at all ages. However, there is substantial variation in terms of levels of education, particularly within the immigrant generation. Slightly less than 50 percent of Chinese immigrants had some form of higher education; about 30 percent had less than a high school education, and 15 percent had obtained only a high school diploma. This educational divide is less stark for U.S.-born Chinese Americans; about one in four had a high school diploma or less and 60 percent had either a college degree or some college education (Weinberg, 1997.) Parental expectations, particularly for immigrant Chinese parents, contribute to high educational aspirations and attainment, regardless of social class. However, social class was associated with different educational strategies that Chinese immigrant parents developed to foster their children's education. Middle-class, suburban parents used private schools or well-funded public schools and were actively involved in their children's studies both in and out of school. In contrast, urban Chinese immigrant parents who worked in the ethnic or mainstream economy drew on ethnic networks to compensate for their structural economic and information disadvantages and were less involved in their children's education due to long working hours and lack of formal schooling and English language proficiency. Often, the children of these parents were motivated by their parents' self-sacrifice, their social and economic struggles, and their expectations for a more hopeful future (Louie, 2001).

Socioeconomically, Chinese Americans span a wide range, with some families living at or below the poverty level and others being among the wealthiest in the general population. Except for Southeast Asian refugees, in 1990 the Chinese had the highest number of persons (13.3 percent) living below the poverty level of all Asian groups in the United States (Asian American Health Forum, 1990). Overall Asian American–Pacific Islander (AAPI) household income was 6.7 percent at $5,000 or less; 13.2 percent between $5,000 and $14,999; 27.0 percent between $15,000 and $34,999; 36.7 percent between $35,000 and $74,999; and 15.8 percent at $75,000 or more (U.S. Bureau of the Census, 1999).

Chinese Migration, Culture, and Family

The history of Chinese migration to the United States is a very sporadic, uneven one. Chinese first arrived in this country in 1820 in extremely small numbers. The catalyst for increased migration was the discovery of gold in California in the 1840s, in conjunction with increasingly harsh living conditions in China due to oppressive, feudalistic control by the Manchu dynasty, repeated floods and famine, and ongoing civil wars. These immigrants and those to follow came with the intent of making a fortune in America—the "Gold Mountain"—and then returning to China (Sung, 1967). Most of these immigrants were from areas around Hong Kong, Macao, and Guangdong (Canton) province and were Cantonese-speaking males.

Patterns of Immigration and Growth of Anti-Chinese Sentiment

These earliest immigrants were received with little animosity and much indifference. However, as the United States entered its own economic downturn in the late 1870s and as the numbers of Chinese immigrants increased into the thousands, anti-Chinese sentiment grew. It culminated in the Chinese Exclusion Act of 1882, which was the first legislation to ban a particular race from entering the United States. In 1924, the Oriental Exclusion Act banned all immigration from Asia. During the period from 1890 to 1945, more Chinese left than entered the United States. Those remaining lived under the oppression of the exclusion laws, suffering innumerable humiliations, racial violence, loss of property and livelihood, and sometimes loss of life. In spite of the hostile environs, many Chinese elected to stay in the United States, but in order to do so they needed to change their status from laborers (who were targets of deportation) to merchants or businessmen. Chinatowns became the basis for this economic conversion, drawing on traditional structures such as clans and family associations to organize an urban economic community built on the service industries, such as restaurants, small shops, domestic work, and laundries (Chen, 1981; Lyman, 1976).

The next wave of immigrants reflected the changing social structure in China. When imperial China fell in 1911, a new middle class consisting of businessmen and entrepreneurs emerged. These families, as well as affluent landowners, began to send their children overseas to obtain an American or European education or to establish an overseas branch of the family business. These new immigrants came from a wealthier social class, usually spoke a different dialect than the earlier Chinese from Guangdong, often originated from such cosmopolitan cities as Shanghai, were better educated, and did not settle in Chinatowns. They had little in common with the earlier settlers, and so the two groups initially had minimal interaction. However, like the earlier immigrants, many of these immigrants were sojourners who intended to return to China and, with their modern education, secure prestigious positions in their province. With the Communist takeover of China in 1949, these immigrants were stranded overseas and became unintended permanent residents in the United States.

In 1965, in the midst of the civil rights movement, the Immigration and Nationality Acts Amendments ended legislated discrimination and resulted in yet another wave of immigrants. Some of these post-1965 immigrants were unskilled laborers, but many were from middle-class or affluent families, speaking Mandarin rather than the Cantonese dialects, sometimes fluent in English, and possessing higher-level skills and education. They usually came via Hong Kong or Taiwan and attempted to establish themselves in businesses, industry, and professions for which they had been trained (Chen, 1981). Although many of these immigrants eventually became successful, they often suffered a period of underemployment or downward mobility because their training or degrees were initially less valued than and noncompetitive with comparable degrees in the United States.

Culture and Family Traditions

Although Chinese American families show much diversity and variation, the following discussion will convey some of the historical and cultural antecedents for Chinese American family structure. The nature and structure of the Chinese family derived from Confucian philosophy, which dictated a sense of order and a prescription for role relationships within Chinese society. Guidelines for specific family relationships, patterns of communication, and negotiations with the outside world were delineated with the goal of harmonious existence in society (Lin, 1938).

Family Roles

Confucian ethics placed a strong emphasis on roles within the family and the proper behavior associated with each role. Obligations, responsibilities, and privileges of each role were clearly delineated according to a vertical, hierarchal role structure, with the father as the undisputed head. His authority was unchallenged, and he was the recipient of total respect and loyalty from all family members. In return, he assumed maximum responsibility for the family's social status and economic well-being. The mother was responsible for the emotional nurturance and well-being of the family, her primary role being to serve the father and raise the children. She was accorded respect from her childdren, although her role was less removed and distant than the father's. She would often intercede with the father on behalf of the children. Mothers were generally discouraged from taking on work roles outside the family (Shon and Ja, 1982).

Gender and birth position were also associated with certain duties and privileges. Sons were more highly valued than daughters; family lineage was passed through the male, while females were absorbed into the families of their husbands. The first-born son—the most valued child—received preferential treatment, as well as more familial responsibilities. The prescriptive roles for daughters were less rewarding, as females often did not come into a position of authority or respect until they assumed the role of mother-in-law.

These family roles were predominant in imperial, feudal China. Of course, as China has modernized, these roles have altered radically. Similarly, in acculturated Chinese families in the United States, only derivatives of these rigidly defined roles remain. For example, females are not entirely relegated to subservient roles. Fathers are often the figurative heads of families, especially when dealing with the public, whereas the mother may in fact be the driving force in the family and the decision maker behind the scenes. First sons continue to be highly valued, but the discrepancies between the sexes in duties and privileges, though still there, are not so glaring.

The extended family, rather than the nuclear family, was the primary family unit in China. The process of migration disrupted these family relationships, but many Chinese in America have attempted to reconstruct this kinship network. For some, the extended family is clearly identified as an important source of social and sometimes financial support. However, for some highly Westernized families, the extended family may also be experienced as a burden and a restriction on one's autonomy.

Patterns of Communication

Congruent with a rigid system of role relationships, rules of communication were governed by the attributes of the parties involved. Within families, usually gender and age governed the degree of open expression allowed, the initiator of conversation, the structure of the language used, and the topics to be addressed. Communication was often indirect, and outright confrontation was eschewed. Even today, expression of emotion is generally frowned on; suppression of undesirable thoughts or emotions is highly valued. These rules for communication contrast markedly with American values of expression and the tendency to "speak your mind" or "let it all hang out" (Shon and Ja, 1982).

Obligation, Shame, and "Face"

In contrast to the Western concept of contractual obligation and reciprocity, the unspoken and obligatory reciprocity in interaction is of paramount importance in Chinese culture and continues to be evident among Chinese in America. Obligations are determined by one's role (for example, the obligation of the child to the parent or filial piety) or incurred through acts of kindness or helpfulness. Behavior is often dictated by a sense of obligation or a desire to avoid being in a position of obligation.

Shame and loss of face are similarly guiding principles of behavior and powerful motivating forces for conforming to societal or familial expectations (Shon and Ja, 1982). Even truthfulness and honesty in the abstract are secondary to "saving face" for oneself and others. Bringing shame on one's family is avoided at all costs. The ability to place the group's or family's wishes above individual desires is held as a virtue. Given that interdependence is the foundation of Chinese culture, everything an individual does is viewed as a reflection on the family as a whole.

Mental Health Issues for Chinese American Children and Adolescents

The literature on psychological and behavioral disorders in Chinese American children and adolescents is limited, as Asian Americans, in general, have not been the focus of systematic inquiry concerning mental health issues. Several studies of Chinese American adults examine psychiatric hospitalization rates, patterns of service utilization, and comparison of inpatients and outpatients (Berk and Hirata, 1973; Brown, Stein, Huang, and Harris, 1973; Sue and McKinney, 1975); however, none of these studies looks at the youth population. The Special Populations Task Force of the President's Commission on Mental Health, which submitted an extensive report on the mental health of Asian and Pacific Americans in 1978, neglected to examine the mental health needs of Chinese American youth. And finally, the Surgeon General's report examining the mental health needs and services for ethnic minority populations highlighted the lack of large-scale studies documenting rates of psychological problems and disorders for Asian American youth.

Only recently have studies begun to examine the mental health needs of Asian American children and adolescents, and most of these studies do not disaggregate the data by specific Asian ethnic group. In a longitudinal study of mental health service utilization rates for ethnic minority youth in California between the years 1983 and 1988, Bui and Takeuchi (1992) conclude that Asian American adolescents were underrepresented in mental health facilities and most were referred by the school system. In contrast to African American and Hispanic adolescents who were more frequently diagnosed with conduct disorder, Asian American adolescents were given nonpsychiatric diagnoses such as organic brain syndrome, drug problems, cognitive impairments, or a deferred diagnosis.

In a survey conducted by the Commonwealth Fund, Schoen and others (1997) found that 17 percent of Asian American boys in grades 5 through 12 reported physical abuse, as compared to 8 percent among white boys. Among Asian American females in the same grades, 30 percent reported depressive symptoms, as compared to 22 percent for Caucasian American females, 17 percent for African American females, and 27 percent for Hispanic females.

The County of Los Angeles Department of Mental Health (1985, 1986) reports serving a total of 652 Chinese American clients during the 1984–85 fiscal year, of whom 97 were children under age eighteen. For the following fiscal year, the number rose to 873, and of these 115 were children under eighteen. The diagnoses of these clients ranged from adjustment disorder to psychotic disorders. Unfortunately, the specific diagnostic breakdown for these Chinese American children is not available.

Racial-ethnic variations in public outpatient mental health services were examined using data from San Diego County mental health services programs from 1996 to 1997 (Yeh and others, 2002). This study included 122 AAPI youth aged seventeen or younger who received outpatient mental health services. Of this sample, 10 percent were Chinese. AAPI youth entered services at a lower rate than other ethnic minority groups and were more likely to do so through involuntary means, with referrals from child welfare or juvenile justice systems. This pattern of service entry contrasts with results from an earlier study (Bui and Takeuchi, 1992) and suggests the need for culturally appropriate outreach services to encourage more timely and voluntary entry into services, which may reduce the need for involuntary treatment and increased service effectiveness. In terms of diagnosis, AAPI youth are more likely to be assigned V-codes and less likely than other groups to have a diagnosis of ADHD (attention deficit–hyperactivity disorder).

Data from various urban community mental health service agencies and programs provide another diagnostic picture. At San

Francisco's Galileo High School Adolescent Program, fifty adolescents (twenty-nine males and twenty-one females, aged fourteen to twenty) were seen during the 1987–88 school year (L. Lee, personal communication, July 28, 1988). Of these, fifteen received a diagnosis of adjustment disorder with depressed mood; twelve, adjustment disorder with mixed emotional features; seven, adjustment disorder with mixed disturbance of emotions and conduct. The remaining sixteen met criteria for a variety of other disorders, ranging from anxiety disorder to schizophrenic disorders. The major precipitating factors appeared to be immigration adjustment and change of school.

At the Asian Bicultural Clinic of Gouverneur Hospital in New York City, fourteen adolescents (aged twelve to nineteen) were seen for suicidal gestures or attempts during the period from 1985 to 1988 (Ma, Cohen, and Yeung, 1988). Six were male, eight female; six were U.S.-born and eight were foreign-born (mostly from Hong Kong). Their diagnoses ranged from affective disorder (seven clients), schizoaffective disorder (two), schizophrenic disorder (one), and atypical psychosis (one) to adjustment disorder (two) and life circumstance problem (one). Eight of the adolescents made one suicidal gesture or attempt during this time period, and the other six made two or three. The precipitating events were family conflicts (four), problem relationships with the other sex (three), school adjustment (three), psychotic delusion (three), and conflict with peers (three).

In a study of a nonclinical population, Lorenzo (1995) found that 99 Asian American ninth-grade students, compared to 404 ninth-grade white adolescents, exhibited less delinquent behavior and performed better academically. However, the Asian American students were significantly more isolated, more depressed and anxious, and less involved in after-school activities than their white classmates. Furthermore, they tended to internalize social problems, were less likely to seek help, and had fewer role models and less social support.

The mental health of Asian American parents has been linked to the mental health of their adolescent children. A family process triggered by mothers' and fathers' depressive symptoms sets in motion parenting practices that are predictive of adolescent depressive symptoms among Chinese Americans (Kim and Ge, 2000).

An effective program for emotionally distressed parents may improve their parenting practices and reduce adolescent depressive symptoms. This entails increased parental involvement, monitoring efforts, and reduction of harsh disciplinary practices. Adolescents' perception of improved disciplinary practices is expected to reduce the psychological distress experienced by these Chinese American youth (Kim and Ge, 2000).

In the past, cultural restraints against aggression have contributed to a relatively low rate of juvenile delinquency. In recent years, however, this rate has been rising, with a particularly marked increase in more aggressive offenses such as assault and robbery (Abbott and Abbott, 1973; Sue, Sue, and Sue, 1983). Arrest statistics published by the U.S. Department of Justice (1990, 1992, 1996) indicate a steady increase in arrests for Asian American youth (ages eighteen and under) from 1987 to 1995, whereas arrests of those over eighteen years were stable in the population at large. In New York City from 1993 to 1996, the number of Asian youths arrested for major criminal activities rose from 399 to 549—a 38 percent increase (New York Police Department, 1998). This was a significant change, given that the city's Asian population increased only 23 percent and the overall number of adolescents of all ethnic groups in the city arrested for major felonies actually declined during this period. A similar trend was noted in Seattle and surrounding King County, where increasing concern about the growth in youth violence and gang activity involving AAPI youth led to the formation of an Asian/Pacific Islander Task Force on Youth. The findings of this task force indicated increasing criminal activity, youth violence, and educational problems among AAPI youth (Asian/Pacific Islander Task Force, 1993). In San Francisco, where approximately 12 percent of the population is Chinese American, 5 percent of the 8,000 juvenile offenders each year are identified as Chinese American (Millard, 1987). As Chinese American youth become more acculturated, parental authority begins to erode and constraints against aggression become less effective. Parents are often distracted from family issues as they try to make a living in the new country; frequently both parents work—a change from the previous role structure—so there is less direct supervision in the home.

A recent study involving 101 Asian adolescents, of which over half were Chinese American, found peer group influence to be the strongest predictor of delinquency (Kim and Goto, 2000). Contrary to previous beliefs, these adolescents reported strong parental social support, in contrast to white adolescents engaging in delinquent behavior who reported lack of parental support. However, the peer groups exerted a stronger influence on these Asian American adolescents. This was attributed to the collectivist ties, based in cultural values, that result in Asian youth being more invested in a peer group and having closer ties to their friends than mainstream adolescents.

In recent years, there has been a resurgence of Asian youth gang activities (Dao, 1992). Gangs, defined as any denotable group of youngsters and young adults who are generally perceived as a distinct aggregation by others in their neighborhood, have been increasingly involved in delinquent incidents. In New York City, youth gang activities around Chinatown have been on the rise (Lee and Zhan, 1998). The process of gang formation in the Chinese community is not unlike that in other communities; however, the gangs' involvement in criminal activities, including assault and extortion within the community, intermittently brings them into the public limelight (Fong, 1968; Lee and Zhan, 1998). It is estimated that AAPI youth constitute 5 to 6 percent of U.S. gang membership, with the highest average proportion occurring in Western urban areas where they make up 11 percent of the gang population (Office of Juvenile Justice and Delinquency Prevention, 1999).

The antecedents for this behavior are similar to the socioenvironmental conditions associated with delinquency, in conjunction with a poor self-image resulting from language problems, poor academic performance in school, self-deprecation internalized from the outside dominant community, and provincial rivalries stemming from place of birth. Youth without adequate parental supervision and communication skills are at increased risk for gang involvement. This is often seen among more recent immigrants from China, Hong Kong, and Taiwan who are either brought to the United States by family members or are sent unaccompanied. These youth are often frustrated in their new country, experience language difficulties, are forced to attend classes with younger students, perform poorly in school, are taunted by youths from other ethnic groups, and are often viewed with disdain by U.S.-born or more acculturated members of their own ethnic group (Cartledge and Feng, 1996).

Chin (1990), in a study of Chinese subculture and criminality, found that Chinese gangs initially began in schools where racial tensions were high and then moved beyond the schools and into the community, engaging in more criminal behavior. These youth indulged in self-destructive behaviors, such as violence and substance abuse, to cope with a sense of alienation. For adolescents living in Chinatown, which has all the characteristics of an urban ghetto, the unemployment rate among youth is high, and the impoverished conditions and poor housing are glaring.

In a comprehensive study of Chinese youth gangs, Lee (1994) suggests that youth join gangs because they are out of options. He contends that due to their minority status, limited economic opportunities, and negative experiences with government institutions, Chinese youth perceive that they have no choice but to join gangs in order to survive in this society. Lee documented some of the distinctive features of Chinese youth gangs:

1. They often have older members, ranging in age from fourteen to thirty-four years old.
2. Their discreet nature makes their existence slow to be recognized in communities and by law enforcement.
3. They are often connected to and controlled by criminal organizations abroad.
4. Some Chinese youth gangs originate in China and spread to the United States through the immigration process.
5. The local, national, and international gang circuits are enmeshed such that a larger organization will rotate its members among different cities in order to confuse law enforcement and local communities.
6. The gang organizational structure is similar to traditional Chinese family structure in its hierarchical rigidity.
7. Recruitment into gangs is coercive or linked to friendships.

These data provide a rough picture of the range of psychological difficulties experienced by Chinese American children and adolescents. However, the relatively small numbers of Chinese American youth in these studies give an incomplete picture. Our limited information on the psychological problems of Chinese American youth makes it necessary to extrapolate from other areas of the literature that may bear on the experiences of these children and their mental health. Three such areas are (1) studies of migration and relocation of youth, (2) self-concept studies, and (3) empirical personality studies.

Touliatos and Lindholm (1980) compared the incidence of psychological disturbance in American-born Caucasian children and in children of foreign-born parents. Within the sample of ninety-seven children of foreign-born parents, forty-two were of Chinese, Japanese, or Southeast Asian descent. Some of these children were American-born, some foreign-born. The types of disorders examined were conduct problems, personality problems, inadequacy-immaturity problems, socialized delinquency, and psychotic symptomatology. In all five areas, the children of foreign-born parents showed less psychopathology than the native-born Caucasian children. Further analysis revealed that children of Chinese, Japanese, or Southeast Asian descent exhibited significantly fewer disorders in the conduct problems and inadequacy-immaturity areas than native-born Caucasian children.

The results of this study are consistent with Aronowitz's review (1984), which concluded that immigrant children do not necessarily show a higher incidence of disorder than their native peers. None of the studies that Aronowitz reviewed focused specifically on Chinese children; however, his conclusions about immigrant children in general may be pertinent. Acknowledging that the incidence of disorder is not greater for immigrant children, he nevertheless documented that when disorders do occur, there is a certain predictability about them. These children tend to present with anxiety and depression and conduct disorders rather than acute psychiatric symptoms. An extensive survey of West Indian children in London revealed that conduct disorders among the immigrant children were manifest almost entirely at school and not at home (Rutter, 1974). The authors suggest that this may be due to possible learning difficulties at school, racial discrimination, and high pupil turnover in the predominantly immigrant schools.

The developmental literature indicates that relocations may be stressful for children (Garmezy and Rutter, 1983). The subjective experience and manner of coping are, of course, related to the developmental stage of the child. For the latency-age child or adolescent, relocations or migrations are experienced directly and may represent a significant loss and, at least, temporary instability and uncertainty. Anxiety and depression may initially outweigh the excitement associated with the move. For the infant and toddler, the relocation is more often experienced through the parents. As long as the parents remain constant figures in the child's life, the impact of a move may be less dramatic. However, the anxiety experienced by the parents may be inadvertently transmitted to the young child. Rutter (1983) indicates that children may be affected by their parents' attitude and psychological state, as well as by an actual event. Thus a relocation may still have a dramatic impact on the very young child, though indirectly experienced.

Children and adolescents may assume passive roles in the early stages of migration and then become quite active and mobilized in the later stages. They generally have little say in the decision-making process and the actual arrangements for migrating; however, once in the new country, they tend to acculturate more rapidly and then assume a more active role in the family. These children become "parentified," assuming roles that previously had been those of their parents. Because of their rapid ease with the new language, they become the negotiators of the outside world for their parents. They do the shopping, pay the bills, and answer the telephone; they are their parents' interpreters. For some children, this new role may be novel and exciting. However, when prolonged, it can become burdensome and tedious and a threat to the traditional configuration of roles within the family.

Ou and McAdoo (1980) examined the self-concept, ethnic preference, and cognitive development of American-born latency-age children of Chinese immigrant parents. The children in this study generally had high self-concept, low anxiety, and high cognitive functioning. A child's mental health was related to the parents' attitude toward their heritage. For the older (fifth- and sixth-grade) boys, the more Chinese spoken between parent and child the higher the boys' anxiety. In addition, the more positive the parents' attitudes were toward Chinese culture, the lower the older boys' self-concept. The researchers concluded that speaking English in the home lowered the boys' anxiety because it lessened the bicultural and bilingual pressure. The findings on self-concept may reflect the uncertainty and difficulty for the latency-age bicultural child in establishing a sound self-concept. Even though the parents may demonstrate a strong attachment to the Chinese culture, the older boys in this sample may be more acculturated to mainstream American society, resulting in some confusion over self-concept.

In a similar vein, Hisama (1980) speculated about the relation between immigrant acculturation patterns and psychological disorders manifested by children. In traditional Asian families, children may be expected to give unquestioning obedience to their parents and strive at any cost for the academic excellence expected of them. Their parents remain unacculturated, creating a substantial gap between the home and school environments. Hisama indicates that the children of these families tend to internalize their distress, thus manifesting more anxiety reactions, psychosomatic disorders, and school phobia. In contrast to these families, the marginal family is characterized by uncertainty in identification with the new and old cultures. Unquestioning obedience to parents is not present in these families. Role relationships within the family have become confused and disorganized. In these families, the children may tend to externalize their anxiety and manifest behavioral disorders.

For adolescent immigrants, problems seem to center on self-concept, identity conflicts, and generational conflicts with parents. Although these are typical issues confronting adolescents, migration seems to exacerbate these normal developmental conflicts (Aronowitz, 1984). Studies of minority immigrants reveal self-depreciation and low self-worth among these adolescents (Nann, 1982; Osborne, 1971), many of whom feel driven to make the difficult choice between the values and identities of their old and new cultures. These conflicts and role stresses may result in deviant behavior and, occasionally, serious psychopathology (Naditch and Morrissey, 1976).

First-born males in Chinese American families are under extreme pressure and may be especially vulnerable to psychological disorders (Hisama, 1980). This point is reiterated by Lee (1982), who states that the positions of oldest son and youngest daughter are associated with the highest rates of psychopathology in Chinese American culture. Oldest sons are expected to provide emotional support to the mother, assume responsibility for the educational and character development of younger siblings, and bring honor and financial support to the family. The youngest daughter may resent being left with responsibility for the parents when her older siblings leave home, as well as the unequal treatment she receives in comparison with her brothers. As the youngest, she may also be the most acculturated and the most vulnerable to cultural conflicts and disagreements with her parents.

Empirical personality studies of Chinese American college students found them to be more inhibited, conventional, and socially withdrawn than their white American counterparts (Sue and Kirk, 1973). A study using the Minnesota Multiphasic Personality Inventory revealed Chinese American college students in Los Angeles to have problems with dependency, inferiority feelings, ruminations, somatic complaints, and limited social skills (Sue and Sue, 1974). Sue and Frank (1973) report that Chinese American college students suffer from more stress than nonminority American students and tend to feel more isolated, lonely, rejected, and anxious. The results of these studies must be interpreted with caution, as the norms for the assessment instruments used were established with white, middle-class populations.

More recent studies have begun to systematically examine the relationship between acculturation, ethnic identity, and adjustment of Chinese and other Asian immigrants. Acculturation may be necessary for successful adaptation and adjustment; however, for both adults and children, developing a sense of Asian identity may serve as a buffer from negative emotions arising from acculturative stress or racism and discrimination (Lieber, Chin, Nihira, and Mink, 2001). Alvarez and Helms (2001) found that individuals do perceive "racial messages" about the value or lack of value in identifying oneself as Asian American, and these messages may be essential to the development of a positive sense of racial self-esteem. This study suggested that Asian Americans, more so than white Americans, may be influential in shaping the development of other Asian Americans' racial identity. Asian Americans' reflected racial appraisals are significantly related to their collective self-esteem. Thus individuals who believed that Asian Americans had a high regard for other Asian Americans were also more likely to have a high regard for themselves as Asian Americans.

This discussion has focused primarily on immigrant and first-generation youth. Later generations of Chinese American youth will be more acculturated; however, they may retain some ethnic traditions and differences in cultural values. Their manifestations of disorder and attitudes regarding mental health may be more similar to those of mainstream American youth, but ethnic identity issues are frequently involved. Identity conflicts may be the primary presenting problem or may be interwoven with other psychological disorders.

Sociocultural Issues in Assessment

Clinicians working with children and adolescents are generally in agreement that working with the family system and the school system facilitates effective psychological treatment (Pothier, 1976; Reisman, 1973). The following ecological approach to assessment focuses on the individual person system, the family system, and, briefly, the school and societal systems. For each of these interacting subsystems, relevant sociocultural factors are presented, as they are key to an accurate interpretation of the data.

The Individual Person System

The categories of data for an assessment of Chinese American youth may be similar to those used with white American youth, with the addition of two dimensions: (1) level of acculturation and (2) immigration history. However, the actual data may have very different meaning when examined in a sociocultural context.

Level of Acculturation
Level of acculturation is an extremely significant factor, as it will affect the interpretation of data obtained throughout the assessment. A recent immigrant child may be very unfamiliar with American customs and values and may possess a distinctly Chinese worldview. Chinese values, traditions, and behavior may be the standards for this child. For a child who is third-generation and very Westernized, however, ethnic differences may be minimal.

English may be spoken in the home, and values may be American-ized. Excessive attention to cultural explanations will be inappro-priate in this situation. Somewhere in the middle range is the bicultural child who incorporates both Chinese and American val-ues and behaviors. For some children, biculturalism engenders stress and even psychopathology when the values come into con-flict. Others, however, negotiate competently between the two cul-tures, mastering both and skillfully employing situation-appropriate behaviors.

Immigration History

The child's age at the time of immigration and resettlement may influence the degree of acculturation and socialization to Ameri-can society. Usually, younger children adjust more rapidly than older children, who may experience more difficulty in acquiring the new language. Country of origin, SES in that country, process of actual migration, and persons accompanying the child may also influence the ease of the transition and the adjustment of the child. Although many children migrate with intact families, many others are sponsored by relatives in the United States and are joined later by their parents. Some children migrate with older siblings and are separated from parents for a long period. Readjustment to nuclear family life or to parents who are recent immigrants and unaccul-turated may be the source of much disharmony in the newly reunited family. Although this factor may not seem to be as critical for American-born Chinese children, it is important to understand the immigration history of their parents or grandparents. Many Chi-nese parents immigrate to America for the futures of their children. This becomes a powerful dynamic in the family, and the burdens and responsibilities placed on the children to justify the parents' sacrifices play an important role in these children's development.

Physical Appearance

For children, any deviation from the norm may garner undesired attention. Conformity in appearance and behavior is highly valued. For the Chinese American child, who differs in physical appearance and, depending on degree of acculturation, may also differ in dress, behavior, and mannerisms, this may be a point of conflict or sensi-tivity. In addition, the generally smaller physique of Chinese American children makes them vulnerable to the "heightism" so prevalent in American society (Okie, 1988).

Speech and Language

The importance of language as an issue will vary, depending on degree of acculturation. It is important to assess the degree of fluency in English and Chinese, especially if this may be affecting competence in school work. For the American-born child, language may not be as critical an issue, although assessing its role in family dynamics would be important. The combination of monolingual parents with bilingual children may upset the traditional role configurations within the family. In addition, a child's rejection of the culture of origin is often associated with refusal to speak the native language—much to the chagrin and displeasure of the parents or grandparents.

Affect

What is often considered excessively restrained or nonexpressive affect in Chinese Americans may in fact be culturally appropriate. Overt expression of feelings is encouraged in Western culture but not in Chinese culture. On the contrary, suppression of emotion, particularly in public situations, is highly valued. Expression of affect, especially negative affect, is thought to reflect poor upbringing. Again, this is related to degree of acculturation. The highly expressive Chinese American child may be behaving in a culturally appropriate way if he or she is from a very Americanized family or is highly adapted to Western manners.

Interpersonal Relations

The quality of relatedness to other children and adults must be examined for appropriate dependence, affection, closeness, and separation. In contrast to the rugged individualism espoused by American society, interdependence (and often prolonged dependence) within the Chinese family is highly encouraged. Acknowledgment of role relationships and associated "proper" behavior contribute to a sense of formality, especially when adults are involved. For example, Chinese children are expected to address all adults by a formal title such as Uncle, Aunt, Mr., or Mrs.—not by first names.

Attitude Toward Self

This category includes one's feelings about oneself, stability of self-identification, self-esteem, and sense of competence. Studies of minority children conducted before the civil rights movement in the 1960s often found negative self-images (Brody, 1968; Clark and Clark, 1947). More recent studies have generated mixed results. Many Chinese American children have experienced some sort of ethnicity-related insult, internal or external, to their sense of self. This may range from simple yet painful teasing at school to recurrent ethnic-derogatory comments by other significant persons, which become internalized by the child and lead to denial of one's ethnicity.

Anxiety and Patterns of Defense

The degree of anxiety, the way it is manifest, and under what conditions are important factors to assess. With children in general and Chinese American children in particular, the earliest manifestations are often somatic concerns and complaints, sleep and appetite disturbances, and disruptions in school performance. Given the importance placed on academic excellence in the Chinese culture, this last is a frequent presenting problem.

Issues of Sexuality

For adolescents, it is important to assess how sexuality is manifest and what its role in family dynamics is. Sexuality remains a taboo subject in many Chinese American families. A therapist must treat this topic with much discretion and develop a strong alliance with the family before broaching issues of sexuality.

The Family System

In working with Chinese American children or adolescents, it is important for the treatment program to involve the family, as this is the critical unit of social organization in this culture.

Acculturation

In addition to the typical generation gap within families, Chinese American families may experience acculturation gaps. Individual members may adapt to a new environment at quite different rates. In recent-immigrant families and even some second-generation families, parents are much more reluctant to accept the values and behaviors of the American culture than their children, who readily become Americanized in dress and behavior and, subsequently, in values. These different rates of acculturation are often the source of family disharmony and have been shown to be associated with negative mental health consequences for both parents and children (Ying, 1999). Migration is often spurred by the desire to provide one's children a better future; thus, when these children begin to express dissenting views and choices incompatible with parental wishes, immigrant parents feel betrayed (Ying and Chao, 1996). Simultaneously, the children are in conflict between their parents and the larger society, experience identity confusion, and often receive little assistance in negotiating these differences. These intergenerational-intercultural conflicts hold negative consequences for the well-being of both generations.

Stage in Migration History

Sluzki (1979) identifies five discrete stages in the migration process, each of which is associated with different types of family conflict and coping patterns. The first two stages are preparation and the actual act of migration. The third stage—a period of overcompensation—is characterized by a heightened level of activity focused on survival and the satisfaction of primary needs.

The fourth stage is a stormy, crisis-ridden period of decompensation. The family is confronted with the task of reshaping its new reality and maximizing its compatibility with the new environment. Family members may also begin to step back and take a more realistic view of their situation. Disappointment may be acknowledged, and a realization of the losses associated with leaving their homeland may penetrate the defense system that initially spawned the period of overcompensation.

The final stage involves a clash between generations, which is often both intercultural and intergenerational. Offspring raised in the United States often clash dramatically with their parents in terms of values, norms, and behaviors. It is in these latter two stages that families are most prone to have contact with mental health services.

Attitudes About Mental Health

When explaining mental disorders, Chinese rarely draw on psychological causes. Explanations usually involve social, moral, or organic factors (Ishisaka and Takagi, 1982; Tseng and McDermott, 1981). In social explanations, the individual is seen as the victim of some unfortunate and uncontrollable circumstance. Fate may be implicated in this event, as opposed to individual factors. In moral explanations, mental disorder is considered a punishment for a violation of values. For example, a violation of filial piety or bringing shame to the family may trigger mental disorder. Guilt arises from transgressions of interpersonal obligations deriving from cultural traditions. Occasionally, the misconduct of one's ancestors may lead to misfortune in later generations. This is exemplified in the popular belief that "one wrong marriage leads to three generations of disorder." Finally, organic and genetic explanations are probably the most common. Physical disease or an imbalance of yin and yang—two basic life forces—is seen as the source of mental disorder. Somatic explanations are consistent with the Eastern concept of unity of mind and body, which links physical and emotional functioning.

Pattern of Help-Seeking

Consistent with the foregoing explanations for mental disorder, Chinese Americans rarely approach formal psychological helpers except as a last resort. Intrafamilial help from family elders or extended family members is often considered more appropriate because of fears of what might happen to the disordered individual if the problems are revealed to outside authorities and also because of the powerful sense of family shame and obligation.

Family Communication

As discussed earlier, what may appear to be formal and somewhat stilted communication may in fact be culturally determined. Patterns of communication are often indirect, not free-flowing, and roles are not egalitarian. A reluctance to disclose family problems may not be "resistance" but culturally appropriate propriety and attempts to save face.

SES

Chinese Americans span the entire socioeconomic range, and one often finds multiple wage earners within a household. This category of data may be important in assessing resources available to the family and may also shed light on the role arrangements within the family as they relate to occupational status. Particularly for recent immigrant families, traditional wage-earner relationships may be disrupted, generating disharmony within the family.

Support System

It is also critical to assess the degree to which the family is isolated or integrated within its community. Is the family most comfortable with traditional Chinese culture? Does it interact with other families with similar values, or is it isolated among primarily non-Asian families? Or, if it is highly assimilated, does it maintain any ties with the Chinese American community and culture? The support network in which a family is embedded may affect identity development and conflict for its children and adolescents.

The School System

Racial-Ethnic Composition

Is the child or adolescent the only Chinese American student in the class? American-born or foreign-born? Is this of significance to the child? For some children, it is isolating and intimidating; for others who are more acculturated, it is of no consequence. However, the way the child experiences peer relationships and internalizes the views of peers is important to assess, as it may strongly influence the child's attitudes toward him- or herself.

Attitudes of the Teacher

The stereotype of the Chinese American student as bright, conscientious, and quiet is extremely pervasive. Although stereotypes may contain seeds of reality, they are nevertheless harmful and limiting to individual growth. Unfortunately, many teachers may have expectations of Chinese students based on these stereotypes. Recently, with the influx of immigrants, many Chinese students are entering school with limited English skills. Teachers in port-of-entry areas are becoming frustrated and annoyed with the difficulties in, and the lack of support services for, dealing with these students. Some teachers are tired of teaching "foreigners." Others minimize cultural differences and expect these students to mirror white, majority students. They would like assertive, active participants in class, not realizing that this expectation may contrast with the child's home environment, where quiet, obedient behavior is expected. The Chinese American student in this situation must negotiate between the conflicting expectations of the two settings.

Societal Issues

The attitude of American society toward its minority populations fluctuates in relation to a number of factors, politics and economics being primary ones. Growth of civil rights, development of affirmative action policies, encouragement of minority businesses, and endowment of scholarships for minority students may be the priority of one administration, only to be rapidly discarded by the succeeding one. Most recently, Asian groups in the mid-1980s have been the targets of considerable anti-Asian sentiment. At the college level, Asian American students are facing a backlash in response to their increasingly successful penetration of exclusive colleges and universities. This has resulted in unofficial yet discriminatory quotas on admissions (Nakao, 1987), as well as negative attitudes and anti-Asian bias among non-Asian students and college personnel. Other sources of hostility include the growth and proliferation of Asian American small business, the mounting trade deficits with Japan and Taiwan, numerous stories heralding Asian American superachievers in education, and the increasing visibility of Asian Americans moving into previously all-white or all-black communities (Fong, 1987). This growing resentment has resulted in a resurgence of violence toward Asian Americans.

Chinese American children and adolescents, though not always immediate victims of this violence, are often unknowing and unintended victims. This hostility penetrates systems in which these children are direct or indirect participants—schools, families, peer groups, parents' places of employment, neighborhood playgrounds, and communities. Even though there may be no obvious link between this societal attitude and a youngster's psychological disorder, it is important to examine the larger societal issues that may form the backdrop for the child experiencing difficulties.

Intervention and Treatment

In the psychological treatment of Chinese Americans, it is necessary but not sufficient to understand sociocultural factors. The therapist must go beyond cultural awareness to an understanding of how these factors translate into concrete therapeutic behaviors. The following discussion uses clinical cases to illustrate pertinent issues in two phases of the therapeutic process: (1) entering treatment and (2) establishing the working alliance. The cases are taken from the caseload of the first author—a Chinese American female psychologist.

Entering Treatment

For many Chinese Americans, contacting mental health services represents a last ditch effort to resolve the problem. Usually, other sources of help have been exhausted, as the following case example illustrates.

> Rose was an eighteen-year-old adolescent who had immigrated from China with her parents as a young child. She was brought to an inpatient mental health crisis unit by her mother and seventeen-year-old brother, with the assistance of a mental health outreach worker. At intake, she was hostile and belligerent and needed to be restrained. She was disheveled and unkempt, was disoriented, and had delusions of meeting Chairman Mao in Chinatown. She was angry with her parents for "incarcerating" her and claimed she had important appointments to keep.
>
> Rose's mother spoke only Toishanese, so a history was obtained using the brother as translator. The mother noted a gradual deterioration in Rose's behavior following completion of high school about one and one-half years earlier. At that time, she became sullen and withdrawn, lost all friendships, and had difficulty maintaining a job in the family's small restaurant. She began using makeup in a garish fashion, staying out late at night, and verbally abusing her mother. The precipitating incident for admission to the crisis

unit was increasingly bizarre behavior in the home, followed by a physical assault on her mother.

During the first six months of Rose's deterioration, the mother had sought help from an acupuncturist, relatives, the family doctor, and a minister. When nothing seemed to relieve the problem, the family, very ashamed and desperate, began to lock Rose in her room. It was during this eight-month period that she would escape at night and wander the streets. Her brother would find her, usually quite delusional, and bring her home. Rose's mother was tearful as she provided this history; the brother seemed nonexpressive but tense. After completion of the intake procedure and medical exam, it was discovered that Rose was six to seven months pregnant. The mother and brother said they were totally unaware of this.

This case vividly illustrates the difficulty with which some Chinese Americans approach formal mental health services. Rather than seek help from unfamiliar sources, this family had lived with their daughter's deteriorating condition for over a year with limited resources and no formal assistance. It was not until she became unmanageable that they sought help. By that time, the daughter had become so psychotic that inpatient treatment was required. The family's reluctance to seek help reflected their feelings of shame and embarrassment, their lack of familiarity with mental health services, and their defensive pattern of denial, which they also mobilized in regard to Rose's sexuality and pregnancy. For the therapist or mental health worker, it is critical to understand the significance of the family's decision to come to the crisis unit: the profound sense of failure, the loss of face, and the exposure of inner-family problems that may provoke feelings of guilt and uneasiness. Conversely, the family may also be yearning for relief and a close supportive relationship. Appreciating this ambivalence may be crucial to the therapeutic relationship.

This case also highlights the role of interpreter. Although family members may often be used for expedience, there is always a potential conflict of interest. It is therapeutically more advantageous to have an interpreter experienced in psychological issues, owing to the difficulty of translating English expressions or emotional terms into Chinese. It is important to use the same interpreter, if possible, and to reassure the client of confidentiality. In addition, it is often useful to schedule pretherapy sessions with the interpreter to establish a relationship, discuss the translation format, and allow the interpreter to raise questions (Lee, 1982).

Another issue in the entering phase of treatment is the *therapist's credibility* in the eyes of the Chinese American client. In the minority mental health literature, there has been much discussion about the therapist-client match: Should Asian clients see Asian therapists? Should blacks see blacks? Sue and Zane (1987) provide a useful reformulation based on ascribed credibility (the position or role one is assigned on the basis of sex, age, and expertise) and achieved credibility (the therapist's skills involving culturally appropriate interventions and general therapeutic skills). Traditionally, in Asian cultures women have been subordinate to men and youth to elders; hence, a young female would have a low ascribed status in contrast to an elderly male. In the entering phase of treatment, the young, female therapist must rapidly demonstrate effective therapeutic skills in order to attain a higher achieved credibility and maintain the client in therapy.

> Mrs. Wong, an immigrant from Hong Kong, traveled one hour to the university mental health clinic for evaluation and treatment of her child, who was manifesting behavior problems. In opposition to a referral from the school, she bypassed the biculturally staffed neighborhood psychiatric clinic. When she was assigned to a Chinese American therapist at the university clinic, she was very disappointed, refused to see this therapist, and indicated that she wanted to see one of the "real" doctors like Dr. Smith.

> Mrs. Chu brought her six-year-old son to the university mental health clinic at the urging of her family doctor, who speculated that the child was developmentally delayed. She was very relieved to be assigned a Chinese American therapist. She immediately and tearfully described her son's problems, as well as her own personal and family difficulties in adjusting to life in the United States.

In these two cases, the therapist's ascribed status had different implications. For Mrs. Wong, expertise was associated with being white, as is the case in Hong Kong, formerly a British colony, where one may be socialized to believe this and where, in fact, British people were "in power." If the therapist's ascribed status as a Chinese

American interferes with Mrs. Wong's attempts to engage in therapy, this should be acknowledged; perhaps another therapist should be assigned the case. An underlying issue is whether to deal with Mrs. Wong's internalized feelings of self-devaluation and ethnic inferiority or to respond to her overt wishes. In this initial stage, the subjective experience of the client is crucial, and if one is to engage the family in treatment, responding to her expressed wishes will be necessary. An additional issue in this case may be Mrs. Wong's concerns with confidentiality, reflected in her traveling beyond her familiar community to one where no one would recognize her.

In contrast, Mrs. Chu valued the opportunity to meet with a Chinese American therapist. This facilitated her rapid self-disclosure and immediate engagement in therapy. For her, the therapist's ethnicity was associated with a high level of ascribed credibility.

Establishing the Working Alliance

A major problem in the treatment of Chinese Americans is their tendency to drop out after the initial sessions. They often do not see the efficacy of "talking"; neither do they experience any sense of personal relief or connection with the helping services. For these reasons, the working alliance needs to be reconceptualized as an *active exchange* in which the clients immediately feel that there is reciprocal giving and receiving and that each is gaining something tangible as a result of their participation in the interaction. For example, extensive evaluations or lengthy history-taking sessions may often result in parents' removing the child from treatment because they feel they have gained nothing in exchange for their time and information. Some of the components in this active exchange, on the client's part, include being willing to come to therapy, disclosing information and feelings, listening to the therapist, and providing some form of payment for services. The therapist's part in this exchange includes willingness to share information about one's credentials and personal qualifications, providing education about the therapeutic process and the mental health system, giving reassurance, empathizing with the client's pain and frustrations, accepting the client's formulations of the problem, and acknowledging appropriate social and cultural etiquette. This reciprocity, or mutual exchange, enables the client to feel an immediate and direct benefit from the treatment. The following case illustrates this reciprocity:

> Wei Lee, a nineteen-year-old male, was referred to the therapist by an inpatient mental health crisis unit for follow-up treatment on an inpatient basis. Wei's diagnosis was paranoid schizophrenia. Many of his delusions were race-related; his feelings of persecution were based on being Chinese American and being rejected by his surrounding community. After one session with Wei and with Wei's consent, the therapist invited his parents to meet with her. Mr. and Mrs. Lee, immigrants from China, had resided in the United States for over twenty years, and both worked as civil servants for the city government. They were a traditional couple, Mr. Lee being the clearly dominant authority and Mrs. Lee being silent, in the background, and considerably more emotional. Wei was their fourth child and had been born in the United States.
>
> Although Mr. and Mrs. Lee recognized the bizarre behavior of their son, they expressed anger and frustration toward the mental health system. They said that very little information had been shared with them and there was no discussion of his diagnosis or treatment plan; after he was discharged, Wei returned home, again became withdrawn, and stopped his medications. They reported that this was Wei's second hospitalization in two years and the pattern was exactly the same. Their questions remained unasked and unanswered, and Wei had refused to continue treatment.

The therapist discussed the diagnosis and range of possible implications, answered questions about the hospitalization and the mental health system, discussed insurance and disability payments, and employed the parents as "collaborators" in the treatment plan. She acknowledged the boundaries and limits of confidentiality in the individual therapy with Wei, but she also invited any calls or questions from the parents. She listened and empathized with their frustrations with their son and the mental health system and acknowledged Mrs. Lee's concerns about possible relationships between events during her pregnancy and Wei's disorder. This meeting went beyond the designated fifty minutes.

For three and one-half years, the therapy with Wei continued with the support of his parents. The payment of a reduced fee was shared by Wei and his parents. Wei learned to identify environmental and personal factors that triggered his delusions and developed methods to cope with them. He began to be able to distinguish reality-based racism from his own projections. No further meetings were held with his parents, although they initiated telephone contact with the therapist about once a month. Wei made considerable gains, lived independently, worked as a grocery clerk, and visited his family regularly.

In working with children and their families, it is important to establish a working relationship with the parents, as they can make or break the therapy. In this case, the therapist exchanged information, education, and supportive empathy for parental support of the treatment. She acknowledged Mrs. Lee's emotion-filled hypotheses about her son's illness while presenting other possible theories and hypotheses, based on her own expertise, for Mrs. Lee to consider. She clarified the treatment process in a nonpatronizing manner and engaged the parents as partners in the treatment. They felt comfortable in calling whenever they had questions or concerns but did not pry into the specifics of Wei's therapy sessions, accepting the therapist's limits regarding that. In contrast to previous therapists who had attempted to disengage Wei from his family with the implication that they were not "therapeutically" good for him, this therapist tried to specify behaviors that would help or hinder Wei's progress. In conjunction with Wei and his parents, she reached the conclusion that an independent residence with regular visits home for meals would be in Wei's best interest and would satisfy the cultural value of family interdependence.

In the active exchange with Wei, the therapist provided the following: support, empathy, and constancy; acknowledgment of his delusions and methods for gaining control over them; acceptance of his belief that racism was partly responsible for his condition; and an examination of his relevant settings—work, residence, and family—and factors in each that triggered his decompensation. Together they outlined methods for coping with those factors. For Wei's part of the exchange, he disclosed conflicts, difficult emotions, and his previously private and protective delusions, and he complied with the overall treatment plan. The alliance with Wei and his parents was grounded in a mutual exchange and a sense of reciprocity. Each participant dispelled any feeling of obligation by actively "giving" and "providing" in the relationship.

The appropriate pacing of self-disclosure and the management of communication are a delicate process with Chinese American clients. Personal disclosure of problems is antithetical to the cultural value of preserving face and keeping one's troubles contained within the family. In group or family therapy, often used with adolescents, this is particularly problematic, as the Chinese American adolescent, perhaps already feeling guilty for needing special treatment, is asked to reveal problems to a group of strangers, in direct contrast to family norms. Thus the adolescent may feel doubly conflicted. Disclosure of family problems may also have different implications for various family members, as is seen in the next case.

> Mrs. Chow requested therapy for her family because of her fourteen-year-old son's outbursts in the home, his poor school grades, and her concerns that he would become a "delinquent." Their first session was with a Chinese American female therapist. Mrs. Chow and her son did most of the talking. She focused on her son's unmanageable behavior, speaking angrily toward him, and then began blaming the father for his inability to control his son. The son, experiencing severe identity conflicts, also seemed angry and accused his father of being too "Chinese-y." His father remained quiet, contributing little to the interaction. However, the family failed to return for subsequent sessions, never directly canceling the session with the therapist but leaving messages with excuses in response to the therapist's inquiries.

In this case, the therapist had lost control of the session, and the rapidity of disclosure had resulted in a loss of face for the father. The public humiliation by his son and his wife made it too difficult for him to return or to allow his family to return. The therapist failed to manage communication with respect to the cultural hierarchy and did not intercede quickly enough to stem the verbal abuse from son to father. The father, receiving nothing positive in this "exchange," refused to participate. In addition, the therapist's low ascribed credibility as a young female further impeded the development of a therapeutic relationship.

In the cases presented so far, using the concept of active exchange to establish a working alliance has focused primarily on the parents. This concept is also pertinent to the therapeutic relationship with the child or adolescent. In this situation, the active exchange may involve using tangible, specific techniques such as role-playing, global assessment scaling, or play therapy.

> Michael, a seventeen-year-old Chinese American high school senior, born in the United States, was referred to an outpatient adolescent crisis unit by his school counselor for depression and suicidal ideation. Michael was failing in several subjects, was repeatedly absent or late for school, and was sleeping much of the time.
>
> Michael's parents were both successful professionals; his mother had immigrated from Taiwan over twenty years earlier; his father was American-born. They said, "There's nothing wrong with us or with Michael's younger brother and sister, so what's wrong with Michael?" The parents expected their children to be doctors and were frustrated and angered by Michael's academic failure. Michael was the first-born son and received the most pressure from the parents.

The therapist arranged a family meeting and then met several times with the parents, met regularly with Michael in individual sessions, and had regular phone contact with his school counselor. In the session with the parents, the active exchange involved the following: in response to their indirect queries, the therapist shared her academic and professional qualifications, knowing that education and advanced degrees were particularly meaningful to this couple and would raise her ascribed credibility; she underscored the importance of diminishing pressure on Michael and gently introduced more realistic expectations for their son (who was not interested in becoming a doctor and lacked the requisite academic record), guiding them toward recognition of Michael's other areas of strength. The parents reciprocated with support of Michael's therapy and attempts to adjust their expectations for Michael. Empathically, the therapist guided them through the process of grieving, as they relinquished their unrealistic aspirations for Michael.

The individual work with Michael involved psychodynamic therapy supplemented with behavioral techniques. It was important that an active exchange with Michael produce meaningful gains early in the relationship. The therapist validated his interests and empathized with the pressure he endured from his parents. Michael became most animated and excited when talking about enrolling in a course to become a volunteer firefighter but would occasionally become unrealistic and impassively state his goal of becoming a neurosurgeon (his parents' wishes). He ventilated his own frustrations and his envy of his younger brother, who was enrolled in an academically exclusive high school. Michael's dreams and fantasies revealed a very active fantasy life, internalized feelings of failure, and much aggression. The therapist noticed much disorganization in his task orientation and problem-solving style. To deal with his disorganization, the therapist used the Global Attainment Scaling (GAS) to accomplish different objectives. This was done with school attendance, focusing on getting to school on time more frequently, which was necessary in order to graduate. This technique was also used in relation to study habits. Michael was a socially awkward, highly introverted adolescent. Role-playing was used to prepare him for upcoming social situations. In general, the therapy focused on discrete behavioral goals (important indicators of progress for both Michael and his parents), as well as in-depth work on emotional areas.

The active exchange was a critical process in this therapy. Both Michael and his parents needed to experience benefits from therapy as soon as possible. Early on, Michael experienced relief from anxiety, understanding from an adult, validation for his interests, and some success using the GAS. As Michael's attendance improved and the number of hours spent sleeping diminished, his parents also noted these changes and continued support of his therapy. Michael's case also illustrates the destructiveness of the media stereotype of the Asian American "whiz kids" (Brand, 1987). Parents expect this stereotype and place unrealistic and injurious academic pressure on their children. For Michael, this was an added stress, compounding already serious emotional problems.

For many Chinese American children, play therapy may be a useful vehicle for dealing with the problem of self-disclosure and saving face, as the following case illustrates:

> Billy was a nine-year-old fourth-grader, referred for disruptive behavior in school, marked deterioration in academic performance, and difficult behavior at home. He had been born in the United States of parents who had immigrated from China as adolescents. Billy was the shortest boy in his class.
>
> Billy repeatedly brought homework into the playroom. He ignored the toys, concentrated on doing his homework, and engaged in minimal

communication with the therapist. He would occasionally ask the therapist to correct his homework. The therapist began to use the homework as a vehicle for communication. Eventually, Billy admitted that he was coming here as punishment and that he thought the therapist was a teacher or some kind of tutor. After the therapist's role was clarified, Billy began to move toward the toys. Over several sessions, he played with army men who were all repeatedly killed by a single "hero." Probing revealed this hero to be "a big white guy and new in town," while the other men were all different colors and not as smart. Symbolically, the play revealed Billy's poor self-esteem and conflicts around being a new Chinese American boy in a predominantly non-Asian, suburban school. Further play revealed anger toward his parents for removing him from his old neighborhood and friends, most of whom were also Chinese American.

Because Billy could not directly talk about these issues or express anger toward his parents to a stranger, play served as a face-saving modality. Unlike verbal disclosure, symbolic play does not provoke guilt or shame for revealing family difficulties or secrets to an outsider. Some children initially have difficulty using the play materials. Most commonly, Chinese American children view the therapist as a teacher, and bringing in homework is sometimes even encouraged by parents, who may not be familiar with the therapeutic process. A decline in academic performance is often a first indicator of problems and, for some Chinese parents who stress academic excellence, a most important symptom to alleviate. When using play therapy, it is important to educate parents about its efficacy, as they may often view it as frivolous and not educational or healing.

Billy's case also illustrates that cultural identity conflicts may be the core problem or may be entangled with the main presenting problem. His feelings of not fitting in and of feeling inferior and different generated much anger and hostility, which, in turn, interfered with his school work and his relations with his parents.

Summary and Conclusion

Chinese Americans are a very diverse population within the United States. They come from different provinces of China and from Hong Kong, Taiwan, and other Asian countries. They speak different dialects; their descendants are variable in their degree of acculturation to American society, and their manifestations and conceptualizations of psychological disorders are numerous. Among Chinese American youth, psychological problems span the entire range from severe psychotic illness to quasi normative adolescent identity conflicts. However, what is striking is the degree to which ethnic and racial issues are interwoven with the presenting disorder. The psychotic delusions often involve themes of racial persecution; the adolescent identity conflicts involve questions such as, "Am I Chinese or American? Where do I fit? Where do I belong?" Consequently, in treating these youth, it is important to understand the dynamic blending of generic and culture-specific features. To a certain extent, the addition of the Cultural Formulation in the *Diagnostic and Statistical Manual-IV* (American Psychiatric Association, 1994) represents a step toward understanding the impact of cultural variants in assessment, diagnosis, and treatment of presenting disorders.

An ecological perspective is conducive to a fuller understanding of the disorders of these youngsters. The individual psychodynamics are intertwined with the primary cultural and social unit—the family; in turn, the family continually negotiates with outside institutions, whether they are schools, offices, neighborhoods, or family associations. As the case studies illustrate, some families experience frustrating and bewildering contact with mental health agencies. Therapists in these situations need to be guides for the youngster and the family, not only collecting data for an assessment but simultaneously unraveling the intersystem conflicts that contribute to the presenting psychological problems.

This chapter has offered a framework for intervention with Chinese American families, children, and adolescents. Although awareness of the culture is important for good intervention, it is not enough. A dynamic understanding of sociocultural factors in assessment, a knowledge of techniques for establishing therapist credibility, and a working alliance based on a reciprocal active exchange and a partnership with the family are essential for effective treatment.

References

Abbott, K., and Abbott, E. "Juvenile Delinquency in San Francisco's Chinese-American Community: 1961–1966." In S. Sue and N. Wagner (eds.), *Asian-Americans: Psychological Perspectives.* Palo Alto, Calif.: Science and Behavior Books, 1973.

Alvarez, A., and Helms, J. "Racial Identity and Reflected Appraisals as Influences on Asian Americans' Racial Adjustment." *Cultural Diversity and Ethnic Minority Psychology,* 2001, 7(3), 217–231.

American Psychiatric Association. *Diagnostic and Statistical Manual of Mental Disorders.* (4th ed.) Washington, D.C.: American Psychiatric Association, 1994.

Aronowitz, M. "The Social and Emotional Adjustment of Immigrant Children: A Review of the Literature." *International Migration Review,* 1984, *18*(2), 237–257.

Asian American Health Forum. *Asian and Pacific Islander American Population Statistics* (Mongraph Series 1). San Francisco: Asian American Health Forum, 1990.

Asian/Pacific Islander Task Force on Youth. *Executive Summary of a Framework for Meeting the Needs of At-Risk Asian/Pacific Islander Youth.* King County, Wash.: Asian/Pacific Islander Task Force on Youth, 1993.

Berk, B., and Hirata, L. "Mental Illness Among the Chinese: Myth or Reality?" *Journal of Social Issues,* 1973, *29*(2), 149–166.

Brand, D. "The New Whiz Kids." *Time,* Aug. 31, 1987, pp. 42–51.

Brody, E. (ed.). *Minority Group Adolescents in the United States.* New York: Krieger, 1968.

Bronfenbrenner, U. *The Ecology of Human Development: Experiments by Nature and Design.* Cambridge, Mass.: Harvard University Press, 1979.

Brown, T., Stein, K., Huang, K., and Harris, D. "Mental Illness and the Role of Mental Health Facilities in Chinatown." In S. Sue and N. Wagner (eds.), *Asian-Americans: Psychological Perspectives.* Palo Alto, Calif.: Science and Behavior Books, 1973.

Bui, T. K., and Takeuchi, D. "Ethnic Minority Adolescents and the Use of Community Mental Health Care Services." *American Journal of Community Psychology,* 1992, *20*(4), 403–417.

Cartledge, G., and Feng, H. "Asian Americans." In G. Cartledge (ed.), *Cultural Diversity and Social Skills Instruction: Understanding Ethnic and Gender Differences.* Champaign, Ill.: Research Press, 1996.

Chen, J. *The Chinese of America: From the Beginnings to the Present.* New York: Harper & Row, 1981.

Chin, K. "Chinese Subculture and Criminality." New York: Greenwood, 1990.

Clark, K., and Clark, M. "Racial Identification and Preference in Negro Children." In T. Newcomb and E. Hartley (eds.), *Readings in Social Psychology.* New York: Holt, Rinehart & Winston, 1947.

County of Los Angeles Department of Mental Health. *Client and Service*

Summary Statistics for the Period 07/01/84–06/30/85. Los Angeles: County of Los Angeles, Department of Mental Health, 1985.

County of Los Angeles Department of Mental Health. *Client and Service Summary Statistics for the Period 07/01/85–06/30/86.* Los Angeles: County of Los Angeles, Department of Mental Health, 1986.

Dao, J. "Asian Street Gangs Emerging as New Underworld." *New York Times,* Apr. 1, 1992, p. B2.

Fong, S. "Identity Conflicts of Chinese Adolescents in San Francisco." In E. Brody (ed.), *Minority Group Adolescents in the United States.* Baltimore: Williams & Wilkins, 1968.

Fong, T. "Asian Small Business Growth Becomes Lightning Rod for Anti-Asian Sentiment." *East/West News,* July 9, 1987, p. 1.

Garmezy, N., and Rutter, M. (eds.). *Stress, Coping and Development in Children.* New York: McGraw-Hill, 1983.

Hisama, T. "Minority Group Children and Behavior Disorders: The Case of Asian-American Children." *Behavior Disorders,* 1980, *5*(3), 186–196.

Ishisaka, H., and Takagi, C. "Social Work with Asian and Pacific Americans." In J. Green (ed.), *Cultural Awareness in the Human Services.* Englewood Cliffs, N.J.: Prentice Hall, 1982.

Kim, S. Y., and Ge, X. "Parenting Practices and Adolescent Depressive Symptoms in Chinese American Families." *Journal of Family Psychology,* 2000, *14,* 420–435.

Kim, T., and Goto, S. "Peer Delinquency and Parental Social Support as Predictors of Asian American Adolescent Delinquency." *Deviant Behavior: An Interdisciplinary Journal,* 2000, *21,* 331–347.

Lee, E. "A Social Systems Approach to Assessment and Treatment for Chinese-American Families." In M. McGoldrick, J. K. Pearce, and J. Giordano (eds.), *Ethnicity and Family Therapy.* New York: Guilford Press, 1982.

Lee, E. "Chinese Families." In M. McGoldrick, J. K. Pearce, and J. Giordano (eds.), *Ethnicity and Family Therapy.* (2nd ed.) New York: Guilford Press, 1996.

Lee, L., and Zhan, G. "Psychosocial Status of Children and Youths." In L. Lee and N. Zane, (eds.), *Handbook of Asian American Psychology.* Thousand Oaks, Calif.: Sage, 1998.

Lee, P. *Out of Options: The Problems of Chinese Youth Gangs.* Unpublished paper. School of Social Welfare, University of California, Berkeley, 1994.

Lieber, E., Chin, D., Nihira, K., and Mink, I. "Holding On and Letting Go: Identity and Acculturation Among Chinese Immigrants." *Cultural Diversity and Ethnic Minority Psychology,* 2001, *7*(3), 247–261.

Lin, Y. *The Wisdom of Confucius.* New York: Random House, 1938.

Lorenzo, M. K. "Emotional and Behavioral Problems of Asian American Adolescents: A Comparative Study." *Child and Adolescent Social Work Journal,* 1995, *12*(3), 197–212.

Louie, V. "Parents' Aspirations and Investment: The Role of Social Class in the Educational Experience of 1.5- and Second-Generation Chinese Americans." *Harvard Educational Review,* 2001, *71*(3), 438–474.

Lyman, S. "Conflict and the Web of Group Affiliation in San Francisco's Chinatown, 1850–1910." In N. Hundley (ed.), *The Asian American: The Historical Experience.* Santa Barbara, Calif.: Clio Press, 1976.

Ma, S. P., Cohen, N. L., and Yeung, W. "Assessing Suicide Risk Among Chinese-American Adolescents." Paper presented at the annual meeting of the American Orthopsychiatric Association, San Francisco, March 1988.

Millard, M. "Problem of Asian Juvenile Offenders Brings Outcry for Better System in S.F." *East/West News,* July 30, 1987, pp. 1, 8–9.

Naditch, M., and Morrissey, R. "Role Stress, Personality, and Psychopathology in a Group of Immigrant Adolescents." *Journal of Abnormal Psychology,* 1976, *85*(1), 113–116.

Nakao, A. "Thorny Debate over U.C.: Too Many Brainy Asians?" *San Francisco Examiner,* May 3, 1987, pp. A1, A12–13.

Nann, B. "Settlement Programs for Immigrant Women and Families." In R. Nann (ed.), *Uprooting and Surviving.* Dordrecht, Holland: Reidel, 1982.

New York Police Department. Office of Management and Planning. New York: Author, 1998.

Office of Juvenile Justice and Delinquency Prevention, U.S. Department of Justice. *Juvenile Offenders and Victims: 1999 National Report.* H. Snyder and M. Sickmund, National Center for Juvenile Justice (comps.). Washington, D.C.: Office of Juvenile Justice and Delinquency Prevention, 1999.

Okie, S. "Children Reach for New Heights in Study of Growth Hormones." *Washington Post,* Oct. 31, 1988, pp. A1, A4.

Osborne, W. "Adjustment Differences of Selected Foreign Born Pupils." *California Journal of Educational Research,* 1971, *22*, 131–139.

Ou, Y. S., and McAdoo, H. "Ethnic Identity and Self-Esteem in Chinese Children." Unpublished report submitted to NIMH Center for Minority Group Mental Health Programs. Columbia, Md.: Columbia Research Systems, 1980.

Pothier, P. *Mental Health Counseling with Children.* Boston: Little, Brown, 1976.

Reisman, J. *Principles of Psychotherapy with Children.* New York: Wiley, 1973.

Rutter, M. "Children of West Indian Immigrants: Rates of Behavioral

Deviance and of Psychiatric Disorder." *Journal of Child Psychology and Psychiatry,* 1974, *15,* 241–262.

Rutter, M. "Stress, Coping and Development: Some Issues and Some Questions." In N. Garmezy and M. Rutter (eds.), *Stress, Coping and Development in Children.* New York: McGraw-Hill, 1983.

Schoen, C., and others. *The Commonwealth Fund Survey of the Health of Adolescent Girls.* Boston: The Commonwealth Fund, November 1997.

Shon, S., and Ja, D. "Asian Families." In M. McGoldrick, J. K. Pearce, and J. Giordano (eds.), *Ethnicity and Family Therapy.* New York: Guilford Press, 1982.

Sluzki, C. "Migration and Family Conflict." *Family Process,* 1979, *18*(4), 379–390.

Special Populations Task Force. *Report on the Mental Health of Asian/Pacific Americans Submitted to the President's Commission on Mental Health.* Washington, D.C.: U.S. Government Printing Office, 1978.

Sue, D., Sue, D. W., and Sue, D. M. "Psychological Development of Chinese-American Children." In G. J. Powell, J. Yamamoto, A. Romero, and A. Morales (eds.), *The Psychological Development of Minority Group Children.* New York: Brunner/Mazel, 1983.

Sue, D. W., and Frank, A. C. "A Topological Approach to the Psychological Study of Chinese- and Japanese-American College Males." *Journal of Social Issues,* 1973, *29*(2), 129–148.

Sue, D. W., and Kirk, B. "Differential Characteristics of Japanese American and Chinese-American College Students." *Journal of Counseling Psychology,* 1973, *20,* 142–148.

Sue, S., and McKinney, H. "Asian-Americans in the Community Health Care System." *American Journal of Orthopsychiatry,* 1975, *45*(1), 111–118.

Sue, S., and Sue, D. W. "MMPI Comparisons Between Asian-American and Non-Asian Students Utilizing a Student Health Psychiatric Clinic." *Journal of Counseling Psychology,* 1974, *21*(5), 423–427.

Sue, S., and Zane, N. "The Role of Culture and Cultural Techniques in Psychotherapy: A Critique and Reformulation." *American Psychologist,* 1987, *42*(1), 37–45.

Sung, B. *Mountain of Gold.* New York: Macmillan, 1967.

Touliatos, J., and Lindholm, B. "Behavior Disturbance of Children of Native-Born and Immigrant Parents." *Journal of Community Psychology,* 1980, *8*(1), 28–33.

Tseng, W. S., and McDermott, J. *Culture, Mind and Therapy.* New York: Brunner/Mazel, 1981.

U.S. Bureau of the Census. *1980 Census of Population: General Population Characteristics, United States Summary.* Washington, D.C.: U.S. Government Printing Office, 1983a.

U.S. Bureau of the Census. *1980 Census of Population: General Social and Economic Characteristics, United States Summary.* Washington, D.C.: U.S. Government Printing Office, 1983b.

U.S. Bureau of the Census. *Statistical Abstract of the United States: 1990.* (110th ed.) Washington, D.C.: U.S. Department of Commerce.

U.S. Bureau of the Census. *1990 Census of Population: General Population Characteristics, United States Summary.* Washington, D.C.: U.S. Government Printing Office, 1999.

U.S. Bureau of the Census. *Census 2000, Summary File 2.* Washington, D.C.: U.S. Government Printing Office, 2000.

U.S. Department of Health and Human Services. *Mental Health: Culture, Race and Ethnicity.* Supplement to *Mental Health: A Report of the Surgeon General.* Rockville, Md.: U.S. Department of Health and Human Services, 2001.

U.S. Department of Justice. *Sourcebook of Criminal Justice Statistics, 1989.* Washington, D.C.: Hindelang Criminal Justice Research Center, 1990.

U.S. Department of Justice. *Sourcebook of Criminal Justice Statistics, 1991.* Washington, D.C.: Hindelang Criminal Justice Research Center, 1992.

U.S. Department of Justice. *Sourcebook of Criminal Justice Statistics, 1995.* Washington, D.C.: Hindelang Criminal Justice Research Center, 1996.

Weinberg, M. *Asian-American Education: Historical Background and Current Realities.* Hillsdale, N.J.: Erlbaum, 1997.

Yeh, M., and others. "Referral Sources, Diagnoses, and Service Types of Youth in Public Outpatient Mental Health Care: A Focus on Ethnic Minorities." *The Journal of Behavioral Health Services and Research,* 2002, *29*(1), 45–60.

Ying, Y. "Strengthening Intergenerational/Intercultural Ties in Migrant Families: A New Intervention for Parents." *Journal of Community Psychology,* 1999, *27*(1), 89–96.

Ying, Y., and Chao, C. "Intergenerational Relationship in Iu Mien American Families." *Amerasia Journal,* 1996, *22*(3), 47–64.

Filipino American Children and Adolescents

Pauline Agbayani-Siewert
Annalisa Vicente Enrile

Prior literature has established that immigrants are especially vulnerable to stress (Padilla, Wagatsuma, and Lindholm, 1985; Saldana, 1994). In addition to everyday life stressors in a highly technological, urbanized society and the universal life transitions faced by the majority of American citizens, immigrants must adjust to new values, norms, and patterns of interaction that may conflict with their previous socialization. They must also contend with the loss of extended family and interpersonal supports and with structural adjustments such as finding employment and housing. As immigrants to the United States, racial prejudice and discrimination may be experienced for the first time. Those who immigrate as families with young children or children born soon after immigration have the further burden of dealing with an intracultural gap that may result in disorganization and conflict within the family.

The aim of this chapter is to examine the mental health status of Filipino American children and adolescents and to assess the impact of sociocultural, ecological, and family influences on their psychosocial adjustment. We also examine the effect of acculturation and intergenerational conflicts between these youth and their parents—major influences on their development.

The acculturation gap between Filipino youth and their families is influenced by such forces as immigration experiences and historical, political, and economic factors. These forces help to shape and influence the interactions among family members.

The information for this chapter was obtained from focus group data, a thorough review of the sparse literature on Filipino mental health issues, and clinical case studies. The focus group, conducted in the spring of 1996, was made up of sixteen Filipino American professional and paraprofessional social service providers representing the Los Angeles Department of Children and Family Services (DCFS), Los Angeles Probation Department, Filipino youth groups, secondary education counseling programs, community activists, and researchers. Participants ranged in ages from their early twenties to middle sixties; the majority had worked ten or more years with Filipino American youth. Males and females were equally represented.

The focus group addressed three major questions in one three-hour session: (1) Who are the youth that you work with? (2) What do you see as the factors that contribute to their problems and to their conflicts with their parents and in the community? and (3) What is going on with their parents? The prominent themes that emerged from the focus group are discussed throughout the chapter.

Sociodemographic Profile of Filipino Americans

The following section presents a brief summary of the sociodemographic characteristics of the Filipino American population in the United States, a large but not highly visible Asian American community.

Geographical Dispersion and Population Size

In the United States, Asian and Pacific Islanders had the fastest rate of population increase between 1980 and 1990 (O'Hare and Felt, 1991). Demographers estimated in 1997 that six groups made up 84 percent of the Asian American population: Asian Americans grew by 179 percent during this period and reached a population total of 9.9 million. Chinese, Filipino, Vietnamese, Asian Indian, and Korean Americans also experienced high growth rates during this period (Lee, 1998). Filipino Americans more than doubled (156 percent) over the last two decades (Pollard and O'Hare, 1999). Next to the Chinese, Filipinos are the second-largest (1.8 million) Asian American group in the United States, or 19.3 percent of all Asian Americans. Nearly two-thirds of Filipino Americans (64.4 percent) are immigrants (Lott, 1997) who have entered the United States under the family preference category (Carino, Fawcett, Gardner, and Arnold, 1990). The majority (70.5 percent) of Filipino Americans have tended to cluster in the western part of the country, with most residing in California (52 percent) and Hawaii (12 percent) (Agbayani-Siewert and Revilla, 1995). Filipino Americans constitute the largest group of Asian Americans in California today. Outside the West, Filipino Americans are generally dispersed evenly throughout the South (11.3 percent), Northeast (10.2 percent), and Midwest (8.1 percent). Along with the growth of large ethnic communities comes an increased social isolation and segregation from white Americans (Pollard and O'Hare, 1999). For example, the average Asian American student has seen a decrease in the percentage of white students in their schools from 1987 (55 percent) to 1996 (45 percent).

Most Filipino American households include extended family members. The average number of people in Filipino American families is larger (4.0) than in all U.S. families (3.1) and in all other Asian American families (3.8) as well (Lott, 1997). Similar to the Vietnamese, Filipino American households have the highest percentage (13 percent) of relatives other than a spouse and children residing in the household (Lee, 1998).

As a group, Filipino Americans tend to be younger than the general U.S. population. Children under the age of twenty make up 29 percent of the total Filipino American population in Los Angeles County (United Way of Greater Los Angeles, 1994). Most (67 percent) of these children are immigrants and are part of the *1.5 generation*—the term used for children who immigrated prior to the age of ten and were raised in the United States. This generation tends to identify more with being American than with their country of origin (Lee and Cynn, 1991). In comparison to the overall Filipino American population, there are relatively few elderly; most reside with their children and grandchildren (Tacata, 1996).

Education and Income

Filipino Americans as a group are highly educated, with 39 percent completing an undergraduate or graduate degree.[1] The high educational level that characterizes Filipino Americans is primarily due to their educational attainment before coming to the United States. Many highly educated Filipinos immigrated to the United States under the occupational preference category, which favored persons with professional skills (Pollard and O'Hare, 1999). Closer examination of census educational data reveals within-group differences based on place of birth and generation. Foreign-born Filipino Americans tend to be more highly educated than those born in the United States (42.3 percent versus 22.3 percent) (Agbayani-Siewert and Revilla, 1995). American-born Filipinos as a group have not achieved as high a level of educational attainment as their immigrant counterparts (Azores-Gunter, 1986–87).

Basing his work on an analysis of the California and Hawaii 1990 Census Public Use Micro Samples, Mar (1999) found a lower rate of return for education for Filipino Americans than white males. Foreign-born Filipino American males earned less than whites and Japanese Americans, whereas American-born Filipino males did even more poorly, with lower earnings than Chinese, Japanese, and white Americans. Conversely, rates of return on education for immigrant Filipino American women were considerably higher than for white women. This is probably a reflection of post-1965 immigration laws, which gave entry to the United States based on the occupational preference for Filipino women in nursing and other professions. Rates of educational return for American-born Filipino women, however, are lower compared to whites. Again, it appears as if the American-born Filipinos do not fare as well as their foreign-born counterparts.

Although many Filipinos have immigrated with higher educational and professional backgrounds, they tend to be underemployed or employed in the secondary labor market (Cabezas, Shinagawa, and Kawaguchi, 1986–87). Similar to Chinese and Japanese, Filipino Americans have higher median household incomes than African, Hispanic, and white Americans (Ng and Wilson, 1995). Census reports of high household income have led many to believe that Asian Americans have "made it" in this country and no longer need protection or special consideration from policies such as affirmative action. Household income, however, is not a good indicator of success for Filipino Americans. Whereas the median 1990 Filipino household income was $43,780, the median per capita income was $13,616; for whites it was $14,900 (Ng and Wilson, 1995; O'Hare and Felt, 1991).

Access to Health Insurance

Access to health care is a problem for many Asian American families. The prohibitive costs of insurance are clearly a major barrier, with 20 percent of all uninsured people working (Families U.S.A., 2001). During 1999, approximately 20 percent of Filipino Americans were uninsured, compared to 14 percent of whites. In a study assessing Asian American health care needs (Zane, Takeuchi, and Young, 1994), it was found that Filipino Americans considered low-cost insurance to be a high priority (Kagawa-Singer, Katz, Taylor, and Vanderryn, 1996). Social policy also serves as an obstacle to obtaining medical insurance for many Asian American immigrants. The Welfare Reform Act of 1996 placed Medicaid restrictions on immigrants who came to the United States after 1996. Even if eligible for Medicaid and other noncash benefits, many are afraid to apply because they fear it will affect their application for citizenship or result in deportation under the Immigration and Naturalization Services (INS) public charge policy. In California, due to a decrease by ethnic minorities in the utilization of health and mental health services, the Department of Public Social Services (DPSS) has distributed flyers to agencies that serve minorities, informing them that INS guidelines permit immigrants and their children to use certain noncash benefits without affecting their immigration status (Department of Public Social Services, 1999).

History and Patterns of Immigration to the United States

Patterns of Filipino migration to the United States are the product of historical, economic, and political policies. Historically, Filipino culture and society is an admixture of numerous influences, most notably American, Spanish, Chinese, and Malaysian. The history of the Philippines is characterized by almost four hundred years of colonized rule under the Spanish, immediately followed by American occupation in 1899 during the Spanish American War (Agoncillo, 1990). American colonialism has had, and continues to have, a profound effect on Filipinos, including children in the Philippines and the United States (Santos, 1997; Lott, 1980; Rimonte, 1997). Filipinos have been inculcated with the American political and cultural ideals of individualism, self-reliance, and equality. It has been said that Filipinos in the Philippines begin the acculturation process before they immigrate to the United States (Santos, 1997). Immigration to the United States has been driven by American immigration policies and needs, as well as immigrants' expectation of occupational and economic opportunities.

It is difficult to offer generalizations that apply to the Filipino community as a whole. Filipino Americans are a diverse population that is divided into five distinct groups that are differentiated by socioeconomic background, education, dialect, geographical origin, social class, and levels of acculturation. The first group of Filipinos to immigrate in significant numbers initially came to Hawaii between 1915 and 1935. They were recruited by the Hawaiian Sugar Planters' Association to work in the sugar and pineapple plantations and later in the agricultural fields of California as migrant farm laborers. The majority of the immigrants were males with little or no education. Life was hard for the first wave of Filipino immigrants, who experienced gross discrimination, exploitation, and even violence.

The average life expectancy for Filipinos in Hawaii was much lower than for whites (Agbayani-Siewert and Revilla, 1995).[2] As with the Chinese and Japanese who worked the fields and plantations before them, hostile sentiments developed toward Filipinos. Although many were offered free passage back to the Philippines if they promised never to return to the United States, very few took advantage of the offer. The Tydings-McDuffy Act of 1935 cut off Filipino immigration to the United States, allowing the entrance of only fifty individuals per year.

American-born children and grandchildren of the first wave of immigrants make up the second group (Kitano, 1997). Many of the children born to the first wave migrated with their families in search of work or lived in farm laborer camps. As discussed earlier, native-born Filipino Americans have less education and household income than foreign-born Filipinos. This group has been ignored by researchers, and very little is known about them.

During World War II, immigration was further suspended from the Philippines, with the exception of Filipino citizens serving in the U.S. Navy who were given an entrance quota of one hundred per year. These navy men generally served in subordinate positions such as stewards and cooks.

The most familiar and largest group of Filipino Americans in the United States today are the post-1965 immigrants. The 1965 immigration law was intended to attract much-needed professionals to the United States, especially in the medical field (Ng and Wilson, 1995). Approximately half of all immigrants entering the country between 1966 and 1976 were admitted under the occupational preference category, often accompanied by their spouses and children. As the need for imported professionals waned, Congress passed legislation in 1976 requiring that professionals can only enter the country at the request of an employer. Further limiting the immigration of professionals, restrictions required that all foreign medical professionals take and pass an examination before they can be admitted into the United States (Ng and Wilson, 1995). If they fail this examination, they cannot be licensed in this country, so many educated Filipino immigrant families experience a downward shift in their economic lifestyle and social status after they settle in the United States.

The final group includes the children from the navy immigrants and post-1965 immigrants who were born or raised in the United States. In addition to a generation gap, these Filipino American youth also have had to contend with an acculturation gap, despite their familiarity with American culture.

Colonial Mentality

Almost four hundred years of Spanish rule and subsequent American interventions and policies have left a legacy in the form of a Filipino American colonial mentality (Campomanes, 1995; Gochenour, 1990; Takaki, 1989; Pido, 1986). Although the Philippines became independent in 1946, the United States has continued to exercise a powerful cultural influence through the media, trade, and educational system. In a 1996 *Los Angeles Times* telephone survey of over seven hundred Filipino respondents, Filipinos were reported to idolize American culture. An idealized perception of the United States, along with political and economic instability in the Philippines, has resulted in a state of readiness to immigrate. Once in the United States, the colonial mentality continues to influence Filipino life and interactions among family members.

A consequence of the colonial mentality is that many Filipinos tend to view anything that is American as superior to Filipino culture (Agoncillo and Guerrero, 1987; Espiritu, 1996). In Strobel's case study research (1996) on the process and experience of deconstructing the Filipino colonial mentality, respondents disclosed feelings of denial, shame, insecurity, loneliness, and inferiority that come with being a Filipino. Rimonte argues that a legacy of colonialism is a "persistent self-hate" that manifests itself in anti-Filipinoism (Rimonte, 1997, p. 41).

Culture and Family Traditions, Values, and Belief Systems

The historical hiatus on precolonial Philippines presents the misleading notion that the Spaniards and Americans were the only influence on Philippine language, beliefs, democracy, and culture. The indigenous population was also heavily influenced by their Malayan ancestors, and this influence is still evident today. Certain traits, separate from Spanish and American influences, characterize Filipinos and seem to define what it means to be Filipino (Agoncillo, 1990).[3]

Family

A distinctive attribute of Filipinos is their close family ties. Like other traditional Asian groups, Filipinos are a collectivist society in which the needs of others, especially the family, are put before individual needs or any other interests (Almirol, 1982). Familial identity is fused with individual identity and may even supersede it. The sense of family obligation is instilled in Filipinos, and it is not uncommon for parents to sacrifice their own needs to meet the needs of their children. Conversely, children will sacrifice for the family. For example, children in traditional Filipino society often live with their parents until marriage and, as a debt of gratitude, often take in their elderly parents (Chan, 1992). This responsibility is accepted as an inherent duty, but it is important to note that most children welcome this responsibility and even view it as an honor. The sense of family obligation encompasses a variety of responsibilities. In general, members of the family strive to improve the family's financial situation. Refusing to assist family members or even distant relatives is a Filipino cultural taboo (Almirol, 1982).

The Filipino family network also extends to fictive relatives (that is, those who are unrelated biologically or through marriage) through the *compadrazgo* (god parents, coparenthood) system (Agbayani-Siewert and Revilla, 1995). Fictive relatives are incorporated into the family through religious rituals that generally mark a significant developmental phase of the individual's life. In this manner, familial ties are expanded, providing a stronger support network and a sense of interdependence among people in the community (Medina, 1991).

Parenting in the United States and the Philippines

Filipino American children are highly valued and referred to as "gifts from God" (Guthrie and Jacobs, 1966). In a cross-national study by Fawcett and colleagues (1974), happiness was listed as the primary advantage of having children by the majority of Filipinos in the Philippines and in Hawaii.

The traditional Asian American socialization of children fosters dependency and interdependency (Uba, 1994; Sue, Sue, Sue, and Takeuchi, 1995; Yu and Kim, 1983). Filipino children are reported to have a "pampered" and prolonged childhood, absolved of adult responsibilities until early adolescence (Andres and Ilada-Andres, 1987). Filipino children are also less autonomous and more dependent on family than are Anglo American children (Keith and Barrando, 1969). In a cross-national study of Filipino and American mothers, Guthrie (1966) concludes that parent-child relationships are organized differently in the two societies. He found that parental control and influence was of greater importance in the Philippines, whereas American mothers were more concerned with establishing their child's independence. The study also reports that Filipino mothers' irritability was associated with a child's assertive behavior in the Philippines and with dependency in the United States. In a comparative study of Filipino American and Caucasian mothers, Flores (1994) reports differences in mothers' expectations regarding their child's behavior. Filipino American mothers more often expect that children will not keep secrets from them and that their children will turn to them for help in solving problems. These parental behaviors function to foster dependency. Flores' findings also report within-group class differences among Filipino American mothers; middle-class Filipinos more closely mirror Caucasian American parenting behaviors.

Children are generally disciplined for bringing shame to the family or being rude (Santos, 1983). Mothers tend to be the primary source of discipline when children are younger (Santos, 1983; Flores, 1994), but fathers take a more active role as children reach adolescence. Discipline of children is both physical and psychological; the latter type takes the form of embarrassment through teasing, derogatory remarks, and gossip to evoke social control (Cimmarusti, 1996; Santos, 1983; Almirol, 1982).

Literature suggests that physical punishment is a primary form of discipline practiced in the Philippines (Paguio, Skeen, and Robinson, 1987; Uba, 1994; Andres and Illada-Andres, 1987). Hitting with a belt, slapping, pinching, beating, and ear pulling are common methods of physical punishment.

Traditionally, authority within the family comes from age, as reflected in a hierarchical system of age-graded roles within the family. Although age is important, under certain circumstances it may be superseded by those with prestige and power such as teachers, priests, and physicians (Santos, 1983). Respect for elders is a notable Filipino characteristic (Chan, 1992; Cimmarusti, 1996).

Decision making is a family affair in which elders, in particular, are consulted. Parents and grandparents are looked upon with honor, and children are expected to respect and obey their commands. Respect toward elders is manifested in the language through the use of special particles such as *po* and *ho* (analogous to the

American *sir* and *madam*). The hierarchical structure extends to sibling relationships; for example, a female sibling has authority over a younger sister or brother. In most Philippine dialects, the use of special kinship terms clearly delineates special ranks of individuals in the family. For example, in Tagalog the word *Ate* (ah-the) indicates first-oldest sister; *Kuya* (coo-yah) means first-oldest brother. The eldest child is expected to behave as though older than his or her years and to shoulder more responsibilities, such as caring for younger siblings and doing household chores (Cimmarusti, 1996). In the absence of a parent, the oldest child often assumes parental child-care and household responsibilities of the same-sex, missing parent (Tompar-Tiu and Sustento-Seneriches, 1995). Generally, the majority of Filipino American parents work, and some even hold multiple jobs (Agbayani-Siewert and Revilla, 1995). As a result, the oldest child may be even more burdened with expectations of childrearing and household responsibilities, as immigrant parents work and cope with adjustments in a new culture.

Parental Role Strain, Stress, and Coping

Literature on the response of Filipino parents to undesirable behavior includes shaming and teasing, gaining the services of a healer (Almirol, 1982; Guthrie and Jacobs, 1966), and physical discipline (Tompar-Tiu and Sustento-Seneriches, 1995). In a survey of Filipino American immigrants, it was found that parents tend to use several styles of coping in response to parental role strain, such as seeking advice, making positive comparisons, and feeling resigned (Agbayani-Siewert, 1993). Coping responses, such as selective ignoring, that function to devalue children to a level of secondary importance, and punitive discipline (scolding and the taking away of privileges) do not tend to be used often. Most parents seek advice from relatives, friends, and neighbors. About one-third of parents reported seeking advice from professional counselors and physicians. However, the most frequently reported type of advice seeking was through the use of literature and not through interpersonal interaction. Vignettes and short stories found in women's magazines that discussed childhood and adolescent problems and presented potential solutions are considered useful. Although the majority of respondents reported regular church attendance, very few sought advice from religious counselors or clergy. However, most respondents indicated that they often used prayer to cope with parental role strain.

Smooth Interpersonal Relationships

The Filipino culture emphasizes calm and cooperative social relations. The value of smooth interpersonal relationships (SIR) discourages direct confrontation and instead encourages harmonious relations by way of passivity (Cimmarusti, 1996). Four indigenous concepts, referred to in Tagalog (the national language of the Philippines), underlie the notion of SIR: *pakikisama, hiya, amor propio,* and *utang na loob.*

Pakikisama (pah-key-key'-sa-mah) is the act of getting along with others and involves maintaining positive social relations. Often, maintaining good relationships includes refraining from overt disagreement.

A second concept of SIR is *hiya* (hee-yah')—to be shy, embarrassed, or ashamed. The Filipino experience of hiya can also be interpreted to mean "a sense of propriety" (Marcelino, 1990). The Filipino culture indoctrinates the importance of appearance and is wholly concerned with what others may think. Very early on, Filipinos are taught to save face, and *hiya* is a form of social control that discourages unrefined behavior through feelings of shyness, embarrassment, or shame. Because Filipino culture upholds self and family honor, *hiya* is the means by which Filipino people regulate behaviors.

The importance of image is further manifested in the Filipino value of *amor propio*—self-respect or self-esteem. *Amor proprio,* in essence, is pride and serves to protect one's ego and image. For example, in the name of *amor proprio,* a Filipino may refuse assistance because of his or her need to present an impression of being self-sustaining.

Finally, a core aspect of Filipino culture involves *utang ng loob*—"internal debt" (Almirol, 1982). *Utang ng loob* dictates social behavior within the family, as well as outside the family. Gratitude and reciprocity of benevolence are the underlying concepts of *utang ng loob,* which is a culturally understood *obligation. Walang utang na loob* (being ungrateful) or *walang hiya* (without shame) are expressions of bad faith and are viewed as extremely distasteful and dishonorable.

Criticisms of SIR

Several Filipino researchers have challenged the concept of SIR as being Western interpretations of "surface values" of Filipino society. As an alternative theoretical perspective, Enriquez (1993) proposes the model of *Sikolohiyang* Pilipino (Filipino Psychology), which uses the indigenous concepts from Filipino languages. The goal of *Sikolohiyang* Pilipino is to examine psychological principles within Philippine life and cultural experience, as well as to contribute to the goal of evolving a universal psychology (Marcelino, 1990). According to Enriquez, concepts underlying SIR derive their significance from the "core" value of *kapwa* (shared identity), which signifies the unity of the "self" and the "others." The concept of *pakikipagkapwa* represents principles of humanity in the acceptance and the treatment of others as equals, and with respect and dignity. In summary, the elaborate structure of Filipino social relations, cultural values, and personality is deeply rooted in the sense of a collective, shared identity. Maintaining this shared identity is an integral aspect of the Filipino culture.

Worldview

Like other Asian American groups, Filipinos have been described as fatalistic; that is, they believe that fate and destiny play large roles in their lives. However, the idea that certain things happen for a reason does not reflect passive acceptance or resignation but a means of enduring difficult circumstances (Chan, 1992). Conversely, empirical research indicates that Filipino Americans are characterized by both an internal and external orientation (Agbayani-Siewert, 1997). Moreover, findings suggest that social class, gender, and religion are significantly related to locus of control. It has also been reported that many Filipinos are very superstitious and, as a result, attribute health problems to the supernatural (Araneta, 1993).

Position of Women

The available information on Filipino gender role structure is inconsistent. Although some researchers have described Filipino gender role structure as egalitarian (Agbayani-Siewert, 1994; Agbayani-Siewert and Yick, 2000; Agoncillo and Guerrero, 1987), others have described it as patriarchal (Alip, 1968; Rimonte, 1991; Aguilar, 1989). The Filipino sex role structure is different from that of other traditional patriarchal Asian groups and is more closely aligned with Western beliefs. In a study examining attitudes toward women, Filipino Americans were similar to whites and significantly different from Chinese Americans (Agbayani-Siewert, forthcoming).

The traditional practice of tracing kinship bilaterally and not patrilineally, as in most Asian cultures, lends support to the argument that Filipino gender role structure is egalitarian (Almirol, 1982). Moreover, before Spanish and American influences introduced chauvinism, the original Tagalog language did not contain sexist biases and, in fact, reflected equal treatment given to both male and female (Marcelino, 1990). Women have generally enjoyed equal status to men in regards to law and to property ownership. Historical accounts of Filipino women's high status in society seem to stem from the ancient myth that woman and man were simultaneously created and emerged together from a bamboo stalk. But according to Aguilar (1989), historical notions of women's superiority in the Philippines do not accurately depict their subordinate status in the society.

Although extant literature suggests that Filipino Americans are characterized by an egalitarian sex role structure, expectations regarding women's sexual behavior reflect traditional patriarchal beliefs. Sex role expectations of Filipino women at times appear to be distributed between two opposing principles—egalitarian and patriarchal. Filipino women are expected to contribute to the social standing and economic well-being of the household similar to males, while simultaneously portraying traditional feminine traits and roles. It is generally expected that males will engage in extramarital affairs, whereas females are expected to remain monogamous (Gilandas, Gastardo-Conaco, and Servilla, 1982). The idealized version of Filipino women as sexually chaste and yet equal to males did not exist prior to Spanish colonialism. Both men and women were free to engage in premarital sex, and trial marriages were encouraged. The expectation of traditional feminine behavior probably stems from vestiges of Catholicism and patriarchal Spanish culture. Consequently, the seemingly inconsistent and paradoxical expectations regarding Filipino women may be a blend of Spanish colonialism and indigenous Filipino culture (Agbayani-Siewert, 2002).

Attitudes Toward Education and Achievement

During 1987, the University of California, Los Angeles (UCLA) Office of Budget, Institutional Planning, and Analysis showed that Filipino students had a dropout rate of approximately 60 percent (Agbayani-Siewert and Revilla, 1995).

Asian American youth are generally perceived as a model minority more involved with high academic achievement and good behavior rather than delinquent activities. Although empirical reports suggest problems in educational achievement for Filipino American youth, they are often mistakenly perceived as similar to the better-known Asian American groups such the Chinese and Japanese, who have achieved educational success similar to or better than the mainstream population (Min, 1995).

Mental Health Issues for Children and Adolescents

The major mental health issues confronting Filipino American youth are delineated in the following section. The lack of epidemiological data and current mental health research on this segment of the Asian American population is evident from the limited amount of data available to document their psychological problems and behavioral disorders.

Mental Health Disorders

In spite of being the second-largest Asian American population in the United States, Filipinos, as a group, have been neglected by scholars. No epidemiological studies have been completed on Filipino American children or adolescents. Moreover, minimal research on adult Filipino American mental health exists. Although an epidemiological study has recently been completed on adult

Filipino American mental health and service utilization, the comprehensive results have not yet been published (Uehara, Takeuchi, and Smukler, 1994). This study represents the first systematic examination of Filipino American mental health and illness. The generalizability of existing research on Filipino American community mental health treatment cases is minimal. Moreover, almost all the research is focused on adults.

To date, epidemiological research that examines Filipino American childhood or adolescent mental disorders or symptomatology does not exist. Research findings on adult Filipino American mental health suggests a greater vulnerability and exposure to negative life events compared to other Asian American groups (Takeuchi and Adair, 1992), high rates of depression (Tompar-Tiu, and Sustento-Seneriches, 1995; Kuo and Tsai, 1986), schizophrenia and affective psychoses (Araneta, 1993; Anderson, 1983; Duff and Arthur, 1973), and heavy alcohol consumption (Lubben, Chi, and Kitano, 1987). Schizophrenia among Filipinos is often diagnosed as the paranoid type.

Several protective factors help to guard against depression among Filipino Americans (Kuo, 1984). Among Filipinos, lower rates of depression were found among married persons, compared to widowed and single persons, and among Catholics as compared to Protestants. Takeuchi and Adair (1992), however, found no difference in distress scores between married and single Filipinos. In comparison to other Asian American groups, Filipino women experience higher rates of depression than Korean and Japanese women (Kuo, 1984).

Once mental health services are obtained, Asian Americans tend to drop out of treatment earlier than most groups. After examining treatment cases of Filipino American and other ethnic-racial groups, Flaskerud (1986) reports that workers' ability to speak clients' language, ethnic match between worker and client, and location of the mental health agency were the best predictors of dropout rates for ethnic-racial minorities. Like other Asian American immigrant populations, Filipino Americans tend to underutilize mental health services during the initial stages of illness. In a study of four community centers, Flaskerud (1986) found a higher proportion of schizophrenia and psychosis diagnoses among Filipino and Vietnamese populations, as compared to whites, blacks, and Hispanics. Because there is little evidence to support a disparity in rates of mental disorders among ethnic-racial minority groups, Flaskerud argues that Asian Americans will use mental health services only when their illnesses are severe. Not only will the afflicted individual put off seeking services, family members may also resist seeking mainstream mental health services because of stigma or a belief that indigenous healing methods will cure the problem.

Suicidal Behaviors

In 1995, an article in the *San Diego Union Tribune* declared, "Filipino Girls Think Suicide at No. 1 Rate" (Lau, 1995). This article cited a study that the Centers for Disease Control and Prevention had done in 1993 that showed an estimated 45.6 percent of Filipino American girls reported thinking about wanting to kill themselves. This is compared to the next-highest group, Latina adolescents, whose rate was 33.4 percent, with lower rates among white girls. Experts quoted in the article attributed the high rates of suicidal ideation of Filipino adolescents to overworked parents, an emphasis on material luxuries, a lack of positive Filipino American role models in both daily life and the media, and low self-esteem among Filipino girls.

Gangs

In 1983, the Los Angeles County Probation Department formed its first caseload of Asian gang probationers and concluded that available resources were not adequate to address the growing problem (Los Angeles County Probation Department, 1994). Based largely on ethnic stereotypes and media portrayals, perceptions of whether or not gangs are a problem in the Filipino American community has been subject to debate.

Stereotypes of an Asian American model minority may interfere with an accurate assessment of Filipino American gangs, due to the overall lack of data on Filipino Americans. Large urban areas throughout the United States have noted the emergence and growth of new Filipino American gangs, who often engage in violent activities to make a name for themselves. These gangs have reportedly been involved in territorial wars, theft, drugs, and murder.

The larger community, however, has tended to associate gang involvement with African American and Latino populations rather than with Filipinos (Thornton, 2000, personal communication).

A community's perception of whether or not a problem exists is a necessary factor in the formal recognition of a social problem. There is evidence to suggest that the Filipino American community does not recognize gangs as an issue (Buenaventura, 1996). Although Filipino American parents may see gangs as a problem in their community, they do not necessarily believe that their children are either likely to join or to be members of gangs. It is not unusual for parents to blame their adolescent's peers for troublesome or deviant behavior. During the focus group discussion, a Los Angeles County probation officer with the Asian American gang unit made the following comment that seems to represent the views of Filipino parents about their own child's involvement in gangs:

> I would like to emphasize that when they come to me they have been through the criminal justice system and this is probably the umpteenth time that they [youth] have gotten caught. I noticed Filipino American [parents] are very over protective with their kids. They have this sense of my kid is not a gang member, he is not doing this, he is not doing that, he is a good kid. It is like there is a denial there. It is like loss of face [for the parents].

Sociocultural Issues in Assessment

Acculturation is a dynamic and interactive process between two cultures that results in changes in cultural values, beliefs, attitudes, and behaviors (Berry, Trimble, and Olmedo, 1986). The educational system in the Philippines that was created by Americans has functioned as a model of forced acculturation, resulting in Filipinos beginning their acculturation prior to immigration (Constantino, 1966). Immigrant families experience a state of social and cultural transition that often results in problems that are not necessarily pathological (Landau and Griffiths, 1981). However, families with children are at a much greater risk for problems, as children typically acculturate at a much faster rate than their parents and elders, resulting in an acculturation gap and an imbalance in family relationships. In a study of Filipino American college students and their parents, Heras and Revilla (1992) found that mothers of culturally traditional students reported higher levels of family satisfaction than mothers of more acculturated students. Children who challenge the cultural norms or reject traditional values and behaviors will experience greater tension and increased dissatisfaction in the family system. In response to such a growing acculturation gap, Filipino parents may intensify their hierarchical stance, which may lead to a breakdown in family communication (Santos, 1983).

Delinquency may be associated with an acculturation gap between youth and their parents. The stress from acculturation strain has been reported as an important factor in producing delinquent behavior in youth (Vega and Rumbaut, 1991). Immigrant youth daily traverse across four cultures—an intergenerational culture, the culture of parents, the peer culture, and transactions between the traditional and new culture. Conflict may emerge as the relatively slower-paced acculturation of parents clashes with the values and behaviors of their more acculturated children (Berry, 1988; Burnam and others, 1987).

As the traditional lines of hierarchical authority become ambiguous, conflict may not only emerge between parents and their children but between grandparents and parents and between grandchildren and grandparents (Buriel, 1993).

The more acculturated youth acquire a new perception of the meaning of discipline that is incongruent with that of their parents and grandparents. For example, Filipino American children socialized in American schools are taught that physical punishment can be a form of child abuse that can be reported to social service agencies and law enforcement. However, parents and grandparents do not necessarily perceive physical punishment as abuse but as a form of discipline that fosters compliance and protects the family from shame.

Children are caught in the middle of a struggle between old and new, whereas parents and grandparents may experience fear and confusion that comes when one's values and beliefs are under attack. Outside the family, traditional Filipino parenting methods may also conflict with mainstream institutions such as schools, law enforcement, and public services for children. A children's services social worker stated that allegations of Filipino American child physical abuse was one of the most frequently reported referrals from schools (Agbayani-Siewert, 1996).

Language

There are more than one hundred different dialects and languages spoken in the Philippines (Tompar-Tiu and Sustento-Sereniches, 1995). Tagalog is the most frequently spoken Filipino language, but in the Philippines and the United States, the majority of Filipino immigrants come to the United States with the ability to speak, read, and write in English. The colonial legacy endures through language preference and use (Rimonte, 1997). In the Philippines, English is as widely understood as Tagalog and has evolved into a slang referred to as Taglish. Although the majority of Filipino immigrants are able to read, speak, and write English, their use and understanding of the language may be limited. Colloquial phrases and words used in the United States may not be familiar to many Filipino immigrants. Language and a lack of culturally competent services may function as barriers to service for many Asians. Prior studies suggest that a lack of culturally sensitive knowledge and service delivery is related to Filipino American underutilization and retention of mental health services (Zane, Takeuchi, and Young, 1994; Flaskerud and Soldevilla, 1986).

Within the Filipino American community, there appears to be a preference for English over a Filipino language. In a study of Filipino American immigrants, the majority reported that they equally preferred English and a Filipino dialect or preferred English over a Filipino dialect (Agbayani-Siewert, 1993). Most parents purposely do not make an effort to teach their children to speak a Filipino language, so fewer than half of all Filipino American youth speak their parents' native language. In a large survey of adolescents, Rumbaut (1994) found that the primary language spoken between Filipino American youth and their parents was English. Moreover, the majority of Filipino youth preferred English over a Filipino dialect.

There is an expectation and hope that children will be accepted and assimilate into the American mainstream through success in education and career. It is believed that part of achieving this success is based on the child's ability to speak good English without an accent. However, many Filipino Americans speak with a strong accent that is associated with a strong sense of inferiority, according to Rimonte (1997) and other scholars. Filipino parents may view an accent as interfering with acceptance by the host culture. Many parents view structural assimilation as tied to upward mobility. Parents do not necessarily want their children to lose or replace their Filipino culture and beliefs, yet they see structural assimilation as being the key to upward mobility. Children are caught in the middle. In order to satisfy parental expectations of success, children must acculturate to a certain degree; if they do not, they will not be able to satisfy their parents' expectations. To achieve these expectations means that they will inevitably alienate themselves from their family (Baptiste, 1987; Berry and others, 1989).

Ethnic Identity

During the fifth stage of Erikson's psychosocial development (1968)—ego identity versus role diffusion—adolescents face the task of developing a sense of self. Without successfully achieving an identity, the adolescent develops identity confusion, which leads to social deviance and conflict. Evidence suggests that developing a sense of identity may be particularly problematic for ethnic minority members (Goodenow and Espin, 1993). The primary challenge for the 1.5 generation is to integrate and unify two disparate cultures (Lee and Cynn, 1991).[4] This task becomes more complex and difficult when parents and youth are ambivalent about their culture. The integration of two cultures is especially troublesome for adolescents who must also cope with the developmental task of an identity crisis (Gibbs and Moskowitz-Sweet, 1991). Adolescent difficulties and intracultural conflict between parents and youth is exacerbated when parents inadvertently deliver contradictory messages. On the one hand, immigrant parents may convey a preference for anything that is American. On the other, they will simultaneously demand an adherence to traditional Filipino cultural norms and values.

Although there is minimal empirical research on the ethnic identity of Filipino American youth, there is substantial anecdotal evidence of negative identity development and shame about being Filipino among Filipino American youth (Quemuel, 1996; Revilla, 1996, 1997).

Identity Conflicts

To develop a healthy ethnic identity, adolescents must resolve conflicts related to their status as members of an ethnic group. These conflicts include issues of ignorance, stereotyping, and prejudice toward the ethnic group and issues of differing norms and values between their own ethnic culture and the dominant American culture (Phinney, Lochner, and Murphy, 1990). Children of immigrants contend with more difficulties during this process of identity development because of the acculturation gap that often exists between them and their parents.

The following excerpt from a university student's essay demonstrates the negative identity and shame experienced by some Filipino youth:

> In the past I was ashamed to admit I was Filipino. I never wanted to learn the language even though I was brought up with my parents and grandparents speaking it. In high school I finally realized that I wasn't the only full-blooded Filipino and I was no longer ashamed to admit it. [Revilla, 1996, p. 9]

Some of the reasons for the shame that young Filipinos feel are illustrated by the following quote of a ninth-grade Filipino girl:

> [O]ur parents don't come [to school functions] because they don't know any English. I don't even tell them when they are supposed to come. They dress so different and I don't want our parents to come because the others will laugh at them and tease us. We are ashamed. [Olsen, 1988, p. 82, as cited in Rumbaut, 1994, p. 120]

Other reasons for shame include demeaning stereotypes of Filipinos (Okamura, 1998), the colonial history of the Philippines, negative media coverage of the Philippines during the Marcos era, and negative portrayal of Filipino American communities (Tizon, 1990). For many young Filipinos today, the internalization of the denigration of Filipinos, Filipino culture, and the Philippines has resulted in an identity crisis that revolves around the lack of pride, self-respect, and self-love as a Filipino.

Culturally Based Attitudes About Health and Mental Illness

With the exception of a few research studies, almost all of the information available on Filipino beliefs and attitudes about mental health and illness is based on the traditional culture in the Philippines. Thus attitudes and beliefs may be more applicable to older immigrants than to their more acculturated children. However, because parents usually decide when or if to seek treatment for their children, it is important for mental health providers to be familiar with traditional Filipino views on mental health and mental illness.

Research in the Philippines (Lapuz, 1978; Sechrest, 1967) and the United States (Flaskerud and Soldevilla, 1986) suggests that Filipino Americans attach a strong stigma to mental illness and that this stigma extends to the entire family system. Similar to other Asian American groups, Filipino Americans will attempt to care for their mentally ill family member; they seek services only when their personal resources are taxed or the disorder becomes severe (Sue and Morishima, 1982).

As with many other Asian American groups, Filipino explanations of mental illness include a blend of the body, mind, and the supernatural (Tompar-Tiu and Sustento-Seneriches, 1995). In a study involving school teachers in the Philippines, half believed in *anitos* (deities embodied in icons), one-third believed that indigenous healers were more effective than physicians, and about a half believed that powerful witches could invoke disease (Sechrest, 1964, in Araneta, 1993). Witchcraft and voodoo are believed to cause anxiety symptoms (Tompar-Tiu and Sustento-Seneriches, 1995). Araneta (1993) presents three categories of Filipino American beliefs about the causes of mental illness—the mystical, personalistic, and naturalistic causation.

The mystical causation denotes individual weakness and is manifested in withdrawal, irrational thought, and bad dreams. It is believed that if the individual is not able to awaken during these bad dreams or nightmares, death may result. Illnesses of personalistic causation are divided into two types—the supernatural and human. Supernatural causes emanate from life forces in animate and inanimate objects that sometimes manifest as ghosts of the dead relatives. The malevolent power of the ghost depends on the circumstances surrounding its death and can cause depression, hallucinations, or suicide. In addition to the dead, other life forces can cause psychophysical disorders if an individual engages in activities that offend the spirits. Naturalistic causation of illness occurs when the individual's balance of basic body elements is disrupted. Natural forces and conditions are found in the environment (cold, hot, stress, wind, and dampness) and diet. Physical and emotional stress can also cause illnesses.

Case Studies

The following section presents two case studies that illustrate some of the common problems reported by Filipino youth who seek mental health treatment. The first case deals with ethnic identity issues in an adolescent; the second deals with cultural conceptions of child abuse in Filipino families.

In the first case study, Joanne fluctuates between embracing her ethnic identity as a Filipina and rejecting it in favor of the mainstream identity, as reflected in the media and among her non-Filipino peers.

> Joanne is a sixteen-year-old high school student, the second child of three girls and one boy in her family. After Joanne's parents were married in the Philippines, they immigrated to the United States where they started their family. Currently, both parents are unemployed. Her father suffers from a kidney-related illness, and because the family cannot afford home health care, Joanne's mother quit her job to provide care for her husband. Although Joanne was born in the United States, she speaks fluent Tagalog at home and has visited the Philippines. She was referred to our program by a school counselor for academic and behavioral problems. Reportedly, she demonstrated low achievement, compounded by chronic "ditching" and disruptive behavior in class. Her teachers also reported that Joanne exhibited frequent mood swings; she often told her parents that she knew she was "acting crazy" but refused to seek counseling. Although Joanne occasionally experimented with drugs such as marijuana and ecstasy, she didn't drink because it made people "act stupid."

When Joanne was referred to me by her school counselor, she seemed pleased to have a Filipina counselor, saying that I would "understand her better" and that it would put her at ease to talk with someone who could identify with her cultural experiences. In our sessions, Joanna constantly compared her life to the lives of her non-Filipino friends and their families. She complained that her parents were too strict, and she fought with them constantly because they always compared her to her older sister who was an honor student and overachiever. She said she didn't feel connected to Filipino culture and preferred to date white boys. She worried that she was too dark and that she had a strong Filipino accent and that her boyfriend's parents didn't like her. Joanne wore blue contacts so she would "not look so Filipino." She believed that the relationship with her boyfriend wouldn't last because of their ethnic and racial differences.

Joanne spent a year in our program, and we focused primarily on her ethnic identity conflict. She fluctuated between feeling "very Filipino" and wanting to fill the traditional role of a Filipina daughter, and wanting to be more "American" like her non-Filipino peers. Joanne's identity conflicts were most apparent in her relationship with her boyfriend. When frustrated in feeling she could never be "white," she would attempt to fit into traditional Filipina roles. For graduation, she asked her parents for blue contact lenses.

In order to address the disconnect between Filipino identity and the mainstream American identity, services need to be developed that are ethnically sensitive and relevant. Joanne was referred to the only ethnic agency in the city that targets Filipino American youth and their families. The agency's traditional individual and family counseling program is supplemented with programs that encourage youth to embrace their ethnic identity and culture, such as involvement in community social and cultural activities. Group work focuses on education and social support. Interacting with other Filipino adolescents helps them understand that they are not alone in experiencing some sort of cultural-ethnic identity issues, regardless of where they live or attend school. Group facilitators raise questions of identity and provide information about Filipino American history and the historical relationship between the United States and the Philippines. Issues of colonial mentality and identity conflicts are brought up in groups, allowing youth to reframe their concepts of identity in a more historical context in order to dispel colonial myths and encourage new definitions of what it means to "be Filipino."

The agency also attempts to address issues of economic status, immigration, and racism and to form a context for youth to participate in their own empowerment, where they will have an opportunity to learn leadership skills. Joanne joined a Filipina youth organization, and soon she reported feeling more in control of her life and not "so ashamed for being so brown." Though she still wears her blue contacts, she also reported that she was doing better in school and getting along better with her parents. Joanne's work in the community created a positive support system for her that had previously been missing. One of her community activities is working in a youth project on the spoken word—a *hip hop* genre of poetry in which individuals write and present their poems, after which the poets compete with one another. The performance part of spoken word allows youth to give voice to and verbalize their issues publicly, building a more positive ethnic identity. Filipino youth blend the traditional *balagtasan,* or "verbal sword play," to participate in spoken word in their own particular style by redefining the cultural tradition of *balagtasan,* popular in the Philippines during the early to mid-twentieth century. Interventions that integrate traditional with mainstream cultural experiences enable Filipino youth to feel comfortable in their ethnic culture yet confident enough to carve out a place for themselves in American culture.

The following case study of Amaya and her grandmother was presented by a Filipino community social worker and exemplifies what can happen when traditional and new values outside of and within the family compete for dominance.

> Two years ago, a Filipino grandmother came to the states and ended up baby-sitting for her grandchild Amaya, a seven-year-old girl. At one point, using the standard of the Philippines, she spanked the child. Amaya then called the police and complained, "Grandma hit me." The police came right away, but this was a real shocker to her grandmother and, I think, even to this point, she still feels negatively toward this granddaughter. The incident really challenged the value of respect for elders. After she was spanked, Amaya even told her mother to send her grandmother back to the Philippines.

Was this a case of physical abuse, as defined by Anglo American norms? Or was it an example of physical discipline, as defined by Filipino norms? There are many conflicting definitions of discipline, depending on one's cultural perspectives. In which situations does a case of parental spanking turn into physical abuse? What are some of the criteria that a social worker or clinician could use to make that assessment, independent of cultural norms?

To answer these questions satisfactorily, effective prevention and intervention requires the partnership of a multitude of systems such as the schools, police, and social service organizations, as well as the Filipino American community. Education would be a necessary first step to inform mainstream organizations about Filipino culture and the immigrant Filipino American community about the differences between American mainstream definitions of child abuse and discipline. An ethnic group's cultural strengths should also be incorporated into any prevention program, such as Filipino American collectivist roots. For example, the cultural value and practice of collectivism can be used to reach out and bring together various organizations in the Filipino community.

Whether providing educational prevention or family intervention in the form of counseling, the content of the material and clinical work should be culturally appropriate (Landau, 1982). For example, many Filipino American families are multigenerational. Thus there is a potential for cultural dissonance across three generations. Considering that elderly grandparents may take responsibility for child care and other domestic chores while parents work requires that problems of child discipline involve the entire household. When first meeting with the family, the practitioner should keep in mind the egalitarian structure of Filipino families. Both males and females should be addressed equally, without deference being shown to the eldest male at the cost of ignoring the mother. Ignoring the mother as an equal will be viewed as offensive and rude.

The cultural practice of *tayo tayo* (just among us) may also affect the practitioner-client relationship. The practitioner can integrate cultural and socially relevant examples of case studies involving Filipino American families, such as a vignette incorporating Filipino cultural material that depicts a family that keeps abuse secret for fear that its members would be shamed (*hiya*). Vignettes may also provide a nonthreatening introduction or a stimulus for discussion on the topic of traditional Filipino versus mainstream

American forms of discipline. In a counseling relationship or group session, vignettes can also be structured as problem-solving exercises.

Summary and Conclusion

Solutions within the Filipino family call for a blending of old and new cultural values and norms. A balance needs to be maintained in which children are given the freedom to be successful in mainstream society and gain the skills and behaviors needed to do so while remaining cognizant of their parents' perspective and concerns. Parents need to be informed that children are growing up in two cultures. Parents can also be educated about the expectations, norms, and pressures faced by their children with peers and at school, as well as alternative methods of discipline. All family members need to develop a tolerance for one another (Agbayani-Siewert, 1994).

This balancing of old and new is difficult because it is the traditional parenting methods and the structure of hierarchical authority that function to maintain Filipino practices and values such as respect for elders and unquestioned obedience from children. As the family attempts to negotiate the problems associated with immigration, it becomes changed. Adjustments must be made to account for changes in the environment. According to this perspective, it is not just the children who are victims but the parents and grandparents as well. Problems within the family are seen within the context of immigrant transition to a new society and a differential rate of acculturation among family members.

Solutions based on this perspective call for changes within and outside of the family. Thus mainstream institutions that work with immigrant families should be culturally and linguistically appropriate (Sue, 1988). For example, teachers and social service agencies should have an understanding of Filipino American culture and knowledge of immigrant parents and their children's experiences and perceptions. Also local resources such as churches and Filipino American organizations provide great potential for community involvement and support of families in cultural transition.

Notes

1. *Highly educated* refers to people who have completed four years of college.
2. For example, life expectancy for Filipinos in Hawaii during the 1920s was 28.1 years and 46.1 during the 1930s. For the same time periods, the life expectancy for whites was 56.5 and 61.9, respectively.
3. The description of Filipino American values and beliefs in this section are traditional and may not be characteristic of all Filipinos.
4. *1.5 generation* refers to individuals born in a foreign country who immigrated to the United States at an early age. These individuals are said to be bicultural and multicultural.

References

Agbayani-Siewert, P. *Filipino American Immigrants: Social Role Strain, Self-Esteem, Locus of Control, Social Networks, Coping, Stress, and Mental Health Outcomes.* Unpublished doctoral dissertation, University of California, Los Angeles, School of Social Welfare, 1993.

Agbayani-Siewert, P. "Filipino American Culture and Family: Guidelines for Practitioners." *Families in Society: The Journal of Contemporary Human Services,* 1994, *75,* 429–438.

Agbayani-Siewert, P. (mod.). "Filipino American Children." Focus Group. University of California, Los Angeles, School of Public Policy and Social Research, Department of Social Welfare, 1996.

Agbayani-Siewert, P. "The Dual World of Filipino Americans." *Journal of Multicultural Social Work,* 1997, *6,* 59–76.

Agbayani-Siewert, P. "Examining the Validity of the BEM Sex Role Inventory for Use with Filipino Americans Using Confirmatory Factor Analysis." Unpublished manuscript, Los Angeles, 2002.

Agbayani-Siewert, P. "Testing the Assumption of Cultural Similarity: The Case of Chinese and Filipino Americans." *Social Work. Forthcoming.*

Agbayani-Siewert, P., and Revilla, L. "Filipino Americans." In P. G. Min, (ed.), *Asian Americans: Contemporary Trends and Issues.* Thousand Oaks, Calif.: Sage, 1995.

Agbayani-Siewert, P., and Yick, A. "Filipino American Dating Violence: Definitions, Contextual Justifications and Experiences of Dating Violence." *Journal of Human Behavior and the Social Environment,* 2000, *3*(3/4), 46–60.

Agoncillo, T. *History of the Filipino People.* Quezon City, Philippines: Garotech Publishing, 1990.

Agoncillo, T., and Guerrero, M. *History of the Filipino People.* (7th ed.) Quezon City, Philippines: Garcia Publishing, 1987.

Aguilar, D. D. "The Social Construction of the Filipina Woman." *International Journal of Intercultural Relations,* 1989, *13*(4), 527–551.

Alip, E. M. *Political and Cultural History of the Philippines* (5th rev. ed.). Manila: Alip and Sons, 1968.

Almirol, E. B. "Rights and Obligations in Filipino American Families." *Journal of Comparative Family Studies,* 1982, *13*(3), 291–306.

Anderson, J. N. "Health and Illness in Filipino Immigrants." *Western Journal of Medicine,* 1983, *139,* 811–819.

Andres, T., and Ilada-Andres, P. *Understanding the Filipino.* Quezon City, Philippines: New Day Publishers, 1987.

Araneta, E. G. "Psychiatric Care of Filipino Americans." In A. Gaw (ed.), *Culture, Ethnicity and Mental Illness.* Washington, D.C.: American Psychiatric Press, 1993.

Azores-Gunter, T. "Educational Attainment and Upward Mobility: Prospects for Filipino Americans." *Amerasia Journal,* 1986–87, *13*(1), 39–52.

Baptiste, D. A. "Family Therapy with Spanish Heritage Immigrant Families in Cultural Transition." *Contemporary Family Therapy,* 1987, *9*(4), 229–251.

Berry, J. W. "Acculturation and Psychological Adaptation: A Conceptual Overview." In J. W. Berry and R. C. Annis (eds.), *Ethnic Psychology: Research and Practice with Immigrants, Refugees, Native Peoples, Ethnic Groups, and Sojourners.* Selected papers from a North American Regional Conference of the International Association for Cross-Cultural Psychology, Toronto, 1988.

Berry, J. W. "Psychology of Acculturation." In R. Dienstbier (ed.), *Nebraska Symposium on Motivation: Vol. 36. Perspectives on Motivation.* Lincoln: University of Nebraska Press, 1989.

Berry, J. W., Trimble, J. E., and Olmedo, E. L. "Assessment of Acculturation." In W. J. Lonner, and J. W. Berry (eds.), *Field Methods in Cross-Cultural Research,* Vol. 8. Thousand Oaks, Calif.: Sage, 1986.

Berry, J. W., and others. "Acculturation Attitudes in Plural Societies." *Applied Psychology: An International Review,* 1989, *38*(2), 185–206.

Buenaventura, R. "Why Do Filipino American Teens Get Involved in Gangs?" *Kalayaan: Issues, Ideas and Information for the Filipino American Community,* 1996, *2*(2), 7.

Buriel, R. "Acculturation, Respect for Cultural Differences, and Biculturalism Among Three Generations of Mexican American and Anglo American School Children." *The Journal of Genetic Psychology,* 1993, *154*(4), 531–543.

Burnam, M. A., and others. "Measurement of Acculturation in a Community Population of Mexican Americans." *Hispanic Journal of Behavioral Sciences,* 1987, *9*(2), 105–130.

Cabezas, A., Shinagawa, I., and Kawaguchi, G. "New Inquiries into the Socioeconomic Status of Filipino Americans in California." *Amerasia Journal,* 1986–87, *13,* 1–22.

Campomanes, O. V. "The New Empire's Forgetful and Forgotten Citizens: Unrepresentability and Unassimilability in Filipino America Postcolonialities." *Critical Mass: A Journal of Asian American Cultural Criticism,* 1995, *2,* 145–200.

Carino, B. V., Fawcett, J. T., Gardner, R. W., and Arnold, F. *The New Filipino Immigrants to the United States: Increasing Diversity and Change* (East-West Population Institute Paper Series Number 115). Honolulu: East-West Center Population Institute, 1990.

Chan, S. "Families with Filipino Roots." In E. W. Lynch and M. J. Hanson (eds.), *Developing Cross-Cultural Competence: A Guide for Working with Young Children and Their Families.* Baltimore: Brookes Publishing, 1992.

Chant, S., and McIlwaine, C. *Women of a Lesser Cost: Female Labor, Foreign Exchange and Philippine Development.* Quezon City, Philippines: Ateno de Manila University Press, 1995.

Cimmarusti, R. A. "Exploring Aspects of Filipino-American Families." *Journal of Marital and Family Therapy,* 1996, *22*(2), 205–217.

Constantino, R. *The Filipinos in the Philippines and Other Essays.* Manila: Malay Books, 1966.

Department of Public Social Services, Los Angeles, County Headquarters. "Important Notice for Immigrants" (flyer), Los Angeles, July, 7, 1999.

Duff, D. F., and Arthur, R. J. "Between Two Worlds: Filipinos in the U.S. Navy." In S. Sue and N. Wagner (eds.), *Asian American Psychological Perspectives.* Palo Alto, Calif.: Science and Behavior Books, 1973.

Enriquez, V. "Developing a Filipino Psychology." In U. Kim and J. W. Berry (eds.), *Indigenous Psychologies: Research and Experience in Cultural Context.* Cross-Cultural Research and Methodology Series, Vol. 17. Thousand Oaks, Calif.: Sage, 1993.

Erikson, E. H. *Identity, Youth and Crisis.* New York: W. W. Norton, 1968.

Espiritu, Y. L. *Filipino American Lives.* Philadelphia: Temple University Press, 1996.

Families U.S.A. "Health Coverage in Asian American and Pacific Islander Communities." Washington, D.C., 2001. Available online at www.familiesusa.org/media/pdf/asian/pdf.

Fawcett, J., Arnold, F., Bulatao, R., Buripkdi, C., Chung, B., Iritani, T., Lee, S., and Wu, T. S. *The Value of Children in Asia and the United States: Comparative Perspectives.* Honolulu: East-West Center, 1974.

Flaskerud, J. H. "Diagnostic and Treatment Differences Among Five Ethnic Groups." *Psychological Reports,* 1986, *58,* 219–235.

Flaskerud, J., and Soldevilla, E. "Filipino and Vietnamese Clients: Utilizing an Asian Mental Health Center." *Journal of Psychosocial Nursing and Mental Health Services,* 1986, *24*(8), 32–36.

Flores, P. "The Philippine American Youth Between Two Expectations: Filipino and U.S. Parenting Standards." *Journal of the American Association for Philippine Psychology,* 1994, *1,* 55–68.

Gibbs, J. T., and Moskowitz-Sweet, G. "Clinical and Cultural Issues in the Treatment of Biracial and Bicultural Adolescents." *Families in Society: Journal of Contemporary Human Services,* 1991, *72,* 579–592.

Gilandas, A., Gastardo-Conaco, C., and Servilla, J. C. "Sex and the Single Filipina: The Omega Woman." Manila: Philippine Education Association, 1982.

Gochenour, T. *Considering Filipinos.* Yarmouth, Me.: Intercultural Press, 1990.

Goodenow, C., and Espin, O. M. "Identity Choices in Immigrant Adolescent Females." *Adolescence,* 1993, *28,* 173–185.

Guthrie, G. "Structure of Maternal Attitudes in Two Cultures." *Journal of Psychology,* 1966, *62,* 155–165.

Guthrie, G., and Jacobs, P. *Child-Rearing and Personality Development in the Philippines.* University Park: Pennsylvania State University, 1966.

Heras, P., and Revilla, L. "Acculturation, Generational Status, and Family Environment of Filipino Americans: A Study of Cultural Adaptation." *Family Therapy,* 1994, *21,* 129–138.

Kagawa-Singer, M., Katz, P., Taylor, D. A., and Vanderryn, J.H.M. *Health Issues for Minority Adolescents.* Nebraska: University of Nebraska Press, 1996.

Keith, R., and Barrando, E. "Age Independence Norms in American Filipino Adolescents." *Journal of Social Psychology,* 1969, *78,* 285–296.

Kimmich, R. A. "Ethnic Aspects of Schizophrenia in Hawaii." *Journal for the Study of Interpersonal Processes,* 1960, *23*(1), 97–102.

Kitano, H.H.L. *Race Relations.* (5th ed.) Englewood Cliffs, N.J.: Prentice Hall, 1997.

Kuo, W. "Prevalence of Depression Among Asian-Americans." *Journal of Nervous and Mental Disease,* 1984, *172,* 449–457.

Kuo, W. H., and Tsai, Y. M. "Social Networking, Hardiness, and Immigrant's Mental Health." *Journal of Health and Social Behavior,* 1986, *27*(2), 133–149.

Landau, J. "Therapy with Families in Cultural Transition." In M. McGoldrick, J. Pearce, and J. Giordano (eds.), *Ethnicity and Family Therapy.* New York: Guilford Press, 1982.

Landau, J., and Griffiths, J. "The South African Family in Transition: Therapeutic and Training Implications." *Journal of Marital and Family Therapy,* 1981, *7,* 339–344.

Lapuz, L. *A Study of Psychopathology.* Quezon City, Philippines: New Day Publishers, 1978.

Lau, A. "Filipino Girls Think Suicide at No. 1 Rate." *San Diego Union Tribune,* Feb. 11, 1995, p. A-1.

Lee, J. C., and Cynn, V.E.H. "Issues in Counseling 1.5 Generation Korean Americans." In C. C. Lee and B. L. Richardson (eds.), *Multicultural Issues in Counseling: New Approaches to Diversity.* Alexandria, Va.: American Association for Counseling and Development, 1991.

Lee, S. M. "Asian Americans: Diverse and Growing." *Population Bulletin,* 1998, *53*(2), 1–40.

Los Angeles County Probation Department. *Report on Asian Gang Task Force.* Los Angeles: Author, 1994.

Lott, J. T. "Migration of a Mentality: The Filipino Community." In R. Endo, S. Sue, and N. Wagner (eds.), *Asian Americans: Social and Psychological Perspectives.* Vol. 2. Palo Alto, Calif.: Science and Behavior Books, 1980.

Lott, J. T. "Demographic Changes Transforming the Filipino American Community." In M. P. Root (ed.), *Filipino Americans: Transformation and Identity.* Thousand Oaks, Calif.: Sage, 1997.

Lubben, J., Chi, I., and Kitano, H.H.L. "Exploring Filipino American Drinking Behavior." *Journal of Studies on Alcohol,* 1987, *49*(1), 26–29.

Mar, D. "Regional Differences in Asian American Earnings Discrimination: Japanese, Chinese, Filipino American Earnings in California and Hawaii." *Amerasia Journal,* 1999, *25*(2), 67–94.

Marcelino, E. P. "Towards Understanding the Psychology of the Filipina." *Women and Therapy,* 1990, *9*(1/2), 105–128.

Medina, B. *The Filipino Family: A Text with Selected Readings.* Quezon City, Philippines: University of the Philippines Press, 1991.

Min, P. G. *Asian Americans: Contemporary Trends and Issues.* Thousand Oaks, Calif.: Sage, 1995.

Ng, F., and Wilson, J. D. (eds.). *The Asian American Encyclopedia.* New York: Marshall Cavendish, 1995.

Novero-Blust, E., and Scheidt, R. "Perceptions of Filial Responsibility by Elderly Filipino Widows and Their Primary Caregivers." *International Journal of Aging and Human Development,* 1988, *26,* 91–106.

O'Hare, W. P., and Felt, J. C. "Asian Americans: American's Fastest Growing Minority Group." *Population Trends and Public Policy, 19,* Washington, D.C.: Population Reference Bureau, 1991.

Okamura, J. Y. *The Filipino American Diaspora: Transnational Relations, Identities, and Communities.* New York: Garland, 1998.

Padilla, A. M., Wagatsuma, Y., and Lindholm, K. J. "Acculturation and Personality as Predictors of Stress in Japanese and Japanese-Americans." *The Journal of Social Psychology,* 1985, *125*(3), 295–305.

Paguio, L. P., Skeen, P., and Robinson, B. E. "Perceptions of the Ideal Child Among Employed and Nonemployed American and Filipino Mothers." *Perceptual and Motor Skills,* 1987, *65*(3), 707–711.

Phinney, J. S. "Ethnic Identity and Self-Esteem." *Hispanic Journal of Behavioral Science,* 1991, *13,* 193–208.

Phinney, J. S., Lochner, B. T., and Murphy, R. "Ethnic Identity Development in Adolescence." In G. M. Breakwell (ed.), *Social Psychology of Identity and the Self-Concept* (pp. 53–72). Thousand Oaks, Calif.: Sage, 1990.

Pido, A. *The Filipino in America: Macro/Micro Dimensions of Immigration and Integration.* New York: Center for Migration Studies, 1986.

Pollard, K. M., and O'Hare, W. P. "America's Racial and Ethnic Minorities." *Population Bulletin, 54(3).* Washington, D.C.: Population Reference Bureau, 1999.

Quemuel, C. *Ethnicity, Identity, and the "Gook Syndrome": Soldiers of Color in the Vietnam War.* Paper presented at the Asian American Studies Joint Regional Conference, Manoa, Hawaii, March 1996.

Revilla, L. "Filipino Americans: Issues of Identity in Hawaii." In J. Okamura and R. Labrador (eds.), *Pagdiriwang, 1996: Legacy and Vision of Hawaii's Filipino Americans* (pp. 9–12). Honolulu: University of Hawaii, Center for Southeast Asian Studies, 1996.

Revilla, L. "Filipino American Identity: Transcending the Crisis." In M. P. Root (ed.), *Filipino Americans: Transformation and Identity* (pp. 95–111). Thousand Oaks, Calif.: Sage, 1997.

Rimonte, N. "A Question of Culture: Cultural Approval of Violence Against Women in the Pacific-Asian Community and Cultural Defense." *Harvard Law Review,* 1991, *43,* 1311–1326.

Rimonte, N. "Colonialism's Legacy: The Inferiorizing of the Filipino." In M. P. Root (ed.), *Filipino Americans: Transformation and Identity.* Thousand Oaks, Calif.: Sage, 1997.

Rogler, L. H. "International Migrations: A Framework for Directing Research." *American Psychologist,* 1994, *49,* 701–708.

Rosenthal, D. "Intergenerational Conflict and Culture: A Study of Immigrant and Non-Immigrant Adolescents and Their Parents." *Genetic Psychology Monographs,* 1984, *109,* 53–75.

Rumbaut, R. "The Crucible Within: Ethnic Identity, Self-Esteem, and Segmented Assimilation Among Children of Immigrants." *International Migration Review,* 1994, *28,* 748–794.

Saldana, D. H. "Acculturative Stress: Minority Status and Distress." *Hispanic Journal of Behavioral Sciences,* 1994, *16*(2), 116–128.

Santos, R. "The Social and Emotional Development of Filipino American Children." In G. Powell (ed.), *The Psychosocial Development of Minority Group Children*. New York: Brunner/Mazel, 1983.

Santos, R. "Filipino American Children." In G. Johnson-Powell and J. Yamamoto (eds.), *Transcultural Child Development: Psychological Assessment and Treatment*. New York: Wiley, 1997.

Sechrest, L. "Symptoms of Mental Disorder in the Philippines." *Proceedings of the Symposium on the Filipino Personality*. Manila: Psychological Association of the Philippines, 1964.

Sechrest, L. "Philippine Culture, Stress, and Psychopathology." *Transcultural Psychiatric Research Review*, 1967, *4*, 18–22.

Strobel, L. M. "The Cultural Identity of Third-Wave Filipino Americans." *Journal of the American Association for Philippine Psychology*, 1994, *1*(1), 37–54.

Strobel, L. M. "Born-Again Filipino: Filipino American Identity and Asian Panethnicity." *Amerasia Journal*, 1996, *22*(2), 31–53.

Sue, S. "Psychotherapeutic Services for Ethnic Minorities." *American Psychologist*, 1988, *43*, 301–308.

Sue, S. "Mental Health." In N. W. Zane, D. Takeuchi, and K.N.J. Young (eds.), *Confronting Critical Health Issues of Asian and Pacific Islander Americans*. Thousand Oaks, Calif.: Sage, 1994.

Sue, S., and Morishima, J. *The Mental Health of Asian Americans*. San Francisco: Jossey-Bass, 1982.

Sue, S., Sue, D. W., Sue, L., and Takeuchi, D. T. "Psychopathology Among Asian Americans: A Model Minority?" *Cultural Diversity and Mental Health*, 1995, *1*(1), 39–54.

Tacata, L. "Sociodemographic Profile of Filipino Americans." Unpublished manuscript. Asian American Recovery Services, San Francisco, 1996.

Takaki, R. *Strangers from a Different Shore*. New York: Penguin Books, 1989.

Takeuchi, D., and Adair, R. "The Exposure and Vulnerability of Ethnic Minorities to Negative Life Events." *Research in Community Mental Health*, 1992, *7*, 111–124.

Tan, M. *Usug, Kulam, Pasma: Traditional Concepts of Health and Illness in the Philippines*. Quezon City, Philippines: Alay Kapwa Kilusang Pangkalusugan, 1987.

Tiongson, A. T., Jr. "Throwing the Baby Out with the Bathwater: Situating Young Filipino Mothers and Fathers Beyond the Dominant Discourse on Adolescent Pregnancy." In M. P. Root (ed.), *Filipino Americans: Transformation and Identity*. Thousand Oaks, Calif.: Sage, 1997.

Tizon, A. "Love and Shame." *Pacific Magazine, Seattle Times Newspaper*, November 18, 1990, 10–46.

Tompar-Tiu, A., and Sustento-Seneriches, J. *Depression and Other Mental Health Issues: The Filipino American Experience.* San Francisco: Jossey-Bass, 1995.

Uba, L. *Asian Americans: Personality Patterns, Identity, and Mental Health.* New York: Guilford Press, 1994.

Uehara, E. S., Takeuchi, D. T., and Smukler, M. "Effects of Combining Disparate Groups in the Analysis of Ethnic Differences: Variations Among Asian American Mental Health Service Consumers in Level of Community Functioning." *American Journal of Community Psychology*, 1994, *22*, 83–99.

U.S. Department of Commerce. *We the Americans: Asians.* Economics and Statistics Administration, Bureau of the Census, 1993.

United Way of Greater Los Angeles. *Los Angeles 1994: State of the County Data.* United Way of Greater Los Angeles, 1994.

Vega, W. A., and Rumbaut, R. G. "Ethnic Minorities and Mental Health." *Annual Review of Sociology*, 1991, *17*, 351–383.

Wolfe, D. "Family Secrets: Transnational Struggles Among Children of Filipino Immigrants." *Sociological Perspectives*, 1997, *40*(3), 457–482.

Yu, K. H., and Kim, L.I.C. "The Growth and Development of Korean-American Children." In G. J. Powell (ed.), *The Psychosocial Development of Minority Group Children.* New York: Brunner/Mazel, 1983.

Zane, N. W., Takeuchi, D. T., and Young, K. N. *Confronting Critical Health Issues of Asian and Pacific Islander Americans.* Thousand Oaks, Calif.: Sage, 1994.

Chapter Six

Southeast Asian Children and Adolescents

Donna J. Ida
Pahoua Yang

The face of the Asian American–Pacific Islander (AAPI) community in the United States has changed considerably over the last twenty-five years. The emergence of Southeast Asians has altered how one looks at and defines what it is to be AAPI. With the exception of indigenous people who were native to Hawaii, most AAPIs historically came to the United States as immigrants. Many left their place of birth for economic reasons. As difficult as the choice was and as hard as the journey has been, it was a journey borne of choice, viewed as a chance to find a better life in this strange new land. Immigrants from Cambodia, Laos, and Vietnam, however, arrived under much different circumstances. As refugees, their journey was involuntary. Seeking an escape from the circumstances of war, they too hoped for a better life.

The trauma the refugees experienced cannot be overstated. The impact goes beyond those who personally witnessed the war in their native land and extends to the sons and daughters who were born and raised in the United States. The mental health issues of these Vietnamese, Cambodian, Laotian, and Hmong adolescents are the focus of this chapter.

Southeast Asian youth present a unique set of factors that place them at particular risk for emotional and behavioral problems. It is important to look at the child or adolescent within the context of his or her environment, social and familial relationships, and place in time. Huang (1998) and Nidorf (1985) have presented similar ecological models; they work well in assessing the experience of Southeast Asian refugee children in the stages of premigration, migration, and postmigration. Although it is extremely important for service providers to recognize and understand the premigration and migration experiences, this chapter focuses primarily on postmigration, as most of the youth in question were born in America and therefore were not part of the earlier migration experiences. Attention to the first two phases, however, will be discussed to the extent that these experiences affect the youth in the form of secondary trauma.

Southeast Asian refugees have migrated in waves over the past twenty-five years, resulting in a wide range of SES, education, acculturation, and levels of ethnic identity development. With the impending fall of Saigon in 1975, 140,000 Vietnamese were evacuated by the U.S. government; of these, 50,000 were children under the age of fourteen (Le, 1983). Most were educated and considered to be in danger because of their association with the United States. The second wave occurred between 1975 and 1978. Although some were unable to escape during the first wave and were vulnerable because of their political connections, the majority came from the middle class or were peasants. The devastation occurring in Cambodia during this period is difficult to comprehend. Up to one-third of the population was executed or died of starvation or disease under the widely feared Pol Pot regime (Loescher and Scanlan, 1986; Ung, 2000).

The third wave has been popularly referred to as the "boat people." Thousands upon thousands of Vietnamese fled the Communist takeover, fearing they would be sent to the "reeducation" camps. Many were ethnic Chinese who were from the merchant class. In August 1978, approximately 6,000 Vietnamese per month sought refuge outside Vietnam. By the spring of 1979, the number increased to 65,000 per month (Reimers, 1985).

The Cambodians were also fleeing on foot to the camps in Thailand. After suffering the ravages of war, they were retraumatized by their camp experience and the subsequent boat trip. Rape, starvation, exhaustion, and robbery were common. Their journey to the United States was precarious at best. It is, indeed, a testament to their strength that so many survived and have thrived in this country. For many, however, the psychological wounds remain silent but no less painful. The war, the camps, and the journey to the United States took a huge emotional toll on this population— a price that is still keenly felt within the community.

This chapter looks at factors affecting the mental health and emotional well-being of Southeast Asian youth living in the United States. Clinical interventions, with case vignettes, are discussed, as well as barriers and challenges to providing culturally competent services. Finally, questions for future discussion of AAPI mental health are presented, particularly as it relates to Southeast Asian youth.

Demographic Profile

Although Latinos and Hispanics have a larger population in terms of actual numbers, AAPIs make up the fastest-growing racial-ethnic population in the United States in terms of percentage increase. From 1980 to 1990, the AAPI population nearly doubled, increasing to 3.7 million persons, or from 1.6 to 2.9 percent of the total U.S. population. The 1990 census reported a 95 percent growth in the AAPI population since 1980, with increases of 102 percent for Chinese, 124 percent for Koreans, 818 percent for Cambodians, and 1,631 percent for Hmong. According to the 2000 census, 11.9 million U.S. residents reported themselves as Asian alone or in combination with one or more other races. This group made up 4.2 percent of the total population. Vietnamese make up approximately 8.4 percent of the total AAPI population; Laotians and Cambodians are 2.0 percent and Hmong 1.2 percent, respectively.

The lack of accurate data is an ongoing issue facing service providers working with the AAPI communities. Treating AAPIs as a homogeneous population is particularly problematic in identifying gaps in services and seeing the necessity for ethnic-specific intervention strategies. This issue was emphasized in a report by the President's White House Commission on Asian Pacific Americans. President Clinton signed Executive Order 13125 on June 7, 1999, to "improve the quality of life of Asian Americans and Pacific Islanders through increased participation in Federal programs where they may be underserved." The fifteen-member commission conducted town hall meetings around the country to listen to the concerns of the AAPI communities. The lack of data was a consistent theme expressed at all levels, regardless of geographical location.

When working with youth, it is critical to look not only at ethnicity but at the generational status and level of acculturation (Huang, 1997; Tanaka, Ebreo, Linn, and Morera, 1998). A fourth-generation Japanese American, a 1.5 generation Korean American, and a Vietnamese youth who has been in the United States for five years all qualify as "Asian American" but have had radically different experiences. To treat all adolescents as belonging to one homogenous population provides little useful information. Historically, statistics and data have been used to work against AAPIs. Citing low utilization rates in mental health settings, AAPIs were seen as having few, if any, problems (Sue and Morishima, 1982; Uba, 1994), thus adding to the myth that AAPIs are the "model minority."

A graphic illustration of how statistics can be misleading is to analyze how hard data can paint a very misleading picture. If one were to look at the aggregate figures for AAPIs, using percent of households with income under $15,000 as a measure of SES, AAPIs look financially well off when compared to the rest of the population. At 19.9 percent, AAPIs have the lowest percentage of households with incomes under $15,000 than any group, including non-Hispanic whites at 21.6 percent. The disaggregated data, however, present a much different perspective. Two distinct economic categories emerge. There are those who are financially stable, such as the Filipinos, Asian Indians, and Japanese at 11.7 percent, 14.1 percent, and 15.6 percent, respectively. At the other end of the economic spectrum are the Hmongs, with 53.1 percent of their population with household incomes of less than $15,000, the Cambodians at 40 percent, Laotians at 32 percent, and Vietnamese at 26.9 percent. All experience poverty at a much higher rate than the national average, thus belying the myth that they are an upwardly mobile, model minority.

The use of aggregated data obscures the differences between groups and gives a false impression of how well the specific communities are doing. Complicating matters is the fact that AAPIs are underrepresented in the provision of mental health services. Although this occurs for a multitude of reasons, such as lack of bilingual-bicultural service providers, stigma, limited hours for services, lack of transportation, and lack of support services, the low visibility at service agencies adds to the misperception that AAPIs do not experience mental health problems. Lower economic status and the lack of culturally appropriate support services frequently add to the stress of the parents.

Brief Historical Perspective

Southeast Asian youth live in a unique world; it is one shaped by events that occurred half-way around the world during a time before most were even born. They are the offspring of parents who cannot understand why their sons and daughters are rejecting traditional Asian values and social practices. One of the most common complaints voiced by the parents is how *Americanized* their children have become. But no matter how Westernized they may be, the lives of Southeast Asian youth are inextricably bound to the experience of parents who fled from Vietnam, Cambodia, and Laos in the aftermath of the war. Some have survived and become quite successful; others have not fared so well.

After the initial wave of refugees who tended to be well educated came the "boat people." Many arrived with little formal education and few resources of any type. They struggled with the language, social practices, and customs and often did not agree with the values they saw their children embrace. Having neither the time nor resources to heal from the emotional wounds suffered during the war, they now must face the stress associated with raising children in a foreign land. It is into this world that many young Southeast Asians are raised. These youth are seen at community-based mental health centers across the country in cities such as Denver, Salt Lake City, San Francisco, San Jose, Oakland, Long Beach, Houston, Dallas, New York City, Seattle, Washington, D.C., Boston, Minneapolis–St. Paul, and Wausau, Wisconsin.

The trauma and multiple losses for refugees have been well documented. It is a well-known fact that many of the refugees experienced severe trauma resulting in serious emotional problems, including major depression and posttraumatic stress disorder (PTSD) (Sack, Angell, Kinzie, and Rath, 1986; Benjamin and Morgan, 1989; Nguyen and Williams, 1989; Prong, 1995; Leung, Boehnlein, and Kinzie, 1997; Moore, Keopraseuth, Leung, and Chao, 1997;

Kinzie and others, 1990; Rousseau and Draper, 1998). The movie *The Killing Fields* brought to the American people's consciousness the atrocities of Pol Pot and what the Khmer Rouge did to the Cambodian people. Loung Ung (2000) poignantly recounted what the war was like from a child's perspective in *First They Killed My Father: A Daughter of Cambodia Remembers*. Personal stories of growing up during the war were told by young boys who eventually moved with their families to Minneapolis in *Dark Sky, Dark Land: Stories of the Hmong Boy Scouts of Troop 100* (Moore, 1989). It is not surprising that the impact of this trauma filtered down to the next generation, affecting the lives of the children of refugees (Lee, 1997).

Between 1982 and 1989, nearly 150 middle-age Cambodian women visited doctors, complaining that they could not see, a complaint that the doctors could not understand (Wilkinson, 1994): they were blind, but medical exams revealed no physical explanation for their blindness. These women did not know each other, nor did they try to conspire to illegally get disability coverage as some had charged. Other than their blindness, the one thing they had in common was that they had all suffered terribly at the hands of the Khmer Rouge. In one interview, a woman said through an interpreter, "I have seen so much, I never want to see again." This type of hysterical conversion reaction is relatively uncommon in the United States, but such a condition can be brought on by severe trauma. This is perhaps one of the most graphic examples of how the refugee population was affected by the war.

The Hmong, known for their tenacity and intimate knowledge of the difficult terrain in Laos, were recruited by the CIA to fight in what has come to be known as the "secret war" or the "quiet war," which the U.S. government denied even existed (Moore, 1989; Prong, 1995; Fadiman, 1997; Zia, 2000). It was the same government that abandoned them in the last frantic days of the war and left them to be killed by the thousands at the hands of those whom they had fought against. There are stories of Hmong soldiers who thought for sure the U.S. government would come back to rescue them, only to hear the helicopters fly overhead as the American soldiers fled the war zone. The terrible realization set in among the Hmong that they were left to face certain death.

There are stories of Vietnamese who endured severe hardships in the refugee camps, where theft, extortion, and rape were not uncommon. Some lived there for a few weeks, others for several years, leaving them feeling vulnerable, depressed, and anxious. Living conditions were unsanitary and chaotic, with children frequently unsupervised (Rousseau and Draper, 1998; Benjamin and Morgan, 1989). Many refugees who resettled in the United States suffered from major depression and PTSD. Others became suicidal and had great difficulty adjusting to life in the United States.

Each spring, newspapers report the accomplishments of young Vietnamese, Cambodian, Laotian, or Hmong students who, in the face of great adversity, managed to rise to the top of the class. The families and communities have every reason to be very proud of them. It is indeed quite an accomplishment, but for every class valedictorian countless others fail to achieve such lofty heights. Increasing numbers drop out of school, join gangs, become depressed and suicidal, get into trouble, or just become lost—the population addressed in this chapter. What makes telling these stories difficult is the fact that the communities wish to forget the pain. They are tired of hearing about problems; many do not want to admit they exist. They need to see a brighter future. Parents have a difficult time accepting that they survived the war only to have their children get into trouble in this land of opportunity. They adhere to cultural values in which it is shameful to acknowledge problems—values that say it is not acceptable to air one's dirty laundry in public. As difficult as it is to acknowledge such problems, it is equally necessary to assess what can be done to alleviate the emotional and behavioral concerns for these youth. It is done with the hopes of sharing information so that we can continue to identify, develop, and implement culturally appropriate intervention strategies.

Sociocultural Values and Norms

There is an inherent danger in giving simple answers as to how any group functions. There are not only differences between groups but also within groups. That having been said, certain sociocultural norms tend to hold true across Asian cultures, including Southeast Asian culture. A core value that is manifested in one form or another is that of the group versus the individual (Sue and Morishima, 1982; Shon and Ja, 1982; Uba, 1994; Lee, 1997; Leung,

Boehnlein, and Kinzie, 1997; Moore, Keopraseuth, Leung, and Chao, 1997; Huang, 1998). A person is viewed within the context of the group and is seen as an extension of his or her family, including one's ancestors (Shon and Ja, 1982; Lee, 1997; Fadiman, 1997). In the United States, great premium is placed on the role of the individual. We use such language as "doing your own thing," "speaking your own mind," "standing up for yourself," and "being a rugged individual." The goal of adolescence is to separate and individuate—to become independent and get ready to set out on your own. This is just the opposite for Asian cultures, which place a premium on the group and family, not the individual. The task of adolescence is to learn one's role in the family, the community, and society. This has great implications for doing family work, which will be discussed later in this chapter.

Southeast Asians tend to be strict in their discipline, expecting filial piety to be the norm. They give daughters less freedom than sons, avoid open, verbal communication between parent and child, and maintain social control through an expectation that there will be family order. Older siblings also share the responsibility of raising younger brothers and sisters and, acting as surrogate parents, have authority over the younger members of the family (Uba, 1994). They are also family-oriented, which includes reliance on the extended family (Le, 1983; Moore, Keopraseuth, Leung, and Chao, 1997; Leung, Boehnlein, and Kinzie, 1997). Parents and grandparents devote their lives to raising their children, who will, in turn, pay their respects to the elders and take care of them in their old age. Life is seen as a cycle in which one is indulged as a child, raised to be part of the larger family unit, then respected and indulged again as an elder.

Traditional Vietnamese culture has been strongly influenced by China (Leung, Boehnlein, and Kinzie, 1997). Confucianism adheres to a strict code of conduct that teaches order and the understanding of one's position in society. It maintains a clear hierarchy, with respect for elders being of utmost importance. Individuals must suppress their personal desires and submit to the needs of the family and society. Traditional beliefs are strongly maintained, as evidenced by the adherence to ancestor worship, even among those who are Catholic or Protestant. There are constant reminders that if a person behaves inappropriately, shame is brought to the entire family, including ancestors. Elders are to be respected, and it is expected that those who are younger remain quiet in their presence. Open disagreement is not accepted. When conflict does arise, other family members are called upon to help resolve the problem. Traditionally, children are seen as the property of their parents, who tend to be strict in their discipline. Sons and daughters are to follow the wishes of their parents, including their choice of spouses and careers (Leung, Boehnlein, and Kinzie, 1997).

The Laotian culture has been influenced by Hindu and Theravada Buddhism. Belief in Hinduism involves appeasing the soul and spirit world (Moore, Keopraseuth, Leung, and Chao, 1997), whereas Buddhism believes in reincarnation and karma. Buddhists also believe in selflessness and in being free from attachment to worldly possessions, even while remaining pragmatic in their approach to life. The Laotians are known to be peaceful, shy, and subdued (Fadiman, 1997; Moore, Keopraseuth, Leung, and Chao, 1997). There is a strong sense of kinship and reliance on extended family. Husbands are the head of the family, and women are expected to take care of the children and the home. Like other Asians, the Laotians place high value on the group and an understanding of one's relationship to others.

The Hmong are probably the least understood of the Southeast Asian populations. They are seen as fiercely independent but also are known to have a gentle side; seen as "unsophisticated and naïve," they can also be very resourceful. Living in the mountains of Laos, they are geographically isolated and have learned how to raise their families and maintain their culture under adverse conditions. They have a strong sense of self and have historically resisted assimilation into other cultures. They believe strongly in the spirit world and rely heavily on the *txiv neeb* (shaman) for help with everyday occurrences, from the birth of a child to helping solve family problems. Beliefs and traditions have been passed down through oral tradition, as they did not have a written language until the 1950s. The U.S. Bureau of the Census (1990) indicates they are the ones who remain most at risk for being linguistically isolated. They also have the highest percentage of individuals living in households at or below the poverty level. Coming from the mountains of Laos, they experienced severe culture shock upon arriving in the United States. This resulted in serious depression, PTSD, anxiety attacks, and other mental health problems. In spite of the many challenges they have had to face, they have taken on leadership roles and been very successful in organizing their communities.

Childrearing Customs

Southeast Asian parents were raised with strict codes of discipline, which may be viewed as abusive in the United States. To parents who have grown up with this philosophy, discipline and physical reprimands are often seen as one and the same. Children seeing their parents through the eyes of peers, child protection services, and school personnel begin to view their parents as abusive. This perception of their parents being unreasonable and overly strict drives yet another wedge between the generations. The issue is not whether the parents condone abuse or not but what constitutes appropriate discipline and who gets to define the parameters. It can be safely assumed that everyone wants what is in the best interest of the child. The question is how this is operationalized. For example, parents may feel it is in the best interest of the child to learn how to be obedient, whereas the case worker may feel it is in the best interest of the child to learn to speak up and express his or her feelings.

In Vietnamese culture, children are supposed to follow their parents' guidance and wishes, including the selection of future mates and career paths. It is the children's responsibility to "fulfill the dreams of the parents, often presented in the name of the 'family'" (Leung, Boehnlein, and Kinzie, 1997). For Laotian children, independent decision making is not a highly valued concept, and becoming an adult is in part measured by how they fulfill their obligation to the family (Moore, Keopraseuth, Leung, and Chao, 1997). For Cambodian families, children are considered independent at birth and then are expected to become increasingly interdependent. It is the child's responsibility to follow the wishes of the parents (Boehnlein, Leung, and Kinzie, 1997).

Early marriage is also a cultural norm in many Southeast Asian cultures and is seen as particularly desirable for females. Although it is changing, there is still pressure to marry young, thus possibly interfering with the girl's educational and career aspirations in this society. Adolescent females feel both direct and indirect pressure to marry before a certain age. Often, well-intentioned parents and relatives have warned young girls with the caution of remaining "on the shelf" too long. Although Southeast Asian communities in America have become more accepting of delaying marriage and encouraging the education of females, this is still an issue that presents great distress to many young Southeast Asian females.

Within the context of living in an agrarian society in Southeast Asia, early matches were desirable for a variety of reasons, including mortality rates, the connections the bride could bring with her, the emphasis on children, and the extra helping hand that was needed in the family. This is particularly true within the Hmong community. Socially, the concept of adolescence did not exist; an individual went from being a child to being an adult. This, coupled with the value placed on matching couples for the good of the family, negated a period when one would date, select a mate based on love, and establish a life separate from one's family. The situation, however, is quite different in the United States; traditional Hmong marriages result in almost certain conflict. A seventeen-year-old Southeast Asian male may complain that his sixteen-year-old wife acts too much like "a child," meaning that she still goes to the mall with friends and doesn't always make supper or do his laundry on time. The young wife, in turn, complains that her husband spends too much time playing video games and not enough time with her. According to the Hmong culture, however, she should make the demands of her husband and in-laws her priority. Because of the strong prevalence of male privilege in traditional Southeast Asian societies, the burden to make the marriage work falls primarily on the female.

Ecological or System Perspective

The ecological or system perspective takes into consideration the fact that an individual does not exist in a vacuum. Variables within one's world affect an individual's thoughts, behaviors, beliefs, emotional well-being, and ability to function competently. Factors include family, community, SES, education, domestic violence, racism, poverty, unemployment, peer influence, gangs, and stereotypes perpetuated by the media.

Another key factor influencing the overall functioning and dynamics of a community is the immigration process itself. When one looks at the Southeast Asian population in the United States, one sees a community in flux. Behavioral patterns, modes of communication, interpersonal relationships, family dynamics, and interactions with the outside community are continually changing. The overt manifestations of a culture (language and dress, for example) are usually the first aspects of a culture to change. The underlying values, however, are less prone to change but may not be as readily identifiable. In other words, as younger generations lose their Asian language abilities, the cultural values may actually exist but are difficult to recognize because they are transmitted in English. Southeast Asian youth may be adhering to traditional Asian values but are doing so in English and following Westernized behavior patterns. Recognizing this dynamic may help break through impasses in the therapeutic process. For example, being a "typical American girl" does not always equate with being a "bad Vietnamese daughter."

Negative, racist images in the media continue to plague contemporary Southeast Asian youth as they did Asian Americans in earlier generations. The stereotypes remain, with variations on a theme reflecting either the evil Ming the Merciless, the exotic Suzie Wong, the subservient Hop Sing, the inscrutable Charlie Chan, or the television kung fu master, Grasshopper, most of whom were portrayed by non-Asian actors. Helen Zia (2000) bemoans the fact that there are few positive role models to reflect back a healthy self-image for Asian American youth. Instead they are stuck with images that portray "gangsters, gooks, geishas, and geeks" (p. 109). Southeast Asian youth complain about getting into fights because they are tired of being called racist names, being teased for being small, having strange names and accents, or looking different.

Southeast Asian youth cannot be viewed outside the context of their family. Although there are tremendous influences outside the home, the experiences of the family cannot be denied. Although the majority of Southeast Asian youth are now born in America, nearly all have foreign-born parents. Communication between family members is hindered by the fact that many of the youth are not fluent in the native language of their parents, and the parents are not fluent in English. Each knows enough to coexist and be understood at a superficial level, but deeper communication is hindered by the fact that neither generation can adequately understand the other, either because of the lack of vocabulary or the lack of common values and behavioral expectations.

Many parents have an either-or perspective: either one disciplines the child (meaning physical punishment) or one does nothing for fear of being reported to the authorities. This dilemma does not go unnoticed by the children, who threaten their parents with, "Go ahead touch me . . . I'll call social services." The power differential has shifted, with children now having more control and authority than the parents in some areas of childrearing. Unaware of child protection laws in this country, the parents are afraid to reclaim their position of authority in the family. This inconsistent or total lack of discipline often results in behavioral problems for young people who do not have adequate supervision and guidance.

In contrast to the parent who feels intimidated and fails to provide adequate discipline is the parent who follows traditional Southeast Asian culture. In that case, parents and elders have absolute authority and expect unquestioned obedience. This respect for authority is extended to adult children in the family as well. To question an elder is highly disrespectful. However, in the United States children are taught to question what they do not understand. When children do this, Southeast Asian parents perceive questioning as a sign of disrespect. The children may not understand why the parents are upset and view them as overreacting and unreasonable. Adolescents point to the "freedom" their non-Asian peers seem to have, citing the fact that friends can date, participate in after-school activities, dress certain ways, wear make-up, and so on. Parents who are fearing that their children are becoming "too Westernized" may resort to excessive control, believing that is the best way to keep their child safe. This, unfortunately, ends up pushing the child even further away toward rebellion. Munzy found that homes with strict parental discipline were often cited by youths as a factor in running away.

And last, but most certainly not least, is the impact of current legislation on the Southeast Asian community. Legislation such as the Welfare Reform Act of 1966 places additional stress on Southeast Asian families. Lacking adequate English skills, many are required to seek employment that does not pay sufficiently to raise a family. Being forced to find employment without having time to gain the necessary language and employment skills almost guarantees that the individual will be trapped in an underpaid position. Citing the lower number of individuals on welfare is misleading; many are still living at the poverty level, even though they are employed. In the Spring of 2002, the current administration is pushing to increase the number of hours an individual must work per week to forty. This means there is even less time for an individual to learn English, improve his or her marketable skills, or take care of the children, leaving many children without appropriate supervision.

Another problem facing many Southeast Asian families is the growing anti-immigrant sentiment. In the Fall of 2000, powerful lobbying groups such as the American Medical Association and the American Psychiatric Association fought against the U.S. Department of Health and Human Services Office of Civil Rights Policy Guidance, which prohibits discrimination against persons with limited English proficiency (LEP) in federally funded health and social services. While "expressing concern" for the care of those with LEP, many in the medical profession stated that provision of services for this population was "too expensive."

The Policy Guidance states that each provider must look at the needs of the persons with LEP that they serve and make sure there are no access barriers based on language. The Policy Guidance goes on to explain that it is not acceptable to ask patients or consumers to bring their own interpreter, to ask untrained family members or staff to interpret, or to charge additional payments for interpreters. Such attempts to deny services only act to further isolate Southeast Asians and other LEP populations and increase the likelihood of additional stress, resulting in emotional and behavioral problems for the family.

Many states have lowered the age to try youths as adults. In Colorado, a youth can be tried as an adult as young as twelve and in Texas at the age of ten. In April 1996, the Anti-Terrorist and Effective Death Penalty Act broadened the categories for what constitutes a deportable offense, and in September of the same year, the Illegal Immigration Reform and Immigration Responsibility Act effectively removed the ability of Immigration and Naturalization Services (INS) to look at the merits of a case on an individual basis. Although most Southeast Asian youth are now born in America, a number of foreign-born youth are currently serving lengthy jail sentences, having been tried as adults. (It is difficult to obtain an exact count, as the Department of Corrections does not provide data based on nationality.) Once released from prison, they are then subject to deportation and reincarceration in the INS facility because the U.S. government wants to get rid of them, and Laos, Cambodia, and Vietnam will not accept them back. An individual could spend years in the INS jail after completing an original jail sentence. This issue is currently being debated in the courts, with no clear outcome in sight.

Mental Health Issues

When looking at the mental health status of Southeast Asian youth, two radically different perspectives begin to emerge. One offers the stereotypical view that Asian American youth have few if any problems. They are the class valedictorians who are held up as shining examples of how to succeed in the face of great adversity. They are living proof that Asians are able to overcome any obstacle and are indeed the model minority. A very different image has emerged over the past few years—that of the troubled youth, the gang banger, the tough, streetwise youth who is involved with extortion, home invasions, guns, and drugs. The reality is that neither picture is completely accurate, yet both exist.

As previously mentioned, the lives of Southeast Asian American youth are greatly influenced by the experiences of their parents. The impact of the war and the resettlement processes on the mental health of Southeast Asian refugees has been well documented (Chung and Okazaki, 1991; Kinzie, 1985, 1993; Lin, Masuda, and Tazuma, 1982). Premigration trauma events and refugee experiences were identified as significant predictors of psychological stress (Chung and Kagawa-Singer, 1993). Clinical studies have found that there are high levels of distress and psychiatric disorders among refugees and that depression and PTSD are the most prevalent disorders for this population (Kinzie and others, 1990). Approximately 50 percent of Southeast Asian refugees in the general population might have PTSD.

Cambodian refugees have been found to have particularly high rates of depression and PTSD (Kinzie and others, 1989, 1990). Many Cambodian adolescents were diagnosed as having depressive disorders and were seen as withdrawn (Sack, Angell, Kinzie, and

Rath, 1986). The trauma experienced in the early years appears to have long-lasting effects, as many Cambodian adolescents showed PTSD over an extended period of time (Abe, Zane, and Chun, 1994). Hmong had a prevalence rate of 80 percent of major depression at a mental health clinic (Kroll and others, 1989).

Although few mental health data on Southeast Asian youth exist, there are ethnic-specific data for juvenile delinquency and gang-related incidents. The fact that these figures even exist attests to the fact that this past decade has seen a sharp increase in juvenile delinquency and gang activity among AAPI youths, particularly Southeast Asians, and gangs now include female members. A few years ago, the number of AAPIs in the juvenile justice system were so few that AAPIs were categorized as "others." Although this still holds true in many instances, larger cities are beginning to collect data, looking at specific ethnic groups in the juvenile justice system.

According to the California Department of Justice, Bureau of Investigations 1998 Report on Gang Activity, there are approximately 25,000 Asian street gang members belonging primarily to Vietnamese, Cambodian, Laotian, and Hmong gangs; each gang varies in size between five to five hundred members. The average gang member ranges in age from fifteen to thirty years old. In the city of Westminster in Orange County, California, approximately 17 percent of all juvenile delinquency and 48 percent of all Asian delinquency offenses involve Asian gangs (U.S. Department of Justice, 2000).

The problem has received so much attention lately that many in the Asian American communities are reluctant to discuss the issue, lest it seem like all Southeast Asian youth are gang members. Like any situation, stereotyping has negative implications and must be treated with caution. Racial profiling occurs in many of the poorer neighborhoods, where the assumption is that if you are Vietnamese, Cambodian, Laotian, or Hmong and live in certain neighborhoods you must be a gang member. Names such as Street Killer Boys, Tiny Rascal Gangsters, Black Dragons, Natoma Boys, Asian Boy Crips, Asian Bloods, Oriental Boys, and Masters of Destruction are names that are well known to the police.

Aside from scattered information on Southeast Asian gangs, few data break information about AAPI youth down by ethnicity.

The following is a sample of data available on AAPI youth who are at risk for emotional and behavioral problems. Because the data are presented in aggregate form, it is not possible to determine the specific prevalence rate for Southeast Asian youth, but one can surmise that, given the known risk factors for Southeast Asians, it would not be surprising if the following data did not bear some relevance to the targeted population.

In a survey conducted by the Commonwealth Fund, 17 percent of Asian American boys in grades 5 through 12 reported physical abuse, as compared to 8 percent among white boys. Using a sample of 3,586, Louis Harris and Associates, Inc., found that 30 percent of Asian American girls in grades 5 through 12 reported depressive symptoms, as compared to 22 percent of white girls, 17 percent of African American girls, and 27 percent of Hispanic girls (Schoen and others, 1997).

Two subpopulations worth special note are those who immigrated during adolescence and adolescent females. Those who arrived in the United States during adolescence are at particular risk for emotional problems (Le, 1983; Nidorf, 1985). They left their home country before they were fully socialized in their native country and arrived too late to be fully acculturated here. The American education system fails to provide an adequate education for these students and merely passes them from grade to grade. Not feeling competent in either world, they experience academic failure and social isolation, which can result in frustration and low self-esteem. One very bright Vietnamese boy who came to the United States at thirteen resented school and the teachers who said he just wasn't trying hard enough. His father also had high expectations of him, which only exacerbated an already tense situation. He dealt with his pent-up frustration and anger by dropping out of school and eventually getting into serious trouble with the law.

Southeast Asian females are particularly vulnerable and are most likely to be caught between the two cultures. Expected to maintain a traditional role within the family, many girls are not encouraged to seek an education or to have a career. Those wishing to be more independent risk disapproval of the family. There are also serious social pressures to be a "good Vietnamese, Cambodian, Hmong, Laotian girl," which means she should not date or wear makeup. Sex education is deemed irrelevant and inappropriate, as being sexually active is completely out of the question. In some instances, this is taken to an extreme, as when a girl is sexually assaulted but no report is filed; this is seen as a way to protect her reputation. The fear is that if it became public knowledge that she had sexual relations of any kind, even if she was a victim, she would not be able to find a good partner for marriage. This may result in the girl remaining in the home with a perpetrator or having to be near someone in the community who has raped her. In one case, the victim was chastised by her mother for not recanting her story and was blamed for the breakup of the family. Needless to say, it is impossible to get accurate prevalence rates, but there have been several instances when incest or sexual assault has occurred and the service provider is unable to file a report due to lack of information. What is known, however, is that the girl will continue to suffer without the support she needs so she can cope with the situation. Adolescent females are at risk for suicide, depression, eating disorders, and substance use as a means to self-medicate or to control weight.

Even those who fit the "model minority" image are not safe from emotional problems. The pressure to be perfect is intense and no longer comes from just the family. Society now expects Asian American youth to excel academically. Not wishing to add to their parents' problems, many Southeast Asian youth feel the added pressure to do well and stay out of trouble—to be the model son or daughter. For some, the pressure becomes too great, resulting in depression. In an unpublished study done by the author, 40 percent of Southeast Asian college students reported they would contemplate suicide if the pressure to succeed became too great. In selected years between 1985 and 1996, AAPI females had the highest rates of suicide for females between the ages of fifteen and twenty-four, with the exception of Native American females in 1993 and 1996 (Centers for Disease Control and Prevention, 1998).

Uba (1994) identifies the Minority Identity Development model as a useful tool to assess the formation of an individual's ethnic identity. She goes on to state that although there are five identified stages of development, an individual does not necessarily pass through them in a linear fashion, graduating to a higher level and never returning to a previous stage. At one end of the spectrum is the Conformity Stage, when an individual wishes to completely adopt the cultural values of the dominant Euro-American culture to the exclusion of Asian values. As a person progresses through different stages, he or she addresses feelings of ambivalence toward both cultures (the Dissonance Stage), rejects the dominant group and becomes immersed in the Asian cultural values (the Resistance and Immersion Stage), and begins to question their previously held rigid beliefs (the Introspection Stage). Finally, in the synergetic Articulation and Awareness Stage, an individual objectively assesses the cultural values of the dominant as well as Asian communities. This means that an individual recognizes that valuing one's own ethnic identity does not require rejecting the value of the dominant society. What stage a Southeast Asian youth finds him- or herself at will depend on multiple factors, including peer pressure, acceptance or rejection by the dominant society, expectations of family, and personality, and will influence both self-perception and emotional and behavioral well-being.

Intervention and Treatment Approaches

Assessment Issues

The first step in working with any person is gaining an accurate picture of the individual in question. In the case of Southeast Asian youth, this also includes gathering information on the family, which may or may not include extended family members. In addition to any medical information that may affect the individual's cognitive or emotional functioning, the minimum information needed would include, age, ethnicity, gender, birth order, and place of birth. If foreign-born, further information should include age of arrival in the United States; native language; English proficiency; language spoken in the home; and family information, including parents' experience during the war; losses due to death, separation, or trauma; and diagnosis if there is major depression, PTSD, and so on. Information on family composition is also important. Is this a nuclear or extended family? Who lives in the household? Do they live in a predominantly Asian community or in a racially mixed neighborhood?

Accurate assessment and diagnosis is critical in putting together an effective treatment plan. It forms the basis for how an individual is perceived, how one views the circumstances that led to the current situation, what resources are available, what potential challenges to therapy exist, what strategies should be used, who gets to define the problem, and what constitutes a successful outcome. For example, it is important to know whether a person hearing voices is "blessed" and able to speak to spirits or is experiencing a psychotic episode. It is not required that the clinician personally believe in spirits, but he or she must respect the fact that this is a legitimate belief in Southeast Asian cultures. These beliefs are still held by many of the youth themselves, no matter how Westernized they have become. What the clinician must do is assess which reality is accurate. Obtaining a consultation is always recommended if there is any question. A basic rule of thumb to follow in providing culturally competent services is that extreme perspectives are usually the least helpful. For example, saying that culture accounts for everything is as dangerous as saying that culture plays no part in an individual's life.

A common situation resulting in the request for an evaluation of a child or adolescent is the fact that he or she is not learning. It is up to the evaluator to determine whether the difficulty in learning is due to a learning disability, auditory or visual perception problems, mental retardation, lack of English proficiency, or emotional-behavioral problems. It could be a combination of any of these, but accurate assessment has important implications for the treatment plan. Tutoring in English for a child with a learning disability may prove to be of little use. Likewise, prescribing Ritalin for a child who appears to be inattentive may be a costly error if the reason the child is not paying attention is that he does not understand English.

The following case studies illustrate the importance of conducting an accurate clinical assessment.

A sixteen-year-old Vietnamese female was brought into the emergency room because of an overdose of pain killers. The attending physician did the mental status exam with the aid of an interpreter and determined that the patient was suicidal. The client had been in the United States for little over a year, was separated from family members, and was very depressed about being here. She was not doing well in school, had few friends, and was suffering from severe back pain caused by an accident in Vietnam. All indications were that she had reasons to be depressed and had the means to harm herself. A few days earlier, the client's doctor had prescribed pain killers. The client was used to taking herbal medication and did not understand how potent Western medicine could be. She dutifully took the pills one at a time, according to the doctor's orders, but did so at five-minute intervals when the pain did not subside. By the time the pills did take effect, she had overdosed. Her boyfriend rushed her to the hospital, where she had her stomach pumped. During the mental status exam, the doctor asked if she was sad and feeling depressed, to which she replied yes. He also asked if she heard any voices; she answered yes. He asked if she had any strange thoughts, and again she replied yes; she said she talks to her dead grandfather. The doctor concluded that she was under severe stress, had become despondent, resulting in the suicide attempt, and diagnosed her as being depressed with psychotic features.

In interviewing her in Vietnamese, it became apparent that she was indeed very depressed but had no intentions of harming herself. She also was not experiencing auditory hallucinations but thought it was a hearing exam when asked if she heard voices. In addition, she was not delusional and indicated that she talked to her grandfather in her dreams. The interpreter failed to interpret the word *dream* accurately, which led to the miscommunication. When it was clear that she was not suicidal, she was released from the emergency room, which was actually traumatizing her and adding to her emotional distress. She was followed up on an outpatient basis by the Vietnamese clinician, who worked with her depression and was able to help monitor her pain medication.

A seven-year-old Hmong boy was brought in for a second evaluation when he continued to have problems in school. He had difficulty learning, was becoming increasingly frustrated, and started acting out in the classroom. The original report indicated that he was not learning because English was his second language and recommended that he get a tutor. That having failed, the teachers concluded that the young boy was just being oppositional and was deemed a behavior problem. The first evaluation was conducted in English at the psychologist's office. The second evaluation was conducted with the assistance of a Hmong caseworker and an Asian American speech pathologist who was familiar with Asian families. The initial meeting was a home visit to gather information from the parents and view the child in a familiar setting. It was quickly apparent that the boy did indeed speak English as he played with his younger siblings but was afraid to speak in the psychologist's office. In addition, the boy felt very uncomfortable being asked to perform tasks that were completely foreign to him. Nothing in the room was familiar to him, including the fact that the psychologist did not look like him or anyone in his family. A follow-up session was scheduled at the school, and the assessment was conducted in both English and Hmong. It was discovered that he had audio-perceptual problems that hindered his ability to process information that required him to listen. Using the tutor only to learn a second language frustrated the student and did not address the underlying cause of his problems. His frustration level and consequent behavioral problems began to decrease when he received appropriate help with the learning disability and was then better able to make use of the tutor.

Home visits are a culturally appropriate assessment and intervention strategy that can help break through an impasse and help foster the therapeutic alliance. This runs counter to many traditional Western forms of therapy, which place a premium on boundaries and require the individual to come to the therapist's office at a set time for a set time, usually for one hour. Although this model can be effective, it is an artificial construct and is counter to how most people communicate. One drawback to home visits is that they are time consuming and cannot realistically be used in all situations. However, they can be cost-effective in the long run by preventing a crisis and reducing the overall number of sessions needed.

Treatment Interventions

There is such stigma associated with mental health in the Southeast Asian community that many will not come in for therapy unless there is a crisis. Coming to the therapist's office only compounds the perception that parents are "bad" and, having failed to raise their children properly, must now turn to a complete stranger to make things better. The shame and loss of face associated with this can drive a silent wedge into the therapeutic process and may keep the parent from returning to future sessions. Doing home visits does not mean that boundaries are not respected. Some situations would be considered inappropriate, and it must be clear why the home visit is being conducted. When done properly, much clinical information can be obtained by seeing the family in the home. The clinician can gain a better understanding of the physical environment that affects the daily functioning of the family. Is there adequate space? Are family members crowded into one or two bedrooms? Is the house clean? Is there adequate food? Is the neighborhood safe? Is there any place for peace and quiet? Is there strong evidence of particular religious or cultural practices?

Traditional Western modes of therapy result in a subtle and sometimes not-so-subtle power differential, which adds to the parents' loss of status. For Southeast Asian parents, this is particularly critical. They have already suffered tremendous losses: the loss of country, the loss of family members, the inability to earn an adequate income, the loss of status in their children's eyes, and the loss of feeling competent in a foreign country. Going on an occasional home visit helps equalize the playing field, particularly in the initial phase of treatment. As soon as the mother offers a cup of tea, she is no longer the "bad" mother but is given the opportunity to be the gracious hostess, thus giving her back some of the dignity she has lost. Seeing the family on their turf also provides an opportunity to talk about things other than problems. The clinician can gather much information by discussing pictures on the walls or objects in the house that have particular significance. The family should also be encouraged to talk about family successes. It is important for the family to share positive moments in the presence of the clinician. This helps reduce the stigma of being a flawed family and may actually highlight that some things are going quite well. Understanding the struggles of their parents can also bring about children's heightened sense of appreciation and respect toward the parents.

> In one case, the trust developed during the home visits was invaluable when a child abuse report had to be filed. Understanding that the clinician was a mandated reporter, the father did not challenge the report, acknowledging that he had hit the daughter, who was defiant and had repeatedly been disrespectful to her mother. Instead of questioning the clinician, the father asked the daughter to be present at the court hearing. The clinician was able to testify on behalf of the father, who was very remorseful over his actions, stating that this was the first time he had touched his daughter and the likelihood of this happening again was slim. The daughter also began to realize how destructive her behavior had become and was able to assume more responsibility for her actions. The crisis could have split the family further apart, but in this instance, the home visits had helped foster communication among family

members so that the crisis could be used to bring them closer; each side was now willing to listen to the other.

Family Treatment

Working with the family is one of the most challenging aspects of working with children and adolescents. Doing home visits is but one way to improve communication with the parents and move the therapeutic process along. Because home visits are not always feasible, it is important to understand family dynamics and how to work within them, regardless of the physical setting. Irrespective of whether the clinician thinks the head of the household, usually the father, is behaving appropriately or not, the proper respect must be shown if there is to be a second session. Until the relationship and trust have been thoroughly established, an open, direct challenge will most likely result in a premature termination of the therapy. Likewise, asking the children to openly express their disagreement or anger toward the parents may result in the parents withdrawing from therapy. They will see the therapist as a person who is insensitive to Asian values and is encouraging disrespect among their children. Only by forming an alliance with the parent and ensuring that their position has been respected can the therapist begin to address the more difficult aspects of therapy.

Sometimes the parents and youth need to have their "private" time so they can openly discuss their feelings and concerns. If the therapy is being conducted in two languages, this may mean the English-speaking clinician works with the child while the clinician works with the parents in their native language. This requires solid coordination and clear communication between the clinicians so they do not inadvertently split the family and add to the miscommunication. When the family is brought back together in the session, it is important to clarify expectations of the family members, as well as what each person will and will not do.

Use of Interpreters

It is frequently necessary to use an interpreter when working with Southeast Asian parents. The most important guideline in this situation is to use qualified, trained interpreters *only*. Far too frequently, someone who is not properly trained to interpret is used. Because the purpose of using an interpreter is to gather information accurately, the use of someone who is not qualified may result in inaccurate information. A family member or untrained interpreter may not translate information he or she deems to be embarrassing or shameful or may not understand what is being asked. This is critical in the event of a mental status exam, in which one needs to get an accurate picture of the individual's mental state and emotional functioning. The use of an inappropriate interpreter can be damaging to establishing a healthy relationship with the parents and can negatively affect the therapeutic alliance.

Under no circumstances, except in a true emergency that requires immediate attention or for very minor information, should the child (including the adolescent) be used as an interpreter. There are numerous reasons for this guideline. First, it is inappropriate to ask the child to speak on behalf of the parent, who is once again placed in a one-down position. This continues the loss of face for the parent and gives too much power and authority to the child. Second, having the child interpret also places him or her in the precarious situation of potentially having to reveal private information about the family. This compromises the child's relationship with other family members and may further damage the relationship with the parents. The child must choose between obeying an authority figure or betraying the privacy of the family. Third, the child may also be asked to interpret information that goes beyond his or her cognitive abilities. There is no guarantee that the information will even be interpreted accurately, which negates the usefulness of the information and may have needlessly jeopardized his or her role in the family.

Similarly, do not use one youth to interpret for another. In one example, the staff at a detention facility felt very resourceful because they had a fifteen-year-old Vietnamese youth sit in on the intake of another Vietnamese boy brought in for theft. The accuracy of any information the youth translated back to the caseworker should have been questioned. Even if the individual had wanted to cooperate, telling the truth may have jeopardized his safety.

Using a holistic approach is important in ascertaining what is really going on. To focus only on the youth as the cause of the problem misses many other factors affecting family dynamics. The parents may be underemployed due to limited English skills; they may be suffering from PTSD or major depression and are therefore not capable of providing adequate supervision; or there might be medical problems that have not been addressed. A case manager may be able to help guide the parents through multiple systems to get the help they need.

Mentorship and Youth Development Programs

The use of mentors is also an effective way of working with adolescents and has been shown to be particularly effective with minority youth (Tierney and Grossman, 2000). A healthy relationship with someone who can positively influence a young person's life is one way to counter the impact of those factors that place a youth at risk for substance use or other delinquent behavior (Hawkins, Catalano, and Miller, 1992; Office of Juvenile Justice and Delinquency Prevention, 1997). The mentor can also help bridge the cultural gap between the youth and his or her parents. Caution must be used, however, not to elevate the mentor in the eyes of the youth at the cost of making the foreign-born parents seem all the more socially inept.

Much has been learned in working with at-risk youth. The most effective programs are those that are multifaceted. Helping a youth manage emotions is only one aspect of working with a young person. It is not sufficient that the individual merely knows what *not* to do; it is also important to learn new skills, build competency, and help the person learn to make healthy decisions. Tutoring and other activities that enhance the individual's academic performance are important. Social learning projects also help the person think beyond his or her own needs. Part of this is to build bicultural competency in the Southeast Asian youth—the ability to function properly in either the world of their traditional parents or the more Westernized world of their peers. Providing multiethnic programs is another way to enhance positive relationships between groups, and they allow the youth to work through cross-cultural conflict and issues of racism—conflicts that frequently result in fights. They learn to communicate with each other and respect the other's culture.

Significant Trends and Future Issues

Working with Southeast Asian youth and their families requires re-evaluating what constitutes culturally appropriate services. The field must continually assess itself in terms of what works and what does not. In order to adequately answer these questions, several areas are of concern and must be addressed:

1. *Collecting appropriate data so as to get an accurate picture of the population in question.* This means disaggregating data to look at ethnicity, gender, and generational status.
2. *Identifying effective programs and providing technical assistance to other communities in need of services.* One must look at both ethnic-specific programs and programs that are multiethnic in perspective. For communities with lower concentrations of Southeast Asians, the latter may be the only feasible model.
3. *Conducting culturally appropriate research and evaluation.* It is important to use appropriate instruments and outcome measures to assess the effectiveness of an intervention strategy and identify what can be done in the most cost-efficient manner possible.
4. *Increasing capacity building.* This is essential and has been identified as a primary area of concern in virtually every community, regardless of size and number of Southeast Asians.

Capacity building includes training bilingual paraprofessionals, as well as retraining professionals who most likely went through programs that did not adequately address cultural competency, particularly as it relates to Southeast Asians. Being bilingual, in and of itself, is not sufficient. What may result is merely insensitivity in two languages.

Blending primary health and mental health, particularly for the adult population, is an important model to look at and was cited in the Surgeon General's report (U.S. Department of Health and Human Services, 1999) as an area that needs further attention. Given the stigma associated with mental health, an individual is more likely to see a physician than a mental health clinician to deal with the stomachache, headache, lack of sleep, or loss of appetite that may be due to depression. As was mentioned previously in this chapter, the experiences of the parents may play a critical role in the emotional functioning of the youth. It is therefore important for the caseworker to also assess and help the parents as they navigate through rough waters. Racism, legislation that is anti-immigrant, trauma associated with the war, and dealing with stresses brought on by the immigration process itself are all factors that can profoundly affect the lives of Southeast Asians. Much has been learned in the past twenty-five years since the Southeast Asians started coming to the United States in large numbers. Many more resources are needed, however, if the field is to be truly effective in implementing a culturally competent service delivery system.

References

Abe, J. S., Zane, N. W., and Chun, K. "Differential Responses to Trauma: Migration-Related Discrimination of Post-Traumatic Stress Among Southeast Asian Refugees." *Journal of Community Psychology,* 1994, *22*(2), 121–135.

Benjamin, M. P., and Morgan, P. C. *Refugee Children Traumatized by War and Violence: The Challenge Offered to the Service Delivery System.* Washington, D.C.: Child and Adolescent Service System Program Technical Assistance Center, Georgetown University, 1989.

Boehnlein, J. K., Leung, P. K., and Kinzie, J. D. "Cambodian American Families." In E. Lee (ed.), Working with Asian Americans: A Guide for Clinicians. New York: Guilford Press, 1997.

Centers for Disease Control and Prevention. *Vital Statistics for Years 1950–1996 and Unpublished Hispanic Population Estimates.* Rockville, Md.: National Center for Health Statistics, 1998.

Chung, R. C., and Kagawa-Singer, M. "Predictors of Psychological Distress Among Southeast Asian Refugees." *Social Science and Medicine,* 1993, *36,* 631–639.

Chung, R. C., and Okazaki, S. "Counseling Americans of Southeast Asian Descent: The Impact of the Refugee Experience." In C. C. Lee and B. L. Richardson (eds.), *Multicultural Issues in Counseling: New Approaches to Diversity.* Alexandria, Va.: American Association for Counseling and Development, 1991.

Fadiman, A. *The Spirit Catches You and You Fall Down: A Hmong Child, Her American Doctors, and the Collision of Two Cultures.* New York: Farrar, Straus and Giroux, 1997.

Hawkins, J. D., Catalano, R. F., and Miller, J. Y. "Risk and Protective Factors for Alcohol and Other Drug Problems in Adolescence and Early Adulthood." *Psychological Bulletin,* 1992, *112,* 64–105.

Huang, L. "Asian American Adolescents." In E. Lee (ed.), *Working with Asian Americans: A Guide for Clinicians.* New York: Guilford Press, 1997.

Huang, L. "Southeast Asian Refugee Children and Adolescents." In J. T. Gibbs, L. N. Huang, and Associates, *Children of Color: Psychological Interventions with Culturally Diverse Youth.* San Francisco: Jossey-Bass, 1998.

Kinzie, J. D. "Overview of Clinical Issues in the Treatment of Southeast Asian Refugees." In T. C. Owen (ed.), *Southeast Asian Mental Health: Treatment, Prevention, Services, Training and Research.* Washington, D.C.: U.S. Department of Health and Human Services, 1985.

Kinzie, J. D. "Posttraumatic Effects and Their Treatment Among Southeast Asian Refugees." In J. Wilson and B. Raphael (eds.), *International Handbook of Traumatic Stress Syndromes.* New York: Plenum Press, 1993.

Kinzie, J. D., and others. "A Three-Year Follow-up of Cambodian Young People Traumatized as Children." *Journal of American Academy of Child and Adolescent Psychiatry,* 1989, *28,* 501–504.

Kinzie, J. D., and others. "The Prevalence Rate of PTSD and Its Clinical Significance Among Southeast Asian Refugees." *American Journal of Psychiatry,* 1990, *147*(7), 913–917.

Kroll, J., and others. "Depression and Posttraumatic Stress Disorder in Southeast Asian Refugees." *American Journal of Psychiatry,* 1989, *146,* 1592–1597.

Kumpfer, K. L. *Strengthening America's Families: Promising Parenting and Family Strategies for Delinquency Prevention. A User's Guide.* Washington, D.C.: U.S. Department of Justice, Office of Juvenile Justice and Delinquency Prevention, 1993.

Le, D. "Mental Health and Vietnamese Children." In G. J. Powell, J. Yamamoto, A. Romero, and A. Morales (eds.), *The Psychosocial Development of Minority Group Children.* New York: Brunner/Mazel, 1983.

Lee, E. "The Assessment and Treatment of Asian American Families." In E. Lee (ed.), *Working with Asian Americans: A Guide for Clinicians.* New York: Guilford Press, 1997.

Lee, L. C., and Zhan, G. "Psychosocial Status of Children and Youths." In L. C. Lee and N.W.S. Zane (eds.), *Handbook of Asian American Psychology.* Thousand Oaks, Calif.: Sage, 1999.

Leung, P. K., Boehnlein, J. K., and Kinzie, J. D. "Vietnamese American Families." In E. Lee (ed.), *Working with Asian Americans: A Guide for Clinicians.* New York: Guilford Press, 1997.

Lin, K., Masuda, M., and Tazuma, L. "Adaptational Problems of Vietnamese Refugees: Three Case Studies in Clinic and Field." *The Psychiatric Journal of the University of Ottawa,* 1982, *7,* 173–183.

Loescher, G., and Scanlan, J. *Calculated Kindness: Refugees and America's Half-Open Door, 1945 to the Present.* New York: Free Press, 1986.

Moore, D. *Dark Sky, Dark Land: Stories of the Hmong Boy Scouts of Troop 100.* Eden Prairie, Minn.: Tessera Publishing, 1989.

Moore, L. J., Keopraseuth, K. O., Leung, P. K., and Chao, L. H. "Laotian American Families. In E. Lee (ed.), *Working with Asian Americans: A Guide for Clinicians.* New York: Guilford Press, 1997.

Nguyen, N. A., and Williams, H. L. "Transition from East to West: Vietnamese Adolescents and Their Parents." *American Academy of Child and Adolescent Psychiatry,* 1989, *28,* 505–515.

Nidorf, J. "Mental Health and Refugee Youths: A Model for Diagnostic Training." In T. Owens (ed.), *Southeast Asian Mental Health: Treatment, Prevention, Services, Training, and Research.* Washington, D.C.: U.S. Department of Health and Human Services, 1985.

Office of Juvenile Justice and Delinquency Prevention. *Juvenile Offenders and Victims: 1997 National Report.* Washington, D.C.: U.S. Department of Justice, 1997.

Prong, L. L. "Childhood Bereavement Among Cambodians: Cultural Considerations." *The Hospice Journal,* 1995, *10*(2), 51–64.

Reimers, D. *Still the Golden Door: The Third World Comes to America.* New York: Columbia University Press, 1985.

Rousseau, C., and Draper, A. "The Impact of Culture on the Transmission of Trauma: Refugees' Stories and Silence Embodied in Their Children's Lives." In Y. Danieli (ed.), *International Handbook of Multigenerational Legacies of Trauma.* New York: Plenum Press, 1998.

Sack, W., Angell, R. H., Kinzie, J. D., and Rath, B. "The Psychiatric Effects of Massive Trauma on Cambodian Children: The Family, the Home, and School." *Journal of the American Academy of Child Psychiatry,* 1986, *25,* 377–383.

Schoen, C., and others. *The Commonwealth Fund Survey of the Health of Adolescent Girls.* Boston: The Commonwealth Fund, November 1997.

Shon, S., and Ja, D. "Asian Families." In M. McGoldrick, J. K. Pearce, and J. Giordano (eds.), *Ethnicity and Family Therapy* (pp. 208–228). New York: Guilford Press, 1982.

Sue, S., and Morishima, J. *The Mental Health of Asian Americans.* San Francisco: Jossey-Bass, 1982.

Tanaka, J. S., Ebreo, A., Linn, N., and Morera, O. F. "Research Methods: The Construct Validity of Self-Identity and Its Psychological Implications." In L. C. Lee and W. S. Zane (eds.), *Handbook of Asian American Psychology.* Thousand Oaks, Calif.: Sage, 1998.

Tierney, J., and Grossman, J. B. "What Works in Promoting Positive Youth Development: Mentoring." In M. P. Kluger and G. Alexander (eds.), *What Works in Child Welfare.* Washington, D.C.: U.S. Child Welfare League of America, 2000.

Uba, L. *Asian Americans: Personality Patterns, Identity, and Mental Health.* New York: Guilford Press, 1994.

Ung, L. *First They Killed My Father: A Daughter of Cambodia Remembers.* New York: HarperCollins, 2000.

U.S. Bureau of the Census. *Profiles of Asians and Pacific Islanders: Selected Characteristics.* Washington, D.C.: U.S. Department of Commerce, 1990.

U.S. Department of Health and Human Services. *Mental Health: A Report of the Surgeon General.* Rockville, Md.: National Institute of Mental Health, 1999.

U.S. Department of Justice. *Fact Sheet.* Washington, D.C.: Office of Juvenile Justice and Delinquency Prevention, February 2000.

U.S. Department of Justice. *Juvenile Offenders and Victims: 1999 National Report.* Washington, D.C.: Office of Juvenile Justice and Delinquency Prevention, 2000.

Wilkinson, A. "A Changed Vision of God." *New Yorker,* January 24, 1994, pp. 52–68.

Zia, H. *Asian American Dreams: The Emergence of an American People.* New York: Farrar, Straus & Giroux, 2000.

Part Four

Hispanic-Latino Population Groups

In this section of the book, we focus on three of the major Hispanic-Latino ethnic groups who have been incorporated into the United States since the U.S. war with Mexico, which took place from 1846 to 1848; two-thirds of Mexican territory was ceded to the United States by the Treaty of Guadalupe Hidalgo in 1848. During the first half of the twentieth century, the Spanish-speaking population increased sharply, as Mexicans moved north to California and the Southwestern states for farm labor jobs and higher wages. Similarly, the population of Puerto Ricans and Cubans on the East Coast, particularly in Florida, New York, and the Northeast, were seeking political and economic freedom for their families after World War II, the Cuban Revolution in 1959, and the Puerto Rican Nationalist Movement in the 1950s and 1960s.

Between 1980 and 2000, the official Hispanic-Latino population in the United States doubled from 14.6 to 35.3 million, or 13.3 percent of the total population (U.S. Bureau of the Census, 2001). Demographers predict that Latinos will make up over 24 percent of the nation's total population by 2050 and one-third of youth under age nineteen.

Since the early 1980s, Central Americans have been the most recent Spanish-speaking group to immigrate to the United States, propelled by a series of civil wars, political violence, and economic instability in countries such as El Salvador, Guatemala, and Nicaragua. They have primarily settled on the East and West Coasts, swelling the ranks of Cubans, Puerto Ricans, Dominicans, Mexicans, Ecuadorians, and Peruvians who preceded them.

As among Asian Americans, there is great diversity among Hispanic groups, ranging from successful Cuban entrepreneurs to Puerto Rican service workers to Mexican American farm laborers. In all of these New World countries, there is also a legacy of racial mixing among the indigenous "Indios," white European colonial settlers, and African slaves, which has produced a heterogeneous population of people with a wide range of skin colors, hair textures, and physical features. As Norita Vlach suggests in Chapter Seven, many Central Americans have "fragmented identities"; they are conflicted about their racial heritage, their social status, and their national identity. This identity conflict is also reflected in the various terms they use to describe themselves (Latinos, Chicanos, Ladinos, Chapines, Salvis), in contrast to the generic term *Hispanics*, which is used by the U.S. government to encompass all Spanish-speaking people. As the authors in this section note, the label *Hispanic* is unwelcome and controversial to many people of Spanish descent.

Sociocultural Characteristics

Central Americans, Mexican Americans, and Puerto Ricans share a number of sociocultural characteristics as Latino population groups (see Garcia-Preto, 1996). First, they share Spanish as a common language; it was transported to the New World by the Spanish explorers and soldiers. Second, the majority are Catholics, although other religions have recently made inroads into these immigrant communities, notably Protestant evangelical denominations. Latino versions of Catholicism have incorporated beliefs and practices of indigenous spiritual beliefs; in several countries, progressive priests have advocated a social and political agenda to improve the living conditions of the poor peasants and working-class laborers.

Third, Latinos have a shared history of "conquest and colonization," which has contributed to their ambivalence about institutional authority, politicians, and Western culture. As Vlach describes in Chapter Seven, the liberation struggles of the late twentieth century in Central and South America, which were aimed at eliminating widespread social oppression by authoritarian governments, displaced millions of people throughout the regions and launched the mass movement of refugees and immigrants to the United States seeking economic and political stability.

Fourth, the family has a very important place in Latino societies; the extended family is seen as a source of social support, financial assistance, and emotional nurturance. In all of these societies, the mother plays a dominant role within the home; maintains close bonds with her children; and defers to the father as the head of the family, responsible for major transactions with the external world. Godparents (*compadres*) are enlisted to assist in child-rearing. Although this varies among the three countries represented here, gender and age roles are fairly rigid, with young males allowed more social and sexual freedom than young females and younger people showing deference and *respeto* to older people.

As Kurt C. Organista notes in Chapter Eight, there are several other values that Latino societies emphasize in childrearing and in interpersonal and family relationships. These include *personalismo* (the ability to build personal relationships with others), *bien educado* (the ability to display good manners and consideration of others), *machismo* (the ability of a man to take care of his children and family obligations), and *simpatia* (the ability to avoid conflict with others).

Finally, as Jaime E. Inclán and Mabel E. Quiñones emphasize in Chapter Nine, despite their growing numbers, Latinos continue to endure high levels of poverty, racial discrimination (especially for dark-skinned, low-income Latinos), economic exploitation (especially for undocumented workers), and lack of access to social, educational, and health resources. Due to the high number of Latino immigrants without health insurance, their children and youth are particularly at risk for disabling health and mental health disorders (see U.S. Department of Health and Human Services, 2001).

Implications for Assessment and Treatment

Latino societies also share some traditional belief systems about health and mental health that have important implications for assessment and treatment. From this perspective, mental illness or emotional distress may be caused by supernatural forces such as the evil eye (*mal de ojo*) or witches (*embrujadas*). Folk illness can be caused by such internal factors as indigestion (*empacho*) or external factors such as fright (*susto*) or envy (*envidia*).

Latinos may seek the services of a *curandera* (folk-healer) for such folk illnesses or turn to a priest to confess their transgressions before they will see a mental health professional for any psychological or somatic symptoms. It is important for clinicians to ask about their conceptions of their symptoms, their help-seeking patterns, and their expectations for help from western-trained professionals.

In their efforts to adapt to an Anglo American society, Latino youth have experienced cultural conflicts in the schools, as reflected in their high school dropout rates; cultural transition in the community, as reflected in their high rates of gang membership; and social marginality in the society, as reflected in their high rates of substance abuse, teen pregnancy, and depression, as Organista documents in Chapter Eight.

The authors of the three chapters in this section recommend family-centered interventions for Latino youth, as well as cognitive-behavior therapy and crisis intervention for those immigrants and refugees diagnosed with posttraumatic stress disorder.

As the youthful Latino populations continue to expand throughout the nation, they will pose a challenge to clinicians who should be knowledgeable about their immigration histories, their cultural values and belief systems, and their bicultural identities, as they cope with cultural transition. Clinicians should also become familiar with the most culturally appropriate and effective modalities of treatment for these youth and their families, who will constitute the largest single group of children and adolescents in American society.

References

Garcia-Preto, N. "Latino Families: An Overview." In M. McGoldrick, J. Giordano, and J. K. Pearce (eds.), *Ethnicity and Family Therapy.* (2nd ed.) New York: Guilford Press, 1996.

U.S. Bureau of the Census. *Statistical Abstract of the United States, 2001.* (121st ed.) Washington, D.C.: U.S. Department of Commerce, 2001.

U.S. Department of Health and Human Services. *Mental Health: Culture, Race and Ethnicity.* Supplement to *Mental Health: A Report of the Surgeon General.* Rockville, Md.: U.S. Department of Health and Human Services, 2001.

Chapter Seven

Central American Children and Adolescents

Norita Vlach

> *When a man dies, people are afraid of his bones. But his*
> *essence is not lost. It remains whole and lives on in his*
> *sons and daughters.*
> POPUL VUH[1]

More than two million Central Americans are acknowledged by the U.S. Bureau of the Census in 2000 as being U.S. residents (Suárez-Orozco and Suárez-Orozco, 2001). Yet it is impossible to count the numbers of Central Americans in the United States accurately because so many are here without legal documentation and do not want to be counted. Many are children and youth whose parents have sought political asylum in the past two decades. Although they share similarities with other Latino youth, Central American youth have in common two important distinctions that are usually overlooked by clinicians and policymakers. One is the legacy of war. Another is a fragmented identity—or an "identity at the crossroads." Since the 1980s, youth from the various countries of the Central American region have become more visible, and questions have been raised as to how they may differ from Mexican and Caribbean youth, who have been the traditional Latino immigrants in American society.

In the past century, a continuing stream of immigrant and refugee families and children has moved north to the United States from the countries of Central America. One large group, primarily of war refugees, arrived in the 1980s. From 1998 to 2000, the U.S. Immigration and Naturalization Service reported apprehending over 1.5 million each year at Southwest border crossings. Close to half of the Central Americans were Hondurans, with Salvadorans and Guatemalans the next-largest groups. Those seeking asylum tended to be mainly Salvadoran and Guatemalan ("INS Border Apprehensions," n.d.).[2]

Central Americans have been a mobile population, dating back to the Spanish conquest and to centuries of political and social upheaval. Contact between diverse racial and socioeconomic groups is, in many cases, the consequence of rape and outrageous violation. Over several generations, racially mixed populations have produced descendants who are heirs to ambiguous social, racial, and cultural positions and identities.

In an earlier era, many Central Americans, especially the professional, educated, and skilled-worker classes, followed the path northward on the heels of economic recessions and political repression; they were seeking opportunities in the United States for economic advancement. The Immigration Act of 1965 reflected the civil rights movement of the 1960s by eliminating the preference for immigrants of European extraction (mostly white) and changing to an equal quota system for all nationalities. Central Americans took advantage of the new welcome mat, and the volume of immigrants and refugees, including children, increased dramatically.

When revolution and war erupted in successive Central American countries in the 1970s, the U.S. response was swift. The national political pendulum had swung to the right, ushering in a new era of immigration policy restrictions. Although overall population size and growth was certainly a concern, it was the darker complexion of new immigrants that alarmed the public more than higher immigration rates per se. These new residents were not familiar, "meltable" Europeans but populations of different races, languages, and cultural traditions (Córdova and Kury, 2001). At a time when the United States was becoming more protective of its borders and less willing to provide services to new immigrants, Central Americans were hastily packing up and crossing frontiers, looking for safe havens.

Refugees of all ages came, fleeing social inequality and disaster, political terror, grinding poverty, earthquakes, and hurricanes.

Endemic civil unrest and low- to high-intensity warfare engulfed the Central American region in waves, leading to kidnappings, massacres, lawlessness, destruction of basic public resources and infrastructure, and the pulling apart of families. The impact of these waves of traumatic events on families and individual children (many of whom came as "unaccompanied minors") was profound. Many came openly as immigrants. Seeking the American dream of prosperity and a better life, they adopted an American identity and left the past behind. For some, this is known as "the cover story"[3] (Schreiber, 1973). Others left only "temporarily," with the intent of going back home as soon as *la situación*[4] improved. Most have not returned, and their children are becoming acculturated in ways that parents have not expected.

Central American youth in the United States struggle today with their "identity at a crossroads." They must resolve both the pressures to acculturate and pressures to come to terms with what they may and may not know of their past. In general, their cultural identity tends to be conflicted due to the powerful influence of the dominant U.S. culture and their already fragmented national identity.

This chapter begins with a review of what the 2000 census data tell us about the demographics of Latinos, particularly Central American populations in the United States. It continues with a discussion of the historical waves of Central American immigration from four countries and the effect of social, ethnic, and other types of status on youth in the United States. Family structure and cultural values are explored, as well as some clinical profiles of problematic functioning, particularly in relation to trauma. How the clinician uses this material in developing a cultural assessment is presented in bulleted guidelines. Some suggested interventions with Central American youth and their families follow. Implications of the foregoing for policy rounds out the discussion. Of particular concern are undocumented status and bilingual education, as well as access to high-quality education, health insurance, health care, and bilingual and culturally competent providers.

Demographic Profile

Demographic data about the diverse Central American population is summarized in the following section.

Geographical and Age Distribution

Predictions by demographers of a dramatic increase in the proportion of Latinos in the United States have been confirmed. Factors contributing to this surge are an aging non-Latino population,
high immigration rates, and higher birth rates (than among non-
Latinos) among a younger Latino immigrant population (Hayes-
Bautista, Schink, and Chapa, 1988). Nationally, 35.7 percent of
Latinos are under the age of eighteen, compared to 29.5 percent
of non-Hispanic whites (Therrien and Ramirez, 2001).

Central Americans are a minority (about 5 percent) of the
total Latino population in the United States; they are more recent
immigrants and are somewhat more scattered geographically.
Central American population centers are slightly different from
those for other Latino groups. Regions of highest Central American concentration are the South (34.6 percent), the Northeast
(32.3 percent), and the West (28.2 percent). The increased diaspora of indigenous Maya throughout Central America, as well
as the United States, has been a contemporary phenomenon of
note (Loucky, Moors, and Moors, 2000). In 1990, the INS detained 8,500 children at the southwestern U.S. border, 70 percent
of whom were unaccompanied; most were from Central and South
America[5] ("Slipping Through the Cracks," 1997; Therrien and
Ramirez, 2001).

Poverty, Income, and Education

In the current census, poverty rates for Central and South American children are now calculated to be 16.7 percent, over twice that
of non-Hispanic white children, whose poverty rates are 7.7 percent. Income levels of $35,000 or more are earned by 24.5 percent
of Central and South American households, compared to 49.3 percent of non-Hispanic whites. Central and South American unemployment rates are lower than those of Mexicans and Puerto Ricans
(5.1 percent compared to 6.8 percent) but are still higher than the
3.4 percent rate of non-Hispanic whites. In addition, compared to
non-Hispanic whites, Central and South Americans are also more

likely to earn lower wages, have lower educational achievement, be unmarried, and not be legal residents or citizens (Therrien and Ramirez, 2001).

Dropout rates for Latino students are four times those of non-Hispanic whites. One and one-half million Hispanic students were dropouts in 2000, and more than half (62.5 percent) of foreign-born Latino youth of high school age never enrolled in school (National Center for Education Statistics, 2001). The Central and South American rates of high school graduation are slightly better than those of Latinos as a whole (64.3 percent compared to 57.0 percent) but are still significantly below the 88.4 percent of non-Hispanic whites (Therrien and Ramirez, 2001). These dropout figures are also in some dispute; depending on how they are calculated, statistical estimates report anywhere from 64.1 percent to only 54.0 percent of eligible Latino youth as completing high school in 1998 (Greene, 2001, 2002). Higher proportions of incarceration for Latino youth are reported than for white youth (U.S. Department of Health and Human Services, 2001).

Health Insurance

The 2000 U.S. census reports that health insurance disparities are high for all Latino children, with 24.9 percent uninsured, compared to 7.3 percent of non-Hispanic white children. The State Children's Health Insurance Program (State Children's Health Insurance Program; Title XXI of the Social Security Act), along with other government and private programs, often use schools as a gateway to access, but they miss many Latino youth because they have dropped out. In general, the rates of uninsured Latino children remain stable at between one-fourth to one-third—a shocking rate of national neglect (Koss-Chioino and Vargas, 1999; Mills, 2002). Such neglect often results in children whose behavioral disorders are criminalized in juvenile and even adult correctional systems rather than identified and treated as mental health concerns. Neglect also results in children and youth whose sense of abandonment may turn to despair, to gang affiliation, substance abuse, and to self-destructive behavior, even to suicide (U.S. Department of Health and Human Services, 2001).

Historical Patterns and Conditions

The following section presents an overview of the historical and social forces that have shaped contemporary economic and political developments in Central America.

Geographical and Historical Highlights

Central America, often called Mesoamerica when combined with Mexico, is a strip of land connecting Mexico to Colombia and South America. Seven small countries make up Central America: Guatemala, Belize, El Salvador, Honduras, Nicaragua, Costa Rica, and Panama. All those countries, except El Salvador and Belize, have a mountain range splitting the strip of land in two, with jungles on one side, mountains on the other, and the Pacific and Atlantic Oceans on either side.

The highly developed Mayans of Mesoamerica built a stunningly complex and hierarchical culture based on cosmologies of beauty, spirituality, power, and privilege. The Spanish conquistadors arrived just after indigenous cultural development had peaked; they set about to systematically destroy the Mayan civilization, leaving the indigenous languages, religious, scientific, and other cultural traditions to function as outlaw, underground, or syncretistic customs, dominated by European Spanish beliefs (Adams, 1970; Adams, 1977; Schele and Friedel, 1990; Coe, 1993). In all things, the societies that grew out of this experience were communities of domination, peonage, slavery, and varying forms of exploitation. European diseases such as smallpox decimated the physical bodies of the Indians, whereas the torture and forced labor of the native populations attacked their bodies and spirits (Vlach, 1992).

The region developed a new ruling class in the nineteenth century following the demise of Spain's colonial empire. These were the *criollos*—children born to the Spanish conquistadors on American soil. Although the *criollos* attempted to forge a new Central American state, a warlord (*caudillo*) mentality prevailed, new European business interests colonized the land, and the region was politically divided into more easily controlled geographical units. The entry of pirates and adventurers from the United States, Britain, and other European countries affected the fate of Belize (a population of former slaves of largely African origin) and Panama, which were seen to have commercial potential because of their proximity to the Panama Canal.

Since this time, the United States has maintained its hegemony in the region by direct and indirect military means (such as the occupation of Nicaragua from 1912 to 1933) and by making strong alliances with the land-owning elites, aiding them in the continuation of the exploitive plantation system. Such an economic system, based on an export economy, has ensured that the dominated majority of the populace cannot maintain self-sufficiency. Those who have lived on their land for centuries have often been forced to migrate as a consequence (Vlach, 1992).

Central American immigration to the United States can be divided into three main waves. The first immigrants came in the late 1800s to work in the food service sector on the West Coast, thus establishing a beachhead for future waves of Central American networks entering the United States. During the 1930s and 1940s, a second wave of immigrants who were fleeing political persecution entered the United States; they tended to be from the intellectual classes, and they helped support social movements throughout Latin America. The third wave began arriving in the 1960s; they were escaping war, and the group encompassed all socioeconomic classes, including indigenous Maya; this migration northward continues to this day (Córdova and Pinderhughes, 1999).

Legacy of War and Migration Waves of the 1980s

The style of war found throughout Central America has been characterized as "LIC" or "low-intensity conflict." This type of conflict is based on small-scale guerilla-style methods applied over a long period of time. The implied threat of a superior force striking at any time has as its goal and consequence mass psychological destabilization of the populace—the weakening of hearts and minds, widespread disruption, accelerated militarism, and constant fear. In Central America, LIC has spilled across borders and disrupted the entire region (Braveman, Meyers, Schlenker, and Wands, 1997). The 1980s were dubbed by the United Nations as "the lost decade" due to resultant massive displacement (Loucky, Moors, and Moors, 2000). The legacy of LIC has had a negative impact on Central American families and youth.

Nicaragua

The latest waves of migration to the United States began in Nicaragua with an earthquake in 1972. The 1978 Sandinista revolution followed five years later, ultimately overthrowing the Somoza dictatorship in 1979. With increasing support from the United States, the counter-revolutionary guerrillas (*contras*) initiated a civil war that forced nearly one-third of that country's population to abandon their homes and seek refuge in the United States during the early 1980s. These higher-status exiles were more likely to be recognized as seeking political asylum and to be welcomed by the U.S. government if they were fleeing the *Sandinistas* (Al-Issa and Tousignant, 1997; LaCayo, 2001).

El Salvador

The "lost decade" of the 1980s saw El Salvador become embroiled in its own civil conflict between the left-wing guerrillas of the FMLN (*Frente Farabundo Martí*—Front for National Liberation) and the government's military forces and paramilitary death squads, which targeted suspected sympathizers of the populist guerrillas. During this bloody conflict, which lasted until a 1992 treaty, a climate of fear and terror prevailed. The government changed its strategy from targeted to wholesale repression in which over 75,000 people were killed and perhaps three times that many wounded. The impact of war dislocated many families, and youth were set adrift, some forming gangs that today are the *salvatruchos* or Salvadoran-born gangs and the *diez-y-ochos* or U.S.-born gangs (relating to 18th Street in Los Angeles). During the same era, 800,000 Salvadorans made their way to the United States (Córdova and Kury, 2001).

Honduras

Honduras, located between El Salvador and Guatemala, became a staging ground for conflicts in all of the neighboring countries. Because of its extreme poverty and total domination by U.S. fruit and railway investments, it became a hot spot for U.S. military bases and a huge military buildup in the region. Refugees from Nicaragua, El

Salvador, and Guatemala poured into the country and into refugee camps, while the area also became the site for the regrouping of various forces on different sides of the regional conflicts. Disappearances and kidnappings became routine there in the decade of the 1980s (Peñalosa, 1986). In more recent years, Hondurans have migrated in large numbers to the United States following the tremendous devastation of Hurricane Mitch in 1998.

Guatemala

Guatemala's experience is similar, both in terms of exploitation by U.S. corporate interests and a caste system (*Ladinos*[6] on top, indigenous on bottom) that underlies its vast socioeconomic, political, and cultural inequalities. Since the 1960s, the resistance of the indigenous Maya majority and the growing Guatemalan middle class has increased. A guerrilla insurgency initially dominated by Ladinos focused on grievances suffered by indigenous Maya. As in other Central American countries, contested land often was the issue. Military, mining, and petroleum interests of the elites combined to keep the growing population landless and the lands free for cattle grazing and prospecting. In the 1960s, repression, disappearances, and terror were centered in eastern Guatemala, then moved to the capital. By the 1980s, the conflict had spread widely throughout the rural countryside. The Guatemalan military and paramilitaries stepped up a policy of genocide; over 400 indigenous villages were pillaged and burned. More than 150,000 Maya were killed during the 1970s and 1980s, and over a million refugees were displaced; many are now living in the United States (Peñalosa, 1986; Loucky, Moors, and Moors, 2000). Along with Salvadorans and Hondurans, they are more likely to be viewed by U.S. authorities as an economic burden; consequently, they have had a harder time qualifying for political asylum.

Fragmented Identities

This section focuses on the conflicts over ethnic identity, social class, and cultural affiliation that influence the process of psychosocial adaptation of Central American youth and their families in the United States.

> I learned to be a Salvi partially through the stories of my
> mother . . . but not completely because she was unintentionally
> becoming Mexican from being around her Mexican husband—my
> dad and the stretch of freeway that connects East L.A. to Bell
> Gardens. It was just easier to say I was Chicana. Technically I am,
> but I actually feel a little more Salvadoran. I wanted something
> more specific than Latina so I could recognize myself and have
> full-time awareness of a part-time identity. I didn't have aunts
> down the street criticizing my mother's *pupusas,* nor cousins to
> grow up with. There weren't any Salvi superheroes or pop cultural
> icons to shine a light on the Salvi self-awareness path. I knew
> there were inherent differences between Mexicanos and Salvis,
> but they were like the wind, and I couldn't really place them.
> [Gutiérrez, 1999]

For Central American youth, the terms most commonly used in the United States to describe ethnic identity are often problematic. Central American national, class, and ethnic identities are fragmented and compartmentalized. This may be an important protective coping strategy, but in many cases, as in the example, the connections to nationality or cultural pride are shallow and shadowy. Much of this situation has to do with the lack of national identity and purpose in Central American countries generally. Although Central American countries have had their revolutions, there has been no effectively concluded national reconciliation in any of these countries in the form of integrated national identities and sense of common purpose, as happened with Mexico and the United States.

The most common terms in the United States used to refer to the pan-ethnic population of Central and South American, Mexican, Cuban, Puerto Rican, and Dominican origin are *Latino* and *Hispanic,* referring to people of Latin American descent. *Hispanic* is promoted by governmental and commercial officials; *Latino* is used as a more grassroots designation. Symbolically, the term *Latino* accentuates ties with countries of Mesoamerica (Mexico and Central America) and South America and distinguishes itself from Spain, the conqueror; *Hispanic* is an ambiguous term that can also refer to a Spaniard from Europe and accentuates the ties to Spain. A historical refrain illustrating the depth of feeling for some of this distinction is "*His* panic, *her* panic, I'm not *anybody's* panic."[7]

Class background is ultimately of greater importance than race because one's standing is then clearly established. However, it is also considered undignified and impolite by most Latinos to talk openly about someone's class or background. Because of the minefield that is so often traversed in ethnic labeling, often the blandest term possible such as *Spanish-speaking* or *Hispanic* is used in order to be inclusive and politically correct. Immigrants and refugee adults tend to identify themselves by nationalities of origin, referring to themselves informally through nicknames such as *Chapines* (Guatemalans), *Salvis* (Salvadorans), or, more formally, through designations such as *Nicaraguan American* or *Panamanian American.*

For Central Americans, there are four main ethnic groups to be found throughout the region. Race and its discriminatory meaning are subsumed within these four groups, and many combinations exist. These four groups, according to de la Cadena (2001), are

1. Descendants of the indigenous Maya, predominating in the highland regions, speaking some twenty-three different and distinct languages such as Kiché, Kaqchiquel, Popti, and Mam
2. Afro-Caribbean populations of mixed black and indigenous heritage, escapees from the slave trade living on the eastern coasts and speaking Garifuna and other languages in addition to Spanish
3. Descendants of European immigrants, mainly Spanish
4. *Mestizos,* or mixed Indian-Spanish origins, creating a positive spiritual and ethnic fusion in some and a sense of skewed, negative, or fragmented identity in others (for example, that implied by the term *half-breed*)[8]

Central American families see hope and faith in education as a way to rise above birth status and social fate. It is even possible to transform oneself into another ethnic identity while keeping one's cultural practices (indigenous to *mestizo*). There are some Mayan youth living in the United States whose family or community connections support them in continuing to observe the Mayan New Year celebration and in maintaining other cultural traditions and ties such as dances and traditional music. However, middle and upper classes tend to see indigenous identity as associated with poverty, sleaziness, and ignorance—an identity with no future. Therefore, indigenous youth often adopt "ladinoization" and, ultimately, U.S. acculturation as a survival strategy.[9] At the same time, some Latin American intellectuals have romanticized the indigenous ethnicity and resisted any attempts by modern Maya to become culturally *mestizo*.

Legal and Illegal Migrants

The following excerpt is from an interview reported by Josúe Gamaliel Rojas:

> People speak bad about us, the undocumented. I don't understand all of it but I know it's bad. Even Mexicans who were once like me—with no papers and no work—think they are better than me. They make others feel like less. I think that's not right.

There is tremendous variation in availability of institutional support for Central American youth, depending on whether the children, adolescents, or family members are documented. Eligibility for health care, the postsecondary school system and scholarships, the ability to work or carry on public activities without fear of being snatched up and deported is different for those who have legal standing in the United States. Often, different family members have different legal standing, making some deportable and some not. If children are born in the United States, they are automatically citizens, in contrast to family members who may be undocumented. This can create tragic family dynamics when the documented child becomes the family's favorite and the undocumented child the family scapegoat (Suárez-Orozco and Suárez-Orozco, 2001).

Since the 1970s, the ability for Central Americans to become legal in the United States has diminished considerably. A contributory factor to inequality of treatment has been the political bias in which certain seekers of political asylum have been seen by U.S. authorities. Nicaraguans, for example, who were fleeing from a *Sandinista* government that the United States was actively attempting to overthrow were legitimized and more readily given official refugee status, whereas Salvadorans and Guatemalans exiled from governments that the United States supported were given little recognition, and, until recently, found it difficult to get political asylum. The risk of applying for asylum is great. If denied, applicants are liable to be returned to their countries of origin or held in detention camps (Al-Issa and Tousignant, 1997; *American Baptist Churches* v. *Thornburgh*, 2002; "Temporary Protected Status," 2002).

In some parts of the United States, children who are detained may still be kept in prisons, where, according to some observers, they receive no legal, psychological, educational, or recreational services. They have been kept in the same confines with adult convicts. A lawsuit dealing with this situation (*Flores* v. *Reno*) was settled a few years ago. Federal authorities are developing a new Office of Juvenile Affairs in response to complaints about the dearth of services and lack of basic human rights often accorded to child refugees ("Slipping Through the Cracks," 1997; Suárez-Orozco and Suárez-Orozco, 2001; "INS Announces Restructuring," 2002). Some children and youth have entered the United States after escaping conscription or massacres or being orphaned. Some end up in orphanages in Central America where U.S. families may adopt them. This practice has led to the widespread fears in Guatemala of child abduction by childless U.S. couples and even trafficking in body parts and organs for the benefit of the U.S. medically privileged. It has resulted in new, more careful oversight by U.S. immigration officials of international adoptions from Central America ("INS Announces Restructuring," 2002).

The political and social environment for immigrants has generally worsened over the past few decades. Since the September 11th attacks of 2001, the George W. Bush administration has promulgated federal emergency orders in which immigrants may be detained without due process, sending shock waves throughout the immigrant rights communities (Sachs, 2002). Antiterrorism fever in the country has only increased an anti-immigrant backlash that was already building. Prior to these new millennium events, the 1990s saw the development of anti-immigrant public initiatives in California. The passage of Proposition 187 in 1994 made immigrants scapegoats for a shifting economy and rising racial tensions in the state; most of its provisions were overturned by the courts.

Nonetheless, its passage demonstrated that many Californians didn't want undocumented immigrants to have equal access to publicly funded schooling and health care. Proposition 187 exacerbated the problem of outreach to Central American immigrant communities who still find it difficult to trust any authorities, be they police or representatives of the health care or educational systems. Proposition 187 was followed in 1996 by a proposition against affirmative action (209) and, in 1998, one promoting English-only in the schools (227). All three propositions targeted immigrants of color, and all were adopted by a majority of the voters (Gibbs and Bankhead, 2001).

Cultural Patterns and Values

Some of the arenas in which Central American families and youth cross the cultural divide fall under the themes of familism, patriarchy and role reversal, parent-child relationships and childrearing practices, rites of passage, spirituality, language and education, and values such as *respeto, simpatía,* and being *bien educado.* Mayan Indian spiritual values and beliefs are influential as well.

Familism

Familism is a central pillar of values and beliefs among Latinos; the idea is that the well-being of the family unit is paramount and supercedes individual needs and goals. The family is a dynamic entity and includes *compadres, comadres, madrinas, padrinos,* and other extended and fictive kin. The reliance on obligation to support family members is great, but the vulnerabilities are also great because of how much families have been affected by *la situación.* In creating clinical profiles of "typical" Central American families and youth, it is possible to overpathologize Central Americans as a result and to miss the strong supportive family ties and ideals that reinforce sacrifice, deference, warmth, and respect. The family ideal is centered on maternal love, extended family support, and paternal protection, with children taking on family and academic responsibilities to achieve success and honor for the entire family and community.

Patriarchy and Gender Role Reversal

Many gender role conflicts exist for Central Americans. Although families are essentially still patriarchal, women are central figures in their homes. *La hembra* or *hembrismo* (the cult of the powerful woman) contrasts to the self-sacrificing *María,* who is deferential in order to respect the *machismo* of her male partner. But women must also work outside the home to make ends meet, which is not traditional in their origin countries. Families must adapt to the diminished power of the patriarchy in the United States, in comparison to its continuing dominance in Central America. Often immigrant or refugee *mothers* are the trailblazers in leaving Central America for the United States; consequently, they become the major breadwinners and providers. Because they can find jobs as housekeepers or restaurant workers more readily than their husbands, they avoid high visibility and liability to deportation, but expectations for maternal love and attention are challenged by such outside demands. These role reversals, as well as a legacy of war and violence from home, incubate the potential for domestic and family violence and abuse. Large numbers of single women raise children alone. There is also a tradition of the *casa chica* (multiple families) that some men take on. Separated families makes it easier to lead double and triple lives (Vlach, 1992).[10]

Parent-Child Relationships and Childrearing Practices

The ideal Central American family, like most Latino families, is child-centered, permissive, and relaxed when children are very young. Babies and toddlers in the family are loved and doted on. Whereas older brothers and sisters are expected to care for their younger siblings, mothers are the central figures of the family; they are expected to care for and love their children above all others, including their husbands. The husband is expected to work hard and provide for the family, play with young children, and provide discipline for older children, but he is not really expected to take an active ongoing parental role. Men may seek a wife who is more traditional from the home country and remain strongly attached to their own mothers after marriage. Although this is a norm in Latin countries, it becomes a "problem" in the United States, where grand-parents are expected to take a back seat. Grandparents are revered figures in Central American families. Often, the dominant (leader-ship) dyad is a grandparent and a parent, not the parental dyad (Fal-icov, 1998).

For children of color, the issue of skin color lives on as a covert legacy of colonialism and slavery, despite heated denial by many Latinos. Many children testify that light-skinned siblings are often fussed over while the darker ones (*prietos*) are seen as less desirable and not as attractive.

Parent-child relations shift when the child reaches latency age—a time when children are expected to take on more respon-sibilities, observe, attend, and participate in family activities and gatherings, including eating out and going to church; this social-izes them into their family roles. Developmental goals are for children to be peaceful, honorable, trustworthy, affectionate, and respectful. Self-expression—a very important developmental goal in the United States—is not so highly valued. Children are kept close to home, as parents perceive the United States as an immoral, more dangerous environment. Concern expressed is about street, racial, and gang violence, as well as looseness of sexual morals and disrespectful behavior of youth to elders.

Threats and fear are common methods of behavioral control. The concept of child abuse is not syntonic for Latino families, al-though this is changing due to the global movement to educate fam-ilies about this problem. It is generally considered acceptable to slap, yell at, or use a belt or switch on disrespectful children who misbe-have, and traditionally there is not so much emotional charge asso-ciated with this. An older child may also discipline a younger child.

Rites of Passage

Adolescents struggle with gender and ethnic identity and sexual orientation in insecure environments where passions run high and negative social mirroring is constant. Rites of passage are ways for youth to transition into adulthood in a culturally sanctioned way. Unfortunately for Central American boys, there are no universal rituals or markers to denote this transition, although for some Catholic girls who are part of a community network there is the *quinceañera*—a formal dinner-dance that is given for a girl by her parents on her fifteenth birthday. Its elaborate nature establishes the "coming out" of a girl who is "becoming a woman." "*Quinces*" have a religious component to them, in which the girl and her family attend church where she confesses to a priest and he gives advice to her and the family (Falicov, 1998).

Values of *Respeto, Simpatía,* and *Bien Educado*

Simpatía is being friendly and warm in relationships with others. It is a highly valued skill and expectation, with the dual objective of making interpersonal interactions go more smoothly and preserving the dignity (*dignidad*) and personal integrity of the persons in a transaction. Connected with *simpatía* is being *bien educado,* or developing the social graces, courtesies, and politeness and *respeto* for others, especially those of professional or high position or authority. It is crucial to understand that avoidance of conflict doesn't necessarily imply agreement. Education, then, has a social harmony component to it. Achievement of certain academic skills is highly valued for deeply rooted cultural reasons as much as for the sake of competitive gain. Central American children often carry the torch of the hopes and the dreams of deceased family members whose self-sacrifice is legendary. Learning a professional skill such as becoming a doctor, lawyer, teacher, or engineer is extremely prized, not so much for personal accomplishment as for the honor it confers on the entire family and even community. Other related values are love of food, music and the arts, crafts, sports (soccer, baseball, and boxing), and storytelling.

Spirituality

Central American families have often gone through great spiritual crises of meaning in coming to terms with how war has polarized them and with the losses they have endured. Suicide attempts can sometimes be understood as expressing a lack of meaning in people's lives following the ruin of war (Frankl, 1965; Maduro and Martinez, 1979). Protestant evangelical versus Catholic rifts are found in families, as charismatic conversions and spritual awakenings are common in youth. The Protestant evangelical movement has made great inroads in the traditionally Catholic Central American countries. Other influential spiritual traditions such as *curanderismo, espiritismo,* and *santería* have influenced Central American health and religious views and practices somewhat, depending on the ethnic group, country, and history of the family.[11] Variations on these themes in the rise of new spiritual leaders, healers, and sects are constantly emerging as a way of coping with a search for community, meaning, and values in the individualistic, mechanistic United States.

Indigenous Central Americans are primarily Mayans from Guatemala who come in family groups when possible. They have an uneasy relationship with Ladinos, even when dependent on them. In some communities, notably Los Angeles, they maintain networks and communities tied together by hometown associations that sponsor such popular Guatemalan pastimes as soccer and marimba playing. Indigenous values and beliefs carry over post-migration. The church is important in maintaining this communal tie to the home country, actually to the home town. Some of these values (see Human Rights Office of the Archdiocese of Guatemala, 1999) are as follows:

- Poetic and metaphorical thinking[12]
- Attention to the traditional calendar (for example, the Mayan New Year, Day of the Dead)
- Serving the past (ancestors) as well as future (new babies)[13]
- Respect for the dignity of *every* person, regardless of position
- Spiritually focused and restorative community activities, ceremonies, and rites

Mayan immigrants are generally trilingual, with Spanish as a second language and English as a third.

Language and Education

The necessity for Central American children and youth to be bilingual often is imbued with an implicit threat to the cultural integrity of the family. First, there are the practical necessities of English fluency—to survive outside the enclave community, to achieve in school, and to work in other than dead-end, low-paying jobs. Some children never went to school in their home countries and are not literate in Spanish or in English, making it more difficult to learn a new language. In some cases, children can readily switch codes from Spanish to English and back again. In other cases, a "Spanglish" hybrid develops. Clearly though, success in the English-speaking world is the goal. However, when children are more comfortable in English than their parents, they often become the translators for their parents and take on a role that is not respectful to their parents. Because the children are acculturating more rapidly, they may be encouraged by well-meaning outsiders to misuse this powerful family role and bypass parents and family completely. This may result in family conflict, disengagement, and alienation.

Second, there is the issue of contested loyalties. The choice of what language the child speaks carries sentiments of loyalty, allegiance, and affinity. If parents are unsure as to whether the United States is a temporary haven or a permanent settlement, cultural commitment may be problematic. Learning disabilities, underachievement, and even elective mutism may be sacrifices that children make as the pressure of English immersion and Anglo-dominated school curricula and personnel confront the language of emotion, familiarity, and comfort (Sluzki, 1983). These same contested loyalties may also play out within a family, as seen in the following case:

> Seven-year-old J. P. was the daughter of a Honduran immigrant single mother who spoke little English. J. P. was withdrawn and uncommunicative in school and was eventually diagnosed as electively mute. Her teacher referred her to a small school-based bilingual play therapy group for traumatized children after it was discovered that she had been sexually abused by her monolingual, English-speaking father, who was now no longer in the home. As the play group progressed, she began to speak in Spanish initially, then also in English. The group facilitated this by giving her nonthreatening opportunities to communicate verbally in both English and Spanish and by using group cofacilitators who spoke both languages.

Mental Health Issues for Children and Adolescents

Although some studies of Latino youth point to higher rates of depression, anxiety, and suicide (U.S. Department of Health and Human Services, 2001), no epidemiological data are available on rates of behavioral disorders among Central American youth. An analysis of the themes found at a Mental Health Day treatment program of mostly Central American teenagers during the early 1990s found six important areas of clinical concern for adolescents and families who were new arrivals.[14] The concerns were family fragmentation, cutting off of the past, abandonment and loss, fending off help, survivor's guilt, and posttraumatic stress.

Family Fragmentation and Reunification

Family fragmentation and reunification were often issues for many reasons. Sometimes the children were not clear as to the reason for the migration to the United States. They may not have been told that they were going until the last moment of departure so as to keep them safe. Families may have been separated for many years, with the children used to living under different family rules and possibly in parenting roles. Parental sacrifice may not be appreciated by children who have felt abandoned or confused by so many years of separation. Fragmented identities are compounded by the existence of these fragmented families.

Cutting Off the Past

Children and youth from Central American countries are often very resilient and adaptable. Looking straight ahead to the future often precludes the backward glance at the past. Children are sometimes also presented with a forced-choice scenario: either stay true to your ethnic background and suffer discrimination or betray your origins by making it in a white world and becoming a "coconut" (brown on the outside and white on the inside). Some students find a "dual frame of reference" adaptive in being able to keep the home country in mind in dealing with obstacles in the United States (Suárez-Orozco and Suárez-Orozco, 1995). But many children learn quickly to dress and talk like American youth. It may only feel skin deep at first, but gradually they may forget who they are (Vlach, 1992).

Abandonment and Loss

The families we see often present with children who are offspring of single mothers, many of whom were abandoned teenage mothers. Many of these poor women never marry. The mothers may be overwhelmed, unable to cope, and vulnerable, dealing with the aftermath of war and family dissolution. Often, drug and alcohol abuse, gang activity, and other ills have contributed to their exhaustion and neediness. Their children may respond by becoming anxiously attached, parentified, and pseudo-mature to an extreme degree. They may act out aggressively themselves, become gang members, internalize the pain and become suicidal, or become teenage mothers themselves.

Fending Off Help

Clinics and social service agencies only come in contact with Central American families who have been unable to solve their problems by themselves and consequently become known to "outsiders." Central American families tend to rely more on church and extended families for support and advice, not formal institutions. Some of the suggested reasons are that mental illness is not pathologized in Latino culture to the extent that it is in this culture; that is, only violent people who are dangerous are referred to professionals for treatment (Romero de Thompson, 1996). Other explanations have to do with experiences of poor treatment, a fear of INS involvement, and a distrust of institutional authorities generally. A related notion is that of the clinical idea of suspicion of the counterfeit—that help is not real, it is only an illusion, and relationships of true *confianza*[15] are rare and difficult to establish.

Survivor's Guilt

Like children of the Holocaust, many of the survivors and second-generation survivors of Central America's "lost decade" are drawn to a search for meaning in the experience of their family. Often, educational achievement is the venue in which restitution or reparation must be made. One young Guatemalan middle school student wanted to become an agronomist to deal with land tenure inequalities that were key to Guatemala's civil war and the death of his uncle. Others feel a sense of despair and become suicidal. Viktor Frankl (1965), after studying concentration camp survivors, asked not "Why do you want to kill yourself?" but "What is keeping you alive?" (p. 85).

When children feel the pressure of high familial expectations, obligations, and sacrifices, they may find that their dreams are buffeted by the reality of marginalization and negative academic labeling. They may take on the social role of "castelike" minorities that are placed in poor educational environments with no familiar cultural referents and low expectations. The cultural-ecological studies of John Ogbu and others have documented the lack of quality found in schooling provided to castelike minorities such as African Americans, American Indians, Mexican Americans, and Puerto Ricans. Many Latino students, particularly boys, accurately perceive the low level of educational opportunity available to them and the inequitable reward structure and opt out of the game (Ogbu and Matute-Bianchi, 1986; Suárez-Orozco, 1989; Ogbu and Simons, 1998; Suárez-Orozco and Suárez-Orozco, 2001). With this type of discriminatory treatment, foreclosed identities may take hold. In addition, these students may develop high rates of anxiety or low self-esteem; they may drop out of school, become gang members, get involved in alcohol and drug use, and engage in other forms of acting-out behaviors (Suárez-Orozco and Suárez-Orozco, 2001).

Trauma and Its Aftermath

The following quote from Adriana Jasmina Castro Guerra (1999) is translated from the original Spanish:

> I was playing with my friends in front of my house under the street lamps that gave off a yellow light. Suddenly, they all went out. This wasn't unusual, but this time I began to hear a lot of [gun]shots. I ran to my house. One of the things that I remember most about El Salvador is the war. I was very small and I didn't understand much about what was going on around me, but it was a very terrible time for me.

Few studies have investigated PTSD in Central American adults living in the United States, let alone among children and youth. The most current epidemiological studies of Latinos are those conducted in the California Central Valley by Vega, Alderete, Kolody, and Aguilar-Gaxiola (1998); Vega and others (1998); and Alderete, Vega, Kolody, and Aguilar-Gaxiola (2000a, 2000b) in which acculturative stress over time is seen to increase the prevalence of psychiatric disorders and substance abuse for Mexican Americans. These studies do not identify PTSD or any culture-bound syndromes such as *susto*[16] that might be particularly applicable to Central American populations.

Cervantes, Salgado de Snyder, and Padilla (1989) found that among a psychiatric adult population of Mexicans and Central Americans, posttraumatic stress rates were highest among the Central Americans. It didn't seem to matter whether they actually saw people who disappeared or were killed during the war-torn era; their reactions included the same set of trauma symptoms qualifying for the *DSM III*-R diagnosis. The Central Americans and Mexicans all described their problems as *nervios*, which is a generic disorder of stress covering a range of mental health symptoms. Basic to the concerns of the Central Americans were fears related to *la situación* and the survival of their families, communities, and country, the hostility of the immigration system, demanding work conditions, substandard living conditions, and problems of reunification with family members. A key worry was fear of assassination in the United States by paramilitaries and political polarization that followed them to the United States. Men reported weakness, fear of falling, nightmares, alcohol abuse, and fear of loss of control. Women reported high rates of anger, loss of tranquility, headaches, pains, and crying.

One of the first studies to note trauma in Central American children in the United States (Arroyo and Eth, 1985) presented case descriptions of children ages five to seventeen who were struggling with serious problems in school. The authors were seeing this clinical population in Los Angeles in the 1980s and stated:

> The war-ravaged child who has experienced traumatic stress is gravely predisposed to further opportunistic insults in the form of separations, a forced uprooting, a tumultuous resettlement. However, having identified their special circumstances, the war-traumatized child's prognosis becomes more favorable with further study and timely interventions. As a growing segment of our society, it is essential that some preparation be made to adequately meet the needs of this special population. [Arroyo and Eth, 1985, p. 117]

Picado (1988) and Chapa (1992) looked at the effects of traumatic stressors on the mental health of Central American children. Death remained "imprinted" on their psyches; they imagined foreshortened futures and, unlike adults, were less able to use denial as a defense. High rates of fear, intrusive thoughts and imagery, nightmares, disturbed sleep, guilt, anger, and attempts to avoid feelings and reminders of traumatic events were reported in comparison to a control group of Mexican immigrant children. Because psychic numbing didn't take place as readily, they were less trusting of people in general. These children did not find parents able to help them cope with their fears because parents were often unavailable or too preoccupied themselves to be able to identify children's symptoms and assist them effectively.

In reviewing the psychosocial functioning of Central American refugee children at the Clínica Oscar Romero in Los Angeles during the early 1990s, another investigator noted common experiences of the children and families she studied (Masser, 1992). Premigration stressors were war-related violence, poverty, loss of family members, physical abuse, and family alcoholism. Immigration process stressors were problems during the journey, separation from caregivers, or problems in dealing with the INS, or *coyotes*. And stressors in the United States were many—poverty, lack of work, inadequate housing, language barriers, worry for family and friends back in Central America, drugs and gang activities in the neighborhoods, anti-Latino racism, lifestyle changes, and unfamiliar values and philosophies. In general, a pile-up of stressful variables produced more symptomatology in the children studied. The combination of home country violence, separation from caregivers, and other adaptation stressors were particularly damaging of children's psychosocial functioning (Masser, 1992).

A nonclinical sample of Central American immigrant children was studied in Tucson, Arizona, to ascertain the level of health problems (Locke, Southwick, McCloskey, and Fernández-Esquer, 1996). Although the sample included only twenty-two children, there was a wide range and frequency of both psychological and physical symptoms and complaints, with only four children rated as "symptom-free." Depression and somatic complaints were common, as were symptoms of social withdrawal and anxiety. A number of children acted out their disturbances through aggression, hyperactivity, and noncompliance.

Important effects of psychosocial trauma on children go beyond the *DSM-IV* symptoms of trauma. Before he was assassinated by death squads in El Salvador, the Salvadoran psychologist and Jesuit priest Ignacio Martin-Barâ (1988a, 1988b) wrote extensively about war trauma in El Salvador. His contention was that war on the scale seen by Central American children and families has pervasive, nonuniform psychosocial effects on the entire society. The major effects he discusses are those of dehumanization: the diminishment of our ability to think, to know and tell the truth, be sensitive to others, and have hope. Some of the cognitive effects are those of ideological rigidity, inability to validate one's own experience, skepticism, paranoia, hatred, and prejudice. Children suffer profound alterations in personality, behavior, and moral development (Martin-Barâ, 1988a, 1988b). A sense of facing up to the conflict may result in emotional growth for some youth; others see antisocial behavior unfairly rewarded with recognition, status, and privileges and identify with these aggressors (Santa Barbara, 1997). One teenager told a school counselor, "If anyone bothers you, I'll kill them for you!" That youth had been a combat participant and found it disconcerting to go from a battlefield to sit in a desk in a U.S. high school classroom. Such symptomatology associated with the war years is no doubt abating in this generation of Central American youth. There are some dramatic changes that can be illustrated by the following story.

> During the 1980s, I collected some photographs of children's drawings from Guatemalan indigenous children (ages 6–12) who were in refugee camps in Mexico. These drawings were graphic in their portrayal of terrorized people running from helicopters that were bombing their villages and from soldiers burning their homes. When I went to Guatemala in the late 1990s, after the Peace Accords were signed, I collected drawings made by children who had grown up in Mexican refugee camps but whose families had recently returned home. By contrast, these new drawings showed a sense of hope and pride in their community.

Although the generation of the lost decade may be aging out of their youth, their experiences are apt to affect the next generation via vicarious or secondary traumatization. Domestic violence has also been a problem for many Central American families, and this situation affects children and youth in many of the same ways.

Finally, the conditions that led to war in Central America have not been resolved, low-intensity conflict continues, and new immigrants and refugees enter the United States every day.

Sociocultural Issues in Assessment

Many investigators have warned of the double-edged consequences of migration and acculturation. Although immigrants are often socially selected as the hardiest of the society of origin, the social stress of the migration and acculturation process may result in frustrated aspirations, higher rates of incidence of psychiatric disorder, and alcohol and drug problems (Vlach, 1992; Al-Issa and Tousignant, 1997).

There are many sociocultural elements of interest in conducting a mental health assessment of Central American refugee and immigrant youth and their families. Some of the key issues of concern are the following:

• *Language spoken and preferred by child and family.* It is helpful to assess which languages are spoken by which family members, including indigenous languages. This will often clue the practitioner in to issues of practical survival (school), as well as contested loyalties.

• *Basic survival needs, including issues of physical illness and documented or undocumented status.* Primary care providers are usually the first practitioners to see Latino family members, including children. It is important to ascertain whether basic needs of food, shelter, and physical and medical needs (including malnutrition) of the child and family are an issue before mental health or other issues are explored. New immigrants and refugees are often very sensitive to accepting charity or anything from "the government," especially if it might affect their legal status. What is your community's attitude to Latino immigrants?

• *Skills, available resources, and independence.* Determine what are the child and family's strengths, including cultural, religious-spiritual, social, and personal strengths. Pertinent factors are the family's skills in English, in work skills, exposure to the United States, and willingness to engage in independent problem solving. Multiple resources predict better resolution of concerns.

• *SES and downward mobility, rural-urban background, age, gender, race, educational status, and general background.* Understanding the issue of class, changes in gender roles, and other types of status helps in determining what interventions to use, what resources would be most congruent, what sense of privilege or stigma exists, and how the child and family might feel about their current situation, as class and other indicators of status are so highly charged. How are they now seen in the community where they are living? Has their economic and social status changed in the United States?

• *Degree of family disruption, obligation, family leadership, organization of family roles, unaccompanied minor issues, attachment issues.* Looking at the child's history of separation from caregivers and the family's style of engagement (cohesive or fragmented) helps to determine interventions and predict what losses have been sustained and what types of relationships the child and family members are needing. A child from a disrupted family is at higher risk. The role of the mother is crucial.

• *Stage of migration and type of acculturation.* The stage of migration[17] may explain the type of coping strategy the child or family is engaged in, for example, overcompensation or crisis (Sluzki, 1979). The type of acculturation the child manifests may be (1) integrated (bicultural), (2) assimilated (melting pot), (3) separated (ethnic community or segregation), or (4) marginalized (alienated), indicating the type of transference or countertransference issues that may be encountered in development of a therapeutic relationship (Dobkin de Ríos, 2001).

• *Health beliefs and practices.* Asking about the child and family's health beliefs, practices, and preferences for help-seeking will help determine culturally appropriate interventions.[18]

• *Sociopolitical context of migration and religious affiliation.* What were the circumstances of migration—the why and how? Any concerns that are related to that experience should be assessed, including the witnessing of violence or experience with or threat of violence in any other form. How have the child and family coped with these concerns? What is the role of religion, rituals, and spirituality in individual and family daily life?

• *Perception of migration and acculturation experience.* Do the child's family members see migration and the necessary adaptations as a positive or negative event in the life of the family (Vlach,

1992)? Do they see family as a support in their lives, or do they actively disengage from each other when under stress?[19] What are the aspirations of child and family? Would the child or family return to the home country?

• *Impact of war and other trauma, expressed symptomatology by children and other family members.* Broad symptom checklists for PTSD for children and parents may be administered. This may be especially significant in terms of overlapping symptomatology with attention deficit–hyperactivity disorder and in terms of vicarious or secondary traumatization.

• *Question for children: If you had three wishes, what would they be? Question for immigrant youth: What are three questions you have about life in the United States?* Children may be slow to share their hopes and fears directly with authority figures but may be more open to questions phrased in terms of projective fantasy. They may also be reluctant to ask questions that relate to their current or future expectations or worries because that is not the usual cultural role of children vis-à-vis adults[20] (Nidorf, 1985).

Interventions and Treatment Modalities

There is a body of literature on work with Mexican American and Puerto Rican adults and families (Falicov, 1998; U.S. Department of Health and Human Services, 2001), but few researchers have given serious attention to work with Latino children and adolescents (Koss-Chioino and Vargas, 1999; Canino and Spurlock, 1994; Gibbs and Huang, 1998). Research on methods of intervention with Central American families and children in the United States is needed. A beginning examination of engagement with Central American children and families and a discussion of selected issues in individual, family, and group treatment will provide some ideas for further research.

Engagement

In intervening with Central American children and adolescents, two major guidelines for engagement may be proposed, whether the intervention is individual, family, group, or residentially based: (1) language matching and (2) sensitivity to multiple experiences.

Language Matching

In engaging with families of Central American children and youth, it is necessary for the therapist to find out what language is preferred by the family (parents or guardians) and what languages are preferred by the child or children, and in what context. In many cases, children are fluent in both languages, and parents are monolingual and Spanish-speaking. There is a tendency for the clinician to move to the language in which he or she is most comfortable and for the family to accommodate the clinician. Although the clinician needs to clarify his or her own linguistic fluency, the family's linguistic *preference* should be respected, *even if they are bilingual.* The meaning of linguistic preference is of clinical significance as well. Often the Spanish language is more associated with emotional depth of feeling, whereas English signifies cognitive defense. The child may want to reject the Spanish language as she or he becomes influenced by school and the mainstream culture.

A clinician should not use a child to interpret for his or her parents. The reversal of the parental hierarchy is thus reinforced, and errors in communication can be made by overempowering the child vis-à-vis his or her parents. The same problems can occur with interpreters, especially if they aren't trained interpreters or if they have some kind of bias (or perceived bias) in relationship to the family being seen. Incompetent interpretation by others who may feel coerced or exploited when asked to step in is also a disservice to children and families.

Indigenous families from Guatemala may raise their children in the United States to speak three languages. Some of the twenty-three indigenous languages are now being taught in Guatemala in indigenous primary schools as part of the resolution of the Peace Accords of 1996.[21] Many children grew up with mothers who did not speak Spanish but did speak to them in their particular Mayan language. English may be preferred as a language with a future for some of these children; some decide to bypass Spanish as the language of oppression now that they are living in the United States. Acknowledgment of the indigenous language and its role in the family can be an important part of the engagement process and confers respect that is rarely given to the indigenous cultural heritage.

A sixteen-year-old Kiché Indian boy was living in the United States as an unaccompanied minor in various foster care homes. His foster care home sought assistance in helping him to tell his testimony about being orphaned after the army had killed his parents and he was raised by the Guatemalan army. As part of the process in which he told his story, he also taught the "witnesses" some Kiché words and phrases, thus providing the interchange more of a sense of reciprocity and respect.

Sensitivity to Acculturation Experiences

Warmth, a handshake, and informal joining are all helpful in initial contacts with Central American children and their families. Many families report having cold, impersonal, and hostile encounters with Western hospitals, clinics, and health practitioners. When a child is hurt by racism and stigma, withdrawal is a common way of coping. Parents may search out cultural healers such as priests and *curanderos* and use pharmacists and home remedies before daring to seek help from an outsider (Dobkin de Ríos, 2001). Opening a dialogue with Central American families and children about cultural and ethnic identity entails some personal disclosure on the part of the practitioner. Although early self-disclosure by the therapist may hasten engagement, it may also hinder it. If the therapist is also Latino, families may have strong feelings about linguistic and class status and certain nationalities. The therapist shouldn't assume that the family's point of view and experiences are identical to his or her own, even if there are many similarities. A neutral political stance is advised as a way of depolarizing strong emotions about war experiences in the family's past. Clinics and agencies should be cautious about displaying Latin American political posters to avoid offending individuals and families for whom the war was more than a slogan.

Individual Therapy

Martinez and Valdez (1992) discuss a transactional contextual model of play therapy with Hispanic minority children in which the play environment facilitates the discussion of sociocultural issues. Multicultural dolls of different hues may help them reflect their own sociocultural world in play. Books in Spanish that address topics of intercultural differences and cultural history, maps, globes, and a variety of music and artwork help to stimulate the openness and cultural curiosity that Central American children may bring as a strength. It will also help them identify what the areas of conflict are. Cultural themes must also be assessed in relation to their priority in the face of other pressing needs of the child and family. The authors also stress the importance of the wider system in reinforcing positive cultural themes beyond the limitations of the therapy hour (Martinez and Valdez, 1992).

> O. L. was an eleven-year-old Guatemalan American girl referred for therapy by her fifty-two-year-old immigrant mother. During a custody dispute when she was three years old, O. L. was "kidnapped" by her Guatemalan father and brought to Guatemala to live. After O. L.'s father was killed in a political assassination when she was six, O. L. was returned to the States to live with her mother. O. L. began acting out by getting in physical fights at school, by not coming home directly after school, monopolizing the telephone, and behaving disrespectfully to her mother, seventy-year-old disabled stepfather, and adult stepsiblings. Fearing that she was seeking the company of gang-affiliated children and other street people in her *barrio* neighborhood, her mother started driving her to and from school and not allowing her to leave the house except to go to school and to her therapy appointment. Initially, the therapist helped mother and daughter negotiate behavioral goals and strategies. Later, in individual play therapy, O.L. re-enacted and drew scenarios of abduction and abandonment. She also drew pictures of her home in Guatemala and wrote letters to her Guatemalan siblings (from her father's partnership with another woman). Symptomatology decreased with the help of a strong therapeutic alliance with her therapist.

Family Treatment

Acculturation pressures may be at the core of family problems with their children. Children learn English quickly, and they also acculturate to U.S. values and behaviors rapidly, sometimes leaving their parents bewildered and resentful. Acknowledging these acculturation pressures and differences between parents and children is an important first step in working with a Central American family. Sometimes the conflicts aren't just with the child but with other institutions with which the family has become involved. The best practices of clinicians in these circumstances are those of education, mediation, negotiation, and philosophical facilitation when the problem is intrafamilial; when the problem stems from interaction with an outside institution, advocacy should be included.

> T. S. was an attractive thirteen-year-old Nicaraguan American girl who came to my attention after she was referred to me for a family evaluation for family reunification. She had made two suicide attempts following her mother's auto accident; she had been expected to become the caretaker. The fact that her father was absent much of the time and had not come to her middle school graduation led her to this crisis. She had developed independent expectations to succeed in the high school she wanted to attend and had a job and activities with friends outside the home. None of these activities were what her family expected from her. T. S.'s acculturation experience made her more vulnerable with respect to the family crisis of her mother's accident and father's disengagement from the family.

Structural family therapy intervention was initiated with this family so that the family could begin to reconstitute as an organized family structure. T. S. had been born in the United States and had many hopes and dreams for her own development that she had taken on in a pseudo-mature fashion. However, she was unable to cope with the pile-up of demands on her in relation to caring for her mother, and her father was disengaging from the household. Bringing in some outside supports such as in-home health care and a relative from Nicaragua diminished the pressure on T. S. She was able to talk to her father in the family session about her disappointments, while pressures on her to care for her mother were reduced with ecological interventions. Family and individual therapy helped T. S. and her siblings grieve the cultural losses her family had experienced and come to terms with the reality of a father who had limited commitment to the household and who appeared to have a *casa chica* arrangement.

Posttraumatic stress symptoms may appear in disguised form, as in this case:

> N. H., a boy almost thirteen years old, was an anxious, bright, hyperactive, impulsive, bilingual Salvadoran refugee who was in the seventh grade in his urban middle school. He had threatened suicide twice and was hospitalized in a children's psychiatric unit when I began to work with him and his mother.

The two had a volatile relationship. N. H.'s mother, the youngest of nine siblings, originally came to the United States in 1981 from El Salvador at the request of her brother B., who lived in Texas. There she became pregnant with N. H. by a Guatemalan national whom she met in Texas, married, and eventually divorced. Returning to El Salvador to raise the child, N. H.'s mother maintained a rather numb attitude to the mutilated and dead bodies she had seen constantly while living in El Salvador. It was left to N. H. to take on a preoccupation with death. N. H. was torn in many respects as to his identity. He was very sensitive to other children denigrating El Salvador in his school. He was also sensitive to issues of skin color, and he identified as a boy attracted sexually to other boys, although not openly as "gay." He enjoyed female-identified activities such as playing with Barbie dolls. His mother and other extended family members are strongly opposed to his sexual preference. N. H. was parentified and worried about his mother's self-destructive relationship with a man who treated her poorly. The political trauma all family members had experienced was intertwined with numerous other clinical and cultural issues that were a part of this family story.

I worked in Spanish with both the mother and son in an ecological and supportive manner as they dealt with basic needs and survival issues. I took on the role of advocate with the middle school in helping find a supportive educational environment for this multiply stigmatized child. I also worked with the mother on how to set limits with her son and with others who were taking advantage of her. In so doing, I modeled positive parenting and at the same time supported her need for positive self-regard and boundaries. A wraparound mental health team provided more in-home services, and work progressed in monitoring N. H.'s preoccupation with death and suicidal ideation. The team met several times to discuss the pros and cons of the family's proposed trip to San Salvador to visit the large extended family.

Group Approaches

In relation to psychosocial trauma, there have been suggestions that for some adults, group treatment is the most effective way to intervene. In these cases, religious or solidarity groups in which *testimonio* (testimony) is given as to experiences in the past may be useful. Some feel this politicizes the process of healing and is counterproductive because people have such idiosyncratic experiences with war trauma. During the height of the wars in Central America, a number of solidarity groups were particularly popular with Salvadorans. However, there was some controversy about this intervention, and it is certainly not for everyone.[22]

Lykes (1994) and others have experimented with running expressive arts workshops with Guatemalan Mayan children in Guatemala. This model incorporates drawing, storytelling, collage, and dramatization as vehicles for the discharge of energy and emotion relating to past traumatic experiences. This approach deserves further study. It may prove to be a beneficial approach in work with Central American children and youth in the United States.

Working with gang-affiliated Latino youth in the United States is challenging because it is based on that youth's readiness to engage, which is variable. Usually if an adolescent is gang-identified, he or she has adopted a new family (the gang), and the therapist must attempt to establish an emotionally corrective relationship that provides support, guidance, nonjudgmental listening, and advocacy (Morales, 1992).

Implications for Mental Health Policy and Programs

A major policy issue for Central American youth is that of gaining documentation through naturalization classes and processes, and for voter education programs for themselves and their family members. Even if they are born here, their parents may be subject to deportation if they are undocumented. Citizenship and the vote are rights and responsibilities that are necessary for true empowerment. Recent immigration policy has been harmful to reunification efforts of Central American families and exacerbates psychological problems associated with family and caregiver stability needs of Central American youth.

A responsive bilingual education policy is vital to move beyond an English-only myopia to the creation of an infrastructure that will support full access to a range of academic resources, technology, support services, classroom teachers, and curricula for our youth. The goal should be to eliminate inequality and institutional racism in education by teaching all students to be able to speak and be literate in more than one language. A variety of new technologies and methods are needed, not just "English immersion." Professional schools (especially medical schools) are beginning to grapple with the problems of training health professionals to work in growing Spanish-speaking communities. One graduate social work program (San José State University) offers "Advanced Social Work Practice in Spanish-speaking Communities," a course taught in Spanish on culturally competent interventions for students who are moderately bilingual.

> Recently, I was contacted by the indigenous hometown *fraternidad* (brotherhood) of the community in Guatemala that I visited after the Peace Accords. The request was that I assist them in organizing toward the goal that schools in a rural Guatemalan community gain access to computers and computer software so that the children there would "have a future."

Without such support and programs in our own local schools, as well as transnationally, Central American children's future options will indeed be foreshortened. A recent change in California law has been the passage of AB540,[23] which opens up postsecondary education to Central American and other undocumented immigrant youth and provides a ray of hope for our youth and their families. Another new initiative has been the opening of the first Central American Studies Program at Cal State Northridge, a California state university. This program will provide an opportunity for students to learn more about what it means to be Guatemalan, Salvadoran, Panamanian, Belizan, and so on. It may also help to integrate fragmented identities.

Summary and Conclusion

This chapter calls attention to clinical and cultural issues faced by Central American youth. The supplement to the Surgeon General's *Report on Mental Health* (U.S. Department of Health and Human Services, 2001) highlights the disparities in mental health services for minorities and problems in access. A severe shortage in residential psychiatric treatment facilities and programs for children and youth exists in California; many of the affected youth are youth of color, Latinos, and Central Americans (California Institute of

Mental Health, 2001). School and community-based youth-oriented services and more mental health services in the juvenile detention centers are urgently needed. Recreation and creative and media arts in community and institutional settings also provide a voice for those youth who are marginalized.

Closing the substantial gap in disparities in quality of care is equally important (U.S. Department of Health and Human Services, 2001). Further research on both preventive and therapeutic interventions and strategies is required to clarify cultural competencies with Central American youth. The lack of available culturally competent providers exists at every level of health and mental health care for Central American youth. More comprehensive training and further research on appropriate quality preventive and therapeutic strategies is needed for all mental health disciplines and professions. Youth and their parents need comprehensive and appropriate health insurance and competent providers who can be both clinically and culturally sound in their assessments and interventions.

Notes

1. This quote is from the animated film *Popul Vuh: Creation Myth of the Maya*, written, directed, and produced by Patricia Amlin and funded by the National Endowment for the Humanities in 1989.
2. Since the terrorist events of September 11, 2001, the U.S. Immigration and Naturalization Service has reported fewer apprehensions at the border. This is expected to be a temporary phenomenon due to (1) fear on the part of potential entrants of terrorism on U.S. soil, (2) heightened security at the border, and (3) anti-immigrant backlash in the U.S. population at large ("INS Border Apprehensions," n.d.).
3. Migration is often a survival strategy precipitated by a family crisis in which the meaning and motive for the action is not clear, so a "cover story" is created.
4. The term *the situation* can euphemistically refer to family or individual experiences of arrest, torture, threatened conscription, seeing dead bodies, rape, traumatic journeys with *coyotes* (smugglers of people), economic exploitation, and undocumented legal status.
5. When the 2000 census gives data on Central Americans, they are lumped together with South American data.
6. "Ladinos" is the term used for Indian-Spanish *mestizos* who have been culturally Hispanicized, seeing themselves as "not Indian."

7. I first heard this as part of a poem written by Concha Saucedo, the long-time executive director and founder of Instituto Familiar de la Raza in San Francisco.

8. In Guatemala, this category is termed *ladinos* because the idea of a positively fused identity is still not widely accepted, and the fiction of Spanish-only descent lives on.

9. "Ladinoization" is a process of replacing indigenous Mayan dress or language and rituals with Spanish dress, language, manners, and identity. Sometimes these identities are layered. Upward social mobility is often the implicit goal.

10. In the past decade, a social movement has emerged in Nicaragua with ties to the United States in which some men are resisting the *machista* stereotype. The situation of Zoilamérica, the famous stepdaughter of Daniel Ortega Saavedra, the one-time Sandinista Nicaraguan president and revolutionary, has raised the stakes on this issue; she publicly accused him of sexual abuse while she was a child. In recent times, she has received support from an organization of Nicaraguan men who are countering violence and abuse of women by adhering to a positive version of machismo—protection of women (Broadbent, 2000).

11. Some followers of these religious traditions seek help for physical and psychological problems from healers and practitioners in these groups.

12. Images in thoughts, language, and dreams have core meanings and purpose.

13. Time (past-present-future) is circular, connected to nature, slow in pace, and connected to community social life.

14. I would like to acknowledge the work of Cheri Coulter-Nava, a social worker who was working at a Mission District agency for adolescent mental health and the Bay Area Spanish Speaking Therapists' Association, where the two of us presented on this topic during the early 1990s.

15. *Confianza* refers to deep trust and respect in a personal relationship rather than in an institution.

16. *Susto* is a culturally defined illness in which a person has been frightened and the soul leaves the body. The person may show symptoms of withdrawal, sadness, anxiety, and physical aches and pains (stomach, headache). The syndrome is etiologically related to PTSD.

17. Carlos Sluzki's important article about the stages of migration and family conflict delineates a number of phases—preparation, act of migration, overcompensation, crisis, and either resolution of crisis

or "transgenerational phenomena." This applies well to the assessment of Central American youth and families.

18. The *DSM IV-R* acknowledges the existence of a variety of "culture-bound syndromes." These psychiatric illnesses are marginalized within the manual. The study of children's disorders is even more marginalized. However some common notions of *ataques de nervios* or *susto* may be similar in nature to PTSD and can be understood in a cultural idiom as being the consequence of the soul leaving the body. Many of these indigenous beliefs are quite suppressed and kept secret, particularly for Central Americans, due to the aforementioned fragmented identities. Other illnesses that may affect young children are *mal de ojo* (listless baby due to "evil eye"), *chipil* (distraught toddler due to mother caring for new baby), and *empacho* (digestive disturbance in young child due to abdominal blockage). These beliefs can be pursued by ethnographic interviewing, inquiring of the parents as to their explanation for the problem and what are the usual remedies.

19. In my own fieldwork on family mental health of Guatemalans in California (Vlach, 1992), I found that most refugee families in my study coped with the early stage of migration through disengagement and conflict. The characteristic profile was that of a disengaged, conflicted, achievement-oriented, and religious family (usually evangelical) that was not cohesive, despite the ideal of family unity. Resilience factors for families who did not fit this profile were loyalty to extended family and to Guatemala, well-organized family roles, maintenance of connection to the Catholic faith, unity of family leadership, and a positive attitude to life in the United States as a challenge and a good thing. Mothers were crucial in making all of this happen.

20. These questions were developed by Jeanne Nidorf as useful in assessment with Southeast Asian refugee children and youth.

21. This information was obtained during the author's field work in Guatemala as a doctoral student in the early 1990s.

22. One anonymous participant told me that there was a need to have structure in the group to help resolve feelings of survivor's guilt and blame. She said that the group helped decrease nightmares and resolve some traumatic memories. As time went on, issues of family separation and culture-generational conflict became stronger, and the group changed. It became a more psychoeducationally focused group in which skills were taught (anonymous personal communication, April 18, 1994; Córdova and Kury, 2001).

23. AB540 allows California high school graduates to pay in-state tuition to attend colleges and universities in California, regardless of immigration status.

References

Adams, R. *Crucifixion by Power.* Austin: University of Texas Press, 1970.

Adams, R. (ed.). *The Origins of Maya Civilization.* Albuquerque: University of New Mexico Press, 1977.

Alderete, E., Vega, W., Kolody, B., and Aguilar-Gaxiola, S. "Effects of Time in the United States and Indian Ethnicity on DSM III-R Psychiatric Disorders Among Mexican Americans in California." *Journal of Nervous and Mental Disease,* 2000a, *188*(2), 90–100.

Alderete, E., Vega, W., Kolody, B., and Aguilar-Gaxiola, S. "Lifetime Prevalence of and Risk Factors for Psychiatric Disorders Among Mexican Migrant Farmworkers in California." *American Journal of Public Health,* 2000b, *90*(4), 608–614.

Al-Issa, I., and Tousignant, M. (eds.). *Ethnicity, Immigration, and Psychopathology.* New York: Plenum Press, 1997.

American Baptist Churches v. *Thornburgh* Settlement Agreement, 2002. Available online at www.ins.gov/graphics/services/residency/abc.htm.

Amlin, P. (prod.-dir.). *Popul Vuh: Creation Myth of the Maya.* Motion Picture. Washington, D.C.: National Endowment for the Humanities, 1989.

Arroyo, W., and Eth, S. "Children Traumatized by Central American Warfare." In S. Eth and R. Pynoos, (eds.), *Post-traumatic Stress Disorder in Children.* Washington, D.C.: American Psychiatric Press, 1985.

Braveman, P., Meyers, A., Schlenker, T., and Wands, K. "Public Health and War in Central America." In B. S. Levy, J. Barry, and V. W. Sidel (eds.), *War and Public Health.* New York: Oxford University Press, 1997.

Broadbent, L. (prod.-dir.). *Macho,* 2000. Motion Picture available from Women Make Movies, 462 Broadway, Suite 500WS, New York 10013; Web site: www.wmm.com.

California Institute of Mental Health. *Psychiatric Hospital Beds in California: Reduced Numbers Create System Slow-Down and Potential Crisis.* Sacramento: California Institute of Mental Health, 2001.

Canino, I., and Spurlock, J. *Culturally Diverse Children and Adolescents.* New York: Guilford Press, 1994.

Cervantes, R. C., Salgado de Snyder, N., and Padilla, A. M. "Post-Traumatic Stress Disorder in Immigrants from Central America and Mexico." *Hospital and Community Psychiatry,* 1989, *40,* 615–619.

Chapa, T. "An Examination of Post-Traumatic Stress Disorder in War Refugee Children from El Salvador, Ages 7 to 11." Unpublished doctoral dissertation. Berkeley/Alameda: California School of Professional Psychology, 1992.

Coe, M. *The Maya.* New York: Thames and Hudson, 1993.

Córdova, C. B., and Kury, F. "Salvadorans." In A. Lopez and E. Carrillo, (eds.), *The Latino Psychiatric Patient*. Washington D.C.: American Psychiatric Association, 2001.

Córdova, C. B., and Pinderhughes, R. "Central and South Americans." In E. R. Barkan (ed.), *A Nation of Peoples: A Sourcebook on America's Multicultural Heritage*. Westport, Conn.: Greenwood Press, 1999.

de la Cadena, M. "Reconstructing Race: Racism, Culture and *Mestizaje*." *Report on the Americas*, 2001, *34*(6), 16–23.

Dobkin de Ríos, M. *Brief Therapy with the Latino Immigrant Client*. New York: Haworth Press, 2001.

Falicov, C. *Latino Families in Therapy*. New York: Guilford Press, 1998.

Frankl, V. *The Doctor and the Soul: From Psychotherapy to Logotherapy*. New York: Knopf, 1965.

Gibbs, J. T., and Bankhead, T. "Preserving Privilege: California Politics, Propositions, and People of Color." Westport, Conn.: Greenwood Press, 2001.

Gibbs, J. T., Huang, L. N., and Associates. *Children of Color: Psychological Interventions with Culturally Diverse Youth*. San Francisco: Jossey-Bass, 1998.

Greene, J. P. "High School Graduation Rates in the United States." November 2001. Available online at www.manhattan-institute.org/html/cr_baeo.htm.

Greene, J. P. "Graduation Statistics: Caveat Emptor." January 16, 2002. Available online at www.edweek.org/ew/newstorycfm?slug=18 greene.h21&keywords=dropouts.

Gutiérrez, R. J. "An Excerpt from 'Part-Time Salvy.' " In K. C. Kim and A. Serrano (eds.), *Izote Vos: A Collection of Salvadoran American Writing and Visual Art*. San Francisco: Pacific News Service, 1999. Available online at www.pacificnews/org/izote/html's/writers_Raquel.html.

Guerra, A.J.C. "An Excerpt from 'La Guerra.' " In K. C. Kim and A. Serrano (eds.), *Izote Vos: A Collection of Salvadoran American Writing and Visual Art*. San Francisco: Pacific News Service, 1999. Available online at www.pacificnews/org/izote/html's/writers_adriana.html.

Hayes-Bautista, D., Schink, W., and Chapa, J. *The Burden of Support: Young Latinos in an Aging Society*. Stanford, Calif.: Stanford University Press, 1988.

Human Rights Office of the Archdiocese of Guatemala. *Guatemala, Never Again: Recovery of Historical Memory Project*. Maryknoll, N.Y.: Orbis Books, 1999.

"INS Announces Restructuring." Available online from United States Immigration and Naturalization Service at www.ins.gov, 2002.

"INS Border Apprehensions." (n.d.). Available online from United States Immigration and Naturalization Service at www.ins.gov.

Koss-Chioino, J., and Vargas, L. *Working with Latino Youth: Culture, Development and Context.* San Francisco: Jossey-Bass, 1999.

LaCayo, A. "Nicaraguans." In A. Lopez and E. Carrillo, (eds.), *The Latino Psychiatric Patient.* Washington, D.C.: American Psychiatric Association, 2001.

Locke, C. J., Southwick, K., McCloskey, L. A., and Fernández-Esquer, M. E. "The Psychological and Medical Sequelae of War in Central American Refugee Mothers and Children." *Archives of Pediatric Adolescent Medicine,* 1996, *150,* 822–828.

Loucky, J., Moors, J., and Moors, M. (eds.). *The Mayan Diaspora: Guatemalan Roots/New American Lives.* Philadelphia: Temple University Press, 2000.

Lykes, M. B. "Terror, Silencing and Children: International, Multidisciplinary Collaboration with Guatemalan Maya Communities." *Social Science and Medicine,* 1994, *38*(4), 543–552.

Maduro, R., and Martinez, C. "Latino Dream Analysis: Opportunity for Self and Social Confrontation." *Social Casework,* 1979, *55*(8).

Martin-Barâ, I. "*La Violencia Política Y la Guerra Como Causa del Trauma Psicosocial en El Salvador*" (Political Violence and War as Causes of Psychosocial Trauma in El Salvador). *Revista de Psicología de El Salvador,* 1988a, *28,* 123–141.

Martin-Barâ, I. *Guerra y Trauma Psicosocial del Niño Salvadereño* (War and Psychosocial Trauma of the Salvadoran Child). Paper presented at the Seminario-Taller for Associación de Capacitación Investigatión para la Salud Mental, Universidad Centroamericana José Simeon Coâs, San Salvador, El Salvador, 1988b.

Martinez, K., and Valdez, D. "Cultural Considerations in Play Therapy with Hispanic Children." In L. Vargas and J. Koss-Chioino (eds.), *Working with Culture: Psychotherapeutic Interventions with Ethnic Minority Children and Adolescents.* San Francisco: Jossey-Bass, 1992.

Masser, D. "Psychosocial Functioning of Central American Children." *Child Welfare,* 1992, *71*(5), 439–476.

Mills, R. J. "Health Insurance Coverage." September 2002. Available online at www.census.gov/prod2001pubs/p60–215pdf.

Morales, A. "Therapy with Latino Gang Members." In L. Vargas and J. Koss-Chioino (eds.), *Working with Culture: Psychotherapeutic Interventions with Ethnic Children and Adolescents.* San Francisco: Jossey-Bass, 1992.

National Center for Education Statistics. "Dropout Rates in the United States 2000." U.S. Department of Education, Office of Education Research and Improvement, 2001. Available online at www.nces.ed.gov/pubs2002/2002114.pdf.

Nidorf, J. "Mental Health and Refugee Youth: A Model for Diagnostic Training." In T. Owan (ed.), *Southeast Asian Mental Health: Treatment, Prevention, Services, Training, and Research*. Washington, D.C.: U.S. Department of Health and Human Services, 1995.

Ogbu, J., and Matute-Bianchi, M. E. "Understanding Sociocultural Factors: Knowledge, Identity, and School Adjustment." In *Beyond Language: Social and Cultural Factors in the Schooling of Language Minority Students*. Sacramento: Bilingual Education Office, California State Department of Education, 1986.

Ogbu, J., and Simons, H. "Voluntary and Involuntary Minorities: A Cultural-Ecological Theory of School Performance with Some Implications for Education." *Anthropology and Education Quarterly*, 1998, *29*(2), 155–188.

Peñalosa, F. *Central Americans in Los Angeles: Background, Language, Education*. Los Angeles: Spanish Speaking Mental Health Research Center No. 21, National Center for Bilingual Research, 1986.

Picado, J. M. "The War in El Salvador: The Child as Witness, Participant, Casualty, Survivor: A Phenomenological Study." Unpublished doctoral dissertation, University of Southern California, Los Angeles, 1988.

Romero de Thompson, S. E. "Hondurans in the United States: Their Perceptions and Beliefs About Mental Health, Mental Illness, and Service Utilization." Unpublished doctoral dissertation, University of Texas, Austin, 1996.

Sachs, S. "A Nation Challenged: Detainees." 2002. Available online at www.nytimes.com.

Santa Barbara, J. "The Psychological Effects of War on Children." In B. S. Levy, J. Barry, and V. W. Sidel, (eds.), *War and Public Health*. New York: Oxford University Press, 1997.

Schele, L., and Friedel, D. *A Forest of Kings: The Untold Story of the Ancient Maya*. New York: Morrow Press, 1990.

Schreiber, J. "The Decision to Move as a Response to Family Crisis." In *Migration: Report of the Research Conference on Migration, Ethnic Minority Status and Social Adaptation, Rome, 13–16 June 1972*. UNICRI Publication Series, no. 5. Rome: Interregional Crime and Justice Research Institute, 1973.

"Slipping Through the Cracks: Unaccompanied Children Detained by the United States Immigration and Naturalization Service." Human Rights Watch Children's Rights Project. 1997. Available online at www.hrw.org/reports/1997/uscrcks/index.html.

Sluzki, C. "Migration and Family Conflict." *Family Process*, 1979, *18*(4), 379–390.

Sluzki, C. "The Sounds of Silence: Two Cases of Elective Mutism in Bilingual Families." In J. Hansen and C. Falicov (eds.), *Cultural Perspectives in Family Therapy.* Rockville, Md.: Aspen, 1983.

Suárez-Orozco, C., and Suárez-Orozco, M. *Transformations: Immigration, Family Life and Achievement Motivation Among Latino Adolescents.* Stanford, Calif.: Stanford University Press, 1995.

Suárez-Orozco, C., and Suárez-Orozco, M. *Children of Immigration.* Cambridge, Mass.: Harvard University Press, 2001.

Suárez-Orozco, M. *Central American Refugees and U.S. High Schools.* Stanford, Calif.: Stanford University Press, 1989.

"Temporary Protected Status," 2002. Available online at www.ins.gov/graphics/services/tps_inter.htm.

Therrien, M., and Ramirez, R. R. *The Hispanic Population in the United States: March 2000 Current Population Reports.* Washington, D.C.: U.S. Bureau of the Census, 2001. Available online at www.census.gov/prod/2001pubs/p20–535.pdf.

U.S. Department of Health and Human Services. *Mental Health: Culture, Race and Ethnicity.* Supplement to *Mental Health: A Report of the Surgeon General.* Rockville, Md.: U.S. Department of Health and Human Services, 2001.

Vega, W., Alderete, E., Kolody, B., and Aguilar-Gaxiola, S. "Illicit Drug Use Among Mexicans and Mexican Americans in California: The Effects of Gender and Acculturation." *Addiction,* 1998, *93*(12), 1839–1850.

Vega, W., and others. "Lifetime Prevalence of DSM III-R Psychiatric Disorders Among Urban and Rural Mexican-Americans in California." *Archives of General Psychiatry,* 1998, *55*(9), 771–778.

Vlach, N. *The Quetzal in Flight: Guatemalan Refugee Families in the United States.* New York: Praeger, 1992.

Chapter Eight

Mexican American Children and Adolescents

Kurt C. Organista

Mexican Americans or Chicanos are historically the oldest and demographically the largest of all Latino groups in the United States. They are also the largest group of U.S. immigrants. With respect to age, Mexican Americans are the youngest of all Latino groups and one of the most rapidly growing ethnic groups in America because of continuous immigration and natural growth (that is, births outnumber deaths). Compared to Anglo Americans, Mexican American families have larger households and more children but are also significantly poorer. The result is a rapidly growing youth population at risk for numerous psychosocial problems.

The purpose of this chapter is to review and recommend state-of-the art, culturally competent mental health interventions with Mexican American children and adolescents. The chapter critically reviews and synthesizes pertinent literature regarding (1) the major psychosocial problems affecting these youth and (2) assessment and intervention strategies that are responsive to the social and cultural experience of Mexican Americans in the United States. Optimal strategies need to span multiple ecosystemic levels of understanding and impact by including sufficient attention to the family and community, as well as the historical and contemporary experience of Mexican Americans in the United States.

Sociodemographic Profile

According to the U.S. Bureau of the Census (Therrien and Ramirez, 2000), two-thirds of all Latinos in the United States are Mexican Americans—a group now estimated at 35.3 million or 12.5 percent of the population. Latinos comprise the following major groups: Mexican American (66.1), Puerto Rican (9.0 percent), Cuban (4.0 percent), Central and South American (14.5 percent), and "Other" (6.4 percent). As can be seen in Table 8.1, SES is considerably lower for Mexican Americans than for Anglo Americans, with serious consequences for children and families. For example, four times as many Mexican American families live in poverty than non-Hispanic white families (26.4 percent and 7.3 percent, respectively), and 40 percent of Mexican American children under eighteen years of age live below the poverty line, as compared to 10.5 percent of Anglo children. Further, the percentages of children below the age of eighteen who live in "deep poverty," which is defined as being more than 50 percent below the poverty line, is 12.4 percent for Mexican Americans versus 4.2 percent for Anglos.

Latinos are generally younger than their Anglo counterparts and have larger families. For example, 38.4 percent of Mexican Americans are below the age of eighteen, as compared to 23.5 percent of Anglo Americans; 35.0 percent of Mexican households consist of five or more members versus 11.8 percent for Anglo Americans (Therrien and Ramirez, 2000). Mexican Americans are also the youngest of all Latinos in the United States (median ages equal 24.6 for Chicanos, 26.9 for Puerto Ricans, and 43.6 for Cubans). Mexican Americans are similar to Anglos with respect to numbers of two-parent households (61 percent and 58 percent, respectively) but have a larger average household size (4.5 and 3.1, respectively) due to higher fertility rates among Mexican American women. In 1990, the number of children born to Mexican women between the ages of fifteen to forty-four was 1,620 per 1,000 versus 1,176 for Anglos and 1,461 for African American women (Frisbie and Bean, 1995).

One-third of all Mexican Americans are immigrants from Mexico, making migration, acculturation, and adaptation significant ongoing concerns. Such economic immigrants are typically from

**Table 8.1. Sociodemographic Profile
of Latino and Anglo Americans.**

Group	Median Income	Percent in Poverty	Percent High School Completion	Percent College Graduation
Latinos	$23,912	22.8	57.0	10.6
Mexican	$23,714	24.1	51.0	6.9
Puerto Rican	$20,310	25.8	64.3	8.0
Cuban	$31,015	17.3	73.0	23.0
Central & South American	$23,649	16.7	64.3	15.1
Other Hispanic	$28,562	21.3	71.6	15.1
Non-Latino Whites	$40,420	7.7	88.4	28.1

Source: Therrien and Ramirez, 2000.

low-SES backgrounds and find work in the secondary labor market with low earnings, no benefits, and little opportunity for advancement. Although labor participation rates for Mexican Americans are generally higher than for their Anglo counterparts, their poverty rate remains four times as high (Feagin and Booher Feagin, 1999).

This social profile suggests significant risk and a need for human services, yet almost 40 percent of Latinos lack health insurance, which is twice the rate of uninsured Anglo Americans (U.S. Department of Health and Human Services, 2001). Further, compared to Asian, African, and Anglo Americans, Latino children are the least likely to be insured. For example, among Latino youth from birth to seventeen years in immigrant families, almost 50 percent of noncitizens are uninsured, as compared to 71 percent of citizens.

Mexican Americans in the United States

The following section presents a brief historical overview of the experiences of Mexican American immigrants in the United States, with a focus on developments since the early twentieth century.

Acculturation and Adjustment

An acculturation framework can help human service professionals understand the development of contemporary Chicano psychosocial problems by placing them within a historical context that considers the dynamics of race relations, the processes of dominance and subordination, and the ways majority and minority groups evolve together over time. Berry's three-phase model of acculturation (Berry, 1997) is used next to outline the historical experience of Chicanos in the United States.

Contact

Although *contact* for the vast majority of Chicanos can be best characterized as *voluntary immigration,* it is important to understand that, like Native Americans, Mexican people were native to what is now the southwestern portion of the United States prior to westward expansion. They are the only other minority group in U.S. history to be annexed by conquest and to have their rights (supposedly) safeguarded by treaty. A pattern of protracted *conflict* with mainstream society and a difficult adjustment has therefore characterized the Chicano experience in America. Historically, this pattern has been characterized by numerous Mexican-Anglo conflicts, beginning with the war between the United States and Mexico in the mid-1800s, the subsequent loss of substantial Mexican land holdings (the present-day Southwest), and a continuous exploitation of labor.

Conflict

Despite the legacy of conflict between Mexicans and Anglos in the United States, significant Mexican immigration to the United States continues to the present day due to the "push" of political upheaval and lack of work in Mexico and the "pull" of tremendous historical need for unskilled labor in the United States. A historical analysis of Mexican labor during the twentieth century reveals a distinct cyclical pattern of importing and exploiting Mexican labor during labor shortages (for example, World Wars I and II) and then abusing Mexican human rights during periods of economic recession (Acuna, 1981).

During the early 1940s, conflict between Chicanos and Anglos again came to a head during the so-called Zoot Suit riots, in which U.S. sailors, off-duty police, and other service men staged mob-style attacks on young Chicano street-gang members. These predominantly second-generation youth formed street gangs and wore flashy zoot suits in response to their growing marginality in America (Mazon, 1984).

Between World War II and the 1960s, Chicano determination to fight social injustice grew into the climax of the Chicano civil rights movement of the 1960s. Beginning in the 1960s, Chicano farm worker activists César Chávez and Dolores Huerta began unionizing farm workers in order to gain bargaining leverage with agricultural growers through lengthy strikes. The United Farm Workers Union in California, unlike other Chicano protests, brought the plight of Mexican and other farm workers to international attention, although they are still fighting that battle.

The events described exemplify the protracted historical pattern of conflict between Chicanos and Anglos in America, most recently manifested in backlashes against Latinos; examples are California's antibilingual education, antiaffirmative action, and anti-illegal immigration initiatives passed in the 1990s (Gibbs and Bankhead, 2001). Although the degree of conflict for Chicanos has not been as extreme or severe as for African Americans and American Indians, it has compromised the adaptation and well-being of Chicanos in America.

Adaptation

The predominant form of adaptation for Mexican Americans, still considerably in evidence today, has been segregation. Segregation in residence, work, and school has historically been the rule for Chicanos, resulting in painstakingly slow but steady progress toward integration and moderate levels of success, as compared to European immigrants. For roughly seventy-five years after the end of the U.S.-Mexico war, Chicanos faced segregation in most public facilities, primary election procedures, and housing (McLemore and Romo, 1998). Bean and Tienda (1990) used census data to calculate a segregation index for Chicanos and found that index for Los Angeles is .57, indicating that 57 percent of Chicanos would need to move out of their residential tracts to produce an even residential distribution of Chicanos and Anglos in Los Angeles. Thus this index indicates moderately high segregation, as do indexes from other heavily Chicano cities such as Chicago (.63) and San Antonio (.57).

Sociocultural Values and Norms of Chicano Family and Culture

Reviews of the empirical literature on the Chicano family (for example, Vega, 1990) describe a variety of organizational and functional characteristics that derive from a blend of traditional Mexican culture and adaptational responses to the social environment, over time, of Chicanos in the United States. Descriptions have evolved from static, stereotypical portraits of the traditional Mexican-based Chicano family to more dynamic descriptions that consider heterogeneity in response to the demands of acculturation to a modern society across various social subgroupings of family members. For example, in her descriptions of the Chicano family, Falicov (1998) uses the term *culture* to refer to a community of people who share, to some extent, the same systems for describing and ascribing meaning to the world (for example, preferred values, norms, behaviors, and role prescriptions). She further asserts that the ecological niche or unique combination of multiple contexts and partial perspectives define each individual's and each family's variation on major cultural themes.

Core Values

Traditional Mexican cultural values that form the basis of norms, behaviors, and role prescriptions and that become modified in response to the American social environment provide a convenient vehicle for describing and discussing Chicano family structures and functioning. For example, although there is currently an expanding variety of Chicano families (for example, single- and two-parent, nuclear and extended, immigrant and multigenerational, gay and lesbian), the families are partially based on the core cultural value of *familismo,* which refers to the central importance of the family as manifested in strong emotional and instrumental interdependence between members, within and across generations, over the life cycle. Whereas more modern Anglo American norms and values stress individualism, competition, independence, and even individuation of members from the family over time, *familismo* nurtures close contact, loyalty, and even a lifelong sense of "self-in-family" that serves as a psychosocial guide for family members with regard to their values and actions.

Reviews of the empirical literature on the Chicano family conclude that research generally corroborates the concept of familism in Chicanos-Latinos, as compared to Anglos, by demonstrating greater participation in family networks within and across generations (for example, emotional and instrumental support and preference for relying on family to cope with problems). Perez and Padilla (2000) studied a three-generation sample of 203 Chicano adolescents and found that, although Mexican cultural orientation decreased from the first to the third generation, and American cultural orientation increased, participants retained their allegiance to Chicano family values.

Mexican American families also share the traditional Mexican value of *respeto* (respect), which refers to deference to those with more hierarchical status in the traditional sense (that is, by virtue of older age or higher social position, including by male gender relative to female). Related values include affiliation and cooperation, which are traditionally stressed in family relations more than independence and assertiveness. *Simpatia* refers to the valuing of smooth, pleasant relationships that minimize and avoid conflict and confrontation. Closely related is the value of *personalismo,* which refers to an emphasis on the personal dimension of relationships, including task-oriented professional relationships in mental health and other social services. As such, the mainstream practice of immediately focusing on the presenting problem can be perceived as impersonal or rude by Latino patients, especially if it is at the expense of the social lubrication needed to build *confianza* or trust (Roll, Millen, and Ramirez, 1980).

It is important not to confuse *personalismo* with informality. That is, it would be a mistake for a service provider to come across too casually or be overly friendly. As described by Roll, Millen, and

Ramirez (1980), the task of the culturally sensitive service provider is to find the balance between task-oriented formality and personalized attention to the patient. To achieve such a balance, it is necessary for providers to engage in sufficient small talk, or *platica*, that includes judicious self-disclosure.

Childrearing

Chicano childrearing practices partially reflect the values just mentioned along traditional age and gender hierarchies; conformity is praised and deviations are disciplined. For example, children are expected to obey and respect parents, and "being right" is secondary to respecting elders by not disagreeing or arguing a point. The term *bien educado* (well educated) refers to children and adults who have been raised properly, as reflected in their adherence to traditional values and interpersonal protocol. *Mal criado* (poorly raised) means the opposite. But childrearing practices also partially reflect modern Anglo American values, resulting in much bicultural variation.

The patriarchal basis of traditional Chicano families can be hard to understand in mainstream America, which stresses more egalitarian and "friendly" relations within and between generations and, increasingly, between the sexes. The clash of values experienced by Chicano youth can become especially difficult when there are no models of flexible biculturality either within their families or in the larger society. The problem is exacerbated by family dysfunction and uneven levels of acculturation between members.

Gender Role Expansion

Falicov (1996) notes that although a patriarchal view of gender roles persists in Chicanos, complexities and contradictions continue to evolve in such a way that traditional family structures and functions coexist with Anglo American norms and behaviors, resulting in varying degrees of biculturality across different cultural dimensions. For example, a double standard in sex role socialization and sexuality has generally persisted in Chicano families, but shared decision making between husbands and wives is evolving, as women enter the workforce in increasing numbers (Ybarra,

1982). Guendleman (1987) found that seasonal migration to the United States expanded the traditional roles of Mexican women to include greater purchasing power, family decision making, division of household responsibilities with husbands, feelings of autonomy, and less stress, as compared to nonworking immigrant women.

Ecological-Systems Perspective

The emerging consensus in the literature is that most of the major psychosocial problems currently affecting Chicano youth result from unmet developmental needs due to the breakdown of conventional social and cultural supports and resources within the family, ethnic community, and greater society. As such, assessment and intervention efforts need to be based on problem conceptualizations that contextualize Chicano youth mental health issues with regard to relevant ecosystemic dimensions such as risk factors related to a combination of poverty and ethnic minority status.

Although it is a major cultural resource, familism alone cannot compensate for the Chicano family's ecological context in which ethnically linked, poverty-related stressors can overtax the family system. For example, Gomel, Tinsley, Parke, and Clark (1998) studied coping strategies in Latino families struggling with economic hardship and found that unemployment, perceptions of economic hardship among members, and the use of the family to cope with such hardship resulted in negative changes in family relations. In contrast, individual coping strategies resulted in more positive relations. With regard to child mental health, Weiss and others (1999) found that emotional and behavioral symptoms in Mexican preschool children were predicted, not by SES or acculturation but by family immigration status, parental dissatisfaction with family functioning, and internal versus external coping strategies.

Natural Support Systems

Many discussions and descriptions of Latino natural support systems have accrued in the literature (for example, Delgado, 1999; Valle and Vega, 1980). Most of the discussion centers on the role of the extended family and informal resources and helping networks in the community that provide a wide range of social support, buffer stress, and boost the enjoyment and meaningfulness of positive events. Service providers are advised to learn about the natural support systems of clients and communities served by agencies. Providers should be cautioned, however, to avoid overtaxing natural support systems that have partly evolved to compensate for social neglect.

Catholicism

The overwhelming majority of Chicanos are Catholic. Falicov (1996) notes that the Catholic Church provides continuity to families across generations, throughout the life cycle, for its central role in rites of passage such as baptism, first holy communion, marriage, and funerals. The church also creates community by providing a central place for Sunday mass, religious and Latino holiday celebrations, and community activities. Parochial school also provides many Chicano children with the rare opportunity for a quality private education to enhance their life chances.

But like Italian Americans, Chicano Catholics demonstrate general allegiance to the church but less active religious participation than Irish Americans (Feagin and Booher Feagin, 1999). As such, Chicanos are able to compartmentalize religion, and their behaviors do not always conform to the church, even though Chicanos may feel "very Catholic." For example, research on contraceptive use in Mexican and Chicano Catholic women consistently reveals high use of a variety of birth control methods, despite church teachings to the contrary (Amaro, 1988; Balls Organista, Organista, and Soloff, 1998). Thus, although the spiritual and supportive dimensions of Catholicism should be used as needed with religious clients, we should not assume their passive conformity to the Catholic Church.

Curanderismo

Almost without fail, writings on Chicano family and culture emphasize the importance of *curanderismo*—Mexican-based folk medicine and healing practices in which *curanderos* (folk healers) perform rituals to rid people of physical and emotional problems of both natural and supernatural origin. However, empirical research with large samples of Chicanos fails to support either widespread or exclusive use of *curanderismo*.

For example, in an early survey of 666 Chicanos from Los Angeles, Padilla, Carlos, and Keefe (1976) found that only 2 percent had consulted a *curandero* for emotional problems during the past year and that only 8 percent had ever done so in their entire life. Furthermore, when asked the first place recommended to someone with an emotional problem, none indicated a *curandero*, as opposed to doctor (25 percent), relative or *compadre* (20 percent), priest (17 percent), friend (14 percent), mental health clinic (14 percent), and psychiatrist-counselor (9 percent). Using a sample of 3,623 Chicanos from the Southwest, Higginbotham, Trevino, and Ray (1990) similarly found that only 4.2 percent reported consulting a *curandero*, herbalist, or other folk practitioner during the past year. The use of folk doctors by this small percentage was predicted by low income and dissatisfaction with modern medical services recently received, indicating the use of *curanderos* as a last resort. Thus Mexican Americans would be better served if we were to concentrate our efforts on promoting accessible, affordable, and culturally acceptable health and mental health services.

Major Mental Health Issues in Mexican American Youth

In their "new framework" for understanding adolescent risk, Burt, Resnick, and Novick (1998) articulate an ecologically comprehensive approach that emphasizes antecedent conditions, early signs of difficulties, and eventual negative outcomes when institutional supports and adolescent competencies are weak or lacking. For Chicano youth, antecedents include excessive poverty, family dysfunction, and deficient community institutions such as schools. Although protective factors include individual, family, and community strengths, such protective factors are frequently undermined by the risk factors just described. As a result, early signs of difficulty such as records of school failure and police records are disproportionately high in Chicano youth, as are more serious and long-term problem behaviors. The most prominent cluster of problem behaviors for Chicano youth includes school failure, risky sexual behavior, substance abuse, delinquency and gang involvement, and depression and suicidality.

School Failure

School failure for Mexican American youth deserves special mention for its important role in all of the aforementioned psychosocial problems. Rumberger's review (1998) of the problem shows that (1) 17 percent of Latino students have dropped out by ninth grade, (2) fewer than 50 percent of Latinos at ninth grade have earned enough credits to be on track for graduation, and (3) by the end of the tenth grade, 31 percent of Latino students have dropped out, and fewer than 21 percent have earned enough credits to be on track to graduate.

Rumberger and Larson (1994) assert that although Chicano dropouts are like non-Chicano dropouts in many respects (dislike for school, low educational aspirations, discipline problems, and so on), they are more likely to drop out before high school and to receive an inferior education. Solorzano and Solorzano's review of the literature (1995) shows that at both elementary and secondary school levels, Mexican Americans are more likely to attend segregated schools characterized by low-quality curricula, less qualified teachers, greater teacher turnover, overemphasis on remedial studies, rigid ability placements and "tracking" in non-college-preparatory courses, low-quality programs for limited English proficiency students, and curricula short on relevance to the Chicano experience. Therefore, theories of Chicano school failure need to focus on the role of school structure, resources, and processes, as opposed to historically misguided searches for genetic and cultural defects within the Mexican American student, family, and community (Rumberger and Larson, 1994).

Research shows that although Chicano students and parents are similar to Anglo counterparts in their educational values and related aspirations, the former have less "instrumental knowledge" regarding scholastic requirements for college and education needed to prepare for desired professional careers; they are also less aware of where to obtain such information (Garcia, 2001). Further, low-SES Chicano parents are less able than Anglo counterparts to provide direct guidance to help their children with homework and vocational aspirations (Azmitia, Cooper, Garcia, and Dunbar, 1996). Without the knowledge and skills to realize educational dreams, it is not surprising that so many Mexican American youth become disconnected from school and consequently involved in risky behaviors and situations, as discussed next.

Risky Sexual Behavior

Risky sexual behavior in adolescents has long been a public health priority for its connection to teen pregnancy and sexually transmitted diseases (STDs), including HIV-AIDS. National survey data indicate a continual rise in the rates of teen pregnancy and live births, with consequent problems such as greater medical risks for mother and child, fewer education and career options for teen mothers, higher poverty and divorce rates for teen parents, and greater potential for wife and child abuse (Berry, Shillington, Peak, and Hohman, 2000; Franklin and Corcoran, 2000). With regard to race and ethnicity, the live birth rate for adolescent Latinas (100 per 1,000) is quickly approaching that of African American counterparts (109 per 1,000), and birth rates for both of these minority groups are more than twice that of Anglo American female adolescents (43 per 1,000).

The little research that has focused on Chicana adolescents indicates two consistent patterns: (1) more acculturated Mexican American females are at greater risk for sexual activity and single motherhood than those less acculturated (Becerra and de Anda, 1984; Darabi and Ortiz, 1986; Reynoso, Felice, and Shragg, 1993), and (2) Chicanas have higher rates of live births than Anglo American girls, despite comparable pregnancy rates and lower rates of sexual intercourse (Aneshensel, Becerra, Fielder, and Schuler, 1990). These findings suggest less knowledge about sex and contraceptives, less contraceptive use, less communication with parents about sexual matters, and fewer abortions among Mexican American females, as compared to their Anglo and African American counterparts (Baumeister, Flores, and VanOss Marin, 1995; Holck, Warren, Morris, and Rochat, 1982).

With regard to STDs, *The Los Angeles County Hispanic Youth Health Assessment Report* (Nuno, Dorrington, and Alvarez, 1998) found that although rates of gonorrhea and syphilis are generally low for Latino and Anglo adolescents, rates of chlamydia are twice as high for Latinos (483.2 versus 234.0 per 100,000, respectively). More alarmingly, even though adolescent AIDS cases are only 1 percent of L.A. County cases, Latinos between the ages of thirteen and nineteen make up almost half of these cases, as compared to 27.2 percent for African Americans and 21.9 percent for Anglos.

Risky sexual behavior in Mexican American youth is yet another problem area that increases with exposure to the United States and is linked to the breakdown of conventional ties to the family and community institutions. Studies of Chicana adolescents show that avoiding sexual activity is predicted by remaining in school, frequent church activity, and family stability (DuRant, Pendergrast, and Seymore, 1990) and that not being pregnant is predicted by intact family and positive attitudes about school, as well as receiving information from parents about sexuality (Baumeister, Flores, and VanOss Marin, 1995). Felice, Shragg, James, and Hollingsworth (1987) also found that dropping out of school was a greater precipitant of pregnancy for Chicanas, as compared to Anglo and African American girls.

The role of Chicano adolescent males is also important to consider. For example, Perez and Duany (1992) report the percentages of sexual activity by the age of nineteen on the part of Latino (81 percent), Anglo (76 percent), and African American (96 percent) male adolescents. Latino adolescent males were also found to have lower rates of effective contraceptive use (50 percent), as compared to their Anglo and African American counterparts (60 percent each).

Substance Abuse

Recent research has begun to document problematic substance use in Mexican American youth. For example, Chavez, Randall, and Swaim (1992) analyzed data from the National American Drug and Alcohol Survey, which spanned twenty-five middle schools and twenty-six high schools. Although the results showed greater current and lifetime substance use in Anglo (n = 2,243) versus Chicano (n = 1,837) twelfth-grade students, Chicano eighth-grade students (n = 2,530) were higher than Anglo counterparts (n = 1,547) in both current and lifetime substance use, as well as related risk behaviors such as using substances alone, using two drugs at the same time, and sharing needles. The authors conclude that sampling twelfth-grade students misses high school dropouts, who are overrepresented among Chicanos and drug users.

Boles and others (1994) found equal rates of alcohol and drug use in Chicano and Anglo high school students, based on data from the California Substance Use Survey, but their study may have missed Chicano dropouts, as asserted by Chavez, Randall, and Swaim, (1992). These researchers also found greater substance use in U.S.-born versus Mexico-born Chicanos, again underscoring the association between exposure to American society and multiple mental health problems.

Recent national surveys such as the 2001 Youth Risk Behavior Surveillance Study (Centers for Disease Control and Prevention, 2002) and the National Household Survey on Drug Abuse Main Findings 1998 (U.S. Department of Health and Human Services, 2000) report that substance use in adolescents ages twelve through seventeen is generally greater in Latino youth than in their Anglo and African American counterparts. Unfortunately, these surveys combine all Latino groups under the category "Hispanic," thereby obscuring important group differences. We can assume, however, that Chicano and Puerto Rican youth account for the high rates of Latino substance use in these surveys, given their SES profiles. For example, a study by Sokol-Katz and Ulbrich (1992) was conducted to compare the influence of single- and two-parent homes on alcohol and drug use in a sample of Chicano ($n = 794$), Puerto Rican ($n = 299$), and Cuban ($n = 144$) adolescents. Results revealed that both Chicano and Puerto Rican adolescents had higher rates of drug use (30 percent and 28 percent, respectively) than Cubans (15 percent), although they did not differ in alcohol use (15, 12, and 16 percent, respectively). Being from a single-parent home predicted drug and alcohol use for both Chicano and Puerto Rican adolescents, but not for Cubans. The authors conclude that Cubans from single-parent backgrounds may still have the advantage of better support networks and generally higher SES—variables that need to be assessed in substance abuse research.

As with adolescents in general, substance-using peers are an especially important risk factor for Chicano youth. For example, Flannery, Vazsonyi, Torquati, and Fridrich (1994) found that peer variables were more powerful than parent variables in predicting substance use in a sample of 1,170 sixth- and seventh-grade students from three middle schools in Tucson, Arizona (24 percent Chicano and 64 percent Anglo). For both Chicano and Anglo youth, peer substance use and peer pressure to engage in antisocial behaviors were the strongest predictors of lifetime alcohol and drug use, as compared to parent-child closeness, involvement in activities, and parental monitoring. Poorer adjustment to school also predicted substance use and Mexican Americans who were generally more poorly adjusted than their Anglo peers.

Although peers do play a central role in adolescent substance abuse, research also supports the central roles of parents and family in the lives of Mexican American adolescents. For example, Coombs, Paulson, and Richardson (1991) found that although peer marijuana use was the most consistent predictor of substance use in both Mexican American and Anglo American students ages nine through seventeen, substance use in the former was predicted by both peer and parent variables, whereas use in Anglo students was predicted almost exclusively by peer variables. Mexican American students were also more likely than Anglo counterparts to choose parents over peers when asked whose ideas they respected more and to whom they would turn and obey during times of trouble.

Brooks, Stuewig, and LeCroy (1998) found that only low family cohesion predicted substance use in male Mexican American middle school students, as compared to peer substance use, peer relations, adjustment to school, family substance use, and level of acculturation. In this study, *family cohesion* referred to low conflict, high parental monitoring, intact family, and time spent together. Family cohesion did not predict substance use in female Mexican American students, which is consistent with the findings of Flannery, Vazsonyi, Torquati, and Fridrich (1994), who found that substance abuse in Chicanas was predicted by poor adjustment to school but not by family factors.

One study examined the separate and combined impact of several risk and protective factors on drug, alcohol, and cigarette use in 516 predominantly Mexican American high school students from Los Angeles (Felix-Ortiz and Newcomb, 1999). Risk and protective factor indicators were constructed from well-substantiated correlates of adolescent substance abuse, including family, peer, community, educational, and psychological factors. Results revealed that risk factors predicted substance use more strongly than did protective factors but that protective factors did mediate the relation between risk factors and substance use for both boys and girls. That is, at high levels of risk, protective factors predicted less substance use; at low levels of risk they did not.

Similar results were reported by Frauenglass, Routh, Pantin, and Mason (1997) regarding tobacco use in poor Latino adolescents in Miami, Florida. They found that when peer tobacco use was high, family support predicted lower tobacco use in participants, whereas at low levels of peer use, family support did not predict tobacco use. Multivariate studies such as these help to elucidate the ecology of adolescent substance use.

Implications of the research cited include the need to increase the quantity and quality of a broad array of protective factors within major adolescent ecological domains (for example, individual, family, peer, community), and vice versa, with respect to risk factors. More attention to female youth is also warranted in view of findings that alcohol and inhalants were the most commonly used substances among Mexican American girls as well as boys and that rates of alcohol use were actually higher for girls (Felix-Ortiz and Newcomb, 1999).

Chicano Gangs and Delinquency

Although Latino youth are 15 percent of all youth in the United States, they make up 18 percent of juveniles in residential placement for crimes committed (Poe-Yamagata and Jones, 2000), and gang membership is an especially problematic area of crime involvement for Mexican American youth.

Although only a small minority of Chicano youth become *Cholos* (gang members), this historically entrenched phenomenon has been a painful and destructive part of the Chicano experience throughout most of the twentieth century, frequently occurring within several generations of the same, *barrio*-dwelling families. Goldstein and Soriano (1994) note that gang data are imprecise because no national-level agency in the United States has assumed responsibility for the systematic collection and dissemination of gang-relevant information. Relying primarily on local police and other criminal justice agencies, Goldstein and Soriano estimate that there are two thousand gangs in America, with twenty thousand members. They also note that the age range for membership has expanded from twelve to twenty-one years of age to nine to thirty years of age and that the ratio of boy gangs to girl gangs has decreased from 20:1 to 15:1, with increasing autonomy in the latter.

Chicano and black gangs predominate in Los Angeles, with an estimated 600 gangs and 100,000 gang members, numbers that translated into 770 gang-related murders in 1991 (Harris, 1994). Gang experts note that four recent trends have made gangs in America more violent and problematic than ever before: (1) access to more lethal weapons, (2) greater availability of drugs, (3) an increase in interracial violence, and (4) an increase in the multi-purpose and sophistication of gang organization and structure (Yablonsky, 1997).

The foundations for a social and culturally sensitive under-standing of Chicano gangs were laid by the pioneering works of Morales (1992) and Vigil (1988), who view gang membership as an extreme response to the failure of family, community, and tradi-tional social systems to meet the developmental needs of Chicano adolescents struggling with the risks inherent in their low-income, minority-status experience in America. Such "multiple marginali-ties" result in compromised development and struggles with dis-torted cognitive maps of the self, family, culture, social systems, and society.

Belitz and Valdez (1994, 1997) emphasize the context of family dysfunction in gang members, as well as the psychological crisis of adolescent and ethnic identity development in response to alien-ation from family and society. They note that in immigrant fami-lies, parent and child role reversals (for example, negotiating in English) and the low-prestige jobs of parents can create images of parents as weak in contrast to neighborhood gang members who appear strong, confident, defiant, and hip. In multigenerational Chicano families, the long-term effects of poverty can erode healthy family functioning needed to guide adolescents through the devel-opmental task of identity development.

Such family dysfunction pushes youth outside the family to struggle with complex issues of identity, purpose, role, and power. The pull of urban gang culture, with its rigidly defined hierarchy, sanctioned roles, and activities for members, along with its symbols of group and cultural identity, can be particularly strong for vulnerable youth. Chicano gang members invariably refer to their gang as their *familia,* to gang members as *carnales* or blood brothers, and to the *respeto* and protection they are accorded as members. They also adopt caricature-like gang names and roles (for example, fighter, artist, leader) and use a mix of gang and Mexican symbols to express their individual and collective identities (tattoos, graffiti, hand signs). Thus the use of gangs to achieve personal and social goals is considerable for these otherwise marginalized outsiders (Gibbs, 2000).

But while gang members claim their "homies" as family, their distorted maps of familism and friendship limit the possibilities for healthy relationships. For example, in a rare empirical study of incarcerated Chicano and Anglo gang members, Lyon, Henggeler, and Hall (1992) found that the gang members' peer relationships were characterized by more aggressiveness and social immaturity than incarcerated youth who were not gang members. Chicano gang members also had more extensive criminal records and reported more hard drug use than incarcerated Chicanos who were not gang members.

In their brief review of the literature, Belitz and Valdez (1997) note that severe family dysfunction is related to gang membership, specifically to substance abuse, domestic violence, and physical or sexual abuse of children and adolescents. The pent-up rage and violence frequently manifested (and valued) by gang members has many roots, including modeling and identifying with an aggressive and abusive parent or street models such as *veterano* (veteran) gang members. The fact that gang members frequently brutalize and kill rival gang members who mirror themselves in almost all respects reflects a deep-seated self-rejection.

Belitz and Valdez (1994) discuss the following case study:

> Seventeen-year-old Benito was from a three-generation, urban, *barrio*-dwelling Chicano family. Benito's father was dominating, aggressive, and physically abusive toward his wife and children. Growing up, Benito avoided, helplessly tolerated, and eventually imitated his father's aggressiveness. Benito loved his mother but did not take her seriously because she was unable to protect him. Academic failure, acting out, and disciplinary action at school

resulted in his hanging out with gang members and eventually joining a local gang. Benito assumed the role of an extremely crazy (*muy loco*) gang member with regard to risk taking (alcohol and drug use, run-ins with the law, fighting). Multiple legal and mental health contacts ensued, with frequent incarceration, where Benito would be victimized by stronger youth and would himself victimize weaker youth. Despite the costs, Benito considered his gang his real family and professed his lifelong loyalty and willingness to die for it. The gang was also where he could claim his Chicano identity, albeit a violent, risk-taking, macho identity.

Vigil (1999) asserts that schools exacerbate the Mexican American gang problem by generally responding with measures of suppression (detention, suspensions), academic tracking, remedial courses, and alternative schools that further alienate gang members from school and nongang peers. The problem is further exacerbated by the current emphasis on simply criminalizing gangs by police; their main objective is to suppress gang activity, often by behaving much like another gang, as depicted in the 1987 movie *Colors* in which police officers adopt ganglike nicknames and interact with gang members in a vicious cycle of provocation, harassment, and brutality.

Females have always been active in Chicano gangs but primarily in an auxiliary role (for example, as girlfriends of male gang members). However, autonomous Chicana gangs have begun to develop, and service providers should not underestimate their toughness and potential for destructive acts. In-depth interviews with twenty-one *Cholas* from the San Fernando Valley in Southern California (Harris, 1994) and forty from Los Angeles County (Felkenes and Becker, 1995) found them to be very similar to their male counterparts in their reasons for joining gangs, using drugs, and engaging in violent acts such as fighting with rival gangs. These girls had weak ties to family, school, and society, and many had experienced abuse in their families. For example, Felkenes and Becker (1995) found that 41.2 percent of the forty girls in their Los Angeles sample had dropped out of school and that only 21.6 were employed full-time. Further, they viewed detention centers more often as safe havens than as deterrents to gang involvement.

Depression and Suicidality

There is mounting evidence that Chicano youth are at greater risk for major depression, depressive symptoms, and suicidality than their Anglo and African American peers. Roberts, Roberts, and Chen (1997) assessed the prevalence of diagnosable major depression in a community-based survey of 5,423 students from five middle schools in Houston, Texas. Impairment related to major depression was also assessed (problems functioning at home, school, and with peers). A comparison of ethnic groups revealed rates of major depression that ranged from a low of 1.9 percent for Chinese students to a high of 6.6 percent for Mexican American students, with Anglo students in the middle (3.9 percent). Although both Mexican and African American students had higher rates of depression than Anglos, only Mexican Americans had significantly higher rates of major depression with impairment, even after controlling for the effects of SES, gender, and age.

These results are consistent with studies of symptoms of depression in adolescents, which consistently show higher rates in Chicano adolescents than in Anglo and African Americans across a wide variety of samples, including a national survey of adolescents between twelve and seventeen years of age (Roberts and Sobhan, 1992), a household area probability sample of Los Angeles County (Siegel and others, 1998), a study of a multiethnic sample of urban high school students (Weinberg and Emslie, 1987; Emslie and others, 1990), and a comparison of Chicano and Anglo middle school students in New Mexico (Roberts and Chen, 1995). With the exception of the study by Roberts and Chen, Mexican American youth rates remained highest, even after controlling for SES, gender, and age.

Depression in Mexican American adolescents appears to be a function of family breakdown due to stressful acculturation characterized by ethnic minority status, excessive poverty, and related risk factors. It appears that the breakdown of traditional stabilizing forces, not poverty per se, renders Chicano adolescents vulnerable. For example, Swanson and others (1992) found higher rates of depression, suicidality, and drug use in 1,775 Chicano high school students than in 2,383 high school students from Mexico. This study links multiple mental health problems in Chicano adolescents to their experience in the United States but not to poverty per se, considering that the Mexican students were much poorer.

Hovey and King (1996) studied the relation between acculturative stress and depression in predominantly poor Chicano high school students and found that both depression and suicidality were predicted by high acculturative stress and low family cohesion (that is, low support, high tension). In turn, acculturative stress was predicted by low family cohesion and low expectations of the future on the part of adolescents. Not surprisingly, suicidality was also predicted by depression and low expectations of the future. This study suggests that the breakdown of the family, coupled with pessimism about the future, can make acculturation depressing and risky for Chicano adolescents.

Family breakdown can impair the ability of parents to guide their children safely through risky environments. For example, in their sample of 121 low-income Chicana mothers of fourth-grade children, Dumka, Roosa, and Jackson (1997) found that maternal support and discipline (protective factors) mediated the impact of poverty and family conflict (risk factors) on child symptoms of depression and conduct disorder. That is, when support and discipline were high, there was no relation between risk factors and symptoms in children and vice versa. Unfortunately, the risk factors contributed to maternal inconsistent discipline and low support for children.

Poverty, as well as family and peer relations, influence depression and acting out in urban youth of color in a variety of ways, according to a study by Seidman, Chesir-Teran, and Friedman (1999). First, the most depressed and antisocial adolescents in their sample came from family relationships characterized by dysfunction (high conflict, low support, and medium parent-child involvement), enmeshment (medium-high conflict, medium-low support, and high parent-child involvement), and conflict (high conflict, medium support, and medium involvement). Second, the most depressed participants also came from peer relationships characterized by rejection. Third, the most antisocial adolescents had peer relationships with engaging but antisocial friends.

It should be noted that even though suicidality increases with age for Anglo Americans, the opposite seems to be true for Chicanos. For example, past research has found Chicano adults to be lower in suicidality than their white counterparts (Sorensen and

Golding, 1988), but research on Chicano adolescents reveals comparable rates to white counterparts and higher rates when comparing Chicanos and whites under twenty-five years of age (Smith, Mercy, and Warren, 1985). Thus suicidality is a "youthful" phenomenon for Chicanos and needs to be recognized and treated as such.

Intervention and Treatment Approaches

In the following section, a range of interventions including primary prevention, individual treatment, family therapy, and group treatment are discussed in terms of their appropriateness and effectiveness for Mexican American youth.

Ecosystemic Map of the Intervention Field

The needs of Mexican American youth affected by the psychosocial problems just reviewed are many and should involve prevention and intervention approaches spanning multiple levels from individual, group, and family therapy to comprehensive school-based programs as reviewed next.

Primary Prevention

Johnson and Walker (1987) conducted a rare empirical and longitudinal study on the primary prevention of behavior problems in young Mexican American children from low-SES backgrounds in Texas. When the children were between the ages of one and three, the parents were provided with home- and clinic-based parenting and family decision-making skills, as well as education about child development. Mother and child interactions were also observed, and services were provided in Spanish as needed. Results are reported for a five- through eight-year follow-up period. Comparisons of experimental and control families revealed dramatic differences in parenting and child development, intelligence, and adjustment. Experimental mothers used less criticism and restrictive control, along with more encouragement and appropriate praise; experimental children scored higher on standard tests of development and intelligence; and experimental boys were less destructive, overactive, and negative-attention-seeking, as well as less emotionally sensitive, than control boys ages four through seven.

Individual Treatment

Cognitive-behavioral therapy (CBT) may be particularly well suited for Latinos and other people of color because of its emphasis on tailoring treatment to the client's particular circumstances, empowering clients through self-change skills, attention to conscious process and specific behaviors, emphasis on action and not just verbal expression, and didactic examination of client problems (Casas, 1988; Hays, 1995). Although these are sound arguments, Wohl (1995) argues that psychodynamic therapy can also be adapted to ethnic minority clients. In Martinez's review of the psychotherapy outcome literature on Latinos, nothing definitive could be concluded about individual therapy.

With regard to gang members, Belitz and Valdez (1997) note that individual therapy needs to involve tolerating the client's intense impulse to act out and to test limits, as well as monitoring the therapist's countertransference with regard to seeing the client as not treatable. Local and general knowledge of Chicano gangs is a basic requirement for sensitive treatment. The role of the clinician blends micro and macro levels by assuming an advocacy and brokering role with respect to accessing resources from multiple agencies such as educational and vocational and court and probation-related resources, as well as supports from natural support systems in the community, including healthy family relations. Ideally, individual therapy for gang members and other Latino youth should happen in conjunction with family therapy.

Family-Focused Interventions

Contemporary Latino family experts increasingly emphasize an ecosystems approach, with the overriding goal of restoring family stability and adaptive functioning by addressing multiple needs, as well as promoting greater bicultural flexibility with regard to understanding and responding to youth and family mental health problems.

Family Therapy

Falicov (1998) views the role of family therapist as an intermediary of family conflict whose job is to reframe troubled children as "nervous" versus bad and family problems as "cultural transitions" in need of better understanding. For example, uneven levels of acculturation between parents and children in families are addressed within the context of migration history and acculturation experience and remedied by heightening mutual understanding and appreciation, as well as improving communication, negotiation, and compromise skills that promote greater flexibility and biculturality.

Szapocznik and colleagues (1997) have developed acculturation-sensitive models of family therapy with Cuban and other Latino immigrant families, with an emphasis on drug-abusing and delinquent adolescents. Like Falicov, Szapocznik attributes adolescent problems to the "acculturation gap" that can exacerbate the normal generation gap between parents and adolescents. For example, in their Bicultural Effectiveness Training, Szapocznik and others (1984) emphasize the goal of aligning family members to work together against acculturation gaps that threaten the family. The goal is to foster cross-generational alliances within families by connecting parents to the positive aspects of more modern American values while connecting children to positive aspects of more traditional Latino values.

> Falicov describes a case vignette of a Mexican immigrant family in which a U.S.-born, fifteen-year-old daughter makes a suicide attempt precipitated by her overprotective father's refusal to let her take a cross-town bus trip to visit a friend who has moved. Therapy focused on helping parents understand their daughter's struggle for greater autonomy in the United States while still trying to be a good Latina daughter and to see that negative consequences can be prevented. Simultaneously, the daughter was helped to see the positive intentions behind her father's strictness (protection from their high-crime, urban environment). Father and daughter were guided through a series of increasingly larger negotiations and compromises such as permission to stay out a little later, providing that the daughter calls home to check in, and permission for the daughter to express her disagreement, providing it is done in a respectful manner.

With regard to evaluation, Szapocznik's summary (1997) of their research shows that their ecosystemic, culture-based family therapies are as effective as more generic forms of family therapy (for example, structural family therapy) in reducing symptoms but superior at engaging and retaining Latino families, as well as preserving family cohesiveness.

Group Treatment

Group therapy is a viable way of addressing Chicano youths' mental health problems, especially in view of the frequently exaggerated importance of peers and urban street culture in response to family dysfunction and the risky multiple marginalities of low-SES and minority status.

Baca and Koss-Chioino (1997) describe a culturally competent group treatment for Chicano adolescents, ages twelve through eighteen, who are experiencing behavioral problems, including substance abuse and gang involvement. Multiple marginalities are addressed by presenting group as a "fourth space" away from home, school, and street—a place where participants can examine their lives in a setting that mimics positive aspects of the home environment (living room furniture, snacks, and so on). The goal of treatment is to promote adjustment by improving the expression of affect, clarifying and affirming ethnic identity, and expanding life choices. Group participants lead pertinent discussions, stimulated by Mexican American–Latino film clips, documentaries, and art or poetry, regarding the pitfalls of gang involvement and alternative ways of meeting their real need for familia, community, and a respected role in the world. Preliminary results reveal improvement in educational problems and family interactions and in decreasing symptoms of depression, conduct disorder, and oppositional defiance disorder.

Belitz and Valdez (1997) also recommend group treatment for Mexican American gang members, often in conjunction with family therapy. The goal of group therapy is to stimulate healthy ethnic identity development by helping gang members see that alienation from both Mexican and American cultures can push marginal individuals toward gangs as a way of addressing legitimate ethnic and adolescent identity needs. In addition to examining the personal and social consequences of gang membership, members are also involved in healthy activities and affiliations designed to replace the positive functions of gangs (for example, community organizations, education programs at school, and probation plans).

Belitz and Valdez (1994) discuss the following case study involving a gang member:

Two years of group, family, and individual therapy were used to help a Chicano gang member named Chris. He had joined a gang at twelve years of age after years of neglect by a substance-abusing mother, sexual abuse by a stepfather, and being shuffled between the homes of his mother and grandparents. At fifteen years of age, the adolescent attempted suicide after threatening to kill his pregnant girlfriend for breaking up with him. Individual therapy focused on processing childhood traumas, related vulnerability, and rage, as well as behavioral consequences (substance abuse, gang involvement, suicidal and homicidal impulses). Group therapy with other gang members focused on exploring adolescent, "gang banger," and Chicano identities. Members were helped to critically examine how their *Cholo* identities, *vato loco* (crazy guy) role models, and gang activities were used to cope with inadequate families, roles, and identities, as well as venting pent-up rage. Consistent with an ecological model, members were helped to distinguish the positive and negative aspects of gang membership and to move into more adaptive roles and identities outside the gang (acquiring a job, being a responsible father, helping community). Chris did not quit the gang for some time but increasingly felt permission to move into other fulfilling roles. Family therapy included helping Chris to express his highly ambivalent feelings toward his mother (resentment for lack of protection yet fantasy of being properly mothered by her), helping his mother apologize, even while expressing appropriate concern about Chris's gang involvement, and involving extended family in treatment in order to construct a more cohesive and traditional Chicano family.

De las Fuentes (2000) advocates the use of group treatment for immigrant Latino adolescents, noting that adjustment to the United States can be especially hard on older adolescents and children who have experienced lengthy separations from parents and siblings prior to migration. She goes on to describe several inner-city, school-based groups that she has conducted in which students can discuss a variety of adjustment issues.

School- and Community-Based Intervention Strategies

The following section describes a school-based intervention project that represents a comprehensive and collaborative approach to prevention and early intervention with Mexican American students at risk of school failure or dropping out.

Comprehensive School-Based Interventions

The Houston Communities in School (CIS) project coordinates a broad range of child and family services in twenty-one schools, with the goal of decreasing dropout rates, improving academic ability, decreasing delinquency, and preparing students for adult work roles (Burt, Resnick, and Novick, 1998). Tailored services generally include personal and pre-employment counseling for students, as well as comprehensive social services for families. For example, CIS in a community known as Little Mexico uses a "club" approach to attract students and gang members to modeling, mariachi, and English as Second Language clubs. The program also includes university student tutors, two caseworkers, a drug counselor, and a community youth service crisis worker. The *Padres con Poder* (Parents with Power) program teaches parenting skills with attention to Latino family themes, as well as community substance and violence prevention. A collaboration between CIS and county juvenile probation provides intensive student and family services to adjudicated youth.

High-risk students are referred to the CIS caseload; lower-risk students are invited to participate in enrichment activities as a way of decreasing stigma. CIS is funded by public and private sources and functions as a broker for local county and community-based services that seek partnerships on behalf of students. Service continuity is maintained by "vertical teams" that follow students through school feeder patterns from elementary through high school. As of 1996, over eighteen thousand students had been served by CIS, with school retention rates between 89 and 100 percent. A similar "full service" school program has been described for Mexican American students in Modesto, California (Dryfoos, 1994).

Specific School-Based Interventions

In the following section, several programs that are targeted for specific problem behaviors among Mexican American youth are described in terms of their culturally relevant features, designed to prevent negative outcomes such as school failure, risky sexual behavior, substance use, and gang involvement.

School Failure Prevention

The ALAS (Achieving Latinos through Academic Success) program aims to interrupt school failure in high-risk Chicano middle school students who have high rates of disciplinary problems, poor grades, and chronic truancy by (1) increasing student problem-solving efficacy with academics and family matters, (2) providing students and their parents with frequent feedback about their school performance and behavior, (3) "hot seat attendance monitoring" to track truancies on a period-by-period basis and to quickly notify parents, (4) involving students in extracurricular school activities with positive peers and adults at school, (5) parent training on how to interact effectively with the school on students' behalf, and (6) problem-solving training around parent-child issues (Rumberger and Larson, 1994). The ALAS program has served two thousand predominantly Chicano junior high students with auspicious results. A report by Rumberger and Larson (1994), following two years of program implementation, shows that ALAS students had better school attendance and grades and lower dropout rates by the end of eighth grade, as compared to no-treatment control students. A follow-up report by Rumberger (1998) shows that by the end of ninth grade, ALAS students continued to out-perform controls (80 percent on track to graduate rather than 50 percent).

The Theme Project (Garcia, 2001) also improved school attendance, academic achievement, and academic preparation in Chicano middle school participants versus a matched control group of students. This program involved a collaboration between teachers and university researchers in the development of a research-based design that included intensive teacher training and enhancement of student learning through collaborative learning groups; all basic subjects were integrated and taught through "themes" of high interest and relevance to student lives (for example, the Olympics, ethnic identity, cultural differences, crime, and nonviolence). The superiority of the Theme Program over the school's normal curriculum was evident on standard achievement test scores (reading, writing, and language subtests); both bilingual and English-only students performed equally well in the program.

Prevention of Risky Sexual Behavior

A recent review of thirty-two teen pregnancy programs, provided mostly to Latino and African American youth, found that those providing contraceptive knowledge and access were superior in increasing contraceptive use and decreasing rates of pregnancy, even though they had no effect on sexual activity (Franklin and Corcoran, 2000). Despite these findings, only 20 percent of the programs provided contraceptives to adolescents. Programs designed to delay sexual activity were found to be effective, but only for younger adolescents.

Programs to prevent risky sex should be provided in schools and churches and should attempt to integrate parents, in view of research showing that stability in these domains is related to less sexual activity (DuRant, Pendergrast, and Seymore, 1990) and less pregnancy (Baumeister, Flores, and VanOss Marin, 1995) in Mexican American and other Latina adolescents. Thus interventions that help parents discuss sexual matters with their children could potentially delay sexual activity and prevent pregnancy, as well as STDs, in Chicana adolescents.

Substance Use Prevention

A meta-analysis of 143 drug prevention programs for adolescents, conducted by Tobler (1986), reveals that (1) the majority of programs are school-based and delivered to white middle-class youth; (2) only 12.6 percent of programs were delivered to at-risk youth, defined as ethnic minority or substance using or maladjusted to school; (3) peer programs (positive peer influence plus drug refusal skills training) were far superior in decreasing drug use than drug knowledge programs, affective programs (that increase variables such as self-esteem, communication, and decision making skills), and combinations of knowledge and affective programs; and (4) at-risk youth benefited most from alternative programs that included remedial tutoring, job skills training, community volunteering, and one-to-one relationships with positive role models. Although no such program for Mexican American youth was found in the literature, a program for Puerto Rican and African American youth in New York was successful at decreasing intention to drink and use drugs at posttest and decreasing drinking at two years posttreatment, as compared to a no-treatment control condition (Forgey, Schinke, and Cole, 1997).

Gang Interventions

Vigil (1999) has long advocated the use of the school as a comprehensive base of prevention and intervention work with Chicano youth at risk for gang membership, as well as their families. Branch

(1997) adds that gang interventions could build on findings from a meta-analysis of interventions for juvenile offenders showing that tight, structured, skills-oriented, behavioral programs are most successful at decreasing delinquent behavior.

Tabish and Orell (1996) describe a school-based mediation program designed to prevent gang violence in *barrio*-dwelling, multigenerational, rival gang members; members are contacted by proactive school staff and gang interventionists who build personalized relationships based on mutual respect, recognition of dignity, and understanding. Regular, formal, participatory mediation sessions include reviewing problems, calling witnesses to clarify and redefine disagreements, and brainstorming to generate solutions. The feasibility of solutions is tested and discussed until consensus is achieved. Although lacking an evaluation component, this program illustrates needed outreach to gang members and their involvement in prosocial, school-based violence prevention.

Significant Trends and Future Issues

Pressing future issues for Chicano youth include (1) the need to do much more of the comprehensive and culturally competent interventions just described, (2) the need for further research to evaluate and document such interventions with rigor, (3) the need to make descriptions and results of exemplary programs available to key policymakers and administrators, as well as service providers, and (4) the persistent need to recruit and train more Mexican American–Latino mental health practitioners and researchers. Regarding the last issue, survey research indicates that only 1 percent of psychologists are Latino and that there are only 29 Latino mental health professionals for every 100,000 Latinos in the United States, as compared to 173 Anglo providers for every 100,000 Anglo Americans (U.S. Department of Health and Human Services, 2001).

In closing, the pernicious cluster of problem areas affecting Mexican American youth are unlikely to improve soon, considering the persistent clusters of risk factors and undermined protective factors that have their roots in historical legacies of racism, subordination, and environmental structures. The emerging trend toward ecosystemically comprehensive, community- and school-based, child- and family-centered, prevention and intervention programs represents a viable way of beginning to address these formidable challenges.

References

Acuna, R. *Occupied America.* (2nd ed.) New York: Harper & Row, 1981.

Amaro, H. "Women in the Mexican American Community: Religion, Culture, and Reproductive Attitudes and Experiences." *Journal of Community Psychology,* 1988, *16,* 6–20.

Aneshensel, C. S., Becerra, R. M., Fielder, E. P., and Schuler, R. H. "Onset of Fertility-Related Events During Adolescence: A Prospective Comparison of Mexican American and Non-Hispanic White Females." *American Journal of Public Health,* 1990, *80*(8), 959–963.

Azmitia, M., Cooper, C. R., Garcia, E. E., and Dunbar, N. D. "The Ecology of Family Guidance in Low-Income Mexican-American and European-American Families." *Social Development,* 1996, *5*(1), 1–23.

Baca, L. M., and Koss-Chioino, J. D. "Development of a Culturally Responsive Group Counseling Model for Mexican American Adolescents." *Journal of Multicultural Counseling and Development,* 1997, *25*(2), 130–141.

Balls Organista, P., Organista, K. C., and Soloff, P. "Exploring AIDS-Related Knowledge, Attitudes and Behaviors in Female Mexican Migrant Laborers." *Health and Social Work,* 1998, *23*(2), 96–103.

Baumeister, L. M., Flores, E., and VanOss Marin, B. "Sex Information Given to Latina Adolescents by Parents." *Health Education Research: Theory and Practice,* 1995, *10*(2), 233–239.

Bean, F. D., and Tienda, M. *The Hispanic Population of the United States.* New York: Russell Sage Foundation, 1990.

Becerra, R. M., and de Anda, D. "Pregnancy and Motherhood Among Mexican American Adolescents." *Health and Social Work,* 1984, *9*(2), 106–123.

Belitz, J., and Valdez, D. "Clinical Issues in the Treatment of Chicano Male Gang Youth." *Hispanic Journal of Behavioral Sciences,* 1994, *16*(1), 57–74.

Belitz, J., and Valdez, D. "A Sociocultural Context for Understanding Gang Involvement Among Mexican-American Male Youth." In J. G. Garcia and M. C. Zea (eds.), *Psychological Interventions and Research with Latino Populations.* Boston: Allyn & Bacon, 1997.

Berry, E. H., Shillington, A. M., Peak, T., and Hohman, M. M. "Multi-Ethnic Comparison of Risk and Protective Factors for Adolescent Pregnancy." *Child and Adolescent Social Work Journal,* 2000, *17*(2), 79–96.

Berry, J. W. "Immigration, Acculturation, and Adaptation." *Applied Psychology: An International Review,* 1997, *46*(1), 5–68.

Boles, S., and others. "Alcohol and Other Drug Use Patterns Among Mexican-American, Mexican, and Caucasian Adolescents: New Directions for Assessment and Research." *Journal of Clinical Child Psychology,* 1994, *23*(1), 39–46.

Branch, C. W. "Race and Ethnicity." In C. W. Branch, *Clinical Interventions with Gang Adolescents and Their Families.* Boulder, Colo.: Westview Press, 1997.

Brooks, A. J., Stuewig, J., and LeCroy, C. W. "A Family Based Model of Hispanic Adolescent Substance Use." *Journal of Drug Education,* 1998, *28*(1), 65–86.

Burt, M. R., Resnick, G., and Novick, E. R. *Building Supportive Communities for At-Risk Adolescents: It Takes More Than Services.* Washington D.C.: American Psychological Association, 1998.

Casas, J. M. "Cognitive Behavioral Approaches: A Minority Perspective." *The Counseling Psychologist,* 1988, *16*(1), 106–110.

Centers for Disease Control and Prevention. "Youth Risk Behavior Surveillance, United States, 2001." *Mortality and Morbidity Weekly Review,* no. 51. Atlanta: Centers for Disease Control and Prevention, 2002.

Chavez, E. L., Randall, C., and Swaim, R. C. "An Epidemiological Comparison of Mexican-American and White Non-Hispanic 8th and 12th Grade Students' Substance Use." *American Journal of Public Health,* 1992, *82*(3), 445–447.

Coombs, R. H., Paulson, M. J., and Richardson, M. A. "Peer vs. Parental Influence in Substance Use Among Hispanic and Anglo Children and Adolescents." *Journal of Youth and Adolescence,* 1991, *20*(1), 73–88.

Darabi, K. F., and Ortiz, V. "Childbearing Among Young Latino Women in the United States." *American Journal of Public Health,* 1986, *77,* 25–28.

de las Fuentes, C. "Group Psychotherapy: Adolescent Latinos." In M. C. Flores and G. Carey (eds.), *Family Therapy with Hispanics.* Boston: Allyn & Bacon, 2000.

Delgado, M. *Social Work Practice in Nontraditional Urban Settings.* New York: Oxford University Press, 1999.

Dryfoos, J. *Full-Service Schools: A Revolution in Health and Social Services for Children, Youth, and Families.* San Francisco: Jossey-Bass, 1994.

Dumka, L. E., Roosa, M. W., and Jackson, K. M. "Risk, Conflict, Mothers' Parenting, and Children's Adjustment in Low-Income Mexican Immigrant, and Mexican American Families." *Journal of Marriage and the Family,* 1997, *59*(May), 309–323.

DuRant, R. H., Pendergrast, R. E., and Seymore, C. "Sexual Behavior Among Hispanic Female Adolescents in the United States." *Pediatrics,* 1990, *85*(6), 1051–1058.

Emslie, G. J., and others. "Depression Symptoms by Self-Report in Adolescence: Phase I of the Development of a Questionnaire for Depression by Self-Report." *Journal of Child Neurology,* 1990, *5,* 114–121.

Falicov, C. J. "Mexican Families." In M. McGoldrick, J. Giordano, and J. K. Pearce (eds.), *Ethnicity and Family Therapy.* (2nd ed.) New York: Guilford Press, 1996.

Falicov, C. J. *Latino Families in Therapy: A Guide to Multicultural Practice.* New York: Guilford Press, 1998.

Feagin, J. R., and Booher Feagin, C. "Mexican Americans." In J. R. Feagin and C. Booher Feagin, *Racial and Ethnic Relations.* (6th ed.) Englewood Cliffs, N.J.: Prentice Hall, 1999.

Felice, M. E., Shragg, G. P., James, M., and Hollingsworth, D. R. "Psychosocial Aspects of Mexican-American, White, and Black Teenage Pregnancy." *Journal of Adolescent Health Care,* 1987, *3,* 330–335.

Felix-Ortiz, M., and Newcomb, M. D. "Vulnerability for Drug Use Among Latino Adolescents." *Journal of Community Psychology,* 1999, *27*(3), 257–280.

Felkenes, G. T., and Becker, H. K. "Female Gang Members: A Growing Issue for Policy Makers." *Journal of Gang Research,* 1995, *2*(4), 1–10.

Flannery, D. J., Vazsonyi, A. T., Torquati, J., and Fridrich, A. "Ethnic and Gender Differences in Risk for Early Adolescent Substance Use." *Journal of Youth and Adolescence,* 1994, *23*(2), 195–213.

Forgey, M. A., Schinke, S., and Cole, K. "School-Based Interventions to Prevent Substance Use Among Inner-City Minority Adolescents." *Health-Promoting and Health Compromising Behaviors Among Minority Adolescents.* Washington D.C.: American Psychological Association, 1997.

Franklin, C., and Corcoran, J. "Preventing Adolescent Pregnancy: A Review of Programs and Practices." *Social Work,* 2000, *45*(1), 40–52.

Frauenglass, S., Routh, D. K., Pantin, H. M., and Mason, C. A. "Family Support Decreases Influence of Deviant Peers on Hispanic Adolescents' Substance Use." *Journal of Clinical Child Psychology,* 1997, *26*(1), 12–23.

Frisbie, W. P., and Bean, F. D. "The Latino Family in Comparative Perspective: Trends and Current Conditions." In C. K. Jacobson (ed.), *American Families: Issues in Race and Ethnicity.* New York: Garland, 1995.

Garcia, E. E. *The Education of Hispanics in the United States: Raices y Alas [Roots and Wings].* Boulder, Colo.: Rowen and Littlefield, 2001.

Gibbs, J. T. "Gangs as Transitional Alternative Structures: Adaptations to Racial and Social Marginality in Los Angeles and London." *Journal of Multicultural Social Work,* 2000, *8*(1–2), 71–99.

Gibbs, J. T., and Bankhead, T. *Preserving Privilege: California Politics, Propositions, and People of Color.* San Francisco: Jossey-Bass, 2001.

Goldstein, A. P., and Soriano, F. "Juvenile Gangs." In L. D. Eron, J. H. Gentry, and P. Schlegel (eds.), *Reason to Hope: A Psychosocial Perspective on Violence and Youth.* Washington, D.C.: American Psychological Association, 1994.

Gomel, J. N., Tinsley, B. J., Parke, R. D., and Clark, K. M. "The Effects of Economic Hardship on Family Relationships Among African American, Latino, and Euro-American Families." *Journal of Family Issues,* 1998, *19*(4), 436–467.

Guendelman, S. "The Incorporation of Mexican Women in Seasonal Migration: A Study of Gender Differences." *Hispanic Journal of Behavioral Sciences,* 1987, *9,* 245–264.

Harris, M. G. "Cholas: Mexican American Girls, and Gangs." *Sex Roles,* 1994, *30*(3/4), 289–301.

Hays, P. A. "Multicultural Applications of Cognitive Behavior Therapy." *Professional Psychology: Research and Practice,* 1995, *26,* 309–315.

Higginbotham, J. C., Trevino, F. M., and Ray, L. A. "Utilization of Curanderos by Mexican Americans: Prevalence and Predictors: Findings from HHANES 1982–84." *American Journal of Public Health,* 1990, *80*(supplement), 32–35.

Holck, S. E., Warren, C. W., Morris, L., and Rochat, R. W. "Need for Family Planning Services Among Anglo and Hispanic Women in the U.S. Counties Bordering Mexico." *Family Planning Perspectives,* 1982, *14*(30), 155–159.

Hovey, J. D., and King, C. A. "Acculturation Stress, Depression, and Suicidal Ideation Among Immigrant and Second Generation Latino Adolescents." *Journal of the American Academy of Child and Adolescent Psychiatry,* 1996, *35*(9), 1183–1192.

Johnson, D. L., and Walker, T. "Primary Prevention of Behavior Problems in Mexican American Children." *American Journal of Community Psychology,* 1987, *15*(4), 375–385.

Lyon, J. M., Henggeler, S., and Hall, J. A. "The Family Relations, Peer Relations, and Criminal Activities of Caucasian and Hispanic-American Gang Members." *Journal of Abnormal Child Psychology,* 1992, *20*(5), 439–449.

Mazon, M. *The Zoot-Suit Riots: The Psychology of Symbolic Annihilation.* Austin: University of Texas Press, 1984.

McLemore, S. D., and Romo, H. D. "Mexican Americans: Identity and Incorporation." In S. D. McLemore and H. D. Romo, *Racial and Ethnic Relations in America.* (5th ed.) Boston: Allyn & Bacon, 1998.

Morales, A. T. "Therapy with Latino Gang Members." In L. A. Vargas and J. D. Koss-Chioino (eds.), *Working with Culture: Psychotherapeutic Inter-*

ventions with Ethnic Minority Children and Adolescents. San Francisco: Jossey-Bass, 1992.

Nuno, T., Dorrington, C., and Alvarez, I. *Los Angeles County Hispanic Youth Health Assessment Report.* Los Angeles: Multicultural Area Health Education Center, 1998.

Padilla, A. M., Carlos, M. L., and Keefe, S. E. "Mental Health Service Utilization by Mexican Americans." In M. R. Miranda (ed.), *Psychotherapy with the Spanish-Speaking: Issues in Research and Service Delivery* (monograph no. 3). University of California, Los Angeles: Spanish Speaking Mental Health Clinic, 1976.

Perez, S. M., and Duany, L. A. *Reducing Hispanic Teenage Pregnancy and Family Poverty: A Replication Guide.* Washington, D.C.: Office of Research, Advocacy, and Legislation, National Council of La Raza, 1992.

Perez, W., and Padilla, A. M. "Cultural Orientation Across Three Generations of Hispanic Adolescents." *Hispanic Journal of Behavioral Sciences,* 2000, *22*(3), 390–398.

Poe-Yamagata, E., and Jones, M. A. *And Justice for Some: Differential Treatment of Minority Youth.* Washington D.C.: Youth Law Center, 2000.

Reynoso, T. C., Felice, M. E., and Shragg, G. P. "Does American Acculturation Affect Outcome of Mexican-American Teenage Pregnancy?" *Journal of Adolescent Health,* 1993, *14,* 257–261.

Roberts, R. E., and Chen, Y. C. "Depression Symptoms and Suicidal Ideation Among Mexican Origin and Anglo Adolescents." *Journal of American Academy of Child and Adolescent Psychiatry,* 1995, *34,* 81–90.

Roberts, R. E., Roberts, C. R., and Chen, Y. R. "Ethnocultural Differences in Prevalence of Adolescent Depression." *American Journal of Community Psychology,* 1997, *25,* 95–110.

Roberts, R. E., and Sobhan, M. "Symptoms of Depression in Adolescents: A Comparison of Anglos, African, and Hispanic Americans." *Journal of Youth and Adolescence,* 1992, *21*(6), 639–651.

Roll, S., Millen, L., and Ramirez, R. "Common Errors in Psychotherapy with Chicanos: Extrapolations from Research and Clinical Experience." *Psychotherapy: Theory, Research and Practice,* 1980, *17*(2), 158–168.

Rumberger, R. W. "Achievement for Latinos Through Academic Success." In P. Gandara, K. Larson, R. Rumberger, and H. Mehan (eds.), *Capturing Latino Students in the Academic Pipeline.* Berkeley: California Policy Seminar, 1998.

Rumberger, R. W., and Larson, K. A. "Keeping High Risk Chicano Students in School." In R. J. Rossi (ed.), *Schools and Students at Risk.* New York: Teachers College Press, 1994.

Seidman, E., Chesir-Teran, D., and Friedman, J. C. "The Risk and Protective Functions of Perceived Family and Peer Microsystems Among

Urban Adolescents in Poverty." *American Journal of Community Psychology,* 1999, *27,* 211–237.

Siegel, J. M., and others. "Adolescent Depressed Mood in a Multiethnic Sample." *Journal of Youth and Adolescence,* 1998, *27*(4), 413–427.

Smith, J. D., Mercy, J. A., and Warren, C. W. "Comparison of Suicide Among Anglos and Hispanics in Five Southwestern States." *Suicide and Life-Threatening Behavior,* 1985, *15,* 14–26.

Sokol-Katz, J. S., and Ulbrich, P. M. "Family Structure and Adolescent Risk-Taking Behavior: A Comparison of Mexican, Cuban, and Puerto Rican Adolescents." *The International Journal of the Addictions,* 1992, *27*(10), 1197–1209.

Solorzano, D. G., and Solorzano, R. W. "The Chicano Educational Experience: A Framework for Effective Schools in Chicano Communities." *Educational Policy,* 1995, *9*(3), 293–314.

Sorensen, S. B., and Golding, J. M. "Suicide Ideation and Attempts in Hispanics and Non-Hispanic Whites: Demographic and Psychiatric Disorder Issues." *Suicide and Life-Threatening Behavior,* 1988, *18*(3), 205–218.

Swanson, J. W., and others. "A Binational School Survey of Depression Symptoms, Drug Use, and Suicidal Ideation." *Journal of the American Academy of Child and Adolescent Psychiatry,* 1992, *31*(4), 669–678.

Szapocznik, J., and others. "The Evolution of a Structural Ecosystemic Theory for Working with Latino Families." In J. G. Garcia and M. C. Zea (eds.), *Psychological Interventions and Research with Latino Populations.* Boston: Allyn & Bacon, 1997.

Szapocznik, J., and others. "Bicultural Effectiveness Training (BET): A Treatment Intervention for Enhancing Intercultural Adjustment in Cuban American Families." *Hispanic Journal of Behavioral Sciences,* 1984, *6*(4), 317–344.

Tabish, K. R., and Orell, L. H. "Respect: Gang Mediation at Albuquerque, New Mexico's Washington Middle School." *The School Counselor,* 1996, *44,* 65–70.

Therrien, M., and Ramirez, R. R. "The Hispanic Population in the United States: March 2000." *Current Population Reports.* Washington D.C.: U.S. Census Bureau, 2000.

Tobler, N. S. "Meta-Analysis of 143 Adolescent Drug Prevention Programs: Quantitative Outcome Results of Program Participants Compared to a Control or Comparison Group." *The Journal of Drug Issues,* 1986, *16*(4), 537–567.

U.S. Department of Health and Human Services. *Cultural Issues in Substance Abuse and Treatment.* (DHHS publication no. [SMA] 99–3278). Rockville, Md.: Substance Abuse and Mental Health Services Administration, 2000.

U.S. Department of Health and Human Services. *Mental Health: Culture, Race and Ethnicity.* Supplement to *Mental Health: A Report of the Surgeon General.* Rockville, Md.: U.S. Department of Health and Human Services, 2001.

Valle, R., and Vega, W. *Hispanic Natural Support Systems: Mental Health Promotion Perspectives.* (no. 80–620047) Sacramento: State of California Department of Mental Health, 1980.

Vega, W. A. "Hispanic Families in the 1980s: A Decade of Research." *Journal of Marriage and the Family,* 1990, *52*(Nov.), 1015–1024.

Vigil, J. D. *Barrio Gangs: Street Life and Identity in Southern California.* Austin: University of Texas Press, 1988.

Vigil, J. D. "Streets and Schools: How Educators Can Help Chicano Marginalized Gang Youth." *Harvard Educational Review,* 1999, *69*(3), 270–288.

Weinberg, W. A., and Emslie, G. J. "Depression and Suicide in Adolescents." *International Pediatrics,* 1987, *2,* 154–159.

Weiss, S. J., and others. "The Impact of Cultural and *Familia* Context on Behavioral and Emotional Problems of Preschool Latino Children." *Child Psychiatry and Human Development,* 1999, *29*(4), 287–301.

Yablonsky, L. "Black and Chicano Gangs: In and Out of Prison." In L. Yablonski, *Gangsters: Fifty Years of Madness, Drugs, and Death on the Streets of America.* New York: New York University Press, 1997.

Ybarra, L. "When Wives Work: The Impact on the Chicano Family." *Journal of Marriage and the Family,* 1982, *44,* 169–178.

Chapter Nine

Puerto Rican Children and Adolescents

Jaime E. Inclán
Mabel E. Quiñones

Puerto Rican adolescents living in the United States experience the developmental tasks of adolescence that have been described in the traditional theories of development (Erikson, 1963). However, Puerto Rican adolescents also struggle with the challenge of imagining a just future that is inclusive of them, and of carving a place in it—or developing an identity. The complexity of Puerto Ricans as a people is the result of that struggle.

Differences in critical contextual variables influence the unique interpretation of the developmental tasks of adolescence. For Puerto Ricans, adolescent questions like Who am I? and Where do I belong? and Where will I be? are intertwined with their unique history. Puerto Rican adolescents confront, directly or through the legacy of their families, dynamics related to their ethnic, cultural, and political identity. This makes being Puerto Rican and growing up in the United States a challenging multidimensional experience.

Colonialism is to Puerto Ricans as slavery is to African Americans; a critical understanding of the reality of the group begins with and is defined by it. Puerto Ricans have a history of over five hundred years of colonialism, from 1492 until 1898 by Spain and from 1898 to the present by the United States (Rodriguez, 1991). The contradiction of colonialism is at the core of common struggles with issues of identity, contradictions between ethnic assimilation or affirmation, adaptation needs versus preservation of the language and the culture, the search for ethnic identity in a country defined by the racial question, the internalized feelings of inferiority of colonialist mentality, and the drive for individual self-esteem, social participation, and reform versus abstention and rebellion. In short, contradictions between respect for one's identity and a society that demands conformity as a condition for dialogue are pervasive.

This chapter provides a picture of the unique sociocultural experience of Puerto Ricans living in the United States. It examines contextual and clinical issues bearing on Puerto Rican adolescent development such as the role of family, acculturation, intergenerational patterns, individuation, and identity development and presents examples of treatment interventions.

The chapter follows the following sequence. First, we present demographic data that describe and locate Puerto Ricans within the reality of the United States. Next, we discuss the different contexts that affect the adolescent's psychology, including social and gender beliefs and roles, socioeconomic and social supports, family issues, and individual and developmental dynamics. And third, assessment issues and clinical interventions are discussed as examples of systemic and contextual interventions in the work with Puerto Rican adolescents in the United States.

Demographic Data

As the Latino population grows in urban areas like New York City (U.S. Bureau of the Census, 2000a), characterizing and differentiating among ethnic groups of Latino heritage in the United States has become more complex. The year 2000 census divided Latino groups by ethnicity, social class, and gender. Although the census gives important information about major trends nationally, it is not as sensitive to mental health variables as we would prefer; it does not differentiate enough between groups and does not provide generational and longitudinal information.

In sharing a cultural heritage and other socioeconomic realities, a common tendency is to identify Latinos as a homogeneous group—as Hispanics or Latinos. What makes Puerto Rican adolescents in the United States different from other Latino groups? What is particular about their experience of growing up?

The 2000 census shows that after 1990 the Hispanic population grew 59 percent. The census estimates that in 2000, 35.3 million Latinos had rough parity with African Americans as the largest ethnic minority in the United States. In Florida and California, for example, Hispanics outnumber African Americans; in California, they account for one-third of the population (U.S. Bureau of the Census, 2000b).

Race is an ongoing and difficult issue for Latinos, as it has been a criterion for discrimination among this ethnic group throughout their history (Hernández, 1999). The 2000 census for the first time provided the option of multiracial identification, which gave Latinos a chance to begin to identify themselves in ways that respond more directly to their racial reality. Provided this opportunity, Latinos identified themselves less as whites and more as racially mixed, shrinking the percentage of non-Hispanic whites from 76 percent to 69 percent.

Latino groups make up 11.5 percent of the total U.S. population. Puerto Ricans, the third-largest group, account for 9.6 percent of the Latino population in the United States, Mexicans for 65.2 percent, Central and South Americans for 14.3 percent, Cubans for 4.3 percent, and other Hispanics for 6.6 percent (U.S. Bureau of the Census, 2000a). There are regional and local differences, for example in the Northeast, where 8.9 percent of the population is of Hispanic origin, of which 3.6 percent is Puerto Rican.

The 2002 census shows that 35.7 percent of the Hispanic population in the United States is eighteen years or younger, in contrast with 23.5 percent of the non-Hispanic white population. Among the Hispanic groups, Puerto Ricans appear to be a younger group. Puerto Ricans below the age of eighteen account for 37.11 percent of the Puerto Rican population in the United States; of those, 18.10 percent are adolescents between the ages of ten and nineteen, from which half (9.4 percent) are between the ages of fifteen and nineteen (U.S. Bureau of the Census, 2000c). According to the March 1999 *Current Population Report* (U.S. Bureau of the Census, 2000a), 56.1 percent of the Hispanic population have a high school diploma or more and 10.9 percent have a bachelor's degree or more. In terms of educational attainment, 63.9 percent of Puerto Ricans obtained a high school diploma or more, and 11.1 percent had a bachelor's degree or more, which qualifies them as more highly educated than other Hispanics. In terms of income, 20.8 percent of Hispanics between the ages of eighteen and sixty-four live below poverty level. In contrast, 43.5 percent of Puerto Rican children (age eighteen and under) and 26.7 percent of Puerto Rican families are below poverty level, which makes them one of poorest groups among Hispanics.

The census does not address why Puerto Ricans as a group, despite their numbers, their educational attainment, their American citizenship, and its related entitlements remain at the bottom of the social ladder. It is proposed that as a group, Puerto Ricans have remained loyal to their ethnic identity and have resisted acculturation, as evidenced by the lower rate of interethnic marriages (Hernández, 1999). In order to better understand the significance of the census data, we cannot limit ourselves to statistical analysis. An appreciation of the effect of lack of access to social and political power and marginalization through generations has to be complemented with an analysis of current social, familial, and individual dynamics and contradictions.

Political participation is a form of community empowerment, and lack of participation contributes to a social context of marginality and disenfranchisement. In spite of the growing numbers, the Latino population remains almost invisible in local and county government (Cooper, 2001). Some of the factors that account for the underrepresentation of Latinos in the government are their young age, limited educational attainment, and lower yearly income—all of which contribute to less political visibility and access to power structures.

In this chapter, we address some issues related to the psychology of Puerto Ricans and, in particular, the psychology of its young people in terms of multiple contexts of assessment.

Contexts of Assessment

A valid psychological assessment of Puerto Rican adolescents requires an understanding of relevant sociopolitical, cultural, family, and individual issues pertinent to the Puerto Rican reality in the United States. The experience of the Puerto Rican adolescent differs from that of Puerto Rican islanders (Garcia-Preto, 1996), mainstream white Americans, African Americans, and other ethnic groups. There is also significant within-ethnic group variation due to race, class, and gender differences.

We posed ourselves the following questions: What makes growing up Puerto Rican different from other adolescent processes? What is unique about it? How can adolescent development be facilitated within the context of culture and identity? To address these questions, we view the Puerto Rican adolescent within several contexts that affect psychosocial and physical development.

Colonization and Immigration

The principal difference between Puerto Rican adolescents in the United States and other adolescents has its root in the sociopolitical history of the United States and Puerto Rico. Puerto Rican adolescents in the United States and in the mainland have not experienced being part of an all-powerful group that can conquer any difficulty. Contrary to their mainstream American peers, Puerto Rican youth's ethnic identity is colored by a sense of powerlessness and resignation resulting from the experience of sociopolitical subjugation and oppression experienced as a group. Puerto Rico was a colony of Spain until 1898, when the United States invaded the Island after taking it as war booty in the Spanish-American War. Until 1917, Puerto Rico had an ambiguous political status, and its inhabitants were considered racially inferior (Skidmore and Smith, 1992). With the 1917 Jones Act, American citizenship was granted and Puerto Ricans gained ease of travel between the United States and the Island, became eligible for some entitlement programs, and were eligible to be drafted into the U.S. military but were not allowed to elect their governor. As an American colony, Puerto Rico continued the struggle it had waged against Spain in order to preserve a national identity.

The decline of the agrarian economy after the American invasion in the 1920s preceded the first wave of migration in the 1930s, mostly of agrarian workers (Rodriguez, 1991). After World War II, Puerto Rico initiated its modernization programs, influenced by the New Deal philosophy. In 1948, Puerto Rico was allowed to elect its first governor, and in 1952 it became a commonwealth. At this time, Operation Bootstrap was launched. It gave tax exemptions and cheap labor incentives to American industrialists wanting to invest capital in the development of the economy (Hernández, 1999). As ways to control an excessive population that would prevent economic growth, massive emigration of Puerto Ricans to the United States and massive sterilization of low-income women were promoted (Facundo, 1991).

The migration from Puerto Rico to the United States became one of the very few choices for economic survival during the period of the Great Migration (1946–1964). In Puerto Rico, migration served to alleviate the structural problem of massive unemployment. In the United States, the immigration of Puerto Rican workers helped to keep the wages low as they assumed low-level jobs with correspondingly meager salaries. In 1967, there was a net migration of 26,000 people (Inclán and Herron, 1998; Facundo, 1991).

During 1972 and 1977, a new sociopolitical climate was prevalent and encouraging of political commitment, in particular the Puerto Rican struggle for independence. Simultaneously, the United States was struggling with an economic recession. Although wanting to commit politically to the movement, many Puerto Ricans were forced to leave the country due to the critical condition of the national economy. This forced a second mass migration to the United States, known as the Revolving Door Migration, which was characterized by a circular pattern of migrating; for the first time, the Island culture was introduced to New York Puerto Rican culture (Hernández, 1999). The immigrants were younger, of diverse class origins, and from different educational and economic backgrounds.

In the 1980s, the migration characteristics changed. The Reagan administration policies in the eighties, the fear of a nuclear war, the growing technology, and the interest in economic power and globalization influenced Puerto Rican thinking (Hernández, 1999). During these years, the migrant population included highly skilled professionals, advanced graduate students, or other professionals who relocated in the United States to improve their financial and social status.

An understanding of the identity conflict experienced by Puerto Ricans in the United States is facilitated by a developmental view of their migration and transculturation within their family experience. Bowen (1976) states that substantial changes in a family system take place over at least three generations. Thus the effects of family migration on the Puerto Rican adolescent can be conceptualized as a multigenerational experience of loss of social status, self-esteem, and mastery, while coping with the ambivalence and contradictions of acculturation (Hernández, 1999). Within this conceptualization, the second, third, and fourth generations, currently the majority of Puerto Ricans we see in our clinics, experience profound difficulties in which stress, failure, and defeat are common (Inclán, 1985).

Puerto Rican adolescents are still outsiders. As Puerto Ricans, they have never been able to control their own destiny. In addition, as immigrants, they carry the burden of being an ethnic minority in North American society. The sense of powerlessness and hopelessness that is often encountered in Puerto Rican adolescents meshes with historical and current social reality.

Culture

For Puerto Ricans, many traditional values are carried through generations, even though they may have little relevance in their everyday lives. Among the ideal traditional values is the value of *familism,* which encourages strong ties among blood relatives and the notion that, no matter what, family comes first (*Mi familia con razón o sin ella* [Family, right or wrong]; Inclán, 1985). The culture and the nuclear family are hierarchically structured and patriarchal. In addition, there is a *compadrazgo* system of godparents and coparents. This system is closely related to the concept of *familismo,* as is a system that involves either members of the immediate or extended family, friends, or significant others that by selection or by petition become the godparents of a child in baptism. This act constitutes a formal agreement among families that, in the absence of the parents, the godparents will be in charge (Inclán, 1985). Through this process, the bond between families and friends is solidified and immortalized, making everyone involved part of the family.

Gender roles, in the ideal sense, are clearly defined in the culture. *Machismo* is a cultural ideology that values male supremacy and encourages men's bravery, unemotionality, hypersexuality, and the role of provider and protector of women and family (Ramos-McKay, Comas-Díaz, and Rivera, 1988; Garcia-Preto, 1996; Stevens, 1973). *Marianismo* is another pivotal cultural ideology that calls for virginity, purity, goodness, sacrifice, resignation, and motherly abnegation (Ramos-McKay, Comas-Díaz, and Rivera, 1988; Garcia-Preto, 1996; Stevens, 1973). Based on the *marianista* value, the woman's primary role is to hold the family together, prioritize the husband, and secure family well-being, even when this involves self-sacrifice.

Personalismo upholds the dignity of the individual. It calls for the development of inner qualities to attain self-respect and offers a guide for the proper way to respect and gain the respect of others. Personalismo involves treating age peers with informal familiarity while treating seniors with deference (Inclán, 1985). Children are taught the importance of respect and the proper way to relate to others on the basis of age, sex, and social class (Ramos-McKay, Comas-Díaz, and Rivera, 1988; Garcia-Preto, 1996).

Aggression is to be controlled, particularly in women. Socially, aggression is supposed to be inhibited. The repression of aggression in women has been associated with the cultural syndrome of *ataques de nervios,* which are characterized by seizurelike patterns, usually psychogenic in nature (Garcia-Preto, 1998). At other times, it is channeled in less dramatic and more "accepted" channels such as somatization, alcohol consumption, indirect verbal aggression, or sarcasm and loud arguments.

Catholicism is the dominant religion, although the individual may experience a personal relationship with God without the institutional rituals (Garcia-Preto, 1996). *Spiritism* is another widespread but not officially sanctioned spiritual belief. Many Puerto Ricans adhere to it and believe that good and evil forces can affect one's life (Garcia-Preto, 1996). "Being" is valued above "doing" and "having"; thus, what you cultivate in yourself is more important than your accomplishments or wealth (Inclán, 1985; Garcia-Preto, 1996). *Racism* is pervasive and greatly denied as an issue, even though race and shades of color have direct implications for social desirability. Puerto Ricans are a racially mixed group, but being black or dark is seen as a disadvantage; racism and race discrimination are prevalent but not spoken about. As a general cultural rule, being darker is associated with a lower status in society, whereas being lighter is associated with a higher status (Ramos-McKay, Comas-Díaz, and Rivera, 1988).

Language is an important cultural value among Puerto Ricans that is emotionally charged as an issue of pride and shame. Third- and fourth-generation Puerto Rican children sometimes refuse to speak Spanish, as they associate it with their seniors and with their lower social status. However, the prevalence of Spanish-English bilingualism among Puerto Ricans in New York City is also seen as a symbol of cultural affirmation and cultural identity (Hernández, 1999).

The process of Puerto Ricans acculturating to their new environment in the United States has taken generations (Inclán, 1985; Hernández, 1999). Although Puerto Rican adolescents continue to struggle to succeed in a culture that is hostile to them, they also struggle to resist assimilation into that culture. The Puerto Rican adolescents seen in our clinics rarely come with an assimilation dream. Instead, they present as a differentiated group who no longer identify with the "classic" Puerto Rican culture of their grandparents; neither do they identify with the host American culture. After at least three generations in the United States, many Puerto Rican adolescents are beginning to identify with a syncretic culture—that of the urban youth of Puerto Rican descent. As is true with any overlapping ideologies, this culture incorporates elements of the traditional Puerto Rican culture (Spanish words, values such as familism) with elements of the mainstream culture (values such as independence, English language) and elements of the urban diverse cultures (rap music, other Latin American music).

Puerto Rican youth, as a disadvantaged group, identify with groups like the Dominican or African American youth (Hernández, 1999). Simultaneously, they differentiate from these adolescent peers by adhering to their symbols of ethnic pride. At the crossroads of developing new cultural representatives and relevant role models, they have identified with a cultural movement or peer idols that represent their "in-between" status: not American, not Puerto Rican, but New York–Puerto Ricans. Examples of the birth of their own "Nuyorican" culture are the Puerto Rican Pride Day Parade in New York City, the Latin groove and Latin hip-hop music movements, and idols such as salsa or pop singers who sing Puerto Rican music with English words (Marc Anthony, Dark Latin Groove, Jennifer Lopez).

Even though cultural ideals tend to persist through time, Puerto Rican traditional cultural values are more like a tradition or moral guide; the group is not necessarily expected to follow it. When dealing with conflicts between parents and children, we are no longer encountering the conflict between the traditional values of the Puerto Rican culture and the acculturated values their youngsters encountered two generations ago. Rather, we are recognizing that the generational conflict occurs in the context of more advanced stages of the U.S.-Puerto Rican process of acculturation; parents tend to be more conservative but somewhat more understanding of the mixture of cultures, and teenagers tend to be more liberal and aggressive in their pursuit of their mixed cultural identity.

Social Class and Community

Clashes between social classes are the social, family, and emotional contradictions that result from being disadvantaged in an affluent society. The 2000 census indicates that 43.5 percent of the Puerto Ricans under the age of eighteen live below poverty level. This translates to a poor quality of life and limited community resources available for the Puerto Rican adolescent. The continuing growing disparity between the "haves" and "have-nots" has grown to major proportions, and the polarization between the two has had a destabilizing effect for the adolescent. The psychological consequences for Puerto Rican youth of this discrepancy include increased feelings of marginalization, a more intense struggle between issues of inferiority and self-esteem, a more complex adolescent crisis, alienation from the "blamed" parents, a dearth of role models, and an ambivalent, often rebellious attitude toward the mainstream society (Koss-Chionio and Vargas, 1999).

In the American society, wealth controls the definition of values in society. Puerto Rican adolescents, generally lacking a trajectory of wealth and entitlement, face the challenge of defining and redefining the social values that will influence their decisions and relationships.

To accept the mainstream path to achievement in this society is not an easy choice for Puerto Rican adolescents. Their parents may coach them but are not available role models. They followed the American Dream fantasy but, in the view of the adolescent, have very little to show for it, just fragmented families, transported and continuous poverty, and broken dreams. The high incidence of school underachievement and dropping out, early marriages and childbearing, and involvement in the criminal justice system are all indicators that we have not yet found good models for guiding Puerto Rican youth into adulthood (Inclán and Herron, 1998). In addition, the current lack of a cohesive, well-organized, active, and critical political force within the Puerto Rican community has limited the possibilities of youth seeking alternative role models of successful Puerto Rican adults.

The problem has reinforcing feedback loops at all levels. For example, given the high prevalence of youth disillusioned with the possibility of success in the American mainstream, schools that serve Puerto Rican communities are disproportionately filled with youth who are looked up to for their tough disregard for cultural values. They constitute a significant peer group influence that competes, often successfully, against the parents' guidance. It is a credit to the resilience of the group that the majority of Puerto Rican youth from poor families stay in the course and break with the powerful forces of history and society that perpetuate the status quo of their ethnic group.

Family

Family dynamics characteristic of adolescence occur in the context of generational clashes experienced among family members. Due to the extended family structure of many Puerto Rican families and the value of familism, the Puerto Rican adolescent is not only confronting differences with their parents but also with their grandparents or other elders.

Within the socioeconomic context of the agrarian culture from which many of the grandparents came, an apprenticeship model of passage into adulthood was functional and adaptive (Inclán and Herron, 1998). The parents of the adolescents seen in our clinics have a different experience from those of the grandparents. Many are second- or third-generation Puerto Ricans who are operating in a more urban context but still preserving part of the ideal cultural values, in particular that of familism and male privilege. In many cases, there is a more latent conflict because as second- and third-generation Puerto Ricans, their experience of acculturation, biculturalism, and ethnic identity remains unprocessed cognitively.

In many Puerto Rican communities, the upbringing of the adolescent is shared by multiple generations and extended family.

These families are often in conflict and have to find a balance between being loyal to the values of the traditional hierarchical and highly structured family and the more individualistic, competitive, personal achievement values of the American urban culture. Being blind to the social and historical roots of this evolution of values often leads therapists to simplistically misinterpret the parents as either overly controlling or overly lenient, depending on the caretaker's generation. This "blame the parent" position can be exacerbated when the therapist fails to recognize the larger social dynamics of being Puerto Rican in the United States (Inclán and Herron, 1998).

One task adolescents have is to expand their social network beyond the family to external resources. This implies a process in which the whole family explores the culture outside the family, the development of new and different sets of values and orientations, and a reintegration of new and old cultural values (Inclán, 1985). For the adolescent, frequently this involves a stressful distancing from one's family, which, lacking the framework to understand the desirability of the individual's movement, is likely to devalue and censure this development. Many find it difficult to accept the adolescent's adoption of the new values and the behavior changes associated with resocialization.

Individual

As all adolescents do, Puerto Ricans undergo biological and psychological changes characteristic of their developmental stage. However, it is the social dynamics and the cultural and community experiences that encourage or hinder the potential that young people have. As stated before, many Puerto Rican youth lack appropriate educational resources and positive role models in their immediate environment. Thus intellectual development is a greater challenge. There is no preparation or training in analytical thinking or relevant strategizing. The school system does not respond to the developmental or social needs they have (Koss-Chioino and Vargas, 1999). This vacuum fosters a reactive approach to intellectual or interpersonal tasks. A vicious circle of isolation and victimization develops, as inner resources are not trained; therefore, the potential for escaping the vicious circle is unavailable (Quiñones, 2000, 2001).

Physical development is also affected. The October 2000 issue of *Time* (Lemonick, 2000) reports that puberty is occurring at an earlier age, with a mean age of twelve for girls. This is particularly true for African Americans and Latinas, who may start to develop secondary sexual characteristics as early as age seven. The figures increase among some Puerto Rican Island groups. Unfortunately, there is limited information and evidence regarding premature male puberty. Some reports indicate the onset of markers of sexual maturity in boys by age ten (Lemonick, 2000), but this evidence is sketchy and controversial. This phenomenon has implications for the psychological and social functioning of the Puerto Rican adolescent.

Girls, expected to act and relate to others as adults based on their physical appearance, are unequipped cognitively and emotionally to respond to their bodies and to others in protective and caring ways. Boys, expected to react to girls in a "manly" way, are also unequipped to respond to this pressure; they do not have the physical and emotional maturity to make informed decisions. Teen pregnancy and failed early and intense romantic relationships are associated with this discrepancy (Koss-Chioino and Vargas, 1999; Lemonick, 2000).

In adolescence, issues of gender also take priority. The cultural ideology of *marianismo* and *machismo* is played out frequently and destructively. First, because the practice differs from the expected ideology, a deficit model is inadvertently set up. Also the expectations can allow for abusive patterns to become part of young people's relationships, as males assume their supremacy and females assume the passivity that may be culturally expected or feel anxiety for not doing so (Quiñones, 2001). Unfortunately, there are not many alternative role models available for these youngsters that could help in breaking the gender relational cycle.

Treatment Modalities with Puerto Rican Adolescents

In this section, we present individual, family, group, and community treatment considerations. The interventions we describe are based on existing theory and techniques but are expanded in order to be more relevant to Puerto Rican adolescents and their families. Specifically, value clashes, migration, and sociocultural factors are introduced as significant intervening variables in treatment. This expanded point of view includes a contextual, historical, and social-systems perspective of problems. Furthermore, it uses and articulates these variables for therapeutic effect. Descriptions and case examples are used to illustrate our treatment approach.

Individual Psychotherapy

Traditionally, individual psychotherapy approaches tend to focus on the psychodynamics of the person, patterns of attachment, quality of relationships, and relationship with the parents, among others. These processes are essential for the understanding and healing of individual conflicts as they represent human aspects shared by everybody, regardless of their background. In working with Puerto Rican adolescents, it is useful to expand the scope of these processes to incorporate other significant contexts that influence their ways of behaving and relating (Malgady, Rogler, and Costantino, 1990). The following case illustrates how historical, cultural, and individual dynamics interact to create in a sixteen-year-old girl a sense of defectiveness that prevents her from feeling worthy and happy.

> Janet was born and raised in New York City, the youngest of three girls. She had been in Special Education for five years, due to a language-based learning disability. Now at age fourteen, Janet requested services because she felt "stuck." Her sisters had run away with their boyfriends, and since then her mother's irrational demands on her had increased. Although Janet complied with most of her mother's expectations, she felt incapable of ever satisfying her.
>
> During Janet's treatment, the therapist focused on family, cultural, and social factors to provide a broader context for understanding the mother-daughter relationship and the symptomatology presented. Janet's mother was incorporated into the treatment, and we focused on her migration history. Asking Mrs. E about her experience growing up, in comparison with Janet's, provided us helpful information.
>
> Janet's mother, whose family was working class, migrated to New York City in the 1960s from a small town on the Island. Mrs. E hoped to become more integrated with the American culture. However, she felt looked down on and segregated by it, so her relationships with Americans were conflicted. As the first person in her family to graduate from college, her college counselor

convinced her that she would have a better chance to succeed in New York City. Contrary to her expectations, Mrs. E did not find a job. She felt embarrassed by her accent and small-town manners and felt threatened by the "all-white, all-American" professional world. Without a job or social support, Mrs. E went to live with relatives in a poor Puerto Rican neighborhood where she met her first husband and had three daughters. But the marriage ended in divorce.

Mrs. E was trapped in self-blame and shameful feelings, so she cut off communication with her family. She did not relate to other women in her ethnic community because she felt they were not "classy enough," nor did she relate to other groups or to Americans because she felt ashamed of who she was.

Although Janet was very close to her mom and her principal goal was to please her, she also felt like a failure, unable to fulfill her expectations. In the family sessions, Janet was asked to discuss her mother's history and encouraged to identify common themes. Janet was surprised to know that her mother felt incompetent and unable to fulfill her goals in life, much like herself. She was also surprised that her mother felt so intimidated by Americans, when in her presence she had valued them incessantly. Perhaps the most difficult thing for Janet was hearing her mother devalue "New York Ricans." Because she identified with that culture, Janet questioned how her mother could appreciate her if she also despised who she was.

At this point in the treatment, we started to challenge the family's values and myths regarding their own ethnic group. Where did these beliefs come from? What made them feel inferior to Americans? What contributed to their limited vision of their past, present, and future? How is it that in this family, gender and ethnicity determine success? How is it that Puerto Rican islanders have a higher sense of self-worth than Puerto Rican immigrants and their descendants? What happens with other Puerto Rican immigrant families in comparison to them?

Mrs. E and Janet started to question their thinking, helping them both to see how the mother's rigidity was associated with her family dynamics. Mrs. E's shame and her need to show her family her success had superceded her relationship with Janet. Mrs. E had identified with the term *minority*. Her difficulty was related to her assumption that her difficulties were entirely her responsibility. She compensated for her inferiority by underestimating and rejecting other Puerto Rican immigrants and did not realize that she and her daughter were part of them. Janet, in an attempt to become visible and assert herself, secretly held on to her Nuyorican identity. However, she felt as if she were violating the family rules and her mother's trust by doing so. These insights and connections helped mother and daughter move from a position of shame and self-blame to a more accepting and empathic view of themselves and their pain.

The focus of the individual sessions with Janet was the analysis of her behavior and feelings. Janet felt defective because she was unable to fulfill her mother's expectations, because she had a learning disability, and also because she was carrying a legacy of shame and unresolved family conflict. Expanding her understanding of herself from a self-centered and defective perspective to a more interpersonal and social one, Janet started to view herself in a different light and to better appreciate herself and the influence of ethnic, cultural, and family background on the type of family she grew up in and the type of person she was becoming.

Family Therapy

The family therapy literature includes some references to treatment issues in working with Puerto Rican families (Garcia-Preto, 1996; Inclán, 1985). In this section, we discuss three issues of importance in treating Puerto Rican adolescents in the context of their families: value differences, the importance of siblings, and questions of role hierarchy.

Although all families experience value conflict between the caretaker and child generations, this clash of values is exacerbated and becomes most intense at adolescence due to the developmental and social changes involved in this stage. When working with Puerto Rican adolescents and their families, we have found the technique of "cultural reframing" useful (Falicov and Karrer, 1984; Falicov, 1998). In this technique, the experience or demand that a parent or adolescent makes is analyzed in relation to the cultural values that constitute the background for the demand or expectation. For example, a mother's request that her daughter interact less frequently with peers is viewed as expressing the traditional Puerto Rican value that the family takes priority over the individual. The adolescent's demand for greater peer contact is viewed as expressing the more acculturated American middle-class value of individuality over family (Inclán, 1985).

Cultural reframing (Falicov, 1998) allows one to shift the focus of blame from the person to the social and cultural processes, which places different demands on the parent and adolescent generations. Contextualization of the problem is achieved when blame of the other has been dissipated or transferred to blame of the socialization and acculturation process as it relates to adolescent expectations. Once this is attained, the therapist may proceed to the next stage of therapy, which involves presenting an objective and impartial model for family progression through the stages of adolescence. This model is based on the process of exchange and negotiation between the parent and adolescent, for greater freedom, trust, and responsibility (Haley, 1980). For most families with adolescents, this is the normal developmental task, and it often needs clarification and therapeutic assistance.

The following case example illustrates the adolescent conflict experienced in the family. It also describes the ways in which the therapist can address the different levels of the conflict and contextualize the presenting problem within the social, cultural, and developmental dynamics.

Four Puerto Rican siblings were in kinship foster care with their aunt. Their father had died of AIDS, and their mother had fallen prey to drug abuse when the children were placed. Jose was sixteen years old and Nicole fourteen; the other two children were seven and eight years old. Nicole had started to explore and act out sexually and was reported to be experimenting with marijuana. The foster mother, a very proud and traditional Puerto Rican woman, reported "having raised model children who never disrespected my household or used drugs, not even smoked cigarettes." She was overwhelmed by Nicole's failure to follow her guidance and threatened the children with return to the foster agency. The older brother, Jose, was angry with Nicole and embarrassed by her behavior because her sexual experimentation included involvement with some of his friends. When treatment was initiated, Jose had withdrawn from friends and family, as he felt impotent to address Nicole's activities.

Treatment options opened up when the foster mother's daughter Carla was included in the treatment. For a period, she attended the sessions instead of the foster mother. Carla's involvement and taking of responsibility de-escalated Nicole's conflict with her mother, as Carla was able to serve as a bridge across the cultures and generations. She could offer useful guidance to Nicole in a way that Nicole was able to hear. Carla's involvement also relieved her mother of her anxiety about feeling ineffective. When Nicole felt listened to, she was more open and participatory in the treatment and sought the advice and support of her brother Jose.

About eighteen months into the treatment, when the initial crisis had subsided, individual sessions were scheduled with Jose. Jose and the therapist (male) explored differences in expectations and in gender role socialization in Puerto Rican young men and women. He was able to identify the cultural and family gender role models that he had internalized and to critically evaluate them. Although he continued to verbalize adherence to some male gender role constructs, specifically "being in charge," he was also able to express change regarding the constructs that men should not be sensitive, cry, or show feelings other than aggressive ones and felt that the hypersexualized, "macho," ready-to-have-sex-at-any-time idea of a Puerto Rican male was an unnecessary burden for men which, in fact, prevents young men from achieving positive self-concepts.

As a result of the redefinition of cultural values and incorporation of another generation as the bridge between the foster children and the foster mother, the communication between the children and the foster mother improved. In sessions and at home, Carla served as the cultural broker, often translating between the two generations. These skills were eventually developed in session by the children and the foster mother, liberating Carla from having to be in the center of each communication transaction and facilitating a more nurturing and oldest-sibling type of relationship between them.

Because more traditional parents have limited ability to serve as a bridge between the old and new cultures, sibling relationships are very important in Puerto Rican families. This is an underutilized resource in family therapy, in general, and in the treatment of ethnic adolescents in particular. Family dynamics and role distributions are usually such that some family member is able to differentiate from the family of origin earlier or more successfully than others. Often young women feel greater pressure to remain at home and help out than male Puerto Rican adolescents do. The sibling who has been able to differentiate successfully from the family of origin can be enlisted in family therapy to serve as a bridge between the parents' and children's generations.

Therapists need to be aware of the importance of siblings in family therapy and move beyond their initial reluctance to include well-differentiated siblings in treatment. Although these siblings may live elsewhere, may be asymptomatic, hold jobs, and have families and other pressing commitments, they remain loyal to the family and tend to respond readily when an appeal is made for their assistance. The case of Marta illustrates this point.

> Marta, age seventeen, had become maladaptively entrenched in the role of executive of the family system—a role she had assumed as a result of the hospitalization of the male head of the household and her mother's very limited social competence. Exploration revealed that an older brother, Ernesto, had moved out of the home but maintained good family ties. Efforts to engage him in the therapy were successful, and Ernesto was instrumental in helping his younger sister reconnect with developmental tasks, issues, and priorities.

In order to accomplish this outcome, the therapist built on the belief systems and values the family adhered to. Upon exploration, it was discovered and articulated that this family placed significant importance on family hierarchy. After the parents, the oldest sibling, particularly if he was male, would make the decisions for the family. After reframing his participation within a cultural and family frame, Ernesto's involvement with the family crisis was seen as only natural. Marta's involvement was reframed as well intended but, due to her inexperience in life and lack of a role model from an elder sibling, she was becoming overwhelmed. A dialogue between the siblings discussing how they could better share responsibilities was encouraged in the sessions.

The family also placed enormous value in traditional roles, which prescribed that the daughter should be the family's caretaker. This time, the therapist decided to respectfully challenge this notion by incorporating developmental and social aspects to the therapeutic dialogue. At seventeen and in the current social organization where the family lived, it would be nearly impossible to be successful as the only caretaker for the family. The role of the man was critically evaluated and expanded by incorporating and normalizing the presence of characteristics other than "being in charge." These included sensitivity, concern, and nurturance, as expressed in the role of the eldest son.

Together, the siblings were able to redefine self and family needs, as well as restructure family affairs so that family functioning could be maintained and Marta's autonomy and differentiation pursued.

Work with Puerto Rican families suggests that traditional approaches to the question of hierarchy within the family be reviewed. The therapeutic approach to the work with these families may require a more flexible and operational basis of role relationship within the family. Although it is standard to support generational hierarchies, the process of rapid social transformation makes the substantive basis for this hierarchy tenuous in many families where the children can quickly surpass parents in technical knowledge and expertise, status, marketability, and income; often they have a greater mastery of the urban Latino and American culture. A therapist who focuses on the family without considering its multiple contexts may operate within a family model that assumes a generational hierarchy that is actually contradicted by the social and familial reality.

Some adolescents, owing to their level of biculturalism, social achievement, or developmental maturity, are able to assume executive or other functional leadership within the family. The clinical criterion to be observed in such situations is whether this role is assumed with the implicit sanction of the parents or in a manner that undermines parental status and role, thus generating family dysfunction and psychopathology (Garcia-Preto, 1996). For example, a socially contextualized family role for a functional and well-differentiated adolescent in a poor Puerto Rican migrant family is one of great responsibility for the family unit as a whole and for the parental and sibling subsystems in particular. In our experience, it is the lack of these types of family responsibilities and expectations that tends to correlate positively with antisocial behavior and social anomie.

Group Therapy

Using group modalities is a good way to obtain a fuller view of the adolescent (Gil, 1996), as it can provide a surrogate extended family and a microcosm of their world in which they may feel safer and more able to trust others. In a group, these adolescents can practice interpersonal strategies and discuss conflicts and dynamics common to their developmental stage without singling out one person as the problem.

In the process of becoming adolescents, Puerto Rican children encounter parental and social demands that are harsh and, on occasion, detrimental to their well-being. For example, based on the cultural expectation of *respeto,* parents expect the adolescent to remain compliant and passive toward the adults, particularly older relatives. However, the social experiences associated with being an ethnic and social minority do not necessarily support the practice of respect; in their experience, many adults in authority discriminate, use, and abuse them based on their ethnicity, race, or gender; this can happen in school settings and workplaces, as well as in other social interactions. The adolescent may not know how to respond effectively to the attacks or even realize that an attack of this nature is taking place. Thus, rather than expect adherence to traditional cultural values such as "giving respect" to adults, regardless of the particular situation, in group therapy adolescents could reconsider and reconceptualize response styles and behaviors in different contexts of development.

Very important among the many pressing issues of adolescence is gender identification. In the case of Puerto Rican teenagers, concepts such as *machismo* and *marianismo,* for example, inform the gender behavior. These notions of masculinity and femininity are passed down over generations without being critically analyzed. In spite of the negative effects it may have on the teenager, the cultural definition of *gender* remains rigid and unchangeable and becomes confused with *ethnicity.* For example, raising a daughter without directly addressing issues of dominance in heterosexual relationships will leave her unprepared to develop a more egalitarian relationship with a male partner. Not addressing cultural aspects supporting the inequality of women in relationships may leave her thinking that to be a Puerto Rican woman she will have to conform to the cultural stereotype. Not addressing cultural homophobia with gay or lesbian teenagers will leave them feeling defective and will facilitate self-hatred.

The process of adolescence for Puerto Ricans also involves the definition of their ethnic identity. Puerto Rican adolescents do not necessarily identify with their parents' idea of being Puerto Rican. Rather than expecting accommodation to the values of the parents (or expecting parents to accommodate to their values), the therapeutic task is one of reframing growing up within the context of the evolving values of the family and of the culture.

We have found that organizing groups around a theme tends to be more effective in working with adolescents. In an attempt to depathologize the experience of Puerto Rican adolescence, the group is organized around themes relevant to their developmental stage rather than around diagnoses. Some examples of these themes are sexuality, issues around being the eldest child, growing up with grandparents, or issues of ethnic identification.

> In a group composed of five girls of Puerto Rican descent between the ages of twelve and fourteen, they all shared the process of becoming women. The girls were second- and third-generation Puerto Ricans living in New York City. According to their parents, their "unacceptable behavior" included outings with boys, disrespectful interactions with the parents or other adults (including yelling, refusing to speak Spanish, rejecting Puerto Rican food), and inappropriate, sexualized dressing. The girls agreed to participate in a group to discuss the difficulties associated with growing up and negotiating freedom with their parents.

The group started by exploring the meaning of being a Puerto Rican woman. They all professed having a clearly New York Puerto Rican identity but had no clear idea of what that meant. They held on to stereotypical notions such as the sexualized Latina or the maternal Latina but had no alternatives to it.

As part of the group process, the girls explored ideas associated with the cultural definitions of womanhood. These involved the definitions based on *marianismo,* the Puerto Rican culture, and the mainstream American definition of Puerto Rican women. Through these discussions, the girls were encouraged to challenge their definitions, behavior, and self-expectations, the expectations of boys, and those of their families. Through exercises and discussion, the group experimented with developing alternative models for their womanhood. For example, what will it be like not to comply with boys' sexual advances? Will that make them less of a woman? What other things are they capable of accomplishing in addition to motherhood? How would they behave if they were not so sexualized?

Issues of shame and pride were very attached to their definitions of being Puerto Ricans. They all felt proud of being Puerto Rican, but they could not identify anything in particular that made them feel good about it. Upon exploration, they all had negatively identified with the stereotypes of Puerto Ricans as welfare recipients, teen parents, or uneducated people, which made them feel ashamed. This contradiction was processed in the group. We explored how being Puerto Rican was often characterized by mainstream American society and by Puerto Ricans as something negative due to the social history of these groups. In our discussion, we talked about how sometimes it was easier to go along with stereotypes than to challenge and question them. We were able to identify aspects that made them proud. The cultural values of familism and friendship, the artistic cultural trends, and Puerto Rican moral codes were among those values they felt proud of.

We also discussed the differences between the cultural values of their parents and those of their own, contextualizing the differences within their historical, cultural, and personal experiences. The emphasis of the discussion was then shifted from criticism of the parents to developing an understanding of evolving cultural values, and to developing ways of negotiating with their parents.

Community Interventions

The following case illustrates the impact of an educational intervention on an older adolescent searching for a positive identity in his transition to adulthood.

> A nineteen-year-old Puerto Rican male was raised in the New York City Public Housing Projects with his mother and three siblings. He had a prior history of school failures and had been arrested three times. After completing the Roberto Clemente Center/Bard College Course in the Humanities, he concluded: "I wasn't interested or noticed where I was, I just got places, did what I had to do,

and got back. Now that's changed. The whole city is open to me. I go places and I'm looking up at buildings all the time. I recognize the Doric columns all around. It's like I was living in that Plato's cave."

The ecological systems perspective not only allows for but calls for expanding interventions from the individual to the family, group, and community levels. Because so many Puerto Rican adolescents and young people come from poor families, their education, as well as the values and worldviews associated with it, is often circumscribed by those in their immediate experience. In addition, many are burdened with the personal consequences that arise from social ills and drop out of school prematurely. Reciprocal feedback loops are built from the societal to the personal level, where education is perceived as "not for me/for you." Over time, the society and the young people begin to articulate discrimination in the form of "what is needed and desired is *job training*."

From the ecological-systems point of view, it is the responsibility of the community center, including mental health centers, to address problems in and of the community such as poverty and social marginalization at the community level also. Study of the humanities can break the isolation and expand one's way of critically understanding society and one's place in it.

It is precisely education that empowers the few in power over the many others who are job-trained. On this basis, in 1996 Earl Shorris (1972) founded the Clemente Course in the Humanities for poor young people who have been marginalized by the mainstream educational system. The Clemente course is a six-credit college-level course offered originally at Roberto Clemente Center in New York City and now throughout the United States. It is offered in academic collaboration with Bard College. At the RCC, every year about thirty young persons from the Lower East Side of Manhattan begin a two-semester college curriculum in the humanities, which offers courses in art history, philosophy, literature, American history, and writing.

The personal transformation that takes place over the nine months of study is a more trusted and enduring outcome than the valuable college credits that Bard College awards. The students' measured self-esteem increases significantly (Shorris, 1972). Community gratitude and feedback is uplifting. An agency director in the community remarked: "You do not have to recruit here or tell me about the program. Lydia (a parent enrolled in their young parents program) used to walk around defeated, with little enthusiasm for life. She questioned all the time why she had her kid, and her fitness as a parent. Last year, while taking the course in the humanities, she began to walk with her head high. It's amazing how proud she now feels. She now participates vigorously and is a leader in our programs; she won't stop talking about it. Can I take it?"

Summary and Conclusion

Puerto Rican adolescents are a significant and expanding at-risk population group. Sociohistorical, cultural, and migration characteristics differentiate Puerto Rican emigrants from previous arrivals. Their role as second- and third-generation youth in their growing-up process is to integrate the culture of their seniors with their own American Puerto Rican culture. As a result of this integration process, a significant number of problems can be expected. Mental health practitioners must be prepared for the challenge that providing services to Puerto Rican adolescents and their families constitutes.

Cultural factors, values, and clashes between parental and adolescent generations cannot be overemphasized as necessary considerations in the assessment and treatment of Puerto Rican adolescents. Neglecting to pay attention to the processes of value orientation and value conflicts can lead to an overemphasis on intrapsychic or family dynamics that may limit the effectiveness of treatment. A contextual approach expands and complements the training in individual, group, and family assessment and treatment of Puerto Rican adolescents. This perspective argues for the need to expand clinical areas of competence to include issues of migration, history, social class, and the role of the community. Therapists working with this group need to understand that more than one worldview competes for these youngsters' attention as a viable life course. Failure to understand this tends to result in ineffective therapy.

References
Bowen, M. "Theory in the Practice of Psychotherapy." In P. J. Guerin, Jr. (ed.), *Family Therapy: Theory and Practice*. New York: Gardner Press, 1976.

Cooper, M. "Diversity Lags Behind Census in Town Halls; Hispanics Are Still Rare in Suburban Government." *New York Times,* Metro Section, Mar. 18, 2001, pp. 33, 36.

Erikson, E. H. *Childhood and Society.* (2nd ed.) New York: W. W. Norton, 1963.

Facundo, A. "Sensitive Mental Health Services for Low-Income Puerto Rican Families." In M. Sotomayor (ed.), *Empowering Hispanic Families: A Critical Issue for the '90s.* Milwaukee, Wisc.: Family Service America, 1991.

Falicov, C. J. *Latino Families in Therapy.* New York: Guilford Press, 1998.

Falicov, C. J., and Karrer, B. M. "Therapeutic Strategies for Mexican-American Families." *International Journal of Family Therapy,* 1984, *6*(1), 18–30.

Garcia-Preto, N. "Puerto Rican Families." In M. McGoldrick, J. K. Pearce, and J. Giordano (eds.), *Ethnicity and Family Therapy.* (2nd ed.) New York: Guilford Press, 1996.

Garcia-Preto, N. "Latinas in the United States: Bridging Two Worlds." In M. McGoldrick (ed.), *Re-visioning Family Therapy.* New York: Guilford Press, 1998.

Gil, E. *Treating Abused Adolescents.* New York: Guilford Press, 1996.

Haley, J. *Leaving Home: The Therapy of Disturbed Young People.* New York: McGraw-Hill, 1980.

Hernández, M. "Puerto Rican Families and Substance Abuse." In J. Krestan (ed.), *Bridges to Recovery: Addiction, Family Therapy, and Multicultural Treatment.* New York: Free Press, 1999.

Inclán, J. "Variations in Value Orientations in Mental Health Work with Puerto Ricans." *Psychotherapy,* 1985, *22*(2S), 324–334.

Inclán, J., and Herron, G. "Puerto Rican Adolescents." In J. T. Gibbs, L. N. Huang, and Associates, *Children of Color: Psychological Interventions with Culturally Diverse Youth.* San Francisco: Jossey-Bass, 1998.

Koss-Chioino, J. D., and Vargas, L. A. *Working with Latino Youth: Culture, Development, and Context.* San Francisco: Jossey-Bass, 1999.

Lemonick, M. D. "Teens Before Their Time." *Time,* Oct. 30, 2000, pp. 66–74.

Malgady, R. G., Rogler, L. H., and Costantino, G. "Culturally Sensitive Psychotherapy for Puerto Rican Children and Adolescents: A Program of Treatment Outcome Research." *Journal of Consulting Clinical Psychology,* 1990, *58*(6), 704–712.

Quiñones, M. E. "On Becoming a Woman: Expanded Role Models for Latina Teenagers." Paper presented at the Family Therapy Network Symposium, Washington D.C., Apr. 1, 2000.

Quiñones, M. E. "On Becoming a Woman: Empowering Adolescents Girls of Color." Paper presented at the Renfrew Foundation Conference, Philadelphia, Nov. 9, 2001.

Ramos-McKay, J., Comas-Díaz, L., and Rivera, L. "Puerto Ricans." In L. Comas-Díaz and E. E. Griffith (eds.), *Clinical Guidelines in Cross-Cultural Mental Health*. New York: Wiley-Interscience, 1988.

Rodriguez, C. *Puerto Ricans Born in the USA*. Boulder, Colo.: Westview Press, 1991.

Shorris, E. *Latinos*. New York: W. W. Norton, 1972.

Skidmore, T., and Smith, P. *Modern Latin America*. London: Oxford University Press, 1992.

Stevens, E. D. "Machiamo y Marianismo: The Other Face of Machismo in Latin America." In A. De Costello (ed.), *Female and Male in Latin America. Transaction Society,* 1973, *10*(6), 51–63.

U.S. Bureau of the Census. *Current Population Reports: The Hispanic Population in the United States 1999. Current Population Reports, Population Characteristics,* Series P20, No. 527. Washington, D.C.: U.S. Department of Commerce, 2000a.

U.S. Bureau of the Census. *Projections of the Resident Population by Race, Hispanic Origin, and Nativity: Middle Series 2001–2005*. Population Projections Program. Washington, D.C.: U.S. Department of Commerce, 2000b.

U.S. Bureau of the Census. *Projections of the Total Resident Population By 5-Year Age Groups and Sex with Special Age Categories: Middle Series 2001–2005*. Population Projections Program. Washington, D.C.: U.S. Department of Commerce, 2000c.

Part Five

Emerging Challenges for Children's Mental Health

In the final two chapters, we address the implications of the mental health issues and psychosocial problems of ethnic minority youth for mental health services, policy, training, and research. Larke Nahme Huang and Girlyn F. Arganza, authors of Chapter Ten, discuss the implications of these issues and problems for mental health services in the major systems of care serving children and young people, that is, education and special education, the child welfare system, the health care and mental health systems, early childhood settings, and the juvenile justice system.

Huang and Arganza discuss each of these systems and evaluate their effectiveness in terms of several factors: their comprehensiveness, their integration and coordination, their appropriateness, and their cultural competence. The authors also look at the degree of access that minorities have to these services, as well as their availability and affordability. Finally, they propose a set of recommendations to improve the delivery of mental health services to low-income minority youth, to improve their access to such services, and to ensure that these services offer culturally competent practitioners who have an adequate knowledge base about the populations they serve, a set of clinical skills that are sensitive to their patients' cultural backgrounds, and a range of clinical interventions that are appropriate for their individual and family problems.

As the authors note, the inequitable and inappropriate mental health services to children and youth in all systems of care have been documented in numerous state and national reports, most recently in the Surgeon General's report *Mental Health: Culture, Race and Ethnicity* (U.S. Department of Health and Human Services, 2001). Their chapter provides an excellent summary of the systemic problems, the barriers to access, and the difficult challenges of creating systems of care that will serve the mental health needs of children and youth of color in a culturally competent manner.

In Chapter Eleven, Larke Nahme Huang and Jewelle Taylor Gibbs examine the implications of the mental health needs of ethnic minority youth in terms of mental health policy options, mental health training programs, and mental health research on ethnic minority populations and communities of color.

Much of the debate over mental health policy focuses on the need to extend health insurance coverage to cover mental health benefits for low-income families. However, such a change would still not reach the millions of uninsured children and youth of color in the United States who do not receive adequate preventive health or mental health services. The authors describe several policy proposals and options that would expand services for low-income youth of color, increase their access to a range of early interventions, and foster health-promoting behaviors among these youth and their families. Formulating policies that acknowledge racial and ethnic diversity and target the needs of ethnic minority communities is a top priority of the Surgeon General's report (U.S. Department of Health and Human Services, 2001).

Training programs for all the mental health professions are woefully inadequate in their curricular offerings and clinical training components regarding the assessment and treatment of minority children and youth. Since the 1970s, numerous surveys have documented the lack of accurate and objective training materials and the lack of clinical resources, internships, supervisors, and even clients to prepare mental health professionals to work with people of color (see U.S. Department of Health and Human Services, 2001). The authors discuss the difficult dilemmas faced by clinical training programs and the challenges of reforming and restructuring traditional professional apprenticeship training methods, particularly in the established disciplines of psychology, psychiatry, and social work. Further, they point out the strong resistance in all of these mental health professional associations to major revisions in training programs that would threaten the status quo of the profession or "weaken" or undermine the intellectual rigor of the training regime—sentiments that frequently mask underlying concerns over increasing access to minority groups.

Finally, the authors discuss the implications of these issues for research on the mental health status, disorders, and treatment needs of ethnic minority populations. The Surgeon General's report on the mental health of minorities delineates several crucial areas of neglected research issues on communities of color. First, there is a dearth of basic epidemiological data on the prevalence of psychological and behavioral disorders among people of color, who are often not included in government-funded research projects. Without such basic data, it is impossible to establish accurate estimates of the mental health needs of these populations, including the proportions of youth of color who are in need of treatment.

Second, there is a lack of information about the effectiveness of various treatment approaches and psychiatric medications used with ethnic minority patients. Well-controlled studies are also needed to determine the effectiveness of ethnic-specific interventions in diverse minority populations, as well as their appropriateness in various clinical settings.

Third, the differential responses to medications for specific psychiatric disorders such as depression and schizophrenia need more research attention to determine the most appropriate dosage levels and treatment durations among patients of different racial-ethnic groups.

A fourth area of needed research is the diagnostic assessment of minority patients, particularly to identify sources of bias in clinical assessment, diagnostic instruments and measures, and assignment to treatment modalities.

Research funding should also be available to identify and evaluate preventive interventions that are effective in reducing the risk of severe disorders among minority youth, as almost no data are available on this topic. Combined with the need for health promotion to increase positive behaviors and coping strategies within these populations, such studies have great potential to improve long-term mental health outcomes for children and youth of color.

In this final section, the authors propose a broad agenda of reforms for minority youth as consumers affected by the mental health delivery system, mental health policy initiatives, mental health training programs, and mental health research strategies. As Huang and Gibbs note in their concluding chapter, the future productivity of the labor force and the future stability of American society are both linked to the health and effective functioning of this generation of children of color, who are destined to become over one-third of the young adult workforce by the year 2020. Improving their mental health status should be both a pledge and a priority for the nation.

Reference

U.S. Department of Health and Human Services. *Mental Health: Culture, Race and Ethnicity.* Supplement to *Mental Health: A Report of the Surgeon General.* Rockville, Md.: U.S. Department of Health and Human Services, 2001.

Chapter Ten

Children of Color in Systems of Care

An Imperative for Cultural Competence

Larke Nahme Huang
Girlyn F. Arganza

In previous chapters, we focused primarily on the individual child, grounding our approach in three frameworks: a developmental, an ecological, and a minority mental health perspective. Through the integration of these perspectives, we have attempted to craft a comprehensive picture of the ecology of the child, the child's cultural background and history, and the culturally determined developmental challenges and mental health issues confronting these children of color. This has been blended with a discussion of culturally appropriate strategies for mental health interventions for these youth, providing guidance for clinical practice. Although this represents a solid beginning for clinical practice and intervention, it is only a beginning and only part of the picture.

An ecological approach examines the context of the practitioner, as well as that of the client, in this case, the child or family. Similar to the child, the practitioner is embedded in a nested array of programs, policies, and systems that have an impact on the clinical work with the child and family. The practitioner is often part of a system with its own culture, values, rules, regulations, and eligibility requirements—all of which enter into the formulation of an intervention plan for the child. Thus the lack of attention to the service system renders our discussion incomplete.

Building on the discussions of clinical interventions in the previous chapters, this chapter examines the systems level, that is, the systems in which these practices occur. For services to improve the mental health outcomes for culturally diverse youth, it is our assumption that both the practice level and the system level must be culturally appropriate and responsive. Researchers have found that culturally relevant clinical treatment targeted for use with ethnic populations is associated with improved mental health (Hall, 1988; O'Sullivan, Peterson, Cox, and Kirkeby, 1989). Ethnic-specific services are also associated with remaining in treatment and with more positive outcomes for culturally diverse youth (Yeh, Takeuchi, and Sue, 1994). In this chapter, we examine the systems of care service delivery model, the relevant child-serving systems, and the status of youth of color in these systems. Disparities of access and outcomes for these youth will be examined. And finally, the cultural competence model is presented as a methodology to improve systems for children of color.

In her book *Unclaimed Children* (1982), Jane Knitzer documents the ongoing failure of service systems to meet the mental health needs of children and adolescents in need of care. Partially in response to this work, the U.S. Congress, in 1983, facilitated the initiation of the Child and Adolescent Service System Program (CASSP), which was to be established by the National Institutes of Mental Health to promote the concept of a system of care. This effort provided funds and technical assistance to all fifty states and several U.S. territories to plan and begin to develop systems of care for children with serious emotional disturbance. In 1992, Congress passed legislation that created the Comprehensive Community Mental Health Services for Children and Their Families Program, which funded a combination of states and local communities to build systems of care. As of October 2002, eighty-five grants have been awarded, thus seeding the restructuring of services in the public sector.

At the same time, during the last two decades the demographics of the United States were rapidly changing, with significant increases in ethnic and racially diverse groups. From 1995 to 2000, there was a 7 percent increase in the total U.S. population; however, racial and ethnic minority populations grew at a much greater rate than the white population, which decreased by 3 percent. Numbers of African Americans increased by 4.7 percent, Hispanics by 30.2 percent, Asian American–Pacific Islanders (AAPIs) by 13.1 percent, and Native Americans by 9.8 percent (U.S. Bureau of the Census, 1998, 2000). Accordingly, youth of color increased in numbers and, in the period from 1995 to 2015, they are projected to increase at the following rates: AAPI youth, 74 percent, Hispanic youth, 59 percent, African American youth, 19 percent, and American Indian youth, 17 percent, compared to white, non-Hispanic youth, whose numbers are projected to decrease by 3 percent (Snyder and Sichmund, 1999). Thus, as service systems were slowly being restructured and the populations being served were undergoing dramatic demographic shifts, new questions arose regarding the appropriateness of services for these increasingly diverse groups of young people and their families. Although Knitzer's work had documented the inadequacies of service systems for youth with complex mental health needs, the situation for youth of color was even more distressing, with glaring inequities in access to services, appropriateness of treatments, and disparities of outcome. In response to these inequities, the designers of the CASSP system of care model then generated an additional framework for examining the cultural competence of these systems of care.

Systems of Care

Children and adolescents with mental health needs often present complex issues that involve different domains of youth functioning. From an ecological perspective, a child's socioemotional struggles may affect behavior in the family, in the school, in the peer group, in the community, and in other domains of the child's life. These domains in a child's life are often addressed by different child-serving systems. For example, psychological concerns are most often detected in the school and in primary health care systems. Or behavioral problems may lead to involvement in special education or with other public sector systems such as the juvenile justice or child welfare systems. A child's mental health issues impinge on multiple aspects of the child's life and, accordingly, multiple domains of the child's functioning. Youth with mental health needs appear in health care, mental health, juvenile justice, education and special education, child welfare, and early-childhood systems. As a result, a comprehensive intervention may involve multiple child-serving systems.

The underlying premise in a system of care is that youth who have or are at risk for mental health problems are best served by a coordinated array of these services that are community-based and provided in the least restrictive environments. In 1986, Stroul and Friedman defined a system of care as "a comprehensive spectrum of mental health and other necessary services which are organized into a coordinated network to meet the multiple and changing needs of children and adolescents with severe emotional disturbances and their families" (Stroul and Friedman, 1986, p. 3). They also delineated the guiding principles for a system of care: care should be individualized, child-focused, and provided in the least restrictive setting; care should be community-based; the family should be involved in the planning and implementation of care; there should be interagency collaboration and leadership; and services should be delivered in a culturally competent manner.

What are the child-serving systems that make up a system of care? Stroul and Friedman (1986) suggest that the components of a system of care include the following services: mental health, education, health, substance abuse, vocational, recreational, juvenile justice, social services, and operational services such as case management, self-help groups, advocacy, legal services, and transportation. Faith-based services, culturally indigenous services, and informal support services may also be part of a system of care. In the absence of an organized system of care, these services may be uncoordinated, fragmented, duplicative, or inappropriate. For youth of color who often do not access a mental health system, many of these other systems become the de facto mental health service, and these youth continue to be unserved, underserved, or inappropriately served by both public and private sector human services (Garland and others, 2001; Hernandez, Isaacs, Nesman, and Burns, 1998; National Technical Assistance Center for State Mental Health Planning, 1997). Or when the mental health needs of culturally diverse youth are misdiagnosed, these youth end up in other, more restrictive systems such as special education, juvenile justice, or child welfare, where their mental health needs may continue to be neglected, overlooked, or of secondary focus (McGarrell, 1993). In addition, in the juvenile justice or child welfare systems treatment may be based more on social control and removal from the family than support for positive growth and development (U.S. Department of Health and Human Services, 2001). Consequently, there are increasing numbers of youth of color with mental health problems experiencing high degrees of unmet need. In order to gain a more complete understanding of these mental health needs, we need to examine the experiences of these youth in some of these other child-serving systems that periodically interface with the mental health system.

The Juvenile Justice System

In the juvenile justice system, it has been estimated that 50 to 75 percent of youth in detention facilities suffer from mental health problems and are likely, without treatment, to become more vulnerable, volatile, and dangerous to themselves and others. The annual report of the Coalition for Juvenile Justice (2000) titled, "Handle with Care: Serving the Mental Health Needs of Young Offenders," indicates that 73 percent of youth in juvenile facilities reported mental health problems during screening; 57 percent had previously received mental health treatment; 55 percent had symptoms associated with clinical depression; 50 percent had conduct disorders; up to 45 percent had attention deficit–hyperactivity disorders, and many had multiple diagnoses. As least half of the youth with psychological disorders also had a co-occurring substance abuse disorder (Coalition for Juvenile Justice, 2000).

In a study of mental health needs among a stratified random sample of youth who were categorized according to level of involvement in the juvenile justice system, a high overall level of mental health needs for all samples was found (Lyons and others, 2001). The study included a community sample of youth on probation, a sample of youth in corrections incarcerated for their crimes, and a sample of youth adjudicated to residential treatment. Significantly higher mental health needs were found in both the incarcerated and residential treatment samples. Diagnosis of serious emotional disturbance using the Children's Severity of Psychiatric Illness scale revealed that 45.9 percent of the community sample, 67.5 percent of the incarcerated group, and 88 percent of the residential treatment sample had serious emotional disturbance diagnoses. The incarcerated group had a higher suicide risk, presented greater danger to others, was more sexually aggressive, and had greater substance abuse problems. The residential treatment group had greater emotional disturbance, more impulsiveness, and more severe past abuse.

For some youth, involvement in the juvenile justice system is the only path to receiving mental health services. According to a 1999 survey conducted by the National Association for Mental Illness, 36 percent of survey respondents indicated that their children were in the juvenile justice system because mental health services outside the system were unavailable to them; 23 percent of parents were told they had to relinquish custody of their children to get needed services; and 20 percent said they actually relinquished custody to get services. This was attributed, in part, to the restrictions of managed care on mental health services and the shifting of populations to the juvenile justice system, which is receiving substantially more mental health referrals without the benefit of adequate treatment capacity (Coalition for Juvenile Justice, 2000).

For youth of color, the situation is worse (Austin, Dimas, and Steinhart, 1992; Pope and Feyerherm, 1993). In 1999, these youth made up two-thirds of the population in public detention and long-term facilities, according to the National Report on Juvenile Offenders and Victims (Snyder and Sickmund, 1999). In 1997, the majority referred to juvenile court were white youth; however, the proportion of cases involving African American youth was twice their proportion in the population (Poe-Yamagata and Jones, 2000). African American youth referred to juvenile court were more likely to be detained than any other groups. In every offense category, a substantially greater percentage of African American youth were detained than white youth. In drug offense cases, African American youth were 32 percent of those referred but 55 percent of those detained. Detention was used more often for African American youth (27 percent) and youth of other minority races (19 percent) than for white youth (15 percent) (Poe-Yamagata and Jones, 2000). Generally, for youth charged with comparable offenses (for example, person, property, drug, or public order offenses), minority youth, especially African American youth, were locked in detention more often than white youth.

Research has indicated that the disparities in treatment at all stages of juvenile justice involvement—referral or arrest, detention, formal processing, waiver to adult court, and disposition—weigh heavily against youth of color. The disparity is most pronounced at the beginning stages of involvement at the intake and detention decision points; however, when racial-ethnic differences are identified, they tend to accumulate as the youth are processed through the system. This "cumulative disadvantage" for minority youth within the juvenile justice system results in disproportionate minority confinement and overrepresentation of youth of color in secure juvenile corrections (Males and Macallair, 2000).

Gibbs (2001) summarizes the major findings from national reports on youth of color in the juvenile justice system.

- First, youth of color are more likely than whites to have contact with the juvenile justice system for a variety of reasons, including neighborhoods with higher crime rates, differential police policies and practices, racial profiling, and racial bias within the system (Poe-Yamagata and Jones, 2000; Snyder and Sickmund, 1999).
- Second, at the initial stages of involvement with the juvenile justice system, African American youth were overrepresented in arrests, in referrals to juvenile court, and in detention, as compared with white youth, although the latter were referred at more than twice the rate of black youth (66 percent versus 31 percent) (Poe-Yamagata and Jones, 2000).
- Third, even when the type of offense is similar, African American youth were more likely to be formally charged in juvenile court than white youth (Snyder and Sickmund, 1999). This is particularly notable in terms of drug-related offenses in which three-fourths of black youth are charged, compared with only half of white youth arrested for drug offenses (Poe-Yamagata and Jones, 2000).
- Fourth, minority youth offenders, in comparison to white youth, were significantly more likely to be waived to adult criminal court in all offense categories (Bazemore and McKean, 1994; Snyder and Sickmund, 1999). For drug offenses referred to juvenile court, this disparity is even more striking, with African American youth experiencing a

24 percent "waiver disadvantage" and white youth a 24 percent waiver advantage (Poe-Yamagata and Jones, 2000).

- Fifth, youth of color were more likely than white youth to receive an out-of-home placement disposition from juvenile court, whereas white youth were more likely to be placed on probation (Snyder and Sickmund, 1999).
- Sixth, minority youth make up only one-third of the adolescent population in the United States, yet they account for two-thirds of the more than 100,000 juveniles confined in local detention and state correctional systems (Snyder and Sickmund, 1999). These youth of color account for the majority of youth detained in both public (67 percent) and private facilities (55 percent). Minority youth are incarcerated in secure facilities twice as frequently as white youth, and African American youth account for the largest proportion of incarcerated youth (Poe-Yamagata and Jones, 2000; Snyder and Sickmund, 1999).
- Finally, in every state youth of color under age eighteen are overrepresented and white youth underrepresented in admissions to adult prisons (Poe-Yamagata and Jones, 2000).

A recent report commissioned by Building Blocks for Youth (Villarruel and Walker, 2002) found that Latino and Latina youth in the juvenile justice system also receive disparate and more punitive treatment than their white peers charged with the same types of offenses. The Latino youth were more likely to be incarcerated; for drug offenses, the incarceration rate for Latino youth was thirteen times the rate for white youth, and the average length of incarceration for drug offenses was five months (143 days) longer than for white youth, almost five months longer for violent offenses, and one month longer for property offenses. Additionally, Latino youth face linguistic barriers resulting in harsher treatment, and profound confusion and frustration for youth and families who speak only Spanish or have limited English proficiency.

Presumption of gang membership may have adverse consequences for youth at all the key decision-making points in the justice system. For example, stereotypes about Latino youth being associated with gangs can affect police decisions about whom to stop and whom to arrest. Alleged gang affiliation may be a determining factor in detaining a youth after arrest (Davis, 1992; Gibbs, 2000). Police and probation departments in some jurisdictions allot "negative points" for alleged gang involvement during the risk assessment of arrested Latino youth.

Clearly, the outcomes for minority youth in the juvenile justice system are distressing and may be attributable to multiple factors (see Snyder and Sickmund, 1999). Although some have argued that this overrepresentation of minority youth in the justice system is merely a result of their showing more delinquency and criminal behavior, an accurate analysis is much more complex. Others suggest that different police policies and practices, location of offenses, reactions of communities, racial profiling, and racial bias within the justice system confirm that juvenile justice systems are not racially neutral. Increasingly, a double standard exists that incarcerates youth of color but rehabilitates white youth who commit comparable crimes (Males and Macallair, 2000).

Combining these findings with studies indicating a high incidence of mental health disorders among the juvenile justice populations (Coalition for Juvenile Justice, 2000) and the lack of effective services to meet the mental health needs of these youth, the vulnerability of youth of color in this particular system is significant. The studies suggest a dual pathway for white and minority youth who commit delinquent offenses, with white youth more likely to be diverted from the juvenile justice system into the mental health system for "treatment," whereas minority youth are more likely to be processed in the juvenile justice system for "punishment" (Dembo, 1988; Krisberg and others, 1987; Mason and Gibbs, 1992). Youth of color in juvenile and adult corrections are less likely than white juveniles to undergo a thorough psychological assessment and less likely to receive any therapeutic treatment (Coalition for Juvenile Justice, 2000; Hutchinson, 1990). However, among those evaluated, youth of color are more likely than white youth to receive a diagnosis of conduct disorder, antisocial personality disorder, or a substance abuse disorder than an anxiety or depressive disorder (Dembo, 1988; Hutchinson, 1990). There is significant concern that as more youth of color with undiagnosed or misdiagnosed mental health issues are entering the juvenile justice system, this particular system is in danger of becoming a warehouse for them (Kotler, 2001). Clearly, there is an urgent need to examine the nexus of mental health and juvenile justice in order to address the mental health needs of these youth.

The Child Welfare System

An examination of the child welfare system reveals two significant findings with major implications for children of color. First, children of color and their families experience poorer outcomes and receive fewer services than their white counterparts in the child welfare system (Courtney and others, 1996). Second, mental health disorders are prevalent and an estimated 30 to 80 percent of children in foster care have severe emotional problems (Blatt and others, 1997; Garland and others, 2001; Schneiderman and others, 1998). The implication of these trends is the need for greater attention and strategies to address the increasing numbers of children of color with mental health needs in the child welfare system—one of the systems in a comprehensive system of care for youth.

First, what do we know about the incidence and experience of children of color in the child welfare system? A thorough assessment of recent trends in child welfare populations (for example, abused and neglected children, children in family foster care, children awaiting adoption) documents the disproportionately large number of children of color (Courtney and others, 1996; Morton, 1999). For example, although African American children constituted only 15 percent of the U.S. child population in 1995, they accounted for 28 percent of substantiated allegations of abuse or neglect and represented 41 percent of the child welfare population (Petit and Curtis, 1997). Racial and ethnic minority youth constitute nearly 20 percent of the national population but represent 40 to 50 percent of the foster care population (Courtney and others, 1996). In a national review, Mech (1983) found that prevalence rates for out-of-home placement per 1,000 children were highest for African American children (9.5), followed by Native Americans (8.8), Caucasians (3.1), Latinos (3.0), and Asian Americans (2.0). A nationwide survey (Plantz, Hubbell, Barrett, and Dobrec, 1989) of Native American children found that they were placed in out-of-home care at a rate 3.6 times higher than the rate for other children. An analysis of prevalence rates in five states with large out-of-home care populations (California, Illinois, Michigan, New York, and

Texas) found the proportion of African American children ranged from three times to over ten times the proportion of white children in care (Goerge, Wulczyn, and Harden, 1994). In contrast, white children constitute 66 percent of the U.S. child population, and they are 57 percent of the substantiated allegations, 46 percent of the child welfare population, 36 percent of the children in out-of-home care, and 52 percent of the child fatality cases.

In a national study of protective, preventive, and reunification services for children and their families in child welfare, researchers found that 56 percent of African American children are served in foster care and 44 percent in their own homes. In contrast, only 28 percent of white children are served in foster care and 72 percent receive services in their own homes. Forty-three percent of white children entering the child welfare system are out in less than three months, compared with 16 percent for African Americans. Similarly, only 31 percent of white children's cases are still open at eighteen months, compared with 64 percent of African Americans (Petit and Curtis, 1997).

These are significant contrasts in population groups, and explanations for these apparent differences in incidence of child maltreatment, service experience, and placement are complex. Lower income, poverty, and sociocultural differences in coping with poverty have been the conventional wisdom for explanations of child maltreatment. However, the relationship between low income and maltreatment does not hold for other lower-income minority groups such as Hispanic families, who are underrepresented in the child welfare system.

Additional studies document a pattern of uneven treatment among groups at different points in the child welfare system. Proportional representation should be expected throughout the system; however, this does not seem to be the case. In fact, for African Americans, disproportionate representation increases with further penetration into the system, suggesting either some direct system bias or a higher rate of failure of interventions with this population. For example, children of color are more likely than white children to be overrepresented in child maltreatment reports, based on the proportion of children of color in the child population. For children of color, these reports are more likely to be substantiated by child welfare authorities than those involving white children.

For physical abuse reports, Eckenrode and colleagues (1988) found that race was the only demographic characteristic having an effect on substantiation rates, such that reports on African American and Latino children were more likely to be substantiated than those on white children. Child sexual abuse cases were the primary form of child maltreatment reported for white children (American Association for Protecting Children, 1988).

Given these differential patterns in incidence reporting and substantiation, do similar differences exist in the types of services provided and the decisions and outcomes for children of color? In a study based on national data sources, Olsen (1982) found that no services were recommended for over half of the families with children in placement, with Native American families having the least chance for service recommendations, and white and Asian American families the greatest chance. African American and Latino children were least likely to have plans for family contact, and Latino adolescents were more likely to be considered behaviorally disturbed than were other adolescents (Olsen, 1982). In another study examining objectives and service plans for children, Close (1983) found that specific family services were less likely to be recommended for African American children and Latino children than white children; children of color had fewer visits with their families, fewer services overall, and less contact with child welfare staff members. The study by Downs (1986) of foster parents in eight states found some evidence of a lack of communication between agencies and African American foster parents. With the recent expansion of child welfare caseloads, kinship foster parents are increasing and are disproportionately African American single parents (Berrick, Needell, and Barth, 1994). However, a comparative study of six hundred kinship foster parents and nonrelative foster parents found that services provided by placement agencies, including respite care, support groups, and training, were much less likely to be offered to kinship foster parents than to nonrelative foster parents (Berrick, Needell, and Barth, 1994).

Much of the research on service use and populations of color in child welfare suggests a pattern of inequity based on race and ethnicity. White families and children receive more services than families and children of color. A number of different factors have been proposed to explain the racial and ethnic disparities reported in service utilization, including systematic biases in referral patterns, differences in the receptivity and accessibility of providers, and cultural influences in help-seeking behaviors (Garland and others, 2000). In part, these inequities reflect historical differences associated with race in access to and utilization of public versus private child welfare services (Billingsley and Giovannoni, 1970). But they may also be related to the current resource allocation in child welfare, which favors more therapeutic services as opposed to concrete services such as employment counseling and preparation (Courtney and others, 1996). Family preservation services provide family-centered, home-based, short-term, intensive services to families at risk of having a child placed in out-of-home care (Wells and Biegel, 1991). The objective of these services is to maintain the child in the family's home.

Given the large number of children of color in out-of-home care, there is renewed interest in examining the effectiveness of family preservation services for families of color. In an evaluation study of family preservation services in Washington state, families of color experienced fewer out-of-home placements (18.2 percent) with the provision of family preservation services than white families (29.8 percent), suggesting that this family preservation model may be more culturally appropriate for families of color than traditional child welfare and mental health services, as it provides a combination of concrete and clinical services in clients' homes (Fraser, Pecora, Haapala, 1991).

In terms of adoption, African American children are adopted at a much lower rate than white children. One study found that of 2,110 children listed in the New York State Adoption Services Photolisting between 1985 and 1989, children of color had longer waits and were less likely to be placed compared with white youth (Mont, 1991). Two pieces of federal legislation, the Multiethnic Placement Act of 1994 and the Interethnic Placement Act of 1996, were passed to attempt to facilitate the adoption of youth of color such that states and other entities involved in foster care or adoption placements, and that receive federal financial assistance under Title IV-E, Title IV-B, or any other federal program, cannot delay or deny a child's foster care or adoptive placement on the basis of the child's or the prospective parent's race, color, or national origin (U.S. Department of Health and Human Services, 2001). One goal of this legislation is the recruitment of foster and adoptive parents who reflect the racial and ethnic diversity of the children in the state who need foster and adoptive homes. Although well-intended, given the higher numbers of minority youth remaining in out-of-home care compared with white youth, the utility of these federal efforts remains to be seen, given the social complexities of transracial adoptions and lack of definitive research on the well-being of youth in transracial adoptions.

This relatively bleak picture of the entry of children of color into the child welfare system and disparities in services and outcomes is merely the backdrop for those children who have mental health problems as well. Children of color with mental health disorders enter the child welfare system from different routes; some are victims of child maltreatment, abuse, and neglect, where mental health problems are identified as secondary to placement in the child welfare system; others are children with serious emotional disorders who are placed voluntarily by their parents, who often must relinquish custody in order to access publicly funded treatment services (even though no abuse or neglect has occurred); and some are children whose parents are in need of mental health or substance abuse services and supports so that the child may return home to a stable environment. There is general consensus that mental health disorders are prevalent among children in the child welfare system (U.S. Department of Health and Human Services, 2001). These children often display disorders in the following areas: attachment and interpersonal relations, depression or anxiety, posttraumatic stress disorder related to trauma or self-regulatory disturbances, functional impairment, and an increase of suicide attempts or violent victimization (Parent Educational Advocacy Training Center, 2000; National Mental Health Association, 2000). Children in foster care have a higher-than-average incidence of emotional and mental health disorders and use both inpatient and outpatient services at rates significantly greater than other children (Halfon, English, Allen, and Dewoody, 1994). In sum, children in the child welfare system confront ongoing challenges arising from multiple risk factors such as chronic exposure to poverty, violence, homelessness, maltreatment, unsafe homes, and poor nutrition; exposure to alcohol or drugs; and the emotional trauma of separation from families, along with inconsistencies in foster care and the emotional turmoil of living in an unpredictable, unstable environment (McCarthy and Woolverton, 2001).

The Special Education System

The overrepresentation of children of color in special education and the quality of their education has been a significant and ongoing issue in public education for the past thirty years. Disproportionate representation of youth of color, particularly African American students, remains a controversial and unresolved issue. The Individuals with Disabilities Education Act (IDEA) (Public Law, 105-17) mandates a free appropriate public education (FAPE) for all individuals with disabilities. The law requires nondiscriminatory assessment, identification, and placement of children with disabilities. These children are entitled to special educational services under IDEA; however, children who achieve poorly because of differences related to environmental disadvantage or ethnic, linguistic, or racial differences are not to be identified as disabled.

The manner in which state and local education jurisdictions implement IDEA and provide educational equity and FAPE has been challenged repeatedly in legal arenas and public discourse. A history of overrepresentation of minority children placed in special education has been documented as discriminatory practice and an infringement of students' civil rights. Yet communities and families of color have also relied on this law to provide special education services for their children who may evidence an emotional, behavior, or learning disorder and require this policy to access appropriate educational and mental health services. Thus the dilemma for special education under IDEA is to identify students with equity and nondiscrimination and to provide the culturally appropriate services for eligible students of color, under IDEA, to achieve good educational and socioemotional outcomes.

Socioeconomic issues play a role in the educational careers of children of color and in their experiences with special education. Poverty affects minority students' preparedness and performance in school (Duncan, Brooks-Gunn, and Klebanov, 1994; Entwisle and Alexander, 1993). Numerous studies have focused on the assessment process and test bias as primary reasons for minority overrepresentation in special education. However, a recent review of the literature attributes bias in educational opportunity to poverty and cultural barriers, citing numerous studies of structural inequality throughout the educational process (Skidba, Knesting, and Bush, 2002). Environmental and sociodemographic factors that contribute to lower achievement in minority students increase their likelihood of referral to and placement in special education (Coutinho and Oswald, 2000; National Research Council, 2002).

In a study examining the reasons for disproportionate placement of minorities in special education, the National Academy of Sciences (Heller, Holtzman, and Messick, 1982) cited student, historical, cultural, and school factors as possible causes of disproportionality but ultimately focused on the issues of quality of services received in regular and special education and the validity of the referral and assessment process. The objectives of the study were to determine an effective educational experience for minority students. Unfortunately, there is limited research on the effectiveness of educational programs and supports for students of color who are identified and served as having a disability. A comparison of strategies for ethnic groups with respect to academic and social progress is necessary in order to clarify how to improve educational services and design appropriate changes in special education programs. This takes on a particular urgency, as the number of children from diverse backgrounds in the nation's schools is increasing steadily. Currently, about one in three U.S. school children are African American, Hispanic, Asian American, or American Indian, and children of color now make up more than 75 percent of the enrollment in numerous urban schools, as white students are becoming a minority. As teachers are identifying more children with emotional and behavioral disorders, better identification, referral, and treatment strategies relevant to youth of color will need to be implemented. Finally, this demographic change underscores a compelling need to link schools and mental health services in order to achieve improved outcomes in the education of youth of color with emotional and other disabilities (Coutinho and Oswald, 2000).

The Primary Health Care System

About 20 percent of U.S. adults and children in any given year have a mental disorder; however, the majority of these individuals do not receive treatment, needlessly suffering from distress and disability. In primary health care, about 25 percent of people have a diagnosable mental disorder, most commonly anxiety and depression (Olfson and others, 1997). In terms of primary care, there are more than 150 million pediatric visits each year (Woodwell, 2000). Most children with mental health problems see their primary care providers rather than mental health specialists. Primary care physicians identified about 19 percent of all children they see with behavioral and emotional problems (Kelleher, 2000). African American and Hispanic children are identified and referred at the same rates as other children. Culturally diverse families with mental health issues often seek care for these problems in the primary health care system. In part, this is due to greater familiarity and less stigma associated with health care settings and culturally based explanations attributing emotional and psychological concerns to a physical basis. Although these children are referred at the same rate to mental health services, they are significantly less likely to receive specialty mental health services or psychotropic medications (Cuffe and others, 1995; Kelleher, 2000).

Currently, there is a lack of information on the psychological problems, services, and treatments for children of color presenting in the primary care system. This information would be critical for understanding better the interface between health care and mental health services. However, there are studies that examine ethnicity in the context of children's general health and use of services. These data highlight striking ethnic disparities in children's health and use of health services. For example, a study based on the National Health Interview Survey (Flores, Bauchner, Feinstein, and Nguyen, 1999) found that Native American, black, and Hispanic children are poorest (35 to 41 percent below poverty level versus 10 percent of white children), least healthy (66 to 74 percent in excellent or very good health versus 85 percent of white), have fewer doctor visits, and are more likely to have excessive intervals between visits. Hispanic subgroup differences on these variables surpass differences among major ethnic groups; nearly all ethnic group disparities for children persisted, even after adjustment for family income and parental education. Specific analyses found that Native American and black children have twice the odds of having suboptimal health compared with white children, followed by AAPI children and Hispanic children. Among the Hispanic subgroups, Puerto Rican and Mexican ancestry were significantly associated with suboptimal child health ratings, in contrast to Cuban ancestry, which was not a significant predictor.

Another recent study surveyed 6,700 adults from ethnically and racially diverse communities about access to quality health care (Collins and others, 2002). The study found that "African Americans, Asian Americans, and Hispanics are more likely than whites to experience difficulty communicating with their physicians, to feel that they are treated with disrespect when receiving health care services, and to experience barriers to care, including lack of insurance or a regular doctor" (p. v). These findings have important implications for the physical and mental health of minority children.

As with other child-serving systems, the status of children of color is related to a multitude of factors, including characteristics of the children and their families, characteristics of the systems, and linkages or access issues. Health insurance coverage is an important determinant of access to health care services. Studies of insurance access for populations of color indicate significantly lower rates of coverage in comparison to the white population. Studies conducted by the Kaiser Commission on Medicaid and the Uninsured (2000) indicate an uninsured rate of 14 percent for the white population, 23 percent for African Americans, 24 percent for American Indians, 21 percent for AAPIs, and the highest uninsured rates of 37 percent for Latinos. Significant within-group variations also exist that are obscured by aggregating this information. For example, within the Asian American population, the percentage of uninsured Japanese is 13 percent, in marked contrast to 34 percent for Koreans and 27 percent for Vietnamese. In 1994–95, Latino children were more than twice as likely as white children to be uninsured, and African American children were almost 20 percent more likely than white children to be uninsured (U.S. Department of Health and Human Services, 2001).

For many of these uninsured youth, Medicaid provides a safety net. In 2001, 22.7 percent of children under the age of eighteen received public insurance through Medicaid (U.S. Bureau of the Census, 2002). The percentage of youth covered by Medicaid was highest for African Americans (38.3 percent), followed by Hispanics (34.9 percent), Asian American–Pacific Islanders (18.0 percent), and non-Hispanic whites (15.3 percent). Although Medicaid appears to be a safety net for minority youth who are not insured through private means, for immigrant youth there are gaps in the net. Between 1995 and 1999 the number of low-income noncitizens on Medicaid fell from 19 percent to 15 percent. Currently, twenty-two percent of children of immigrants are uninsured (Kaiser Commission on Medicaid and the Uninsured, 2000). The immigrant population is especially vulnerable to inadequate insurance due to welfare reform and other policy changes that created a five-year ban on Medicaid eligibility for newer immigrants (after 1996). Other prohibitive factors include language barriers, confusion and apprehension on the part of noncitizens regarding becoming a public charge, and concerns regarding eligibility for citizenship (Kaiser Commission on Medicaid and the Uninsured, 2000).

These disparities in health access and outcome for children of color further complicate the identification and treatment of mental health disorders. Primary care services, similar to schools, are frontline providers for these children and their families. However, already confronted with these significant disparities in general health access and utilization, it is expected that prevention and intervention for mental and behavioral health problems will be even more limited.

The Mental Health System

In one of the largest national studies to date on children's use of mental health services, Pottick (2002) reports that more than 1.3 million children under the age of eighteen (or 1 of 50 youth) received mental health services in the United States during 1997. This is nearly double the number of children who received treatment in 1986, although the extent of unmet need in the United States is still unknown. This increase in rate of service used may not be reflected equally among poor or minority children or those in socially stressed or resource-deprived communities. In terms of race and ethnicity, more white (65 percent) than black (19 percent) or Hispanic youth (14 percent) received mental health services. In addition, the majority of youth (51 percent) who received mental health services in 1997 were adolescents thirteen to seventeen years old; 40 percent were between six and twelve; and a surprising 9 percent were preschoolers. Primary presenting diagnoses were disruptive behavior disorder (31 percent), mood disorder (21 percent), and adjustment disorder (16 percent); almost 40 percent of the total sample were seriously emotionally disturbed (Pottick, 2002).

The Surgeon General's report *Mental Health: Culture, Race and Ethnicity* (U.S. Department of Health and Human Services, 2001) highlights the mental health needs and service utilization of the four racial-ethnic populations in the United States. Although issues related to the child population in each group were presented, these discussions were extremely limited, reflecting the lack of systematic research and attention given to the mental health concerns of children of color.

In a California study of 12,106 youth with serious emotional disturbance, Mak and Rosenblatt (2002) found that ethnic minority youth were more likely than white youth to receive severe diagnoses such as psychosis or disruptive behavioral disorder. Epidemiological research is inconclusive about whether there are definitive differences between mental health disorders of African American and white youth; however, African American youth were more likely to have unmet need than were white youth (Shaffer and others, 1996). African American children received outpatient mental health services at a lower rate than white children. They also received less treatment in the schools and in psychiatric inpatient care; however, they were well represented in residential treatment centers for emotionally disturbed youth (Firestone, 1990). These centers are more likely to be funded from public sources. In many cases, child welfare authorities initiate treatment for African American children, as opposed to their parents, and seem to be a principal gatekeeper for African American mental health care (U.S. Department of Health and Human Services, 2001).

In the Great Smoky Mountains Study (Costello and others, 1997) American Indian children were found to have fairly similar rates of disorder (17 percent), in comparison to white children from surrounding counties (19 percent). Rates of anxiety disorders, depressive disorders, conduct disorders, and attention deficit/ hyperactivity disorder were not significantly different. In a school-based psychiatric epidemiological study of Northern Plains youth, more than 15 percent had a single diagnosis; 13 percent met criteria for multiple diagnoses (Beals and others, 1997). The five most common disorders were alcohol dependence or abuse (11 per-

cent), attention deficit/hyperactivity disorder (11 percent), marijuana dependence or abuse (9 percent), major depressive disorder
(5 percent), and other substance dependence or abuse (4 percent). In this population of youth, there was considerable comor-
bidity involving substance abuse.

In terms of service utilization, the few studies examining this
variable indicate that American Indian children rarely receive services in the specialty mental health system but more likely through
juvenile justice and inpatient facilities and in schools (Costello and
others, 1997; Novins, Fleming, Beals, and Manson, 2000). Services
for substance-related problems were most commonly provided in
residential settings.

Studies of mental health problems for Latino youth reveal a
consistent pattern of significantly more mental health problems
than white youth. More anxiety-related problems, delinquency
problem behaviors, and depressive symptoms and disorders were
reported in multiple studies (Vazsonyi and Flannery, 1997; Roberts
and Chen, 1995; Roberts and Sobhan, 1992). However, the few
studies that examine the use of mental health services indicate that
Latino youth use these services significantly less than white youth,
have fewer lifetime counseling visits, and are underrepresented in
the use of outpatient mental health facilities (Pumariega, Glover,
Holzer, and Nguyen, 1998; Bui and Takeuchi, 1992).

There are few epidemiological studies on the mental health disorders of AAPI children and adolescents. The few studies that have
been conducted with small samples of Asian Americans find few differences between this population and that of white youth, although
in a study conducted by the Commonwealth Fund, Schoen and others (1997) found depressive symptoms in girls in grades 5 through
12 to be highest in Asian American females (30 percent), as compared with white females (22 percent), African American females
(17 percent), and Hispanic females (27 percent).

Even though the overall prevalence of mental health problems
and disorders is not different from that of other groups, Asian
Americans have the lowest rates of utilization of mental health ser-
vices among ethnic populations for both adults and youth (U.S.
Department of Health and Human Services, 2001). When Asian
Americans do utilize services, they are generally more severely ill

than white Americans who use the same services. This pattern is true for Asian American adolescents as well (Bui and Takeuchi, 1992) and suggests a high level of unmet need for services.

The Status of Children of Color

This review of the status of children of color in selected child-serving systems that constitute a "system of care" for youth reveals a dismal picture. These youth experience major disparities in needs, services, and outcomes and are doubly jeopardized by their mental health disorders and their minority status. The currently inadequate state of culturally anchored services challenges state and local providers to develop policies and practices to ensure that the interactions and outcomes between children of color and service systems will be productive. Focusing on and incorporating issues of culture in service provision and policy development ensures opportunities for practitioners, agencies, and systems to respond more appropriately to the unique needs of culturally diverse populations (Hernandez, Isaacs, Nesman, and Burns, 1998). To begin to reduce these disparities would require a multipronged, multisystem, comprehensive strategy that would necessitate significant system reform from the policy to the practice level.

Cultural Competence Model

A beginning step toward creating more culturally responsive service systems for children of color is delineated in the cultural competence model developed by Cross, Bazron, Dennis, and Isaacs (1989). In this model, cultural competence is defined as a "set of congruent behaviors, attitudes, and policies that come together in a system, agency or among professionals and enables that system, agency or those professionals to work effectively in cross cultural situations"; *culture* is defined as "the integrated patterns of human behavior that includes thoughts, communication styles, actions, customs, beliefs, values, and institutions of a racial, ethnic, religious or social group" (Cross, Bazron, Dennis, and Isaacs, 1989, p. 13). The term *competence* implies action and assumes that the skills needed to interact in cross-cultural situations can be acquired, learned, and utilized. In most situations, human service providers are not people of color. This concept of cultural competence implies that all providers, regardless of their ethnicity or socioeconomic status, are capable of becoming culturally competent and effective in working with culturally diverse children and their families. In this sense, the responsibility for the provision of culturally appropriate services is placed on all employees of an organization, not just the employees of color who would otherwise assume an unrealistic burden. Cultural competence must be integrated at all levels: the clinical provider level, the program and administrative level, and the larger organizational and systems level (Fong and Gibbs, 1995).

Systems, organizations, and individuals that are culturally competent demonstrate five essential elements at all levels of functioning: (1) valuing diversity, (2) engaging in cultural self-assessment, (3) being aware of cross-cultural dynamics, (4) institutionalizing cultural knowledge, and (5) adapting to diversity (Cross, Bazron, Dennis, and Isaacs, 1989). Valuing diversity is accepting that each culture has preferred behaviors, interactions, and values that may differ from one's own preferences. Understanding this may enable providers to interact more successfully with differing cultures. Particularly in a system of care, awareness and acceptance of differences in communication, life view, and definitions of health and family are critical to the successful delivery of services (Cross, Bazron, Dennis, and Isaacs, 1989). For example, gross underutilization of mental health services may be a result of the system's inability to value a diverse culture's "comfort zones" and the way different cultures seek help. Locating mental health services in primary care clinics may better reflect the ability to value different culturally preferred and less stigmatizing routes to care. Differential acceptance of psychiatric medications is another example. Although medication is an empirically supported treatment for ADHD, some ethnic minority groups are reluctant to use these medications.

Ongoing assessment of an agency's or one's own cultural perspectives and biases and how they interact with those of other cultures enables organizations and individuals to choose policies and practices that minimize cross-cultural barriers and maximize understanding, exploration, and an attitude of inquiry (Evans and Lee, 1998; Fong and Gibbs, 1995). For example, what is the agency's capacity to provide services in the languages represented in their area? Does the agency do an ongoing assessment of this capacity?

Organizational hiring practices and diversity policies must mirror the changing demographics of a target population. The major inequities in treatment decisions and outcomes discussed earlier must be examined in regard to institutional bias and racially based practices that yield negative outcomes for children of color.

In cross-cultural interactions, differences are inevitable, as each party brings to the relationship unique histories and culturally prescribed patterns of communication, behavior, and problem solving, as well as stereotypes or implicit feelings about the other (Canino and Spurlock, 1994; Paniagua, 2001). Tensions and missteps in these interactions are to be expected and contribute to this two-way process of understanding and anticipating the dynamics of difference. An organization or system of care incorporates cultural knowledge into the service delivery framework. Each level of the system needs accurate and ongoing information. For example, the practitioner must know the client's concepts of health and family and be able to communicate effectively; the supervisor must understand how to provide cross-cultural supervision; the administrator must know the character of the population and how to make services accessible and welcoming. Processes must be incorporated within the system to obtain the cultural knowledge it requires. Networks and communication strategies must be developed to respond better to the needs of children of color.

Adaptation to diversity involves the institutionalization of cultural interventions as a legitimate helping approach or the incorporation of activities and policies designed to counteract negative stereotypes and prejudices encountered by children of color at school or in the media. Ongoing adaptation to emerging cultural needs and information contributes to building a more culturally competent service delivery system (Cross, Bazron, Dennis, and Isaacs, 1989). For example, more collaboration and partnering between mainstream services and ethnic-specific services or ethnic providers may reduce some of the access issues and inequities of care in child-serving systems discussed earlier in this chapter. Good models exist of family resource centers and natural cultural helpers working collaboratively with mainstream agencies to link children of color with mental health or child welfare resources (Joseph and others, 2001). For some cultures, faith-based institutions are more familiar, accessible, and welcoming and are good "escorts" into systems that are culturally distant and historically mistrusted (Koss-Chioino, 2000; Neighbors, 1984).

This framework of cultural competence allows organizations and individuals to assess and set goals for themselves as they provide services to diverse children and families. Becoming culturally competent is a developmental process that evolves over time. In the preceding chapters, the information provided on specific ethnic and racial groups and strategies for culturally responsive psychological interventions contributes to the understanding and valuing of differences and to the process of becoming more culturally competent. The goal of this process is for systems, agencies, and practitioners to develop an effective capacity to respond to the unique needs of diverse cultures and to be aware of policies and practices that may be discriminatory, devaluing, or culturally offensive. Through this process, the quality of service may be improved, and disparities in outcomes for children of color may gradually be reduced.

References

American Association for Protecting Children. *Highlights of Official Child Neglect and Abuse Reporting, 1986.* Denver, Colo.: American Humane Association, 1988.

Austin, M. J., Dimas, J., and Steinhart, D. *The Over-Representation of Minority Youth in the California Juvenile Justice System.* San Francisco: National Council on Crime and Delinquency.

Bazemore, G., and McKean, J. "Minority Overrepresentation." In L. S. Thompson and J. A. Farrow (eds.), *Hard Times, Healing Hands* (pp. 99–119). Arlington, Va.: National Center for Education in Maternal and Child Health, 1994.

Beals, J., and others. "Psychiatric Disorder Among American Indian Adolescents: Prevalence in Northern Plains Youth." *Journal of the American Academy of Child and Adolescent Psychiatry,* 1997, *26,* 1252–1259.

Berrick, J., Needell, B., and Barth, R. "A Comparison of Kinship Foster Homes and Foster Family Homes: Implications for Kinship Foster Care as Family Preservation. *Children and Youth Services Review,* 1994, *16*(1–2), 33–64.

Billingsley, A., and Giovannoni, J. M. *Children of the Storm: Black Children and American Child Welfare.* New York: Harcourt Brace Jovanovich, 1970.

Blatt, S., and others. "A Comprehensive, Multi-Disciplinary Approach to Providing Health Care for Children in Out-of-Home Care." *Child Welfare,* 1997, *87*(2), 331–347.

Bui, K.V., and Takeuchi, D. "Ethnic Minority Adolescents and the Use of Community Mental Health Care Services." *American Journal of Community Psychology*, 1992, *20*(4), 403–417.

Canino, I. A., and Spurlock, J. *Culturally Diverse Children and Adolescents: Assessment, Diagnosis, and Treatment.* New York: Guilford Press, 1994.

Close, M. "Child Welfare and People of Color: Denial of Equal Access." *Social Work Research and Abstracts*, 1983, *19*(4), 13–20.

Coalition for Juvenile Justice. *Handle with Care: Serving the Mental Health Needs of Young Offenders.* Washington, D.C.: Coalition for Juvenile Justice, 2000.

Collins, K. S., and others. *Diverse Communities, Common Concerns: Assessing Health Care Quality for Minority Americans. Findings from The Commonwealth Fund 2001 Health Care Quality Survey.* Boston: The Commonwealth Fund, 2002.

Costello, E. J., and others. "Psychiatric Disorders Among American Indian and White Youth in Appalachian Mountains Study." *American Journal of Public Health*, 1997, *87*, 827–832.

Courtney, M., and others. "Race and Child Welfare Services: Past Research and Future Directions." *Child Welfare*, 1996, *75*, 99–135.

Coutinho, M., and Oswald, D. "Disproportionate Representation in Special Education: A Synthesis and Recommendations." *Journal of Child and Family Studies*, 2000, *9*(2), 135–156.

Cross, T., Bazron, B., Dennis, K., and Isaacs, M. *Towards a Culturally Competent System of Care: Volume 1: A Monograph on Effective Services for Minority Children Who Are Severely Emotionally Disturbed.* Washington, D.C.: Georgetown University Child Development Center, National Technical Assistance Center for Children's Mental Health, 1989.

Cuffe, S. P., and others. "Race and Gender Differences in the Treatment of Psychiatric Disorders in Young Adolescents." *Journal of the American Academy of Child and Adolescent Psychiatry*, 1995, *34*, 1536–1543.

Davis, M. *City of Quartz: Excavating the Future in Los Angeles.* New York: Vintage, 1992.

Dembo, R. "Delinquency Among Black Male Youth." In J. T. Gibbs (ed.), *Young, Black, and Male in America: An Endangered Species* (pp. 129–165). Dover, Mass.: Auburn House, 1988.

Downs, S. "Black Foster Parents and Agencies: Results of an Eight-State Survey." *Children and Youth Services Review*, 1986, *8*, 201–218.

Duncan, G. J., Brooks-Gunn, J., and Klebanov, P. K. "Economic Deprivation and Early Childhood Development." *Child Development*, 1994, *65*, 296–318.

Eckenrode, J., and others. "Substantiation of Child Abuse and Neglect Reports." *Journal of Consulting and Clinical Psychology*, 1988, *56*(1), 9–16.

Entwisle, D. R., and Alexander, K. L. "Entry into School: The Beginning School Transition and Educational Stratification in the United States." *Annual Review of Sociology*, 1993, *19*, 401–423.

Evans, B., and Lee, B. K. "Culture and Child Psychopathology." In S. S. Kazarian and D. R. Evans (eds.), *Cultural Clinical Psychology: Theory, Research, and Practice*. New York: Oxford University Press, 1998.

Firestone, B. *Information Packet on Use of Mental Health Services by Children and Adolescents*. Rockville, Md.: Center for Mental Health Services Survey and Analysis Branch, 1990.

Flores, G., Bauchner, H., Feinstein, A., and Nguyen, U. "The Impact of Ethnicity, Family Income, and Parental Education on Children's Health and Use of Health Services." *American Journal of Public Health*, 1999, *89*(7), 1066–1071.

Fong, L., and Gibbs, J. T. "Facilitating Mental Health Services to Multicultural Communities in a Dominant Culture Setting: An Organizational Perspective." *Administration in Social Work*, 1995, *19*(2), 1–24.

Fraser, M., Pecora, P., and Haapala, D. *Families in Crisis: The Impact of Intensive Family Preservation Services*. New York: Aldine De Gruyter, 1991.

Garland, A., and others. "Racial and Ethnic Variations in Mental Health Care Utilization Among Children in Foster Care." *Children's Services: Social Policy, Research, and Practice*, 2000, *3*(3), 133–146.

Garland, A., and others. "Prevalence of Psychiatric Disorders in Youth Across Five Sectors of Care." *Journal of the American Academy of Child and Adolescent Psychiatry*, 2001, *40*(4), 409–418.

Gibbs, J. T. "Gangs as Transitional Alternative Structures: Adaptations to Racial and Social Marginality in Los Angeles and London." *Journal of Multicultural Social Work*, 2000, *8*(1–2), 71–99.

Gibbs, J. T. "The Criminalization of Minority Youth: Implications for Mental Health Issues in the Juvenile Justice System." Paper presented at the annual meetings of the American Psychological Association, San Francisco, August 25, 2001.

Goerge, R., Wulczyn, F., and Harden, A. *Foster Care Dynamics: California, Illinois, Michigan, New York and Texas—A First-Year Report from the Multi-State Foster Care Data Archive*. Chicago: Chapin Hall Center for Children, University of Chicago, 1994.

Halfon, N., English, A., Allen, J., and Dewoody, J. "National Health Care Reform, Medicaid, and Children in Foster Care." *Child Welfare*, 1994, *73*, 99–115.

Hall, L. "Providing Culturally Relevant Mental Health Services for Central American Immigrants." *Hospital and Community Psychiatry*, 1988, *39*, 1139–1144.

Heller, K., Holtzman, W., and Messick, S. (eds.). *Placing Children in Special Education: A Strategy for Equity*. Washington, D.C.: National Academy Press, 1982.

Hernandez, M., and Isaacs, M. (eds.). *Promoting Cultural Competence in Children's Mental Health Services*. Baltimore: Paul Brookes, 1998.

Hernandez, M., Isaacs, M., Nesman, R., and Burns, D. "Perspectives on Culturally Competent Systems of Care." In M. Hernandez and M. Isaacs (eds.), *Promoting Cultural Competence in Children's Mental Health Services*. Baltimore: Paul Brookes, 1998.

Hutchinson, J. "Mental Health Issues for Incarcerated Black Youth." In J. A. Farrow and R. Jenkins (eds.), *East Coast Scientific Symposium on the Health of the Black Adolescent Male* (pp. 19–20). Rockville, Md.: U.S. Department of Health and Human Services, 1990.

Joseph, R., and others. *Neighborhood Governance in the Annie E. Casey Foundation Mental Health Initiative for Urban Children: Summary of Findings and Lessons Learned*. Tampa, Fla.: University of South Florida, The Louis de la Parte Florida Mental Health Institute, Department of Child and Family Studies, 2001.

Kaiser Commission on Medicaid and the Uninsured. *Key Facts: Immigrants' Health Care Coverage and Access*. Washington, D.C.: Kaiser Family Foundation, 2000. Available online at www.kkf.org.

Kelleher, K. "Primary Care and Identification of Mental Health Needs." In U.S. Public Health Service, *Report of the Surgeon General's Conference on Children's Mental Health: A National Action Agenda*. Washington, D.C.: U.S. Public Health Service, 2000.

Knitzer, J. *Unclaimed Children: The Failure of Public Responsibility to Children and Adolescents in Need of Mental Health Services*. Washington, D.C.: Children's Defense Fund, 1982.

Koss-Chioino, J. D. "Traditional and Folk Approaches Among Ethnic Minorities." In J. F. Aponte and J. Wohl (eds.), *Psychological Intervention and Cultural Diversity*. Needham Heights, Mass.: Allyn and Bacon, 2000.

Kotler, J. "Mental Health and Juvenile Justice: Seeking Common Ground." Networks, summer newsletter. Alexandria, Va.: National Technical Assistance Center for State Mental Health Planning, 2001.

Krisberg, B., and others. "The Incarceration of Minority Youth." *Crime and Delinquency*, 1987, *33*, 173–205.

Lyons, J., and others. "Mental Health Service Needs of Juvenile Offenders: A Comparison of Detention, Incarceration, and Treatment Settings." *Children's Services: Social Policy, Research, and Practice*, 2001, *4*(2), 69–85.

Mak, W., and Rosenblatt, A. "Demographic Influences on Psychiatric

Diagnoses Among Youth Served in California Systems of Care." *Journal of Child and Family Studies*, 2002, *11*(2), 165–178.

Males, M., and Macallair, D. "The Color of Justice: An Analysis of Juvenile Adult Court Transfers in California." Washington, D.C.: Building Blocks for Youth, 2000.

Mason, M., and Gibbs, J. "Patterns of Adolescent Psychiatric Hospitalization: Implications for Public Policy." *American Journal of Orthopsychiatry*, 1992, *62*(3), 447–458.

McCarthy, J., and Woolverton, M. *Issue Areas for Summary Article on the Mental Health Needs of Children in the Child Welfare System.* Unpublished manuscript. Washington, D.C.: Georgetown University, 2001.

McGarrell, E. "Trends in Racial Disproportionality in Juvenile Court Processing: 1985–1989." *Crime and Delinquency*, 1993, *39*, 29–48.

Mech, E. "Out-of-Home Placement Rates." *Social Service Review*, 1983, *57*, 659–667.

Mont, D. "The Adoption of Special Needs Children in New York State." Unpublished manuscript. Ithaca, N.Y.: Cornell University, 1991.

Morton, T. "The Increasing Colorization of American's Child Welfare System: The Overrepresentation of African-American Children." *Policy and Practice*, 1999, December, pp. 23–30.

National Mental Health Association. *Child Welfare and Mental Health: Connections and Concerns for Mental Health Advocates.* (draft). Alexandria, Va.: National Mental Health Association, Prevention and Children's Mental Health Services Department, 2000.

National Research Council. Committee on Minority Representation in Special Education. *Minority Studies in Special and Gifted Education.* (M. S. Donovan and C. T. Cross, eds.). Washington, D.C.: National Academy Press, 2002.

National Technical Assistance Center for State Mental Health Planning. "Cultural Competence in Children's Mental Health." Networks, spring newsletter. Alexandria, Va.: National Technical Assistance Center for State Mental Health Planning, 1997.

Neighbors, H. "The Use of Informal and Formal Help: Four Patterns of Illness Behavior in the Black Community." *American Journal of Community Psychology*, 1984, *12*, 551–566.

Novins, D., Fleming, C., Beals, J., and Manson, S. "Quality of Alcohol, Drug, and Mental Health Services for American Indian Children and Adolescents." *American Journal of Medical Quality*, 2000, *15*, 148–156.

Olfson, M., and others. "Mental Disorders and Disability Among Patients in a Primary Care Group Practice." *American Journal of Psychiatry*, 1997, *154*(12), 1734–1740.

Olsen, L. "Services for Minority Children in Out-of-Home Care." *Social Service Review,* 1982, *56,* 572–585.

O'Sullivan, M. J., Peterson, P. D., Cox, G. B., and Kirkeby, J. "Ethnic Populations: Community Mental Health Services Ten Years Later." *American Journal of Community Psychology,* 1989, *17,* 17–30.

Paniagua, F. A. *Diagnosis in a Multicultural Context.* Thousand Oaks, Calif.: Sage, 2001.

Parent Educational Advocacy Training Center. *Mental Health and Hope: Foster Care Issue Brief.* Springfield, VA: PEATC, 2000.

Petit, M., and Curtis, A. *Child Abuse and Neglect: A Look at the States.* Washington, D.C.: CWLA Press, 1997.

Plantz, M., Hubbell, R., Barrett, V., and Dobrec, A. "Indian Child Welfare: A Status Report." *Children Today,* 1989, *18*(1), 24–29.

Poe-Yamagata, E., and Jones, M. *And Justice for Some: Differential Treatment of Minority Youth in the Justice System.* Washington, D.C.: Youth Law Center, 2000.

Pope, C., and Feyerherm, W. *Minorities in the Juvenile Justice System.* Washington, D.C.: Office of Juvenile Justice and Delinquency Prevention, 1993.

Pottick, K. "Children's Use of Mental Health Services Doubles: New Research-Policy Partnership Reports." Update: Latest Findings in Children's Mental Health, Vol. 1, No. 1. Rutgers, University, The U.S. Department of Health and Human Services, and The Annie E. Casey Foundation, 2002.

Pumariega, A., Glover, S., Holzer, C. III, and Nguyen, H. "Utilization of Mental Health Services in a Tri-Ethnic Sample of Adolescents." *Community Mental Health Journal,* 1998, *34,* 145–156.

Roberts, R., and Chen, Y. "Depressive Symptoms and Suicidal Ideation Among Mexican-Origin and Anglo Adolescents." *Journal of the American Academy of Child and Adolescent Psychiatry,* 1995, *34,* 81–90.

Roberts, R., and Sobhan, M. "Symptoms of Depression in Adolescence: A Comparison of Anglo, African, and Hispanic Americans." *Journal of Youth and Adolescence,* 1992, *21,* 639–651.

Schneiderman, M., and others. "Mental Health Services for Children in Out-of-Home Care." *Child Welfare,* 1998, *77*(1), 29–40.

Schoen, D., and others. *The Commonwealth Fund Survey of the Health of Adolescent Girls.* Boston: The Commonwealth Fund, November 1997.

Shaffer, D., and others. "The NIMH Diagnostic Interview Schedule for Children, Version 2.3 (DISC-2.3): Description, Acceptability, Prevalence Rates, and Performance in the MECA Study. Methods for the Epidemiology of Child and Adolescent Mental Disorders Study."

Journal of the American Academy of Child and Adolescent Psychiatry, 1996, *35,* 865–877.

Skidba, R. J., Knesting, K., and Bush, L. "Culturally Competent Assessment: More Than Nonbiased Tests." *Journal of Child and Family Studies,* 2002, *2*(1), 61–78.

Snyder, H., and Sickmund, M. *Juvenile Offenders and Victims: 1999 National Report.* Washington, D.C.: Office of Juvenile Justice and Delinquency Prevention, 1999.

Stroul, B., and Friedman, R. *A System of Care for Children and Youth with Severe Emotional Disturbance.* Washington, D.C.: Georgetown University Child Development Center, National Technical Assistance Center for Children's Mental Health, 1986.

U.S. Bureau of the Census. *Overview of Race and Hispanic Origin and Population Estimates Program, Population Division.* Washington, D.C.: U.S. Department of Commerce 1998.

U.S. Bureau of the Census. *Overview of Race and Hispanic Origin and Population Estimates Program, Population Division.* Washington, D.C.: U.S. Department of Commerce, 2000.

U.S. Bureau of the Census. *Current Population Survey. Annual Demographic Supplement.* Washington, D.C.: U.S. Department of Commerce, 2002.

U.S. Department of Health and Human Services. *Mental Health: Culture, Race and Ethnicity.* Supplement to *Mental Health: A Report of the Surgeon General.* Rockville, Md.: U.S. Department of Health and Human Services, 2001.

Vazsonyi, A., and Flannery, D. "Early Adolescent Delinquent Behaviors: Associations with Family and School Domains." *Journal of Early Adolescence,* 1997, *17,* 271–293.

Villarruel, F., and Walker, N. *Donde Esta la Justicia: A Call to Action on Behalf of Latino and Latina Youth in the U.S. Justice System.* Washington, D.C.: Building Blocks for Youth, 2002.

Wells, K., and Biegel, D. E. (eds.). *Family Preservation Services: Research and Evaluation.* Newbury Park, Calif.: Sage, 1991.

Woodwell, D. *National Ambulatory Medical Care Survey: 1998 Summary.* Advance data from vital and health statistics, No. 315. Hyattsville, Md.: National Center for Health Statistics, 2000.

Yeh, M., Takeuchi, D., and Sue, S. "Asian-American Children Treated in the Mental Health System: A Comparison of Parallel and Mainstream Outpatient Service Centers." *Journal of Clinical Child Psychology,* 1994, *23,* 5–12.

Chapter Eleven

New Directions for Children's Mental Health Services, Policy, Research, and Training

Larke Nahme Huang
Jewelle Taylor Gibbs

Just over ten years ago, we published the first edition of this book, *Children of Color: Psychological Interventions with Minority Youth* (Gibbs and Huang, 1989). In part, that book was a product of our frustration with the lack of resources, materials, research, and focused attention on the mental health issues of society's most vulnerable citizens. We wanted to provide "sketches" of the mental health issues of youth of color as an initial attempt to increase our understanding of the challenges they encounter and the competencies they display. As we stated in our closing paragraph in the 1989 edition, we provided merely sketches, which were far from a finished picture. Now, thirteen years later, where are we? Is the picture more complete? Are the sketches finished portraits?

We begin this discussion with two excerpts from a California newspaper, the *Fresno Bee,* the first from August 11, 2002:

> *Lost in America: Hmong Parents Grieve for a Lost Generation.*
>
> Since late 1998, eight Hmong teens have killed themselves, devastating Fresno's Hmong community. The string of suicides accounted for nearly half of Fresno County's teen suicides in the

last four years, though the Hmong (refugees from Laos) are just 3 percent of the region's population. Four Hmong students killed themselves in the first six months of last year. The teens are among the first generation to be raised in America. Their parents had hoped they could restore honor and pride to a displaced people, but the teens struggle to balance their American lifestyle with Hmong traditions. Hmong parents, raised in a primitive, agrarian society, expect their children to follow and respect their culture. They also want them to succeed in American society. Sometimes these expectations conflict, sometimes with tragic results . . . many of these teen-agers feel lost. They do not really belong to the Hmong community or to the mainstream community either. Many have no one to talk to, feel the older generation doesn't understand. . . . While Hmong-Americans have become high school valedictorians, graduated with college degrees and ventured into many professions with success, gang activity and now teen suicides have plagued this new generation in Fresno. . . . Hmong leaders concede their community has not come to grips with the problems of its children, and the topic of suicide is rarely discussed in Hmong families . . . the Hmong community generally refuses to discuss the issues, but adds that something must be done: "We cannot let another kid die like this, another parent go through this." In the string of suicides that began in late 1998, the teens used various methods: gunshot, hanging, drowning, and tshuaj ntxuav nyiaj, a cyanide-based cleaner used on the silver coins that decorate traditional Hmong costumes. Three of the teens killed themselves by drinking tshuaj ntxuav nyiaj. The teens, while struggling with the traditions of their Hmong heritage, reached back to it as they sought death. [Ellis, 2002a]

And this also appeared August 11, 2002:

Breaking the Silence

There is no Hmong word for "I feel." There is no Hmong word for "depression." There is no Hmong word for "suicide". . . . The complex word problems between the Hmong parents and their children are well documented. Too often, they don't talk to each other. In many ways, it is an intense version of the typical immigrant generational breakdowns we laugh about. The Hmong generational problem is much more serious. It's life and death—and hope. There is hope in the voices heard in today's special report. The fact that so many Hmong parents, friends and family members were willing to bare their private pain to the community's daily news-paper is a big step toward ending the isolation that feeds despera-tion. One father who lost his son to suicide heard there were others. He appealed to the Fresno Unified School District for help in preventing this heartbreak for other parents, but no one knew what to do or how to do it. When the district did make a plan, the bureaucratic inertia was excruciating. Four more children killed themselves while the district assembled its program, applying for money in the slow-moving grant process. One would think this should have set off an emergency task force from the Fresno County mental health department, just as a cancer cluster would have sent researchers running to the area in their lab coats. Yet the Hmong cries were just one of dozens of minority voices competing for money and time. . . . Fresno Unified initially put together an ambitious plan, asking for five Hmong mental health clinicians to spread among middle and high schools. That idea was scrapped because of a lack of applicants. Still, the district has put together a working program. . . . The parents are responding nicely, grateful for the help. The crisis is not over. Though there has not been a Hmong suicide in 15 months, at least three Hmong teens have attempted to kill themselves in the past year. . . . And the grant money runs out in April. Clearly, we should move closer to the district's original plan, with Hmong clinicians taking the lead. We may have to grow our own clinicians, encouraging young Hmong women and men to pursue mental health careers.

This story of tragedy and hope captures the trajectory of men-tal health for children of color in the past ten years. The mental health tragedies continue: poor outreach, lack of access, under-utilization of services, culturally inappropriate services, struggles to reduce the power of stigma, lack of human and fiscal resources, lack of language capacity among providers—all contributing to dev-astating outcomes for these children. Yet, as also conveyed in this story, there have been important areas of progress:

• Minority families and youth are realizing they are critical part-ners in developing appropriate treatment and intervention plans and, in turn, this contributes to breaking the silence engendered by stigma.
• There is increasing recognition that the traditional systems of mental health delivery may be too limiting for children of

color and that other, more accessible systems such as schools, churches, and community organizations may be more effective points of service delivery.

- Workforce shortages are being highlighted.
- New forms of financing services are being sought.

Thus, although the task of providing appropriate mental health services for children of color remains daunting, there are isolated pockets of hope.

New Hope for a National Agenda

Two landmark events provide new impetus for a compelling national agenda to address the mental health needs of children of color. In September of 2000, the Surgeon General's Conference on Children's Mental Health, "Developing a National Action Agenda," was convened in Washington, D.C. This conference brought together a broad cross-section of mental health stakeholders, including youth and family members, professional organizations and associations, advocacy groups, faith-based practitioners, clinicians, educators, health care providers, academic researchers, and the health care industry. This group acknowledged that the burden of suffering experienced by children with mental health needs and their families has created a health crisis in this country. Increasing numbers of children are suffering or at risk of suffering needlessly because their emotional, behavioral, and developmental needs are not being met by the institutions explicitly created to care for them. Eight specific goals for an action plan were put forth at this conference: (1) promote public awareness of children's mental health issues and reduce stigma associated with mental illness; (2) continue to develop, disseminate, and implement scientifically proven prevention and treatment services in the field of children's mental health; (3) improve the assessment of and recognition of mental health needs in children; (4) eliminate racial-ethnic and socioeconomic disparities in access to mental health care services; (5) improve the infrastructure for children's mental health services, including support for scientifically proven interventions across professions; (6) increase access to and coordination of quality mental health care services; (7) train frontline providers to recognize and manage mental health care issues and educate mental health providers about scientifically proven prevention and treatment services; and (8) monitor the access to and coordination of quality mental health care services.

Each of these goals has significant implications for children of color. Stigma is a major barrier to the treatment of mental health disorders. Coupled with a culturally different understanding of mental disorders and mistrust or unfamiliarity with the mental health systems, stigma is an even more serious problem for minority youth. Stigma prevents them from seeking help or even acknowledging a problem. For example, since 1980 suicide rates have doubled in young black males; American Indians, with high incidences of alcoholism and despondency, die by suicide at an alarming rate (Satcher, 2000). The sense of shame or fear associated with mental disorders impedes these youth and their families from seeking appropriate services, particularly among Asians and Latinos, as noted by Huang, Ying, and Arganza in Chapter Four and by Organista in Chapter Eight. Stigma also affects policy, and it is on this level that stigma-induced discrimination and prejudice may be most devastating, reaching past individuals, families, and communities to policymakers and federal and state leaders who make decisions about equity of treatment and parity of access (Satcher, 2000).

A second landmark event was the Surgeon General's report, *Mental Health: Culture, Race and Ethnicity* (U.S. Department of Health and Human Services, 2001). This was a remarkable supplement to the first-ever Surgeon General's report, *Mental Health: A Report of the Surgeon General* (U.S. Department of Health and Human Services, 1999), underscoring the significant disparities in mental health care and outcomes for the four most recognized racial and ethnic minority groups in the United States. This report detailed striking disparities in mental health services for racial and ethnic minorities, compared to whites. Minority populations had less access to and availability of mental health services, were less likely to receive needed mental health care, often received poorer quality of mental health care when in treatment, and were underrepresented in mental health research (U.S. Department of Health and Human Services, 2001). Many of the barriers that deter communities of color from accessing and engaging in treatment operate for all populations: fragmentation of services, lack of availability of services, cost of services, and societal stigma toward mental illness (U.S. Department of Health and Human Services, 1999). However, additional barriers deter people of color from seeking services, including mistrust and fear of treatment, different cultural conceptualizations of illness and health and help-seeking, differences in language and communication, and racism and discrimination. As a result, racial and ethnic minorities experience a greater disability burden from emotional and behavioral disorders than do whites. This higher burden arises from receiving less care and poorer quality of care rather than from disorders being inherently more severe or prevalent, as documented in the Surgeon General's report noted earlier.

A key message in this report was the pivotal role of culture in mental health, mental illness, and mental health services. Culture is important because it determines what people bring to the clinical settings, how they express and report their symptoms, how they seek help, what they develop in terms of coping styles and social supports, and the degree to which they attach stigma to mental health problems (see, for example, Guerra and Jagers, 1998; Kazarian and Evans, 1998). This concept, however, is not limited to the child and his or her family. It also applies to the providers in that each group of providers and each system of service delivery embodies a "culture," with shared beliefs, norms, values, and patterns of communication. There is a culture of the provider, which is shaped to some degree by the cultures of the service systems in which they work. The health care provider, the educator, the social service worker, and the juvenile court judge all work in a system and a professional discipline that has its own organizational or discipline culture. Each of these providers may view symptoms, diagnosis, and intervention in ways that diverge from each other and from the view of the child and family consumers.

The previous chapters in this book highlight the influence of culture and point out the various ways that each group may understand psychological disorder, manifest help-seeking, and encounter different barriers and opportunities when seeking services. There are many similarities among the various racial and ethnic groups, such as the value of interdependence over independence, the primacy of the group over the individual, the emphasis on extended family networks rather than nuclear family units, and the clashes of roles and values with those of mainstream society. There are also significant differences. The bottom line, however, is that for each of these groups, culture matters. Culture is at the heart of their behaviors, and although much of any given culture is stable and consistent, shifts and clashes occur throughout the vicissitudes of human development, and culture is modified over time in its transmission between generations.

To highlight visually the significance of culture, we are proposing an ecological model for assessment and intervention that draws heavily from Bronfenbrenner's model (1979) of the person in the environment. This individual is embedded in a complex array of systems dynamically interacting with the individual and with one another. The individual and the environmental systems are mutually shaping systems, each changing over time and each adapting in response to changes in the other (Garbarino, 1982). The interaction is reciprocal and ongoing throughout development. Figures 11.1 and 11.2 depict the two levels of interaction.

Figure 11.1 displays an ecological network for a developing child or adolescent; the significant microsystems are the family, the school, the faith-based community, and the community and social peer group. For the child with emotional and behavioral disorders, we've added two other microsystems: mental health providers and indigenous or natural helper systems. As the bidirectional arrows symbolize, the direction of influence is two-way, although the distribution of power and the strength of the influence are not distributed equally. The culture of systems and organizations generally exerts more influence over the individual and family than vice versa. The geometric shapes around each microsystem and the individual symbolize the different cultures of the various systems. The culture of each system represents a blend of the subculture of race, ethnicity, social class, or institutionalism. These shapes are distinct for each microsystem in order to highlight the differences and the potential for conflict among the various systems. For example, returning to Figure 11.1, the individual ethnic minority child comes from the "culture of the triangle," attends a school in the "culture of the rectangle," and participates in a peer group and neighborhood characterized by the "culture of the pentagon." In this sense, the child negotiates three distinct cultural systems. Eventually, in order to develop a coherent sense of self, the child must meaningfully integrate these diverse cultural systems. The experience of this child would differ significantly from an Anglo Ameri-

Figure 11.1. An Ecological Model for Assessment and Intervention: First-Order Interactions.

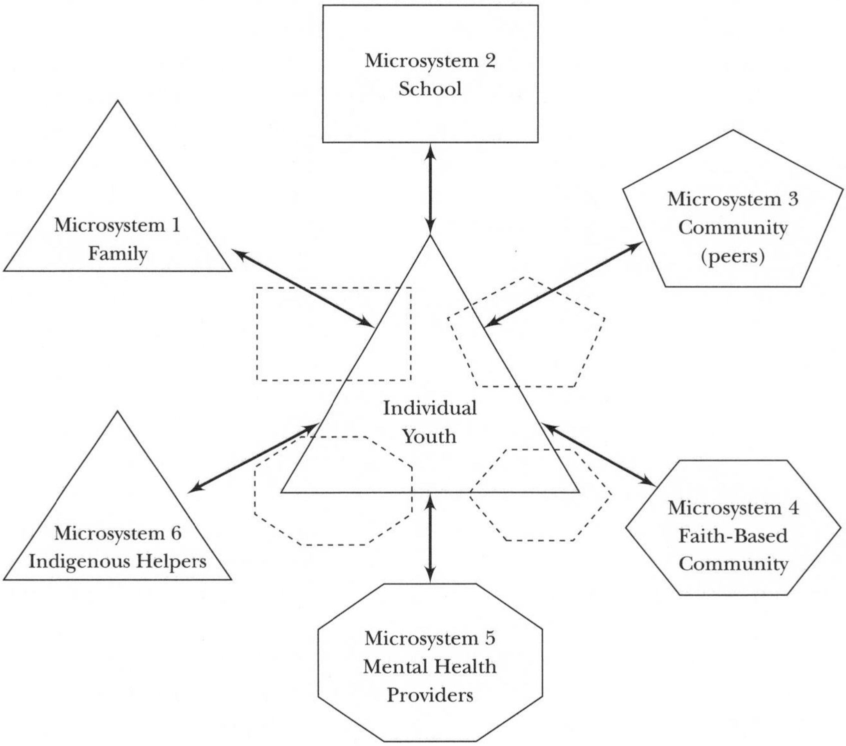

can child whose family, school, community, and peer networks all emanated from the same cultural basis.

This ecological map also targets the points for intervention. Although the child or adolescent is most frequently the focus of the intervention, in some instances this may be inappropriate. Rather, the school, the family or the peer network, or some combination of these systems and the individual, may more appropriately be the focus of an intervention. For some children, an approach may involve all of these systems wrapping services around the child. Inherent in this wraparound approach is the need to attend to culture in order for all the involved systems, providers, friends, and family to work together toward a shared treatment goal.

Figure 11.2. An Ecological Model for Assessment and Intervention: Second-Order Interactions (Solid Lines).

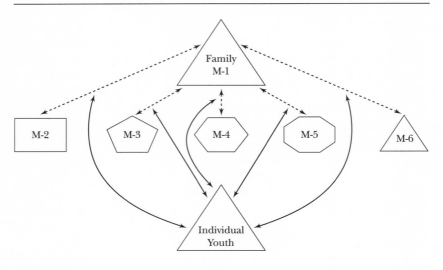

The second-order interactions, or what Bronfenbrenner (1979) calls the mesosystem (interactions between the various microsystems that have an impact on the individual child) are shown in Figure 11.2. For example, the interaction between the school and the family system, whether mutually supportive, absent, or hostile, will have an impact on the child. Reciprocally, the child will also have an effect on this relationship. Similarly, the relationship between the family and the peer group or between the family and the mental health provider will affect the child or adolescent. As in the previous first-order interactions, the consonance or dissonance of cultures may affect the nature of these interactions. The cultures of each system are represented again by the various geometric shapes denoting distinctive cultural perspectives.

As mentioned throughout this book, mental health providers working with children and adolescents need to be familiar with the total ecology and the cultural experiences of the child. Without knowledge of the settings that foster or impede healthy social and emotional development, our understanding of ethnic minority youth will remain limited and incomplete, and our system of service delivery will continue to be fragmented and poorly coordinated (Garbarino, 1982; McLoyd, 1998; Stiffman and others, 1999). For example, there are specialists who work with children in medical settings, in school settings, in recreational settings, in family settings, in juvenile justice settings, and in advocacy. Rarely is a specialist trained or given the opportunity to work with the whole child or gain access to the child's total environment. Services are delivered on the basis of pieces of the child's life; providers and case workers become "setting specialists," as opposed to child specialists (Namir and Weinstein, 1982). This serves to promote "professional preciousness" (Sarason, 1974)—the conceptualizing of problems in ways that professionals have been trained to treat them. It impedes the coordination of multiple and disparate services and leads to further polarization and fragmentation.

The model for assessment and intervention that we have proposed is based on the ecological map of the child and supports the concept of a system of care for children who have, or are at risk of having, psychological disorders. For the child of color, providers must be familiar with more than one setting, engaged in interdisciplinary collaboration and information sharing, sensitive to the cultures of each setting, competent in learning about the culture of the particular child, and aware of the child's functioning in these various cross-cultural situations. In addition, it is critical to be aware of how the culture of the provider, the clinician, or the larger health care system governs the societal response to a child with a psychological disorder. The culture of the provider, as well as of the child, influences delivery of care, including diagnosis, treatment, and the organization and reimbursement of services. Service systems and clinicians are naturally immersed in their own culture and are often ill equipped to meet the needs of children and youth from different backgrounds and, in some cases, have displayed bias in the delivery of care. This may be why so many youth of color with emotional and behavior disorders end up in juvenile justice or child welfare instead of mental health care.

New and Not-So-New Priorities

In Chapter Ten, Huang and Arganza document the need for a more comprehensive, coordinated, and culturally appropriate system of care to meet the mental health needs of low-income families and youth of color. As the Surgeon General's report points out, improving the availability, accessibility, and affordability of mental health services for this underserved population is one of several major health care priorities that are critical to improving the health and mental well-being of our increasingly ethnically and culturally diverse society. Most important, youth of color will constitute 56 percent of that society by the year 2050, according to demographic projections (National Center for Health Statistics, 2000). These priorities are briefly summarized in the areas of mental health policy, mental health research, training and workforce development, ethnic-specific services, and civil rights.

Mental Health Policy

In the area of mental health policy, the Surgeon General's report delineates a number of policy issues that need to be addressed in order to ensure access and equity in mental health care for youth of color and their families. First and foremost, health insurance for uninsured children and youth must be expanded through federal and state funding sources so that all families will be able to obtain needed health and mental health care for their children. As noted in the previous chapter, uninsured rates for the four racial and ethnic minority populations in the United States are extraordinarily high, ranging from 21 to 37 percent of the particular population group. This severely limits access to services for children of color. There are several model state, county, and local programs, such as those in the state of Minnesota and in three counties in Northern California, that provide health coverage for all children in the community through local tax initiatives.

Two federal programs, Medicaid and the State Children's Health Insurance Program (SCHIP), serve low-income children and their families and children with disabilities who have exhausted other sources of insurance coverage. In 1998, the 21 million children served by Medicaid constituted over 51 percent of its recipients, making it a significant provider of mental health services (Levant, Tolan and Dodgen, 2002). Eligible recipients are children under age nineteen living in families at or below the poverty level, children under six years of age whose families are at or below 133 percent of the federal poverty level, children in foster care, and other criteria selected by individual states (Health Care Financing Administration, 2001). SCHIP, created in 1997, is a significant expansion of the federal role in providing health care coverage. SCHIP extends Medicaid-equivalent benefits to children in families who are at or below 200 percent of the federal poverty level. It allows flexibility to states in how they set up their programs as long as they provide mental health coverage equal to at least 75 percent of the value of benchmark plans in each state.

Medicaid and SCHIP represent important steps in providing mental health benefits to children; however, states often provide fewer benefits than expected, and the impact on accessibility to mental health services for children has been limited (Levant, Tolan, and Dodgen, 2002). In fact, with states increasingly moving toward Medicaid managed care, services for children are lagging further behind adult services, with limited provisions for children, curtailing of existing services, and cost shifting to other systems (Brown, 2000). These trends significantly affect children of color who tend to be overrepresented in the low-income population. SCHIP has fared little better, as states have used their flexibility to limit mental health services and have had difficulty in outreach to and enrollment of culturally diverse families, particularly where language is a barrier. In addition, low reimbursement rates discourage providers from accepting Medicaid clients. Expansion of Medicaid eligibility for near-poor families may not be sufficient to increase access to mental health services unless it is tied to increased provider availability and provider incentives to treat low-income minority children.

Although Medicaid is an invaluable funding source for public mental health services, it is founded on a medical model of treatment that is not designed for mental health treatment built on community-based services and supports. For children, this is especially critical, as they often require an array of services that may be school-, family-, or community-based, not necessarily hospital- or inpatient-based. Consequently, what Medicaid covers may not match with the needs of the child. Yet in terms of flexibility of coverage, Medicaid is often more flexible than private insurance and covers such services as transportation or child care to assist with access to mental health treatment. Thus revisiting the structure of Medicaid reimbursement may be critical to enhancing care for low-income children of color.

The major federal program specifically designed to support community-based public mental health services—the Community Mental Health Services Performance Partnership Block Grant—is currently funded at $433 million, approximately 1.6 percent of state mental health agency expenditures (Glover, 2002). Although this is a relatively small portion of mental health dollars, these state plans need to address more explicitly how they will increase access, availability, and appropriateness of care for their ethnic-racial minority populations and, in particular, their youth of color with mental health needs.

Current state prioritization for mental health funding represents a significant barrier to mental health care. In 2001, only seven states ranked mental health as a top priority (Lutterman, Hirad, and Poindexter, 1999). State appropriations for mental health have increased at a much lower rate than total state spending and spending for corrections. From 1990 to 1997, the percentage growth in state spending on mental health was 33 percent, whereas total state spending grew 56 percent, and spending on corrections grew 68 percent. For example, in 1996 California's corrections budget exceeded the funds allocated to public education and mental health services in a state where youth of color make up nearly two-thirds of public school students (Gibbs and Bankhead, 2001). These funding policies portend poorly for children of color with mental health needs. With an erosion of state general revenue funds for mental health, a growing reliance by states on Medicaid and other federal programs, and an expanding budgetary allocation to corrections, the task of meeting the Surgeon General's challenge to provide better access and care to ethnic and racial minorities seems elusive. Without efforts to change these funding priorities, it seems inevitable that disparities will persist and youth of color will lack necessary services and end up in juvenile justice and corrections.

As the momentum for parity of coverage for mental health treatment in commercial health insurance plans grows, it is not clear how this will affect children of color, given that they are among the most highly represented in the uninsured populations. For example, for Latino youth in immigrant families, only 47 percent of noncitizens were insured. In addition, commercial plans often have the least flexibility in their benefit design. Health plans are based on medical necessity and may be constrained in obtaining nonmedical services that are an essential component of mental health care for minority children in schools, juvenile justice settings, or child welfare agencies. This issue needs to be examined further to ensure the development of policies that will address the needs of ethnic minority children.

The past decade has been marked by an increasing focus on accountability and results in the field of mental health. Outcome data, performance requirements and indicators, standards of care, and benchmarks have become an integral part of the operation of mental health and other human service agencies and organizations (U.S. Department of Health and Human Services, 1999). In keeping with this effort, there should be a systematic evaluation of the quality of services received by youth of color and their families. Minority and low-income populations are vulnerable to discriminatory practices and poorer-quality treatment in health and human services. Policies and procedures must be developed to document systematically and consistently the service access, plans, and outcomes for children of color. Although grievance and appeals procedures are an integral part of managed care technologies, minority families tend not to use these mechanisms for fear of reprisals, termination of services, or lack of familiarity with or information regarding how to file a grievance.

Perhaps the most critical finding from the Surgeon General's National Action Agenda for children is the need for a primary mental health care system for children. As highlighted in Chapter Ten, the responsibility for children's mental health care is disjointed and fragmented, as services are dispersed across multiple systems, including education, primary health care, juvenile justice, child welfare, and specialty mental health care. These child-serving systems each lack the financial infrastructure to support the full range of services needed by children and their families. They lack a full range of prevention, early identification, early intervention and treatment, and follow-up supportive care. Each system lacks the ability to exchange information and coordinate treatment planning across system boundaries. Furthermore, each system has its own eligibility criteria for treatment and reimbursement. These issues, pertinent to all children with mental health concerns, are heightened for children of color when language, culture, unfamiliarity and mistrust, lack of financing, and systemic racism and discrimination provide even greater barriers to quality care.

A primary mental health system would focus on early identification and intervention. The frontline providers for children are the schools and primary health care providers such as physicians and nurse practitioners (Cunningham and Freiman, 1996; Kaplan, Cologne, Guernsey, and Hanrahan, 1998). It is in these systems that mental health disorders are most frequently identified. In schools, mental health services are often channeled through special education under the Individuals with Disabilities Education Act (IDEA). Rethinking of mental health models for schools should move beyond special education as the source of intervention and use mental health resources in a different manner than traditional clinical models. A more comprehensive public health model would combine schoolwide (universal), targeted (for students at risk), and intensive interventions for those with serious emotional and behavioral disturbance. Similar to the public health model that includes early and periodic screenings and immunizations, a system of mental health screenings may prevent later, more serious full-blown emotional and behavioral disorders for children. Such a system would converge well with patterns of help-seeking among racial and ethnic minorities. As pointed out in each of the previous chapters, children of color are not readily brought to specialty mental health care service by their families or communities (Hoberman, 1992; McMiller and Weisz, 1996). Rather, they are more likely to seek treatment in schools or primary health care settings. Currently, these systems are not well integrated with mental health services. One study reported an average delay of three to four months between referral to a mental health professional by pediatricians and the first available appointment for mental health services; two-thirds of referring primary care physicians noted substantial delays when attempting to obtain mental health services for their patients (Behar and others, 1996). For ethnic minority clients, there is even less follow-through on referrals from primary care to mental health providers. Thus policies that integrate culturally appropriate mental health care services into schools and primary health care settings and build partnerships between primary care providers and mental health specialists may be a first step toward building a primary mental health care system for children.

Mental Health Research

As noted in the introductory chapter, there are numerous issues in the area of ethnic minority health that need to be researched. The Surgeon General's report supports the need for expanding the research base, as noted here:

> Because good science is an essential underpinning of the public health approach to mental health and mental illness, systematic work in the areas of epidemiology, evidence-based treatment, psychopharmacology, ethnic- and culture-specific interventions, diagnosis and assessment, and prevention and promotion needs to be developed and expanded. [p. 59]

We still lack a national epidemiological study of child psychological disorders, although several large-scale studies approach consensus indicating about 17 to 25 percent of children experience a diagnosable mental health disorder (Costello and others, 1996). For children of color, however, we have few epidemiological data. More minority youth need to be systematically included in study populations for mental health research. In 1994, the National Institutes of Mental Health (NIMH) adopted guidelines regarding the inclusion of minority populations in federally funded research projects; however, researchers have been slow to respond to this policy. In addition, minority populations have remained guarded about participating in government- and academic-sponsored research, given a history of exploitative research (see, for example, James Jones's 1982 book about the Tuskegee syphilis study from 1932 to 1972). Thus the generalizability of these studies is limited to a shrinking white population base. The rapidly increasing diversity of the U.S. population, with Latinos soon to replace African Americans as the largest minority group and Asians currently the fastest-growing nonwhite group, will render current epidemiological data obsolete. To address these changing demographics, several large-scale studies funded by NIMH have been recently undertaken, including the National Survey of American Lives, the National Latino and Asian American Study, and the American Indian Services Utilization, Psychiatric Epidemiology, Risk and Protective Factors Project. It is expected that these studies will yield rich data about rates of psychiatric disorder, patterns of symptomatology, access to services, and psychosocial functioning of these diverse population groups (U.S. Department of Health and Human Services, 2001).

The increasing diversity within these population groups also needs to be addressed, as was reflected in the year 2000 census, which more carefully delineated ethnic, racial, and multiracial categories in order to obtain more accurate population counts. For example, within the Asian American populations, the newly emerging groups such as Southeast Asians, who have encountered more recent trauma and relocations, as described by Ida and Yang in Chapter Six, will present a markedly different mental health picture than the fourth-generation Japanese or Chinese Americans. As Organista points out in Chapter Eight, studies of Mexican Americans on both sides of the Texas-Mexico border reveal the impact of immigration status, with higher rates of depressive symptoms, drug use, and suicide for those youth living in the United States (Swanson and others, 1972; Vega and others, 1998). In Chapter Three, Gibbs discusses the unique developmental challenges faced by biracial and bicultural youth in the formation of positive self and ethnic identities.

There is increasing emphasis on developing, implementing, and disseminating evidence-based practices in mental health care (Drake and others, 2001; Bernal, Bonilla, and Bellido, 1995). Numerous research endeavors are documenting the efficacy of various treatment modalities for different child and adult psychiatric disorders. Consistent with the trend toward increased accountability, payers and purchasers of mental health services want to know what they are paying for and whether it works. The Surgeon General's report documents effective treatments for selected psychiatric disorders. Two recent publications (Burns and Hoagwood, 2002; American Psychological Association, 2001) described effective clinical and community-based treatments for child emotional and behavioral disorders. However, for children of color, these efforts fall short in several ways. First, youth of color are rarely included in efficacy and effectiveness studies. For psychosocial interventions that may be sensitive to social and cultural circumstances, it is not clear whether these evidence-based practices are effective for culturally diverse minority populations (Bernal and Scharrón-Del-Rio, 2001). Some preliminary studies have indicated that cognitive-behavioral therapy is equally effective in reducing anxiety among African American and white children (Friedman, Paradis, and Hatch, 1994; Treadwell, Flannery-Schroeder, and Kendall, 1995). Studies of multisystemic therapy that engages a network of supportive individuals in a helping effort have found this intervention to be equally effective with African American and white juvenile offenders (Borduin and others, 1995). These studies are the exceptions. More research needs to be conducted in well-designed, systematic, replicable studies with multiethnic samples of youth.

As the list of evidence-based practices continues to grow, there is increasing concern about the gap between what is known and what is actually practiced. Many of the interventions studied have not been transported to real-life, real-world settings. Studies conducted in academic settings with single diagnoses and controlled variables have not translated readily to clinic settings where co-occurring diagnoses are more prevalent and complex social and environmental factors are not experimentally controlled. This dissemination gap is even more glaring for minority populations who are neither the participants in nor the recipients of the findings of the research studies. For example, recent data suggest that Latinos are less likely to receive treatment according to evidence-based guidelines, and African Americans are less likely than white Americans to receive appropriate care for depression or anxiety (see U.S. Department of Health and Human Services, 2001). African Americans are less likely to receive an antidepressant when their depression is diagnosed, and those who do receive antidepressant medication are less likely to receive the newer, selective serotonin reuptake inhibitor (SSRI) medications, which have fewer troubling side effects than the older antidepressants (Melfi, Croyhan, Hanna, and Robinson, 2000).

Community-based and ethnic-specific agencies have been providing services to minority populations since the late 1960s (Akutsu,

Snowden, and Organista, 1996; Snowden, Hu, and Jerrell, 1995). These programs emerged in response to the need for more culturally appropriate interventions and services that would be more responsive and welcoming to an ethnic minority clientele. Research needs to be conducted on the programs that have been meeting the needs of minority populations for several decades (Sue and others, 1991; Takeuchi, Sue, and Yeh, 1995). The "evidence" needs to be built on these programs. In addition, proven evidence-based practices need to be disseminated to the programs that have an established infrastructure for delivery of mental health care that is accessible, acceptable, and affordable to communities of color.

In the area of psychopharmacology, research is urgently needed on the differential effects of psychotropic drugs on children of different ethnic groups. Recent findings suggest that there may be different rates of metabolism and different physical responses to drugs for different ethnic groups. For example, there is emerging evidence that some ethnic minority groups metabolize some antidepressants and antipsychotic medications more slowly and might be more sensitive than whites (Bradford, Gaedigk, and Leeder, 1998). This sensitivity may be manifested in a high rate of response and more severe side effects. This finding has particular relevance to youth of color who present in substance abuse treatment programs and psychiatric emergency rooms where excessive dosages of psychoactive drugs may induce toxic effects that may be misdiagnosed or mistreated (Lin, Cheung, Smith, and Poland, 1997; Segal, Bola, and Watson, 1996; Walkup and others, 2000).

The area of diagnosis and assessment is a particularly crucial area of research due to a long history of controversy about racial bias in clinical assessment and treatment disposition for minority patients (Paniagua, 2001). For many years, minority patients have been assigned more severe diagnoses yet have consistently received less therapeutic treatment. Studies of youth in clinical settings found that African American and Latino youth were more likely than white youth to receive diagnoses of conduct disorder and personality disorder; they were more likely to be overrepresented in public mental health services but less likely to be referred for psychotherapy or private inpatient psychiatric treatment (Bui and Takeuchi, 1992; Mason and Gibbs, 1992). It is important to understand the influence of ethnocultural factors on behaviors and symptoms of minority youth in order to avoid either underdiagnosing or overdiagnosing them. There are also specific culture-bound symptoms and disorders that immigrant and refugee youth may present, such as high rates of posttraumatic stress symptoms (Kinzie and others, 1989; Paniagua, 2001). It is important for the clinician to understand the cultural meaning of these symptoms and the experiences that precipitate them (Lopez and Guarnaccia, 2000).

In Chapter Ten, we discuss the need for more culturally appropriate practice, programs, and policies. Although cultural competence has received increasing attention nationwide, it is primarily an ideology and a set of guiding principles that lack empirical validation. The cultural competence model presented earlier is based on sound principles and values and consensus among expert clinicians and academicians in the field. It has been the basis for state cultural competence policies, standards, and guidelines for practice, as well as a proposed methodology to reduce disparities. However, research is needed to determine the utility and effectiveness of any cultural competence approach. Given the many aspects of cultural competence (language skills, clinician's knowledge and values, "cultural" skills, adaptive communication, cross-cultural relationships) researchers may need to target the aspect of cultural competence that has the most impact on quality of care (see U.S. Department of Health and Human Services, 2001). Thoughtful conceptualizations of culture, quality mental health care, cultural competence, and meaningful outcomes may advance such research (Isaacs and Benjamin, 1991).

Research on cultural competence is beset by a persistent dilemma. The pressing demand for culturally competent care requires immediate attention, yet research-based approaches require clear operationalization and empirically based guidelines that take time to develop (Sue and others, 1991). Efforts to implement cultural competence guidelines prematurely may risk failure in implementation or in outcomes, thus creating a setback in efforts to incorporate cultural competence in mental health practice. Conversely, waiting until guidelines have been formally tested may miss a political and social window of opportunity. The challenge is to establish and maintain dialogues between those in the policy arena who want immediate action with those in the research arena who require more time and deliberation (Vega and Lopez, 2001).

In all of the research endeavors proposed, ethnic minority communities need to be involved in the planning, design, and implementation of these studies. These communities are the end users of the services, and it is critical to obtain buy-in from both their explicit and implicit leadership. Participation from community leadership in the research enterprise may enhance the validity of the research and the acceptability of the findings. Inclusion of service providers, families, and consumers in the research process facilitates its future implementation and the dissemination of its products.

Training and Workforce Development

Ethnic and racial minorities are underrepresented among mental health providers, researchers, administrators, policymakers, advocates, and consumer and family organizations. In addition, providers and researchers from all backgrounds lack awareness of the impact of culture on mental health, mental illness, and mental health service delivery and utilization (U.S. Department of Health and Human Services, 2001). Mental health professionals and providers in the systems of care that interface with mental health problems need to develop their understanding of the roles of age, gender, race, ethnicity, and culture in research and treatment, as well as the skills to work with culturally different populations (American Academy of Pediatrics, Committee on Pediatric Workforce, 2000; Morris and Hanley, 2001). Preservice and inservice training programs need to prepare practitioners to serve ethnic minority youth and their families more effectively. Although the major mental health training programs require at least one course in "diverse populations," it is usually not integrated well into the curriculum and often not highly valued by students. Information about cultural diversity and its impact on health and mental health should be mainstreamed throughout these training programs, not only in the academic curricula but in the internship experiences, the supervisory relationships, and in research assignments, as well as in the postdoctoral, continuing education courses and workshops for clinicians (Ridley, Chih, and Olivera, 2000; Speight and others, 1995; Yutrzenka, 1995).

One of the objectives of this book is to increase the understanding of the role of culture in mental health care delivery for children of color and improve the access to services. If access to services is increased, it becomes imperative that the services be culturally appropriate and provide quality care. In part, this quality of care depends on the individuals providing the care. Training and capacity development are therefore essential to quality care for culturally diverse youth. Although it is recognized that minority providers are not the only providers who can treat persons of similar race or cultural background, minority providers tend to treat a higher proportion of minority patients than do white providers. Also, ethno-cultural matching between provider and client encourages minority consumers to enter and stay in treatment (Sue and others, 1991). These trends heighten the need to recruit more racial and ethnic minorities into the mental health field, possibly through more targeted federal training or grant programs, outreach by graduate and professional schools, and educational programs for high school, college, and graduate students (U.S. Department of Health and Human Services, 2001).

Culture- and Ethnic-Specific Services

Confronted with discrimination, exclusion, and inaccessible services, ethnic and racial minority communities have established their own parallel systems of care. Using faith-based services, natural healers, extended family, and neighborhood supports, these communities have developed infrastructures to handle the mental health problems of their children and families (U.S. Department of Health and Human Services, 2001). Sometimes this works; sometimes it doesn't. Nevertheless, these community structures may be important partners in developing systems of care for culturally diverse children. For example, some communities have developed Family Resource Centers that provide a variety of services in a readily accessible, nonstigmatizing venue; others have trained bilingual paraprofessionals to be escorts to more mainstream mental health services. More linkage needs to be done with these naturally existing community helpers in order to meet the mental health needs of culturally diverse youth.

Mental Health and Civil Rights

Access to quality mental health for people of color is not only a health issue but a civil rights issue. Under Title VI of the Civil Rights Act of 1964 and the Americans with Disabilities Act, there are protections to ensure that those who seek mental health services receive such services, free from discrimination based on how they look, how they speak, their national origin, or their mental health status. In August 2000, the Office of Civil Rights issued guidance to assist health and human services providers who receive funding from the U.S. Department of Health and Human Services to understand their obligations to provide language assistance to individuals with limited English skills. This guidance outlines four elements usually contained in effective programs: (1) an assessment of the language needs of the population served, (2) a comprehensive written policy for oral interpretation and written translation, (3) a staff training plan, and (4) procedures for regular monitoring. The four racial and ethnic groups discussed in this book each present growing linguistic challenges, given the increasing number of immigrants and refugees from Africa and the West Indies, Asia, and Central America. Language accessibility is a critical component of access and quality of care, and it is a civil right not always known to these populations.

Where Do We Go from Here?

The sketches we began of children of color in 1989 are more complete but far from finished. New populations have arrived since 1989, bringing more pressures and needs to an already struggling mental health system. The complexities of mental health issues for children of color have increased, and the unmet needs remain high. We have described selected cultural groups in some detail, including their cultural beliefs, mental health concerns, and service utilization patterns. We have provided culturally based approaches to clinical interventions for each group with case examples. In Chapter Ten, we provided an overview of the current status of children of color in the major child-serving systems, as well as a widely cited cultural competence model for assessment and intervention. And in this final chapter, we have outlined important priority areas for continued initiatives. So, what are the next steps?

Rosalynn Carter answered this cogently in her closing statement at the Carter Center's Annual Mental Health Symposium in November 2000 (Carter Center, 2000):

We in the mental health community know the tremendous need for adequate mental health care for all people. From our study of the Surgeon General's supplemental report, we have learned so much more about the barriers that particularly face minority individuals seeking treatment for mental illnesses. It is up to us and our organizations to raise public awareness and ultimately improve access to quality care that is ethnically appropriate and culturally sensitive. It is a challenge, but it is also a great opportunity.

And finally, in the words of David Satcher, the former U.S. Surgeon General, at the symposium (2000, p. 13):

> To the extent that we meet the health needs of the most vulnerable among us, we actually do the most to promote and protect the health of the nation. Whether we're talking about children or ethnic minorities, the extent to which we respond to the needs of our most vulnerable citizens and the degree to which we make changes to alleviate the unique needs of our least protected says a great deal about how well we are promoting and protecting the health of the nation. In that spirit, I approach this task to deal with mental health issues related to ethnic and racial minorities.

Dr. Satcher and Mrs. Carter have eloquently delineated the challenges we, as mental health practitioners, researchers, and policymakers, must confront and the dilemmas we must solve in order to achieve the goal of equal access, equitable treatment, and culturally appropriate services for children of color and their families in the twenty-first century.

References

Akutsu, P. D., Snowden, L. R., and Organista, K. C. "Referral Patterns to Ethnic-Specific and Mainstream Mental Health Programs for Hispanics and Non-Hispanic Whites." *Journal of Counseling Psychology,* 1996, *43,* 56–64.

American Academy of Pediatrics, Committee on Pediatric Workforce. "Enhancing the Racial and Ethnic Diversity of the Pediatric Workforce." *Pediatrics,* 2000, *105*(1), 129–131.

American Psychological Association. "Developing Psychology's National Agenda for Children's Mental Health." Working Group on Children's

Mental Health. Washington, D.C.: American Psychological Association, 2001.

Behar, L., and others. "The Fort Bragg Child and Adolescent Mental Health Demonstration Project." In M. C. Roberts (ed.), *Model Programs in Child and Family Mental Health* (pp. 351–372). Mahwah, N.J.: Lawrence Erlbaum Associates, 1996.

Bernal, G., Bonilla, J., and Bellido, C. "Ecological Validity and Cultural Sensitivity for Outcome Research: Issues for the Cultural Adaptation and Development of Psychosocial Treatment With Hispanics." *Journal of Abnormal Child Psychology*, 1995, *23*, 67–82.

Bernal, G., and Scharrón-Del-Rio, M. R. "Are Empirically Supported Treatments Valid for Ethnic Minorities? Toward an Alternative Approach for Treatment Research." *Cultural Diversity and Ethnic Minority Psychology*, 2001, *7*(4), 328–342.

Borduin, C., and others. "Multisystemic Treatment of Serious Juvenile Offenders: Long-Term Prevention of Criminality and Violence." *Journal of Consulting and Clinical Psychology*, 1995, *63*, 569–578.

Bradford, L., Gaedigk, A., and Leeder, J. "High Frequency of CYP2D6 Poor and 'Intermediate' Metabolizers in Black Populations: A Review and Preliminary Data." *Psychopharmacology Bulletin*, 1998, *34*, 797–804.

"Breaking the Silence." *The Fresno Bee*, August 11, 2002b, 1.

Bronfenbrenner, U. *The Ecology of Human Development: Experiments by Nature and Design*. Cambridge, Mass.: Harvard University Press, 1979.

Brown, J. *Mandatory Managed Care: Children's Access to Medicaid Mental Health Services*. Washington, D.C.: U.S. Department of Health and Human Services, Office of the Inspector General, 2000.

Bui, K. V., and Takeuchi, D. T. "Ethnic Minority Adolescents and the Use of Community Mental Health Care Services." *American Journal of Community Psychology*, 1992, *20*, 403–417.

Burns, B., and Hoagwood, K. *Community Treatment for Youth: Evidence-Based Interventions for Severe Emotional and Behavioral Disorders*. North Carolina: Oxford University Press, 2002.

Carter Center. *Reducing Disparities: Ethnic Minorities and Mental Health*. The Sixteenth Annual Rosalyn Carter Symposium on Mental Health Policy. Atlanta, Ga.: The Carter Center., 2000, pp. 13, 66.

Costello, E., and others. "The Great Smoky Mountains Study of Youth: Functional Impairment and Serious Emotional Disturbance." *Archives of General Psychiatry*, 1996, *53*, 1137–1143.

Cunningham, P. J., and Freiman, M. P. "Determinants of Ambulatory Mental Health Service Use of School-Age Children and Adolescents." *Mental Health Services Research*, 1996, *31*, 409–427.

Drake, R. E., and others. "Implementing Evidence-Based Practices in Routine Mental Health Service Settings." *Psychiatric Services*, 2001, *52*, 179–182.

Ellis, A. D. "Lost in America: Hmong Parents Grieve for a Lost Generation." *The Fresno Bee*, August 11, 2002a, 1.

Friedman, S., Paradis, C., and Hatch, M. (1994). "Characteristics of African-American and White Patients with Panic Disorder and Agoraphobia." *Hospital and Community Psychiatry*, 1994, *45*, 798–803.

Garbarino, J. *Children and Families in the Social Environment*. Hawthorne, N.Y.: Aldine, 1982.

Gibbs, J. T., and Bankhead, T. *Preserving Privilege: California Politics, Propositions, and People of Color*. Westport, Conn.: Praeger, 2001.

Gibbs, J. T., and Huang, L. *Children of Color: Psychological Interventions with Minority Youth*. San Francisco: Jossey-Bass, 1989.

Glover, R. *The Testimony of the National Association of State Mental Health Program Directors to the President's New Freedom Commission on Mental Health*. July 8, 2002, Washington, D.C.

Guerra, N. G., and Jagers, R. "The Importance of Culture in the Assessment of Children and Youth." In V. C. McLoyd and L. Steinberg (eds.), *Studying Minority Adolescents: Conceptual, Methodological, and Theoretical Issues* (pp. 167–181). Mahwah, N.J.: Lawrence Erlbaum Associates, 1998.

Health Care Financing Administration. *Medicaid: A Brief Summary*. Retrieved June 1, 2001, from www.hcfa.gov/pubbforms/actuary.orm edmed/default4.htm.

Hoberman, H. M. "Ethnic Minority Status and Adolescent Mental Health Services Utilization." *Journal of Mental Health Administration*, 1992, *19*, 246–267.

Isaacs, M. R., and Benjamin, M. P. *Towards a Culturally Competent System of Care*. (vol. II). Washington, D.C.: Georgetown University Child Development Center, CASSP Technical Assistance Center, 1991.

Jones, J. H. *Bad Blood: The Tuskegee Syphilis Experiment*. New York: Free Press, 1982.

Kaplan, D. W., Cologne, B. N., Guernsey, B. P., and Hanrahan, M. B. "Managed Care and School-Based Health Centers: Use of Health Services." *Archives of Pediatrics and Adolescent Medicine*, 1998, *152*(1), 25–33.

Kazarian, S. S., and Evans, D. R. (eds.). *Cultural Clinical Psychology: Theory, Research, and Practice*. New York: Oxford University Press, 1998.

Kinzie, J. D., and others. "A Three-Year Follow-Up on Cambodian Young People Traumatized as Children." *Journal of the American Academy of Child and Adolescent Psychiatry*, 1989, *28*, 501–504.

Levant, R., Tolan, P., and Dodgen, D. "New Directions in Children's Mental Health Policy: Psychology's Role." *Professional Psychology: Research and Practice*, 2002, *33*(2), 115–124.

Lin, K., Cheung, F., Smith, M., and Poland, R. "The Use of Psychotropic Medications in Working with Asian Patients." In E. Lee (ed.), *Working with Asian Americans: A Guide for Clinicians* (pp. 388–399). New York: Guilford Press, 1997.

Lopez, S. R., and Guarnaccia, P. J. "Cultural Psychopathology: Uncovering the Social World of Mental Illness." *Annual Review of Psychology,* 2000, *51,* 571–598.

Lutterman, T., Hirad, A., and Poindexter, B. *Funding Sources and Expenditures of State Mental Health Agencies, Fiscal Year 1997.* Alexandria, Va.: National Association of State Mental Health Program Directors Research Institute, 1999.

Mason, M. A., and Gibbs, J. T. "Patterns of Adolescent Psychiatric Hospitalization: Implications for Public Policy." *American Journal of Orthopsychiatry,* 1992, *62*(3), 447–458.

McLoyd, V. C. "Socioeconomic Disadvantage and Child Development." *American Psychologist,* 1998, *53,* 185–204.

McMiller, W. P., and Weisz, J. R. "Help-Seeking Preceding Mental Health Clinic Intake Among African American, Latino, and Caucasian Youths." *Journal of the American Academy of Child and Adolescent Psychiatry,* 1996, *35*(8), 1086–1094.

Melfi, C., Croyhan, T., Hanna, M., and Robinson, R. "Racial Variation in Antidepressant Treatment in a Medicaid Population." *Journal of Clinical Psychiatry,* 2000, *61,* 16–21.

Morris, J., and Hanley, J. "Human Resource Development: A Critical Gap in Child Mental Health Reform." *Administration and Policy in Mental Health Reform,* 2001, *28*(3), 219–227.

Namir, S., and Weinstein, R. "Children: Facilitating New Directions." In L. Snowden (ed.), *Reaching the Underserved: Mental Health Needs of Neglected Populations.* Newbury Park, Calif.: Sage, 1982.

National Center for Health Statistics. *Health, United States, 2000.* Hyattesville, Md.: Centers for Disease Control, 2000.

Paniagua, F. A. *Diagnosis in a Multicultural Context.* Thousand Oaks, Calif.: Sage, 2001.

Ridley, C. R., Chih, D. W. and Olivera, R. J. "Training in Cultural Schemas: An Antidote to Unintentional Racism in Clinical Practice." *American Journal of Orthopsychiatry,* 2000, *70*(1), 65–72.

Sarason, S. *The Psychological Sense of Community: Prospects for a Community Psychology.* San Francisco: Jossey-Bass, 1974.

Satcher, D. *Reducing Disparities: Ethnic Minorities and Mental Health.* Report of the Sixteenth Annual Rosalyn Carter Symposium on Mental Health Policy. Atlanta: The Carter Center, 2000.

Segal, S., Bola, J., and Watson, M. "Race, Quality of Care, and Antipsychotic Prescribing Practices in Psychiatric Emergency Services." *Psychiatric Services*, 1996, *47*, 282–286.

Snowden, L. R., Hu, T., and Jerrell, J. M. "Emergency Care Avoidance: Ethnic Matching and Participation in Minority-Service Programs." *Community Mental Health Journal*, 1995, *31*, 463–473.

Speight, S. L., and others. "Operationalizing Multicultural Training in Doctoral Programs and Internships." *Professional Psychology: Research and Practice*, 1995, *26*, 401–406.

Stiffman, A. R., and others. "Impact of Environment on Adolescent Mental Health and Behavior: Structural Equation Modeling." *American Journal of Orthopsychiatry*, 1999, *69*(1), 73–86.

Sue, S., and others. "Community Mental Health Services for Ethnic Minority Groups: A Test of the Cultural Responsiveness Hypotheses." *Journal of Consulting and Clinical Psychology*, 1991, *59*, 533–540.

Swanson, J., and others. "A Binational School Survey of Depressive Symptoms, Drug Use, and Suicidal Ideation." *Journal of the American Academy of Child and Adolescent Psychiatry*, 1992, *31*, 669–678.

Takeuchi, D. T., Sue, S., and Yeh, M. "Return Rates and Outcomes from Ethnic Specific Mental Health Programs in Los Angeles." *American Journal of Public Health*, 1995, *85*, 638–643.

Treadwell, K., Flannery-Schroeder, E., and Kendall, P. (1995). "Ethnicity and Gender in Relation to Adaptive Functioning, Diagnostic Status, and Treatment Outcome in Children from an Anxiety Clinic." *Journal of Anxiety Disorders*, 1995, *9*, 373–384.

U.S. Department of Health and Human Services. *Mental Health: A Report of the Surgeon General*. Rockville, Md.: U.S. Department of Health and Human Services, 1999.

U.S. Department of Health and Human Services. *Mental Health: Culture, Race and Ethnicity*. Supplement to *Mental Health: A Report of the Surgeon General*. Rockville, Md.: U.S. Department of Health and Human Services, 2001.

Vega, W., and Lopez, S. "Priority Issues in Latino Mental Health Services Research." *Mental Health Services Research*, 2001, *3*(4), 189–199.

Vega, W., and others. "Lifetime Prevalence of DSM-III-R Psychiatric Disorders Among Urban and Rural Mexican Americans in California." *Archives of General Psychiatry*, 1998, *55*, 771–778.

Walkup, J. T., and others. "Patients with Schizophrenia at Risk for Excessive Antipsychotic Dosing." *Journal of Clinical Psychiatry*, 2000, *61*, 344–348.

Yutrzenka, B. A. "Making a Case for Training in Ethnic and Cultural Diversity in Increasing Treatment Efficacy." *Journal of Consulting and Clinical Psychology*, 1995, *62*(2), 197–296.

About the Authors

Jewelle Taylor Gibbs is the Zellerbach Family Fund Professor Emerita of Social Policy, Community Change, and Practice at the School of Social Welfare, University of California at Berkeley. She received her A.B. degree *cum laude* from Radcliffe College and later received an M.S.W. degree in social welfare and an M.A. and a Ph.D. degree in psychology from the University of California at Berkeley. Gibbs is the editor of *Young, Black and Male in America: An Endangered Species* (1988), author of *Race and Justice: Rodney King and O. J. Simpson in a House Divided* (1996), and coauthor of *Preserving Privilege: California Politics, Propositions and People of Color* (2001), as well as numerous book chapters, articles, and essays. She has received many awards for her research and advocacy on behalf of youth of color, including the McCormick Award from the American Association of Suicidology in 1987 for her research on minority youth suicide. Gibbs has served on the board of directors of the American Orthopsychiatric Association, several editorial boards, and the Committee on Children, Youth, and Families of the American Psychological Association. Gibbs is a fellow of the American Psychological Association and a founding member of the advisory board of the National Center for Children in Poverty. A former fellow of the Mary I. Bunting Institute at Radcliffe College, Gibbs has also been a visiting professor at the University of Toronto and a visiting scholar at the University of London, at McGill University, and in the Claremont College system. In 2001–02, she was a visiting fellow at the Research Institute for Comparative Studies in Race and Ethnicity at Stanford University. Gibbs currently serves as a consulting psychologist to foundations, nonprofit organizations, schools, and social agencies on the mental health issues of low-income and minority youth and families.

Larke Nahme Huang is currently the director of research at the Center for Child Health and Mental Health Policy at the Georgetown University Center for Child and Human Development in Washington, D.C. She is also a senior policy associate at the National Technical Assistance Center for Children's Mental Health. She conducts research, training, and consultation in the areas of child development, systems of care for culturally diverse youth, cultural competence in behavioral health and education systems, outcome measurement, and acculturation for multicultural youth. She has published many articles and chapters on these topics and has been a practicing clinician in both private and public settings. She is the coauthor of *Using Evaluation Data to Manage, Improve, Market and Sustain Children's Services* (2000). Huang received her A.B. degree with highest honors from the University of Maryland Honors Program and her M.S. and Ph.D. degrees in psychology from Yale University. She completed a two-year clinical fellowship at the Langley Porter Psychiatric Institute at the University of California, San Francisco. Huang has also served as cochair of the advisory board for the National Asian American Psychology Training Center, as consultant for the Head Start Validation Program, as chair of the advisory board of the American Psychological Association Minority Fellowship Program, and as a member of the American Psychological Association's Committee on Children, Youth, and Families. She served on the Governor's Advisory Committee on the Policy Implications of California's Increasing Minority Populations. In June 2002 she was appointed a commissioner on the President's "New Freedom" Commission on Mental Health.

About the Contributors

Pauline Agbayani-Siewert, associate professor at the University of California at Los Angeles, holds a joint appointment with the School of Public Policy and Social Research, the Department of Social Welfare, and the Asian American Studies Center. Agbayani-Siewert received her B.A., M.S.W., and Ph.D. degrees at UCLA and currently serves as a consultant to the first epidemiological study of Asian American mental health, funded by the National Institutes of Mental Health.

Girlyn F. Arganza is a policy associate at the Center for Child and Human Development at Georgetown University in Washington, D.C. Arganza received her M.A. in community psychology at Georgia State University in Atlanta.

Marivic R. Dizon is a doctoral student in counseling psychology at the School of Education at Stanford University, Stanford, California. Dizon received her B.A. degree *magna cum laude* from Wellesley College and her Ed.M. degree from the Harvard University Graduate School of Education.

Annalisa Vicente Enrile is currently a doctoral student in the School of Public Policy and Social Research at the University of California at Los Angeles. As a Fulbright fellow in the Philippines, Enrile became interested in the mental health issues of Filipino youth and their families.

Donna J. (D. J.) Ida, a clinical psychologist, serves as the executive director of the National Asian American Pacific Islander Mental Health Association in Denver, Colorado. Previously, Ida served for ten years as director of child and adolescent services at the Asian Pacific Development Center, where she was a member of numerous mental health advisory boards and committees.

Jaime E. Inclán, a clinical psychologist, serves as director of the Roberto Clemente Center in the Bronx, New York, where he specializes in working with low-income Latino and immigrant families. He is also a clinical associate professor of psychiatry at the New York University School of Medicine. A native of Puerto Rico, Inclán received his B.A. degree from Georgetown University and his Ph.D. from New York University.

Teresa LaFromboise is the director of training in the Community-Based Counseling Psychology Program at Stanford University, Stanford, California. She is also an affiliated faculty member in Native American Studies in the Center for Comparative Studies in Race and Ethnicity at Stanford University. LaFromboise received her M.A. in education from the University of North Dakota and her Ph.D. in counseling psychology from the University of Oklahoma.

Kurt C. Organista is an associate professor in the School of Social Welfare and director of the Center for Latino Policy Research at the University of California at Berkeley. A clinical psychologist, Organista received his B.A. from the University of Southern California and his M.A. and Ph.D. degrees from Arizona State University. His research focuses on the health and mental health issues of Latino populations.

Mabel E. Quiñones, a clinical psychologist, serves as the director of the Multicultural Child and Family Psychology Training Program at Beth Israel Medical Center in New York City. She is also a part-time faculty member in the Department of Psychiatry at Albert Einstein College of Medicine, the New York University School Psychology Program, and the New School for Social Research. Quiñones received her B.A. and M.A. degrees from the University of Puerto Rico and her Ph.D. in clinical psychology from the City University of New York.

Norita Vlach is an associate professor in the College of Social Work at San Jose State University in San Jose, California. Vlach holds an M.S.W. degree in clinical social work and a Ph.D. in medical anthropology. She is the author of *The Quetzal in Flight: Guatemalan Families in the United States,* which documents her community development work with Guatemalan refugees in the San Francisco Bay Area.

Pahoua Yang is a psychotherapist with the Children's Service Society in Wassau, Wisconsin. Yang, who received her M.S. in social work from the University of Wisconsin, also serves as director of the Hmong Mental Health Institute in Wisconsin.

Yu-Wen Ying is a professor at the School of Social Welfare and adjunct professor in the Department of Psychology at the University of California at Berkeley. A clinical psychologist, she conducts research on Asian American mental health and maintains a private practice in the San Francisco Bay Area. Ying received her B.A. degree *magna cum laude* from Barnard College and her Ph.D. in psychology from the University of California at Berkeley.

Name Index

Subject Index